CLEOPATRA THE GREAT

CLEOPATRA THE GREAT

The Woman Behind the Legend

Dr. Joann Fletcher

HARPER

An Imprint of HarperCollins*Publishers*
www.harpercollins.com

HarperCollins books may be purchased for educational, business, or sales promotional use.
For information, please write: Special Markets Department, HarperCollins Publishers,
10 East 53rd Street, New York, NY 10022.

This book was originally published in Great Britain in 2008 by
Hodder and Stoughton, a Hachette Livre UK company.

FIRST U.S. EDITION

Library of Congress Cataloging-in-Publication Data has been applied for.

ISBN: 978-0-06-058558-7

11   12   13   14   OFF/RRD   10   9   8   7   6   5   4   3   2   1

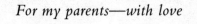

For my parents—with love

Contents

THE ANCIENT WORLD,
FEATURING SITES RELEVANT
TO CLEOPATRA
AND HER PREDECESSORS

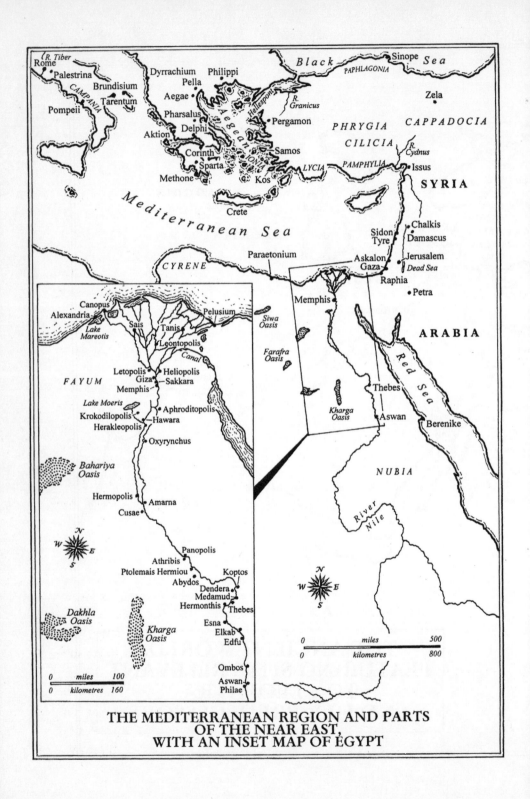

THE MEDITERRANEAN REGION AND PARTS
OF THE NEAR EAST,
WITH AN INSET MAP OF EGYPT

Introduction

As the most famous woman in ancient history, Cleopatra is intimately associated with ancient Egypt and is perhaps its best-known monarch. What is rather less well known is that she was actually European by descent and, like her illustrious predecessor Alexander the Great, traced her origins back to Macedonia in northern Greece. She spoke Greek, her name was Greek and her life was bound up in the fate of the Hellenised world as it struggled for survival against the expansion of Rome.

She was a key player in events which shaped Western civilisation, and even her death was a turning point in Europe's history. Yet the general belief prevails that her life can only be traced through the well-documented careers of the Roman men with whom she dealt. Indeed, it was recently claimed that 'her celebrity seems to have been due primarily to the fact that she slept with both Julius Caesar and Mark Antony – the two most powerful men of her day – and that she was credited with being extremely ambitious'.

Cast in their shadow as little more than an exotic yet flawed appendage, a convenient scapegoat for the men's own shortcomings, Cleopatra appears in Roman sources only when affecting Roman interests. There is little to suggest that she restored Egypt to its former glories by re-creating a great empire at Rome's expense: her astonishing achievements were ignored in Rome's official version of events, with most of the documentary evidence deliberately destroyed, texts suppressed and her name erased from the records.

Having done everything it could to destroy all evidence of the woman herself, Rome's hate-filled propaganda created its own version of Cleopatra which resonates to this day. She was one of only two people whom the Romans ever truly feared, so they repaid her defiance with a blend of lies and misogyny so powerful that she has passed into Western consciousness as little more than a femme fatale, clinging to power until her seductive charms failed her and a dramatic snakebite suicide elevated her to the status of ultimate tragic heroine. With a name now synonymous with tragedy and excess, the popular image of Cleopatra is based on little more than Roman propaganda, Elizabethan drama and Elizabeth Taylor, while the real Cleopatra, for all her fame, was almost completely obscured. For a long time classical scholars seemed unwilling to venture into the 'exotic' world of ancient Egypt, and Egyptologists were largely dismissive of an era they regarded as 'un-Egyptian'. Even in the 1960s, her reign was described as 'a blacked-out landscape illuminated by occasional flashes of lightning when Egypt impinges upon world events'. Yet by this time things had finally started to change in certain quarters. In his landmark biography of Cleopatra first published in 1953, Hans Volkmann referred to the beginnings of new research which had 'torn away the deceptive web which the hate of her enemies had spun around Cleopatra, and ascertained the truth'. And by the 1980s so much new information had come to light that scholars began to collaborate for a major US exhibition in 1988 followed by a more recent version in Europe in 2001.

Some astonishing new evidence was assembled, ranging from commemorative texts, epitaphs and eulogies to tax records, astrological charts and personal correspondence; even Cleopatra's own handwriting was identified only a few years ago. With the Roman sources now more evenly balanced with Greek and Egyptian evidence, vital clues in archaeological reports from sites now lost can be combined with details of sites which have only recently come to light, including Cleopatra's own palace quarters. Just as her coins, statuary and architecture contribute to the overall picture, so the jewellery, clothing, cosmetics, food, furnishings and all the minutiae of daily life as it was lived in the first century BC are able to add a further rich layer of detail to what is now known about the woman herself. By re-creating life within her seaside palace in Alexandria, at her splendid estate by the Tiber or on board her golden cruise ship, details of her famous banquets, vast libraries, exotic wardrobe and even beauty regime can be used to explore and indeed explode a number of long-standing myths, from her first appearance on the world stage as she emerged from a rolled-up carpet to her legendary death by snakebite.

Having replaced such myths with more rational explanations, the same range of evidence also makes it possible to pinpoint Cleopatra's specific whereabouts at precise moments in her life. On 25 March 51 BC, only days into her reign, she appeared as a precocious seventeen-year-old astutely reviving ancient rites by rowing the sacred bull, the earthly incarnation of the sun god, along the river Nile. Then at midnight on 28 December 47 BC, having given birth to her first child, she would have stood within the rooftop shrine of Dendera temple and in moonlit rites assumed the powers of the mother goddess Isis. Even her death on 10 August 30 BC, accompanied by a full supporting cast, was designed to leave the very longest of lasting impressions. Very much the performer staging spectacular events to emphasise a divinity she had held since birth, Cleopatra literally transformed herself into a goddess for every occasion. Adapting her image to appeal to audiences at home and abroad, she appeared as Venus in the heart of Rome, sailed across the Mediterranean as Aphrodite and restored Egypt's former empire as Isis, having absorbed all the attributes of the feminine divine.

She was a frequent traveller, and detailed examination of the ancient sources makes it possible to follow her from Egypt to Greece, Asia Minor, Arabia and Italy. For although Cleopatra had been born and raised in the Greek city of Alexandria on Egypt's Mediterranean coast, she had also lived in Rome for two years and spent many months in Athens, Ephesus, Antioch and Tarsus. Her regular journeys by sea reflected her upbringing within the ancient world's busiest and wealthiest port. Created by Alexander the Great in 331 BC to transform Egypt from an inward-looking backwater into a vibrant cosmopolitan centre, the magnificent city of Alexandria lay at the heart of world affairs and its greatest asset was unquestionably Alexander himself. His mummified body on permanent display was a constant symbol to Cleopatra of her own potential greatness, and her determination to reassemble his vast empire stretching as far as India saw her withstand Roman expansion for over twenty years, successfully maintaining Egypt as the last of Alexander's kingdoms to remain independent.

Although much of Cleopatra's reign was devoted to the world beyond Egypt, her ancient kingdom formed the exotic backdrop for the traditional rites needed to maintain her status as divine monarch. Appearing before her subjects on regular state journeys up and down the Nile ensured both their support and the financial resources necessary to implement her ambitious foreign policies. Even her coinage, depicting a stern, almost masculine-looking profile and purposefully manufactured to appeal to vast areas of a world ruled by men, was valuable propaganda. Such images are regarded by the modern world as evidence that Cleopatra was no great beauty, and in the apparent absence of any true portraits it was even claimed that while 'Nefertiti is a face without a queen, Cleopatra is a queen without a face.'

But this is no longer true of Nefertiti, and the case for Cleopatra too has changed in recent years. Her image has been identified in a whole variety of media, including at least three stunning marble portrait busts which compare most favourably with contemporary images of women then considered leading beauties. Yet Cleopatra's impact was based on far more than facial aesthetics and, fully deserving the same epithet as her predecessor Alexander, Cleopatra the Great can now finally be acknowledged as 'a figure whose brilliance and charisma matched Alexander's own'.

My own fascination with Cleopatra began, like so much else, in childhood. I began to develop an abiding interest in those individuals in history who had made their mark, especially if they had had a mixed press or indeed acquired a negative public image. Cleopatra's close connections with Alexander only increased my desire to learn more. As I grew up I continued to read all I could about both of them, visiting the places they visited and trying to get my head around their special relationships with ancient Egypt. My interest went into overdrive when I began studying for my first degree in ancient history and Egyptology in 1984. It was then that I was introduced to Cleopatra's flamboyant family the Ptolemies, the Greek dynasty who controlled Egypt for the three centuries between Alexander and Cleopatra herself. And, although these rulers are usually passed over as effete, ineffectual and of little relevance to Egypt's true pharaonic past, the Ptolemies' contribution to Egyptology was immense.

With their mania for historical research, the Ptolemies created the Great Library at Alexandria and employed teams of scholars to collect and study texts from all over the ancient world. It was here the Egyptian scholar Manetho compiled a list of names of every pharaoh from the beginning of Egyptian history three thousand years earlier, organising them into a system of dynasties which is still used today. Written details of that most Egyptian of practices, mummification, only survive in two Greek accounts, one of which was composed in Cleopatra's lifetime, and even the names used for the country and its ancient culture are predominantly of Greek derivation; they range from the standard Egyptological terms 'hieroglyph', 'obelisk', 'pyramid' and 'sarcophagus' to the names of their gods Isis, Osiris and Anubis, their kings Tuthmosis, Amenophis and Sesostris, the river Nile and even the land of Egypt itself.

As generous patrons of their adopted heritage the Ptolemies also implemented a massive building programme throughout the country, including most of the temples still standing in Egypt today. Their wall inscriptions detail rituals often unknown from any other source, and it was the Ptolemies' frequent use of multilingual inscriptions, in Greek and Egyptian, that provided the modern world with the means by which hieroglyphs were finally translated. The names 'Ptolemy' and 'Cleopatra' were, appropriately, the first to be read aloud since ancient times.

Using riches from their foreign empire, Egypt's Greek monarchs greatly embellished their kingdom; and, although Rome's inexorable expansion saw their eventual decline, Ptolemaic fortunes were dramatically reversed by Cleopatra. As the last of their line, yet the first to learn the Egyptian language, it was she who restored Egypt's empire to the size it was over a thousand years earlier; Egypt was once again a world superpower, and its people were rightly proud of a pharaoh whom they worshipped for centuries after her death.

Although she is still very much an icon in modern Egypt, a significant number of Egyptologists remain unconvinced. Recently it has been claimed that Cleopatra might be the most famous woman from ancient Egypt, but 'far more significant was Hatshepsut, a female pharaoh who reigned for nearly twenty years in the 15th century BC'. Yet significant for whom?

Not only did Cleopatra reign for the same length of time, she transformed Egypt from a petty client kingdom within Rome's grasp into a power so great that she almost gained the whole of the known world. So while Hatshepsut was indeed a phenomenal character who was certainly influential to her Ptolemaic successors, her significance to both Egypt and the rest of the ancient world was far less than that of Cleopatra, whose impact and influence were felt over great swathes of the region for centuries.

This influence has become increasingly apparent during our own extensive research at the University of York, combined with long-standing involvement with television. One of our first projects examined Egypt's links across North Africa as we followed the fortunes of Cleopatra's daughter, whose sophisticated court owed much to her mother's lifestyle, and whose pyramid-inspired tomb in modern Algeria once contained the closest physical link with Cleopatra to survive.

Subsequent projects took us to southern Arabia, a land famous for its own female ruler the Queen of Sheba, where Cleopatra is said to have visited in brief exile and whose long-term trade with Egypt almost certainly inspired their own mummification practices. Then in Rome, where Cleopatra lived for several years, the mummified burials of a wealthy Isis devotee and her son from the first century AD provided further evidence for Egypt's not inconsiderable influence in Europe. Even beyond the limits of the known world, the first eyewitness description of Britain and its people were written by Cleopatra's partner Julius Caesar.

The long-running search for Nefertiti has also thrown up significant clues. As we continue to discover ever more about this earlier female pharaoh, evidence from the Valley of the Kings and its environs has revealed that such women were long remembered and indeed venerated by their female successors down to Cleopatra's time. But whereas my own research into Nefertiti began with an unidentified body rather than any particular interest in her as an individual, the fascination with Cleopatra lies firmly with the extraordinary abilities and achievements of the woman herself.

As more and more pieces of the historical jigsaw appeared, the desire to try to piece them all together finally became too strong to resist. I had already collaborated on a popular biography of Alexander but my fascination with Cleopatra was not so easily dealt with, bound up as it is with three millennia of female pharaohs who are key to an understanding of their ultimate successor. Although many biographies of

Cleopatra begin with the woman, then examine the way she has been portrayed in later centuries from Plutarch via Shakespeare to Hollywood, this approach can often reveal more about subsequent cultures than about hers. The historical Cleopatra is best sought out among contemporary historical evidence.

Yet even then it is always a struggle to root out the real personality, especially in the case of Cleopatra who even in her own lifetime was many different things to many different people. This determined leader, brilliant politician, erudite scholar and mother of four was a multi-faceted character who could really be all things to all people: to the Romans she was a deluded and drunken whore, to the Greeks and Middle Eastern peoples a beneficent and glorious liberator, to the Egyptians their living goddess and monarch, and in her own mind Alexander's true successor. And in amongst the spin and propaganda from so many diverse sources, attempts to reach the woman herself have proved challenging to say the least.

Ultimately only a saga covering several millennia, three continents and a whole range of diverse evidence could ever hope to make sense of this incredibly complex yet endlessly fascinating woman. Rightly dubbed a 'great potentate' by Yorkshireman George Sandys in 1615, writing soon after the reign of Elizabeth I, even his contemporary William Shakespeare was forced to acknowledge that the great Cleopatra truly had been 'a lass unparalleled'.

Yorkshire
2007

PART ONE

I

The Spirit of Alexander: Europe and Egypt

In March 51 BC, with the death of her father the pharaoh, the girl must have contemplated her situation as she stared through the hazy crystal glass into the face of the mummified god. It was well known that his blood ran through her veins, and although she was a mere seventeen years old he had been even younger when he led the first of his military campaigns which ultimately conquered the known world. By reviving his empire to its former greatness, she would prove herself his true heir.

As light from the flickering torches of the burial chamber hit the crystal coffin, Alexander's distinctive features would have been plainly visible as she contemplated past and future. Although the man before her had been dead for almost three hundred years, the skill of the embalmers had ensured his permanent physical presence, while the rites of mummification had reunited his soul with his body according to ancient lore in which he himself had so passionately believed.

The greatest prize of ancient times, his body had been fought over by successors unable to function without him until eventually he had been laid to rest here in Alexandria in a splendid tomb close to the palace. Following Egypt's long tradition of venerating royal remains he was worshipped as Alexander Ktistes, 'Founder of the City', whose body contained the city's 'daimon' or spirit attended by its own priesthood. He was the focus of the reigning dynasty and its source of inspiration, and his royal descendants who led these rites were incredibly proud of their shared blood – something which Cleopatra felt more keenly than any of her predecessors.

Although her plans to take sole possession of the throne would have been easier to implement if she too had been male, she was fully aware that many other women had ruled Egypt before her. Indeed, from the fabled female pharaohs of ancient times to the women of her own dynasty her half-sister had ruled as sole monarch until their deposed father had regained his throne and ordered her immediate execution. By a very early age, Cleopatra knew all too well that within the royal house of the Ptolemies one's closest family were the most dangerous enemies of all. And at that moment, the main obstacles to her own ambition were two small boys and a young girl, her remaining siblings, who thoroughly despised their elder sister. Although all of them had been considered divine since birth, she had always been their father's favourite and, prior to his death, he had named her his heir alongside the elder of her two brothers as family tradition dictated. Yet her decision to seize sole control and ignore the ten-year-old boy and the ambitious advisers who controlled him meant that even now they were busily plotting her downfall.

If life inside the labyrinthine palace with its intrigues of cliques and courtiers posed a constant hazard for all four children, life beyond its fortified walls was little better. The volatile citizens of Alexandria had repeatedly demonstrated their feelings for previous rulers through rebellion, revolution and regicide, on several occasions storming the palace and removing the royals by force. Only seven years earlier they had driven Cleopatra's father from his throne; his eventual return, with Rome's military backing, had drained most of the contents of Egypt's treasury. And given the Alexandrians' hatred of Roman intervention, not to mention the money it was costing them, only the permanent presence of Roman troops within the palace had been able to guarantee the survival of the newly restored king.

With its forces already in place, Rome was simply biding its time before Egypt fell into its hands as easily as the rest of the Mediterranean kingdoms of Alexander's once mighty empire had done – Macedonia and Greece in 146 BC, Cyrene in 96 BC, Asia Minor and Syria in 65 BC and finally Cyprus in 58 BC. And following the recent death of the Egyptian king during a partial solar eclipse, surely a most terrible omen, all that stood between mighty Rome and world domination was a teenage girl and her young brother.

Against such ridiculous odds, this was the moment when the seventeen-year-old first revealed her right to the epithet 'Great'. Determined at all costs to keep her country independent, she began by taking power directly into her own hands with the support of her closest advisers. Although the Alexandrians wanted the expulsion of all Roman troops stationed in their city, such a blatant move would simply have led to all-out military conflict which an impoverished Egypt was in no position to win. With no choice but to maintain the status quo, Cleopatra became a collaborator in the eyes of the anti-Roman Alexandrians, and as unpopular as her father had been. Yet she also realised that true power lay beyond this volatile Greek city on the Mediterranean, and was to be found at the heart of her antique kingdom. And so began the enduring relationship between Cleopatra the Great and the people of Egypt.

The new monarch's ability to win hearts and minds had been greatly enhanced by her ability to speak to them directly in their own language, and as the first of her dynasty to learn Egyptian she had a deep understanding of their ancient culture. Brought up in a palace where education had been raised to an art form, she was well versed in a heritage which would help unlock the vast resources necessary to rebuild Egypt's capabilities and restore its fortunes. Guided by her close circle of Greek and Egyptian advisers, Cleopatra's opportunity to demonstrate her devotion to native tradition arose only days into her reign with the auspicious birth of the divine Buchis bull, the sun god's earthly incarnation, far to the south at Thebes. The installation of the god in his temple was an event that had been celebrated for over a thousand years. And although it was something of a formality for many of her predecessors, who understood little of the esoteric proceedings and were present in name only, Cleopatra decided she would not only attend the ceremony but would lead the rites in person.

She was the first monarch in several centuries to take such an active part in the rituals which gave Egypt its strength, and her decision had been inspired by Alexander's own attitude. He too had celebrated traditional rites during his six months' stay in Egypt, honouring the ancient deities and paying homage to the sacred creatures that contained the souls of the very gods themselves. Yet Alexander had also brought his own Greek culture with him, establishing his city on Egypt's Mediterranean coast and filling it with all the elements of traditional Greek culture, which gradually filtered south to transform the entire country for ever.

Although Greek culture took permanent root in Egypt under

Alexander, cross-cultural contact had first begun over two thousand years earlier between Egypt and Crete. Foreign influences gradually penetrated south along the Nile valley, as long-haired Minoans in bright-coloured kilts had appeared as far south as Thebes by 1500 BC, bearing Greek-style gifts in tribute and taking home Egyptian concepts of architecture, technology and animal-based religion.

Egypt's royal family even claimed dominion over parts of the Greek world, from the warrior queen Ahhotep (*c.* 1550 BC), named 'Mistress of the Shores of the Northern Islands' of the Aegean, to the fourteenth-century BC Amenhotep III, 'Amenophis' in Greek, who laid claim to Knossos, Rhodes and Mycenae. Imported Mycenean pottery found at his family's royal city, Amarna, enabled early archaeologists to date the site to *c.* 1350 BC, while the presence of such pottery on Egypt's western Mediterranean coast revealed a thriving trading colony around the end of the second millennium BC.

Following the end of the Bronze Age around 1200 BC, widespread unrest around the Mediterranean led to displaced populations migrating through Asia Minor, down through Syria and Palestine and eventually reaching Egypt. Dubbed 'Peoples of the Sea' by the Egyptians, their reports of Greek 'Ekwesh' Achaeans, 'Denyen' Danaans and piratical 'Lukka' of Lycia reveal they joined forces with the Libyans to invade Egypt on several fronts.

Although repelled by the last great warrior pharaoh, Ramses III, many of the invaders settled in Egypt's Delta region and were redeployed as mercenaries by an increasingly ineffectual monarchy. When Egypt finally split in two in 1069 BC, the pharaohs relocated north to the Delta city of Dja'net (better known in its Greek form, Tanis), opting for burial within the precincts of the city's main temple where their gold-filled tombs remained intact. Yet their predecessors' sepulchres in the Valley of the Kings far to the south in Thebes were plundered apparently with the collusion of the local priests of Amun, who now controlled the south as self-styled priest-kings. Reburying the royals in more secure parts of the Valley, they used the opportunity to enhance their own status, holding some mummies back for burial alongside themselves while settling old scores on others, damaging the bodies of those monarchs who had in life undermined their priestly authority.

When the northern pharaohs came to a power-sharing arrangement with their southern counterparts, their former Libyan adversaries who had settled in the Delta eventually took the throne for themselves. Their northern location gave them direct access to the Mediterranean, a region so dominated by Greek trading colonies the Egyptians called it 'the Sea of the Greeks'. Egypt began to appear in Greek literature, and the eighth-century BC epic poems the *Iliad* and the *Odyssey* claimed that 'hundred-gated Thebes' was the place 'where the houses are furnished in the most sumptuous fashion.'

Greeks routinely travelled over to Egypt to see its splendours for themselves, but the two cultures were also drawn together in mutual defence against the Assyrian empire as it expanded west from the region of modern Iran. Having invaded Egypt in 671 BC, the Assyrians returned two years later to execute all local rulers except Necho I of Sais, retaining him as a client king to rule Egypt on Assyria's behalf. His son Psamtek I, better known by his Greek name Psammetichus, built up his power with thirty thousand Greek mercenaries permanently stationed along Egypt's eastern frontier, forming a vital defence against foreign invasion and repelling one launched by the Babylonian king Nebuchadnezzar II in 601 BC.

Psammetichus' son Necho II (610–595 BC) created Egypt's first navy with Greek triremes, the most up-to-date warships of their time, and forced Egypt's inward-looking culture to face out across the Mediterranean. Supporting Greek trading colonies in the Delta, this Saite monarch transformed Egypt's stagnant economy with a great canal linking the Nile to the Red Sea, and is even said to have sent an expedition to circumnavigate Africa. His successor despatched an expedition of Greek, Egyptian and Jewish troops to the far south of Egypt in 592 BC, and after founding a temple to Isis on the island of Philae travelled on to the ancient rock-cut temple at Abu Simbel where his soldiers' graffiti is the oldest Greek inscription in Egypt.

Their visit to a monument already over six hundred years old underlines the Saite practice of revisiting a time when Egypt had been a world power second to none, and, in obvious reaction to the succession of foreign invasions which had destroyed much of Egypt's heritage and pride, the Saites did all they could to restore its former glories. They revived ancient titles and rituals, created exact replicas of ancient tomb scenes and restored ancient monuments, even the pyramids and the fabled monarchs buried within. Mummified remains found inside Sakkara's Step Pyramid were rewrapped and reburied in the belief that they were those of its builder, King Djoser, while a mummy within the third pyramid at Giza which they identified as Mycerinus was reburied in a brand-new coffin. Such face-to-face contact with long-dead predecessors clearly inspired the Saites as they transformed mummification practices for both humans and animals. Although individual creatures such as sacred bulls had long been embalmed, the practice was vastly expanded as literally millions of each god's sacred creature were transformed into mass-produced, linen-wrapped offerings for purchase by the devout. An important part of Egypt's economy, animal mummies soon became the means of demonstrating a unique culture to foreigners in a vigorous if somewhat peculiar demonstration of patriotism.

Yet links with Greek culture remained strong, particularly under the Saite king Amasis. Described as a man 'fond of his joke and his glass, and never inclined to serious pursuits', he was dubbed the 'Philhellene' after marrying a Greek woman, expanding the navy with Greek help and moving the thirty thousand Greek mercenaries into Egypt's traditional capital, Memphis. Within this great city at the apex of the Delta Amasis extended the great temple of the creator god, Ptah. Its name, Hut-ka-Ptah ('house of Ptah's soul'), pronounced 'Aiguptos' by the Greeks, provided the modern name Egypt.

Amasis also embellished his home town of Sais, where the tombs of his dynasty were built within the temple complex of Neith, the creator goddess. Worshipped as mother of the sun, who had created the world with her laughter and could at any time destroy it with her ear-splitting voice, Neith was also worshipped at the Greek trading settlement of Naukratis, where her cult received 10 per cent of all goods coming into Egypt via the only officially sanctioned route from abroad.

Not only the centre of trade with a monopoly on Greek imports, Naukratis was also a magnet for foreign visitors. Some of the biggest names in Greek history travelled to Egypt to learn something of its fabled wisdom. They included statesmen such as the Athenian law-giver Solon and the Spartan Lycurgus, the literary giants Pindar and Euripedes, and the philosophers Pythagoras, Eudoxos, Plato and

Anaxagoras, the last-named particularly interested in the phenomenon of the annual Nile flood. It is therefore most appropriate that the Greeks were the ones to name Egypt's great river, which until then had been called just that, 'the great river' or 'pa iteru aa'. At the Delta it divided up into smaller branches to become 'the rivers', na-iteru, from which the 't' was eventually dropped and the Egyptian 'r' replaced with the Greek 'l'. The result, 'Neilos', formed the river's eventual name. Even the over-used phrase 'Egypt is the gift of the Nile' was composed by the Greek historian Hekataios, who, in his lost work *Aegyptiaca*, was the first to observe that Egypt's Delta region was 'the gift of the river'.

Like many of Hekataios' observations repeated by his fellow Greek Herodotus some fifty years later, both men visited the same sights where they were shown around by the native priests, the custodians of the ancient culture who were able to interpret the mysterious picture writing which curious Greeks dubbed 'sacred carvings', or 'hieroglyphs'. Both men had been shown the 'Hall of Statues' at Karnak temple, where figures of each high priest had been set up in an unbroken lineage: the priests claimed there had been 341 generations since the first pharaoh, Menes. Stressing such antiquity to imply cultural superiority, the priests at Sais even told one Athenian politician that he and his countrymen were merely children since their own history was so short.

Although the Greeks continued to regard Egypt as the cradle of civilization whose priests held powers passed down from the gods themselves, they nevertheless found certain things completely un-fathomable, for 'the Egyptians themselves in their manners and customs seem to have reversed the ordinary practices of mankind'. This was particularly so in the case of women, for in contrast to the restrictions imposed on respectable Greek women who only went out of the house as a last resort and even then fully covered, their Egyptian sisters were not only allowed out, but attended market and 'are employed in trade while the men stay at home and do the weaving'. Further unnatural practices meant that Egyptian 'women pass water standing up, men sitting down', with similarly amusing overtones in the Greeks' descriptions of the Egyptians as 'crocodiles' and 'papyrus eaters'. The characteristic triangular tomb structure 'mer' was dubbed 'pyramis' after the small Greek cake, and the tall stone monolith 'tekhen' became an 'obelisk', or kebab skewer.

Yet as the massive Persian empire, successor to Assyria and Babylon, began its inexorable expansion west, the scattered peoples of southern Europe and the eastern Mediterranean suddenly became very aware of their 'Greekness'. They assumed superiority over all non-Greek-speaking 'barbarians', so that the Persians became denigrated as effeminate trouser-wearing cowards and the Trojan War wheeled out as proof of Greek superiority over their weaker eastern neighbours. On occasion these even included Egypt, whose mystique had been undermined by long-term familiarity, although there remained the need for mutual support against a common enemy.

When the Persian king Cambyses invaded Egypt in 525 BC and executed the last Saite king, he exhumed the mummy of his predecessor Amasis to have it tortured and beaten, but since 'the corpse had been embalmed and would not fall to pieces under the blows, Cambyses ordered it to be burnt' to deprive the pharaoh's soul of its physical home. He then ridiculed the sacred Apis bull, asking the priests, 'Do you call that a god, you poor creatures?' before mortally wounding the beast and having the priests flogged.

Despite such Greek accounts, the Persians successfully ruled Egypt through an efficient civil service, leaving most officials in their posts and replacing the pharaoh by a governor ruling on the Persian king's behalf. Military garrisons were installed as far south as Elephantine, and with the Saite canal between the Nile and Red Sea reopened and camels used in increasing numbers, trade and communications were greatly enhanced.

Although Persia also took over Greek colonies in Asia Minor, the city-state of Athens pulled off an amazing victory at the battle of Marathon in 490 BC and, despite their city being sacked in a revenge attack, struck back to defeat the Persians soundly by land and sea. The Greeks then assisted Egypt to throw out its Persian occupiers, as commemorated by the Egyptians in Homeric-style battle epics, but the Persians soon came back. With the Greeks embroiled in their own internal conflicts as Athens and Sparta slugged it out during the Peloponnesian War of 431–404 BC, an isolated Egypt slipped back under Persian control and suffered serious cultural decline until renewed Greek help once this war was over gave the Delta courage to rise again.

The cities of Sais and Mendes declared independence, fighting off Persian attacks with assistance from Athenian forces headed by the Greek general Chabrias. In 380 BC a real renaissance began when the Egyptian general Nakhtnebef – better known by his Greek name, Nectanebo – proclaimed himself pharaoh (380–362 BC). From its base at the Delta town of Sebennytos this last native dynasty restored national pride, revived ancient art forms, built an astonishing number of temples and promoted the cults of the sacred animals headed by the Apis bull of Memphis. And although the Persians invaded again in 373 BC, they were defeated once again.

Nectanebo I was distinctly pro-Greek and, having married a Greek woman named Ptolemais, a relative of Chabrias, produced a daughter sufficiently powerful to be sent as his representative heading an expedition south to Akhmim to obtain new sources of building stone. Although her name is lost, her official titles are preserved in a rock-cut chapel originally decorated by the fourteenth-century BC pharaoh Ay, father of the famous female pharaoh Nefertiti, whose inspirational titles were duplicated by Nectanebo I's daughter: 'hereditary princess, held in high esteem, favoured with sweet love, the mistress of Upper and Lower Egypt, of gracious countenance, beautiful with the double feather, great royal consort, Lady of the Two Lands'.

Nectanebo I was briefly succeeded by his son Djedhor, the first pharaoh to issue coins in Egypt's barter-based economy, but he was deposed by his cousin Nectanebo II (360–343 BC). After beating back a vast Persian invasion force in 350 BC with help from Athens and Sparta, Nectanebo II was worshipped throughout Egypt. His attempts to restore his country's glories by resurrecting the power of its past were part of a nationwide effort to create 'a magic defence' against the Persian menace. Yet for all this ritual protection, the legendary Nectanebo II was finally defeated in 343 BC and Egypt taken back into the Persian empire. Cities such as Heliopolis and Mendes were destroyed, along with the tombs of the kings who had rebelled against Persian rule, and many members of the ruling classes were deported to Persia. Nectanebo himself managed to flee south into Nubia, although it was rumoured that at some stage during his reign he had also sailed to northern Greece. Having predicted that the Macedonian queen Olympias would soon give birth to the son of Zeus, greatest of the gods of Greece, Nectanebo then donned the mask of the god and himself fathered her child, which was very much in the Egyptian tradition of divine conception legends. The myth also neatly claimed the child, whom she named Alexander, to be the successor of the last native pharaoh.

Despite the harshness of their regime, the Persians remained in Egypt for little more than a decade before Alexander himself arrived in Egypt in 332 BC to claim his fabled birthright. Welcomed as a saviour and the rightful heir of Nectanebo II by a populace desperate to be rid of the hated Persians, he initiated three centuries of Greek rule which would culminate in the extraordinary figure of Cleopatra herself.

Born in Egypt of Macedonian descent, Cleopatra had a traditional Macedonian name which, in its original Greek form, began with a 'k'. And although the name is generally translated as 'glory to her father', its meaning may be more accurately understood as 'renowned in her ancestry'. And it was quite an ancestry. At least thirty-three Cleopatras are known from ancient times, and with the origins of her famous name rooted in myth and the forces of nature, the first Cleopatra was daughter of the North Wind Boreas. The name's mythological origins are also associated with a daughter of the legendary King Midas, and the first historical Cleopatra may have been a sister of the real Midas, King of Phrygia (central Turkey), who married Macedonia's first historical king Perdikkas (670–652 BC). Considered to exist at the very edge of the civilized world, both geographically and culturally, the Macedonians originated in the northernmost part of Greece, close to the lands of Scythia and Thrace where tattooed warriors still collected severed heads. When not participating in warfare themselves, Macedonia's elite in-dulged in hunting, feasting and drinking bouts that lasted days at a time.

Still ruled by Homeric-style kings when much of Greece had adopted democracy, Macedonia's southern neighbours found their northern accent hard to understand and dismissed them as semi-barbarian, even though the Macedonians were Greek speakers, had Greek names and worshipped the traditional gods of Greece whose fabled home atop snowy Mount Olympus lay at the heart of Mace-donia's rugged landscape. From their mythical founder 'Makedon', believed to have been a son of Zeus, Macedonia's earliest royal rulers traced back to the seventh century BC were both polygamous and apparently incestuous. The choice of royal heir, normally the king's eldest son, was made by the Assembly made up of warrior elite, and the succession was typically affected by threats, bribes and murder. A king's first task, therefore, was to remove all rivals and then to produce an heir.

After marriage to Macedonia's first historical king, Perdikkas I, the first historical Cleopatra became the mother of the royal house, faithful vassals of Persia until Athens' great victory in 480 BC allowed them to switch sides. Over the next century nine kings ruled over a volatile Macedonia until Archelaos (413–399 BC) brought a degree of stability and moved his capital from Aegae to Pella on the Aegean for much-needed access to the sea. As Pella became a cosmopolitan royal capital, its marble palace embellished with murals and mosaics created by Athenian craftsmen, Archelaos invited the greatest minds of the age to his court. Although the Athenian philosopher Socrates turned down the offer, those who did accept royal patronage included the poet Pindar, Hippocrates, known as the father of medicine, and the leading dramatist Euripides, whose great masterpiece the *Bacchae* was inspired by his new home and its bloody history.

Following Archelaos' murder and intermittent civil war, Amyntas III (389–369 BC) strengthened Macedonia's defences against Illyria to the west and married the Illyrian princess Eurydike, who bore him three sons. Amid the royal family's constant feuding, the deaths of Amyntas and his eldest son were apparently caused by the ambitious Eurydike and her lover, and when her second son died from wounds sustained fighting the Illyrians, the third and youngest son Philip, then twenty-four, was elected king in 359 BC. After eliminating other rivals to the throne in time-honoured fashion, Philip II (359–336 BC) decisively crushed the Illyrians and embarked on years of campaigning which resulted in the loss of his right eye, a maimed arm and crippled leg. Yet it transformed Macedonia from a feuding, feudal kingdom into a world superpower.

He also found time for a most complicated bisexual love life, including a youthful fling with his second cousin Arsinoe and no fewer than seven wives. The most famous of these was Myrtale of Epirus (modern Albania), first encountered during nocturnal fertility rites on the windswept island of Samothrace and at marriage given the Macedonian name Olympias to reflect the divine landscape of her new home. Able to trace her own ancestry back to the sea goddess Thetis, mother of the Greek superhero Achilles, Olympias paid particular respect to Zeus and his son Dionysos, god of wine and embodiment of vitality. Dionysos' female acolytes achieved states of complete possession, and Olympias undertook her own Dionysiac rites with tame snakes which 'terrified the male spectators as they raised their heads from the wreaths of ivy . . . or twined themselves around the wands and garlands of the women'.

Yet regardless of her power as queen, Olympias had to co-exist with her husband's other families. These included a son, Philip Arrhidaios, born to his third wife, and a daughter, Cynane, who fought alongside her father, born to the second. Although Olympias produced an equally formidable daughter called Cleopatra, her crowning achievement was her son Alexander, known to history as 'the Great' and raised by his mother to believe himself the son of Zeus.

Born in July 356 BC on the same day that the great temple of Artemis at Ephesus burned down, since the goddess was apparently away assisting at his birth, Alexander was already in military training by the age of seven and had gained his first experience of battle at fourteen. An androgynous-looking youth, with long curling hair and a smooth complexion, 'fair-skinned, with a ruddy tinge', the young Alexander modelled himself on his ancestor Achilles, the lead character of the *Iliad*, in which the quote 'ever to be best and stand far above all others' became something of a personal mantra. As a bibliophile well versed in history, even as a child Alexander had an understanding of cultures far beyond the Greek world. Once, receiving a Persian delegation in his father's absence, he had 'talked freely with them and quite won them over, not only by the friendliness of his manner but also because he did not trouble them with any childish or trivial inquiries, but questioned them about the distances they had travelled by road, the nature of the journey into the interior of Persia, the character of the king, his experience in war, and the military strength and prowess of the Persians', a precocious curiosity supplying vital intelligence for his future plans.

For his son's higher education, Philip had selected a little-known Thracian philosopher called Aristotle who had studied under Plato in Athens and whose father had been doctor to Philip's family. Moving to Macedonia, the new tutor was given a fine house and teaching facilities, and despite the discrepancy between his republican beliefs and the monarchy he served, Aristotle recommended that 'a wise man should fall in love, take part in politics and live with a king'.

Aristotle's political teachings provided Alexander with a solid background in statecraft, and the ideal of the highly principled 'great-souled man' provided the student with a model to emulate. Given Alexander's obvious love of Homer, Aristotle's well-thumbed and annotated copy of the *Iliad* became his student's prized possession. A shared fascination with scientific exploration was reflected in the specimens of flora and fauna the prince sent back to his old tutor when on campaign.

Yet Aristotle's advice to look after the Greeks 'as if friends and relatives, and to deal with the barbarians as with beasts or plants' reflected the Greek view of their superiority over other races. In much the same way that slaves were 'animated tools', Aristotle claimed that men were superior to women, whose high-pitched voices shared with eunuchs reflected an inherently deviant nature. Women were separated by the Greeks into three basic groups,: it was said that 'courtesans we keep for pleasure, concubines for attending day-by-day to the body and wives for producing heirs, and for standing trusty guard on our household property', which explained why in Greek society all 'respectable' women were largely confined to the home.

Although Aristotle maintained that a man's most important relationships should be with other men, Alexander's commitment to his lifelong companion and fellow student Hephaistion was equally likely to have been a reaction to his father Philip's promiscuity and the problems caused by so many offspring from so many relationships. It was certainly believed that another fellow student, Ptolemy, was Alexander's half-brother, since his mother Arsinoe, a princess of the royal house and Philip's second cousin, had also been one of his many lovers until married off to a lowly squire named Lagus. The ancient sources admit that 'the Macedonians consider Ptolemy to be the son of Philip, though putatively the son of Lagus, asserting that his mother was with child when she was married to Lagus by Philip'. It was claimed that 'Ptolemy was a blood relative of Alexander and some believe he was Philip's son', and even 'Olympias, too, had made it clear that Ptolemy had been fathered by Philip', a paternity that Ptolemy himself kept low-key out of respect for his mother.

In 340 BC Philip appointed the sixteen-year-old Alexander regent. After forces commanded by the teenager put down a Thracian rising, father and son fought together to unite the rest of Greece in preparation for a war against the traditional enemy, Persia. This long-held dream of a Pan-Hellenic crusade in revenge for the invasion of Greece had always ended in internal feuding, and with Athens and Sparta each considering itself the leader of any such plan they now opposed Macedonia's attempts to lead them. An Anti-Macedonian League was set up, ironically financed by the old enemy, Persia. It was led by the Athenian orator Demosthenes, who, in his vitriolic *Philippics*, denounced Philip as not a true Greek nor even from a 'respectable' country. Yet Philip soon defeated the League and secured their support against Persia in return for the release of Athenian prisoners. The ashes of the fallen were also returned by Alexander on his only visit to Athens, where new statues of his father and himself were dedicated to 'Philip and his heirs in perpetuity'.

With everything ready for the great crusade, Philip's plans suddenly changed when his kingdom's stability was threatened by internal feuding. His estranged relationship with Olympias had developed into open hostility after Philip had married a courtier's young niece, Eurydike, and the bride's uncle had announced the hope there would soon be an heir of pure Macedonian blood. This had so enraged Alexander he had started a fight, then left court with his mother for Epirus where her brother was king. As Philip and his new bride began producing a fresh batch of royal heirs, the Epirite king complained bitterly to his Macedonian brother-in-law that his family's honour had been offended. Philip then played a masterstroke by offering him marriage to Princess Cleopatra, Alexander's eighteen-year-old sister and the Epirite king's own niece.

When the offer was accepted, things were sufficiently secure at home to allow Philip to send an advance force over to Asia Minor, and ask the Oracle at Delphi if he would conquer the Persian king. On receiving the ambiguous answer 'Wreathed is the bull. All is done. The sacrificer awaits', he misinterpreted this as confirmation of his imminent success. In fact the one to be sacrificed was Philip himself. As guests gathered at Aegae in the hot summer of 336 BC to witness uncle marry niece Philip was cut down by the captain of his bodyguard, who in turn was speared through by his fellow guards. Although some believed he had acted alone to avenge a personal grudge, others felt that Olympias must have initiated the murder to free the throne for her son. Whatever her guilt, she left no doubt about her feelings by publicly crowning the killer's corpse with a gold wreath and presenting it with offerings. Certainly it seems more than suspicious that the plot had been so widely known that the orator Demosthenes was able to announce the news in faraway Athens almost as it happened. As word of the assassination spread rapidly, it became imperative to elect a new king. So the army chose Olympias' son, who was duly installed as Alexander III.

At his funeral, which according to Macedonian tradition was led by his son, the new king, Philip was cremated. His remains were then collected up and placed in a gold larnax chest decorated with the star of the Macedonian house, to be buried with lavish funerary goods in the royal necropolis at Aegae. His entourage were then put on trial before Alexander and the Assembly of warriors, and while the remaining guards were acquitted, the male relatives of Philip's last wife, Eurydike, were found guilty and executed at his tomb. Although the Assembly spared Eurydike herself, she and her child were killed on the orders of Olympias − who had them roasted alive if later accounts are to be believed. She may also have had a hand in the fate of one of Philip's older sons Arrhidaios, whose retarded nature 'was neither hereditary nor was it produced by natural causes. On the contrary, it was said that as a boy he had shown an attractive disposition and displayed much promise, but Olympias was believed to have given him drugs which impaired the functions of his body and irreparably injured his brain.'

With his position established at home, Alexander turned his attentions to securing the rest of Greece, where many cities refused to acknowledge him until he arrived at their gates with the Macedonian army. Despite Demosthenes' attempts to spread false rumours that he had been killed subduing Celtic lands by the Adriatic, Alexander returned to reimpose control and, with Athens in no position to argue, was finally recognised as Supreme Commander of Greek Forces by all but Sparta, who still insisted that it should have the military leadership. Alexander then consulted the Delphic Oracle. Despite arriving on an inauspicious day when the Oracle could not be approached, he took the priestess by the arm and propelled her toward the shrine, taking her exasperated comment, 'You are invincible, my son!' as confirmation of his future success.

Having installed the capable general Antipatros as regent of Macedonia, Alexander finally set out against Persia in early 334 BC with a combined allied force of forty thousand infantry and six thousand cavalry. Marching them east to the Hellespont where they were transported across the narrow waters from Europe into Asia, he sacrificed a bull to the sea god Poseidon, poured wine for the Nereid sea nymphs and was first to leap from the ships on to the beach. Hurling his spear into the sand, he declared all Asia 'spear-won land' before making a detour to Troy, fabled city of Homer's *Iliad*, where he exchanged his own armour for an ancient set used in the Trojan War. He then made a pilgrimage to the tomb of Achilles, laying a wreath on his grave as he prayed for some of his ancestor's legendary powers in the battles to come.

With sight-seeing cut short by news that the Persians were already massing on the banks of the river Granicus east of Troy with the sole aim to take him dead or alive, Alexander led the charge on his famous horse Bucephalus (meaning 'Bull's Head'). After fierce fighting, the Persians were routed, and Alexander sent three hundred of their abandoned shields to Athens as an offering to the goddess Athena with the inscription 'Alexander, the son of Philip, and all the Greeks with the exception of the Spartans won these spoils of war from the barbarians who dwell in Asia'. The rest of the lavish plunder was sent back to his mother in Pella, and instantly reversed the 500 talents of debt which Philip had left. (1 talent = 26 kg silver)

As he marched south through the Greek colonies of Asia Minor Alexander was welcomed as a liberator, and at Ephesus he transferred all the taxes formerly paid to Persia to the cult of Artemis, whose great temple was still being rebuilt after burning down on the day of his birth. The only significant opposition was encountered at Miletus, whose faith in the Persian fleet proved misplaced once Alexander had blockaded and stormed the city.

With most of the coast now his and the enemy fleet virtually impotent, he reinstated Queen Ada as ruler of Halicarnassus after her brother had deposed her. He also honoured her with the official title 'Mother', while his own mother Olympias continued to wield power in an unofficial capacity back in Macedonia, much to the annoyance of its male regent Antipatros.

Having marched south across Anatolia to the Cilician plain, Alexander was sufficiently recovered from fever and a Persian-backed attempt to poison him to be ready to face the Persian king himself. For Darius III had decided that this Greek upstart had penetrated far enough into his empire, and, with an army of six hundred thousand under his personal control, outnumbered Alexander by an astonishing ten to one.

As the two armies faced each other at Issus near Tarsus on a November morning in 333 BC, Alexander once more led the cavalry charge into the Persian lines, fighting his way toward Darius who stood tall in his golden war chariot surrounded by his elite bodyguard. Yet 'in military matters the feeblest and most incompetent of men', Darius soon lost his nerve and, as he 'led the race for safety', his troops fell into confused disarray. The battle was lost, and the death toll of 110,000 Persians in that one day's conflict remained unequalled until the beginning of the twentieth century. Darius had also abandoned the amazing sum of 3000 talents, loose change to the king of Persia but more money than Alexander had ever seen. Darius' royal tent was still 'full of many treasures, luxurious furniture and lavishly dressed servants'. With 'the whole room marvellously fragrant with spices and perfumes', a battle-weary Alexander took full advantage of its huge gold bath before having dinner, reclining with his companions on magnificent dining couches.

Darius had even left behind his mother, his sister, to whom he was married as was Persian custom, and their children, whom Alexander treated with every courtesy; however, he declined Darius' offer of an alliance in exchange for returning them. He also decided against pursuing the enemy into the Persian heartlands, preferring to secure the eastern Mediterranean where Egypt was still under Persian control and would be able to mount a counter-attack. So he would need to capture the Phoenician coast and Egypt before he could even consider marching east. Although most Phoenician cities along the coast of modern Syria and Palestine were keen to be rid of Persian control, Tyre required a six-month assault with siege engines, catapults and ship-borne battering rams, while similar siege further south at Gaza produced some 16 tons of frankincense and myrrh amongst the spoils.

When a second envoy from Darius offered him all Asia Minor west of the Euphrates, his daughter's hand in marriage and 10,000 talents, Alexander pointed out that he already held the lands and the money and could marry the princess regardless of her father's permission. Knowing that it would also take Darius considerable time to form a new army, Alexander felt sufficiently secure to press on south into Egypt where he remained a full six months. Yet this was no eccentric diversion. His time here was crucial to both his strategic and commercial plans, since a strong coastal base was vital for communications across the Mediterranean and would allow him to take over the seaborne trade previously controlled by Phoenicia.

So as his closest friend Hephaistion and the navy tracked him along the coast, Alexander covered the 130 miles of desert between Gaza and the Egyptian border in a week. Late in October 332 BC he marched into the fortified frontier town of Pelusion (Pelusium), but found no resistance: Egypt's Persian governor simply handed over the treasury. Ordering his fleet to follow him by sailing south down the eastern branch of the Delta, Alexander set out at the head of his troops, passing through a landscape of temples and tombs not built to human scale. Yet for all its mystique, Egypt was not an unfamiliar place. Raised with his mother's tales of exotic gods, Alexander, like many of his fellow countrymen, was well versed in the works of previous Greek travellers whose writings were the guidebooks for subsequent generations.

After passing the ruins of the first Greek mercenary camps the Macedonians came to Bubastis, Egyptian Per–Baster or 'house of Bastet' the cat goddess, whose female devotees drank, danced and shook their sistrum rattles in fertility rites shared with the goddess Isis. Beyond lay Iunu, the Greek Heliopolis or City of the Sun. Although much of this once magnificent city had been destroyed a decade earlier by the Persians when reasserting their control, toppling its granite obelisks which now lay scorched and fallen, much of the massive temple beyond seems to have escaped unscathed. Within its multiple-columned interior dating back to the Pyramid Age, the primeval creator sun god Ra had been worshipped three times daily for the last three thousand years and his soul was still present within his sacred Mnevis bull.

Crossing over the Nile to the west and the land of the dead, the

Macedonian army reached the most famous wonders of the ancient world, the great pyramids of Giza, still covered in their shining white limestone. Alexander was so impressed by these two-thousand-year-old monuments that he declared he would erect one over his father's tomb back home 'to match the greatest of the pyramids of Egypt'. But Giza was only the beginning of a pyramid field which stretched for many miles, and as his troops pressed on south past the pyramids and sun temples of Abusir they could see the pyramids of Sakkara perched high on the desert escarpment above their final destination, Egypt's traditional capital, Memphis.

Amid scenes resembling VE day, Alexander marched into the great city and received a rapturous reception. Hailed as saviour and liberator by the Egyptians after two periods of Persian domination when an absent king had exploited their wealth, demonstrated scant respect for tradition and put down rebellion with ever harsher measures, he was a tangible, visible king doing all he could to demonstrate his respect for them and their country. Even rumoured to be descended from the gods themselves, Alexander was legitimate pharaoh of Egypt simply by right of conquest and was officially recognised as such by the city's high priest, Maatranefer. As Egypt's highest native aristocrat, the hereditary high priest of Memphis was the country's spiritual leader whose close relationship with the monarchy brought true stability to the land. It was an alliance that wise kings were careful to promote, for, as Plato himself had noted, 'in Egypt, it is not possible for a king to rule without the help of the priests'.

Their power base at Memphis was the cult centre of the creator god Ptah, whose vast temple was filled with the images of pharaohs still worshipped at the site alongside Imhotep, architect of Egypt's first pyramid. Honoured by the Greeks as Imouthes, whose reputation for wisdom equalled that of Egypt's own goddess Isis, she was also regarded as the mother of the Apis bull and worshipped as the sacred Cow of Memphis. Both cow and bull were housed in a golden stall within the temple and honoured with a constant stream of offerings while musicians and dancing dwarves performed before them.

Keen to pay his own respects just like the last native king, Nectanebo II, Alexander would have been equally keen to honour each of the bull's predecessors who at death became one with Osiris, god of the

Underworld. As Osiris-Apis, or Serapis, already a popular god in Alexander's day, each successive bull had been mummified and interred within a vast network of catacomb tombs known as the Serapaion (Serapeum), which lay beneath the sands of Sakkara high above the city. In order to reach it, pilgrims such as Alexander had to follow its 2-km-long sphinx-lined causeway as it left the city and the lush green valley to rise up the cliffside to the dusty desert above. Yet Sakkara was no silent graveyard. Its pyramids, tombs and chapels were surrounded by elements of the funerary trade as far as the eye could see. Groups of foreign tourists mingled with trinket sellers hawking their wares as *theagoi* or 'bearers of the gods' trundled past with carts of small-scale animal mummies en route to burial, and the droning of funerary priests was intermittently drowned out by the wailing of professional female mourners, tugging their hair and beating their chests in time-honoured fashion.

Passing the earliest of the pyramids created by the divine Imhotep, the long causeway wound on beyond clusters of smaller pyramids and long streets of tombs until finally reaching the Serapeum. As bright sunlight gave way to the gloom of its subterranean chambers, great galleries stretching out 100 metres into the darkness incorporated huge recesses within which the sacred bulls were interred inside great granite sarcophagi. Each one was adorned with jewellery and flowers, and the walls were covered with the prayers of kings and commoners paying homage to the collective souls of Apis.

Yet bulls' tombs were not the only ones here, and, in the grand tradition of royals buried deep within temple courtyards after the decline of the Valley of the Kings, the precincts of the Serapeum that had been so magnificently embellished under the last native dynasty contained the sepulchre of Nectanebo II, its last native king. Empty and unused after of his flight into exile in 343 BC, his green stone sarcophagus inscribed with finely wrought images of the sun god Ra in the Underworld stood in the centre of the burial chamber as a poignant reminder of Egypt's lost glories.

Now confirmed as Nectanebo II's successor, Alexander was deter-mined to initiate a new golden age, and on 14 November 332 BC 'in the Throne Chamber of the Temple of Ptah' was formally named pharaoh of Upper and Lower Egypt. Crowning him with the combined white and red crowns of the two respective regions, the high priest Maa-tranefer proclaimed him 'Horus, the strong ruler who seizes the lands of the foreigners'. He was also given the name 'Meryamun Setepenra', 'beloved of Amun and the chosen one of Ra', written in hieroglyphs enclosed within a pair of protective oval cartouches. As 'chosen one of Ra' he became part of a tradition stretching back to the Pyramid Age, while the epithet 'beloved of Amun', the great state god identified with the Greek Zeus, reinforced his belief that his own divinity was more than wishful propaganda. The coronation was followed by Macedo-nian-style feasting and drinking, Greek games and literary contests featuring leading performers from across the Greek world. Then Alexander took up residence in the palace at Memphis, becoming 'the one in the great house' or 'perwer', from which the term 'pharaoh' derives.

Over the following two months he formulated his military and economic plans. Holding meetings with native priests and academics to discuss Egypt's laws and customs. He was, like every pharaoh before him, the country's nominal high priest, and set out plans to build and embellish temples dedicated to Egypt's traditional gods. He also took time to study native beliefs and even attended lectures by the Egyptian philosopher Psammon. This respect for native tradition was revealed by the chance survival of one of the papyrus notices posted up around Memphis by Alexander's officer Peukestas, which states 'By order of Peukestas: no one is to pass. The chamber is that of a priest.'

In January 331 BC, Alexander set out from Memphis to find possible locations for a new commercial site and sailed north down the western branch of the Nile to the old Greek trading colony of Naukratis. Deciding that the landlocked site offered little scope for development, he pressed on 45 miles further to the Mediterranean coast and reached Per-gwati, the Greek Canopus, where Osiris was worshipped as a human-headed jar believed to contain pieces of his dismembered body. Although the narrow strip of hilly land between the sea and Lake Mareotis to the south housed little more than a few fishing commu-nities, Alexander recognised this part of Egypt's windswept coast from the description given by Homer, remembering that 'there is an island called Pharos in the rolling seas off the mouth of the Nile, a day's sail out for a well-found vessel with a roaring wind astern. In this island is a sheltered cove where sailors come to draw their water from a well and can launch their boats on an even keel into the deep sea.'

With the constant north-west wind, Zephyros, blowing in fresh from the Mediterranean Pharos was regarded as a sacred site, home to Poseidon's protégé Proteus, the Old Man of the Sea. It was here that the Greek king Menelaus had been stranded on his way home from the Trojan War until Proteus' daughter Eidothee had helped him set sail before disappearing beneath the waves. And now Alexander himself had a similarly spiritual encounter when an old man appeared to him in a dream, reciting Homer's very lines. When Alexander viewed the site on waking he declared Homer to have been not only a great poet but also a knowledgeable and far-seeing architect.

For the stretch of land before him resembled 'the top of a bull's head with two straight peninsular horns jutting out into the open sea just beyond the two ends of the island'. Alexander was 'at once struck by the excellence of the site, and convinced that if a city were built upon it, it would prosper. Such was his enthusiasm that he could not wait to begin the work; he himself designed the general layout of the new town, indicating the position of the market square, the number of temples to be built and which gods they should serve – the gods of Greece and the Egyptian Isis – and the precise limits of its outer defences.'

Alexander also envisaged a great library, a fitting creation for a city founded on a literary quote, and five districts named after Greek letters: the Alpha district to be set around a great central crossroads, Beta the 'Basileia' or 'palace quarter', and Gamma, Delta and Epsilon housing the city's mixed population. Supplied with an underground system of pipes and cisterns to bring in fresh water, the city was arranged around a grid pattern of roads which would funnel the sea breezes between buildings to provide cool air in summer, taking advantage of a climate likened to the French Riviera, 'generally sunny, but sometimes rather cold and rainy in winter, and not intolerably hot in summer, there being an almost continuous northern breeze from the sea'.

As Alexander paced rapidly up and down the shoreline, his cloak flapping behind him as he built the city in his mind, his architect Deinokrates followed along its invisible roads and avenues with increasing difficulty until it was suggested that the dark ground should be marked out using barley meal from the soldiers' rations. When a large snake suddenly appeared in their midst, Alexander's advisers identified it as the city's guardian spirit or 'Agathos Daimon'; then an eagle spotted overhead and sacred to Zeus was likewise regarded as auspicious. But then a great flock of seabirds suddenly descended and ate all trace of the fledgling city, and Alexander's fears were only allayed when his trusted seer Aristander pronounced that the city would flourish and provide abundant resources to nourish its people.

Named Alexandria after its founder, it would soon become the most famous and successful of the seventy or so settlements he founded throughout his growing empire, each created along traditional Greek lines and populated with a mixture of pensioned-off Macedonian troops, Greek settlers and people from the local region. Although Alexandria also attracted thousands of immigrants from all parts of the ancient world, it would always stand apart as 'Alexandria ad Aegyptum', 'Alexandria-adjacent-to-Egypt', and people would speak of making the journey 'from Alexandria to Egypt'.

After sending Aristotle's nephew Kallisthenes down to Aswan in the far south to investigate his uncle's revolutionary theory that the Nile flood was not sent forth by a subterranean god but caused by rains further south, Alexander himself decided to travel west to the remote oasis of Siwa to consult the oracle of Zeus-Ammon, the Libyan form of Amun. Set deep in the Sahara some 400 miles west of Thebes, the renowned oracle was believed to be an offshoot of Amun's temple at Karnak, created at the same time as Zeus's oracle at Olympias' home town of Dodona in Epirus. With a reputation for infallibility, Siwa's distant oracle had once been visited by a delegation from Nectanebo II whom Alexander was keen to emulate, and although he never revealed the precise reason for his own visit, the question of his own divinity was still at the forefront of his mind. On a more practical note, he may also have been testing the viability of ancient caravan routes which passed through Siwa and neighbouring oases to link central Africa to his new city on the coast, whose future success would presumably have been another question to put to the god.

So in late January 331 BC Alexander set out west along the coastal road and, after receiving envoys from the Greek colony of Cyrene (modern Libya), his small group turned south into the Sahara. After a sudden violent sandstorm obliterated the track and disorientated their native guides, disaster was only averted when two black ravens miraculously appeared and led them to safety. Although his likely half-brother Ptolemy later recalled that their saviours had been snakes rather than birds, Alexander's apparent ability to summon such guardians must have reinforced rumours that he might just be the son of a god he claimed to be.

As the first pharaoh ever to complete the journey in person, Alexander emerged from the desert and made straight for the temple of Ammon high on a rocky outcrop. He was met by its high priest, greeting him in faltering Greek, 'O, paidion', 'Oh, my son', but mispronounced 'O, pai dios', 'Oh, son of god', a linguistic slip which no doubt delighted his visitor. Then, amid clouds of incense, the veiled image of Ammon, resembling a 'phallic-looking mummy . . . draped in cloths and jewels', was brought out into the light and carried around the temple forecourt before returning to the darkness of its inner sanctuary, followed by Alexander.

When he finally emerged into the daylight some time later and was asked what had transpired, he would only say that he had been given 'the answer which his heart desired'. Presumably discussing the nature of his divine paternity, he was adamant he would only reveal the secret to his mother on his return to Macedonia; but when asked if his father's murder had been avenged, 'the high priest commanded him to speak more guardedly, since his father was not a mortal'. Although such notions tend to be dismissed as little more than self-delusion, Alexander's belief that he really was the son of a god was quite acceptable in the ancient world where the line between mortal and divine was at best blurred and where millions worshipped as gods those who had once been human, and in some cases still were.

Whatever the answers had been, Alexander was sufficiently satisfied to present rich offerings to the oracle. After returning to Memphis he ordered new shrines for the god's divine image in his main cult centre, Thebes, as well as commissioning a granite shrine at Karnak temple and a limestone version at Luxor. He also drew inspiration from earlier pharaohs by incorporating the horns of Amun's sacred creature, the ram, into his own royal regalia, and when the city of Mytilene offered him divine honours, he was portrayed on their coinage with the horns curling through his hair. The legend of the all-conquering 'Two-horned One' was born.

When finalising his plans for Egypt's government in his absence Alexander decided against placing power in the hands of one man. Instead, he followed Aristotle's advice that a king must hold an even balance between all parties by appointing a committee of Egyptians, Macedonians and Persians to rule along traditional lines, headed by Kleomenes of Naukratis as governor. And now, having secured Egypt and the entire eastern Mediterranean, Alexander could finally set out in pursuit of Darius.

Leaving Egypt in the spring of 331 BC a changed man and living god, he pursued and defeated Darius for the third and final time later that year. At the age of only twenty-five, Alexander, King of Macedonia, Hegemon of Greece, Overlord of Asia Minor and Pharaoh of Egypt had now become Great King of the Persian Empire by right of conquest, and married Darius' beautiful daughter. He had also become the richest man in the world by inheriting 180,000 talents, around 375 tonnes of gold, much of which he transformed into coinage and changed the entire world economy forever.

As trade flourished across a vast network of new markets, Greek culture arrived in the wake of a campaign route stretching a further 11,000 miles. Over the next eight years Alexander travelled east from Babylon and through Persia to Afghanistan (ancient Sogdia), where he acquired another wife. He and his men then crossed the snows of the Hindu Kush to reach India's monsoon lands where he fought against rajahs and their fearsome war elephants, celebrating his victories by adopting the elephant-skin headdress. Declaring himself an invincible god, he returned west via the blazing deserts of Gedrosia (southern parts of Pakistan and Iran), navigating routes through the Indian Ocean and Persian Gulf to arrive back in Babylon where he began to plan his next campaign into Arabia, then on across North Africa to the Straits of Gibraltar and into the unknown.

Since setting out from Macedonia in 336 BC, thirteen years of endless campaigning without a single defeat had gained him an empire covering 2 million square miles across three continents. His superhuman achievements had changed the face of the known world, and his reign had been a turning point in world history. Greek culture had been irrevocably transformed by the many others encountered during his ceaseless campaigning. It is all the more extraordinary that Alexander was only in the early part of his career when he died suddenly at the age of thirty-two before ever returning to Egypt and the city he created but never saw.

2

In the Blood: the Ptolemies and Their Cleopatras

On 10 June 323 BC, Alexander the Great was declared dead in the ancient palace of Nebuchadnezzar in Babylon. Set on the banks of the river Euphrates close to the Hanging Gardens built for Nebuchadnezzar's queen, the city was also home to the temple ziggurat known as the Tower of Babel. Yet these fabled landmarks had been eclipsed by the 70-metre (230 feet) high-step pyramid that Alexander had commissioned as a lavish funerary pyre for his closest friend, Hephaistion, who had died from fever late in 324 BC, whose body had presumably been embalmed since he was not cremated until the pyre's completion in May 323 BC.

Following the funeral, Alexander had toured the Euphrates' canals and marshlands, brushing aside a number of bad omens as he returned to Babylon to continue with plans for his forthcoming Arabian campaign. Yet, starting to feel feverish, he had slept in his palace bathroom to keep cool, drinking heavily as was his custom as his fever increased. When the army heard of his condition they demanded to see him, filing past his bed to greet him one last time. Then, bequeathing his personal possessions to Ptolemy and his official signet ring to the highest-ranking general, Perdikkas, he whispered that his empire should go 'to the strongest' and his body should go to Amun, signifying burial in Egypt whose ancient funerary rites would guarantee him eternal life. Throughout the night of 9 June, Ptolemy and Alexander's closest friends held a vigil in the temple of Serapis, the Egyptian god whose cult Alexander had taken on campaign. Yet even Serapis was unable to save him, and, most likely suffering from cerebral malaria, he finally lost consciousness.

As his death was announced, the shock reverberated around the ancient world. His courtiers stood around the deathbed, not quite knowing what to do for the best, until Perdikkas called an Assembly to debate the succession. Although he and the cavalry wanted to await the imminent birth of Alexander's child by his Sogdian wife Roxane, the infantry demanded that Alexander's half-brother Arrhidaios be made king at once; although mentally impaired, he was a Macedonian male of royal blood, whereas the unborn child would be half-barbarian and, even worse, might be female. With neither side willing to back down, fierce fighting broke out around Alexander's body until the infantry ringleaders were permanently silenced.

In the midst of this power struggle, the body had remained untouched for almost a week. Yet, despite the extreme summer heat, it was in pristine condition, its suspiciously lifelike complexion taken as evidence of Alexander's divinity. Most likely, however, he had been in a terminal coma and had only just died – or was perhaps even still alive as the embalmers began their work. After removal of his brain and major organs to prevent putrefaction, the body was crowned with Macedonia's royal diadem and placed within an Egyptian-style coffin 'made of hammered gold, and the space about the body they filled with spices such as could make the body sweet-smelling and incorruptible'. The sealed coffin, draped in a rich pall of gold and purple, then took centre stage in the Assembly as his men debated their next move.

Following the birth of the baby Alexander IV in autumn 323 BC he became joint king with Arrhidaios, although both were simply figure-heads for the army. Yet with none of its officers capable of taking sole control of such a vast empire, they decided to divide it between them. With Perdikkas in control of the army, Antipatros would retain Macedonia while Lysimachos took Thrace, Antigonas Asia Minor, Seleucus Babylonia and Ptolemy, probably at his own suggestion, 'was appointed to govern Egypt and Libya and those lands of the Arabs that were contiguous to Egypt; and Kleomenes who had been made governor by Alexander, was subordinated to Ptolemy'.

Ptolemy and the others swiftly left Babylon for their new lands, having ordered a magnificent hearse to transport Alexander's precious body back west. It consisted of a six-metre-high golden temple adorned with scenes showing him on the move as he had always appeared in life, travelling by chariot, with his cavalry and navy, and even depicting the Indian war elephants he had adopted. With gold statues of Nike, winged goddess of victory, standing over a tolling bell at each corner of the jewelled roof, a great purple banner flying high from the apex marked the progress of the glittering cortege as it finally left Babylon and slowly headed west, attracting great crowds.

Yet disagreements over its final destination soon escalated into all-out war because, despite the fact that Alexander had wanted burial in Egypt, Perdikkas had plans of his own. Already regent for the joint kings and engaged to Antipatros' daughter, he had also received a marriage proposal from Alexander's widowed sister, Cleopatra. As he contemplated the throne for himself, he realised he would need Alexander's body, not only to appease his prospective bride and mother-in-law Olympias but also to offset the belief that Macedon's royal line would cease if its kings were not interred in the traditional burial ground at Aegae.

Although the other Successors were all keen to halt Perdikkas' ambition, it was Ptolemy who acted decisively by instigating a hijack at Damascus and substituting a fake mummy as 'Alexander's real body was sent ahead without fuss and formality by a secret and little used route. Perdikass found the imitation corpse with the elaborate carriage and halted his advance, thinking he had laid hands on the prize. Too late he realized he had been deceived.' So began the first of the Successors' many wars when Perdikkas invaded Egypt in 321 BC in an attempt to retrieve the body and terminate Ptolemy. Yet when two thousand men were lost trying to cross the Nile at Memphis, over half of them falling victim to crocodiles, the rest mutinied, killed Perdikkas and offered the regency to Ptolemy.

Nevertheless he declined, preferring to keep hold of Egypt and the all-important body which he 'proceeded to bury with Macedonian rites in Memphis'. Fulfilling Alexander's last wish for burial with Amun, who had a temple here too, it seems highly likely that Ptolemy honoured Alexander's desire to be seen as Nectanebo II's successor by placing the gold coffin within Nectanebo's unused stone sarcophagus in the Serapeum. The entrance was embellished with a new causeway terminating in a semi-circle of famous Greeks, statues which over time have been heavily sandblasted by the desert winds. They are most likely to have portrayed Alexander alongside the likes of Homer, Pindar, Plato, Aristotle, Ptolemy and Dionysus himself, appropriate companions for Alexander's temporary resting place while construction of a permanent tomb continued in Alexandria.

Ptolemy certainly took his responsibilities to Alexander very seriously, not only writing his biography but also, alone of all the Successors, building and renovating temples in the names of the joint kings Arrhidaios and young Alexander IV. Although Egypt's priests appreciated Ptolemy's efforts, declaring that 'this great governor searched for the best thing to do for the gods of Upper and Lower Egypt', the joint monarchs never saw the work carried out in their names since both were kept hostage in Macedonia by the ageing regent Antipatros and his son Kassandros.

With Arrhidaios married off to his able cousin Eurydike, daughter of Philip's warrior daughter Cynane, the couple supported Kassandros' plan to succeed his father until rumours that Kassandros had poisoned Alexander roused his mother Olympias to action. After defeating Eurydike's army in 317 BC she forced her to commit suicide and ordered Arrhidaios' execution, finally clearing the way for her six-year-old grandson Alexander IV to become sole king. Then in 315 BC Kassandros took Olympias captive and, having handed her over to her victims' relatives for execution, he eventually poisoned the young king and his mother Roxane and took the throne of Macedonia for himself in 310 BC. Alexander's forthright sister Cleopatra, imprisoned to prevent her bestowing power by marriage, was murdered by Antigonas when she accepted a proposal and sanctuary from Ptolemy in Egypt.

Although Alexander's immediate family had all been killed, Ptolemy himself managed to survive, still acting as governor for the murdered Alexander IV when his fellow Successors had declared themselves kings. Only in 305 BC, at the age of sixty, did he finally become king, but he always refused divine honours in his lifetime and accepted only the Greek title 'Soter', 'Saviour', which Rhodes awarded him for military support. To compete with the other Successors, his rivals, he also began to issue his own coinage, bearing an image that depicted his Alexander-like large eyes and tousled hair encircled by a diadem countered by his determined chin and prominent, eagle-like nose. The latter feature was the likely inspiration for his personal badge, the eagle, which became the Ptolemies' emblem and is still the central motif of Egypt's national flag.

By November 311 BC Alexandria was sufficiently complete to become the new royal capital, its position on a coastline with few discernible features marked by plans for a huge lighthouse on Pharos Island. Connected to the mainland by a mile-long causeway, the city's harbour would then be divided into an eastern and western side, while a third, smaller harbour linking the Mediterranean to Lake Mareotis and the Nile would give access to the rest of Egypt.

The city's Greek and Jewish citizens settled in various parts of the city, but the Egyptians preferred the western sector which they called Raqed, Greek Rhakotis, meaning 'building site'. They also referred to their new Greek neighbours as the 'girdlewearers', although the distinct lack of ethnic tension was maintained through a unique system of Greek, Egyptian and Jewish laws rather than imposing Greek legislation on the native population. The same toleration was extended to religion when Ptolemy combined the Egyptian Serapis – the ancient combination of Osiris and Apis – with the Greek gods Zeus, Asklepios and Hades to create a Greek-looking deity of Egyptian origin acceptable to all as state god. Although Serapis' cult centre became the most prominent of Alexandria's many temples, Ptolemy I also planned a Macedonian-style Temple of the Muses or Mouseion (Museum) in which knowledge was elevated to a religion. This great research centre, funded by the crown, would house leading academics whose research would benefit the kingdom and enhance its status abroad. It would have its own library under the care of Aristotle's former student Demetrios of Phaleron, whose failing eyesight, restored by entreaties to Serapis, was a glowing endorsement for his patron's new state god.

Ptolemy I also employed a team of Greek and Egyptian experts to advise on matters of culture and religion, and, as the new regime continued to build and renovate temples throughout Egypt, ancient land creation schemes were revived to increase productivity and provide land for veteran troops. With the settlers housed in new Greek towns, existing Egyptian settlements took new names based on the Greek divinity closest to the local cult. So, as places such as ancient Henen-nesut became 'Herakleopolis', city of Herakles, Shedet 'Krokodilopolis', city of the crocodile and Edfu 'Apollonopolis', 'city of Apollo', ancient Egypt slowly disappeared beneath the emerging kingdom of the Ptolemies.

During a long and well-travelled career Ptolemy I had fathered large numbers of children. A short-lived marriage to a Persian noblewoman named Artakama and affairs with several courtesans were followed by marriage to Antipatros' daughter Eurydike and then Antipatros' grand-niece Berenike, who became 'the most powerful of Ptolemy I's wives and the one with the most virtues and intelligence'. Despite having at least nine children by other women, including six with Eurydike, those born to Berenike I would form the basis of the dynasty. When Eurydike and their eldest son Ptolemy Keraunos ('Lightning') were exiled in 287 BC the old king made his genial younger son Ptolemy II his co-regent, allowing him to spend his remaining years pottering about his palace. Finally dying in his bed at the age of eighty-four, the last of the great Successors, Ptolemy I had lived half a century longer than his beloved Alexander but was buried with him. Following his orders to be cremated according to Macedonian custom, Ptolemy I's ashes were gathered up and placed in the newly completed alabaster tomb when Ptolemy II 'brought down from Memphis the corpse of Alexander' for joint interment.

The late king had already arranged a wife for his twenty-eight-year-old successor, the daughter of his old ally Lysimachos of Thrace. She dutifully produced three children before their marriage was abruptly terminated by the unstoppable ambitions of the new king's extraordinary sister, Arsinoe II. As the most capable of Ptolemy I's children, she had been married off at sixteen to sixty-year-old Lysimachos, giving him three sons and in return being made queen of Thrace and Macedonia. But, wanting more power, she had used false allegations to remove her stepson, the heir apparent, whose followers fled to Seleucus for help. After Seleucus killed Lysimachos in battle he was assassinated by Keraunos, whose claims to Thrace, Macedonia and Egypt were strengthened by marrying his ambitious half-sister Arsinoe II, now Lysimachos' widow. Yet even she baulked when her new husband's elimination of rivals began with her own sons, and she fled to Samothrace until Keraunos' death in battle left her free to marry for a third time.

With her sights still fixed on the throne of Egypt, Arsinoe moved to Alexandria and, after engineering the exile of her brother Ptolemy II's first wife, married him herself in 275 BC and became his co-regent, the first of a long line of Ptolemaic royal women to hold exactly the same status as their male counterparts. Although some Greeks were shocked by the marriage, if not the co-regency, Arsinoe II had already been married to her half-brother Keraunos. Marriage between close relatives was a tradition of the Thracian, Epirite and Macedonian rulers, and indeed brother-sister marriage was regular practice amongst Persian royalty and certainly for some of ancient Egypt's previous monarchs.

Clearly Arsinoe II found inspiration in her fifteenth-century BC pharaonic predecessor Hatshepsut, who had married her half-brother before taking power as pharaoh herself. Adopting Hatshepsut's titles, Arsinoe II was referred to as 'Daughter of Ra', the female equivalent of the traditional pharaoh's title 'Son of Ra', and also took her predecessor's title 'Daughter of Geb', the earth god and father of Isis. Like Hatshepsut, she wore Geb's distinctive red crown embellished with the ram's horns of Amun and the double plumes, cow horns and sun disc of Hathor-Isis. Equally symbolic headgear was adopted for her Greek-style portraits. A huge cameo celebrating the marriage featured her brother in a Greek helmet, while Arsinoe II wore the diadem of Dionysus and the marriage veil of Zeus' sister-wife Hera draped over her fair hair styled in a bun. In addition to their shared blond hair, the siblings had the same long nose, plump cheeks and eyes sufficiently large to be taken as evidence for an exophthalmic goitre yet most likely an exaggerated physical trait that they shared with their putative uncle Alexander. It was certainly a family resemblance that Arsinoe II fully exploited for her own political ends and, vigorously promoting the image of a divinely inspired dynasty, the couple deified their deceased parents Ptolemy I Soter and Berenike I as twin 'Saviour gods', worshipped with Alexander at the new Ptolemaia festival to showcase their dynastic power.

Celebrated every four years, the Ptolemaia was perhaps the most lavish public festival ever held in the ancient world, steeped in the outrageous opulence or 'tryphe' which became the Ptolemies' trademark. Based on the ancient Greek Dionysia festival, it presented Dionysos as god of the Ptolemaic house, returning from India just like Alexander and accompanied by the same unimaginable wealth in a day-long procession. Eyewitness accounts describe eighty thousand soldiers in shining armour followed by great crowds in sumptuous costumes and troops of elephants and camels bearing exotic goods from Africa, Arabia and India. Never-before-seen giraffes and rhinoceroses caused the same consternation as the huge automata figures that magically rose up to receive libations amid rivers of wine. Gold statues of the gods were followed by god-sized suits of golden armour and crowns; a 120-foot-wide gem-encrusted myrtle wreath, ancient slang for female genitals, was accompanied by an 80-foot-long gold penis tipped by a star to emphasise none too subtly the mechanics of royal succession.

Following their parents' deification their children too became divine: Arsinoe II's Greek title 'Philadelphus', 'sibling lover', extended to her brother-husband Ptolemy II to create twin gods likened to married siblings Zeus and Hera. The same comparison with Egypt's Isis and Osiris was even closer to the mark, for the goddess Isis was the active partner in that relationship too. In much the same way that Arsinoe II had steam-rollered her way to the top, Isis had taken over the roles of all the other female deities, including Hathor, goddess of love, whom the Greeks called Aphrodite. Born from the sea, Aphrodite was the perfect goddess for the new coastal capital: her whose earthly incarnation was described as 'rising from the flashing sea and laughing, striking lightning from her lovely face'.

Yet all-nurturing, all-powerful Arsinoe herself seems to have had little genuine regard for her subjects and beneath a carefully crafted public image was prone to sneering at them, commenting of one festival gathering, 'that must be a very dirty get-together. For the assembly can only be that of a miscellaneous mob who have themselves served with a stale and utterly unseemly feast.' She, by contrast, lived in the greatest luxury and was fabulously wealthy in her own right at a time when most women in the ancient world had no financial independence whatsoever. Wielding financial and political power akin to her pharaonic female predecessors, Arsinoe II's tremendous talent for government resulted in great improvements at home and abroad.

Able to create a Domesday-style inventory of Egypt's assets, aided by an efficient royal postal system and meticulous records, tremendous wealth was created and collected on behalf of a monarchy whose strict revenue laws established royal monopolies on everything from linen and papyrus to perfume and vegetable oil. The royal finance minister undertook regular inspection tours up and down the Nile, and local agents oversaw day-to-day business ranging from the training of Greek gymnasts to dealing with local entrepreneurs. They also procured slaves from Palestine, Syria and Nubia, for in contrast to the lower levels of slavery in ancient Egypt, the Greeks relied on this form of labour for their households, farms and factories. And, of course, they had to pay taxes and import duty on them. Foreign trade was further boosted by reopening the old Saite canal connecting the Nile to the Red Sea, whose main port, Berenike, formed the gateway for trade with Arabia, India and the Orient. The Ptolemies also traded with Arab merchants such as Zayd'il bin Zayd, an importer of 'myrrh and calamus for the temple of the gods of Egypt' who worked around Memphis.

Yet the Ptolemies' vast wealth was 'not heaped up to lie useless, as if the wealth of ever-industrious ants; much is lavished on the shrines of the gods' to enhance their status as benefactors, and to guarantee the loyalty of priests and people to whom they appeared as traditional rulers making offerings and performing ancient rites. The burials of sacred animals were a further costly undertaking for the crown, with a staggering 100 talents' worth of myrrh (the equivalent of 2,600 kg of silver) requested for the burial of a single sacred cow. Large sums were also expended on the armed forces to keep Ptolemaic territory intact, and to foil invasion from Cyrene to the west by the couples' older half-brother Magas, a son of Berenike I by an earlier marriage. The couple also put down an incursion by Nubians to the south, quelled a rebellion of Celtic mercenaries in northern Egypt and defended the eastern Delta against Seleucid invasion before the two sides finally made peace in 271 BC.

The Ptolemies' reach across the Mediterranean was reflected in a huge marble statue of Isis on the Acropolis in Athens, along with buildings on Delos and a temple to Ptolemy II at his birthplace on Kos. On Samothrace Arsinoe II erected a monument in gratitude for her earlier period of sanctuary here, commemorating the place where Alexander's parents first met with an enormous rotunda temple of Doric columns and carved bulls' heads.

At the other end of the Mediterranean the couple also expanded trade links with Italy, whose Greek colonies were gradually being taken over by Rome. Although this small Italian city is said to have sent a delegation to Alexander himself, Arsinoe II and her husband were the first of the Successors to make official contact, sending an embassy to Rome in 273 BC. In response, 'the Romans, pleased that one [sic] so far away should have thought so highly of them', sent ambassadors to Alexandria. The resulting treaty was commemorated with Rome's first silver coins, so similar to those of Arsinoe II that the Ptolemies must have supplied the necessary expertise. They could never have guessed that their new allies were nothing less than a ticking time bomb which would push its way to the heart of Egypt's affairs with fatal results.

Yet for now the Ptolemies ruled supreme, their pole position in the Mediterranean marked by the completion of their great Pharos lighthouse which was immediately regarded as one of the wonders of the world. At 135m, almost as tall as that other wonder, the Great Pyramid of Giza, its blazing beacon reflected by polished metal mirrors for almost 50 miles in every direction was regarded as a man-made star through which Isis illuminated the world. Her presence on Pharos was also marked by a colossus beside the lighthouse, the Nile's static goddess transformed into a lively windswept figure appropriate to her new coastal setting. Striding forward as a kind of 'action version' of the Statue of Liberty, great Isis Pharia held out her billowing mantle ('pharos') to catch the breeze, emphasising her invention of navigation and her role as 'Mistress of Winds' inherited from Hathor and Aphrodite.

Visible to all who approached by sea, great Isis was flanked by colossal companion figures of the royal couple, who used pharaonic statues to give ancient kudos to their modern city. With its wide boulevards and marble colonnades shaded by green awnings it anticipated many of Europe's later cities; comparisons have also been drawn with New York, based on a shared grid pattern of high-rise buildings, financial houses, passenger terminals, fast-food outlets, theatres, libraries and parks adorned with ancient Egyptian obelisks. Alexandria even had automatic doors and steam power courtesy of leading scholar Heron, who invented the steam turbine simply as a means of opening and closing temple doors. It was just one of many inventions that the monarchs funded within their Mouseion (Museum), with its lecture halls, laboratories, observatories, gardens and zoo, although its best-known feature was the Great Library. Designed to hold all the world's knowledge under the Ptolemies' sole control, rival Successors to

Alexander decided to set up their own library at Pergamom in western Anatolia (modern Turkey) until the Ptolemies' immediate ban on papyrus exports forced their rivals to invent parchment ('pergamenon') as a means of sustaining the race for knowledge.

Anxious to obtain Greek translations of all known texts in the ancient world, Ptolemy II set his scholars to work on everything from a complete translation of the Hebrew scriptures to the fabled knowledge of ancient Egypt. He commissioned his father's Egyptian adviser, Manetho, to compile a complete history of every known pharaoh since records began, and also wrote to him on matters of religion; one of Manetho's replies to the king, comparing the gods of Egypt and Greece, explained that Thoth, represented by the ibis and the ape, was the same as the Greek Hermes.

Yet Ptolemy II also made staff changes, sacking the head librarian, Demetrios, who had supported a rival claimant to the throne, and replacing him with the Homeric expert Zenodotus, whose assistant, Callimachus of Cyrene, composed the first library catalogue. It listed 120,000 scrolls of poetry, history, rhetoric, philosophy, law and medicine, copies of many of which were housed in a second, 'daughter' library within the Serapeum temple. The Serapeum's medical centre was staffed by 'pastophor' physician priests who were able to consult ancient Egyptian medical texts and the works of Hippocrates and Aristotle. The latter's grandson, Erasistratus, and a fellow medical student, Herophilus, carried out human vivisection. With royal permission they 'cut open criminals received out of the kings' prisons, and they studied whilst the breath of life remained in them', working out the function of arteries and discovering that the brain, not the heart, was the centre of the nervous system. With Ptolemy II himself regarded as 'the most august of all princes and devoted, if any one was, to culture and learning', the Mouseion and Library soon became the stuff of legend, 'and concerning the number of books, the establishing of libraries, and the collection in the Hall of the Muses, why need I even speak, since they are in all men's memories'.

The legendary buildings formed part of the royal palace which extended along the Lochias promontory, each monarch extending the complex with his or her own personal quarters and following Macedonian tradition by building in imported marble. Interior water features and mosaics were also de rigueur, and further adorned with sumptuous furnishings; even the tentlike royal dining pavilion housed 'marble figures, a hundred in all, the work of foremost artists, and paintings by artists of the Sicyonian school alternating with a great variety of selected portraits'. At the apex of its scarlet ceiling perched a pair of great gold eagles, the symbol of the Ptolemaic house, now duplicated to represent the twin monarchs; below, gold and silver tables paired with a hundred golden couches were laden with jewelled tableware.

Such opulence was certainly to Arsinoe II's taste, and Ptolemy II seems to have been as content to let her make decisions about interior design as in every other area of his life. Her tremendous eye for detail was certainly appreciated by those who passed through public parts of the palace at festival time. One housewife told her friend, 'Come on! Get your cloak. Let's go to the house of the king, rich Ptolemy. I hear the queen has done a beautiful job of decorating it . . . And when you've seen it, what won't you be able to say to someone who hasn't!' Yet some were clearly less impressed, claiming that 'everything in Egypt was play-acting and painted scenery', a comment which cut to the heart of this melodramatic monarchy for whom image was everything.

Having transformed the Ptolemaic house into a dazzling bastion of conspicuous consumption in only five years, Arsinoe II died at the age of forty-six just before the full moon on 9 July 270 BC. Following her lavish Macedonian-style cremation, the Greeks imagined that their sun god Apollo had sent down his golden chariot to raise her to heaven, whereas the Egyptians preferred to imagine her heavenward soul as Isis' star Sothis, which appeared annually between 17 and 19 July. Worshipped in a city where streets were named after her, the deified woman was now commemorated at the annual Arsinoeia festival, when her clergy led the crowds through the city, and people drank from wine jugs adorned with her image.

On Alexandria's blustery Cape Zephyrion, a new temple dedicated to Arsinoe II as Aphrodite Zephritis, Lady of Winds, featured a giant drinking vessel in 'the form of the Egyptian Bes the dancer, who trumpets forth a shrill note when the spout is opened for the flowing wine', to emphasise the dynasty's ritual use of alcohol. Close to the harbour lay a second lavish sanctuary, the Arsineion, its site marked by a great stone obelisk of Nectanebo II and inside it a six-foot-high statue of Arsinoe II covered in glittering sea-green peridots below an iron statue, said to have been suspended magically in space by the temple's magnetic roof to capture the moment when Arsinoe rose to heaven.

Throughout the country Ptolemy II decreed 'that her statue be set up in all the temples. This pleased their priests for they were aware of her noble attitude toward the gods and of her excellent deeds to the benefit of all people'. Named as 'Beloved of the Ram', she was worshipped at Mendes, the place 'where bitch-mounting goats go mating with the women'. This aspect of ritual behaviour was described by the historian Herodotus, who reported with some understatement that 'a goat tupped a woman, in full view of everyone – a most surprising event'.

Arsinoe II was shown with the same ram's horns as Alexander, and like him called 'child of Amun'; the god Amun himself informed Arsinoe II that 'I will make you a god [sic] at the head of the gods on earth'. She was indeed worshipped throughout Egypt as the female counterpart of Osiris, Ra, Ptah, Min, Montu and Sobek, the ancient crocodile god of the Fayum. The capital of the Fayum was renamed Arsinoe and the whole of this fertile lakeside region south-west of the Delta reclassified as the Arsinoite nome (province). A port on the Red Sea was also named Arsinoe, and her worship extended as far afield as Cyprus, Delos and Thera, reflecting Ptolemaic influence across the eastern Mediterranean.

Although Ptolemy II clearly missed his sister-wife's capable govern-ment, her physical presence seems never to have been a prerequisite since the king, like his father, had always maintained relationships with large numbers of women, including the exceptionally beautiful Bilis-tiche of Argos. Usually termed 'mistresses', they followed the Egyptian tradition of minor wives and, provided with their own palaces, resembled the large female households of pharaohs of the past.

Recognised as 'a man of wit and taste, partial to the ladies', Ptolemy II loved the good life and it eventually took its toll. Perhaps as overweight as his obese half-brother Magas, he certainly suffered from drink-induced gout in his final years. He was able to do little more than sit by his palace window and observe his subjects enjoying picnics on the sands below, gloomily declaring, 'Unlucky devil that I am! To think I cannot even be one of those fellows.' The second Ptolemy died at the age of sixty-two in January 246 BC and, after cremation in accordance with Macedonian tradition, his ashes were buried in Alexandria in ceremonies led by his son and successor, the thirty-eight-year-old Ptolemy III.

The new king was crowned by the high priest Anemho II in 246 BC, the same year that he married his cousin Berenike of Cyrene, only child and successor of the portly Magas. The acquisition of Cyrene's fleet proved crucial in the Ptolemies' renewed war with the Seleucids. Berenike II ruled Egypt in her husband's absence, and was even said to have gone into battle beside him on at least one occasion. The campaign was lengthy but successful, extending Egypt's reach as far east as Babylonia, from where Ptolemy III retrieved Egyptian treasures looted long ago by the Persians.

Awarded the Greek title Euergetes, 'Benefactor', the couple were worshipped as 'Benefactor Gods' and Berenike II identified with Isis and Aphrodite. She was an attractive woman with 'deep-set long eyes, a nose wide at the nostrils, a ball-chin – a face slightly reminiscent of Nefertiti . . . it looks as though the Hellenistic Greeks, like the moderns, admired the Nefertiti profile' which Berenike II further emphasised by drawing back her blonde hair in a bun. She also wore long corkscrew ringlets characteristic of her homeland Cyrene, and her hair even achieved its own immortality after a lock which she dedicated in the temple of Arsinoe Zephritis mysteriously disappeared, presumably blown away in the continuous sea breeze, until identified in the night sky by the court astonomer as the constellation Coma Berenikes ('the curl of Berenike').

Using her striking appearance for political purposes, she adopted an unusual ship's prow crown to commemorate naval victories and also wore an anchor-shaped brooch; a connoisseur of perfumes, she wore them to great effect in the manner of her pharaonic predecessors. Far more than a decorative queen, however, Berenike was the first female Ptolemy to hold full kingly titles during her lifetime; named 'ta per-aat Bereniga', 'the pharaoh Berenike', and hailed as 'female Horus', she was clearly 'perceived as the equivalent of an Egyptian king. There could be nothing clearer than the idea of a female Horus.'

During her twenty-five-year reign she also produced six children, her two daughters receiving the same privileges and education as their male siblings. Following the death of one princess in childhood, the native priests decreed that 'a sacred statue for her, of gold and set with precious stones' should be set up in every temple, their classical equivalents featuring the veiled Berenike II mourning the child who leans against her knee, looking up in an Alexander-like pose of deification.

Such figures were erected within the colonnades of Alexandria's new Serapeum, 'adorned with great columned halls and statuary which seems almost alive'. The new temple contained royal quarters and subterranean chambers for the cult of Apis, the monarchs showing 'constant concern, combined with heavy outlay and expense, for Apis and Mnevis and the other renowned sacred animals in the land'. Equally generous endowments to the Great Library included the original scripts of the great Athenian dramatists, taken out on loan for 15 talents' deposit so that they could be copied and returned (until it was decided to keep the priceless originals and return the copies). In 235 BC, Berenike III's countryman Eratosthenes of Cyrene became head librarian and put forward the revolutionary suggestion that the earth was round. Calculating its circumference by measuring the distance between Alexandria and Aswan, he worked out its diameter to within 80 km (50 miles). He even calculated the length of the year, although his calendar of 365 1/4 days was dismissed by the Egyptian priests, who preferred their own 360-day year with five days left over as birthdays of the gods.

The relationship between crown and clergy gave the Ptolemies a direct line to their pharaonic past, and when the high priest Anemho II was appointed 'priest of the Royal Ancestors' a huge temple was begun at Horus' cult centre, Edfu, under his guidance. Intended as a shrine to the kingship embodied by Horus, 'the one who has his being before the ancestors', the new temple would allow the cumulative powers of the country's pharaonic ancestors to be drawn down into the hands of the Ptolemies. But only with the priests as intermediaries.

For in reaction to the Ptolemies' mass translation of Egypt's ancient wisdom into easily accessible Greek, six thousand new symbols had been added to the existing eight hundred to make the hieroglyphic script impenetrable to all but the initiated. Allowing the new temple to act as a huge ritual document, certain words were deliberately chosen for their alliterative effect when read aloud by the priests. So, the straightforward phrase 'offerings shall be made in your shrine, O Falcon, O you of the dappled plumage!' was vocalised as the tongue-twisting 'shespu er shespet ek shenbet sab-shuwt'. Warnings that the goddess 'Nekhbet stabs him who violates your inviolable soil' or 'shatat her shemy shash shaw ek shata' were accompanied by violent scenes of the pharaoh spearing Horus' enemies, declaring, 'I hold my harpoon! I drive back the hidden ones, I stab their bodies, I cut them up, I deflect their attack against Horus of the dappled plumage.'

This obsession with spearing, stabbing and generally annihilating the powers of darkness presented the king as the defender of the gods who in turn defended Egypt. And the gods were certainly receptive, for the Ptolemies had gained territory encompassing Egypt, Libya, Israel, Jordan, Syria, Lebanon, Cyprus, Cilicia, Pamphylia, Lycia, Caria, parts of Ionia in modern Turkey, parts of Thrace and the Greek Peloponnese and Aegean.

Having lived up to his Egyptian epithet 'strong protector of the gods and mighty wall for Egypt', sixty-two-year-old Ptolemy III died in the winter of 222 BC. He was cremated in ceremonies led by his widow and successor, Berenike II, who took her twenty-year-old son, Ptolemy IV (221–205 BC) as co-ruler. The new Ptolemy's title of Philopator, 'father-loving', was nevertheless at odds with his feelings for a mother whose public popularity was an obstacle to the ambitions of her wayward son's powerful courtiers. In a terrifying purge, Berenike II and her remaining children were all killed except for fourteen-year-old Arsinoe, spared for marriage to her brother after which they became the 'father-loving gods'. Although young Arsinoe III was also identified with Aphrodite and Isis, her portraits' permanently melancholy expression captured something of the trauma surrounding her accession and her brother-husband's long-term relationship with Agathoklea, daughter of Ptolemy III's ambitious mistress Oinanthe.

Sharing the new king's sumptuous lifestyle, Agathoklea and her brother Agathokles were a malevolent influence, for despite an unusually stable childhood and superb education Ptolemy IV was 'a loose, voluptuous, and effeminate prince, under the power of his pleasures and his women and his wine . . . while the great affairs of state were managed by Agathoklea, the king's mistress, [and] her mother and pimp Oinanthe'. Even the Spartan king Kleomenes, living in exile at court and a royal counsellor under the last regime, became 'an eyewitness of the sickness of the realm'. He was killed, and his flayed body displayed in public.

In 217 BC the Ptolemies faced crisis point when the Seleucid king Antiochos III took back Syria and marched towards Egypt with seventy thousand troops and 102 Indian elephants. In order to field an army of equal strength, large numbers of Egyptians were quickly trained in Macedonian tactics and seventy-three somewhat jumpy African elephants transported up the Red Sea coast in huge 'elephantagoi' ships. After following her mother's example by dedicating a lock of hair to invoke the gods, the slight figure of Arsinoe III addressed the troops – she is even shown wielding a spear in contemporary images – before the two forces clashed at Raphia on 22 June. Most surprisingly, the Egyptians won the day and, after taking back the whole of Syria, the victorious monarchs were welcomed home with great festivities. Yet as it began to dawn on the Egyptians just exactly where the power lay, serious bouts of internal unrest broke out in middle Egypt and spread to the Delta.

Nor were things any easier for the Ptolemies' allies in Rome. After the invasion by Hannibal of Carthage and his famous elephants they requested, and received, emergency supplies of Egyptian grain. In gratitude the Romans issued gold coins featuring their war god Mars and the Ptolemies' royal eagle, then sent a delegation to Egypt, 'taking presents to the king and queen to commemorate and renew their friendship'.

Although the ambassadors' gifts included a smart Roman toga for the king, this mode of dress is unlikely to have appealed to Ptolemy IV who, like his predecessors, preferred to emphasise his power through an ostentatious show of wealth. He paid regular homage to the god of the royal house, styled himself 'Neos Dionysos' (the new Dionysos) and had himself tattooed with the god's sacred ivy leaves; wearing an ivy wreath, 'carrying a timbrel and taking part in the show', he participated in rites which involved large quantities of wine.

Ptolemy IV modelled himself on Alexander – whose own involvement with the wine-fuelled cult was such that he has often been dubbed an alcoholic. It is therefore fitting that Ptolemy IV's greatest achievement, possibly begun by his parents, was Alexander's mausoleum. Built on the northern side of the Canopic Way, Ptolemy IV 'built in the middle of the city a memorial building which is now called the Sema ['tomb'] and he laid there all his forefathers together with his mother, and also Alexander the Macedonian' after exhuming their remains from the original marble tomb in the city.

It was also said that 'the Soma also, as it is called, is part of the royal district. This was the walled enclosure which contained the burial places of the kings and that of Alexander' (with Soma meaning 'body' and Sema meaning 'tomb'). All trace of both the body and the tomb vanished centuries ago, although it was said that the tomb was 'worthy of the glory of Alexander in size and construction'. Scattered evidence also suggests a tall, imposing structure, possibly circular and topped by a pyramid-shaped edifice; its subterranean burial chamber or inner sanctum would have housed the urns of Ptolemies I, II and III and their female counterparts Berenike I, Arsinoe II and Berenike II, interred beside Alexander's mummy within his gold coffin and stone sarcophagus.

The Sema drew down the ancestral powers of Alexander for the good of the Ptolemies in much the same way that the temple at Edfu brought together the powers of the royal ancestors for the good of Egypt. With work on the inner parts of the Edfu temple soon complete, a new temple to Horus further south in Nubia named Arsinoe III in its inscriptions. She was honoured for producing a son, the first Ptolemaic child to be born of a full brother–sister marriage. A rather pensive child who took after his mother, the boy, named Ptolemy, was made co-regent soon after his birth in October 210 BC. His status as an only child presumably reflected the fact that Arsinoe III is said to have regularly pleaded with her brother-husband to stop using the palace for his drinking parties. Yet 'his shameful philanderings and incoherent and continuous bouts of drunkenness, not surprisingly found in a very short space of time both himself and his kingdom to be the object of a number of conspiracies'.

In 207 BC Herwennefer of Thebes declared himself pharaoh with the backing of the Karnak priests, who set themselves in direct opposition to the Ptolemies and their priestly allies in Memphis. The south broke away and Egypt slid towards anarchy. By the end of 205 BC Ptolemy IV, not yet forty, was dead. His courtiers hushed up his death, murdered Arsinoe III and secretly cremated the couple, placing their matching silver urns close to Alexander in the tomb they had completed for him.

Their six-year-old son was now declared Ptolemy V and Agathokles and his family became his guardians, holding on to their power through intimidation and violence until matters came to a head when the imperious Oinanthe ordered her bodyguard to attack fellow worshippers who had cold-shouldered her. As the violence escalated, the Alexandrians responded and stormed the palace, seizing Agathokles and taking him to the Gymnasion law courts for execution. His sister, mother and remaining female relatives were likewise taken to the Gymnasion and handed over to the mob, where 'some bit them, some stabbed them, others cut out their eyes. Whenever one of them fell, they ripped their limbs apart, until they had in this way mutilated them all. For a terrible savagery accompanies the angry passions of the people who live in Egypt.'

As a succession of Greek courtiers now vied for power in Alexandria royal authority in the rest of Egypt ebbed away, and by 200 BC the Seleucid king Antiochos III had reversed his defeat at Raphia and, allied to Macedonia, was preparing to invade Egypt. Faced with this threat, Ptolemy V's ministers sent an emergency delegation to Rome asking for help. Having finally defeated their own great enemy, the Carthaginian Hannibal, the Romans were only too pleased to assist by attacking Macedonia, which initially fell to them in 197 BC.

That same year the thirteen-year-old Ptolemy V celebrated his coming of age by moving the royal capital away from Alexandria to the relative security of Memphis, much to the delight of the native priesthood. After royal troops took back Thebes, rebellion in the Delta was ruthlessly put down and its ringleaders condemned by their fellow countrymen within the clergy. The king then 'had them slain on the wood' in public executions at Memphis – no doubt they were bludgeoned to death with a stone mace in time-honoured fashion. This graphic display formed the climax of the king's traditional-style coronation which was finally held at Memphis on 26 March 196 BC some eight years after his actual accession. The high priest Harmakhis placed the red and white crown of a united Egypt on his head as Ptolemy V 'Epiphanes', 'the One who manifests himself', was named a 'god, the son of a god and goddess and being like Horus, son of Isis and Osiris', in direct reference to his parentage.

Then Egypt's native clergy and the Greek priest of Alexander came together to issue a joint decree declaring that Ptolemy V had established order and spent large sums on the temples and the 'sacred animals that are honoured in Egypt'. Written out in both Greek and Egyptian to be as widely understood as possible, copies of the decree were set up all around the country. The most famous version was set up in Neith's temple at Sais and later reused as building stone at Rosetta, became the means by which hieroglyphs were finally translated some two thousand years later.

The coronation was soon followed by a royal marriage after Antiochos III changed his plans. Instead of invading Egypt he requested an alliance, offering the teenage pharaoh his ten-year-old daughter Cleopatra and the whole of Coele-Syria ('Hollow Syria', between Lebanon's mountain ranges from Cilicia down to Gaza) as her dowry. When the couple were married in 194 BC at Raphia, Egypt gained Seleucid territory by marital rather than martial means.

The couple took the titles 'Manifest and Beneficent Gods'. Cleopatra I was named 'Female Horus' as her husband's equal, and even Rome acknowledged 'Ptolemy and Cleopatra, rulers of Egypt'. Known as 'The Syrian', the first Cleopatra to rule Egypt is said to have 'brought the only important intrusion of foreign blood' into the Ptolemaic house, being a descendant of the Persian Apama, wife of Macedonian Seleucus I, and having a mother from the royal family of Pontus in Asia Minor (modern Turkey). Yet inheriting neither her father's sharp features nor the 'ill-favoured looks and boxers' noses' of her mother's side, Cleopatra I had an attractive profile which was further enhanced by her adoption of Berenike II's Cyrene-inspired ringlets combined with the robes of Isis for the full goddess ensemble.

Following a daughter named Cleopatra, the couple's son Ptolemy was born as the royal forces ended twenty years of anarchy by retaking Thebes. Its priests fled to Nubia and the rebel pharaoh was taken prisoner but, on the advice of the Memphis priests, was pardoned to initiate reconciliation. As part of the same PR campaign the royal couple embarked on a state progress up the Nile, making personal appearances before their reconquered subjects before finally reaching Philae in the far south, where the priests formally congratulated them for their success against the Theban rebels and the birth of their son.

Remaining on good terms with the Romans, the royal couple also renewed their alliance with the Greek city states. At the formal banquet renewing the treaty, the main topic of conversation was the pharaoh's physical prowess and his ability to hit a bull with a javelin from horseback. Yet in his last years Ptolemy V became increasingly unpopular with his subjects, taking back financial concessions made to the Egyptians and seeking hefty donations from his Greek courtiers to fund a campaign against Syria. In the spring of 180 BC, still only twenty-nine, he was poisoned by his generals. The first of his dynasty to be mummified, and presumably interred within the mausoleum of Alexander and the Ptolemies, he was succeeded by his widow, the twenty-four-year-old Cleopatra I, who maintained the male–female dual monarchy by taking her eldest son, six-year-old Ptolemy VI, as her co-regent. Formally acknowledged as 'the Pharaohs Cleopatra the mother the manifest goddess and Ptolemy son of Ptolemy the manifest god', he took the Greek title 'Philometor', 'Mother Loving', and the pair were equated with Isis and her son Horus.

Terminating all plans for a campaign against her Seleucid relatives in Syria, Cleopatra I pursued a peaceful domestic policy and became a greatly loved figure. Her Macedonian name became a popular choice for children around the country: one proud new grandmother wrote to her daughter, 'Don't hesistate to name the little one "Cleopatra", your little daughter.' When she died suddenly in April 176 BC, aged only twenty-eight, Cleopatra I was honoured with her own clergy based at Thebes in contrast to the Alexandrian-based cults of her predecessors, suggesting that some in the royal city had not supported her pro-Syrian stance.

Courtiers swiftly married off the ten-year-old king Ptolemy VI to his slightly older sister Cleopatra II so as to prevent marriage to any foreigner with designs on Egypt. The young monarchs' advisers then recommended war on Syria where Antiochos IV, brother of the late Cleopatra I, was preparing to use his position as the monarchs' uncle to seize their throne. Then, to prevent him using the youngest Ptolemy as a pawn, the child was made co-ruler with his two older siblings in a three-way rule presenting a united front.

After invading Egypt in 169 BC, Antiochos IV swiftly took Memphis, placed his teenage nephew Ptolemy VI under the 'protection' of his Seleucid family, and had himself crowned co-regent 'following Egyptian custom'. Yet the Syrian pharaoh had a very short reign and would be mainly remembered for his outrageous parties at which he 'was brought in by the mime performers entirely wrapped up . . . when the symphony sounded, he would leap up and dance naked and act with the clowns.'

Following his coronation, this colourful monarch then marched on Alexandria where Cleopatra II and her younger brother had set up a rival monarchy, backed by the citizens who were able to repel Antiochos' attack. Needing Egypt and Syria to remain neutral while they reconquered Macedonia, a Roman delegation then arrived in Alexandria and, ordering Antiochos IV to leave Egypt at once, drew a circle around him in the sand and demanded that he agreed before stepping out. Left with little choice, he pulled out of Egypt on 30 July 168 BC, leaving the country a virtual protectorate of Rome. The Roman ambassadors told the young monarchs somewhat ominously that they 'should always consider the trust and good will of the Roman people the supreme defence of their kingdom'.

Under the theatrical-sounding epithet the three 'Theoi Philome-tores' (Mother-loving Gods), the trio of young monarchs Ptolemy VI, Cleopatra II and Ptolemy VIII worked together until famine started to cause widespread unrest and Thebes again declared independence. Marching south to deal with the rebels, Ptolemy VI was overthrown in a coup led by his younger brother Ptolemy VIII and the Alexandrians. Although ex-king Ptolemy travelled to Rome to put his case for unfair dismissal before their governing body, the Senate, it proved unneces-sary since the Alexandrians soon deposed the power-mad Ptolemy VIII and begged their former king to return. Yet, having seen for themselves how weak Egypt had become, the Romans ensured the kingdom remained divided by insisting that Ptolemy VIII should receive Cyrene while Ptolemy VI and Cleopatra II kept Egypt.

Resuming their co-rule, 'Pharaohs Ptolemy and Cleopatra, manifest gods' were keen to maintain relations with their Egyptian subjects: they took up residence in the royal palace at Memphis, received petitions at the 'window of appearances' and dined with the local elite. During a progress south in 156 BC they attended ceremonials for the Buchis bull in Thebes, carried out work at Edfu, Esna and Philae, and founded a new temple at Ombos (Kom Ombo). It was dedicated jointly to the crocodile god Sobek and Horus the Elder ('Haroeris'), and its sanctuary was partly paid for by the local garrison, demonstrating their loyalty to the popular royal couple.

Similar feelings were displayed by their Jewish troops after the couple gave sanctuary to the Jewish high priest Onias IV following the sacking of Jerusalem's Temple by their mutual adversary Antiochos IV. Ptolemy and Cleopatra gave him the ancient Delta site of Leontopolis (modern Tell el-Yahudiya, 'Mound of the Jews') and permission to replace an ancient temple of the cat goddess Bastet with a scaled-down version of the Jerusalem Temple. This clever move brought Jewish settlers into the vulnerable border region and harnessed their military prowess to guard the route to Memphis.

With military bases around the Aegean, the couple were held in high regard throughout the Greek world, although over in Cyrene their younger brother Ptolemy VIII continued to gain Roman support by leaving his possessions to Rome in his will; he even proposed marriage to a hugely wealthy Roman matron, but she turned him down. Becoming a father when his partner Eirene gave birth to his eldest son, Ptolemy Apion, the eighth Ptolemy was nevertheless written out of the Egyptian succession when his elder siblings produced children of their own, appointing their eldest son Ptolemy Eupator ('of distinguished lineage') as their heir and then, on his early death, his younger brother Ptolemy VII. Yet it would be the couple's two daughters who produced the future monarchs of the Ptolemaic and Seleucid houses in a family tree so complex that it is best described as a 'genealogical cobweb'.

After a determined Ptolemy VI finally took Syria he married his eldest child, Cleopatra Thea, to the Seleucid king Balas – who proved so ineffectual that Ptolemy VI annulled the marriage and accepted the throne for himself. Crowned at a great ceremony in Antioch, he then gave his daughter away for a second time to Balas' rival; Balas himself was soundly defeated by Ptolemy VI and his new son-in-law. But at the moment of his greatest triumph the forty-one-year-old Ptolemy VI, king of Ptolemaic Egypt and Seleucid Syria, was thrown from his horse and fell into a coma, only gaining consciousness to see Balas' severed head just before he died.

Although Cleopatra II immediately made her seventeen-year-old son Ptolemy VII co-regent, news soon reached Cyrene. So Ptolemy VIII invaded Egypt, his promise to spare the new king if Cleopatra II married him ending at the wedding feast when the young king was murdered 'in his mother's arms'. Then, in a mass purge of all those who had supported the previous regime, Ptolemy VIII 'murdered many of the Alexandrians; not a few he sent into exile, and filled the islands and towns with men who had grown up with his brother'. Inevitably Ptolemy VIII has been portrayed as a monster of epic proportions. His official title of 'Euergetes' or 'Benefactor' became 'Kakergertes', 'Malefactor', and although the Alexandrians also knew him as 'Tryphon', meaning 'the Opulent' or 'the Decadent', they usually called him 'Physkon', 'Fatty'.

Spectacularly obese and very short of stature, Physkon's unfortunate physique was on full display when receiving a Roman delegation in 139 BC. Having magnanimously refused his usual carrying chair, he had personally met his visitors at the harbourside to accompany them the short distance to the palace. Yet, far from being humbled in the presence of the pharaoh, the Romans were highly amused, declaring that 'already the Alexandrians have derived some fun from our visit. Thanks to us they're finally seen their king walking!' And instead of admiring the quality of royal robes made of the finest gauzy linen, his guests recoiled at the sight of a body 'utterly corrupted with fat and with a belly of such size that it would have been hard to measure it with one's arms'.

Following the removal of Rome's own monarchy almost four centuries earlier, its Republican ideals were completely at odds with the Ptolemies' opulent display, not to mention the make-up, perfume, wigs and jewellery which had long been favoured by Egyptians of both sexes. As the delegation reported back to the Senate, they had been 'astonished at the number of inhabitants of Egypt and the natural advantages of the countryside', adding that 'a mighty power could be sustained – if this kingdom ever found capable leaders'.

Yet for all his obvious flaws, Ptolemy Physkon realised that the future lay within Egypt. Whereas his brother had lived by Greek values, he promoted native culture by placing Egyptians in the highest offices and bringing the crown's relationship with the priests of Memphis to its ultimate conclusion with a dynastic marriage between church and state. As an internal matter ignored in the classical sources, Physkon seems to have married one of his younger daughters, Berenike, presumably born to a minor wife, to the son of the high priest Petubastis I who had crowned him at Memphis in 145 BC. And when Physkon's co-ruler

Cleopatra II gave birth to a son, they named him Ptolemy 'Memphites' to strengthen the ties with Egypt's spiritual capital. The lad then appears as their heir in wall scenes at Edfu temple, a place which was finally inaugurated on 9 September 142 BC in the presence of brother and sister monarchs 'the Two Horus'.

Yet co-rule with his older, more popular sister had never suited Physkon, and in a psychological masterstroke he replaced her not only with a younger model but with her own ambitious daughter Cleopatra III. When uncle and niece produced their first child on 18 February 142 BC, the same day that a new Apis bull was born, Cleopatra III began her blatant self-promotion as Living Isis to counteract any divine associations claimed by her mother.

Although Physkon married his niece once she had delivered the goods, the couple's attempts to neutralise Cleopatra II proved ineffective. She was determined to hold on to power which was hers by birth rather than marital status, and her popular support meant that uncle and niece were forced to accept their co-ruler in a three-way monarchy. Differentiated as 'the sister' and 'the wife' when appearing together, it was 'the wife', Cleopatra III, who proved the most productive for by 135 BC she had five children – the future Ptolemies IX and X and their three sisters Cleopatra Tryphaena, Cleopatra IV and Cleopatra Selene.

Fearing for her one remaining son, Memphites, as he approached adulthood, the forty-something Cleopatra II sent him to Cyrene before launching her solo bid for the throne. Following pitched battles around the palace, her Jewish troops and the Alexandrians finally ousted Physkon and his brood in 132 BC. Stripped of his titles, his statues pulled down, Physkon fled to Cyprus as Kleopatra II declared herself sole ruler of Egypt under the deeply provocative title 'Mother-Loving Saviour Goddess'. She had not only reverted to her former husband's title 'Mother Loving', but the 'Saviour' part of her title derived from the first Ptolemy in order to reveal her dynastic ambitions, for, as Physkon rightly suspected, she was going to recall fourteen-year-old Memphites and make him her co-ruler. So Physkon acted first, summoning their son to Cyprus where he killed him. He then mutilated his body and sent the pieces back to his mother, who displayed them to the Alexandrians to show what their former king had done.

Although Cleopatra II then reigned alone for a year, she fled to Antioch with the royal treasury when Physkon eventually retook Alexandria, killing her key supporters by burning them alive inside the Gymnasion arena. Yet, as widespread unrest once more broke out around Thebes, Physkon had little choice but to agree to a reconciliation and Cleopatra II resumed her official role as 'the sister' alongside her despised brother and daughter.

As part of their attempts to regain control abroad Physkon and Cleopatra III sent their eldest son, Ptolemy IX, to govern Cyprus. In Seleucid Syria they continued their game of dynastic one-upmanship against Cleopatra II, whose eldest child, Thea, had ruled here following marriage to three Seleucid kings. Having proposed to one, killed another and even shot one of her sons with a bow and arrow, Thea had reluctantly accepted her teenage son Antiochus VIII Grypus, 'hook-nose', as her co-ruler until it was suggested that he should marry Physkon's eldest daughter, Tryphaena, and make her queen. This time trying poison to kill her son and prevent the union, Grypus insisted that his mother drank it first, with fatal results.

Having lost four of her five children to her brother Physkon's ambitions – two of her sons murdered by him, her daughter Thea now dead and her youngest child her deadly rival – Cleopatra II at least had the satisfaction of outliving her detested younger brother, who died in his bed on 28 June 116 BC. She would have been unsurprised to be left out of his will: Physkon left Cyrene to his eldest son, Ptolemy Apion, and Egypt and Cyprus to Cleopatra III 'and whichever of her sons she would make co-regent'. In fact she preferred her younger, more pliable son, but her mother and the Alexandrians insisted that the elder became king. So, in a new three-way monarchy spanning three generations, the two Cleopatras, mother and daughter, were joined by twenty-six-year-old Ptolemy IX Soter nicknamed 'Lathyrus' or 'Chickpea', whose long curly hair was often topped by an eagle-skin headdress. But although the old lady had finally imposed her will on the succession, Cleopatra II died soon afterwards, having spent almost sixty eventful years on the throne.

Finally free of the two monarchs who had dominated her life and most of the second century BC, Cleopatra III became pharaoh, 'Female Horus' and 'daughter of Ra', her name always written before that of a co-ruler she was planning to be rid of, and the ancient sources admitting that 'we know of none of the kings so hated by his mother'. Yet Cleopatra III used all her children for political ends. With her eldest daughter Tryphaena finally married to Grypus of Syria, her middle daughter Cleopatra IV, who had been married to her brother Ptolemy Chickpea, was forced to divorce him when he became co-ruler, for their mother did not want her headstrong daughter as a rival. The furious Cleopatra IV then moved to Syria and married her cousin Antiochus IX, whose war with his half-brother Grypus and his wife Tryphaena soon had the sisters at war too. When Tryphaena ordered the murder of her younger sibling who was hiding out in a shrine of Apollo, her hands hacked off as she clung desperately to the god's statue, Antiochus IX took his revenge by sacrificing Tryphaena to the spirit of her sister, his dead wife.

Back in Egypt Cleopatra III still had one daughter left, the young Cleopatra Selene, whom she married off to Chickpea to create a triple monarchy of mother, son and daughter, with Cleopatra III always taking precedence. Chickpea and Selene produced several children. Chickpea concentrated on his religious duties as priest of Alexander and supporter of the sacred animal cults, and in 115 BC he travelled through his kingdom to celebrate the Festival of the Inundation at Elephantine. Seizing her chance to exchange Chickpea for her younger son, Cleopatra III claimed that Chickpea had tried to kill her. The mob went for him, and he only just managed to escape with his life. Forced to leave behind his sister-wife Selene and their children, two of whom seem to have been named Ptolemy, Cleopatra III was now free to rule with her obedient youngest son Ptolemy X, who emphasised his official title 'Alexander I' by borrowing his illustrious namesake's distinctive helmet with white feathers. He also took over the role of Alexander's priest from his deposed brother, at least until his mother fancied this previously male role for herself, even adopting Alexander's elephant-skin headdress. Although her use of traditional male attire followed that of her pharaonic female predecessors, Cleopatra III's presentation of herself on equal terms with a male king often resulted in overtly masculine portrayals, with some of her images so far from the feminine ideal as to appear decidedly grim.

Also taking over traditional male roles within Egypt's temples, it was she who stood alone before Horus at Edfu, while at the rock-cut temple of el-Kab she performed solo rituals under the extraordinary title 'Female Horus, Lady of Upper and Lower Egypt, Mighty Bull'. So not only was she now divine, she had defied gender 'to become both king and queen, both god and goddess', and was worshipped as the Living Isis Cleopatra-Aphrodite with no fewer than five personal cults. But her rampant megalomania was clearly too much for the Alexandrians who referred to her as 'Kokke', 'the scarlet one', a slang term for female genitals and surely the most unpleasant of all the Ptolemies' unofficial epithets.

Certainly her eldest son Chickpea had real cause to hate her. He had escaped to Cyprus with little more than his life but his mother had sent a hit squad after him, forcing him to flee to the Seleucid court of his brother-in-law Antiochus IX with whose backing he managed to retake Cyprus and plan his invasion of Egypt. Yet his relentless mother really knew how to twist the knife, gaining the support of the widowed Grypus by sending him her remaining daughter, Chickpea's abandoned wife Selene. It seems she even took away their two sons, together with a son of Ptolemy X. They were packed off by ship with all that Cleopatra III really held dear – her will, a vast treasure of coins, works of art, precious stones and 'women's ornaments' – to the safety of Asklepios' shrine on Kos.

Mother and son then faced each other in the so-called 'War of the Sceptres'. Cleopatra III's Egyptian land forces, led by the Jewish generals Chelkias and Ananias and supported by Ptolemy X in command of the navy, managed to defeat Chickpea and won back much of Syria. Yet within a few months of her greatest victory Cleopatra III was dead, just short of her sixtieth birthday, and said to have been murdered by Ptolemy X, her younger son. Ptolemy X now married his niece Berenike III, who took the dynastic name 'Cleopatra' on marriage to an uncle who very much resembled his notorious father Physkon. Although the tenth Ptolemy was so fat that he needed at least two people to support him, 'when it came to the rounds of dancing at a drinking party he would jump from a high couch barefoot as he was and perform the figures in a livelier fashion than those who had practiced them'. Much preferring his elder brother Chickpea, the Alexandrian Greeks dismissed him as 'Kokke's child'.

His relations with the Egyptians were very different, however, particularly since the royals and the Memphis priests were now related after 'the younger sister of the King Ptolemy men called Alexander' had married the high priest Pasherenptah. When their teenage son and 'half-Ptolemy' Petubastis II succeeded his father he was anointed high priest by his uncle Ptolemy X in Alexandria, and 'drank in the presence of the king. He [the king] handed out unto him the golden crook, mace, robe of linen from the southern house and the leather garment according to the ritual of Ptah's festivals and solemn processions. He [the king] placed his golden ornaments on his head according to the custom of his forefathers in the 17th year of his age.'

Clearly revealing the intimate relationship between the country's secular and religious leaders, Ptolemy X and Cleopatra-Berenike III paid regular visits to Memphis and granted increased privileges to many native temples, particularly Horus' temple at Athribis which the king himself described as 'a first-class and remarkable temple, one of the most ancient and most famous'. Yet the regular turnover of monarchs had caused such problems for the stonemasons that they began to leave the royal cartouches blank, and when rebellion broke out in Thebes yet again they abandoned work altogether.

The huge territory of Cyrene was lost in 96 BC after Ptolemy Apion had bequeathed it to Rome, and with the Romans right up against its western border Egypt's fortunes looked so bleak that Ptolemy X was deposed by his Greek troops in 89 BC and fled to the court of his powerful sister Selene. After her husband Grypus had been assassinated in 96 BC she had proposed to his half-brother Antiochus IX, and at his death made her twenty-year-old stepson and nephew Antiochus X husband number four. Then aged forty, she gave her young husband two sons, the last Seleucid kings, and now helped her brother Ptolemy X assemble a mercenary army and march back into Egypt.

Yet, unable to pay his troops, he had turned in desperation to his namesake, entering the Soma's subterranean burial chamber in Alexandria and approaching the mummy of Alexander. He then committed the most terrible act of sacrilege, for 'Ptolemy X Alexander I removed the gold sarcophagus of Alexander the Great and substituted one of glass'. When they found out that the precious gold coffin of their beloved Alexander had been melted down to pay those who had fought against them, the Alexandrians were so incensed that they drove Ptolemy X from Egypt, pursued him north to Cyprus and killed him in a sea battle.

With his younger brother killed literally on his doorstep, a jubilant Chickpea immediately set out to Egypt to become pharaoh for a second time. Celebrating a second coronation at Memphis, led by his nephew Petubastis II, he retained his daughter Cleopatra-Berenike III as co-ruler since she was, as even the Romans knew, 'extremely popular with the Alexandrians'. Then he turned his attentions to the ongoing rebellion in the south. Those still loyal to the crown were reassured that 'the greatest god, Soter the king, has reached Memphis, and that Hierax has been despatched with considerable forces to bring Thebes under control. We wanted to inform you so that you, knowing this, take courage. Farewell.'

Although the 'considerable forces' proved effective and Thebes was thoroughly sacked, the threat from abroad suddenly became very real when the Romans claimed that Ptolemy X had made a will leaving Egypt to them. Yet, immersed in their own problems, many Romans felt that anyone sent to Egypt as governor might prove a serious threat to the stability of their already shaky Republic. So, under the leadership of Cornelius Sulla acting as official Dictator, it was decided to let Chickpea carry on as king for now.

To keep a close eye on events, Sulla's general Lucullus arrived in Alexandria in 86 BC and was warmly received by Chickpea, who presented him with an emerald carved with the royal likeness. Housed in the palace guest quarters, Lucullus was so impressed by his rich and cultured surroundings that he began to acquire books for his own house in Rome and incurred 'great expenses in collecting Greek art', copying his master, Sulla, who had stripped out the Greek sites of Olympia, Delphi, Epidaurus and Athens to bring some much-needed, albeit borrowed, culture to Rome. Yet as the Republic disappeared beneath piles of eastern wealth, many Romans blamed its inevitable decline on 'loose foreign morals' and the 'filthy lucre' brought in from abroad.

This same foreign wealth had also come from Rome's war against Mithridates VI of Pontus, who had seized the island of Kos in 88 BC and taken the treasure of Cleopatra III back to his court along with her three grandsons. When Sulla came to Pontus for peace negotiations, one of these princes, the son of Ptolemy X, managed to reach Sulla's camp and, returning with him to Rome, became a most useful informant on all matters Ptolemaic.

Chickpea died at the age of sixty-one in 81 BC, leaving Cleopatra-Berenike III his sole heir, and Rome seized its chance to intervene. Exploiting the Ptolemaic tradition of co-rule between a male and female monarch, Sulla sent over his young protégé Prince Ptolemy to take the throne alongside his popular, albeit elderly, stepmother and cousin. Although the Alexandrians dubbed him 'Pareisactus', 'the Usurper', Ptolemy XI was fully entitled to the position of co-regent. But, clearly unwilling to be junior partner to a woman after so many years away from court, he murdered her after eighteen days' co-rule. As any adviser could have told him, this was not a wise move: in time-honoured fashion the Alexandrians stormed the palace, dragged the king to the Gymnasion and tore him to pieces with a violence not seen since they avenged the deaths of Berenike II and Arsinoe III back in 203 BC.

Then, despite the dubious claim that young Ptolemy XI had left everything to Rome in his will, the Alexandrians exercised their Macedonian rights in selecting the next king and sent a delegation to Pontus to offer the crowns of Egypt and Cyprus to the two remaining prince Ptolemies, the 'heir and the spare'. They were most likely the sons of Chickpea and Selene, but the Romans, wishing to bolster their own claims to Egypt, declared them illegitimate. Even if they had been born to one of Chickpea's minor wives, usually termed 'mistresses' or 'concubines' by a monogamous culture like Rome, such accusations were a nonsense in Egypt or indeed Macedonia, where the modern interpretation of legitimacy was not a prerequisite to royal office.

Regardless of Rome's opinion the newly appointed King Ptolemy of Egypt, a rather gaunt, hook-nosed individual in his mid-twenties, arrived at the end of 80 BC in Alexandria, a city he had not seen since infancy. In January 79 BC he married Cleopatra V Tryphaena, most likely a daughter of Chickpea and perhaps Selene, for the new couple were named 'the Father-Loving Gods' and 'the Brother-and-Sister-Loving Gods'. They clearly took this divinity very seriously, for whereas previous kings were addressed 'our lord the king', petitions to Ptolemy XII were headed 'our god and lord the king'. He also took the title 'Neos Dionysos', first used by Ptolemy IV whose Dionysiac skills were now displayed by the new king who played the pipes with such skill he was 'not a man but a piper [auletes] and magician [magos]', and was known as 'Auletes' (Piper), an honorific title in Dionysos' cult. Such musical abilities were greatly admired among even the military-minded Spartans, and music suffused Greek culture in much the same way as drama, which had also begun as a rite of Dionysos. Dramas were regularly staged by Auletes, dressed in flowing mantle, ivy wreath and small horns, and he expected those attending court to join in with him to pay homage to the god of the Ptolemaic house. Yet the Romans found such practices offensive, and, believing men should never dance or get drunk in public and should never wear anything less than proper male attire, the writer Livy voiced the opinions of many Romans who felt the Macedonians in Egypt 'degenerarunt' – 'have degenerated'.

Degenerate banquets aside, the first five years of Auletes' reign were comparatively uneventful, although there seems to have been some distance between the king and his cousin, the high priest Petubastis II, who certainly had a claim to the throne himself. Yet, since Auletes' claim was stronger, it seems that Petubastis II was content to observe the rightful order of succession, remaining the spiritual leader of the Egyptians from his power base at Memphis until his death in 76 BC. The accession of his fourteen-year-old son and successor Pasherenptah III seems to have brought about a reconciliation since he was invested as new high priest in a grand ceremony in Alexandria. 'The king himself halted his war chariot. He arrayed my head for me with the glorious chaplet of gold and all the genuine precious stones, the royal effigy being in its midst. I was made his prophet.'

Suitably empowered by his royal cousin Auletes, Pasherenptah III returned the favour with a belated coronation at Memphis at which Ptolemy XII Philopator Philadelphos Neos Dionysos was given the traditional Egyptian epithets 'Heir of the Saviour God, Chosen One of Ptah, the Image of Truth'. As the teenage high priest proudly announced, 'It is me who placed the uraeus [royal serpent on the crown] upon the king on the day of Uniting-the-Two-Lands for him and also carried out for him all the ceremonies in the Mansion of the Jubilee. It is me who conducted all the offices concealed from the public eye.' The same obscure sources then state that the royal family undertook a progress of their country before returning to a state banquet in Memphis where the king, 'with his courtiers, his wives, the royal children with his lordly possessions were sitting at meal and were spending a pleasant time while assisting at festivals of all gods and goddesses'.

Although Auletes and Cleopatra V Tryphaena had produced a daughter, Berenike IV, some time between 80 and 75 BC, reference to 'his wives' and 'the royal children' reveal that there were other women whose children were formally recognised as legitimate by the Egyptians, despite Roman claims that Berenike IV was Auletes' only 'legitimate' issue simply because she had been born to his first wife, Cleopatra V Tryphaena. Yet Tryphaena then fell from favour for some reason, since her name is omitted from official records after August 69 BC when a second daughter is known to have been born to a woman whose identity, age and even nationality are unknown.

And it is a mystery made all the more frustrating because that child was Cleopatra the Great.

PART TWO

3

The Goddess Comes Forth: Cleopatra's Early Life

It has been suggested that Cleopatra's mother, presumably one of Auletes' minor wives mentioned in Egyptian sources, was a noblewoman of Memphis' priestly dynasty. If so, it would certainly explain Cleopatra's deep understanding of both the native culture and its language. Yet with no direct proof for such an attractive suggestion, others have estimated that Cleopatra was 32 parts Greek, 27 parts Macedonian and 5 parts Persian. And despite intermittent pairings of brothers and sisters throughout the Ptolemaic line, in which morbid obesity and mental instability did occur from time to time, Cleopatra herself seems to have exhibited no such traits.

She shared her earliest years with her elder sister Berenike IV and three younger siblings – a sister called Arsinoe born some time between 69 and 65 BC, and two brothers, both named Ptolemy, who were born in 61 BC and around 59 BC respectively. The elder boy is known to have been placed in the care of a eunuch named Potheinos, who was his nurse ('nutricius'). All born to a mother or mothers unknown, Auletes' four youngest children were regarded as completely legitimate in Egyptian eyes and collectively hailed 'Our lords and greatest gods'. So, addressed as a 'goddess' ('thea') from birth, Cleopatra would have been well aware of her divine status, particularly on royal visits to the Soma where her father, resplendent in his official regalia of gold crown and purple cloak as Alexander's high priest, led the rites before the body of their fabled ancestor.

The family's status was also enhanced by blood ties with Pasherenptah III, high priest of Memphis, who acted as 'the eyes of the king of Upper Egypt the ears of the king of Lower Egypt'. His status as royal confidant was shared by Horankh, high priest of Letopolis, whose family had long intermarried with the Memphis priesthood and who was sufficiently supportive of Auletes to be called the 'god's beloved and friend of the King'.

Rewarded by generous tax exemptions, Auletes' priestly supporters maintained stability throughout the country. In a new wave of temple contruction, at Tanis, Medamud and Kom Ombo, a monumental pylon gateway at Edfu had been decorated with huge figures of Auletes smiting his enemies, together with companion figures of his sister-wife Cleopatra V Tryphaena, 'daughter of the sun god', later covered over after her apparent fall from favour.

To fund such projects, a depleted royal treasury compounded by recent bad harvests was partly refilled when Auletes re-established direct trade with India. He appointed a 'military overseer of the Red and Indian Seas' to deal with attacks by the Nabatean Arabs (from the region of modern Jordan), who resented that they were no longer required as middle men, and resumed the export of textiles, wine, glass and slaves from the Horn of Africa. Traded for spices, resins, precious stones, ebony, ivory and silk, and processed in the factories of Alexandria, such commodities were re-exported to the rest of the world for huge profits.

Yet such wealth made Auletes' kingdom even more attractive to the Romans, particularly since Sulla's protégé Ptolemy XI was said to have left Egypt to Rome in his will. When Sulla's dictatorship ended in 78 BC power came to be shared by three ambitious generals, Gnaeus Pompeius (Pompey) Magnus, Gaius Julius Caesar and Marcus Licinius Crassus. Crassus demanded that Egypt should be taken.

Forced to buy time and keep his kingdom safe from invasion with a series of well-placed bribes to various members of the Roman Senate, Auletes also helped fund Pompeius' campaign against Mithridates VI of Pontus. Mithridates suicide allowed Rome to strip his kingdom of assets, including the former treasury of the Ptolemies which Mithridates had originally seized from Kos. Such was the booty Pompeius brought back to Rome that the Senate awarded him a Triumph, a Roman version of the Ptolemaia festival but dependent on at least five thousand of the enemy having been killed in the conflict. Mithridates' widow and two daughters were paraded through the city as the climax of the triumphal procession, and the accompanying portrait head of Pompeius made entirely from looted pearls caused a public sensation. Conscious that he was being overshadowed in the popularity stakes, Caesar began to look for ways to compete with Pompeius who had not only assumed Alexander's epithet 'the Great', but even his distinctive hairstyle with its raised lock of hair over the brow, a feature that Caesar's famously receding locks could never hope to replicate.

Rome then turned its attentions to the once mighty Seleucid empire, whose widowed monarch Selene had sent her two sons to Rome in 75 BC to claim the thrones of Syria and Egypt as their birthright. Yet Rome had no intention of supporting any such claim: Pompeius was sent east to take Judaea with Auletes' financial support and Egypt was effectively surrounded, with Roman troops permanently stationed on its north-eastern as well as its western borders after Physkon's son Apion had handed over Cyrene in 96 BC.

As the piecemeal conquest of Alexander's former empire brought the Romans ever closer, the young Cleopatra would have grown up fully aware of the danger they posed to her family's future. Yet, as her father continued to bankroll Pompeius, she would also have witnessed how their inexorable advance could be halted by financial means. The traditional Ptolemaic display of wealth, exemplified by the lavish banquets held in Pompeius' honour, confirmed Auletes an easy source of cash, and as the handouts continued only fear of a Roman takeover prevented the Alexandrians from staging outright rebellion.

They were forced instead to vent their frustrations in sporadic violence. One eyewitness reported that when 'one of the Romans killed a cat and the multitude rushed in a crowd to his house, neither the officials sent by the king to beg the man off nor the fear of Rome which all the people felt were enough to save the man from punishment, even though his act had been an accident'. This event, usually interpreted as evidence that the Egyptians were a nation of animal lovers, takes a far more significant twist when set against the anti-Roman atmosphere of 60 BC.

That same year Pompeius, Crassus and Caesar formed the first Triumvirate, a three-way power-sharing arrangement cemented by Pompeius' marriage to Caesar's daughter. As effective rulers of Rome's Republic, they exploited Auletes' position to the hilt and in a 'cash-for-thrones' scam offered him the all-important title 'friend and ally of the Roman people' in recognition of his help in conquering Seleucid territory.

Although this was the closest thing to a guarantee that Egypt would not be invaded, the title came at a cost of 6000 talents which was most of Egypt's annual revenue. Given the series of low Nile floods leading to bad harvests, famine and strikes, the money could not be met through trade alone, and tax increases would have caused outright rebellion. Left with little choice, Auletes was forced to borrow vast sums from the wealthy Roman banker Gaius Rabirius Postumus in order to pay Caesar for the long-coveted title. Then when the Romans seized Cyprus from Auletes' brother Ptolemy in 58 BC, claiming that he had helped pirates disrupt Roman shipping, the proud ruler declined the alternative post of high priest and, preferring to die a king, took poison.

Having been unwilling to jeopardise his new and costly title 'friend of Rome', Auletes had refused to help his brother, and as the Romans seized Cyprus' treasury the Alexandrians finally rebelled. Exercising their ancient right to implement a change of monarch, they replaced Auletes with his eldest child, Berenike IV, and as co-ruler recalled Cleopatra V Tryphaena from 10 years' exile from court. Although later historians assumed she must have been another of Auletes' daughters and numbered her 'Cleopatra VI', it seems she was simply the fifth one returning to replace her brother and former husband Auletes.

Deposed in late summer 58 BC and fearing for his life, Auletes had fled both his palace and his kingdom, although he was not completely alone. For one Greek source reveals he had been accompanied by 'one of his daughters', and since his eldest, Berenike IV, was monarch and the youngest, Arsinoe, little more than a toddler, it is generally assumed that this must have been his middle daughter and favourite child, eleven-year-old Cleopatra.

Leaving Alexandria by ship, father and daughter sailed north and within a week arrived in Rhodes to a warm reception. The inhabitants were long-term allies of the Ptolemies and devotees of Isis. Their celebrated Colossus of Rhodes, a 120-foot bronze sculpture of the Greek sun god Helios with the unmistakeable features of Alexander, had been felled by an earthquake but 'even lying on the ground it is a marvel', which must have made a huge impression on the young princess.

Yet Auletes' main reason for visiting Rhodes was to meet with the Roman statesman Marcus Porcius Cato, on Rhodes en route to oversee the annexation and asset-stripping of Cyprus. Having summoned the Roman into the royal presence, Auletes was told that on the contrary he must go to Cato, who was then undergoing a laxative treatment of 'purging medicine' and seems to have received him on the latrine. For 'Cato neither went forward to meet him, nor so much as rose up to him, but saluting him as an ordinary person, bade him sit down. This at once threw Ptolemy into some confusion' as the living god of Egypt was reduced to holding audience in the toilet.

With little achieved, father and daughter travelled on to a suitably reverential welcome in Athens, a centre of culture and learning second only to Alexandria. Here the Ptolemies had long been worshipped as gods and their statues adorned the Acropolis. The royal visit of Auletes and his daughter was commemorated by an official inscription, and then they set out for Rome. By this time Rome had taken every other part of Alexander's western empire – Macedonia, Greece, Cyrene, Asia Minor, Syria and most recently Cyprus. Only Egypt remained, which Auletes was determined to get back at any price.

On arrival in Italy the royals were formally received by Pompeius, who reciprocated their support by offering them one of his sumptuous villas some 30 miles south-east of Rome among the wooded slopes of the Alban Hills. Presumably they would have paid at least one visit to the new temple of Isis on nearby Monte Ginestro near Praeneste (modern Palestrina) – the worship of Isis had already spread as far as Rome, where her temple, destroyed in nationalist riots in the second century BC, had soon been rebuilt on top of the Capitoline Hill, the city's most prestigious location. And even though foreign gods had been banned only six months before the royal visit, the people had restored them 'by force', since Egypt's deities clearly had a special place in many a Roman heart.

Although the city's brick buildings must have proved quite under-whelming to an Alexandrian, Rome's military power meant that the members of its Senate were now the world's ultimate power-brokers. They were lobbied and bribed by Auletes until his money ran out and he was forced to borrow more in his attempts to regain his throne. Cleopatra V Tryphaena and Berenike IV were just as determined to prevent his return and sent a delegation of one hundred leading citizens to put their own case to the Senate; but they were either bribed, threatened or some even killed on Auletes' orders before they ever got the chance. Then came a challenge from Pompeius' colourful rival Julius Caesar, who tried to have himself elected Governor-General of Egypt by popular vote. Failing to do so, he then headed west with a five-year command of Gaul, leaving Pompeius to dictate the pace in Rome.

As debate about 'the Egyptian question' rumbled on, with little achieved except increasing amounts of cash changing hands, a frustrated and bankrupt Auletes decided to cut his losses and in 57 BC returned east to Ephesus. Once part of the Ptolemies' empire and the wealthiest city in Asia Minor, Ephesus was an exciting, cosmopolitan place, home to the goddess Artemis whose original temple, burned down on the day Alexander the Great was born, was still being rebuilt when he passed through twenty-two years later en route to Egypt. Having taken a full 120 years to complete, her new marble temple dominated the approach from the sea. A sweep of marble steps led up to a multi-columned structure where Artemis' smiling colossus looked down, hands of ivory outstretched beneath gold-studded robes to receive a constant stream of offerings, from necklaces of shining pearls and polished amber to the plump testicles of bulls slaughtered on her altar.

In a temple populated by statues ranging from bronze Egyptian priests to marble Amazon warriors, a portrait of Alexander by his favourite painter Apelles, would have been admired by his Ptolemaic successors who wished to make their own offering. Auletes commissioned a pair of great ivory doors to embellish a temple considered one of the seven wonders of the ancient world. His daughter Cleopatra had seen four of these wonders by the age of twelve, from the Pharos lighthouse and pyramids in her own country to Rhodes' colossal Alexander-Helios and now Artemis' temple at Ephesus. Her personal connection with each confirmed both her own importance and that of her dynasty within the ancient world.

Her father's choice of temple embellishment may also have been a response to news that his sister-wife Cleopatra V Tryphaena and their daughter Berenike IV had completed his pylon at Edfu with 45-foot-high doors in Lebanese cedar encased in shining bronze. The inaugural ceremony was held on 5 December 57 BC. Yet this seems to have been Cleopatra V Tryphaena's final state appearance. Her death soon afterwards left Berenike IV sole ruler, and the news came through to Ephesus that she was actively seeking a husband as co-regent.

Disregarding her half-brothers, Auletes' two sons who were little more than babies, Berenike IV turned to the last of her Seleucid relatives, to Selene's youngest son who had unsuccessfully lobbied Rome for the thrones of Syria and Egypt some twenty years before. But his chance to rule Egypt at last was terminated by his mysterious death. Berenike IV's subsequent attempts to join with the other branch of the Seleucid house by marrying the grandson of Grypus and Tryphaena was blocked by Syria's new Roman governor, Aulus Gabinius, who declared it was 'not in Rome's interests' nor those of Auletes, who was bribing him too.

Becoming increasingly desperate, the Alexandrians tracked down a minor Seleucid royal whom they named Seleucus Kybiosaktes ('Salt-fish Seller'), but he was not to Berenike IV's taste and she had him strangled after a week. Not to be put off, they then produced a man named Archelaos who claimed to be a son of Mithridates VI of Pontus but was actually the son of one of his officers. Sufficiently adept to learn quickly from Auletes' modus operandi, he bribed Gabinius, reached Egypt and married Berenike IV, who fortunately for him seems to have been happy with her new husband. Yet Gabinius' superior Pompeius had other plans. Having defeated Pontus, and wanting Egypt's wealth for himself, he finally decided in Auletes' favour and ordered Gabinius to reinstate Auletes in return for 10,000 talents.

And so, in the spring of 55 BC, a triumphant Auletes and his daughter Cleopatra were met at Ephesus by Gabinius and his troops, the Gabiniani cavalry led by their twenty-eight-year-old commander Marcus Antonius (Mark Antony), who fell in love with the fourteen-year-old princess 'at first sight', according to later romantics. Flanked by their Roman troops, Auletes and Cleopatra marched south into Egypt and after Antonius had captured Pelusium advanced on Alexandria where Archelaos was killed in battle. Disregarding Auletes' orders, Antonius gave him an honourable burial, but 'in his rage and spite against the Egyptians' Auletes executed his own daughter, Berenike IV, and all her supporters. Total carnage was only prevented when Antonius intervened, for which 'he left behind him a great name among the Alexandrians' on his return to Rome. Most of the Gabiniani were posted permanently in Egypt to protect Auletes from the Alexandrians, if not vice versa; these tall, fierce warriors from Gaul and Germany adapted to life in the royal city and even married local women.

Sufficiently secure in his second term in office, Auletes re-established his reign with a traditional jubilee festival and a resumption of temple-building at Koptos, Hermonthis, Edfu and Philae. He also set in motion plans for a whole new temple complex for Hathor-Isis at Dendera, just north of Thebes; as the most senior female royal left alive, Cleopatra must have accompanied her father to lay the official foundation stone on 16 July 54 BC. Planned for the most auspicious day of the year, when the rising of Isis' star Sothis heralded the start of the Nile flood, the event also commemorated the divine Arsinoe II's rise to heaven, a potent gesture designed to entice both goddesses to bring forth the waters.

Despite previous poor harvests, Auletes had also managed to clear his huge debts to the banker Rabirius who had turned up in Alexandria looking for his money. Appointed Minister of Finance and kitted out in Greek dress to blend in as he went about his duties creaming off profits, Rabirius became so rich and so unpopular during his year in office that Auletes was forced to take him into protective custody. He then let him escape back to Rome, where he was immediately prosecuted for illicit gains alongside Gabinius. Both men were also accused of 'unRoman' behaviour because they had worn foreign dress. The Republican lawyer Marcus Tullius Cicero described Gabinius as a 'thieving effeminate ballet boy in curlers', while his defence of Rabirius rested on the fact that Alexandria was well known as 'the home of all tricks and deceits'.

Yet it was also the home of all culture and learning, and in the cultural renaissance which accompanied Auletes' second term, his four remaining children continued to benefit from a truly wide-ranging education. With access to the incredible educational facilities of the Library and Mouseion, home of cutting-edge research for the past two centuries, each of the children had his or her own staff: the elder prince Ptolemy was taught by his personal tutor Theodotus of Chios, while Arsinoe was taught by the eunuch Ganymedes.

Following her European tour, elder sister Cleopatra likewise resumed her education back in Alexandria, and of all the Ptolemies made by far the greatest use of it. Her Greek title 'Thea' meant 'sage' as well as 'goddess', and indeed Cleopatra's intellect was her most important quality for later Egyptian historians, for whom she was 'the most illustrious and wise among women . . . great in herself and in her achievements in courage and strength'. As 'the last of the wise ones of Greece' she was 'the virtuous scholar', the polymath monarch 'who elevated the ranks of scholars and enjoyed their company'.

Benefitting from her father's renewed patronage of the Mouseion and the emergence of several new philosphical schools, she attended the lectures of Philostratus and joined in philosophical debate, discussing the ancient pharaonic 'Ancestor Ritual' in which she described 'the dead lying in Hades, waiting for the waters of rebirth to come and revive them so they can be reborn and flower again in the springtime'. She may also have studied under the astronomer royal Sosigenes, and took an active interest in astrology and the new-fangled Zodiac introduced from Babylon.

Able to consult works in the Royal Library, which housed Alexander's personal journals and books including his copy of Homer's *Iliad* given to him by Aristotle, Cleopatra could have read the famous plays of Athens' great tragedians Aeschylus, Sophocles and Euripides in their original hand, thanks to the wheeling and dealing of her canny Ptolemaic predecessors. And although they had been told that 'there is no Royal Road to geometry' by the mathematician and royal tutor Euclid, his successors Katon and Photinus both dedicated their works to Cleopatra.

Following the family literary tradition, which included Ptolemy I's biography of Alexander, the tragic plays of Ptolemy IV and Ptolemy VIII Physkon's natural history of birds in the royal zoo, Arab historians claimed that Cleopatra too 'wrote books on medicine, charms and cosmetics in addition to many other books ascribed to her which are known to those who practiced medicine'. First-century BC Alexandria was a centre of medical expertise where the court physician Dioskurides studied plague, Apollonius researched the works of Hippocrates, and the gynaecological surgeon Philoxenus specialised in the treatment of uterine cancer. Cleopatra's experiments into foetal development, anticipating her future role, are said to have influenced the Greek doctor Galen. Toxicology was another area of interest for Cleopatra and, perhaps tutored by the pharmacologist Zopyros who Auletes employed to produce antidotes, she is said to have observed the effects of the various poisons used within the Gymnasion's execution ground and written up her findings.

Later sources named her 'Theosebia', 'scribe of the god' – all written works were believed to be inspired by Thoth, the Egyptian god of wisdom and patron of scribes. Her epithet may also refer to the fact that Cleopatra was the first Ptolemy to learn the Egyptian language known as the 'words of Thoth', which the god himself had invented. A linguist who could converse in at least nine languages, from the Ptolemies' familiar Greek to the languages of the Syrians, Hebrews, Medes, Parthians, Arabs, Ethiopians and Troglodytes, Cleopatra had a fluency in the Egyptian tongue which suggests that she may have had an Egyptian mother. She certainly had an Egyptian half-cousin in Pasherenptah III, high priest of Memphis, whose wife, Taimhotep of Letopolis, was described as 'a worthy young woman, skilled in speech, whose advice is bright'.

Although such talents would have been deeply unappreciated in most parts of the ancient world, the elite women of Ptolemaic Egypt enjoyed life in a society based on principles of equality which had long suffused the ancient culture. The Ptolemies' main guide through this culture was the native priest Manetho, whose comprehensive list of every pharaoh since the beginning of Egyptian history included many of the female pharaohs omitted from official lists, but now reinstated alongside their male counterparts as a direct result of Ptolemaic policy. It seems no coincidence that Manetho was working for Ptolemy II and his formidable sister-wife Arsinoe II, the first Ptolemaic female to take equal powers to her brother-husband and assume pharaonic titles.

Although Herodotus had claimed Nitocris to have been Egypt's only female king, Manetho knew otherwise. He listed a second as Scemiophris, a Greek corruption of Sobekneferu, who had changed the traditional king's title 'son of Ra' to 'daughter of Ra' and had worn the royal headcloth and male-style kilt over her female dress in an innovative case of royal cross-dressing. His third female king was Amensis, the Greek mispronunciation of the title 'daughter of Amun'

used by Hatshepsut, who succeeded her half-brother husband to rule as
regent for his son by a minor wife. With greater claim to the throne, she
ruled as king for a further fifteen years, re-establishing trade along the
Red Sea coast and initiating a huge building scheme which made Luxor
temple the place where each monarch united with Amun in a
programme of royal regeneration which included Alexander himself.
At nearby Karnak the golden tips of the pink granite obelisks she
erected flashed sunlight across the river to her multi-terraced funerary
temple at Deir el-Bahari, where scenes portrayed Amun impregnating
her mother made Hatshepsut 'his daughter in very truth'. She wished to
be buried with her mortal father in the Valley of the Kings directly
behind her Deir el-Bahari temple, and although her body was removed
from their joint tomb in ancient times, a mummy found elsewhere in
the royal valley was identified as Hatshepsut over a century ago.

Having drawn on the male garb, false beards and innovative titles
of her female predecessors, Hatshepsut herself was the role model for
Manetho's subsequent female pharaohs. The next was named
Acencheres in a garbled Greek version of Ankhkheperura, the throne
name of Nefertiti, whose masculine-style attire fooled many historians
into assuming that she was a he. Nefertiti became king in her own
right after the death of her husband Akhenaten, although the couple's
attempts to reduce the power of the Amun clergy caused these priests
to obliterate Akhenaten, Nefertiti and their immediate successors of
the so-called Amarna Period (c. 1352–1323 BC) from their official
records. So Manetho's evidence for a female ruler at this time was
presumably obtained from Thebes' rival Memphis. A hint that these
female rulers were still highly regarded in the northern capital is
suggested by the fact that Memphis' high priests continued to marry
women with similar names, from the high priest Neskedty who
married Sobeknefer and produced a daughter named Nefer(t)iti to the
high priest Horemakhet, wed to a woman named Nefer(t)iti who
produced a daughter with the same name.

Nefertiti herself was buried in the Valley of the Kings, most likely in
tomb KV.56 close to the Amarna-period tombs of her husband
Akhenaten (KV.55) and his successor Tutankhamen (KV.62), but
her body was at some stage reburied by the priests of Amun. Brutally
damaged around the face, it was placed in a side chamber of another

tomb, unwrapped and anonymous, in an attempt to ignore an identity that was too politically sensitive. In fact the entire Amarna period is generally interpreted as a cut-off point whose rulers were intentionally forgotten by succeeding kings.

Yet women of the Amarna dynasty continued to marry into the royal house, to kings from Horemeheb to Seti II, which explains the jewellery found in Nefertiti's likely tomb, KV.56, the 'Gold Tomb'. Inscribed with the names of Seti II and his wife Tawosret, the jewellery was not made for wearing since the rings were far too small for adult fingers and the royal names would have appeared upside-down when worn. So they were presumably votive offerings for an illustrious predecessor: the jewellery's motifs show Tawosret in the same formal pose adopted by Nefertiti, even standing in front of her husband to take precedence.

With a name meaning 'the Mighty One', Tawosret ruled as regent until 1888 BC before taking full kingly titles as 'Strong Bull beloved of Maat, Daughter of Ra, beloved of Amun, Tawosret', combining male and female in names modelled on those of her grandfather Ramses II, whose official dress she also adopted. During a period of civil war, her memory was attacked after her death, her burial in the Valley of the Kings plundered and her empty tomb left open in a final epitaph to the last female pharaoh for almost a thousand years. Yet even though her name had been removed from the official records on the orders of a male successor claiming to have restored order, Manetho still found evidence for 'King Thuoris' 'in whose time Troy was taken', placing his fifth and final female pharaoh within a timeframe familiar to his Ptolemaic patrons.

Having clearly learned much from her pharaonic as well as Ptolemaic predecessors, the bookish Cleopatra soon followed them in Auletes' plans for the succession. In a great public ceremony held in Alexandria on 31 May 52 BC he presented all four remaining children with the title 'Philadelphos', 'sibling-loving', although only the sixteen-year-old Cleopatra was named Thea Philopator, 'Father-Loving Goddess', when she became full co-ruler and her father's female counterpart.

Auletes' thirtieth regnal year was her first, so official documents covering mid-52 BC to mid-51 BC were dated 'the thirtieth year which is also the first'. The co-rulers' Macedonian-style marble portraits set up around Alexandria reveal the same gaunt face, wide Alexander-like eyes, prominent aquiline nose and rounded chin. The determined expression of one example identified as the young Cleopatra reveals a teenager who took her new role very seriously, with her Macedonian-style diadem worn low towards her face in the manner of a rather severe-looking Alice band. Yet her first official portraits had been made at Dendera, where work had progressed at such a pace that the subterranean crypts designed to house the temple treasury were finished and decorated within two years. Their walls were adorned with figures of the sixteen-year-old ruler Cleopatra, simply dressed in the finest linen robes and a plain broad collar necklace, the tall feather, horn and sun disc crown of Hathor-Isis over her long hair swept back behind her shoulders. The keeper of the all-important ankh 'key of life' symbol, which she held in one hand, she protectively raised the other to support her father as he made offerings to the temple's gods.

Stating in his will that Kleopatra should remain ruler at his death and that the position of co-ruler should be taken by her eldest half-brother Ptolemy, Auletes called on the Senate to ensure the stipulated co-regency was carried out. Yet as Rome's Republican government headed for political meltdown, Julius Caesar noted that 'one copy of the will had been taken to Rome by his envoys to be placed in the treasury, but had been deposited with Pompeius because it had not been possible to place it there owing to the embarrassments of the state; a second duplicate copy was left sealed for production at Alexandria'. And then, having proved the most tenacious of monarchs by clinging to the throne of Egypt despite spending half his life abroad, Auletes died in Alexandria in his mid-fifties. A partial solar eclipse on 7 March 51 BC dramatically marked his passing.

Cleopatra immediately suppressed news of her father's death to all but her inner circle. Her royal cousin Pasherenptah III was given the title 'prophet of King Ptolemy, justified', indicating Auletes' deceased status, and as he oversaw the funerary arrangements, the body underwent the traditional ten-week mummification process which, as always, would have been carried out in private. She herself continued to issue official documents in the joint names of herself and her late father, with no mention of her ten-year-old brother Ptolemy whose advisers, if they had known the true position, would simply have assumed power and ruled through him. She also knew that Rome would immediately intervene and force her to accept her brother as co-ruler, so the Senate only received official confirmation of Auletes' death on 30 June 51 BC, almost four months after the event.

Meanwhile Cleopatra had brought together her own group of advisers, whose seal rings would have been engraved with her cartouche and portrait to signify their loyalty. Encouraged by Pasherenptah and his fellow priests, she established her position as her father's true heir by continuing and refining his building projects at Dendera and Hermonthis. Her generous patronage of the temples would be a vital means of maintaining the loyalty of a native population who were heavily taxed for the first five years of her reign to keep her regime viable. So, to keep them on side, she decided to risk leaving Alexandria while her young brother's courtiers were still unready to challenge her, and travel south to make personal appearances before her Egyptian subjects.

On reaching Memphis, she would surely have made a state visit to the city's temple for some form of official recognition by Pasherenptah, and, despite there being no surviving record of her coronation, Cleopatra Thea Philopator was given the official title 'King of Upper and Lower Egypt'. Clearly the equivalent of a male king, she was named as 'Female Horus, the Great One, Mistress of Perfection, Brilliant in Counsel, Lady of the Two Lands, Cleopatra, the Goddess who Loves her Father, the Image of her Father', with a specially created title hailing her 'Upper Egyptian King of the land of the white crown, Lower Egyptian King of the land of the red crown'.

As a means of emphasising her direct link with the land, she publicly demonstrated this title by adopting the red and white combined crown of a united Egypt in place of the simple Macedonian diadem. Another traditional form of headgear which she favoured in appearances before her Egyptian subjects was the ancient crown of the earth god Geb, featuring Amun's ram's horns and the cow horns, sun disc and two tall feathers of Isis-Hathor. It reflected her status as 'daughter of Geb': Geb, being the father of Isis, was a means of underscoring Cleopatra's links with the goddess. Her use of both the crown and the title also linked her to three previous female pharaohs, Arsinoe II, Nefertiti and Hatshepsut.

Beneath such elaborate headgear, and equally essential to her power dressing, Cleopatra's hair was maintained by her highly skilled hair-dresser Eiras. Although rather artificial-looking wigs set in the tradi-tional tripartite style of long straight hair would have been required for appearances before her Egyptian subjects, a more practical option for general day-to-day wear was the no-nonsense 'melon hairdo' in which the natural hair was drawn back in sections resembling the lines on a melon and then pinned up in a bun at the back of the head. A trademark style of Arsinoe II and Berenike II, the style had fallen from fashion for almost two centuries until revived by Cleopatra; yet, as both traditionalist and innovator, she wore her version without her pre-decessors' fine head veil. And whereas they had both been blonde like Alexander, Cleopatra may well have been a redhead, judging from the portrait of a flame-haired woman wearing the royal diadem surrounded by Egyptian motifs which has been identified as Cleopatra.

Although her wavy red hair swept back in the melon-style bun and topped by the band-like royal diadem would be complemented by the simple lines of her Greek dress, Cleopatra's role within the Egyptian world would have required the assistance of her wardrobe mistress, Charmion, to create intricate costumes of ancient design – traditional-style, tight-fitting sheath-dresses of finest linen embellished by gold sequins, precious stones, beading and feathers. One of the ancient costumes particularly favoured by the Ptolemaic royal women was the iridescent vulture-feather dress; the bird's wings enfolded the torso and abdomen to offer symbolic protection to the area responsible for producing the next generation.

As a form of dress worn by figures of Isis herself, it was presumably adopted by Cleopatra when early in her reign she further underlined the links with her father by paralleling his title 'Neos Dionysus' with her own 'Nea Isis'. From then on, she 'gave audience to the people under the name of the New Isis' and 'appeared in public dressed in the habit of the goddess Isis', the traditional white linen worn by both goddess and acolytes covered with an outer layer of black to transform her into Isis 'the black-robed queen'. Her 'black raiment' was duplicated by her clergy, the Melanephoroi or 'Wearers of Black'. The Ptolemies' invention of mordants to fix dyed colours transformed ancient Egypt's off-white linens into the sea-greens, violets, hyacinths, flames and crimsons described in contemporary texts. Isis herself was imagined as wearing a voluminous black mantle over a 'many-coloured robe of finest linen . . . but what caught and held my eye more than anything else was the deep black lustre of her mantle. She wore it slung across her body from the right hip to the left shoulder, where it was caught in a knot resembling the boss of a shield; but part of it hung in innumerable folds, the tasselled fringe quivering.'

Although the Greeks worshipped the goddess as Isis, the Egyptians still knew her as Aset, whose name, meaning 'throne', evoked her role in maintaining the kingship. The Ptolemies had long realised this when invoking 'Isis the Great, Mother of the God, the Great One, the powerful, sovereign of the gods without whom no one accedes to the palace, it is at her command the king ascends the throne'. Isis' takeover of every goddess' identity had made her 'Myrionymos', 'the one of countless names', and this assumption of sovereignty over deities and monarchs alike allowed Cleopatra as Nea Isis to claim tremendous power over both the mortal and divine worlds.

As the most effective way of connecting with subjects who were largely illiterate and had little or no access to the formal portrayals set up within the temples, she would have appeared before them as a spectacular-looking yet instantly recognisable figure. Yet, far more than a silent icon upon a golden throne, Cleopatra spoke to them directly in their native tongue, the first monarch to do so since the last native pharaoh, Nectanebo II, three centuries before. Clearly this was no Macedonian, speaking only Greek to the Mediterranean world, but a true pharaoh who spoke directly to them as Egyptians in their land of the Nile. Her cause was their cause, and, by actively participating as goddess–monarch in rites which had for so long sustained their country, she secured their loyalty.

Cleopatra travelled on upriver, inspecting the rapid progress of work on the temple at Dendera. When she finally arrived at Thebes on 22 March 51 BC she became the first monarch in living memory personally to oversee the installation of the new Buchis bull, which had been born in Thebes at the end of her father's reign. Regarded as the earthly embodiment of the sun god Ra, Buchis was also sacred to the war god Montu and fertility god Min, both of whom were aspects of Amun. He represented these 'male gods united in a bull', his name Buchis simply the Greek version of Ba-her-khet, meaning 'soul on body'. The Egyptians called the bull 'the living spirit of Ra born of the great Cow united with the creator gods, he is Amun who goes on his four feet, the image of Montu, lord of Thebes, the father of fathers, the mother of mothers, who renews the life of every one of the gods'.

Selected at birth for specific markings on a white body and black head, Buchis, it was claimed, 'changes colour every hour and is shaggy with hair which sprouts outward contrary to the nature of all animals'. Covered by a beadwork net to discourage flies, he wore a golden crown of sun disc and feathers, and, with his horns gilded and eyes adorned with cosmetics, was liberally doused with ritual perfume. Fortunately for the monarch and those in close proximity, he was also fumigated with precious incense in ceremonials lasting three days and nights.

His installation ceremony would have been the perfect opportunity for the male gods within the bull to combine with Cleopatra as supreme goddess, their combined powers then being harnessed by the priests to restore the country's much-needed fertility. Given the ongoing low flood levels and famine, something rather extreme would certainly have been required to kick-start this process. Classical descriptions from Cleopatra's time describe a forty-day period of ritual incubation for each new bull when 'only women may look at it; these stand facing it and pulling up their garments show their genitals.'

Using their sexuality en masse to stimulate and balance this most overt manifestation of male fecundity was a practice that the Greeks called 'anasyrmenê'; it was something that Herodotus had observed among women's bawdy revels en route to fertility festivals. The sun god's daughter Hathor had employed this tactic to liven him up, and, to stimulate the sun god's hidden powers, royal women down the centuries had performed similar rites, from a topless Nefertiti being caressed by the sun disc's many hands to the 'Hand of god' priestess performing manual stimulation for her divine husband Amun-Ra, recreating the moment when the god 'took his phallus in his fist and ejaculated' to ultimately create the world. The reigning queen is also known to have starred in Egypt's ancient harvest rites alongside the sacred bull, dancing around the king with her arms upraised in imitation of cow's horns, before pressing her hands to her breasts. Then, to the priestly strains of 'Hail Min who fecundates his mother, how secret is that which you have done to her in the darkness', the sexual powers of queen and bull came together to create new life. Explicit references to the 'Bull who copulates with fair ladies' in the Coffin Texts (funerary spells inscribed on Egyptian coffins) were paralleled by Greek myths of the Minotaur, half-man, half-bull, born to the Minoan queen Pasiphae after her union with a bull. Even at the cultural heart of Greek civilisation, Athens' most ancient temple contained a sacred cattle shed or 'bukolion', in which the high priestess or 'queen archon' ritually mated with the bull of Dionysos. Zeus, King of the Greek gods, was even believed to take animal form to impregnate mortal women.

Although belief in the fecundity of the divine bull remained so strong in Egypt that as recently as 1851, local women still straddled one of the life-size statues of the Apis bull at Sakkara in their attempts to conceive, the act itself in ancient times involved penetration by divine heat or light. This might range from a lightning-type heavenly fire to 'generative light falling strongly from the moon', the celestial body identified with Isis whose horned crown linked her to the moon's lunar crescent. It seems, therefore, that some form of nocturnal ritual would have been required to activate the hidden powers of fertility during Cleopatra's three-day event at Thebes and Hermonthis.

Although previous bulls had been installed with little more than a perfunctory ceremony at Thebes, led by officials acting in the king's name, on this occasion Cleopatra was not only present in person but took an active part, bringing with her some of the famous Ptolemaic glitz she would employ for theatrical-style events throughout her reign. Following the preliminary ceremonials at Thebes, the Egyptian sources state that 'the Lady of the Two Lands, the goddess Philopator, rowed him in the barque of Amun, together with the royal boats, all the inhabitants of Thebes and Hermonthis and the priests being with him and he reached Hermonthis, his dwelling-place'.

This astonishing description of Cleopatra rowing the sacred bull along the 9 km stretch of the Nile from Thebes to Hermonthis would suggest considerable physical strength, since she would have had to row against the prevailing south–north current. Yet even if her role was simply a ceremonial one involving little more than touching an oar – in much the same way that official tree planting in our own times involves little more than waving a shovel while minions do the physical work – the event nevertheless reveals a clear understanding of Egypt's multi-layered mythology. For Cleopatra was re-enacting the legend of King Snofru, Egypt's greatest pyramid builder, who was worshipped for centuries after his death as the earthly representative of the sun god. In one story, he was propelled across the waters by a rowing crew of young women, priestesses of the sun god's daughter Hathor – a goddess inextricably linked with Isis, goddess of sailing par excellence and Cleopatra's alter ego.

So after the glamorous black-garbed teenager had boarded the golden boat of Amun and taken her place beside the great shaggy bull with its painted face and crown, perhaps reaching out to touch a golden oar to signal the start of the proceedings, the rowers themselves would have manoeuvred the sacred vessel out on to the water, accompanied by a flotilla of priests and local officials. As the local population crowded the banks for a glimpse of this extraordinary regatta, it was said that 'Hermonthis and beautiful Thebes were united in drunkenness and the noise was heard in heaven', and 'as for the ruler, everyone was able to see her'.

When the vessels finally reached the quayside at Hermonthis, a welcoming party of priests would have accompanied Cleopatra and the bull up to his new home within the war god Montu's magnificent temple. Purified with sacred water and incense, Cleopatra would have performed the necessary rites before Montu, Buchis' mother the sacred cow, and finally Buchis himself, whose anthropomorphic, Minotaur-like figure on the temple's wall scenes suggests that his part was played by a masked priest. There was even a sound-bite from Cleopatra herself, announcing, 'I adore thy majesty and give praise to your soul, O great god, self created', recorded in a small vertical column of text placed between the figures of god and ruler.

Yet there was still no mention of her supposed co-ruler and brother Ptolemy XIII in any of the Hermonthis events of late March 51 BC, and he was also missing when Wennefer, chief priest of Isis the Great, erected a Greek stela (inscribed stone slab) in the Fayum's Arsinoite region on 2 July 'on behalf the female king [basilissa] Cleopatra, goddess Philopator'. Presenting offerings to the seated Isis feeding her son Horus, Cleopatra was shown as sole ruler here too, this time as a traditional pharaoh with double crown, stiffened linen kilt and flat, bare torso in a form of female monarchy not seen for more than a thousand years.

She was again named sole ruler on a document dated 29 August 51 BC and this seems to be how things remained for the first eighteen months of her reign. Although Rome did not pose an immediate threat on account of its own internal problems, it was certainly a difficult time for Egypt when resources were at full stretch. Having inherited no money from her father, a series of low Nile floods and bad harvests had forced her to bring in a period of heavy taxation which only her strong relationship with priests and people prevented from turning into rebellion. Yet, combining tax revenues with the profits from ongoing foreign trade, Cleopatra was eventually able to recoup around 12,500 talents per year, demonstrating a skill for wealth creation which equalled if not exceeded the fiscal achievements of her Ptolemaic predecessors.

Yet her brother's advisers remained as determined as ever to remove her from sole power, and his former nurse Potheinus and tutor Theodotus joined forces with the Egyptian military commander Achillas to launch a coup. Despite a lack of detail, the unlikely combination of temple architecture and documents dealing with bean cargoes gives clues to a likely scenario, since recent examination of a Zodiac scene from Dendera temple has revealed a portrayal of the night sky as it appeared in August 50 BC. Cleopatra is likely to have travelled south to inaugurate this spectacular piece of innovative carving, and her absence may well have been used as the perfect opportunity to demote her.

It would have taken little effort to convince the Alexandrians that Auletes' daughter spent far too much time with her Egyptian subjects while neglecting them, and, as food shortages led to rationing in the royal capital, Ptolemy's advisors had managed to gain control of food supplies by 27 October 50 BC, depriving Cleopatra's supporters in the rest of Egypt. All wheat and pulse cargoes were to be diverted to the great warehouses of Alexandria 'on pain of death' by order of Ptolemy XIII and Cleopatra, who now was named second. Official documents naming 'Pharaoh

Ptolemy and Pharaoh Cleopatra, the gods who love their father', were also dated to 'year 1 which is also year 3', as Ptolemy placed his first year as king in prime position.

Yet, regardless of these ongoing difficulties in her power struggles with her brother's faction, Cleopatra did not forget her responsibilities to the native religion. When the Apis bull died at Memphis in her third regnal year, 49 BC, she funded the funeral rites and paid 412 silver coins to cover votive offerings for the bull's spirit and supplies of food for its clergy. Thousands of people from all walks of life came together at Memphis' great cemetery Sakkara as the bull's great body was taken from its golden stall, washed and cleansed in a tent of purification, then transferred to the house of embalming within the temple complex. Accompanied by the dirges of mourners who held a constant vigil outside, the body was placed on a great limestone embalming table for evisceration. After forty days drying out beneath natron salts the carcass was anointed and wrapped in best-quality linen from the temples of the Fayum, with specific amulets inserted into the wrappings at key points. Then, laid out in an unnatural kneeling position, the bull was lowered into its coffin.

As one of the priests of the god Ptah who apparently undertook the bull's embalming went outside and tore a cloth to signal to the faithful to intensify their grief, the coffin was brought out in procession on a heavy golden barque, pulled along to its Serapeum tomb by the country's highest officials and accompanied by two priestesses representing Isis and her sister-goddess Nephthys. A tantalising hint that Cleopatra herself may once again have taken a direct role as Isis in the sacred bull cult is possibly revealed by an uninscribed limestone stela portraying the mummified Apis mourned by Isis and Nepthys. Although the fact that Isis wears the red crown of northern Egypt has previously been dismissed as a sculptor's mistake, it seems equally possible that this was meant to show Cleopatra as Living Isis, appearing in public ceremonials and wearing the red crown to symbolise her determination to keep hold of the region it represented. Although her presence at such rituals ensured native support, she remained locked in a vicious power struggle against her brother's advisers in Alexandria. In Rome too, matters had reached crisis point and the fall-out would soon reach Egypt.

Julius Caesar had by now returned from his long absence in Gaul to challenge Pompeius' supremacy. No longer connected by marriage, the two men began to form new alliances, appointing relatives and supporters to key government posts. In Caesar's case these appointees included the young Marcus Antonius, who 'grew up a very beautiful youth' and became 'the firebrand and tornado of the age' but had been forced to flee Rome to escape his debtors. After studying in Athens and Rhodes, he had been taken on by Gabinius as cavalry commander in Antioch. Setting out from here to Ephesus and his first meeting with the teenage Cleopatra in 55 BC, he had made a great name for himself in Alexandria before returning west to serve with Caesar in Gaul. His youthful looks, much admired by at least one tribune and most of Rome's female population, were matched by his 'gladiatorial strength' – one of the few positive things Cicero could find to say about him during a long-standing feud initiated by Cicero's execution of Antonius' childhood guardian following a political conspiracy, but temporarily patched up by Caesar to maintain political harmony.

As the arms race between Caesar and Pompeius spiraled out of control, the Senate ordered both to give up their powers. When Pompeius failed to respond, Caesar decided to force the issue and march on Rome. Leaving his Italian HQ at Ravenna on the night of 10 January 49 BC, he ordered offerings for the gods to counter fears that they were about to invade the homeland, then led a single legion across the River Rubicon, sacred boundary between Gaul and Italy and the point at which all campaigning generals were required to disband their forces. Once over the border, they met up with Antonius who had managed to escape from Rome disguised as a slave after his support for Caesar had proved unpopular.

As Caesar began his rapid advance on Rome, Pompeius' indecision was taken for weakness and the Senate refused him the post of commander-in-chief of Rome's forces. Although these far outnumbered those of Caesar, the speed of his invasion had taken everyone off guard, and as Pompeius made a tactical withdrawal south to Campania, many senators, mindful of previous civil wars, kept a low profile. Yet Caesar decided against mass executions of his political opponents, and adopting the novel approach of leniency explained that 'this is a new way of conquering, to strengthen one's position by kindness and generosity'.

Not only a superb general in the mould of his hero Alexander, Caesar was also a gifted writer whose *Commentaries on the Civil War* covering the events of 49–47 BC were published in annual instalments. He wrote as he spoke, in the style of an official communiqué, and even Cicero was forced to admit that 'Caesar wrote admirably: his memoirs are cleanly, directly and gracefully composed, and divested of all rhetorical trappings.' He also kept official transcripts of Senate meetings, public gatherings and key political speeches; fascinated by the politics of past regimes, he was keenly aware of history and his own place within it, using his writing to answer critics who claimed that his ambition alone had destroyed the Republic.

When Caesar failed to bring Pompeius and the Senate into discussions he lost patience, stating, 'I earnestly invite you to join with me in carrying on the government of Rome. If, however, timidity makes you shrink from the task I shall trouble you no more. For in that case I shall govern it myself.' Rome was on the brink of civil war.

In order to take Caesar on, Pompeius went east to build up his forces: once again he requested military support from Egypt, sending his eldest son Gnaeus to the brother and sister monarchs in Alexandria. Later Roman sources hinted at a romantic liaison between Cleopatra and Pompeius's son, although friendly relations had probably begun in their childhood when Auletes and Cleopatra had been Pompeius' guests in Rome. So to honour this debt of guest-friendship Cleopatra and Ptolemy contributed five hundred Gallic and Germanic cavalry from the Gabiniani and a squadron of sixty warships to be used against Caesar, the man who had once tried to take Egypt from their father.

While Pompeius gained ground in the east, Caesar did so in the west. After taking Spain he crossed to North Africa to tackle Pompeius' other African ally, King Juba I of Numidia (Algeria). Although Juba had supplied Pompeius with the grain that Rome needed to feed its growing population, many Romans regarded him as a sadistic barbarian who had defeated two Roman legions and executed the survivors.

By the summer of 49 BC, the power balance in Egypt had shifted yet again. Cleopatra was no longer co-ruler and had been deposed by her brother's courtiers, who declared Ptolemy XIII sole monarch. His former nurse Potheinos promoted himself to minister of finance to get his hands on Egypt's purse-strings. And within a couple of months, the duplicitous Pompeius personally recommended that his remaining colleagues in the Senate should formally thank Ptolemy XIII for his military help and recognise him as Egypt's sole legitimate ruler.

Unwanted by the Alexandrians and officially unrecognised by Rome, 'pharaoh Cleopatra' was nevertheless still recognised by the Egyptians. After retreating south to her loyal supporters around Thebes and their powerful military commander, Kallimachos, she seems to have travelled across the Eastern Desert to the Red Sea. Leaving Egypt at the beginning of 48 BC, she 'took up residence in Arabia and Palestine' where her ability to speak Hebrew and Aramaic helped her plan her strategy. A court was established in Askalon, near Gaza, where she built up an army paid for with coins from the Askalon mint. Her coin portraits show her wearing a characteristic melon hairstyle and diadem and reveal a careworn, rather gaunt face with deep-set eyes, a very aquiline nose, a rounded chin and a bowed lower lip. All these features bore a striking similarity to her father, Auletes, with something of the dynasty's founder, Ptolemy I; Cleopatra's masculine-style coin images were purposely designed to show her as a capable successor to such men as she prepared to do battle and retake the throne.

Caesar likewise had been busy. In order to take the war to Pompeius he sailed east to Greece in January 48 BC to join Antonius, then marched on Pompeius' base at Dyrrhachium. Although rations ran so low that Caesar's troops were forced to eat bread made of grass as he led parties of raiders in disguise across the enemy lines, Pompeius failed to follow up his victories in their sporadic encounters. This left Caesar free to face him again.

At Pharsalus on 9 August, in blazing heat, Caesar prayed to his ancestor Venus, Greek Aphrodite, whose armed image he always wore on a ring. Promising her a great temple if she brought him victory, his rousing battle-cry of 'Victrix' carried the day. Although he rode up and down the lines ordering his men to kill as few of the enemy as possible, fifteen thousand of Pompeius' men still died, with another twenty thousand surrendering and Pompeius himself only just managing to escape.

As the largest battle ever fought between Romans, Pharsalus was also one of the most decisive in history, making Caesar the master of Rome and gaining him many new 'friends'. After taking on to his staff two staunch Republicans, Gaius Cassius Longinus and Lucius Junius Brutus, son of Caesar's long-term mistress Servilia, Caesar went east to Anatolia to find money to pay his victorious troops. In Ephesus, he made a point of leaving Artemis' rich temple treasury intact and in return received the title 'Manifest God', 'descended from Ares [Roman Mars] and Aphrodite [Venus] and Saviour of Mankind'. Caesar's progress was reported to Cleopatra down the coast at Askalon, where she no doubt rejoiced at news of Pompeius' defeat. Caesar's reaction to divine honours would have given her a real insight into the character of a man happy to exploit a divine persona to further his political ends.

His desire to emulate his hero Alexander gave them further common ground, and when he travelled on to Troy for another PR opportunity he paid homage to his ancestors the Trojan Prince Aeneas and the goddess Venus. For as he had said himself, his family 'reckon descent from the goddess Venus' and 'can claim both the sanctity of kings who reign supreme among mortals, and the reverence due to gods, who hold even kings in their power'. Echoing Alexander's own beliefs, this was clearly someone with whom Cleopatra could do business. So she sent him a detailed report of her own situation and told him she was about to take back her throne by force of arms.

Her brother's ally, Pompeius, had been defeated. The Nile flood, on which Egyptian agriculture was dependent, had failed again. Since the amount of water was seen as a measure of the gods' goodwill, the fact that these were the lowest levels ever recorded made great propaganda. The return of Living Isis would restore divine favour. All things considered, it was the perfect time to launch her invasion. She set out at the head of her army on the six-day march south to the Egyptian border.

Ptolemy's advisers Potheinos and Theodotus encouraged the fourteen-year-old pharaoh to go to meet her, dressed in his golden armour and military cloak woven with the images of gods and ancestors. He was accompanied by his general Achillas and the Gabiniani among a force of twenty thousand men. After arriving at Mount Kasios, some 30 miles east of Pelusium, Ptolemy's army set up camp on the sandy mounds to await Cleopatra. Then, as sister and brother finally faced each other on 28 September 48 BC and prepared for hostilities, a small flotilla of Roman ships appeared off the coast, carrying the defeated general Pompeius, his wife Cornelia, their youngest son and two thousand men who had remained loyal. True to form, a cash-strapped Pompeius had returned to his usual source, seeking help from his ally Ptolemy XIII of Egypt.

His arrival was greeted with little enthusiasm. Not only were the royal coffers close to empty, but Ptolemy's advisers had no desire to be placed at a disadvantage with the victorious Caesar, already in the east. And there was always the real possibility that the Gabiniani troops might go over to their former general and weaken Ptolemy's forces against Cleopatra. Deciding that 'a dead man cannot bite', Potheinos and Theodotus agreed that Pompeius' elimination would placate his enemy Caesar, who would then return to Rome, grateful to the Egyptian king, who would be allowed to remain in power.

So as Pompeius' ship pulled close to land, Ptolemy XIII granted his formal request to land and waited in full military regalia, watching as Achillas and two Roman officers of the Gabiniani were sent over to row him ashore. As he climbed down into their boat, Pompeius recognised one of the officers as having served under him – although his greetings were cut short when the same man stabbed him in the back. Ptolemy then ordered that Pompeius should be beheaded, his body cremated on the beach and his severed head embalmed to preserve it. After seizing most of Pompeius' fleet, Achillas remained with the troops in Pelusium to keep Cleopatra at bay while Ptolemy returned to Alexandria with Pompeius' head to await Caesar's arrival.

They did not have long to wait. Just a few days later the general, distinctive in his purple cloak, arrived off the coast of Alexandria with a small fleet and a modest force of four thousand. Hoping to catch up with the defeated Pompeius and extend his famous clemency, Caesar too needed money, claiming that Auletes' heirs still owed him 6000 talents. In an attempt to discourage him from landing, Theodotus sailed out to meet him with Pompeius' head as a gift – the presentation of a relative's body parts to make a political point had long been part of the Ptolemies' modus operandi. But Caesar was appalled. Although he later wrote with characteristic detachment that 'he learns of the death of

Pompeius', he was seen to be so overcome with grief at the time that he wept openly, for, regardless of recent battles, the severed head before him belonged to his son-in-law and the father of his short-lived grandchild. His genuine feelings for Pompeius were also revealed by the fact that he took the head from Theodotus and kept it safe until such time as he could give it appropriate burial ashore.

This was certainly not the reaction Theodotus was expecting. Much to his alarm and that of Potheinos, who was watching closely from the shore, Caesar reverted to his official status and, declaring his intention to carry out his duty as executor of Auletes' will, proceeded to disembark. Mindful of how this might appear to the famously volatile Alexandrians now lining the harbourside, he decided against a show of force and took only a small group of officers led by the two lictors carrying the fasces, the bundles of axes and reeds that served as traditional symbols of consular office.

Stirred up by Potheinos, the crowds assumed that Caesar was asserting Rome's power over their territory and started to grow restless. Then, 'undaunted, with looks that ever masked his fears', Caesar brazened it out and made for the nearby palace quarter within which lay the fortified Inner Palaces and the home of the monarchs themselves. Stretching for half a mile or so along the breezy seafront, this 'amazing building complex comprised multiple colonnaded courts of different shapes and dimensions' that marked the way each generation had added their own personal palace. Passing through its adjoining administrative buildings, Caesar finally reached the guest quarters and took up residence.

Posing as simply another Roman tourist doing the sights, he nonchalantly viewed the Library and Museum and 'visited the temples of the gods and the ancient shrines of divinity which attest the former might of Macedonia. No thing of beauty attracted him, neither the gold and ornaments of the gods, nor the city walls; but in eager haste he went down into the vault hewn out for a tomb. There lies the mad son of Macedonian Philip', this description of Alexander by a Republican sympathizer revealing he was hated almost as much as Caesar for their shared imperial ambitions.

But Caesar's real reason for visiting Alexander's city was to settle the Ptolemies' dynastic dispute to the best advantage of Rome and himself, so he ordered brother and sister to dismiss their armies and appear before him. Retaining his forces at Pelusium to keep Cleopatra at bay, Ptolemy XIII arrived with the customary pharaonic splendour and accompanied by the ever-present Potheinos. Ptolemy informed the Roman general that his sister had taken power for herself, then raised an army against him, so had forfeited all rights to the throne and left him sole ruler. Caesar then pointed out that any successor of Auletes still owed him 6000 talents, at which point Potheinos, in his role as treasurer, intervened to suggest that Caesar must surely have more pressing business elsewhere. The Roman was unimpressed with Potheinos' insolence, particularly in light of his role in Pompeius' murder. Potheinos for his part resented the challenge to his behind-the-scenes authority and made sure the Alexandrians continued their hostility, even ordering royal meals to be served on the poorest-quality tableware to imply that Caesar had stolen all the gold and silver plate.

Surrounded by the Alexandrians within the confines of the Palace quarter, Caesar then waited for Ptolemy's former co-ruler. Although she had already written to him, Cleopatra wanted to plead her own case in person. But she realised she would have to take great care if she were to make her way through the city without being recognised and avoid the guards whom Potheinos had stationed all around the palace to prevent her reaching Caesar alive. Yet against overwhelming odds, the twenty-two-year-old managed to pull off one of the most daring wartime missions ever staged, successfully crossing enemy lines with the greatest panache.

4

A Veiled Proposal: Cleopatra Meets Caesar

Having dismissed her troops at Pelusium, Cleopatra left camp for Alexandria in the company of a Sicilian courtier named Apollodorus, whose title, 'Philos', was the official Macedonian term for a high-ranking confidant. With the presence of her brother's troops making an approach by land impossible she decided to take to sea, travelling west along the Delta coast towards the Pharos lighthouse. Reaching Alexandria's Great Harbour under cover of darkness, her small vessel with Apollodorus at the helm attracted little attention. As the boat approached the steps of the royal harbour beside the palace she concealed herself to avoid her brother's guards.

According to the famous version of events related by the first-century AD Greek historian Plutarch, Cleopatra 'was at a loss at how to get in undiscovered' until she hit upon the idea of stretching herself full-length on a carpet which Apollodorus rolled up, tied and carried in to Caesar. Her 'piquant wrapper' has been imagined by some to have been nothing less than a full bale of oriental rugs; other translations have suggested an alternative mode of transport after 'she thought of putting herself into the coverlet of a bed and lying at length, whilst Apollodorus tied up the bedding and carried it on his back through the gates to Caesar's apartments'. This has been interpreted as some sort of 'linen bag of the kind used to carry carpets' or a 'bed-linen sack'. Certainly, a brilliantly staged piece of political daring has been reduced to little more than knockabout comedy. Yet it seems somewhat unlikely that a pharaoh of Egypt and living goddess would allow herself to be rolled up, trussed up and manhandled in such a manner, or indeed that the sudden appearance of a late-night carpet salesman touting for business around the palace would fail to raise suspicion from a guard already on high alert.

It may be that confusion was caused by the way ancient bedlinen doubled as clothing – the Greek word 'himation' refers to a piece of material used as a bedsheet, wrapped around the body on waking to form the standard outer garment worn by both sexes throughout the day. In similar fashion, cloaks were often used as blankets and 'coverlets and bedclothes were considered as clothing by the Romans'. The scenario of a heavily cloaked Cleopatra would certainly seem to make far more sense in the context of first-century BC Alexandria, where the fashion for heavy drapery would have formed the perfect disguise – particularly since the himation and more tent-like pharos mantle were often used by women to cover the face in public. By no means a recent invention, face veiling dates back thousands of years. Although never used by the ancient Egyptians, it was a widespread custom amongst elite women from Assyria in the east right through to the Greek colonies of Asia Minor and even in Athens. In Cleopatra's day it was standard practice for Greek women: 'they wrap their heads in their himatia such that the garment seems to cover the whole face like a little mask; the eyes alone peep out; all the other parts of the face are covered by the mantles'. It was a form of dress imposed by husbands who wanted to hide their possessions from other men; one second-century BC Roman consul even divorced his wife for going outdoors without being fully covered, telling her that 'by law, only my eyes should see you'.

Although classical sculpture did not show the face covered either by veils or helmets, both of which were pushed back to reveal the subject's face, veiling was occasionally represented on a small scale: there are scenes on Greek vases showing women with their himatia pulled over their faces as they dance before their menfolk and the deities Dionysos and Artemis. The face veil also appears on small-scale sculpture, the most accomplished example being a bronze figurine from Alexandria of such quality that she may well have been one of the royal favourites or 'minor wives' passing through the palace en route to the king. With only her painted, elongated eyes visible, she is completely swathed in her sheetlike mantle. The outline of her hair is pulled back into a bun just visible through ample drapery which makes her body appear 'fluid and like a whirlwind', recalling the way the sea breezes caused the mantles of Alexandria's ladies to blow about them like the billowing mantle of Isis Pharia, whose colossus stood guard close to the palace.

It is therefore quite intriguing to imagine a similarly clad Cleopatra on her daring mission to reach Caesar, silently moving through the harbour's dark waters beneath the towering figure of her alter ego. As her boat reached the seaward side of the palace she must have pulled her dark mantle tight about her, concealing her well-known face as she followed Apollodorus swiftly up the white stone steps and across the limestone esplanade before disappearing into the shadows. They would have entered by one of the palace entrances no doubt used by the steady stream of favoured female courtiers on their visits to successive kings. It has reasonably been suggested that, should the need have arisen, Latin-speaking Apollodorus would have been able to communicate with any Roman guards they encountered – either Ptolemy's Gabiniani or Caesar's personal bodyguards – allowing his royal charge to pass un-hindered through the passages of the labyrinthine palace she knew so well.

Slipping into Caesar's quarters, Cleopatra then famously revealed herself. But, rather than springing unceremoniously out of an unrolled carpet, dizzy and unkempt, it is far more likely that she simply pulled back her heavy dark mantle to reveal her face in a gesture recalling the way gods' statues were concealed from profane eyes within temples. For even the Romans knew that in Egypt the sacred inscription accompanying the bejewelled statue of Isis stated, 'I am that which is, which hath been, and which shall be, and none have ever lifted the veil that hides my Divinity from mortal eyes.'

As Living Isis now revealed her own divinity before Caesar's eyes, her appearance as the many-named goddess brought together multiple strands of mythology in a superbly stage-managed event, laden with meaning and innuendo which only the limits of Caesar's intellect would prevent him from understanding. Veiling had been a key part of marriage ceremonies dating back to at least the sixth century BC, and the unveiling of a bride by her husband in both Greek and Roman ceremonies signified the surrender of her virginity to him. Since the concept of a woman unveiling herself in front of a man whom she did not know was completely alien within these cultures, Cleopatra's highly suggestive gesture may therefore have been an invitation to some sort of union or alliance.

Her unveiling must also have revealed inner clothing made of the ultra-fine linen that the Ptolemies so favoured, from Arsinoe II's gauzy veils to the transparent robes of Physkon whose visibly obese physique had so horrified his Roman guests. Yet as Cleopatra's 'white breasts were revealed by the fabric of Sidon,' a popular tale of the time described how its hero 'could see her whole body in it, and her desire grew even greater than it had been before' – feelings no doubt shared by the Roman who stood before her.

Cleopatra certainly seems to have been deeply attractive to Caesar, despite current notions that she was no great beauty, based on interpretations of coin images whose masculine-type features were deliberately exaggerated to compete with those of male rivals. A form of propaganda also employed by her female predecessors Hatshepsut, Nefertiti and Cleopatra III, the masculine-type portraits of the seventh Cleopatra have nevertheless been added to the ambiguous statement that 'her beauty was not in and for itself incomparable'. This has been taken to mean that she simply was not beautiful, rather than that there were other women whose beauty could compare with hers. But the same ancient source clearly states that Cleopatra was able to rely on 'the power of her beauty' while another clearly admits she 'was a woman of surpassing beauty, and at that time, when she was in the prime of her youth, she was most striking. Being brilliant to look upon and to listen to, with the power to subjugate every one, even a love-sated man already past his prime, she thought that it would be in keeping with her role to meet Caesar, and she reposed in her beauty all her claims to the throne'.

Certainly her surviving portrait busts seem to support her legendary beauty, despite doubts that they may represent Cleopatra because they are not inscribed – but then there are only three known statues of Ptolemaic royal women which do bear an identifying inscription. Even the famous bust of a royal woman in a tall blue crown from Amarna has no convenient name tag, yet no one has so far suggested that this is not Nefertiti. And given their characteristic features and iconography, it is usually possible to identify images of the Ptolemies, including the seventh Cleopatra herself.

Yet even if it is accepted that she was beautiful, perceptions of what constitutes beauty have varied tremendously throughout history – from

Rubenesque to Twiggy-thin, from noses long and aquiline to small and retroussé, the ancient ideal of beauty seems far from the artificially enhanced glamour of modern times. Certainly one high-class courtesan portrayed on an ancient Greek vase, looking at her face in a mirror with the tag line 'she is beautiful', seems rather wide of the mark to modern eyes, as does the image of the legendary courtesan Phryne who was renowned down the centuries as an all-time beauty. She was the model for Praxiteles' famous sculpture of Aphrodite, regarded as breathtaking by all who saw it, but the statue has at best a mediocre face, which is far outshone by the aesthetic qualities of Kleopatra's sculpted features, at least from this twenty-first-century Western female's perspective.

Clearly, in the eye of the beholder, images of Cleopatra have been subjected to an incredibly wide range of descriptions. One female writer has claimed she was 'pretty neither by the standards of [her] own day nor by those of ours', while discussing one of Cleopatra's marble heads another female historian believes that 'whilst it does not flatter her it bears a close relationship to the portraits of Alexander the Great'. Then again, male commentators claim the same head 'suggests her great physical beauty' and 'is infinitely more beautiful than the unflattering coin portrait, and it does convey an image of the great queen's personality'. As for these coin portraits, which have led some experts to declare that 'even the famously attractive Cleopatra VII of Egypt is shown with a flabby neck that suggests a goitre', they have variously been described as portraying someone who looks like a man 'in drag' and 'a cruel, hook-nosed hag' whereas to others the face is both 'attractive' and 'radiant'.

Regardless of such widely differing opinions of her physical beauty, the ancient sources agree that Cleopatra's character exerted a force all of its own. It was said that 'contact of her presence, if you lived with her, was irresistible; the attraction of her person, joining with the charm of her conversation, and the character that attended all she said or did, was something bewitching'. She was also blessed with 'a most delicious voice', in contrast to the high pitch of most female voices which apparently deviated so far from the masculine 'norm' they made men feel uncomfortable. Nor was the Greek belief that 'silence is the ornament of women' likely to have been a view held by Cleopatra.

Able to converse easily on all matters of culture and politics, enhanced by travel to places in Greece, Italy and Syria that were also familiar to Caesar, 'she had the facility of atuning her tongue, like an instrument with many strings, to whatever language she wished. There were few foreigners she had to deal with through an interpreter, and to most she herself gave her replies without an intermediary – to the Ethiopians, Troglodytes, Hebrews, Arabs, Syrians, Medes and Parthians. It is said she knew languages of many other peoples too, although the preceding kings had not tried to master even the Egyptian tongue, and some had indeed ceased to speak Macedonian.' Although there are no references to her speaking Latin, it seems hardly credible that she would not have been able to understand the language of those with whom she had to deal throughout her life, for not all Romans could speak Greek. Yet Caesar, trained in Greek and Latin rhetoric, is known to have conversed in Greek, the medium of scholars.

A modern psychiatric profile has claimed that Cleopatra had a borderline psychological disorder and a 'narcissistic personality seems consistently to be the best description for her'; but she had been raised as a goddess from birth, and such traits are hardly surprising in a descendant of Alexander and three centuries of monarchs who believed themselves divine and were worshipped by their people. Yet the supreme self-confidence that such belief gave Cleopatra was clearly most attractive: Caesar must have greatly admired her youthful vitality and fearless nature, graphically demonstrated by the means she used to reach him and perhaps inspired by his own well-publicised methods of crossing enemy lines. For only a year earlier he had run the blockade of Pompeius' fleet in the Adriatic, having 'muffled his head with a cloak and secretly put to sea in a small boat, alone and incognito', as she had just done.

Despite the age gap, the twenty-two-year-old Greek pharaoh was not so different from the fifty-two-year-old Roman general, who may well have been something of a father figure. His sculpted images certainly show a man not dissimilar in appearance to Auletes, and for all their differences the two men shared some distinct characteristics. Both were flamboyant, both were pragmatic, and when necessary both were completely ruthless.

Born in 100 BC, Gaius Julius Caesar – pronounced in the same way as the German 'Kaiser', which, like the Russian term 'Tsar', is a derivative – was named after his father, a government official. The family were descended from an exclusive group of aristocrats who used dynastic marriage to increase their wealth and social status. Educated by a tutor who had himself studied Greek and Latin rhetoric in Alexandria, the young Caesar became a keen poet and writer. Already ambitious, he broke off his first betrothal to make a more politically useful marriage with Cornelia, daughter of the powerful statesman Lucius Cornelius Cinna; their only child, Julia, was born in 76 BC.

After originally training for the priesthood Caesar became a lawyer. Sent east on a mission to Bithynia, near Pontus, he returned as something of a dandy inspired by Hellenistic fashions. It was said that 'his dress, it seems, was unusual: he had added wrist-length sleeves with fringes to his purple-striped senatorial tunic, and the belt which he wore over it was never tightly fastened – hence Sulla's warning to the aristocratic party "Beware of that boy with the loose clothes".'

By contrast, he became well known for his plain speaking. Once his rather high-pitched delivery had been improved by a speech coach from Rhodes, Caesar became a great orator, emphasising his points by vigorous gesticulation. Even the hypercritical Cicero was moved to ask, 'Do you know of any man who, even if he has concentrated on the art of oratory to the exclusion of all else, can speak better than Caesar? Or anyone who makes so many witty remarks? Or whose vocabulary is so varied and yet so exact?'

On his way to study in Rhodes, Caesar had been kidnapped by Cilician pirates who put a ransom of twenty talents on his head. Claiming to be worth at least fifty, he told the pirates that once free he would track them down and kill them; this caused much amusement among his captors, who let him go on payment of the ransom. Unfortunately for them, the twenty-six-year-old Caesar had been serious and set great store by keeping his word. He obtained some ships, caught up with the pirates and executed them by the standard Roman method of crucifixion – albeit cutting their throats as an act of mercy because they had treated him well.

Following a spell of military experience for which he received the oak wreath for valour, Caesar joined the staff of the millionaire general Crassus. After the death of his first wife whom he honoured with a public obituary, most unusual for a Roman woman, Caesar married Pompeius' cousin Pompeia and was posted to Spain, where the sight of

Alexander the Great's statue at the port of Gadir (Cadiz) made him deeply despondent. Comparing his own achievements at the age of thirty-two with those of Alexander who had already conquered much of the known world, Caesar also felt upstaged by Pompeius who had taken Alexander's epithet 'Great' and most of the east.

Yet Caesar had decided on an alliance and, marrying his daughter Julia to Pompeius, joined with him and his old boss Crassus to form the first Triumvirate in 60 BC. As effective rulers of Rome, they sold the title 'friend and ally of the Roman people' to Cleopatra's father Auletes, and when he was deposed the following year Caesar decided to try his luck there.

But when he failed to be elected Governor-General of Egypt he went instead to Gaul in an attempt to pacify the unruly northern parts, make a name for himself, compete with Pompeius – and plunder with impunity.

In his own accounts Caesar dispassionately describes his encounters with a whole host of peoples, from the ferocious Suebi of Germany, whose elaborately tall hairstyles enhanced their stature in battle, to the Gallic religious leaders he termed 'druides', an elite ruling class he equated with the Roman Senate. He also produced the first eyewitness account of Britain, a land in such unchartered territory that many Romans doubted it even existed.

Yet Caesar may well have known that the Greek sailor Pytheas had circumnavigated Britain in the 320s BC, and with his subsequent account 'On the Ocean' housed in Alexandria's royal library and familiar to its head librarian Eratosthenes, at least one Ptolemaic merchant ship had traveled to 'Britannike' in the second century BC.

In his account, written as always in the third person, Caesar claimed to have invaded Britain in August 556 BC 'because he knew that in almost all the Gallic campaigns the Gauls had received reinforcements from the Britons. Even if there was no time for a campaign that season, he thought it would be of great advantage to him merely to visit the island, to see what its inhabitants were like, and to make himself acquainted with the lie of the land, the harbours and the landing-places' – not to mention its rumoured sources of pearls, a commodity for which Pompeius had already received great plaudits in Rome.

Disembarking at Walmer in Kent in August 55 BC, Caesar and 10,000 troops were met by the locals, armed and ready in chariots, with bristling hair and their bodies stained with blue woad plant dye 'which gives them a more terrifying appearance in battle'. It was also well known that the Celts, like the Thracians, severed the heads of fallen enemies, and in a practice not unfamiliar to Kleopatra's relatives, 'embalm in cedar-oil and carefully preserve in a chest, and these they exhibit to strangers'.

Consisting of little more than a fortnight in Kent, this first invasion had largely been a means of winning support in Rome where it proved an incredible propaganda success. As the first time the Roman army had successfully ventured into unchartered territory, the senate voted a twenty-day period of thanksgiving, the longest ever awarded a Roman general.

Spurred on by his success, Caesar initiated plans for a repeat performance the following year. Some of his ships were pounded to pieces by the waves off the Kent coast, as they had been on the first occasion, but with the reinforcement came tragic news. His daughter Julia had died giving birth to Pompeius' child, Caesar's grandchild, which itself survived for only a few days. Although Pompeius had wanted to bury them on one of his lavish estates, the crowds had intervened and given Julia a great cremation on the Field of Mars as a gesture to her popular father.

In typical fashion, Caesar took the news stoically, revealing little of the grief he must have expressed in private and pressing on with matters at hand as a welcome distraction. After taking a major hill fort near St Albans in late July, he heard that rebellion had again broken out in Gaul, so moved back to the coast. From here he wrote up his report and sent a number of letters back to Rome. Knowing full well that whatever he told the gossip-loving Cicero would be swiftly relayed to everyone else, Caesar described his time in the land with 'astonishing masses of cliff', noting the island's supplies of iron, tin, beef and grain.

Caesar finally left Britain in late September, accepting the surrender of the tribal leader Cassivellaunus and taking hostages and tribute, including freshwater pearls which 'he weighed with his own hand to judge their value'. Both his British invasions had been a massive PR success, even if his critics claimed there had been little plunder. Despite the freshwater pearls, Cicero told his friends that there wasn't a single ounce of silver in Britain and he doubted whether any of the British slaves had any literary or musical taste. Yet the fair appearance and blue-stained skin of these 'sky-blue Britons' did cause a minor fashion craze as Roman ladies tried to replicate their 'azure beauty'.

With a third of Rome's population made up of slaves, Caesar himself took pains to buy the best: 'So high were the prices he paid on slaves of good character and attainments that he became ashamed of his extravagance and would not allow the sums to be entered in his accounts'. He was also able to provide many of his troops with a slave each following the surrender of Gaul, but news of the terrible massacres which had accompanied his conquests of Gaul and Germany was seized on by his opponents in Rome. They demanded he face trial as a war criminal until his huge territorial gains overruled such concerns. Yet, unlike many of his accusers, Caesar had little racial prejudice and numbered Gauls amongst his associates.

In the manner of Alexander, Caesar 'always led his army, more often on foot than in the saddle', advising them to 'keep a close eye on me!' and expecting them to follow. Again like his hero, he was extremely popular with his troops whom he addressed as 'comrades', as opposed to other Roman leaders who felt the term too familiar. He judged his men for their fighting abilities rather than their morals and allowed them to relax off duty however they wished, answering critics by claiming that, 'My men fight just as well when they are stinking of perfume'. Yet he did expect them to be well turned out. As a well-known dandy himself, his customized toga with eastern-style fringing which echoed Alexander's penchant for foreign attire was complemented by a number of rings, and he also liked to wear the wreaths of laurel or oak leaves awarded for military successes. Apart from displaying his status, they disguised his thinning fair hair more effectively than his usual method. For 'he used to comb the thin strands of his hair forward from his poll' since his baldness was 'a disfigurement which his enemies harped upon, much to his exasperation'.

Yet despite a receding hairline and thirty-year age gap, the man who appeared to Cleopatra that night in Alexandria as she pulled back her veil was still 'tall, fair and well built with a rather broad face and keen dark brown eyes'. There was clearly a sexual attraction between them, and given Caesar's incredibly promiscuous track record it seems highly unlikely that the two simply shook hands. Having done her homework, Cleopatra had already 'discovered his disposition which was very susceptible, to such an extent that he had his intrigues with ever so many women – with all, doubtless, who chanced to come his way'.

For in addition to his one betrothal and marriages to Cornelia and Pompeia, he had next married Calpurnia, daughter of the influential and very wealthy Lucius Calpurnius Piso. He also maintained a long-term relationship with Servilia, mother of the staunch young Republican Brutus, and 'his affairs with women are commonly described as numerous and extravagant: among those of noble birth who he is said to have seduced were Servius Sulpicius' wife Postumia; Aulus Gabinius' wife Lollia; Marcus Crassus' wife Tertulla; and even Gnaeus Pompeius' wife Mucia'. The wives of his closest colleagues were a valuable source of information to him. Yet he divorced his second wife, Pompeia, after she herself was alleged to be having an affair. Her lover's attempts to infiltrate Caesar's house, heavily disguised as a woman, caused such a scandal that Caesar claimed he had little choice but to terminate the marriage, since 'Caesar's wife must be above suspicion'.

With no such qualms himself, there were claims of him fathering children as far away as Gaul. His soldiers were so proud of their leader's reputation that whenever they returned to Rome they marched along to the strains of their favourite ditty: 'Home we bring our bald whoremonger, Romans lock your wives away! All the bags of gold you lent him went his Gallic tarts to pay!' In Spain, he made the acquaintance of numerous local women in the company of his like-minded chief of staff, who went by the delightful nickname of 'Mentula', 'Penis'. Persistent rumours surrounding Caesar's time in Bithynia claim that he even had an affair with its king, Nicomedes. The details were salaciously relayed by Cicero: 'Caesar was led by Nicomedes' attendants to the royal bedchamber, where he lay on a golden couch, dressed in a purple shift . . . So this decendant of Venus lost his virginity in Bithynia'. His troops found this most amusing, as did, the young poet Catullus, calling Caesar a 'pansy Romulus' until his father made him apologise.

Yet despite his well-deserved reputation as 'every woman's husband and every man's wife', most Romans would remember the episode in which their noble general was the one who was seduced. Claiming that Cleopatra had entered the palace 'without Caesar's knowledge – the disgrace of Egypt, promiscuous to the harm of Rome', they ignored the fact that she was simply returning to her own home. Running with their theme of 'lecherous prostitute queen', they described her as a woman 'worn among her own household slaves'. As their stories grew in the telling, 'she became so debauched that she often sold herself as a prostitute; but she was so beautiful that many men bought a night with her at the price of their own death'; reluctant to dismiss such lurid images, modern accounts still claim that Cleopatra had 'the power of the courtesan – and she exploited it professionally'.

Although the recent claim that Cleopatra was 'willing to use her body to gain her political ends' is intriguingly never made of Caesar or indeed any other male leaders, political matters of an intimate nature were certainly high on his agenda that night. It may well be that as a descendant of Aeneas of Troy, forefather of Rome, whose steamy romance with the North African ruler Dido of Carthage was an entente cordiale he wished to revive, Caesar was obviously attracted to Cleopatra's status as one of the very few surviving descendants of Alexander the Great. And as a prominent *philalexandrotatos*, 'lover of Alexander', Caesar no doubt fancied his chances with his hero's equally attractive descendant. As dreams of future dynasties may already have emerged in their increasingly intimate conversation, the two figures were certainly drawn together by their precarious situation and, both effectively trapped within the palace, became the closest of allies within a single night.

Recognising Cleopatra's abilities in all their forms, Caesar swiftly reversed Pompeius' recommendation that she be excluded from the throne and before the morning she was fully reinstated. Since Caesar himself states simply that he 'was particularly desirous of settling the disputes of the princes [sic] as a common friend and arbitrator', many historians seem to doubt that he had any romantic attachment to her. They support their claim with the fact that he rarely mentions her in his official commentaries, only twice by name and even then in the third person; but this ignores another fact, that Caesar always wrote in the third person and in the same objective style. Since his words were intended as propaganda, gushing prose would have been highly inappropriate and he never revealed his emotions in his work.

So Caesar's feelings for Cleopatra must be sought in his actions, and these speak volumes. Knowing full well that the Alexandrians had no desire to have her back, because their feelings had been stirred up by Potheinos and were reinforced by Ptolemy XIII's forces who greatly outnumbered his, Caesar took a massive gamble reinstating her. When her brother arrived at Caesar's suite the following morning and saw his despised sister relaxing in the Roman's company, the young pharaoh was so incensed that he rushed from the palace and tore off his diadem, dashing it to the ground in a dramatic display of teenage rage. No doubt encouraged by Potheinos, he shouted that he had been betrayed, rousing up the ever-predictable Alexandrians who once more prepared to storm the palace.

Yet this time Cleopatra did not have to flee her home before the mob, because she was saved by Caesar's famous powers of eloquence. Calmly walking out before the crowds, he dramatically produced the last will and testament of Ptolemy XII Auletes, which he had no doubt located with Cleopatra's help the night before. As he began to read aloud its contents in fluent Greek he made it clear that brother and sister were to rule together, revealing that Auletes had called upon Rome to ensure that the will was implemented and that it was his own intention as Roman consul to carry out the late king's wishes.

As arbitrator in the family's disputes he announced that the siblings would co-rule in Egypt, and in a masterstroke of quick thinking assuaged public feeling even further by bringing into the succession the two remaining children: the younger Ptolemy and Arsinoe were made joint rulers of Cyprus. Although Rome had taken the island only ten years earlier, Caesar now gave it back to the Ptolemies – a reversal of policy which caused outrage in Rome but bought Caesar valuable time to try to establish a power base within the city. It also showed Cleopatra how former Ptolemaic territories could easily be handed back at the word of one man.

Although Ptolemy XIII and Potheinos were far from happy with Caesar's dynastic solution, public opinion was placated. To celebrate the restoration of the monarchy a great ceremony was held which marked the formal union of Cleopatra VII and Ptolemy XIII as co-rulers and presumably also a husband and wife in accordance with three centuries of Ptolemaic tradition. Despite no evidence that an actual marriage took place, this is hardly surprising, for while Ptolemaic marriage contracts do exist, it was not necessary to have a religious ceremony to legalise Egyptian marriage. It was brought about by little more than the couple living together, as noted in one second-century BC text which stated that 'it is a good thing for me to sit down with Tanous so that she may be my wife'. Yet it seems that sitting down together was all that transpired, with Ptolemy XIII's presence at the celebrations simply for appearance's sake. Although he, his younger brother Ptolemy and their sister Arsinoe were all officially recognised as monarchs by Rome, all three knew that power really lay with their despised elder sister and her new friend Caesar, partners in every sense of the word.

So Cleopatra once more reigned over her court and its lavish celebrations, presumably held in the formal quarters of the palace. Expanded by each generation of monarchs since its founding by Alexander three centuries earlier, the palace of Auletes and his successors was of such legendary magnificence that its fame was known throughout the world. With its precincts and colonnades embellished by five-foot-long sphinxes in granite and diorite bearing Auletes' own features, 'the surge of the breakers was ever to be heard in its airy halls' where windows of translucent glass overlooked open sea.

Beneath the watchful eyes of the two gold eagles of the Ptolemaic house, set at the highest part of a roof supported by agate columns, 'the rafters were hidden beneath a thick coating of gold. The walls shone with marble', the gleaming white stone imported from Turkey, the green and white-veined marble from the Pyrenees, yellow and white from Haute-Garonne in western Gaul and at least two varieties from Greece. Marble and alabaster also covered the floors, and although this was cool in summer, the Romans had to take particular care since their regulation hobnailed footwear was quite unsuited to such surfaces and slipping on duty was not unknown. Further embellished with additions of Arabian onyx, lapis lazuli from Afghanistan, turquoise from Sinaii and the newly fashionable purple porphyry stone from the Egyptian desert, the stone floors were inset with exquisite Macedonian-style mosaics of mythological scenes alternating with still-life studies such as a first-century scene of a small terrier with a red collar sitting beside an overturned wine jug. The similarly inlaid marble walls glittered with inlaid gems, gold leaf and tiny multicoloured sections of millefiori glass. Walls coated in rich red cinnabar were embellished with meticulously executed trompe l'oeil scenes of cityscapes and gardens intersected by ivory panels and doors inlaid with Indian tortoiseshell studded with sparkling green emeralds. An extra layer of brilliance was added by family portraits, statues of the royal family and the gods, carved in marble and bronze inlaid with precious stones and set alongside antique pharaonic pieces.

In a scene glittering in the light cast by elaborate candelabra and chandeliers, guests, reclining on dining couches covered in purple and crimson tapestry coverlets shot with gold, gathered for a spectacular formal banquet. Royal protocol at the Ptolemaic court demanded that the monarchs were placed in the highest position and their most important guests placed closest. Caesar himself followed this Eastern practice of grading diners and 'while stationed abroad, he always had dinner served in two separate rooms: one for his officers and Greek friends, the other for Roman citizens and the more important provincials'; although it has been suggested that he used this arrangement as a means of distancing himself from his more tiresome guests.

Known to have been on the 'top table' couches that night were Caesar, carefully turned out as always, the elderly Memphite priest Acoreus in his finest white linen robes, and possibly the high priest Pasherenptah III and the astronomer royal Sosigenes. The royal party would also have included Ptolemy XIII, his sister Arsinoe and their youngest brother Ptolemy, all hating the obvious relish with which their elder half-sister Cleopatra would have been revelling in her restored status.

Stunningly dressed and covered from head to toe in lavish jewels, Cleopatra's appearance that night was in complete contrast to the plain-looking matrons of Caesar's Rome. Permitted a maximum of half an ounce of gold jewellery by law, such women made a virtue of their lack of adornment – the fabulously wealthy Cornelia, once wooed by Physkon, famously claimed that her children 'were her jewels'. It is therefore no surprise that subsequent descriptions of Cleopatra by

Republican sympathisers referred to 'her baleful beauty painted up beyond all measure: covered with the spoils of the Red Sea, she carried a fortune round her neck and in her hair, and was weighed down by her ornaments', her body semi-visible through her finest linen robes.

According to Roman etiquette when dining in public, women were expected to 'take the food with the tips of your fingers; and you must know that eating is itself an art', although they were also advised 'to eat a little less than you feel inclined to' and 'don't drink more than your head will stand. Don't lose the use of your head and feet; and never see two things when only one is there.' Then, to counteract the effects of wine or spicy food, they should add small amounts of perfume to their drink. The perfume theme was greatly expanded in Ptolemaic dining rooms, where the heady fragrance of incense was complemented by carefully chosen flowers, the floors were strewn with petals 'like an extraordinarily beautiful meadow' and guests were presented with floral wreaths.

As a key feature of Egyptian banquets down the millennia, the traditional lotus headband had been partly superseded by chaplets of roses sacred to Aphrodite-Venus and to Isis, the 'Rose-breasted Lady' who was honoured with offerings of wine and roses. Initiation into her cult involved a festival banquet 'in honour of lady Isis', accompanied by invitations to dine at the table of 'Lord Serapis' within the temple precincts. The 'pleasant social intercourse and conviviality' which marked the Isis-and-Serapis dining experience seems an apt description of the first formal banquet Cleopatra held for Caesar.

With all manner of exotic foods piled high on jewel-studded gold plates and Memphis-made silverware, vintage wines chilled in silver wine buckets were decanted into goblets of crystal and agate cups. Presented with the best-quality linen napkins, guests were then served by an attentive staff of Greeks, Libyans, Nubians and northern Europeans 'so fair haired that Caesar said he had never seen hair so red in the Rhine country.'

Yet for all the delicacies on offer, Caesar was apparently quite indifferent to food: at one dinner party in Milan he had been unconcerned that his asparagus had been dressed in rancid oil, and he even rebuked his more discerning staff when they failed to follow his example. But although 'he once put his baker in irons for giving him a different sort of bread from that served to his guests', this was probably a reaction to the risk of being poisoned – an occupational hazard for prominent figures in the ancient world, where some claimed that Alexander himself had been killed by drinking poisoned wine. Many employed an official taster, and Ptolemy I once acted as such to Alexander early in his career. The Greek physician Galen claimed that 'walnut and rue at the the start of the meal counter all poisons', while Mithridates VI of Pontus commissioned his own designer-made antidote from the pharmacologist Zopyros. When his kingdom was seized by Pompeius Mithridates' suicide by poison proved impossible and he was forced to resort to a sword. The now unemployed Zopyros was then taken on by Auletes to help avoid his own assassination within the court at Alexandria.

Having narrowly escaped a similar fate himself Caesar, a man who cared as little for alcohol as he did for food, was described as 'the only sober man who ever tried to wreck the Constitution', and 'not even his enemies denied that he drank abstemiously'. For him, the most interesting part of any meal was the post-dinner discussion in the grand tradition of the Greek dinner or 'deipnon' where like minds came together to eat, drink and discuss in a group of 'deipnosophists'. Translated as 'philosophers at dinner' or 'the partying professors', this was also the title of a multi-volume work by the Egyptian-born Athenaeus of Naukratis. It comprised an entertaining collection of anecdotes, quotations and philosophical debate set against the background of a dinner party and covering subjects from food and drink to Alexander's Successors and events from Athens, Rome and Egypt to Asia Minor and the Celtic world.

On many such evenings that Caesar shared with Cleopatra, 'he often feasted with her until dawn', although at this first state event he fell into deep conversation with her adviser the priest Acoreus. Keen to learn more about the source of the country's great wealth, the annual Nile flood that made agriculture possible, Acoreus told Caesar the traditional explanation that the waters were sent forth by a ram-headed god from his subterranean cave. The priest then informed him that this had been superseded by the research of Greek scholars, which revealed the flood was actually caused by snows melting in the highlands of Ethiopia. As the conversation moved on to Egypt's culture and religion, Caesar may well have consulted Acoreus about the ritual ramifications of a formal union between a descendant of Venus-Aphrodite with the Living Isis-Aphrodite.

While the discussion continued long into the night, Cleopatra and Caesar had no idea that they were only moments away from death at the hands of Potheinos' assassins. Considering whether to 'slay our cruel mistress in her very bed' and 'take Caesar's life' or to launch their attack at the banquet when 'it was possible that the blood of Caesar might be shed over the king's drinking cups and his head fall upon the table', they decided such an attack would also place their charge Ptolemy XIII in danger.

But as they wavered over the ideal time to strike, deciding in the end to delay the assassinations until the following day, they were overheard by a figure lurking in the shadows, 'a busy listening fellow whose excessive timidity made him inquisitive into everything'. Unfortunately for them this was Caesar's barber, who immediately passed on the news, and 'Caesar, upon the first intelligence of it, set a guard upon the hall where the feast was kept and killed Pothinus', avenging Pompeius' fate by ordering his beheading.

In the ensuing chaos, Achillas managed to escape from the palace and reach his men, the twenty-thousand-strong force newly arrived from Pelusium. They joined up with the Alexandrian Greeks who had formed a people's militia and surrounded the palace walls, whose fortifications were further reinforced as Caesar set up his headquarters in the adjoining Theatre of Dionysos.

Intense and vicious fighting began in November 48 BC. Caesar quickly realised that his modest force of four thousand could never risk a pitched battle against this far larger enemy, particularly one which included large numbers of Gabiniani, trained in Roman warfare. Left with little choice, Caesar and Cleopatra, with Ptolemy XIII as a hostage, were forced to remain within the relative safety of the palace, hemmed in between the hostile city and the open sea.

Caesar defended the area as best he could, awaiting the reinforcements he had summoned from Anatolia and the Levant when he first landed. But he knew that Achillas would try to block their arrival with ships already in the harbour and so, after no doubt consulting with Cleopatra, 'he burnt all those ships and the rest that were in the docks' including the Roman triremes, Egyptian warships of the royal fleet. Yet as the flaming torches were applied to ships, the wind rapidly spread the blaze to the dockside warehouses where many books in temporary storage awaited transfer to the Great Library.

In the smoke and confusion which enveloped much of the palace Arsinoe and her eunuch tutor Ganymedes managed to escape to Achillas' army and the Alexandrians, who declared her 'basilissa', female equivalent of 'basileus', the Greek for king, in place of the hated collaborator Cleopatra. Appointing Ganymedes her chamberlain, she decided to change Achillas' siege tactics, and when the general disagreed she had him killed and replaced with Ganymedes. He sprang into action, cutting off the palace with roadblocks and armed guards amid vicious street-to-street fighting. He also used his detailed knowledge of the palace layout to contaminate its freshwater supplies, pumping seawater into the pipes and underground reservoirs until the equally resourceful Caesar and Cleopatra, who both seem to have known their Homer, remembered descriptions of the region's freshwater springs and ordered the digging of new wells.

With the Alexandrians demanding their king back, Caesar decided to buy time and handed him over, perhaps hoping for conflict between the petulant young pharaoh and his sister Arsinoe. Yet so united were they in their opposition to their half-sister and her Roman champion that the pair joined forces, and with their dual monarchy reinstated, the Alexandrians fought with even more vigour than before.

With the situation looking increasingly bleak Caesar's first wave of reinforcements finally appeared at sea, allowing him to take Pharos Island and its lighthouse and to move all his men to the mile-long causeway linking the island to the city. Caesar himself directed operations, purple cloak flapping in the wind and detailed notes in hand, as the men began to fortify the causeway. Then a sudden enemy attack caused panic. As the men crowded into all the available boats in their attempts to escape, the overloaded vessels began to sink and many drowned. Caesar himself managed to swim some 200 yards to land, keeping his papers dry by holding them in his left hand above the water – not bad going for a man in his fifties still wearing his armour. Despite this setback he continued to fight to protect the palace and, however dire the situation became, he never handed Cleopatra over to her enemies. For not only was he determined to retain her as his ally, if not partner, but in the thick of the war she had discovered she was pregnant.

Much to the couple's great relief, the rest of the reinforcements from Anatolia, Syria and Arabia finally arrived in early March under the leadership of Caesar's ally the prince of Pergamon. Joined by three thousand men under Antipatros, father of the future King Herod and prime minister of the Jewish high priest who had wisely changed sides after the battle of Pharsalus, the prince marched across the Egyptian border and took Pelusium by storm, skirting south down the eastern edge of the Delta towards the site of modern Cairo. As Ptolemy XIII took his large army south along the opposite branch of the Delta to halt the enemy advance, Caesar followed at a distance before mounting a pincer movement with his princely ally. In fierce fighting they defeated Ptolemy XIII and his troops; the teenage king, resplendent in his heavy gold armour, drowned in the Nile after a most determined campaign. After retrieving his body to prove his death to any doubtful supporters and to undermine the credibility of any future pretender, Caesar rode back to Alexandria that same evening to give Cleopatra the news of their victory.

It seems she already knew. Approaching the city's eastern Canopic Gate, he was met by a great procession of 'Sacred Emblems', divine figures, the statues of gods and royal ancestors carried on the shoulders of their priests. Chief amongst them no doubt was the Living Isis, resplendent in her carrying chair as she came out of her royal city to meet her conquering hero.

During the great ceremonies of thanksgiving for their victory, Cleopatra and Caesar must have visited the Soma, as much a place of pilgrimage for him as it was for her. As Alexander's living successor, and now sole pharaoh, she would have paid homage to his guardian spirit (*daimon*) within his mummified body; and with the couple's shared dream of re-establishing his empire now a real possibility, the dynastic ramifications of the child she was carrying would not have been lost on either of them.

After leaving offerings, perhaps in Caesar's case his rings and one of his purple cloaks in the manner of later Roman leaders, he seems to have used the opportunity to conduct proper funerary rites for his former son-in-law Pompeius. His embalmed head was now buried in the Nemeseion, a tomb within the grove of Nemesis by Alexandria's newly extended eastern city wall. Then, to thank his Jewish allies including those in the city who had remained loyal throughout the fighting, 'Julius Caesar made a pillar of brass for the Jews at Alexandria and declared publicly that they were citizens of Alexandria', confirming traditional rights which had been undermined following their support for certain rulers in previous royal feuds.

Peace restored, Caesar resumed his official role, but, despite four months of civil war and against all Roman expectations, he did not absorb Egypt into the Roman empire. This would have meant installing a governor who might well take power for himself, and since Cleopatra was his most trustworthy ally he once more implemented Auletes' will, explaining that 'the elder of the two boys – the late king – being now no more, Caesar assigned the kingdom to the younger one and to Kleopatra, the elder of the two daughters who had remained his loyal adherent'. So substituting one Ptolemy for another, twelve-year-old Ptolemy XIV became Kleopatra's nominal co-ruler, the couple assuming the title 'Theoi Philopatores Philadelphoi', 'the Father-loving, Sibling-loving Gods' – although her name once again took precedence.

Nevertheless, formal co-rulership with her youngest brother does not seem to have prevented Cleopatra from marrying Caesar 'according to Egyptian rites'. According to the earliest Arabic source, Caesar 'fell in love with her, married her and had a son with her'; a chalcedony gem bearing Caesar's image, his laurel wreath embellished with a festive flower garland, was perhaps made to commemorate such a happy event.

Because Caesar was still married to Calpurnia, his polygamous marriage to Cleopatra was unrecognised in Roman law – as, indeed, was marriage between a Roman citizen and a foreigner. This explains why Roman sources refer to Cleopatra as Caesar's 'mistress' rather than his 'wife'. Although this is something that most modern historians still choose to follow, it ignores the fact that Egyptian marriage was traditionally little more than cohabitation.

Since the status of the two people involved in this particular case must surely have required the gods to formalise their union, a visit to their respective cult centres at sites throughout Egypt could only be undertaken with a journey along Egypt's main highway, the Nile. And according to the ancient sources, this is indeed a journey which Cleopatra and Caesar undertook.

PART THREE

5

The River of Life: the Progress down the Nile

Although it is certain that Cleopatra and Caesar embarked on a Nile cruise following their victory in the Alexandrian War, historians have long been divided about its duration. Some claim that it 'could have been scarcely more than a day trip', or at best a week, while others believe they cruised south for several months. The Roman historian Appian added that details of their cruise 'are related more particularly in my Egyptian history', which although sadly lost, does suggest a journey of considerable duration.

It would certainly not have been the first such riverborne progress made by the Ptolemies, who had often used the journey as a means of maintaining their profile among their Egyptian subjects – to suppress unrest or celebrate a victory, marriage or birth. Ptolemy IV and Arsinoe III had travelled upriver to celebrate military success in 217 BC, while the first Cleopatra and her husband had sailed as far south as Philae in 186 BC to announce their defeat of rebels and the safe delivery of a son. Cleopatra's own grandfather, Ptolemy IX Chickpea, had similarly traveled the length of the country to perform sacred rites in the deep south, and her father, Auletes, had cruised 'through the whole country, and back to Memphis where he attended the performance of religious festivities and was on that occasion escorted by his nobles, his wives, and his royal children.'

Now Caesar too 'ascended the Nile with 400 ships, exploring the country in company with Cleopatra and generally enjoying himself with her,' although rather more than a simple holiday, their cruise would have been something like a waterborne Triumph to celebrate the successful outcome of the recent hostilities. With their huge military escort of warships and troop carriers displaying the full extent of Rome's military powers, it was also a means for Cleopatra to show off her antique land to Caesar, who would finally see for himself the vast resources at his disposal through the good offices of his good lady. Now that she was visibly back in power and victorious alongside the world's most powerful man, who was clearly her partner, Cleopatra's pregnant state had completed her transformation into Living Isis. She was now the quintessential mother goddess carrying her successor as she sailed upon the waters, and her presence among her people would be the means of ensuring the successful flood they all so desperately needed.

As repair work began on the war-torn land-based palace the victorious couple would have embarked at the royals' private harbour on to Cleopatra's great ship of state, a home from home. Most likely a version of the famous 'thalamegos' ship constructed for Ptolemy IV, this graceful two-level floating palace some 300 feet long was surrounded by its own gardens and walkways and fitted out in the most sumptuous manner. Ancient accounts described an upper storey with windows and balconies housing 'saloons for dining parties, with berths, and with all the other conveniences of living'. Large enough to hold twenty couches, its main dining room was panelled in fragrant cedarwood adorned with inlays of gold and ivory, below a coffered ceiling of gilded and sculpted wood supported by columns of finest cypress. Another of the dining rooms was fitted out in Indian marble, and there was even a novelty 'ancient Egypt'-themed dining room with traditional-style columns which 'bulged as they ascended, and the drums differed, one being black and the other white, placed alternately. Some of their capitals were circular, resembling rose blossoms slightly opened, . . . calyxes of water-lilies and the fruit of freshly-budded date-palms.'

That such luxurious craft really existed is borne out by similarly lavish facilities discovered aboard a pair of first-century AD pleasure boats, each around seventy metres (230 feet) long originally moored on Lake Nemi in the Alban Hills south-east of Rome. The Italian dictator Mussolini, also an amateur archaeologist, described these 'immense and superb vessels with rooms and gardens and fountains, ornamented with marbles and precious metals and rare woods, all shining with gold and purple' which he recovered from the bottom of the lake on his orders. Further kitted out with mosaic flooring, bathing facilities and areas for the cults of Isis and Artemis, the craft were clearly influenced by the Ptolemies, several of whom – including Cleopatra and her father – had apparently once resided in this very region.

With a rotunda-shaped shrine housing a marble statue of Aphrodite-Isis, the Ptolemies' state vessel also housed a columned chamber of Dionysos large enough to hold thirteen couches before a jewel-studded gold recess housing portrait statues of the royal family in finest Parian marble. On the upper deck, an open-air dining room and seating area covered by purple and gold-spangled awnings provided the optimum vantage point from which to view and be viewed – perfect for those warm evenings on the Nile. Above rose the great mast to a height of more than 100 feet, supporting the dyed linen sail decorated perhaps in the manner of previous pharaohs, who used patterns of stars and their names and titles as a means of heralding their arrival by river. Alexander and his generals certainly favoured brightly dyed sails and ensigns; the Ptolemies' purple topsail was a particular trademark of Cleopatra, and her alter-ego Isis Pharia, the inventor of sails, was the image adorning the ensign of many a royal boat.

Unfurling the purple sails to catch the northerly winds, Cleopatra's captain, traditionally known as the 'Director of the Royal Ship', maneouvred her state vessel through the causeway's swing bridge to reach the smaller Kibotos ('coffer') harbour. There they were joined by Caesar's four-hundred-strong naval escort to travel down the 12-mile-long canal which cut through the centre of Alexandria's native Egyptian quarter, Rhakotis. Planned by Alexander and built by Ptolemy I, the route nevertheless became known as 'Cleopatra's Canal' in memory of the monarch who used it on her regular journeys between her Greek city and Egyptian kingdom.

Then the ships passed into the open water of Lake Mareotis, whose small islands of brightly planted pleasure gardens were a favourite haunt of Alexandrians on days off. The banks, fringed with groves of cultivated papyrus, housed waterside villas whose vineyards produced high-quality wine, exported as far afield as Italy and France. Perhaps Caesar and Cleopatra picked up some of it for the journey ahead. As the vast flotilla finally reached the Nile itself, it travelled south down the Canopic branch towards the old trading colony of Naukratis some 45 miles inland, continuing on past Terenuthis whose fine temple to

Hathor-Termuthis combined powers serpentine and bovine within a single goddess. The Delta's flat landscape now spread out green as far as the eye could see. Cleopatra and Caesar would have seen the same endless fields of lush crops watered by *shadufs*, patient donkeys trotting along beneath impossible loads, women carrying their burdens on their heads and groups of small children waving excitedly from the banks, that the tourist sees today – a timeless landscape changed only by the mosques of Islam and the modern world's electric supplies.

Possibly docking at Khem, the Greek Letopolis, near the southern apex of the Delta, Cleopatra is likely to have met with its hereditary priests. Related by marriage to the Memphite clergy, and close supporters of her father who had given their high priest the title 'god's beloved and friend of the King', the Letopolis clergy would be useful allies in Cleopatra's plans for the future. On the opposite bank lay Heliopolis, ancient Iunu, cult centre of the sun god Ra whose power had supported the monarchy since the Pyramid Age. First stop for Roman tourists after Alexandria, the ancient city sited on a great mound surrounded by the lakes and waterways of the Nile had been sacked by the Persians in 342 BC. It was now something of an ancient reclamation yard: the Ptolemies had taken away sections of its statuary and gold-tipped obelisks to embellish their new city on the coast.

Yet much of the city's vast sun temple had remained intact. It was the place where Ptolemy II had set up colossal granite figures of himself and his sister-wife Arsinoe II, perhaps in exchange for the obelisk he took. Both they and their successors continued to honour the temple's sacred Mnevis bull, described by one ancient Greek tourist as 'the Ox Mneuis kept in a sanctuary as a god'. Travelling around Egypt with a particularly useless guide he had picked up in Alexandria, he dismissed the temple's multi-columned halls and vast expanses of decorated wall as 'a display of vain toil with nothing pleasing or picturesque about it'. Yet its elaborate precincts were also the pre-eminent place to worship the sun god in the incense-fuelled rites which had been held three times a day for the previous three thousand years. The presence of a gold-clad Cleopatra as the sun god's own child would have added a powerful extra dimension to the solar-based proceedings.

The sun god himself sank down into the western horizon each evening to do battle with the forces of darkness before appearing renewed the following dawn. Cleopatra and Caesar would have followed him when crossing over the Nile to the west bank, traditional land of the dead and the world's most familiar tombs at Giza – one of the seven wonders of the ancient world, and the highlight of every tourist itinerary then as now. The Ptolemies had kept back the drifting sands from the pyramids and their guardian Sphinx, whose paws, covered in the Greek and Latin graffiti of numerous travellers, revealed that Roman officials came to pay homage to the Sphinx and were 'pleased with the Pyramids', which presumably impressed Caesar as much as they had Alexander.

As the couple sailed on, the outlines of many more pyramids became visible along the high desert escarpment all the way to Sakkara. Here the oldest of all such monuments had been created more than two thousand years earlier by the great sage Imhotep, subsequently deified and adopted into the family of the creator god Ptah. The Greeks worshipped him as Imouthes, whose hymns announced that 'every person who is Greek shall worship the son of Ptah, Imouthes'. Along with Thoth and Isis, pre-eminent deities of wisdom, he was worshipped within the Imensthotieion temple down the valley in Memphis, the most important destination for any royal progress south.

At the time of Cleopatra's visit with Caesar Memphis was described as 'large and populous, ranks next after Alexandria, and is made up of mixed races like those who have settled together at Alexandria. Lakes stretch before the city and palaces' which had been greatly embellished in the second century BC when the Ptolemies had made Memphis their temporary capital. Since its clergy were among her most trusted advisers, Cleopatra must have undergone a full-blown coronation or formal renewal of her powers here at the hands of her powerful relative Pasherenptah III, who had similarly crowned her father, Auletes, some four years after he had actually become king. Cleopatra's pregnancy, fulfilling her title 'Mother of the God', made it imperative to surround her unborn child with all the magical protection that Egypt's gods could bestow.

The presence of Nea Isis, literally 'Isis Incarnate', at the very place within Ptah's complex where the goddess was said to have passed from among mankind would have been tremendously significant for the Egyptians. And while Ptah was the traditional god of the city, Isis was his female equivalent, worshipped as the ever-fertile 'Cow of Memphis' in rites so famous that Roman poets could talk of 'the altars where incense is offered to the sacred Cow of Memphis'. Even the Greek traveller who had been unmoved by Heliopolis fulsomely described how 'the bull Apis is kept in a sort of sanctuary, regarded as a god. His forehead and certain other parts of his body are marked with white, but the rest is black, and it is by these marks that they always choose the bull suitable for the succession after the death of the one holding the honour. Before his sanctuary lies a court, in which there is another sanctuary allocated to the bull's mother', where she and Apis were brought out to meet their adoring public at a set time each day.

The way the animals behaved before their visitors was interpreted by the priests. The Greek philosopher Eudoxus of Knidus, for instance, had visited 'the bull with the beautiful horns' and 'standing sideways by him, it licked his robe', a gesture interpreted by the priest to mean that the philosopher would be famous but short-lived. Entertainment for these creatures was supplied by the temple's musicians, singers and dancing dwarves – the importance of keeping them happy reflected their role as bringers of fertility, and their golden stalls were sited close to the temple's sacred lake where priests monitored the rise and fall of the annual flood levels. Although repeated attempts to encourage the waters to rise over previous years had proved unsuccessful, the lowest-ever level being recorded during Cleopatra's exile the previous year, her return as the ultimate fertility figure meant that her powers could be combined with those of the bull to invoke the full force of the flood and so bring fertility to a land still in crisis.

From judicious use of moonlight to the heady fumes of incense, the Ptolemaic clergy had begun to draw on increasingly cryptic sources of magic as a means of manipulating the world around them. After summoning up Greek, Persian, Jewish and Babylonian gods and spirits with exaggerated 'popping and hissing noises' and tongue-twisting texts read out from the walls around them, they incinerated magical figures in the temple furnace. One ancient account claimed that the Memphis furnace had been used for alchemy, the means of trying to turn base metal into gold as perfected by Cleopatra and her circle of priest-philosophers. Monarch and clergy had certainly attempted to transform the mundane into the spectacular by working their secret magic for the good of Egypt.

Pasherenptah III would presumably have hosted the same kind of formal state banquet for Caesar and Cleopatra that he had previously given for Auletes and his entourage, recalling them all 'sitting at meal and spending a pleasant time while assisting at festivals of all the gods and goddesses'. They would have dined on gold and silver tableware specially commissioned from the metalworkers of Memphis in the kind of surroundings described as 'elegant and decorated,' with 'its floor decorated with genuine lapis and genuine turquoise. There was a great deal of furniture in it, which was covered with royal linen, and there were numerous gold cups on the sideboard . . . incense was put on the brazier, and perfume was brought.'

Although in his youth Pasherenptah had claimed to be 'a noble resplendent of possessions of every kind. To me belongs a harem of fair maidens', subsequent marriage to Taimhotep of Letopolis had failed to produce a son to succeed him. So perhaps the couple had slept in Sakkara's incubation chambers, whose erotic wall paintings and fertility-god figures were believed to help in such cases. Or they may have spent the night in Ptah's temple, as had a priest's barren wife in one Ptolemaic tale, there receiving a dream telling her to give her husband a preparation of melon vine to receive from him 'the fluid of conception'; the plant's root was recommended in later Arab pharmacopoia as a powerful aphrodisiac and stimulant to sperm production. But ultimately, Taimhotep and her husband turned to Imhotep, 'who gives a son to him who has none', and this time it was Pasherenptah who received the dream, telling him to set up a new statue of Imhotep in his shrine at Sakkara.

Since the shrine had undergone a makeover following royal approval from Cleopatra, herself probably in Sakkara only two years earlier when she seems to have accompanied the funeral of the Apis bull, she may well have revisited the site with Caesar to view the great tomb of the Mothers of Apis cows whose powers she shared, and no doubt the Serapeum where previous Apis bulls were interred. The sacred spirits of both cows and bulls were honoured with gilded stelae and statuary: Cleopatra's Ptolemaic predecessors had commissioned superb-quality statues of the creatures in dark serpentine and limestone, setting up figures of themselves at the former sepulchre of Alexander to maintain the royal presence in this most significant of dynastic sites.

Finally the visitors left Memphis. As they progressed upriver the outlines of successive pyramid fields at Dahshur, Mazghuna, Lisht and Medum dominated the west bank's horizon to their right, while the valley floor began to narrow and hug the river. Groves of fragrant mimosa gave way to Aphroditopolis, city of Hathor-Aphrodite and her sacred white Hesat cow whose priests proudly declared 'Know that Hesat is Isis!' Cleopatra, as Living Isis, may well have undertaken sacred duties at Aphroditopolis.

Yet the couple's attention was likely to have been drawn to the opposite bank of the river, where a minor branch of the Nile led to the great Fayum region(the renamed Arsinoite home) around Lake Moeris. The early Ptolemies, employing reclamation schemes several millennia old, had created nearly 500 square miles of extra agricultural land able to produce huge quantities of grain, pulses and wine. Visitors were particularly impressed by 'its development for it alone is planted with olives, of which there are many large trees bearing fine fruit'. The Ptolemies' achievements in the Fayum clearly impressed Caesar, who began to contemplate how such a scheme in Rome might allow the city to support itself and free it from its reliance on foreign grain.

Nevertheless the Fayum, like other parts of Egypt, had clearly suffered during the run of low floods. Patches of stagnating swampy ground increased malaria levels, and medical texts which described those suffering 'from every shivering fit and fever' could recommend little more than costly imported black pepper as a remedy. It would therefore have been imperative that Living Isis made her presence felt in the Fayum, just as she had at the very beginning of her reign when, still finding her pharaonic feet, she had been depicted in the guise of a male pharaoh making an offering to Isis. Yet now she appeared in the guise of Isis herself, alongside the region's chief deity, Sobek the crocodile god, in a kind of double-act, her own charms balanced by those of Sobek as 'Pneferos', 'He with the beautiful face'. Greek hymns in praise of Isis, her crocodile consort and their little-known child Anchoes may have been specially written by the Egyptian priests for the visit of their pregnant monarch and her party. Cleopatra is believed to have initiated new building activity in the northern Fayum at this time and, continuing the royal funding of the sacred crocodiles' funerary expenses, may well have had direct contact with those of the Fayum, the regional equivalent of the sacred bulls.

One temple discovered in 1912 had the cult equipment laid out alongside a mummified crocodile reclining on its processional stretcher. Housed in the temple's sacred lake, each live creature had been adorned by 'putting rings made of glass or gold into its ears and bracelets round its front feet'; they proved enormously popular with foreign visitors, few of whom had ever seen such a creature. When Cleopatra's grandfather, Chickpea, had been preparing for the visit of a Roman senator in 112 BC, local officials were told to 'make ready guest-chambers and landing-stages and presents, and to take every care that he should be satisfied' with a trip to see the sacred crocodiles at feeding time. Usually they were 'fed on grain and bits of meat and wine, which are always offered to it by visiting foreigners', as one Greek tourist reported, going on to say that 'we came upon the creature as it lay on the edge of the lake and when the priests went up to it some of them opened its mouth and another put the cake in, then the meat, and poured the honey-mixture down'. As the sated crocodile then swam off across the lake, another visitor arrived with offerings and the priests sped round to reach them and repeat their no doubt lucrative performance.

Since close contact with a crocodile was incredibly risky, some Fayumi temples employed 'sauretai' or crocodile keepers. The Romans noted that those living around Isis' cult centre of Dendera further south were particularly skilled at handling them; they were certainly sufficiently confident to balance on the crocodiles' backs in a pose skilfully captured in first-century BC marble statuary. It may be more than coincidence that such crocodiles and their fearless handlers who were able to haul them in and out of their tanks first appeared in Rome in 58 BC, the year Auletes and Cleopatra visited the region.

Isis was believed to be capable of calming and taming crocodiles, as reflected in one of her titles, 'Wet-nurse of the Crocodile', and as a result rites which brought together the female monarch and the Fayum's sacred creature in their roles as Isis and Sobek were deliberately misinterpreted in certain quarters. Much like the monarch's mystic union with the sacred bulls, such a performance was never going to be understood by those in Rome who regarded Egypt as the home of everything unacceptable, from their bizarre worship of animals to their equally strange ideas of sexual equality. It is therefore unsurprising that oil lamps of Roman manufacture often featured the image of a naked woman with her hair in a bun, holding the palm branch associated with the worship of Isis and squatting on the phallus of a large crocodile, a vulgar portrayal which seems to be 'a satirical reference to Cleopatra VII of Egypt'.

Yet, keen to see the place where such behaviour was believed to go on, first-century BC Roman tourists flocked to the Fayum, comparing its main monument, the so-called Labyrinth at Hawara (from 'Hut-weret', 'great temple'), with the Giza pyramids. The Labyrinth was the funerary complex of pharaoh Amenemhat III (1842–1797 BC), completed by his dutiful daughter and successor Sobekneferu whose name appeared as frequently as her father's throughout the complex. Given its long winding passages and secret subterranean crypts filled with statues of Sobek and the mummies of his sacred crocodiles, the Greek historian Herodotus wrote that this temple was the most amazing thing he had seen in Egypt. Cleopatra's dynasty added 'a large statue of Serapis, 9 cubits high, made of smaragdus', emeralds, whose glistening green associating Serapis with the region's mighty green crocodile god would almost certainly have been worn by Cleopatra as crocodile consort.

The hallowed area all around the Labyrinth had long been regarded as the optimum area for burial, and mummification was performed by the hereditary embalmers who lived along Hawara's King Street. Like many members of Egypt's mixed population, they were in regular dispute with their Greek neighbours. Hostilities also existed between the Fayumis and their southern neighbours in Henen-nesut, whose ram-headed god Herishef, identified with the Greek Herakles, was the origin of the town's more familiar name, Herakleopolis.

The town had been home to kings who had fought a long civil war in 2100 BC against the Thebans further south, its later association with Herakles certainly apt for a combative population still demonstrating their rivalries two thousand years later. Demonstrating their devotion to specific sacred animals, whose images would have acted as totems in territorial disputes, the Herakleopolitans honoured the ichneumon, whereas the jackal god Anubis was held in special reverence by their southern neighbours in Kynopolls, 'Dog City'. They in turn had long-running disputes with those over the Nile who venerated the pike, its distinctive features giving rise to their town's name Oxyrhynchus, meaning 'sharp snout'. As the fish believed to have swallowed the phallus of Osiris after he had been dismembered and thrown in the Nile, the sacred Oxyrhynchus fish became closely associated with Isis, who was honoured with one of many temples in a town whose main thoroughfare was Cleopatra-Aphrodite Street.

Like most big towns, Oxyrhynchus featured 'a mixture of religious buildings in traditional Egyptian style rubbing shoulders with the classically designed public buildings that defined the Greek polis – the bath complex, the gymnasium and the theatre. But on leaving the centre, one would have moved into a large and dirty Egyptian village showing comparatively little change from previous eras' and reflecting the dusty surroundings of life as it has always been lived on the desert edge. As the couple sailed deeper into the heart of Egypt, the ever-observant Caesar must also have noticed how the towns and villages had started to change: the Greek influence, which radiated so strongly from Alexandria and reached as far as the Fayum, was becoming far less obvious the further south they sailed.

When they reached the ancient site of Khmun, main cult centre of Thoth whose affinity with Hermes led to its Greek renaming as Hermopolis, this great focus of pilgrimage for both Egyptians and Greeks must have witnessed Cleopatra disembarking to pay her respects to the deity whose reputation for learning she is known to have honoured. Having brought knowledge and writing to humans, Thoth had also taught the magical arts to Isis, whose fine Ptolemaic shrine was part of Thoth's great complex filled with his sacred bird the ibis, bred on specialist farms or 'ibiotrophion' and fed on clover. A series of colossal quartzite baboons, representing Thoth's other sacred creature, led to a large column-filled hypostyle hall planned by Alexander. Here a classical 'Ptolemeion' with a cylindrical altar formed the focus of a ruler cult so strong that Cleopatra would be venerated here for four hundred years in rites administered by the priestly Petosiris family, whose burials in the nearby cemetery accompanied the mummified remains of thousands of Thoth's sacred ibis and baboons (*Papio hamadryas anubis*), their souls honoured by the Ptolemies with offerings of lavish jewellery.

Just to the south of Hermopolis, where the distinctive eastern hills formed an unusual landscape which appeared to give birth to the sun each dawn, the open plain held a cemetery of sacred dogs or jackals whose living counterparts could occasionally be seen slipping through ruins stretching far into the distance. Curious statues in the hillside flanked royal decrees ordering the burials of the royal family and the sacred Mnevis bull to be relocated to this remote place, while rows of tombs further along the hillside were covered in extensive Greek graffiti. The presence of elaborate goldwork of Ptolemaic date in the very valley containing the tombs of Mnevis and former royals was intriguing evidence that the wealthy of Ptolemaic times were clearly familiar with a site now known as Amarna, city of Akhenaten and Nefertiti.

Caesar and Cleopatra and their entourage pressed on upriver to Cusae, where earlier Ptolemies had embellished the temple of Golden Hathor, the sun god's daughter whom the Greeks knew as Aphrodite Ourania, the 'heavenly one'. Here the hillsides, dotted with the rock-cut tombs of previous generations, gave way to subterranean caves housing many thousands of mummified crocodiles stacked up in huge piles. They ranged in length from 12-inch babies to giants of over 30 feet, wrapped singly, in family groups or even in the mating position, and their combined souls were venerated by priests wearing cuirass-like costumes of crocodile skin, presumably to take on some of the creatures' sacred powers.

The splendid progress would then have reached two large settlements on either side of the river. Athribis, on the east bank, was a corruption of the ancient 'Hut-Repyt', literally 'house of Repyt', the lioness goddess whose 230-foot-wide temple had been built by Cleopatra's father and grandfather. Keen to follow them, she commissioned another wave of building work to expand the goddess' complex as a fitting balance for that of Repyt's consort Min which lay across the river.

The priapic nature of the fertility god Min meant that the Greeks regarded him as their own god Pan; his cult centre of Khent-Min (modern Akhmim), dubbed Panopolis by the Greeks, was the home town of an influential family whose intermarriage with the royals had led to the so-called Amarna period. The family's cliffside shrine had been embellished by a daughter of the later pharaoh, Nectanebo I, and paralleled by a shrine of Auletes. The centre of the ritual activity, however, was Min's great temple, whose façade, nearly 300 feet wide, fronted a mazelike layout of such magnitude and complexity that later visitors were warned that 'only by loud screaming can one lead one another's way' – a practice far removed from the peaceful, ordered routine of the ancient clergy. At the heart of its echoing interior of columned halls, corridors, ramps and staircases lay the mystical 'House of the Moon' where Min received his leonine consort Repyt for their annual union, her statue being carried in festive procession in the same way that Cleopatra would have been carried aloft in her gold carrying chair before performing the sacred rites.

Beyond Min's stronghold lay Ptolemais Hermiou, something of a Greek oasis in an otherwise Egyptian desert and founded as a counter-balance to Thebes. It soon developed into one of the largest cities in the region, from where royal officials kept the monarchy informed of events. Cleopatra's own 'men on the ground' were her key officials Hephaistion and Theon, and their regular correspondence revealed that a temple of Isis had been built at Ptolemais Hermiou in Cleopatra's honour. Perhaps she and Caesar paid a visit on their progress south, for in a letter dated the following year, 7 March 46 BC, she wrote, 'To Theon. Let the relevant persons be told that the temple of Isis built on behalf of our well-being by Kallimachos the military commander south of Ptolemais is to be tax-free and inviolable together with the houses built around it as far as the wall of the city. Let it be done!'

Business concluded, the royal party would have carried on to Abedju (Abydos), home of the famous temple of Osiris which, like many others, was linked to the Nile by a small canal. Groves of acanthus gave way to the paved quayside of the temple, a 'remarkable structure of solid stone' that was yet another great draw for Greek and Roman tourists who called it the Memnonion after the throne name of its builder, the thirteenth-century BC pharaoh Seti I 'Menmaatra'.

Certainly royal names were of tremendous importance in a temple housing the cult of Seti's royal predecessors. The so-called Chamber of Ancestors, which listed all the monarchs from the beginning of Egypt's history c.3100 BC down to Seti's own day, revealed how his no-

nonsense militaristic dynasty had rewritten Egypt's history to suit their own agenda. Although it omitted the names of such undesirables as the female pharaohs Hatshepsut, Nefertiti and her fellow 'heretics' Akhenaten, Tutankhamen and Ay, Abydos' list was still an important part of the ancestor rituals which seem to have been familiar to Cleopatra. Now, carrying her own successor, she may well have visited the temple with Caesar to view and indeed read out the royal ancestor list for herself. The place was certainly a tourist highlight, with hundreds of graffiti in Greek, Cypriot, Carian, Aramaic and Phoenician paying homage to famous pharaohs of the past, to Osiris, Serapis and all 'the gods in Abydos'. Pilgrims were allowed to sleep within the temple's incubation area to receive therapeutic dreams, but it seems that some pilgrims had dreams of a rather different nature. One of the graffiti outlining the charms of a local working girl was amended in a second hand, verifying the initial comments but adding that 'to my mind, she is too short'.

In the vast desert necropolis beyond the temple of Abydos lay Egypt's last-known royal pyramid. It was a cenotaph to Queen Tetisheri, honoured down the centuries as the founder of the XVIII royal dynasty and mother to married brother-and-sister rulers Tao II and Ahhotep. And as the final resting place of Egypt's earliest kings, the necropolis was still in the burial business in Ptolemaic times.

Yet its greatest tomb was the mythical burial site of Osiris, Lord of the Underworld, making this a place of pilgrimage for many centuries. It was always packed out during the annual 'Mysteries of Osiris', which took place amid the tombs during the Egyptian month of 'Koiakh' (from 'Ka-her-ka' or 'soul-upon-soul', ancient Egypt's equivalent of 'All Hallows'). It remained one of the most important festivals in the Ptolemaic calendar, when Osiris' death and resurrection were commemorated by the living remembering their own deceased relatives.

The priests undertook secret nocturnal rites within the temple's innermost sanctum before stepping out into the darkness of the great desert graveyard. As their torch-lit procession commemorating Isis' search for Osiris was echoed by lamps lit in homes across Egypt, it was believed that she reunited his dismembered body parts through mummification and, using her great magic, raised the dead god to conceive her son Horus. With Osiris' burial on 21 December followed by Horus' birth on 23 December, linked to the winter solstice and similar cross-cultural legends of death and resurrection, both the site and the story would have held tremendous resonance for Cleopatra whose impending motherhood was only a few months away. Perhaps she ventured down into Osiris' subterranean Osireion temple, whose monolithic construction was intentionally sited below ground level to receive the annual floodwaters, in order to invoke the waters as Living Isis.

As her royal party progressed further upstream, the valley floor shrank to nothing when the cliffs pulled right up to the Nile as it veered north-east. The point where the river bent back again to resume its southerly course was the site of Iunet, Greek Tentyris (Dendera), the very birthplace of Isis, born to the sky goddess Nut but already 'older than her mother'. The goddess' beautiful new temple was certainly one of the places Cleopatra was keen to see following her last visit almost two years before.

Since Auletes laid the foundation stone on 16 July 54 BC in the company of his female other half, most likely his daughter Cleopatra, work had proceeded incredibly swiftly thanks to generous royal patronage and regular inspections by the regional governor Pa-ashem, or Pakhom to the Greeks. Yet it had not been a straightforward task, since Auletes' initial plans had been embellished to create what some regard as Egypt's most complex temple. Its multi-storey interior concealed stairways and secret rooms accessed through a series of sliding blocks in walls and pavements, while the hieroglyphs covering the surfaces were the most decorative of all temple inscriptions. The figure of every female monarch in the interior represented Cleopatra, performing sacred rites, and on the exterior a massive sculpted head of Hathor was covered in precious gold leaf to reflect the goddess' role as 'the Golden One'. Cleopatra's lavish use of gold, silver and precious stones to cover the temple's wall scenes, shrines and statues was described in first-century BC temple records listing all sorts of building work undertaken on shrines, including 'the naos shrine of Hathor resplendent in silver, gold and every kind of precious stone without measure' and 'the statue of Isis which is hidden, made of finest gold'.

With Isis-Hathor addressed as 'Mistress of Wine' and presented with the appropriate libations, she returned the favour by providing the monarch with the means and power to rule, adding, 'I give you happiness daily, without distress for your majesty.' Offering 'drunkenness upon drunkenness without end' as a means of communing with the gods, the other key feature of Dendera's rites was music, particularly the region's favourite African music or 'nigro tibicine' which may well have accompanied the words of a wonderfully evocative hymn to Isis-Hathor inscribed on the walls of the Offering Hall.

Perhaps a tribute from Auletes' daughter, the lyrics seem particularly apt given his love of music which he used to express his own devotion to gods Greek and Egyptian. The words describe how 'Pharaoh comes to dance and comes to sing, Mistress, see his dancing, see the skipping! He offers the wine jug to you, Mistress, see his dancing, see the skipping! His heart is pure, no evil in his body, Mistress, see his dancing, see the skipping! O Golden One, how fine is the song, like the song of Horus himself, which Ra's son sings as the finest singer. He is Horus, the musician! He hates to see sorrow in your soul, he hates the bright goddess to be sad! Oh beautiful One, Great Cow, Great Magician, Glorious Lady, Gold of the gods, he comes to dance, comes to sing with his sistrum [sacred rattle] of gold and his menat [ritual necklace] of malachite, his feet rush toward the Mistress of Music as he dances for her and she loves all he does!'

Although she too may have performed such rites, the pregnant Cleopatra must have proceded most carefully on her inspection tour of the temple. She would have slowly ascended the gentle incline of the smooth stone steps to reach the rooftop shrines where the sky goddess Nut, stretched out on the ceiling, prepared to give birth to her divine children Isis and Osiris amid the blood-red of the dawn sky.

Contemplating her forthcoming labour, the ruler seems also to have visited the temple's separate Mammisi Birth House, built by the earlier pharaoh Nectanebo I for the rites in celebration of Isis-Hathor's safe delivery of her child Horus. Its priests would surely have performed protective rites for their monarch, invoking the powers of the dwarf god Bes as chief protector of pregnant women and employing the specially infused amulets of Bes that they were known to produce for women to wear during childbirth.

Sufficiently primed and protected to continue on her royal progress south, she would have reached the next key site, Koptos, where the safe birth of Isis' child was marked by an annual flower festival. It was the place where Isis was said to have cut off a lock of her hair in mourning for Osiris, and the very hair was displayed as a holy relic in the temple at Koptos for over a thousand years. One soldier wrote home, 'I hope that you are in good health, and without cease, for you, I worship close to the hair at Koptos.' Other pilgrims seem to have been rather more demonstrative, and in the grand tradition of Egyptian fertility worship inebriated women exposed themselves to the accompaniment of temple musicians in honour of Isis' phallic consort Min, an aspect of Osiris, before Min's sacred bull and Isis' dainty gazelle.

Having established her own presence within Min and Isis' temple with a limestone statue of herself wearing the crown of double plumes, sun disc and cow's horns, Cleopatra also commissioned a new stone shrine for Isis' cult statue; a small crypt or 'priest hole' at the rear of the shrine enabled priests to conceal themselves in order to make divine pronouncements on the deity's behalf. It was decorated with images of herself leading the rites as sole monarch with no male consort, and the accompanying hieroglyphs named her 'Lady of the Two Lands, Cleopatra Philopator, beloved of Min of Koptos, King's Daughter, King's Wife' in the only acknowledgement of the formal union with her youngest brother, Ptolemy XIV. In a further innovative touch, the shrine's rear wall featured a uniquely realistic view of Isis' sacred barque as it would have appeared within the shrine, viewed from the front rather than the traditional profile view.

During her time at Koptos, Cleopatra is likely to have followed tradition by presenting Isis and Min with gold and agate vessels containing myrrh and cinnamon oil, part of the wealth imported through the eastern desert they guarded. For Koptos was the place where the main Red Sea trade route connected with the Nile valley, and its priests had become very powerful from their cut of the wealth which came into their temple.

Politically aligned to Thebes, the Koptos clergy operated a kind of clerical exchange system in which their god Min-Osiris was worshipped in Thebes, and Theban priests were in charge of the Osiris cult in Koptos. Similar arrangements covering other temples in the region allowed the Theban priests to control much of the south from their base at Karnak, and as Cleopatra and Caesar came nearer to Thebes they would have come first to its outpost at Madu (Medamud), sacred to the great war god Montu whom they must have wished to thank for their recent success in the Alexandrian War.

From the temple quayside they would have seen an avenue of sphinxes leading up to Montu's great temple, its façade built by Cleopatra's father Auletes, its fine portico by her grandfather Chickpea and its multi-columned hypostyle hall by her great-grandfather Physkon. Lively wall scenes depicted the temple musicians playing their harps, lutes and barrel drums for the dancers, the accompanying lyrics of an ancient XVIII-dynasty favourite, 'Come, Golden Goddess', proclaiming, 'it is good for the heart to dance! Shine on our feast at the hour of retiring, and enjoy the dance at night. Come! The procession takes place at the site of drunkenness, drunks play tambourines for you in the cool night, and those they awaken bless you.'

Further within the temple's depths, a series of Minotaur-like statues with bull's heads on human bodies represented Montu, paired with companion figures of his human-featured consort Rattawy, 'Female Sun of the Two Lands'. Caesar now came into his own as the living embodiment of the war god alongside his goddess consort Cleopatra. They must have paid their respects to Montu's Buchis bull in its sacred area immediately behind the temple. Its epithet 'lord of Medamud, Thebes, Tod and Hermonthis' reveals that the same bull did the rounds of a ritual circuit encompassing Montu's four cult sites, so this would not have been Cleopatra's first encounter with the shaggy black and white creature she had rowed between Thebes and Hermonthis in her first act as monarch four years earlier.

Although such divine journeys traditionally took place on the Nile, it seems that the 3-mile journey between Medamud and Thebes could also be undertaken along the ceremonial canal which connected Montu's Medamud temple with his shrine at Karnak. Yet the likely dimensions of Cleopatra's royal ship suggest that, on this occasion at least, her arrival in Thebes would have been by river.

Once Thebes's political power had been finally smashed by her grandfather Chickpea, the ninth Ptolemy, back in 88 BC after decades of conflict with the crown, the formerly great city had been reduced to little more than a series of scattered villages. But as a known supporter of the region's cults from the very start of her reign, Cleopatra had been given refuge in the region when ousted from power by her eldest brother, Ptolemy XIII. Now, restored to her throne, she would have received the same positive welcome from the powerful military commander Kallimachos, who controlled the entire Theban region on her behalf.

Having produced a succession of powerful dynasties in the past, the Thebans had always had difficulty taking orders from their nominal masters in the north. They regarded themselves as a people apart and expressed the north–south divide with their own customs, even piercing their left ears to mark themselves out in contrast to the Alexandrians and certainly the Romans, who considered earrings for men effeminate and a sign of slavery. Rightly proud of their past glories, the Thebans were quite used to the tourists who came to see their sights, sailing down the ancient canal route towards the Theban hills and the temples and tombs of the ancient pharaohs.

First stop on any itinerary was an astonishing pair of 60-foot-high colossi seated sentinel-like before the ruins of a vast funerary temple of the fourteenth-century BC sun king Amenhotep III ('Amenophis' in Greek). Earthquake damage to the northernmost figure subsequently caused it to emit a musical sound as it warmed up in the morning sun, and the phenomenon clearly struck a chord with the Ptolemies who were familiar with the practice of exposing cult statues to the sunlight to reactivate the spirit within. Although one Greek visitor somewhat shattered the magic by asking if the sound was 'deliberately made by one of the men standing all around and near the base', or at the very least was enhanced by human effort, Manetho had told the Ptolemies that the sound was a means of communication from Amenhotep III, 'considered to be Memnon and a talking stone'. The king's throne name was 'Nebmaatra', pronounced Nimmuria or Mimmuria, and the Greeks had equated him with their own hero Memnon, killed in the Trojan War. The statues' legs had since been transformed into an ancient visitors' book recording appreciative comments including those of subsequent Roman rulers. Cleopatra may well have brought Caesar here to listen to the statue's dawn chorus and explain its links both to her pharaonic predecessors and to Caesar's own family connections with Troy.

Beyond the Memnon Colossi the Ptolemies had clearly been active around the towering cliffs of Deir el–Bahari, where the famous multi-terraced funerary temple of the female pharaoh Hatshepsut was well known for its famous scenes of Amun impregnating Hatshepsut's mother. It had been conserved and expanded by Cleopatra's dynasty: its innermost shrine became a chapel to Imhotep-Asklepios, his daughter Hygeia and the ancient Egyptian sage Amenhotep, son of Hapu. It was also a place where the ailing came to pray and find comfort; a priest would project his voice through a small opening to advise the supplicants beyond. Their grateful graffiti revealed an impressive success rate, from a Macedonian labourer cured on the day of his visit to a dedication by a Greek couple thanking Amenhotep for the birth of their child. The whole area was regarded as holy, and was still used as a burial ground. The nearby funerary temple of Ramses II was similarly described by one of Cleopatra's contemporaries as the 'tomb of Osymandyas', the Greeks' pronunciation of Ramses' throne name Usermaatre. He was worshipped here after his death, even though the pharaoh himself was actually buried, like virtually every other pharaoh of the New Kingdom era (1550–1080 BC), in the nearby Valley of the Kings. Even then it was a major tourist destination, described by one Greek visitor as 'marvelously devised, a spectacle worth seeing', and graffiti left in the tombs agreed that 'those who have not seen this place have never seen anything: blessed are they who visit this place'. At least six of the royal tombs were easily accessible in Ptolemaic times, although the most popular was the 'tomb of Memnon' that the Greeks associated with the builder of the great singing colossi but had actually been built by a later pharaoh who, in a confusing act of hero worship, adopted the same throne name, 'Nebmaatra'.

The valley might have ceased to be a royal burial ground over a thousand years earlier, but it nevertheless remained a most sacred place: the cult statue of Amun of Karnak still made its annual procession across the Nile to visit the tombs and temples of the royal ancestors. It was a place where private individuals had long sought burial in their attempts to capture some of that ancient magic for themselves, and in Cleopatra's time their mummies continued to stack up inside much older tombs. The son of a powerful local official, Menkare, even retrieved the five-hundred-year-old sarcophagus of Psammetichus II's daughter from her ransacked tomb for his own burial.

Across the river on the east bank, despite the wartime devastation wrought on the city of Thebes many of its sacred shrines remained intact, including Luxor's 'temple of the divine soul'. With an inner sanctum decorated with scenes of Amun impregnating the mother of yet another mortal king in a story predating the alleged paternity of Alexander by more than a thousand years, the temple's holiest shrine, commissioned by Alexander himself, was covered in his image, making offerings as a traditional pharaoh before his impressively endowed father Min-Amun. Marking the spot where each monarch had come to revitalise his or her spiritual powers through secret congress with his or her spiritual father Amun, the temple muct have held considerable allure for both Cleopatra and Caesar. Their state visit may have continued along the impressive sphinx-lined processional way which connected the temple with the great Karnak complex with its 70-foot-high Ptolemaic gateway – the place where justice was dispensed, executions carried out and offerings made by those unqualified to venture any further into the temple's vast precincts.

Living Isis, however, would almost certainly have been carried through her ancestor's great gateway in her carrying chair, quite possibly towards the subterranean 'tomb of Osiris' built by Ptolemy IV and decorated by scenes of the same king performing resurrection rites before the Apis bull. This may well have been the southern counterpart of the Soma burial chamber in Alexandria completed by the same king. The nocturnal vigils held in the Karnak chamber hint at attempts to revive Alexander's soul at the cult centre of his divine father Zeus-Amun using the power of Egypt's supreme funerary deity, Osiris. And with Isis taking a starring role in such rites, the Karnak chamber must have been a key place for Cleopatra to visit with Caesar, both of whom were familiar with its counterpart burial chamber in Alexandria.

Despite the damage inflicted on parts of Karnak during the earlier civil war, sufficient had remained of its northerly precinct of Amun-Montu for Cleopatra to have personally installed Montu's sacred Buchis bull there, imbuing the event with her divine presence before rowing him to Hermonthis. Now, with her return visit to Hermonthis' 'magnificent' temple allowing an inspection of new wall scenes naming her 'King of Upper and Lower Egypt' and 'Female Horus', Cleopatra would also have seen the images of herself worshipping Buchis, Montu and Rattawy, whose name was literally 'Female Sun of the Two Lands'. Reflecting Cleopatra's own title 'Lady of the Two Lands', Rattawy was a deity she seems to have cultivated, for at Hermonthis she 'was there because Cleopatra wanted her to be there'.

Clearly an important element in Cleopatra's grand design, a new Mammisi Birth House was commissioned behind the exisiting temple in a layout corresponding exactly with that of the Birth House and temple at Dendera. Certainly Cleopatra's Hermonthis Mammisi was a superb building whose 'luxuriant decoration represented an excellent example of the baroque style of [Ptolemaic] architecture'. As work began on its three chambers surrounded by a colonnade of slim columns, 'the play of light and shadows at the capitals, and the effect of the huge, window-like openings that created beautiful connections between interior and exterior spaces, must have been stunning'. Statues of Montu's sacred bull adorned an interior featuring unprecedented scenes of the actual birth-ing process. To complete the Mammisi there would be a sacred lake with its own Nilometer for measuring the annual flood levels, a wide stone staircase rising directly from the lake to the Mammisi entrance allowing those who were performing ritual ablutions to rise untainted into the temple to perform their rites in a purified state.

Leaving the sacred lands of the Buchis bull, Caesar and Cleopatra would have reached Tasenet (modern Esna), a site the Greeks called Latopolis or 'Fish City' after its sacred *Lates niloticus* fish. Yet its main temple, built by the Ptolemies, was dedicated to the ram-headed creator god Khnum, the god long believed to have caused the Nile to flood and to have fashioned humans on his potter's wheel – the very wheel still displayed in its own shrine. Khnum's annual ceremonies were listed on the surrounding temple walls. The 'Mystery of the Birth' contained the 'Spell for establishing the Wheel in the bodies of all female beings' which involved placing 'the egg in the bodies of women, to provide the country with younger generations for the favour of the King of Upper and Lower Egypt, beloved of Khnum'. This was followed by a rite involving a trio of young women representing the various stages of pregnancy.

As the couple sailed south to Nekheb (El-Kab), the birth theme intensified at the great labyrinth-like temple of the vulture goddess

Nekhbet, one of the principal assistants at royal births. Embellished by the Ptolemies, who had also added to Nekhbet's shrines in the surrounding hills, this temple was where Cleopatra III had built her own rock-cut shrine to the local lioness goddess Shesmetet. Appearing alone as 'Female Horus, Lady of Upper and Lower Egypt and Mighty Bull', the sweeping amalgamation of king, queen, god and goddess would not have been lost on her great-granddaughter Cleopatra VII.

If Cleopatra and Caesar did venture as far south as the ancient sources claim, they would certainly have reached Horus' cult centre, Edfu. As a site of incalculable importance for the Ptolemies, Edfu was the pre-eminent place to celebrate the cult of the royal ancestors in which each dead king was represented by Osiris, and the living pharaoh by Osiris' son Horus. It was founded by the third Ptolemaic couple and inaugurated by the eighth, while Cleopatra's father had also made a very definite mark at the site with his huge front pylon gateway. A maze of internal stairways recalled those of Dendera, while its façade was adorned with massive figures of Auletes smiting the enemies of Egypt alongside two pairs of huge flagpoles of imported Lebanese cedar, which set the pennants of the gods fluttering 130 feet above the ground. Then, at the centre, a pair of 45-foot-high doors of the same timber, covered in highly polished copper, reflected the sunlight and literally dazzled all who approached.

Far more than a colossal gateway, Auletes' pylon and adjoining court beyond had been skilfully designed to exploit the use of light and dark, so that the pylon's shadow at the winter solstice on 21 December covered the courtyard in darkness, while at midsummer on 21 June it cast no shadow and instead acted 'as a giant sundial'. This subtle exploitation of sunlight was also employed within the temple, and in an ancient form of special effects designed to heighten the atmosphere the light decreased towards the darkness of the innermost santuary, where a monolithic shrine of highly polished syenite dating back to Nectanebo II had been retained as a link with the last native pharaoh. It held within it a smaller gilded shrine whose delicate doors opened to reveal Horus' gold cult statue set with semi-precious stones. A live falcon was housed alongside as the living incarnation of both Horus and the current monarch. Kept well fed with meat provided by the crown, and presumably with its wings well clipped, the sacred falcon was worshipped alongside its sculpted equivalent in daily rites each morning, noon and dusk, and every year both were taken up to the roof to unite with the sun.

Falconry duties aside, Edfu's clergy were also employed in the temple's small perfume 'laboratory' whose walls were inscribed with the costly materials once housed within, from the frankincense used as the gods' wake-up call in the morning ceremonies, via the sixteen different kinds of myrrh burned at the main midday service, to kapet, the Greek 'kyphi', a sweet, cinnamon-based incense employed in evening rites. Then there were specific perfumes designed to anoint the gods' statues, from the 'best quality oil' used to illuminate the face of the sculpted Horus to the traditional 'sacred oils' which had been in use since the Pyramid Age. By Ptolemaic times there were nine of these, ranging from the frankincense and fir seeds of 'Festival Scent' to the carob, lotus and white frankincense of 'Madjet'.

While other side rooms housed sacred vestments and equipment, the temple library held such ancient works as *The Book of Conducting the Cult*, *The Secret Forms of the God* and *Knowing the Periodic Return of the Stars*, along with scripts for the sacred drama *The Triumph of Horus* in which the god avenges his father Osiris by slaying his murderer Seth. The drama was performed to a musical accompaniment which no doubt appealed to the Ptolemies' love of theatre, and the story was replicated in highly detailed scenes on the temple walls alongside those of Horus' sacred marriage to the goddess Hathor.

For a ceremony known as the 'Festival of the Beautiful Union', Hathor's golden statue was brought 110 miles south from Dendera to Edfu each year. Surrounded by flowers and doused in her signature 'tisheps' unguent used exclusively 'for anointing the Golden Goddess Hathor', she was carried in stately procession towards the darkness of the temple's inner sanctum and joined to Horus in sacred marriage.

It certainly seems possible that the 'Festival of the Beautiful Union' was repeated for Caesar and Cleopatra, earthly representatives of the divine couple Hathor, the Roman Venus, and Horus 'the faraway conquering god'. Perhaps they exploited the gods' atypical marital arrangements, in which they retained their independent status and continued to live some distance apart despite their union. The iconography of Hathor also fitted Cleopatra's requirements. In keeping with

Egyptian tradition the goddess was both Horus' partner and his mother, to emphasise the endless cycle of regeneration. The name Hathor, 'Hut-Hor', meaning the 'house' or 'womb' of Horus, highlighted Cleopatra's pregnant state, which the Edfu priesthood would have done all they could to safeguard through traditional protection rituals. For, as the temple's god declared, 'I am Horus whom Isis has brought forth and whose protection was guaranteed in the egg.'

Protection ceremonies formed a key part of most ceremonials, from coronations, jubilees and gods' installations to ensuring safe delivery of the next generation of royals. As described in the temple's *Book of the Magical Protection of the Ruler in the Palace*, a lengthy rite required the monarch to be covered with protective amulets and surrounded by the same kind of seal images of previous rulers found in storage at the site. Then, with the accumulated powers of gods and ancestors forming a kind of divine force field, a live falcon, goose, hawk and vulture were each made to spread their wings around the ruler, who was also anointed with tears extracted from the falcon's eyes – the Eye of Horus was the most potent of the amulets found throughout Egyptian culture. With such spells as the 'Formula for Repelling the Evil Eye' read out, execration rites were performed to neutralise harmful forces. The ceremony ended with the birds being taken up to the temple roof and released to the four cardinal points to mark the renewal of royal protection.

Yet all this meant far more than simply ensuring Cleopatra a safe delivery. The unborn child's role as the future Horus would have been particularly significant at Edfu, where Horus the 'Great God' was believed to have had 'his being before the ancestors', and whose rites were celebrated immediately after the main daily ceremony in all temples. The ancestors' presence at coronations, jubilees, harvest rites and sacred marriages also raises the intriguing possibility that the main purpose of Cleopatra's long cruise south with Caesar was largely to visit Edfu, where their sacred union, followed by protection rites for an heir to guarantee divine continuity, was central to Cleopatra's dynastic plans.

Although it is not known whether the couple ventured any further south, where the steep sandstone cliffs reaching down to the river made the Nile difficult to navigate, they may well have continued, albeit with a smaller naval escort, since one of Caesar's Roman biographers was adamant that they 'would have sailed together in her state barge nearly to Ethiopia had his soldiers consented to follow him'. In her attempts to alleviate the serious famine ravaging her kingdom Cleopatra would surely have wanted to continue south towards the legendary source of the Nile as previous Ptolemies had done, both to invoke the annual flood and to keep an eye on a border region vital to Egypt's security. There was an important military base at Pa-Sebek, 'the land of Sobek', the crocodile god known to the Greeks as Ombos (Kom Ombo). Its beautiful temple, built on a promontory on the Nile, had been a favourite with Cleopatra's father, whose monumental gateway gave direct access from the river.

Perhaps Auletes' daughter and unborn grandchild passed through with Caesar, viewing the progress on wall scenes showing Cleopatra solo before the gods, or the temple crocodiles in their stone pool with its elaborate system of fountains. The people of Ombos, like the Fayumis, regarded the creatures as divine and treated them with great respect. Yet at a time when such animal cults had become emotive symbols of regional status, stage-managed fights between neighbouring temples were a form of worship: rival supporters travelled to away matches to get drunk and taunt their rivals. Since the people of Edfu and Dendera regarded the crocodile as evil, their visits to Ombos could sometimes get out of hand, and when the Dendera crowd became increasingly drunk on one visit the mood is said to have turned nasty; spurred on by religious hatred, the Ombites began a fist-fight ending in a murder, the man's body torn to pieces as 'the victorious crowd, gnawing his bones, ate all of him' in an apparent act of ritual cannibalism.

Most Nile journeys ended at the ancient trading post of Swenet, the Ptolemaic Syene (modern Aswan), which was a magnet for scholars. Eratosthenes had come here from Alexandria to calculate the circumference of the earth from the angles of shadows, since at midsummer the sun cast no shadow at noon. Other researchers had come to study the Nile floods and investigate Egyptian beliefs that the ram-headed creator god Khnum sent forth the annual flood from his cave beneath the large island in the middle of the Nile. Caesar's own desire to discover the true source of the flood must have made this a place of great interest for him, and studying the island's well-built Nilometer, he may have quizzed the priests about the new theories concerning rains further south as he had discussed with one of the Memphis clergy. He may also have accompanied Cleopatra on her state visit to the island's red granite temple of Khnum, built by the first Ptolemy on behalf of Alexander's son Alexander IV, and where the visit of her grandfather Chickpea was commemorated on a large red granite stela. The temple complex also housed Khnum's sacred rams, whose vigorous powers of fertility were preserved at death when each was mummified and buried within the island where Khnum himself resided. Their powers would have combined with those of Cleopatra as she presumably celebrated a version of the annual Festival of Inundation as her grandfather is known to have done. Perhaps this was followed by a visit to the island's temple of Isis housing the goddess' oracle, whose priests are likely to have sought royal assurance that their privileges would not be reduced in the face of the crown's growing support for Isis' main cult centre only a little way south at Philae.

Founded by the last native dynasty, so only a few centuries rather than millennia old, Philae had certainly been the destination for the first Cleopatra, who came with her husband in 186 BC to celebrate both a military victory and the birth of her son. Now it was the likely end point for Cleopatra and Caesar's own journey, using a smaller vessel to negotiate the narrow channels dug out of the river's rocky outcrops (known as cataracts). Philae's gleaming temple on the 'Island from the time of Ra' would then have appeared to rise up from the waters before them.

No doubt greeted by its priests as Living Isis, 'Queen of the South', Cleopatra is likely to have adopted the multi-horned crown of Geb to emphasise continuity with her great predecessor Arsinoe II, portrayed in Philae's relief scenes in the same crown she in turn had borrowed from Hatshepsut in a reassuring continuity of female monarchs combining with Isis to become 'Mistress of Life, as she dispenses life. Men live by the command of her soul'. In further scenes bestowing the milk of life to her infant son Horus in the temple's Mammisi, Isis received myrrh, jewels and even a sacred gazelle from Ptolemy Physkon and his two wives Cleopatras II and III. The same rulers had provided Philae with its library, perfume laboratory, three granite shrines for Isis' statues and a pair of stone obelisks, behind which the first great pylon gateway once more featured the huge figures of Cleopatra's father Auletes smiting Egypt's enemies.

Auletes had also created a beautiful temple for Osiris on the nearby island of Biga, the 'pure mound', where local tradition claimed he was actually buried surrounded by a sacred grove of trees. Here the clergy sang their daily dirges and poured their libations of milk, sacred to Isis whose cult statue was regularly ferried over from Philae to lead her husband's funerary rites. Pilgrims from as far afield as Italy collected the sacred waters Lourdes-style to use in Isis' worship back home. Many threw gold coins into the waters or brought rich offerings, and as the crown diverted large amounts of their own wealth into Isis' sacred coffers neighbouring temples fought a losing battle to retain their traditional spheres of influence against the powerful priests of Philae.

With the imminent motherhood of Living Isis destined to create a new golden age in which they would surely play a key role, the Philae priesthood commemorated the time when their goddess appeared amongst them with a golden figure that would be venerated and cherished for centuries to come. As she sailed down the Nile Cleopatra had been worshipped as the most powerful deity incarnate, and the impact of some two million people paying heartfelt homage to his partner clearly made a lasting impression on Caesar, who was already contemplating the way in which his own divinity might be used to bring Rome even more completely under his sole control.

6

Great Mother Isis: the Birth of Caesarion

Following the couple's return to Alexandria after their cruise south, Caesar began preparations for his return to Rome where Pompeius' sons were still at large and their supporters growing in strength. Although his failure to return immediately after the Alexandrian War was criticised by those in Rome who blamed his protracted stay on Cleopatra, accused of ensnaring the noble Roman with her feminine wiles, factors beyond even his control had been at play, from the onslaught of the Alexandrians to the onset of unfavourable coastal winds which made sailing hazardous for several months, and all of which he described himself in his own accounts. Caesar had therefore used the winter and spring of 48–47 BC to maximise support in the East, replacing an uncooperative regime with a loyal ally and guaranteeing himself a potential heir, a steady cash flow and a reliable source of grain for the people of Rome, whose backing would be vital if he was to push his policies through the Senate.

To ensure Cleopatra's safety and maintain her position, he left three legions in Alexandria under the reliable command of his favourite freedman, Rufio. Their presence would also demonstrate to his critics back in Rome that he had made Egypt a Roman protectorate. Not only that, it would offset any suggestion of seizing the country and simply making it a province, something which Caesar would certainly have done had he not been romantically involved with its persuasive monarch.

Although theoretically Cleopatra still ruled alongside her remaining half-brother Ptolemy XIV and had the twelve-year-old firmly under her control, her half-sister Arsinoe IV was still causing problems. By declaring herself monarch in Cleopatra's place when the Alexandrians were besieging the palace she had committed a treasonable act which

Cleopatra would not forget. Yet, rather than imprison her in Alexandria as a focus of potential resistance, or risk the backlash that her execution would cause, it was decided that Caesar should take Arsinoe back to Rome as his prisoner.

Having presumably said their farewells in private, the heavily pregnant monarch in her golden carrying chair must have accompanied him in procession the short distance from the palace to the Great Harbour keen to demonstrate their alliance in the full glare of the Alexandrian public. Perhaps they clasped each other's right hands in the formal gesture of farewell, as Caesar finally boarded ship and left Egypt. The occasion surely affected Cleopatra. Since him had given her her throne, her heir and indeed her life, she decided to create a suitably impressive monument to honour him – the Caesareum which in Greek was 'Kaisaros Epibaterios', 'Embarking Caesar', hinting at its inspiration.

Sailing out of Alexandria's Great Harbour past the palaces, the Pharos and the colossus of Isis, Caesar did not go straight back to Rome. Needing to shore up Jewish support for his forthcoming struggles against Pompeius' sons, he sailed along the coast to Acre to reward Pompeius' former supporters Antipatros and Hyrcanus for their valuable help in the Alexandrian War. As Rome's representative, he confirmed their regime, excused them all tribute, allowed them to rebuild Jerusalem and gave them the port of Joppa (Jaffa) which Cleopatra had wanted herself as part of her plans to regain the Ptolemies' former territories. Caesar had instead restored Cyprus to her, and the revenues from that island allowed her to relax the heavy taxes she had been forced to impose at the beginning of her reign in order to keep Egypt afloat.

With the economy gaining ground and Roman troops available for military support if needed, Cleopatra was in an increasingly secure position as she finally prepared to give birth to her first child on 23 June 47 BC. Yet a pharaoh in labour was no everyday occurrence. Her own life and that of her successor were of such paramount importance to the future of the country that the birth would have been accompanied by every form of protection that the gods of Egypt and the rest of the ancient world could bestow. Isis the Great Mother was repeatedly invoked along with Hathor – her classical equivalents Greek Aphrodite and Caesar's own ancestor the Roman Venus. Artemis was another vital member of the divine birth team. As the 'Reliever of the birth pangs of women' and revered as Artemis 'Polymastica' (meaning 'the Many Breasted'), Artemis had left her own great temple in Ephesus to attend Alexander's birth in Macedonia. She was linked to the Greek goddess Eileithyia, and portrayed like Isis with a torch to help mother and child in the darkness. The combined Artemis-Eileithyia declared, 'I have brought forth the new-born baby at the tenth orbit of the moon – fit light for the deed that is consummated'.

Given the child's paternity, the polytheistic Egyptians may well have invoked the Roman deities associated with childbirth, from Alemona who guarded the foetus to Partula who presided over the birth itself. And given the presence of Caesar's troops within the palace quarter, it seems likely that at least one of their number would have performed the ancient, albeit bizarre, rite in which a light cavalry spear which had already been used to kill in battle would be thrown over the house in which the birth was taking place in order to ease the delivery. Known as the 'hasta caelibaris' or 'celibate spear', it was thought to have magical powers over life and death, although its purpose was the very opposite of that of the Roman spears which had rained down around the palace only six months before.

The highest echelons of the Egyptian priesthood, including Cleopatra's closest advisers, would have gathered within the palace. Incense-fuelled rites and prayers would have featured religious personnel wearing the mask of Bes, god of childbirth. According to the third-century BC legend of Alexander, Nectanebo II wore the mask of Zeus-Ammon when impregnating Alexander's mother Olympias. Still there nine months later, he attended her labour with a divining dish, assorted wax figurines and all his inherent powers as a pharaoh of Egypt to achieve the most auspicious time for his son's birth by 'measuring the courses of the heavenly bodies; he urged her not to hurry in giving birth. At the same time he jumbled up the cosmic elements by the use of his magic powers, discovered what lay hidden in them and said to her "woman, contain yourself and struggle against the pressure of Nature"' in order that Alexander would be born at exactly the most propitious moment.

Although this description comes from a work of fiction, it nevertheless hints at the kind of rites which may have been employed when Cleopatra gave birth to a child regarded as Alexander's descendant, although the kind of esoteric rites long employed in Egyptian medical practice had been refined and improved by the medical schools of Alexandria. Specialist obstetricians, some of whom were female, were available to the wealthy. Details of the obstetric treatments available from those trained in Alexandria's enlightened schools were preserved in the second-century AD works of Soranus of Ephesus. He was the most famous gynaecologist until modern times, and during Europe's Middle Ages his works were consulted widely. Soranus' *Gynaecology* covered everything from pregnancy and labour to childhood illnesses, even listing the qualities required in a good midwife who must be 'literate with her wits about her . . . sound of limb, robust and according to some endowed of long slim fingers and short nails. . . . She will be unperturbed, unafraid in danger and able to state clearly the reasons for her measures, bringing reassurance to her patients and be sympathetic. . . . She must also keep her hands soft, abstaining from wool working which would make them hard, and she must acquire softness by means of ointments if it is not present naturally.'

Trained in gynaecology and obstetrics, some midwives were clearly authorities in their own right and wrote on the subject, while the Greek doctor Galen (c. AD 129–210) dedicated his *On the Anatomy of the Uterus* to a midwife. Later Arabic sources claimed that Galen had even been taught by a female gynaecologist named Cleopatra, and although Galen himself certainly recommended treatments advocated by 'Cleopatra', this most likely referred to his use of medical knowledge obtained by those working under the patronage of the monarch to whom they dedicated their work. Nevertheless, Jewish Talmudic texts claimed that Cleopatra VII was actually involved in medical experiments to determine the stages of development of the foetus, no doubt reflecting her tremendous interest in matters concerning her own all-important fertility. Certainly Alexandrian-based Herophilus had identified the ovaries and Fallopian tubes by the early third century BC; and even though the actual process of ovulation and conception remained relatively mysterious, Soranus' descriptions of the female anatomy were sufficiently accurate to have been based on the dissection of human corpses made possible by the Ptolemies' patronage.

Prior to this, the Egyptians had thought the uterus responded to external forces; after the Egyptian god Seth, murderer of Osiris, had threatened Isis and her unborn child during her pregnancy, his name was used in spells to scare the uterus into submission. Presumably influenced by his time with the priests and doctors of Heliopolis, the Greek philosopher Plato likewise believed that the uterus had its own 'animal-like existence'; even Hippocrates, known as the father of medicine, referred to the 'wandering womb' which caused 'hysteria', a specifically female condition to be treated by internal fumigation.

Challenging these earlier ideas, those trained at Alexandria realised that hysteria was based on some form of seizure of the senses, in most cases brought on by recurring miscarriage and premature birth which was the lot of many women in antiquity. Demonstrating a most admirable bedside manner, Soranus therefore recommended laying the patient in a warm room, gently rocking her and massaging her lower body with sweet olive oil, although therapeutic massage had been used in pregnancy in Egypt since at least 1500 BC.

Having identified the three stages in caring for pregnant women, Soranus stated that to preserve the 'injected seed' the woman must avoid stress, shocks, heavy lifting and falling, together with drunkenness, drug taking and malnutrition. Doing everything possible 'to appease the soul', he also noticed that some women developed unusual food cravings for charcoal, earth and unripe fruit, and although he advised a careful diet to build up strength for the birth, he warned that 'one must not pay attention to the popular saying that it is necessary to provide food for two organisms'. In addition to gentle exercise and frequent relaxing baths, he recommended alleviating discomfort by using a broad linen bandage 'if the bulk of the abdomen is hanging down under its weight'. All this is excellent advice still followed today.

In preparation for the birth, which invariably took place in the home, the woman would ideally call on the services of a midwife, several attendants and a physician, who in the case of Cleopatra was probably her personal physician Olympus. Perhaps also assisted by her two devoted maids, Charmion and Eiras, she would have bathed, tied up her hair and fastened protective amulets around her neck, forehead or arm in the same way that Isis had prepared for the birth of Horus by 'fastening an amulet about herself'. Soranus himself had no time for such superstition. He nevertheless acknowledged the comforting placebo effect, advising fellow practitioners that 'one should not forbid their use, for even if the amulet has no direct effect, still through hope it will possibly make the patient more cheerful'.

Certainly amulets were still popular in Ptolemaic times, many made of haemetite or bloodstone which was believed to prevent excessive blood loss. They featured images of Isis, the knife-wielding hippopotamus goddess Taweret or the ram-headed Khnum, 'god of the House of Birth who opens the vagina', but the most popular of all was Bes, 'greatest god of the womb of women', whose mass-produced amulets manufactured at the Dendera temple were available for pilgrims to take home. If used with the spell to 'bring down the womb or placenta to be said four times over a dwarf of clay tied to the woman's head', it was guaranteed that the 'good dwarf' himself would attend the birth to combat all dangers. The renowned potency of Egyptian-made birth amulets presumably explains their distribution across the ancient world. One example featured multiple images of Bes and Isis together with a uterus and a key to symbolise its unlocking; it was embellished by a Greek invocation to Seth and the triplicate writing of Jahweh, the one god of the Jews, in a potent blend of Egyptian, Greek and Semitic beliefs familiar in Cleopatra's Alexandria – yet in this case found as far afield as a Roman villa in Hertfordshire.

With the woman suitably protected by a host of unseen forces, the initial stage of labour took place in bed. Then, when the midwife had confirmed that the dilation was sufficiently large, the woman would be required to get out of bed and, supported by the midwife's assistants, take her position on a birthing chair. This replaced the somewhat rudimentary birth bricks upon which Egyptian women had traditionally squatted. With handles at the sides to grip and a back against which to push, an open front gave access to the midwife crouching before the woman, though Soranus advised that she 'should beware of fixing her gaze steadfastly on the genitals of the labouring woman, lest being ashamed, her body becomes contracted'. After the woman had been encouraged to 'make every effort to expel the child', the baby eventually slid out into the midwife's hands. Her assistants were on hand with 'warm water in order to cleanse all parts; sea sponges for sponging off; pieces of wool in order for a woman's parts to be covered; bandages to swaddle the new born; a pillow to place the newborn infant below the woman until the afterbirth has also been taken care of; and things to smell, such as pennyroyal, apple and quince'.

Certainly painkillers had long been available for the wealthy, from a decoction of henbane (*Hyoscyamus*), a mild narcotic of the belladonna family, to the opium juice or 'poppy tears' obtained from the heads of poppies (*Papaver somniferum*), known to the Greek botanist Dioscorides. The root of the white mandrake boiled in water was also used to make a draught to be drunk 'before surgical operations and punctures to produce anesthesia', and it also seems that cannabis (*Cannabis sativa*) was available. Recommended in ancient Egyptian medical texts in connection with treatments for 'mothers and children', cannabis was also used by the Assyrians, Greeks and Romans, its use in obstetrics due to its 'remarkable power to increase the force of uterine contractions, concomitant with a significant reduction of labour pain'. Quite likely available for Cleopatra to inhale in order to alleviate her first birth, cannabis had certainly been used to ease the excruciating labour of a fourteen-year-old in fourth-century AD Jerusalem. Although her attempts to deliver a full-term foetus through her immature pelvis had ruptured her cervix and caused a fatal haemmorrage; the carbonised drug was found in her burial.

In different circumstances, the unfortunate girl might have had access to the sophisticated abdominal surgery certainly being performed by the first century BC, when Caesar himself is said to have been delivered this way during his mother Aurelia's difficult labour. The family name of Caesar was perhaps based on the Latin word for womb, 'caesus'.

Such procedures were certainly possible with advances in medical equipment, 'expertly-made precision instruments' such as the first-century BC dioptra or bronze speculum used for internal examination. It was much smoother than its Renaissance equivalents, and Alexandria's medical texts even gave instructions to warm and lubricate such cold metal implements as well as the hands of the practitioner.

Yet despite every available procedure and painkiller, Cleopatra still faced a labour which may have been complicated by problems both psychological and physical. Had she developed an abnormal pulse and breathing, it was usual practice to lubricate the neck of the uterus with oil or grease; if the child had shifted position, physical manipulation would have been used to prevent a dangerous breach birth. But although Soranus told practitioners that 'one should do everything gently and without bruising', some truly horrific instruments were available to extract the child in cases of stillbirth or where the mother's life was regarded as more important, even if this was not always necessarily the case.

Traction hooks could be inserted into the foetus to pull it out whole, or hooked knives employed to decapitate and pull it out piece by piece. Soranus preferred to offset such extreme risks to the mother by amputating as the body parts appeared. Then, if the head was too large to come out naturally, a cranioclast made up of metal forceps with jagged teeth, quite similar to its modern equivalent, was used to break and remove the skull.

Since giving birth was, unsurprisingly, the most dangerous time in a woman's life, the fact that many married in their early teens when their bodies were simply not equipped to deal with the process expected of them caused many of them to die from ruptures, uterine haemorrhage or infection. The epitaph of one eighteen-year-old Egyptian asked, 'Who died here? Herois. How and when? Heavy-wombed in pained labour she set down her burden – a mother she was for a moment, but the child died also. Light may the earth be on her, may Osiris bestow cool water.' In equally moving correspondence to a father, he was told 'on receiving my letter please be so good as to come home promptly because your poor daughter Herennia has died. And to think she had already come safely through a miscarriage. For she gave birth to a still-born child in the 8th month, but herself survived 4 days, and only after that did she die . . . so if you come and you so wish, you can see her.' Caesar himself had received such a letter when campaigning in Kent, informing him that his only daughter Julia had died in childbirth and that her baby, his only grandchild, had died a few days later. But in the hot August of 54 BC, both had been cremated before he was able to pay his own last respects. So it must have been with enormous relief to both Caesar and indeed the whole of Egypt that Cleopatra finally gave birth to a healthy child, not only validating her claim to be the 'Great Mother

Isis', 'Great Mother of the Gods', but truly the mother of Horus, for her first-born was a boy.

Instantly she was transformed into the maternal figure par excellence – the image of Living Isis breast-feeding her new son cannot be underestimated. Yet despite the impact of such massively powerful propaganda, maternal breast-feeding was only recommended after a period of three weeks to allow the mother to regain her strength. Although babies could be bottle-fed using small pots with thistle-shaped strainers, cow's or goat's milk could cause fatal diarrhoea or dysentery. Women with sufficient means therefore tended to employ a wet nurse or 'nutrix'. They were advised to seek out a woman who was healthy, between twenty and forty, with several children of her own and preferably Greek.

After any birth, both mother and child traditionally remained secluded in the bedroom for seven days, the time when they were most vulnerable to the supernatural forces blamed for high rates of infant mortality – most children were unnamed for at least a week after birth. The incense used by Isis to drive away evil forces following the birth of Horus would also have been burned for Cleopatra, whose surroundings would have been thick with the costliest frankincense, myrrh and pistacia resins to counter all harm.

Then, on the seventh day, the new mother was traditionally presented with cosmetics and a mirror. Once she was suitably attired, a celebration of thanksgiving would be held and the child named at a special ceremony. So, after the careful attentions of Eiras and Charmion, a splendidly attired Cleopatra was able to issue the public announcement that a new pharaoh had been born.

The decree was set up in Egyptian demotic script at Sakkara's Serapeum, as throughout the country, and this great-great-great-great-great-great-great-great grandson of Ptolemy I was inevitably given the same name, Ptolemaios, to continue the dynasty descended from Alexander's half-brother. The additional titles 'Philometor' and 'Philopator', 'Mother and Father Loving' in honour of both his parents were also reflected in the Egyptian form of his name, 'Ptuwlmis djed tuw en ef Kisrs', 'Ptolemaios named Caesar', for Cleopatra was determined that 'the child's parentage was not in doubt. He combined Egypt and Rome in his lineage.' This was something the Alexandrians fully acknowledged when they nick-named him Caesarion, meaning 'son of Caesar' or 'Little Caesar', the name by which he is still best known.

Cleopatra's production of a son must have been a particularly proud achievement in Caesar's Roman world, where male children were considered far superior to girls. Announcing the news of his fatherhood to his close associates Gaius Matius and Gaius Oppius, Caesar also began to contemplate plans for a new law which would make it legal for him to have more than one marriage for the purpose of producing an heir – clear evidence of the serious nature of his relationship with Cleopatra and his intentions for their son.

He issued coinage featuring the head of his ancestor Venus-Aph-rodite holding her distinctive sceptre, as well as a series of coins from her Cyprus mint showing Cleopatra as Aphrodite holding the same type of sceptre and nursing her tiny baby. As the coins circulated in the Mediterranean world and announced the news abroad, Cleopatra's royal decree sent throughout Egypt was followed up by Caesarion's name and titles being carved upon the walls of key monuments.

Extraordinary scenes of the birth were completed at her Hermonthis Mammisi, where Cleopatra was portrayed as the goddess helped by female attendants as she gave birth to Horus 'the Sun Child', fulfilling the famous inscription in the temple at Sais which stated that Isis would give birth to the sun. Sustained by the potent milk of Isis, Hathor and Rattawy, the Sun Child was also portrayed as the son of Montu the war god in a subtle compliment to Caesar, Montu's living representative, and, as stated in the accompanying hieroglyphs, in public acknowl-edgement that he was Caesarion's father.

As scenes of Caesarion's divine birth continued, Cleopatra was then shown alongside Amun-Ra, whose habit of impregnating royal women by assuming the guise of their husbands was well known; the Hermonthis clergy declared that the god had indeed impregnated their living goddess Cleopatra by assuming the form of Caesar. Yet this complex theological motif stressed an even deeper link with Amun, whose role as father of Alexander as well as Caesarion made the child Alexander's true successor, and like him the bringer of a new golden age.

The repeated stressing of paternity and ancestry at Hermonthis is also revealed in Cleopatra's choice of titles. Alongside her epithets 'Female

Horus, the Great One, Lady of the Two Lands' she was also 'the Goddess who loves her father' and 'Image of her father', the Egyptian word 'father' being interchangeable with 'ancestor'.

This connection with previous generations, be they father or great-great ad infinitum dating back millennia, was emphasised in the Mammisi's very curious architecture, in which Cleopatra had borrowed from tomb design by commissioning a false door. It was built against the wall of the temple's second room to allow communication with the spirit world, and its presence within her Hermonthis Mammisi suggests the same desire to communicate with the dead as revealed in rites undertaken in Alexandria in the burial chamber of the Soma.

Although new mothers were not allowed inside any temple during a forty-day period of purification after giving birth, such rules can hardly have applied to Cleopatra as pharaoh, nominal high priest of every temple and living incarnation of the deity herself. Wishing to present lavish offerings once sufficiently recovered, she, like most Egyptian and Greek women, would have offered up clothing and jewellery. These would have ranged from the silver uterus-shaped amulets offered to Great Mother Isis to the decorated textiles presented to Hathor-Isis and Artemis-Eileithyia, honoured with various items of clothing in heartfelt thanks for 'keeping dreadful death far away when in labour'. Similar relief was expressed by a second-century BC grandmother at the birth of a baby girl: 'From your mother, greetings. We received the letter from you in which you announce that you have given birth to your child. I kept praying to the gods every day on your behalf. Now that you have escaped, I am spending my days in the greatest joy. I sent you a flask full of olive oil and several pounds of dried figs.'

Exuberant thanksgiving celebrations would have accompanied the birth of the pharaoh's first son and heir as the Nile flood began less than a month later in mid-July; just as she had brought forth a son, Living Isis now brought forth the waters. To mark her country's renewed fertility, Cleopatra adopted a double form of the cornucopia horn of plenty only previously associated with Arsinoe II. She placed the distinctive emblem on her coinage with the words 'Kleopatras Basilisses', 'of Cleopatra the Female King', showing herself as mother to her new son on one side and mother of her country on the other.

While continuing work at the Caesareum on Alexandria's shoreline to honour her baby's absent father, it seems highly likely that, in keeping with pharaonic tradition, she began plans for her own tomb at this time, to ensure it would be complete when needed. She made the revealing decision to have a tomb separate from the Soma, wanting a monument of equal standing to perpetuate her status as legendary goddess in tandem with Alexander's as legendary god. One of the few remaining ancient sources states that 'she had caused to be built joining the temple of Isis several tombs and monuments of wonderful height and very remarkable for their workmanship.' Although the city had many Isis temples, some believe Cleopatra built her tomb in the eastern Hadra quarter of the city based on remains of a temple with sphinxes and royal statues. But as a further ancient reference refers to 'the tomb which she was building in the grounds of the palace', it is possible that her tomb was in fact built at the edge of the sea beside an Isis temple on the eastern side of the Lochias promontory and 'actually formed part of the temple buildings; and if this be so Cleopatra must have had it in mind to be laid to rest within the precincts of the sanctuary of the goddess with whom she was identified'.

During these weeks when Cleopatra was busily embellishing her city and planning Caesarion's inheritance, his father Caesar had travelled through Syria to Anatolia in order to obtain money from those who had supported Pompeius. He had also received reports that Pharnaces II of Pontus, son of Rome's old opponent Mithridates VI of poison antidote fame, had expanded into Roman-held northern Anatolia and killed Roman-appointed tax collectors. Even though Caesar needed cash, he dismissed Pharnaces' offer of a huge crown of gold and his daughter, and on 1 August 47 BC their forces met at Zela in southern Pontus. As the very place where his father had once beaten Rome with the aid of scythe-wheeled chariots, the son's deployment of the same deadly equipment failed to produce the same result and Caesar won a great victory. Borrowing a pithy epithet from the Greek writer Democritus, Caesar sent the Senate the telegram-like message 'veni vidi vici' – 'Came. Saw. Conquered.'

Having spent around nine months in Egypt, he had managed to sort out the rest of the East in two before sailing back to Italy. Landing in the south at Tarentum on 24 September he met with the former

Pompeius supporter Cicero, who had been kept under house arrest by Antonius ever since the battle at Pharsalus the previous year. Following another one of their 'courteous, insincere conversations in which the two men specialised', Caesar agreed to free Cicero on condition that he lent him money.

Yet Caesar also discovered that his deputy Antonius had been exploiting his position by seizing Pompeius' property; Caesar now demanded Antonius paid the going rate for it. In addition he found out that Antonius had alienated the elite by his behaviour, carousing in public with the actress Volumnia, driving her through Rome in a chariot drawn by lions and drinking so heavily that he had thrown up in the middle of the Forum the morning after a friend's wedding. Dropping Antonius as a public liability, Caesar replaced him with his former, more reliable if less flamboyant deputy Marcus Aemilius Lepidus as he now prepared to take on Pompeius' pugnacious sons Gnaeus and Sextus, who had been building up their power base in the region of modern Tunisia.

So, after marching down to western Sicily, Caesar set sail for the North African coast on 25 December, arriving at Hadrumetum (Sousse) three days later. Falling as he disembarked, quick as a flash Caesar reversed the ill omen and, clutching firmly at the sand, exclaimed, 'Africa! I have tight hold of you!' And on the same day, from her own part of North Africa, his wife Cleopatra, as part of the great Mysteries of Osiris, was directly invoking the gods to protect him.

With the inauguration of the second roof chapel at Dendera planned for the 26th of the Egyptian month Khoiak (28 December) 47 BC, precisely calculated by the temple astronomers as the moment when the full moon passed right over the centre of the temple's roof in 'a very rare occurrence', it is unthinkable that Cleopatra would not have been present to take advantage of the moment when maximum moonlight infused her new chapel with the full powers of Isis. Attended by torchbearers, she would have first purified herself in Dendera's sacred lake, which became known as 'Cleopatra's Bath'; perhaps she used the very silver jugs and basins housed in the temple treasury. The millennia-old rituals then required her to be anointed with specific perfumes. Of the thirteen kinds of myrrh resin stored in the temple's perfume laboratory, it was claimed that the gold-coloured resin 'springs from the Eye of Ra', the red 'from the left eye of Osiris' and the white 'from the eye of Thoth'. The earlier female pharaoh Hatshepsut took advantage of its protective qualities appearing 'with the best of myrrh on all her limbs', which may also have been worn by Cleopatra. She was additionally anointed with extract of lotus (*Nymphaea caerulea*) whose hyacinth-like fragrance, popular with both royals and clergy, was listed in the temple's *Book of Unguents* as being specifically prepared for use in Osiris' ceremonials.

Cleopatra would then have had her eyes outlined with black eye-paint, embellished with the green malachite shade associated with the eye of Horus to bestow his divine protection. In scenes in the temple's crypts she and her father Auletes were shown presenting the goddess with these colours, listed as 'green eye paint for the right eye and black kohl for the left eye'.

Within the temple's robing room, Cleopatra would have adopted the dress of Isis whose finest of linen gowns was a 'many-colored robe . . . part was glistening white, part crocus-yellow, part glowing red and along the entire hem a woven border of flowers and fruit clung swaying in the breeze'. Its rainbow colours were then concealed by a lustrous black mantle which hung 'in innumerable folds, the tasseled fringe quivering. It was embroidered with glittering stars on the hem and everywhere else, and in the middle beamed a full and fiery moon'; these were the same stars and sacred animals of the Zodiac found on the stoles of devotees of this 'Black-robed Queen'.

With her clothing complete, Cleopatra's pinned-up hair would similarly have been transformed into the coiffure of Isis whose long hair 'fell in tapering ringlets on her lovely neck'. Introduced by Cyrene-born Berenike II as a style popular in her homeland, its distinctive ringlets had then been adopted by the first Cleopatra 'the Syrian' who combined it with the robes of Isis to create the full goddess ensemble. Since this hairstyle subsequently became associated with Isis and her devotees, the seventh Cleopatra may also have had her auburn hair styled this way – or she may simply have worn a long dark wig for an instant transformation.

She would have finally been crowned in the regalia of tall feathers, horns and solar disc which 'shone a round disc like a mirror', the 'vipers rising from the left-hand and right-hand partings of her hair' alluding to the sacred uraeus snakes which were a key part of the royal image. As portrayed on the rear wall of the temple, Cleopatra also wore a broad collar of traditional design, fringed with small beads, inlaid with carnelian, lapis and turquoise fastened with Ptolemaic-style hook and loop fastener, and matching gold bracelets. The ensemble was completed by the presentation of a pair of silver sistrum rattles 'which sang shrilly when she shook the handle' and an accompanying menat necklace of multiple malachite beads, either worn or carried with the sistra as sacred implements which formed her badge of priestly office.

All these magnificent ornaments were stored in caskets brought from the security of the temple's crypt. Dendera's lavish treasury was 'filled with every kind of real precious stones, every kind of perfume, every kind of grain', which Cleopatra would have presented to her divine alter-ego in thanksgiving for the safe birth of Caesarion and the continuity of the Ptolemaic house. And all were exempt from tax. Guarded by the temple treasurer Petearsemtheus and Cleopatra's own images on the surrounding walls, there were golden globular vessels for offering wine and milk, silver censers and large 'thymiateria' incense burners decorated with Greek and Persian designs interspersed with figures of Bes, and large quantities of silver plate inscribed in both Greek and Egyptian to 'Ptolemy living forever beloved of Ptah' and to Hathor-Isis, 'Lady of Dendera, Lady of Heaven, Mistress of All Gods'.

The treasury even contained scaled-down versions of the crowns and jewellery for the goddess' cult statues, which were attended to daily by the temple 'stolist' or dresser. Make-up was applied to them along with various sacred oils designed to reactivate the divine essence within, in much the same way that they were used to reactivate the soul within the mummy at the funeral. By Ptolemaic times the standard set of seven oils used since the Pyramid Age had increased to nine, from 'Festival Scent', made of frankincense, fir seeds and bitumen, to 'Madjet', made of carob, lotus and white frankincense. Specific unguents were also manufactured for specific rites, one complex recipe taking 365 days to produce half a litre (less than a pint). There was also the 'secret unguent' made specifically for cult statues which blended carob pulp, myrrh and bitumen with finely ground gold, silver, lapis, turquoise and carnelian, a sparkly, sweet sticky mixture to be applied to the divine limbs whilst still warm and pliable. Yet on this occasion, spicy Tisheps unguent 'for anointing the golden goddess Hathor, great mistress of Dendera' would no doubt have been the one selected.

As the main cult statue, dressed in identical manner to the monarch, was brought out from its inner sanctum on the shoulders of the shaven-headed priests, the procession, led by Cleopatra playing her sistrum rattles, proceeded up the temple staircase. Its winding walls, portraying the same journey, showed the monarch skilfully negotiating her way upwards while looking over her shoulder to face the goddess. A similar ceremony was held each New Year's Eve, when Hathor's gold statue was brought up the western staircase and placed in the 'Kiosk of the Union with the Sun Disc'. The shrine's curtains were pulled back precisely at dawn on New Year's Day to allow the solar power to re-energise the spirit within the statue, which was then taken back down into the darkness of the inner sanctum via a second, straight staircase to the east. Cleopatra was now performing a similar ceremony in which Hathor's solar powers were balanced by the lunar energies of Isis.

Monarch and priests travelled up the temple staircase and out towards the roof chapel, following the path of the moon in an anti-clockwise direction. They passed the western chapel with its innovative Zodiac ceiling that she had inaugurated some three years before, and reaching the newly completed eastern chapel, stepped through its open-air court and into the darkness of its inner chamber beyond. As Cleopatra's eyes adjusted to the limited light, the secret – 'mysterion' – of Osiris' resurrection would have appeared on its walls, from the ritual chants to be sung at each hour to the list of all 104 amulets required for his mummification.

Given its very specific layout her chapel 'may have had a performa-tive function' – this seems to have been part of Cleopatra's policy of using theatre as a means of enhancing her divine status. And as her presence filled the entire temple, from her earliest image within the subterranean crypts far below to her physical form high on its roof, she now stood alongside Isis' sacred statue awaiting midnight when the pure moonlight would flood in through the narrow opening in the ceiling and bathe them both in its glowing rays.

As the moon slowly reached its zenith and the chamber became increasingly brighter, its detailed wall scenes portraying the mystical union of Isis and Osiris were slowly brought to life by its pure white light. Given that 'generative light falling strongly from the moon' was felt sufficiently powerful to impregnate the virgin cows who brought forth the sacred bulls, the prone image of Osiris awaiting rebirth would similarly have been filled with lunar energy. As Isis helped him achieve erection and resurrection, bringing forth all the spirits of the ancestors in his wake, he then impregnated her with his essence, as described some twenty-three centuries earlier in the Pyramid Texts, the world's oldest collection of religious literature: 'your sister Isis comes to you, rejoicing in love for you, she placed your phallus on her vulva and your seed issues into her, she being as alert as a star'.

Isis was also as bright as the moon, and was believed to emit her own generative force. Cleopatra harnessed such divine powers by taking the title Isis Selene, 'the Moon'. The goddess-monarch appeared in the light of a dazzling full moon at midnight because, it was claimed, 'at that secret hour . . . the Moon-goddess, sole sovereign of mankind, is possessed of her greatest power and majesty. She is the shining deity by whose divine influence not only all beasts, wild and tame, but all inanimate things as well, are invigorated; whose ebbs and flows control the rhythm of all bodies whatsoever, whether in the air, on earth, or below the sea.'

Yet at that very moment the goddess-monarch's partner and father of her child was facing serious danger to the west, where he had embarked on a long-drawn-out war with Pompeius' sons and supporters. Face-to-face combat had been avoided by their use of guerilla tactics until Caesar took their supply base at Thapsus, after which they were finally forced to fight him on 6 April 46 BC. Ranged against Caesar and his Mauretanian allies were ten legions and a combined cavalry force of Gauls and Germans, together with his old adversary, the bearded Juba I of Numidia, who brought further troops including his crack cavalry, some mounted on camels to deal with the desert terrain. Juba also had thirty war elephants, but the initial barrage from archers and slingers scared them so much that they turned and fled, trampling their own infantry and causing a rout in which Pompeius' sons' supporters, including Juba, were forced to retreat.

Although Pompeius' sons themselves managed to escape, they lost ten thousand men. Pompeius' father-in-law Metellus Scipio and

Caesar's sworn enemy Cato, whose asset-stripping of Cyprus had followed the suicide of Cleopatra's uncle, both committed suicide, while Juba planned his own death on top of a huge funerary pyre consisting of his capital city as a last grand gesture. But when the city's inhabitants made it clear they were none too keen on his plan and refused him entry, he made a deal with his remaining Roman ally Petreius: resigned to their fates, they had a final dinner then a duel to the death, when Juba, as victor, was killed by a slave.

Caesar sold off Juba's treasures at auction and then divided up his kingdom of Numidia among the Mauretanian princes who had supported him; these included Bogudes and his wife Eunoe, rumoured to have been another of roving Caesar's conquests according to his critics back in Rome. The rest of Numidia became the Roman province of Africa Nova; Juba's impressive cavalry were absorbed into the Roman army, and the region's plentiful grain supplies diverted to Rome where they were eventually able to feed the city for eight months of the year.

Finally leaving Africa, tremendously relieved after a lengthy and stressful campaign which had brought on an attack of the epilepsy which had always dogged him, Caesar travelled back to Rome in the company of Juba's four-year-old son, also named Juba. The boy would form part of Caesar's forthcoming Triumph, along with the thirty elephants and twenty-two camels captured at Thapsus – the earliest record of these creatures west of Siwa.

Back in Rome with his exotic cargo, Caesar was received by an uneasy yet sycophantic Senate who awarded him a whole string of unprecedented honours. He was already Pontifex Maximus or chief priest, and now they made him Dictator for a period of ten years.

During a forty-day period of thanksgiving, he was also awarded a series of four Triumphs to celebrate his victories in Gaul, Egypt, Pontus and Africa; the Senate diplomatically ignored the fact that many of these battles had been fought against his fellow countrymen. Despite the official calls to cut down on both overt displays of wealth and foreign influences, Caesar's lavish Triumphs came close to the Ptolemies' legendary excesses. The fixtures and fittings were made from different themed materials for each: citrus wood for Gaul, acanthus for Egypt, tortoiseshell for Pontus and ivory for Africa; 2822 gold crowns sent from all over the empire brought in an astonishing 20,414 lb of pure bullion – just over 9 tons. There was sufficient wealth to give every infantryman 240 gold pieces, around 6000 denarii at a time when the average soldier earned one denarius a day. Even so, one man complained there could have been even more had not the Triumphs been so lavish. Unfortunately this was overheard by Caesar, and the disgruntled soldier became one of the human sacrifices to Rome's war god Mars, whose heads were hung from Caesar's official residence as the high priest Pontifex Maximus.

At the first Triumph, the one for Gaul, widely regarded as the most magnificent of the four, incense bearers marched along to sweeten the proceedings as crowds lined the streets to see a procession of tableaux highlighting key episodes in the war. Exploiting the fact that most Roman women were politically clueless and understood little of the endless procession of paintings and models, men in the crowds were advised to impress such women with their superior knowledge of what each figure represented, even if it required a good deal of skill to work out that the golden statue bound in chains represented Caesar's cross-Channel conquest of Britain.

Yet everyone would have recognised the victor in his elaborate gold chariot, dressed in purple cloak and red leather parade boots with the gold crown of Jupiter held over his head by a slave. Although it was also the slave's role to repeatedly whisper in Caesar's ear the traditional words 'Remember, you are a mortal', to counteract the mass adulation, he must have started to have his doubts as the deafening shouts and cheers bordered on worship.

Alongside a marching band of oboe and zither players the army added their own form of tribute, 'chanting ribald songs as they were privileged to do, this was one of them – ' "Gaul was brought to shame by Caesar, by King Nicomedes he. Here comes Caesar, wreathed in Triumph for his Gallic victory," ' a very public allusion to their leader's alleged homosexual affair earlier in his career. Presumably none too happy with the serenade, Caesar's mood cannot have been improved when the axle of his chariot suddenly broke, a terrible omen as a result of which he was obliged to climb the steps to the Temple of Jupiter (Zeus) on top of the Capitoline Hill on his knees in an ancient rite of supplication. He ascended the hill once more that evening 'between two lines of elephants, 40 in all, which acted as his torch-bearers' and accompanied him home in grand procession. The Gallic triumph then ended with the traditional execution of the enemy leader, in this case brave Vercingetorix the Gaul, strangled after six years in captivity.

Victory against Egypt, or more correctly against Ptolemy XIII, his advisers and the Alexandrians, was the theme of Caesar's second Triumph, in which a parade of floats carried huge models of the pyramids, the famous Pharos lighthouse with a beacon of impressively lifelike flames and a great reclining statue of the Nile as a male god. The crowds also cheered large paintings of the deaths of Pompeius' murderers Potheinos and Achillas, but the appearance of Arsinoe in her golden chains at the Triumph's big finish visibly upset them. No doubt remembering the fate of Vercingetorix, the crowd grew so uneasy that Caesar displayed his famous clemency to win them back and exiled her to Artemis' sanctuary at Ephesus. The destination hinted at the involvement of her half-sister Cleopatra, who herself seems to have lived there in exile some ten years earlier.

For Triumph number three, humour was employed in scenes showing Mithridates' son Pharnaces running away from Caesar, the accompanying placard proclaiming, 'veni, vidi, vici' – Came. Saw. Conquered – in a repetition of his message to the Senate to indicate his victory and emphasising the tremendous speed with which the battle had been won. In the final Triumph for 'Africa', relating to his most recent victory at Thapsus against Pompeius' supporters, the defeated and now deceased king Juba I was represented by his four-year-old son Prince Juba while Pompeius' Roman allies appeared in gruesome paintings showing each one commiting suicide. Although Caesar refrained from actually naming them, the sight of Cato disembowelling himself, Pompeius's father-in-law throwing himself into the sea and Petreius being stabbed was an unwelcome and very public reminder to some in the Senate that Caesar's main opponents had been fellow Romans. Yet, regardless of their feelings about the endless twists and turns of a power struggle raging among an elite minority, Caesar's fourfold Triumph had been a great success with the masses who were completely won over by a whole series of lavish entertainments.

After military prizes had been awarded to Caesar's supporters, including his sister Julia's puny but precocious sixteen-year-old grandson Gaius Octavius (Octavian), the sons of client kings from Asia Minor and Bithynia performed sword dances. Among dramatic performances was a piece by the leading dramatist Decimus Laberius who made political digs at Caesar in his plays, this time ad-libbing 'see how easily an old man slips' and 'the man who many fear must also fear many himself'. Caesar feigned his usual public indifference and presented him with five thousand gold pieces for the performance.

For racing fans, horse racing at the newly extended Circus track was followed by chariot racing, the most popular sport in the ancient world, much loved by Cleopatra's predecessor Berenike II whose own horses had won the chariot race at the Nemean Games in Greece. It was a sport that the Romans loved too, and some celebrity charioteers generated such strong emotions that when one famous exponent was cremated, a distraught fan threw himself on the pyre.

Three days of athletic events were staged on the Campus Martius, the Field of Mars, followed by gladiatorial contests which, before the creation of Rome's first arena in 29 BC, were held here or in the Forum itself. Originally a means of displaying aristocratic valour, they had by now degenerated into ever more gory displays sponsored by public figures as a means of gaining support from the masses. After being entertained by fights to the death, the public could visit the refreshment stalls and souvenir sellers offering engraved beakers or terracotta figurines of favourite fighters. Some women were so enamoured that they would pay congratulatory visits after a successful show. Gladiators were famed for their sexual potency, and even senators' wives were known to give up everything to elope with such a man, for, even scarred and disfigured, 'he was a gladiator!' Even if their favourite was killed and his body dragged away by slaves dressed as the Roman god Mercury or Egypt's Anubis, the blood spilled was in great demand for its healing and aphrodisiac powers; even the spear which had killed him was used in ceremonies of birth and marriage.

Influenced by the various cultures absorbed into Rome's growing empire, gladiatorial styles ranged from the heavily armed 'myrmillo', generally pitted against the 'retiarus' net-thrower with his trident, to the 'essedarii' who fought from chariots and whom Caesar himself is thought to have introduced from Britain. There were even female gladiators dressed as Amazons, some of whom seem to have been devotees of Isis and Anubis; although their behaviour was criticised by those who asked 'what modesty can be looked for in some helmeted hoyden, a renegade from her sex, who thrives on masculine violence', they nevertheless had a popular following.

Certainly Caesar's 320 pairs of silver-clad gladiators proved a huge hit, as did a pair of Roman nobles who fought to the death in the Forum. There were also the 'bestiari' animal fighters, the North African Telegenii using their crescent-shaped goads to provoke a succession of exotic wild animals including 400 lions and giraffes sent over from Africa Nova's new governor.

With Caesar dedicating the proceedings to the memory of his daughter Julia in the manner of funeral games, the shows culminated in a pitched battle fought between two armies each made up of five hundred infantry, thirty cavalry and twenty elephants, the central part of the Circus' chariot track removed to allow the armies to advance toward each other and fight. The grand finale was a spectacular naval engagement between multi-oared Egyptian and Tyrian ships floating on an artificial lake created especially for the occasion.

Clearly inspired by his time with Cleopatra in Egypt, where lavish display had long been used to win over the masses, Caesar had the whole of Rome's city centre decorated with lengths of Gallic linen, silk from Cos and, apparently, the cotton ('carbasus') first brought back from India by Alexander. All were made into spectacular awnings stretching from his mansion down the Sacred Way, over the entire Forum and right up to the Capitol in 'a display recorded to have been thought more wonderful even than the show of gladiators which he gave'. Again inspired by the large dining pavilions of Alexander and the Ptolemies, Caesar used costly fabrics to cover an area where no fewer than twenty-two thousand couches were laid out for the crowds to enjoy a free banquet of various meats and thousands of costly sea eels provided by the fish farms of his wealthy cousin, all washed down with the finest Falernian wine.

Unsurprisingly, news of such events brought vast numbers of people to Rome. Many were forced 'to sleep in tents pitched along the streets or roads, or on rooftops', and the pressure of such crowds inevitably inflicted casualties. Two senators were among those crushed to death during the stampede to reach these unmissable spectacles.

Rome had certainly seen nothing like it, and with his carefully designed events making Caesar 'an overnight celebrity' backed by the mob, his unrivalled power as Dictator rendered the Senate virtually impotent. Although Cicero made a series of fulsome speeches praising the returning hero's great achievements while hinting that he should nevertheless restore the Republic as soon as possible, Caesar had other plans. To implement them fully would need the help of his ally Cleopatra of Egypt. And to this end he summoned her to Rome, where she would live for almost two years.

PART FOUR

7

Caesar's Palace: Cleopatra in Europe

As Cleopatra prepared for her state visit to Rome, she spent the spring of 46 BC organising government. She would be accompanied overseas by her co-ruler brother Ptolemy XIV, maintaining the façade of a traditional dual monarchy while preventing any takeover bid in her absence. The day-to-day administration would be overseen by her most trusted officials, her minister for current affairs, Theon, and possibly a finance minister named Seleucus. Kallimachos of Thebes would retain control of the south as governor, and her royal cousin Pasherenptah III would continue to oversee matters from Memphis.

The continuity of the latter's priestly dynasty would soon be guaranteed by the birth of his long-awaited son following prayers to Imhotep. New mother Taimhotep was able to report that 'he was born in regnal year 6, day 15 of Epiphi [15th July 46 BC], in the 8th hour of the day under the majesty of the Sovereign, Lady of the Two Lands, Cleopatra. The child's appearance was like that of the son of Ptah and there was jubilation over him by the people of Memphis. He was called Pedubastis and all rejoiced over him.'

Yet, as all offered their heartfelt thanks to Isis the Great, her living counterpart had already left Egypt for Europe in the early summer, taking her one-year-old son Caesarion, and a great retinue of servants as well as her thirteen-year-old brother. This was possibly Ptolemy XIV's first voyage across the Mediterranean, the Egyptians' 'Great Green', 'the sea of the Greeks' and the Romans' 'Mare Nostrum', 'our sea'.

Resembling the legendary sea-going vessels of her Ptolemaic predecessors, Cleopatra's great ship of state, necessarily of different design from her river-going vessel, may well have replicated the proportions of the ocean liner built by the fourth Ptolemy. At a time when the average Athenian trireme with three banks of oars and sails was around 120 feet long, this royal ship was 420 feet long, had forty banks of oars and was constructed from the same amount of imported timber as fifty trireme-type vessels. It was nevertheless 'extraordinarily well proportioned – wonderful also was the adornment of the vessel besides; for it had figures at stern and bow not less than 18 feet high, and every available space was elaborately covered with encaustic painting; the entire surface where the oars projected, down to the keel, had a pattern of ivy leaves and Bacchic wands' of Dionysos.

It was launched 'by a crowd to the accompaniment of shouts and trumpets', and the same pomp and ceremony no doubt marked the departure of Cleopatra's entourage on a sea crossing previously undertaken by several of her predecessors, from feuding brothers Ptolemies VI and VIII to Sulla's protégé Prince Ptolemy XI and her own father Auletes, with whom Cleopatra seems to have travelled some twelve years earlier.

The direct journey between Alexandria and Rome's main seaport which was then Puteoli took less than a fortnight, while the Alexandria mailboat could do the crossing in a single week. Cleopatra's great ship, however, would have travelled at a more stately pace, first reaching Italy's south-west coast and the fertile region of Campania. Lying as it did on the main trade route with Alexandria, and first settled by Greek traders in the eighth century BC, the region had a hybrid Greco-Italian culture suffused with Egyptian influences. Isis herself was worshipped in temples with sacred pools to replicate the Nile, and the 'Navigium Isidis' or Voyage of Isis festival was celebrated every March with oil lamps shaped like the ship of Isis. But it was the real thing that now sailed into the Bay of Neapolis (Naples), passing Mount Vesuvius' vine-clad slopes. Former Greek trading colonies such as Pompeii, taken over by Rome, had been transformed into fashionable resorts on a coastline dubbed 'the Colony of Venus', playground for Rome's rich and famous where Sulla, Cicero and Caesar all had holiday homes. Sailing on past Neapolis, another former Greek colony with a strong Isis following, Cleopatra finally reached Puteoli, Rome's main seaport until the first century AD. Here she disembarked to a suitably lavish reception laid on by an official delegation sent out by Caesar, if not by Caesar himself.

After perhaps visiting Puteoli's long-established temple of Isis to give thanks for her safe crossing, Cleopatra would have made her onward journey to Rome along the famous Appian Way by carriage. The lack of springs would presumably have been offset by a plentiful supply of cushions, while fine linen drapes would have kept out the potentially fatal mosquitoes of the Pontine marshes. En route, Cleopatra is likely to have visited the temple of Isis-Fortuna built into the side of Monte Ginestro at Palestrina, a place of pilgrimage both for women wanting children and for those who had recently given birth. Life-giving spring water gushed up within the temple's man-made grotto in the same way that the Nile's floodwaters lapped the polished silver pavements of Egypt's carefully sited temples. In thanks for the birth of Caesarion, Cleopatra may well have embellished the place probably visited as a teenager, commissioning the great mosaic of her kingdom across its submerged floor. Based on parts of the mosaic that have survived, supplemented by drawings of areas damaged in the seventeenth century, it portrays the full length of the Nile bordered by its many temples. It has recently been suggested that the mosaic commemorated her Nile cruise with Caesar, and may even have once portrayed Cleopatra herself in part of the scene which originally depicted trumpeters heralding the arrival of a Ptolemaic royal disembarking from a ship under a large red parasol with long gold fringing. And since Roman military figures awaited the royal arrival beneath a temple awning while drinking wine at some sort of festival, it is just possible that the Palestrina mosaic may once have constituted the equivalent of Cleopatra and Caesar's wedding photograph.

Cleopatra's entourage finally reached the city walls of Rome where a kind of early park-and-ride scheme instituted by Caesar 'decreed that from sunrise until dusk, no transport, cart wagon or chariot of any form would be allowed within the precincts of Rome.' With 'no exceptions to this order', Cleopatra must have arrived after dark or more likely proceeded by litter, a mode of transport as popular for the Roman elite as it was for the pharaoh of Egypt, who used it in Rome to see and be seen beneath the shade of her royal canopy.

As invited heads of state, Cleopatra and her co-ruler Ptolemy XIV were formally received by Caesar and awarded the official title 'reges socii et amici populi Romani', 'friend and ally of the Roman people'. This was the same title that Auletes had worked so hard to achieve some thirteen years earlier, and for which privilege he had been forced to pay so dearly. His daughter was given both 'high titles and rich presents', likely to have included the large pearls that Caesar is known to have given previous lovers such as Servilia, whose gift was reportedly 'worth 60,000 gold pieces', around one and a half million denarii. So how much more must Caesar have presented to Cleopatra as mother of his only living child, whom he could now see for the first time?

Perhaps he gave her some of the freshwater pearls from Britain, or the great pearls which had once been part of the Ptolemies' royal treasury, sent to Kos for safekeeping where they were seized by Mithridates of Pontus, then by Pompeius, whose lavish Triumph of 61 BC was famed for the sheer number of pearls on display. It would certainly have been appropriate if Caesar chose to right past wrongs by returning property seized by Pompeius to its rightful owner.

Following the bestowing of these honours, Caesar housed Cleopatra and her royal party in his grand villa on the Janiculum Hill in the fashionable Trastevere district on the west bank of the Tiber. Enjoying spectacular views across the city, the villa, set in its own parkland extending down to the river, was one of the first things seen by those entering Rome after arriving by sea. Its landscaped grounds were no doubt influenced by Greek culture, since many Romans 'do not think they have a real villa unless it rings with many resounding Greek names' and the groves and walkways of Aristotle's Temple of the Nymphs in Macedonia where Alexander had studied were particularly admired. Alexandrian technology now allowed gardens once designed around natural springs to be created anywhere they were required, from the Nile-style water gardens, ridiculed by Cicero's set, to bronze and marble figures such as the ubiquitous boy on a dolphin, gushing their waters into pools of fish and water lilies, which were sometimes used when dining alfresco to keep drinks and food trays cool.

Reclining beneath shady pergolas and awnings, Cleopatra must surely have enjoyed the great expanses of gardens at her disposal – gardens described as being filled with colourful spreads of lilies, narcissi and oleander, beds of white, pink and red roses and highly scented purple, yellow and white violets. These were laid out between ever-green hedges of laurel, myrtle and box clipped neatly into ornamental shapes. There would also have been fig trees, mulberry bushes and no doubt that novelty the cherry, brought back from Pontus in 74 BC, among the exotic plunder. Fashionable antique statuary was placed in the most appropriate positions within the gardens of the wealthy, with statues of Artemis as Great Hunter set in woodland areas modelled on the 'paradeisos' game parks of Alexander's Successors, populated by the same shrill, strutting peacocks imported from India along with more mundane creatures reared in artificial fishpools, warrens and dovecotes. Usually placed in the sunniest spot to enhance his connection with the Greek sun god Helios, Artemis' brother Apollo was another favourite garden figure, and Caesar's relative Julia, mother of Marcus Antonius, was said to worship before a shrine of Apollo in her garden.

Far more than decorative, garden statuary was also placed near trees considered holy in the same way that Egyptian sycamores and tamarisks were sacred to Hathor, and it seems no coincidence that the most important deity in any Roman garden was Hathor's Roman equivalent Venus, whose comely image was often placed beside water to re-create the goddess' birth from the sea. Her maritime links were ultimately absorbed by Isis, similarly honoured in Roman garden shrines where devotees underwent initiation. The goddess' ability to resurrect them at death in the same way that she revived Osiris' phallus to conceive their son was echoed by the phallic imagery which suffused Roman life. As the male-dominated culture's ultimate talisman, phallic mobiles dangled in the breeze to protect against evil spirits while well-endowed figures of the gnome-like Priapus waved their attributes to attract all-round fertility.

Caesar's wealthy father-in-law Lucius Calpurnius Piso had been accused of looting antique statues from Greece to embellish his Italian gardens and Caesar's own extensive grounds were no doubt adorned with a whole range of such figures. He had certainly acquired a taste for luxurious living early in his career, when a country mansion that he had had built at Nervi so disappointed him he had it demolished. So his villa on the Janiculum Hill must have met his demanding specifications and been sufficiently grand to house a monarch and her impressive entourage.

Its multiple-roomed interior may have been specially decorated for Cleopatra's visit with the same trompe-l'oeil fantasy architecture of cityscapes and mythical creatures believed to have adorned her own palace in Alexandria. Egyptian imagery of sun discs, crowns and serpents gradually appeared in neighbouring villas, inspired by the oriental monarch in their midst. There must certainly have been mosaic flooring, since Caesar was such a fan that 'he carried tessellated and mosaic pavements with him on his campaigns'. No doubt his marble floors and veneers resembled those in the villas of his military colleagues, perhaps overlaid with the same richly patterned Persian carpets that adorned the palace at Alexandria or even the more exotic 'tossae Britannicae', rug-like floor coverings known from Roman homes in various parts of Europe and which Caesar may have picked up on his visits to the far north.

Greatly appreciated at the onset of winter temperatures sufficiently chilly to freeze the Tiber, raised floors allowed heat from a furnace to circulate in a system of underfloor heating known by the Greek name of *hypokaust*. Lighting was provided by tallow candles or exquisite oil lamps of bronze or gold, decorated with lotus leaves, dolphins' heads and sea shells and placed in elaborate candelabra or on wall-mounted lamp brackets. Those in the form of ships' prows, alluding to the nocturnal Festival of Isis in which the waterborne goddess appeared surrounded by lights, would have been a most suitable choice for the fittings in Cleopatra's new home.

Although a Roman villa was not cluttered with furniture, couches, first introduced from second-century BC Greece, were ubiquitous, and well upholstered in fabrics dyed a range of scarlets, greens, yellows and the gleaming purples imported from Tyre on the Phoenician coast. They were very similar in appearance to first-century BC Roman beds which had curved legs and sometimes horse-head terminals, inlaid Egyptian-style with ebony, ivory and gold; Caesar was alleged to have slept with a previous royal lover, the king of Bithynia, on a golden bed. The Egyptian influence only extended so far, however, since the Romans much preferred pillows to the traditional wooden headrests of the Egyptians, which were still used by the priests of Isis.

As 'a keen collector of gems, carvings, statues and Old Masters', Caesar displayed his objets d'art in specially made cabinets, while images of the gods and family members, which in his case could be one and the same, adorned the traditional household shrine with its small bronze altar for burning incense. Another of the city's villas, owned by one of Sulla's staff, was 'crammed with gold and silver vessels from Delos and

Corinth, an "automatic cooker" which he had bought at an auction, embossed silver, coverlets, pictures, statues and marbles'. Sulla himself had lived in a villa on the Palatine Hill close to the immense mansion of Caesar's former deputy Antonius, while Caesar as Pontifex Maximus also 'used the official residence on the Sacred Way', where his Roman wife Calpurnia also lived.

In contrast to the majority of Romans, who lived in slum housing and high-rise apartment blocks in the overcrowded city centre, the rich avoided the summer heat by relocating to their country homes; many of them also owned one of the new 'villa marittimae' springing up along the Campania Riviera south of Rome. It was a place where Cleopatra may well have spent some time, since Caesar and many of his associates had homes in the region. Cicero particularly loved his house at Pompeii, while one of Caesar's officers had a fine villa known as the 'House of the Faun', which was 'more imposing than any known palace or villa of contemporary Hellenistic kings'. Rightly famous for its superb mosaic floor created c. 100 BC, its portrayal of a wide-eyed Alexander at the battle of Issus so closely resembled the early Ptolemies it is thought to have been modelled on an Alexandrian original. Equally recognizable to Cleopatra would have been Nile-side landscapes and images of Isis and Horus, favourite themes for both villas and temples including the rich red walls inside Isis' temple at Herculaneum. Portraying lively images of her priests and priestesses, dancing masked figures and Osiris' mummy upright in his open coffin, similar red walls in the Pompeiian villa known as the 'House of the Mysteries' featured the festivities accompanying religious initiation before Dionysos and a giant phallus hidden beneath a veil.

One of the region's most lavish homes belonged to Caesar's father-in-law. Its 800-foot-wide marble frontage, with a high tower affording superb sea views, boasted a columned portico containing his collection of antique bronze portraits including at least one of Cleopatra's relatives, together with a superb library of almost two thousand works. A slightly later villa built over a promontory at Laurentum similarly exploited its coastal location with huge windows, flecked by the waves on stormy days; folding doors between the windows could be drawn back to take advantage of milder weather.

Although every Roman home of quality also housed the type of elaborate bathing facilities first developed in the East, limestone-lined bathrooms with drains had been available to the Egyptian elite for several thousand years. Also part of palace life in Bronze Age Greece, the piped water which was a key feature in the palaces of Macedonia and Alexandria had spread to Rome by 312 BC, when the first aqueduct bringing fresh water to the city was circulated via a system of earthenware and lead piping. Certainly a plentiful water supply was required for Rome's public baths, whose popularity rose dramatically during the first century BC in response to a growing population living closer together.

Water was known to have therapeutic qualities, and various forms of hydrotherapy included a new cold-water treatment developed by one of Antonius' Greek slaves, Antonius Musa. So beneficial did it prove that Musa's statue was eventually set up beside Asklepios and his fellow health-bestowing deities Hygieia and Fortuna. And since Isis-Fortuna was also patron goddess of baths in the West and Aphrodite was the deity most associated with bathing in the East, it is no surprise that Cleopatra, as the Living Isis-Aphrodite, would become so intimately linked with the process and immortalised in the place name 'Cleopatra's Baths' found commonly throughout the ancient world.

Cleopatra would certainly have felt at home in the luxurious surroundings of most Roman bathing facilities, for it was said that 'people regard baths fit only for moths if they haven't been arranged so that they receive the sun all day long through the widest of windows, if men cannot bath and get a tan at the same time and if they cannot look out from their bath tubs over stretches of land and sea'.

The villa at Laurentum featured baths 'surrounded by glass windows overlooking the sea', made from the translucent selenite stone known as 'petra specularis'. Roman descriptions of glass ceilings, large mirrors, mosaic and marble surfaces, multiple statues and silver taps with 'masses of water that fall crashing down from level to level' are borne out by the silver basins with lion-head taps known from Egypt and the first-century BC seaside palace at Caesarea Maritima in Palestine. The palace's marble-lined bathrooms with a *hypokaust* system featured a caldarium hot room which cleansed the skin, while the invigorating plunge pool of the frigidarium cold room closed the pores and refreshed the body.

In her own daily regime, presumably wearing the standard woo-den-soled bathing shoes to prevent slipping on the wet marble floors,

Cleopatra would have been attended by a small army of servants bringing supplies of fluffy towels with absorbent looped threads, natural sea sponges and pumice stones with a bronze handle to provide a good grip. And although the Romans had no soap, a form of hard soda detergent had long been known in Egypt and was certainly available to the Alexandrians, who also used a preparation of soapwort root known as 'oeno'.

Among various forms of cleansing cream, 'brechu' was made of ground up lupin seeds soaked in water; its Roman equivalent, 'lomentum', made of broad-bean flour and applied before entering the bath, was 'not without use to a wrinkled body'. The same ground beans and lupin seeds also formed the basis of a 'certain cure for spots and pimples' enhanced by 'the glutinous matter wherewith the Halcyon cements its nest', a poetical description for kingfisher droppings whose enzyme guanine, an amino acid which heals the skin and was recommended in the first-century BC Roman beauty manual *Medicamina Faciei Femineae* ('The Art of Beauty'), is currently used in facials for sun-damaged skin offered by the upmarket beauty salons of London's Knightsbridge.

Along with mineral-based skin treatments such as the clay-based 'creta fullonica', 'nitrum' made from ash, and concoctions of chalk and vinegar, Cleopatra is famously said to have bathed in asses' milk. It was a practice followed by many a wealthy Roman woman who 'freshens her complexion with asses' milk to smooth wrinkles and soften the skin. The fatty emulsion of milk protein improved the texture of dry complexions, while the lactic acid provided an 'ancient form of chemical peel, the cosmetic procedure used to straighten out wrinkles or even out pigmentation' in much the same way that acidic bulls' bile was used to treat blotchy complexions.

Upper-class Roman teeth were kept clean with a mixture of soda and bicarbonate and pistacia gum and perfumed pastilles were chewed as popular breath fresheners. They also employed toothpicks, and kept their nails manicured with pumice and bronze nail cleaners. Often part of a standard 'pocket set' resembling a Swiss army knife, there were also fine bronze spoon-type implements to clean the ears and, for the wealthiest individuals, tweezers of silver and gold. Caesar, however, is said to have employed an 'alipilus' or 'hair-plucker' along with his ever-present barber who kept 'his head carefully trimmed and shaved', no doubt using a thin iron razor.

Yet in contrast to the ancient Egyptian practice of complete body depilation for both sexes, the classical world regarded male depilation as effeminate. Only women were expected to be hair-free, and told to 'see that your legs are not rough with bristles'. Hairs were softened with red-hot walnut shells or removed with depilatory mixtures of pitch, resin or wax to which were added various caustic substances.

In addition to such products designed to remove unwanted body hair, various substances to encourage a luxurious head of hair were often credited to Egypt's royal women. They ranged from an oily preparation dating back to the Pyramid Age to several hair restorers credited to Cleopatra herself and quoted by the second-century AD Greek doctor Galen, who states that 'medicines for hair loss are recorded in her own words, more or less as follows. "Against hair loss: make a paste of realgar [arsenic monosulphide] and blend it into oak gum, apply it to a cloth and place it where you have already cleaned as thoroughly as possible with natron [salts]", adding that 'I myself have added foam to natron to the above recipe, and it worked nicely.'

Even though it was Caesar rather than Cleopatra who needed such help, he preferred to disguise his receding hair with a wreath. Wigs and hairpieces were also used to conceal hair loss or augment what remained. Drawing on the expertise of the Egyptians' three-thousand-year-old wigmaking industry, the Romans imported black hair from India and blond and red from northern Europe, either to add detail to existing styles or to create complete wigs such as that made for one Roman follower of Isis, set in a ready-made bun coiffure for an instant 'Cleopatra look'. Yet in contrast to the Egyptians' blatant use of very obvious and often highly stylised wigs, amusement and even a sense of stigma accompanied their use in the Roman world. One young woman was so surprised at the unexpected arrival of her suitor that 'she put her wig on back-to-front in her confusion'.

For despite the social pressures to attain the beauty demanded of them, Roman women were expected to pretend that their beauty was entirely natural and 'on no account let your lover find you with a lot of 'aids to beauty' boxes about you. The art that adorns you should be unsuspected . . . Let your servants tell us you are still asleep, if we arrive before your toilet's finished. You will appear all the more lovely when you've put on the finishing touch. Why should I know what it is that makes your skin so white? Keep your door shut, and don't let me see the work before it's finished. There are a whole host of things we men should know nothing about!'

So it would generally be behind the privacy of the closed bathroom door that the body would be cleansed, depilated and oiled, after which the combined oil and sweat would be scraped off using a metal implement known as a strigil. Trained masseurs performed massage techniques dating back several millennia in Egypt; their therapeutic effects were enhanced by substances chosen for their specific medicinal qualities, and believed to provide protection from unseen forces. Gods and royalty alike were routinely doused in such costly oils, and courtiers were even portrayed massaging the royal feet at various state cere-monies – Cleopatra herself is known to have had her own feet massaged on at least one such occasion, perhaps with costly Mendesian unguent made up of myrrh, cinnamon and resin which was rubbed into the feet after bathing.

Equally costly ingredients were used for her hands. Once she spent 400 denarii on a single pound of moisturiser whose honey-and-oil base would have been enhanced by the addition of kyphi, the sweet and spicy blend of cinnamon, honey, wine and resin that was known to have a soporific effect on the body. Its distinctive aroma 'seductively brings on sleep, so that without getting drunk, the sorrows and tensions of daily anxieties are loosened and untied like tangled knots' – the perfect way to unwind at the end of a busy day.

Although several of Cleopatra's female predecessors had promoted Egyptian perfumes before an ancestor of Caesar's had banned 'foreign essences' as a corrupting influence, they were now the height of fashion. Brand names such as 'Aphrodite's Elixir' or 'Bloom of Youth' gave no clue to their ingredients, but great insight into ancient marketing techniques which even then used aspirational images in the age-old quest for beauty. During her time in Rome, Cleopatra may also have worn Rhodinon perfume made from roses, a favourite of her Cyrene-born predecessor Berenike II and the sacred flower of both Venus and Isis the 'Rose-breasted Lady'. Rose fields north of Neapolis (Naples) supplied the local perfume houses, and the intensive cultivation of olives and flowers around Pompeii's 'House of the Perfume Maker' was borne out in the images of perfume production in local wall paintings, which even showed the end product sniffed on the tester's wrist.

Given the battery of cosmetic equipment that Cleopatra would have required to sustain her high-maintenance public image, her private quarters must have been filled with all manner of compartmentalised caskets and chests holding her bottles, pots, phials and mixing dishes. Manufactured in rock crystal, veined agate, silver, gold and coloured glass, cosmetic and perfume vessels ranged from simple test-tube-shaped 'unguentaria' of iridescent colour to miniature amphorae, blue glass aryballos flasks with dolphin-head handles, bunches of blue glass grapes and blue bird ampullae, trademark bottles of the north Italian glassmakers. And although perfume is generally assumed to have been worn only by women, its bottles are so commonly uncovered on former military sites that 'one cannot escape the conclusion that on some occasions, Roman soldiers were pleasantly sweet-smelling!'

Roman barracks were also well equipped with bath-houses and toilet facilities; even the public toilets at Ostia featured marble seats, mosaic floors, painted walls and an altar to Isis-Fortuna as ever-present goddess. Saite and Ptolemaic royals used gold chamber pots, whose contents were disposed of via a sophisticated system of underground sewers which took the waste out to sea. Personal hygiene was tackled with a sponge on a stick, while menstruation was generally dealt with using pieces of linen, from the 'bands of the behinds' in ancient Egyptian laundry lists to the Greek 'rhakos', recycled old cloth that was also used in a form of tampon. The problem of PMT at the onset of menstruation was regarded as a problem best cured by getting pregnant.

Judging by literary works of the time, including the graffiti on bath-house walls, this would certainly have happened within the relaxed environment of the bathroom, where mixed bathing for all classes had become normal practice by the later first century BC and was a popular pastime for couples. It was traditionally followed by dinner ('cena') which, since breakfast was minimal and lunch a light snack at most, was the main meal of the day, usually enjoyed late in the afternoon or evening.

With social dining used to express one's status, the impressive surroundings of the dining room, often painted a strong cinnabar red or dramatic black, might be further adorned with still-life images of food. Even the mosaic floors could have a food-based theme, from the Eastern-inspired colours of glistening fresh seafood to the trompe l'oeil 'Unswept Hall' which showed a floor littered with the debris of a banquet in full swing. Then, in contrast, Italian-produced mono- chrome mosaics of a skeleton carrying wine jugs advised the living to 'eat, drink and be merry' in much the same way that, according to Herodotus, small models of the dead were taken around diners at Egyptian banquets to emphasise the transitory nature of life.

Guests reclined on couches around a central dining table, a linen napkin at their neck and another to wipe their fingers – forks had yet to be invented, although the Romans were particularly fond of imported Eastern silverware. And after the gods had been invoked in an ancient form of grace, a procession of servants brought in gold and silver platters laden with food.

With bread the basis of most ancient diets, the wealthy enjoyed light 'artophites' bread made from best wheat flour in contrast to the soldiers' dried 'buccellatum' bread or the coarse bran loaves fed to slaves and dogs. And although, through economic necessity, most Romans added little more to their bread than eggs and vegetables, plain food was a means for some to demonstrate Republican credentials in the face of increasingly exotic fare from the East. One third-century BC Roman general required nothing more than a dish of home-grown boiled turnips, since 'a man for whom such a dinner sufficed had no need of gold'. Yet Caesar and Cleopatra, like most wealthy Romans, expected a much wider range of fare on their dining tables than bread and turnips.

Beginning a meal with the traditional 'gustatio' starters, asparagus was a favourite dish commonly served at Caesar's table with an olive oil- based dressing or perhaps incorporated into some form of mousse. Served alongside were such dishes as mushrooms in red wine, celery in raisin sauce, lentils with mussels and herbs, olives in herb-flavoured oil, bread and tapenade (olive paste), vegetable fritters and small balls of fried cheese-pastry known as Globi.

When in Rome, Cleopatra may have done as the Romans did and enjoyed an early form of tagliatelle known as lagana, a great favourite of Caesar's associate Cicero, along with a polenta or porridge called pulmentus to which cheese might be added to create 'Puls Punica', Carthaginian porridge. There were various types of cheese, from ricotta to softer cream cheeses blended with herbs or nuts; Sicilian cooks were well known for their enthusiastic use of cheese, although their cheesy fish recipes were a little too much for some palates.

Yet fish, both plain and highly flavoured, appeared frequently at the Primae Mensae, the main course. A favourite of Greeks and many Italians, all manner of seafood could be caught around the Bay of Naples, although Caesar was also supplied by his wealthy cousin's fish farm whose speciality, sea eels, would have been presented at Cleopatra's table when she was in Rome. Eels were among the most expensive of fish, and the belief that the Egyptians worshipped then was referred to in one Greek comedy which claimed that 'the eel you consider the greatest divinity, and we the greatest dish'. But then, the Greeks' extreme love of seafood also bordered on the religious.

One recipe for eels dressed in beet leaves compared the fish to nubile goddesses in the same way that a pair of Greek sisters were referred to as 'the anchovies' on account of their 'pale skin, slender figures and large eyes'. 'Some men's lust for fish was so great that they were described as 'opsomanes', 'fish-mad'; rather than those who were simply 'gunaikomanes', 'girl-mad', and, since they were able to wield such power, fish were commonly used in love spells. With the red mullet associated with the classical goddess Hekate and the Nile perch sacred to Hathor, the Egyptian association between fish and reproduction is reflected in the words of a girl rising from the waters, inviting her lover to 'see the red fish playing between my fingers'. Then as now, certain seafood was regarded as an aphrodisiac: Venus herself was said to consume giant oysters at midnight. It would not be too difficult to imagine Caesar and Cleopatra sharing a dish of the oysters imported into Rome from as far afield as the Red Sea and Britain, presumably well packed with ice or vinegar.

For the wealthy minority, exotic imports might also include British beef imported via Gaul; 'Numidian birds' or guinea fowl from North Africa; Egypt's smoked quail, which were a favourite of Alexander; and even the Indian peacocks kept for their ornamental value but very occasionally served at table as the ultimate in conspicuous consumption, even if they were so tough that they had to be made into rissoles and then stewed in a broth. Served alongside them were the more widely available roast lamb, sucking pig, roast duck and pigeon, with a range of elaborate sauces. Caesar's secretary Aulus Hirtius was famous for the sauces his chef produced, from lamb stewed Lydian-style with feta cheese to beef and veal cooked in a sweet and sour sauce.

It is questionable whether Cleopatra ever tucked into famous Roman delicacies such as dormice in honey or milk-fattened snails served in liquamen, a sauce made from fermented fish entrails. But liquamen was certainly a firm favourite with the Romans, who added it liberally to most savoury dishes and it was a staple of the dining table along with its more concentrated version, garum. The frequent use of salt, wine vinegar and costly black pepper imported via Egypt's Red Sea ports, along with ginger, cinnamon and turmeric from south-east Asia, all earned the Romans a well-deserved reputation for highly flavoured food.

A selection of grapes, apples, pomegranates and figs usually formed the last course. Cleopatra had a taste for large, juicy figs and may well also have been fond of Egyptian dates, which were imported by the sackload from Thebes. The soft fruits of Campania were available too, stewed in wine or made into jelly along with an early form of ice cream made from honey, nectar and ice, a favourite of Alexander's that was no doubt available to his successors. Honey was also added to stewed fruit, egg custards and a whole array of confections such as sesame and honey wafers, nut and poppy-seed biscuits, a panforte-type fruit and nut cake, and the distinctive pyramid-shaped cakes or 'pyramis' made of honey-soaked wheat in an amusing tribute to Cleopatra's homeland.

After dinner came the 'drinking course' symposium, and although Caesar drank little himself he and Cleopatra may have shared the odd glass of vintage Caecuban, 'the Roman equivalent of the modern champagne', drunk from the finest crystal goblets. With performances by the 'perfumed singer and musical virtuoso' Marcus Tigellius Hermogenes, and the occasional recitation from the Mytilene poet Crinagoras who visited Caesar in 45 BC, the couple's symposia brought like-minded philhellenes together in a combination of floor-show and philosophical debate, sometimes led by Cleopatra's philosopher friend Philostratus.

Although the original Greek symposia tended to be all-male drinking parties at which women were only there to provide some variety to the standard homosexual proceedings, the mixed gatherings of Rome clearly intimidated some men who claimed 'worse still is the well-read menace, who's hardly settled for dinner before she starts . . . comparing, evaluating rival poets . . . she's so determined to prove herself eloquent, learned . . . Avoid a dinner partner with an argumentative style . . . choose someone rather who doesn't understand all she reads. I hate these authority-citers . . . who with antiquarian zeal quote poets I've never heard of'.

Although Roman women's drinking habits would have been strictly policed at such events, Cleopatra's court by the Tiber would have been governed by the very different traditions of the Ptolemies and their patron deity Dionysos, god of wine, whose previously banned rites were reintroduced into Rome by the famously abstemious Caesar. No doubt he restored the god as a gesture to Cleopatra, but the reappearance of a cult featuring public drinking and dancing must have proved unpopular with many of the more straitlaced Romans. It was certainly true of those who wanted the old Republic back, and who as the enemies of Caesar could have had little love for the woman presiding over her foreign court at the heart of Rome.

Although Caesar lived with his Roman wife Calpurnia in his official residence on the Sacred Way, the ancient sources suggest that he appeared with Cleopatra fairly openly. Some modern commentators suggest he was far too busy to have seen much of her, only dropping in from time to time; on the contrary, Cleopatra's influence on Caesar cannot be underestimated.

It was certainly not lost on the Republicans, who had long blamed anything they didn't like on the nearest 'non-Roman' source, be it Greek or Egyptian. Having already declared Alexandria 'the home of all tricks and deceits', Cicero paid Cleopatra at least one visit to acquire certain literary works he claimed she had promised him. In the end her efficient network of spies and informers presumably discovered his true opinion, and the books were never forthcoming. This clearly upset Cicero – but with several failed marriages suggesting some sort of problem with women, not to mention his loathing for most things Greek, exemplified by his use of the term Graeculus, 'dirty little Greek', and his deep hatred of monarchy, it seems unlikely he could ever have forged a close friendship with a woman he refused even to name, referring only to 'the queen' in an intended insult.

His attitude certainly revealed the enormous divide between Egyptian monarchy and Roman Republicanism, although Cleopatra's presence in Rome was at odds not only with Republican ideals but also with the status of Roman women. At a time when the best epitaph a Roman woman could hope for was that she was 'charming in conversation, yet her conduct was appropriate. She kept house, she made wool', a woman wielding more power than the men around her was simply unacceptable. So too was a woman covered in all the trappings of royalty which the Romans associated with men, and while a man in women's clothes was simply regarded as effeminate, Roman women were forbidden by law to wear male clothing.

Certainly Cicero had claimed that 'our ancestors established the rule that all women, because of their weakness of intellect, should be under the power of [male] guardians', although he presumably never voiced such sentiments in the presence of the intellectually superior Cleopatra. Yet in an extraordinary letter to a friend, Cicero wrote, 'I hate the queen! And the man who vouches for her promises, Ammonius, knows I have good reason to do so; although the gifts she promised me were of a literary nature and not beneath my dignity – the sort I should not have minded proclaiming in public. Her man Sara too, beside being a rogue, I have found impertinent towards myself. Once, and only once, have I seen him in my house; and then, when I asked him politely what he wanted, he said he was looking for Atticus. And the queen's insolence, when she was living in Caesar's house in the gardens across the Tiber, I cannot recall without indignation. So no dealings with that lot!'

Although his intriguing reference to 'her man Sara' has been assumed to be a shortening of the Egyptian name Serapion, it may just as likely refer to Cleopatra's brother Ptolemy XIV whose royal title 'son of Ra' would have been vocalised as 'sa ra' when read out at audiences in Rome. If he did visit Cicero's house, his belief in his own divine status would also explain his perceived 'impertinence' in much the same way that his half-sister was described as insolent.

As Cicero and his fellow Republicans discussed how they should deal with this unnaturally powerful woman who wielded so much influence over Caesar and the future of Rome, they expressed equal suspicions of Antonius, a long-standing enemy of Cicero's. Referring to him as a 'loathsome man', Cicero ridiculed Antonius' love of all things Greek and lampooned his exotic dress sense, from his penchant for the white 'phaikasion' footwear of Athenian officials and Alexandrian priests to his choice of local clothing when working in Gaul. From time to time Antonius also dressed as Herakles, his family's divine ancestor, whom he resembled in build 'and also by the fashion of his dress. For whenever he had to appear before large numbers, he wore his tunic girt low about the hips, a broadsword on his side, and over all a large coarse mantle'.

Yet the things that Cicero so despised about Antonius were the very things which made him so attractive to Caesar and Cleopatra. He had mended his former ways with the help of his ambitious third wife, Fulvia, and the couple may well have paid court to Cleopatra in an attempt to heal the rift with Caesar. Antonius once lost interest in a speech when Cleopatra passed by in her carrying chair, whereupon 'Antonius started up and left them in the middle of their cause, to follow at her side and attend her home.' Knowing him to be a philhellene and a great admirer of Alexander, Cleopatra realised his cause was theirs, drawing him back into their circle of allies as she embarked on her quest to bring Caesar supreme power in Rome to complement her own position as supreme monarch in Egypt.

Their young son Caesarion was destined to be the new Alexander, to rule over a united East and West. His early years in Rome may well have followed Soranus' indispensable advice on weaning, teething, swaddling and even nappy rash, together with recommendations for a small 'push-cart' or chair on wheels when the baby started to walk. It was said that the boy not only looked like Caesar but walked like him, and now that they were able to spend time together in the privacy of the villa a bond must have developed between father and son, his only surviving child in a culture which prized male heirs above all else.

Although the time was not yet right for Caesar to make a public announcement of his paternity, he had nevertheless told Antonius and several close associates as he began work on a new law which would make it legal for the Dictator to have more than one marriage for the purpose of producing an heir. This was clear evidence of the serious nature of his relationship with Cleopatra and his intentions for their son. Cleopatra herself was highly popular among Caesar's faction, as well as an object of tremendous curiosity to the general public.

Having recently enjoyed the dazzling splendours of Caesar's Triumph for Egypt, the people of Rome must have regarded Cleopatra's arrival in their city as adding to this exotic allure: she was the most glamorous individual most Romans had ever seen; every detail of her appearance and lifestyle was scrutinised and copied. From her Egyptian-themed surroundings to her melon hairstyle and pearl jewellery, so many Roman women adopted the 'Cleopatra look' that their statuary has often been mistaken for Cleopatra herself.

Yet superb sculpted images of Cleopatra were certainly created during her time in Rome, where she sat for sculptors both Roman and Greek as they attempted to capture her likeness in marble and metal. Although some have doubted if any of these likenesses survived, at least two such heads exist which represent Cleopatra when she resided in Rome; both are made of imported Greek marble and closely resemble her coin portraits. And, though both are uninscribed in the manner of most ancient portraits, in first-century BC Rome there would have been no mistaking who this woman was.

Chief among them was 'a beautiful image' which Caesar himself set up at the very heart of the city. Having vowed to his divine ancestor that if she brought him victory against Pompeius he would build a new temple in her honour, he fulfilled his vow with a temple dedicated to 'Venus Genetrix', 'Venus who brings forth life', bringing the ancestress of the Julian house directly into his plans. He selected his new temple's statuary with the utmost care in order to demonstrate his policies publicly. The temple was fronted by an antique statue of Bucephalus, Alexander's favourite horse, to which Caesar added his own figure as rider, literally in the saddle as Alexander's successor. Behind this most eloquent of equestrian statues, a flight of steps ascended to a high podium of Corinthian columns, beyond which lay Venus' gleaming shrine housing a spectacular collection of sparkling gems and cameos. In their midst stood a superb statue of Venus commissioned from the Greek sculptor Arcesilaus, adorned with a pectoral-like breastplate of the choicest British pearls and Cleopatra's gift of her own pearl necklace. Yet the tableau was only completed when Caesar added the finishing touch, 'a beautiful image of Cleopatra by the side of the goddess'.

Played down by some historians as little more than a 'polite' gesture, this blatant move has been described by others as 'open acknowledgement of marriage between a descendant of a prestigious dynasty and the daughter of a god'. Figurines of Venus were traditionally presented to brides at marriage, and this life-size golden version may well have been Caesar's very public announcement about his relationship with Cleopatra and his dynastic intentions. But whereas the Ptolemies had always set up statues of themselves and their families alongside those of the gods in their temples, this was certainly not the case in Republican Rome where living individuals were never portrayed in this way. And as a statue giving divine authority to a woman in the very centre of their city, it was political dynamite.

Although the original gold statue of Cleopatra disappeared long ago, it was copied in yellow-toned Parian marble sometime between 46–44 BC, ending up in the second-century AD statuary collection of the wealthy Quintili brothers in their villa on the Appian Way. Now known as the 'Vatican Head' after its current home, it was long believed to represent a Roman priestess until it was noticed her 'infula' ritual headband was actually the broad diadem of the later Ptolemies. Its large eyes and small mouth were very similar to those found on Cleopatra's coin portraits, and the head, despite its lack of nose, was finally identified as Cleopatra in 1933.

With her braided hair set in the melon coiffure, a clue that this might just be a copy of Caesar's original gold statue of Cleopatra was the appearance of a small nodule over the forehead that the Roman sculptor who copied the original didn't quite understand. It may have been meant to represent 'a lotus crown or uraeus, or even the remains of a large knotted lock of hair', most likely a type of lampadion 'top-knot' as featured on a first-century BC marble head of a woman from Pompeii's Isis temple, or even a stylised version of Alexander's own distinctive raised lock of hair over the brow. A second detail that the copyist was unsure about was a kind of blemish on its left cheek which may once have been the traces of a child's fingertip. Equating Cleopatra with Aphrodite-Venus, the child on the original statue was likely to have been Caesarion as Eros-Cupid in the same mother-and-son pairing used on Cleopatra's Cypriot coinage, in which her infant son looks up towards her face.

The second such head of Cleopatra, just under life-size and again made in Rome of the same Parian marble, was found in a villa along the Appian Way south of the city. The abrasive action of a chemical cleaner applied at some stage has produced a soft-focus, vulnerable quality not shared by the more defined features of the Vatican Head, creating a 'slightly more flattering portrayal' about which male scholars seem particularly enthusiastic. As 'perhaps the finest and most beautiful portrait sculpture' of all Ptolemaic rulers, eventually bought by Berlin's Antikensammlung, the Berlin Head 'speaks for itself . . . it is infinitely more beautiful than the unflattering coin portrait, and it does convey an image of the great queen's personality'. Two further male commentators give the same rave reviews of its 'great physical beauty'. A less effusive female opinion claims that 'whilst it does not flatter her, it bears a close relationship to the portraits of Alexander the Great', and the head does indeed demonstrate a slight tilt in a mirror image of Alexander, whose well-known images tend to show his head tilted slightly to the left. The Berlin Head once again shows the hair gathered up in the melon coiffure topped by a diadem; tiny curls frame the face, while the same small tuft of hair over the brow seems to replicate Alexander's distinctive locks.

There is even a third life-size head of Parian marble which presents a stylised image of a Ptolemaic royal female of divine status. Wearing the same vulture headdress and tripartite wig of echeloned curls portrayed in Cleopatra's Egyptian temple reliefs and duplicated on gold signet rings perhaps worn by the pro-Caesar faction, this image, known as the Capitoline Head', most likely reflects the period when Living Isis resided in Rome as partner to the warrior Caesar. Certainly Isis had a strong military dimension for the Romans: 'Isis-Victoria' was equated with both Venus Victrix and Rome's national war goddess Bellona, partner of war god Mars. And when Rome's main Isis temple on the Capitoline Hill was destroyed by order of the Senate in 48 BC, Caesar and Cleopatra may well have outlined plans for a new Isis temple to be rebuilt on Mars' sacred site, the Campus Martius. The resulting 'Iseum

Campense' completed a few years later housed all manner of Egyptian-inspired statuary and pieces imported from Egypt, some discovered as recently as 1987.

Caesar's image too was now erected in temples as part of a policy of self-promotion backed by the Senate, which voted him 'temples, altars and divine images and a priest of his own cult'. One particular statue of Caesar, dedicated 'to the Unvanquished God', lifted its title from a statue of Alexander in Athens. So Caesar's message could really not have been clearer – he was the new Alexander, his partner Cleopatra was Alexander's living successor and their son Caesarion, conceived in Alexander's own city, would succeed them both in a new world order.

Nor was it a coincidence that this particular statue of Caesar as god was placed in the temple of the deified Romulus, founder of Rome, a city inaugurated back in 753 BC but which still paled against the opulent cities of the East. So Caesar took it upon himself to transform the eternal city by diverting part of the vast wealth obtained from his military successes into a grandiose programme of redevelopment.

Having learned much from his time in Egypt, a land sustained by its knowledge of hydraulics, Caesar planned to reroute the river Tiber and create an artificial harbour at its mouth to give Rome direct access to the sea. Surely inspired by the Fayum's vast reclamation scheme, he also planned a canal to drain the Pontine marshes in order to reduce the incidence of malaria which affected the city every summer and autumn. The vast quantities of grain produced on the agricultural land gained by draining the Fayum almost certainly influenced his decision to drain the Fucine Lake, east of Rome, to increase the amount of arable land and make Rome more self-sufficient. For in such a small city with almost one million inhabitants and 'as crowded, probably, as modern Bombay or Calcutta,' Rome's daily grain dole to 320,000 people was unsustainable. So as well as increasing local grain supplies, Caesar decided to send many of the unemployed claimants to other parts of Italy and some to Greece, including Corinth. That city's fortunes as a trading centre would be revived by his ambitious scheme to cut a canal through the Isthmus of Corinth, the shortest route between the Ionian and Aegean seas and most likely influenced by Egypt's trade-enhancing canal between the Nile and Red Sea.

As Cleopatra and her advisers assisted Caesar in developing his grand designs, the old brick-built city of Rome began to give way to a marble-clad metropolis modelled on Alexandrian lines. Caesar's new Forum of Julius, incorporating his imposing temple of Venus and its gold statue of Cleopatra, was officially opened in 46 BC. The nearby Basilica of Julia, named after his daughter, housed Rome's law courts within the same magnificent porticoes as Alexandria's Gymnasion. As Cleopatra visited such sites beneath the fine linen drapes of her royal canopy, plans were drawn up for a new election building on the Campus Martius measuring an astonishing mile in circumference, together with the world's largest theatre beside the Tarpeian Rock on the Capitoline Hill; both followed Alexander's practice of dominating with scale and were ultimately based on the same colossal Egyptian architecture which had so impressed Caesar.

Yet the most lasting area in which Cleopatra influenced Caesar was their mutual passion for scholarship and, despite recent stock depletions during the Alexandrian War, Cleopatra still owned the world's largest library. It was surely with her advice that Caesar envisaged similar facilities for Rome, having appointed a head librarian the year he returned from Egypt, 47 BC. The librarian was given a remit to collect copies of all the Greek and Latin works in existence, a task which required direct cooperation with Alexandria.

Having so emphatically affected Rome's culture, religion, politics and even its landscape, Cleopatra also provided Caesar with the means to shift time. In a move which still regulates the Western world – albeit with minor modifications by the Pope in 1582 – Cleopatra's astronomers presented Caesar with the Egyptian calendar to replace their defective Roman version. Egypt had invented the 365-day year, their ancient solar calendar of 360 days provided with an extra five days added at the end of each year to bring it into line with the movement of the sun. Each temple's astronomer priest ensured that the rites and festivals were performed at exactly the right moment by using a combination of astronomical observation, obelisks, sundials and a sophisticated mechanical water clock invented by an Alexandrian barber-turned-engineer. The Alexandrian scholars had also refined the ancient Egyptian calendar by taking on board the calculations of Kallippus of Cyzicus, a colleague of Aristotle, who had reformed the Greek calendar in 330 BC by harmonising the solar and lunar calendars using information gleaned by Alexander's scholars in Babylon.

By contrast, Rome's 355-day lunar-based calendar involved the insertion of an extra month every other year to produce the annual average year of 366 days; the excess day was eliminated if the extra month was left out of the calendar every twenty years. But since the Roman priests who monitored such complexities had failed to do their job during Caesar's long absences in Gaul during the fifties BC, Rome's calendar had gradually drifted two months ahead of the seasons. So when it was a summery July the calendar read an autumnal September, and with festivals now falling at inappropriate times Cleopatra's advisers were fortunately on hand to correct this serious discrepancy.

Under the guidance of her astronomer royal, Sosigenes, Rome's unwieldy lunar calendar was discarded in favour of Egypt's more straightforward solar version. It became known as the Julian Calendar and was made up of 365 days, with an extra day added every four years to create what is now known as a leap year. The fifth month, Quinctilis, was renamed 'Mensis Julius' or July in honour of Caesar's birthday, which was publicly celebrated in the manner of Eastern rulers.

In order to introduce their new calendar on 1 January 45 BC, Caesar and Sosigenes added two extra months between November and December in 46 BC as a one-off measure. This made 46 BC the longest year on record at an astonishing 445 days, so Cleopatra's stay in Rome became rather more lengthy than the simple dates '46–44 BC' would suggest. The extension also had serious political ramifications, since those in annual office remained in power for longer.

But as Rome's entire way of life was being transformed by the vision of one man under the influence of not just a foreigner, or even a woman, but a monarch too, die-hard Republicans were already discussing ways to put an end to the reforms. Rumours circulated that Rome was no longer good enough for Caesar, that he wanted to transfer the government to Alexandria and even make himself a monarch alongside his foreign partner. It must have been clear that the couple, who appeared openly together in Rome, regarded them-selves as married regardless of Roman law and Caesar's existing marriage to Calpurnia, particularly as Caesar was drawing up legislation to amend his marital status by making it legal for him to have more than one marriage.

Yet, regardless of the changes afoot in Rome, the civil war rumbled on as Pompeius' sons hiding out in Spain continued to evade all attempts to deal with them. So once more the task fell to Caesar, and although details of Cleopatra's whereabouts at this time were later destroyed, along with almost every other description of her time in Rome, she may well have returned briefly to attend to Egypt's affairs when Caesar left for Spain in November 46 BC.

Pompeius' sons and their allies managed to avoid direct conflict for several months until Caesar finally drew them out in the spring. Battle commenced on 17 March 45 BC some 40 miles east of modern Seville at Munda. The fifty-four-year-old was soon in the midst of fierce hand-to-hand combat on the front line, genuinely fighting for his life until the battle started to turn. In the rout that followed, his one thousand losses could be set against the thirty thousand enemy dead, with a further twenty to thirty thousand rebels killed following their continued resistance at Cordoba. And although Pompeius' younger son Sextus managed to escape yet again, his wounded brother Gnaeus was caught, executed and his severed head put on public display.

Yet Caesar was far from feeling triumphant. His exertions had taken such a toll on his health that his epilepsy resurfaced with a fainting fit at Cordoba. Filled with horror at the thought that the same should ever happen in front of his enemies and shatter his omnipotent image, he was deeply unsettled by the event. After reorganising Spain, he set out for Italy in August but did not go straight to Rome. Instead he made for his estate at Lavicum (Labici), south-east of the city, where on 13 September, contemplating his own mortality, he changed his will.

This stated that he now left three gold pieces to every Roman citizen as well as bequeathing them his Janiculum villa gardens as public parkland. Money was also earmarked for Antonius, although the bulk of his immense fortune, once intended for his son-in-law Pompeius and then to any son of Calpurnia, was left to his seventeen-year-old great-nephew Octavian. As grandson of Caesar's sister Julia and his nearest male relative as recognised in Roman law, he was to take the name Gaius 'Julius Caesar' Octavianus – but only after Caesar's own death.

Since Roman law still prevented any bequests to foreigners there was no mention of Cleopatra or Caesarion, whose paternity would not be legitimised until Caesar's new law concerning marriage came into force. Nevertheless the will contained a clause appointing guardians for 'a son being subsequently born to himself', and since this was clearly not by the barren Calpurnia it seems highly likely that Caesar was hoping for more children with Cleopatra, who if she had left Rome in Caesar's absence had now returned to witness his Spanish Triumph in October 45 BC.

Towards the end of the year Caesar and his staff travelled to Puteoli, and on the night of 19 December stayed with Cicero to gauge the level of Republican feeling from his host's gossipy conversation. As Cicero described to a friend, Caesar had been 'a formidable guest, yet no regrets! For everything went very pleasantly indeed . . . On the 19th he stayed with Philippus until one o'clock and let no one in – I believe he was doing accounts with Balbus. Then he went for a walk on the shore. After two he had a bath . . . He had an oil-massage and then sat down to dinner . . . His entourage were very lavishly provided for in three other rooms. Even the lower-ranking ex-slaves and the slaves lacked for nothing; the more important ex-slaves I entertained in style. In other words, we were human beings together. Still, he was not the sort of guest to whom you would say 'do please come again on your way back''. Once is enough!'

Perhaps he was still contemplating his own mortality as he walked on the beach that December afternoon; thoughts of Caesarion, Cleopatra and perhaps the news that she was once again pregnant, to judge from later elusive clues, may well have been at the forefront of Caesar's mind. For he was about to leave on yet another campaign, to take on the mighty Parthian Empire in the East. This was his greatest challenge yet: he wanted to halt Parthian raids on the Roman province of Syria, avenge the defeat and death of his former political ally Crassus back in 53 BC, but perhaps most of all emulate his hero Alexander, whose defeat of Parthia's predecessors, the Persian Empire, had brought him his own immortal fame.

Since it was said in the oracular Sibylline Books that 'only a king can conquer the Parthians', Caesar may well have expected the title as a leaving present from the Senate. This had recently doubled in size when he had changed the law to allow in provincials from all over Italy and southern Gaul, to push through his reforms with the help of the consuls for the following year, one of whom was Antonius. It must have been quite clear Caesar was never going to reinstate the Republic which he considered an unworkable system of government when set against the Alexander-style monarchy exemplified by his partner Cleopatra.

Having learned from her potent blend of politics and religion, Caesar as Dictator controlled the state government and as Pontifex Maximus the state religion. He was already declared 'Saviour God' in the East, following in a long tradition of ruler cults. Rome's stark divide between mortal and divine was rapidly coming to an end as the divine statuary of Caesar and Cleopatra was paralleled on their coinage. Cleopatra was the only female Ptolemy to issue coins on her own behalf, some showing her as Venus-Aphrodite. Caesar now followed her example and, taking the same bold step, became the first living Roman to appear on coins, his rather haggard profile accompanied by the title 'Parens Patriae', 'Father of the Fatherland'.

The Senate then transformed the traditional, temporary title of Dictator into permanent office by declaring him 'dictator perpetuo', Dictator for Life; they awarded him the purple robes of the toga purpurae, the dress of Rome's former kings, and even a throne of gold – he was king in all but name. The public took over by crowning one of his statues and shouting, 'Long live the King!' Encouraged by such popular support, Caesar, no doubt supported by Cleopatra and Antonius, decided to launch his bid for the throne at the annual Lupercalia Festival on 15 February.

Caesar took up his position in the Forum, dressed in his purple robes and seated on his golden throne. Then Antonius, bare-chested in the festival's traditional goatskin loincloth, publicly offered him a garland of bay twined around a royal diadem. Since such emblems of kingship were unlikely to have been widely available in Republican Rome, the diadem may well have been supplied by Rome's monarch-in-residence, and 'it is likely that Cleopatra made her contribution, even if she was not present'.

Yet the stage-managed event did not exactly go as planned. Cicero, blaming Antonius, described the moment when 'your colleague sat on the rostra, wearing his purple toga, on his golden chair, his garland on his head. Up you come, approaching the chair . . . you display a diadem. Groans all over the Forum! Where did the diadem come from? You hadn't found it in the gutter. No, you'd brought it with you, a planned, premeditated crime. You made to place the diadem on Caesar's head amid the lamentations of the people – he kept refusing it, and the people applauded. You had been urging Caesar to make himself king, you wanted him your master rather than your colleague'.

No doubt very much in on the act, Caesar became so exasperated when the crowd applauded his refusal of the crown that he 'got up, took off his mantle and shouted that he was ready to have his throat slit if someone wanted to do it'. He declared that he had lived long enough – his health was perhaps still worrying him, combined with 'a tendency to nightmares', but his despondency eventually began to lift as he worked on his forthcoming campaign.

After sending an advance force east to Macedonia together with his great-nephew Octavian, who was to make up for his poor grasp of Greek by enrolling at the local university, the region was placed under the control of Antonius. Lepidus was given Spain and southern Gaul and Publius Cornelius Dolabella Syria. Caesar guaranteed Jewish support by reducing their annual tribute, and as he mapped out his strategy, his ally and partner Cleopatra of Egypt was 'no doubt' actively involved in the consultations with Caesar and his officers.

His departure date was set for 18 March. Cleopatra would also return to Alexandria at this time, accompanied by one of Caesar's most trusted men to command the three legions charged with protecting her and their son Caesarion. And since the campaign would be a lengthy one, Caesar fixed the appointments of Rome's main officials for the next two years, when he would continue to rule as Dictator even in his absence.

Yet this remote control by a virtual monarch was more than a step too far, and as Caesar's departure date drew closer so too did his enemies.

8

Death and Resurrection: Osiris Avenged

As Caesar made his final arrangements before leaving on his Parthian campaign, the Republicans were conspiring to send him on a very different journey. The plot was ostensibly led by the son of Caesar's old friend and former lover of Servilia, Lucius Junius Brutus, who had been a supporter of Pompeius until his defeat at Pharsalus. Then, as a favour to his mother, Caesar had employed both him and his brother Decimus. Yet the family had a long tradition of Republicanism: their ancestor Lucius Brutus had expelled Rome's last king in the seventh century BC. And when graffiti appeared on one of Caesar's statues claiming that 'Brutus was elected consul when he sent the kings away, Caesar sent his consuls packing and Caesar is our king today', the words 'If only you were alive now!' were soon added to the base of a statue of Lucius Brutus.

Like many of the Republican elite his descendant had been raised to believe it was his duty to remove tyrants (usually defined as those regarded as having seized power illegally) and restore liberty. Brutus' romantic notions of regicide were soon exploited by his more pragmatic brother-in-law Cassius, who had also switched to Caesar's side after Pharsalus. Married to Servilia's daughter, the dour Cassius had been given several important posts, but despite previous military experience in Parthia with Crassus he had been passed over for Caesar's forthcoming campaign.

As the rather naïve Brutus became the figurehead of Cassius' plot to assassinate Caesar they were joined by around sixty fellow conspirators, around twenty of whom are known by name. They included nine former allies of Pompeius; the rest bore personal grudges. All were sufficiently misguided to genuinely believe that the removal of Caesar, Antonius and their key supporters would bring about the immediate return of the Republic. Brutus decided to make the most of their grand gesture and at the last moment decided against killing Antonius, despite the advice of Cicero who wanted him dead too.

Having become increasingly offended that he could not always gain an audience with an increasingly busy Caesar, Cicero claimed he 'no longer refuses to be called a tyrant, in fact he practically demands it, and that is exactly what he is', remarking that he was glad Caesar chose to compare himself with Rome's deified founder Romulus because he too had been killed by senators when he became a tyrant. Although he maintained that Caesar must fall, 'either through the agencies of his enemies, or of himself', Cicero himself was excluded from the plot since he lacked the courage of his convictions and was such an appalling gossip.

As the rest of the conspirators formulated their plot, which soon became public knowledge, Caesar perversely began to act as if he was beyond danger, cultivating an aura of divine invulnerability by dismissing his Spanish bodyguard in February 44 BC. Despite pleas from Antonius and no doubt Cleopatra, the Father of his Country never imagined that any of his children could seriously wish him harm, particularly since past events had repeatedly shown that only he was capable of bringing Rome victory. For, as he used to say himself, 'It is more important for Rome than for myself that I should survive. I have long been sated with power and glory; but should anything happen to me, Rome will enjoy no peace. A new civil war will break out under far worse conditions than the last.' He should have been a prophet.

The first day of March, the month named after the war god Mars which marked the beginning of the campaigning season, was also sacred to Juno, the Greek Hera, wife of Zeus. On this date wives were traditionally given presents by their husbands. So perhaps Cleopatra, like Calpurnia, may have received even more gifts from Caesar on one of the last occasions she would ever see him.

Despite a series of bad omens, including a warning from the augur (soothsayer) Spurinna that Caesar would only be safe after 15 March, known to Romans as the Ides, he ignored it all and concentrated on the business at hand. Having ordered a statue of his former son-in-law Pompeius to be restored after it had been toppled by the crowds following Pompeius' fall from grace, Caesar had had it re-erected in the

Assembly Rooms, and it was here that he called a meeting of the Senate for the morning of the 15th. Given the presence of that pithy statement in the Sibylline Book that 'only a king could conquer Parthia', which Caesar would be setting out to do in only three days' time, the conspirators concluded that this would be their last opportunity to strike a blow for liberty and restore their beloved Republic.

On the evening of 14 March Caesar dined at Lepidus' home with a group of associates who asked him his opinion on 'the best sort of death', to which he replied, 'let it come swiftly and unexpectedly'. That night when he returned to his official residence, the home he shared with Calpurnia, he dreamed he floated above the clouds and shook the hand of Jupiter (Zeus) himself; Calpurnia, clearly fearful of recent gossip and rumour, told him of her dream in which their temple-like roof gable crashed down and he was stabbed to death in her arms.

Perhaps worried about a renewed attack of epilepsy in such stressful circumstances, Caesar decided to cancel his 9a.m. meeting with the Senate, maybe to enable him to consult his doctor, Antistius. But Brutus' brother Decimus dropped by and managed to persuade him otherwise. So, dressed in his purple toga, Caesar finally left home an hour late and, travelling by sedan chair, arrived at the Assembly Rooms where the Senate were already in session.

As he was about to enter, Brutus' former tutor, the Greek scholar Artemidorus, gave him a note which he said contained important information about an imminent attack. Adding it to his pile of paper-work and letters to read through later, Caesar passed the augur Spurinna to whom he bullishly claimed, 'the Ides of March have come', to which Spurinna replied, 'Ay, they have come, but they have not yet gone.' And although Antonius, still jumpy at the lack of bodyguards, was waiting at the entrance to accompany Caesar in, one of the conspirators took him aside and struck up a conversation with him so that Caesar would have to enter the Senate alone.

After the gathering rose to greet him, he took his golden seat in front of Pompeius' re-erected statue where a group of senators approached to talk to him. Tillius Cimber was the first to speak, coming close to plead for the return of an exiled brother. Caesar told him he would have to wait, whereupon Cimber grabbed Caesar's shoulders with both hands. As Caesar pulled away shouting, 'This is violence!', the pack sprang upon him. One of the Casca brothers stabbed him sideways in the throat and Caesar retaliated by stabbing him in the arm with his sharp metal writing stylus, the only weapon he had to hand. But this time Caesar's pen proved no match for the blades of his enemies, and as one dagger thrust followed another and another, Cassius wounded him in the face before Brutus finally came at him. '*Kai su teknon?*', 'You too my son?' asked Caesar in Greek rather than the usually quoted '*Et tu Brute?*' Latin version.

Dignified to the end, Caesar had not cried out, and wanting no one to see him die, had covered his head with his toga while loosening his belt to let the lower part fall over his feet. He had effectively formed his own shroud as the assassins continued their attack, and finally his lifeless body slid, covered, to the ground at the foot of Pompeius' statue. Of the hundreds of senators present, only two had made any attempt to intervene. Despite the oath that of them all had taken to guard Caesar's safety, the rest simply froze before scattering in terror.

Although the murderers planned to drag Caesar's body to the Tiber and confiscate all his property amid scenes of popular rejoicing, they had severely miscalculated public feeling. Their attempts to address the gathering crowds as 'liberators' met with such outright hostility once the news got out that they were forced to flee to the Capitoline Hill. After the bloodstained corpse had been left on the floor of the empty Assembly Rooms 'for some time', three of Caesar's household slaves carried it back to his house in a litter, one lifeless arm hanging down at the side. With Calpurnia's nightmare now a reality, Caesar's doctor, Antistius, conducted a post mortem and discovered that of all the twenty-three wounds only one, the second to the chest, had been fatal.

As the news spread quickly through Rome, Cicero expressed his complete admiration for the deed, telling a friend that 'our heroes most splendidly and gloriously achieved everything that was in their power.' Yet such joyful emotions were certainly not shared by the majority of those in Rome.

It would have been a matter of hours at most before the news reached Cleopatra, who must have been genuinely distraught. Tearing at her clothes and pulling at her hair in traditional gestures of mourning, she had finally become the ultimate Isis as she lived the myth, mourning for her husband the dead ruler who had been so brutally cut down.

As the masses, who had also loved Caesar, began demanding

vengeance, Antonius as consul and Caesar's deputy took charge in the absence of the Senate. Acting firmly in the days after the murder, he followed Caesar's example to become only the second living person to appear on Rome's coinage. That issued shortly after the Ides of March carried the earliest known portraits of Antonius: he was shown in mourning, bearded, with his head covered in priestly fashion to stress piety toward the dead man he intended to succeed. He appointed Lepidus Pontifex Maximus to fill the priestly vacancy left by Caesar, and Lepidus returned the favour by backing him with troops.

After Calpurnia and her father Piso had handed over Caesar's private papers, his well-briefed secretary and Caesar's personal fortune to allow the implementation of Caesar's will, Antonius called a Senate meeting on 17 March. He had them ratify Caesar's plans to carry out any outstanding matters, then ordered a general amnesty and met with the assassins, knowing full well that if he punished them the civil war would begin again. But leaving them unpunished would be an admission that they had been right to kill Caesar, and so began a period of 'armed neutrality, whilst Antonius carried on the government along Caesarian lines', using Caesar's papers, his secretary and no doubt Cleopatra's continuing advice to guide him.

When Caesar's will was read at Antonius' house on 17 March Cleopatra would have been unsurprised that, as foreigners, neither she nor Caesarion was included, although Antonius later informed the Senate that Caesar himself had acknowledged Caesarion's paternity. Yet the recent addition of a clause appointing guardians for 'a son being subsequently born to him' seems almost certainly to have referred to Cleopatra, who was most likely pregnant again at the time of Caesar's murder.

After the will had been read out, the magistrates carried Caesar's shrouded body in public procession to the Forum where it lay in state for several days on a finely carved ivory bier spread with gold and purple cloth. With his torn and bloodied purple toga emotively displayed at the head of the couch, the temporary memorial was topped by a wax effigy bearing the twenty-three stab wounds which could be observed when the image was turned by means of a macabre mechanical device. Such effigies were a Roman practice commonly featured in Triumphal processions.

Yet the body and effigy were also laid out within a golden funerary shrine 'modelled on the temple of Venus Genetrix', the counterpart of Isis-Hathor 'the Golden One', and since golden funerary shrines were an ancient Egyptian tradition Cleopatra may well have been involved in Caesar's funeral rites. For although nothing could bring back the living Caesar, his transformation into Osiris according to Egyptian belief would strengthen her role as Isis, while his full deification would enhance her status and that of their son Caesarion. No doubt working closely with Antonius to promote Caesar's divine powers to their mutual advantage, an announcement was made by his former deputy that Caesar would be awarded all human and divine honours. Then Antonius led the funeral procession of officials, musicians and masked professional mourners to the Forum, where huge crowds had been holding candle-lit vigils.

Dispensing with the formal eulogy, Antonius drew on his Greek-style oratorical training and immediately won over friends, Romans and countrymen alike. After reiterating the oath taken by all senators to guard Caesar's safety, he gave an emotive reading from a popular drama in which Alexander's hero Achilles asked, 'Did I save these men that they might murder me?' Then, as feelings spilled over, the Roman people took matters into their own hands. Despite the fact that arrangements had been made to take the body to the huge pyre on the Campus Martius, the bier was ignited where it lay in the Forum. The crowds ripped up magistrates' benches, judges' chairs, tree branches and whatever came to hand to add to the blaze; his troops threw on the arms they had carried at his Triumphs; while women offered their jewels and even the tunics and amulets of their children to encourage the flames to consume Caesar's body and release his soul.

Although Cicero would claim that Antonius had first lit 'the torches which charred the very body of Caesar', at least one eyewitness account described two 'divine forms, perhaps the Twin Brethren' suddenly appearing with 'javelin at hand and sword at thigh' to set light to the pyre. And given Cleopatra's track record for stage-managed state events, including the attempted crowning of Caesar at the recent Lupercalia, it seems highly likely the two 'divine forms' could have been actors dressed as Castor and Pollux, the twin deities popular in both Alexandria and Rome. The tale was embellished by court poets describing the gods themselves coming down for Caesar, the goddess Vesta, guardian of Rome's eternal flame maintained in her temple by the Vestal Virgins, claiming that 'I myself carried the man away, leaving only his image behind: what fell by the sword was Caesar's shade'.

As public grief turned into mass hysteria, some of the crowd tried to burn down the homes of Brutus, Cassius and other known conspirators. One man, mistaken for an assassin, was killed and his head paraded around the streets on a spear. It was only Antonius' control of the city that prevented mass slaughter. Many of the conspirators fled Italy in fear of their lives, Brutus' brother admitting that 'we must give place to fortune; I think we must leave Italy and go to Rhodes or somewhere else. If the best happens we shall return to Rome. If ordinary fortune, we shall live in exile, if the worst, we shall employ the last resort . . .'. Their genuine amazement that the people had not supported their actions revealed just how remote the Republican elite were from the feelings of the people whom Caesar himself had so effectively exploited and who continued to mourn his passing and honour his memory.

The burnt bones and ashes were collected up and placed in an urn beside those of his daughter Julia in the family tomb, the Tumulus Iuliae. In the Forum a 20-foot-high column of Numidian marble was set up, simply inscribed 'For the Father of the Country'. Antonius then ordered the Assembly Hall to be walled up and never used again, and the title of Dictator to be abolished for ever.

Although he would also have protected Cleopatra and Caesarion had they wished to stay in Rome, she seems to have had no desire to remain once Octavian had received his mother's letter telling him about his great-uncle's murder and the contents of the will. For as he sped back from student life in Macedonia to claim his inheritance, Cleopatra knew only too well that he would be a threat to the life of Caesar's true son, Caesarion.

Yet Cleopatra may also have lost their second child around this time, in much the way that Caesar's daughter Julia had suffered the same fate in 55 BC, losing Pompeius' child after seeing his cloak covered in blood after a violent public meeting and imagining the worst. Although heavily censored by Octavian in his later rewriting of history, there is some evidence in Cicero's copious correspondence that Cleopatra suffered a miscarriage in the month following Caesar's death. Writing with regret about the miscarriage suffered by Cassius' wife after her husband's part in Caesar's murder, Cicero added immediately afterwords, 'I am hoping it is true about the queen and *that* Caesar.' The possibility that this cryptic comment may refer to a second child of Caesar and Cleopatra is backed up by references to Caesar's non-Roman children in the plural and his own provision for a son 'who might be born' to him.

Yet, regardless of such a loss, some Romans had suddenly become brave enough to say what they had only thought when Caesar had been alive, Cicero commenting that 'I see nothing to object to in the flight of the queen.' And indeed Cleopatra had left Rome by 15 April with her son, her brother and her entourage. Presumably she would have worn the dark head cover or ricinium that Western widows had adopted as early as Homer's time. But for the Egyptians black had always been the colour of new life and rebirth. So, dressed in her usual dark robes of Isis, Cleopatra's appearance would have served a dual purpose.

Yet the black-robed monarch did not sail straight to Alexandria, but travelled east to Cyprus to restore Ptolemaic authority. Although Caesar had returned the island to Egypt in 48 BC after ten years' harsh Roman rule, it had technically been given to her two younger siblings, Ptolemy XIV and Arsinoe IV. Since Arsinoe was still alive in nearby Ephesus, where Caesar had exiled her, and stirring up dissent, Cleopatra was more than keen to appear before the Cypriot people as their rightful female monarch alongside their acknowledged ruler Ptolemy XIV – even if he had been airbrushed from the official coinage, which depicted only Cleopatra with young Caesarion.

Having ensured that Cyprus' wealth was once more directed to Egypt, Cleopatra appointed the official Serapion as governor before setting sail for Alexandria. It was possible to cross the Mediterranean in as little as six days if the Etesian winds were blowing from the north, and, managing to avoid the sudden spring storms, Cleopatra's ship finally reached the shelter of the Great Harbour.

Backed by the three legions that Caesar had stationed there, she picked up the reins from her caretaker government and was firmly back in power by July 44 BC. Although a document dated 26 July was issued in the joint names of Cleopatra and Ptolemy XIV, by September he had ominously disappeared from the records. Having reached fifteen, notional adulthood, he may well have wanted more power for himself, and Caesar's death meant there was nothing to prevent Arsinoe resuming co-rule with him. The pair would have posed a real threat to Cleopatra and her three-year-old son, so he was eliminated, reputedly poisoned by Cleopatra in time-honoured royal tradition.

Retaining her title Thea Philopator, 'the Goddess who loves her Father', Cleopatra then dropped the now redundant title 'Philadelphus', 'Brother Loving', while upholding the Ptolemaic tradition of dual rulers by immediately making Caesarion her co-ruler. As Ptolemy XV Caesar, Theos Philopator Philometor, 'the God who loves his Father and Mother', he became the Living Horus in every sense, his mother Cleopatra the Living Isis and his father Caesar Osiris. For in the well-known Egyptian saga, Osiris was resurrected at the hands of his all-powerful wife Isis and took his place as Lord of the Underworld, while their son Horus was successfully raised by Isis to take his father's place on earth.

As Egypt's most potent legend became Cleopatra's political policy, the contemporary Roman historian Diodorus Siculus related that 'Isis lived with her brother and husband Osiris, and when he died she vowed she would never accept the partnership of another man. She avenged her husband's murder and continued thereafter to rule entirely according to the laws. In sum, she was responsible for the most and greatest benefactions to all mankind.' The arrangement allowed Cleopatra to assume Isis' all-encompassing male–female duality in which she claimed, 'I have acted as a man although I was a woman in order to make Osiris' name survive on earth', and as far afield as the Greek islands Isis' devotees claimed 'she has made the power of women equal to that of men'.

From nurturing mother goddess to a deity believed to be more powerful than a thousand soldiers, Isis appeared with her sacred creature, the snake, wrapped round her forearm 'in her role as supreme magician slaying Osiris' enemies'. This was no doubt replicated by means of a pair of golden snake bracelets – such jewellery was tremendously popular throughout Ptolemaic and Roman times, often worn in matching pairs on the forearms so that the snakes might appear to travel up the right arm and down the left. Perhaps it was teamed with jewellery incorporating Caesar's portrait in the same way that the Ptolemies' gold coin images were placed on richly bejewelled necklaces and girdles. Caesar's own golden image was certainly worn on rings featuring a small offering jug for the libations made to his divine soul.

Even though his ashes were buried in the family tomb in Rome, his soul was sustained within Egypt where Cleopatra, sharing Isis' power of raising the dead at least in spirit, resumed her programme of temple building. Caesar's memory was maintained in time-honoured Egyptian fashion within her magnificent Caesareum, reinforcing Caesarion's paternity in stone.

Built close to the royal palace complex on Alexandria's seafront, it resembled in some ways the temple the second Ptolemy had built in memory of his own deceased and deified partner Arsinoe II. Cleopatra seems to have been sufficiently inspired by the ancient obelisk set up before her ancestors' temple that she planned to duplicate the feature using a pair of 200-ton rose granite obelisks from Heliopolis. The 1400-year-old 'Cleopatra's Needles' were eventually erected 60 metres apart at either side of the Caesareum's grand entrance, and the temple's 150m-wide frontage facing the harbour stretched back 70 metres within its own manicured parkland. With massive foundations supporting some sort of multi-level superstructure such as a terraced sanctuary, it was by far the most impressive of Cleopatra's Alexandrian buildings, 'the like of which had never been seen before'. The Jewish philosopher Philo later claimed 'there is elsewhere no precinct like this temple, situated on an elevation facing the harbours renowned for their excellent moorage; it is huge and conspicuous, decorated on an unparalleled scale with dedicated offerings, surrounded by a girdle of pictures and statues in silver and gold, forming a precinct of enormous breadth, embellished with porticoes, libraries, chambers, groves, gateways, broad walks and courts and everything adorned with the beauty that the most lavish expenditure could provide'.

Based on fragments of an inscription from the Caesareum which stated 'when climbing the second staircase, below the right-hand portico, next to the temple of Venus, in which stood a marble statue of the goddess', it seems highly likely that Cleopatra replicated the programme of statuary set up in Caesar's Venus temple in the Forum. But alongside figures of the goddess and Cleopatra, the central figure of the Caesareum was 'the image of the god Julius', perhaps comparable with another statue of Caesar carved from southern Egyptian schist, its green colour evoking Osiris' green skin to represent resurrection. Newly discovered granite figures of Caesarion may also have been part of such a family group.

Cleopatra was also planning a complementary building known as the Cleopatreion, presumably one of her cult centres within Alexandria still known as Cleopatra's Baths, and the two buildings emphasising the connection between the individuals they honoured. Caesar's earlier support for the city's Jewish community was reflected in the synagogue built during Cleopatra and Caesarion's joint reign and dedicated to 'the Great God that heareth'. Cleopatra and her son also renewed a grant of asylum to Jews, issuing the decree 'on the orders of the female king and the male king' in both Greek and Latin, the use of Latin a nod to Caesar's pro-Jewish feelings and underlining the monarchs' relationship with Rome.

Cleopatra is likely to have toured her kingdom again, this time in the company of her new co-ruler Caesarion to show herself to her people as mother of Horus, and they may well have travelled to the heart of the Delta to Leontopolis (modern Tell el-Muqdam). Its name meant 'City of the Lions' and its temple to the lion god Mihos (Greek Miysis) was adorned with limestone sculptures of the recumbent creatures, embellished with bronze lion-themed furniture, fittings and offering vessels. There was even a live lion, the god's sacred creature, kept within the temple precincts: it was entertained by the clergy who recited poetry, chanted, played music and even danced for the animal's pleasure. Elaborate ceremonials involving the monarch referred to the pharaoh as 'nisw pa maai', 'the Lion King', and each sacred creature was equated with both Mihos and Horus. At death the lion then became Osiris and was mummified. A limestone stela dated to the joint reign of Cleopatra and Caesarion emphasises the way in which the mummified lions were revered by the royals, evidence of yet another animal cult used by Cleopatra as part of her religious and political strategy.

Yet Cleopatra concentrated most of her building projects in the south, where she presumably travelled with Caesarion to oversee more work on the Isis-Hathor temple at Dendera. As draughtsmen were set to work on the vast expanse of outer wall, massive yet meticulous scenes of Cleopatra and Caesarion offering to Isis and Horus were duplicated with an almost mirror image in which the royal pair also made offerings to Hathor and her son Ihy. Such towering propaganda equated Cleopatra with the temple's chief deity, Isis-Hathor, the single-parent goddess whose union with an absent father had produced a single son named here as 'Uniter of the Two Lands', a traditional phrase referring to northern and southern Egypt which might now equally apply to Egypt and Rome. Cleopatra also had her son shown in the dual crown of a united Egypt, and most significantly of all, she placed the images of her son in front of her own, announcing to the world the order of rightful succession.

High above these potent scenes, Cleopatra's elaborate suite of rooftop shrines created for Osiris' resurrection had suddenly taken on particular significance. She carried out her sacred duties within their walls, intoning words dating back twenty-three centuries as she encouraged her dead husband to 'live, Osiris, live! May the listless one rise up – I am Isis!' Reassuring him that 'Horus comes at your call Osiris, you will be placed upon his arms, you will be safe in your power', Cleopatra-Isis resurrected the powers of the dead Caesar-Osiris who would live for ever through their son Caesarion-Horus in an eternal cycle of continuity.

More than likely progressing south to Thebes, Cleopatra must have been keen to acknowledge the part played by her capable governor Kallimachos during her absence and no doubt also to show that she was back in control. At the sandstone temple of Hathor-Isis on the west bank at Deir el-Medina, where her father Auletes had undertaken work, a large granite stela inscribed in both Greek and Egyptian demotic was set up, its accompanying images showing Caesarion worshipping Amun-Ra while Cleopatra in the distinctive Geb crown of horns and feathers worshipped the war god Montu, both male deities representing aspects of Julius Caesar previously acknowledged in his lifetime.

This same identification was also clear at Montu's cult centre of Hermonthis a few miles to the south, where Cleopatra's daringly innovative birth house had been embellished with extraordinary scenes of Caesarion's divine conception and birth in which Caesar actually appeared as Amun-Ra in order to impregnate Cleopatra in the time-honoured fashion of the pharaohs. The building had by now entered a second phase of construction, in which a high entrance kiosk with elegant multiple columns was added to an already imposing façade. Cleopatra's plans for a final phase of construction featuring a second such kiosk would raise the height to over 50 feet. With a series of slim columns featuring the repeated figure of the dwarf god Bes, favourite deity of women in labour, accompanied by cartouches of Cleopatra VII and Ptolemy XV Caesarion, this stunning creation was typical of Cleopatra's architectural vision.

Finally in the deep south at the Ptolemies' spiritual home, Edfu, Cleopatra knew it was vital to make her son's presence felt as the living representative of all Ptolemies past. In the shade of the great entrance pylon of Auletes, where his towering images brought order to the land, two majestic Horus falcons in granite flanking the temple entrance protected the small male figure recently identified as the young pharaoh Caesarion.

Such active policies not only ensured Caesarion's birthright; the invocation of Egypt's traditional deities would bring maximum protection to the boy at a time when childhood ailments were commonly fatal. It was an acknowledged fact among the ancient medical profession that dysentery 'carries off mostly children up to age of 10', and the environment was also filled with hazards ranging from the extreme climate to the prevalence of snakes, scorpions and crocodiles. One inscription mourned the loss of a one-year-old boy whose 'body lies in the sand, but his soul has gone to its own land', such baby burials often including their toys and even feeding bottles.

Yet Caesarion was considered to be in the very safest of hands, since Living Isis was regarded as the pre-eminent deity of healthcare and able to cure everything from snakebite to blindness. By Ptolemaic times the clergy of Isis were medical practitioners who knew by heart the six-part medical treatises covering anatomy, pathology, surgery, pharmacology, ophthalmology and gynaecology, all contained in temple texts known collectively as the *Book of Thoth*. Spells many centuries old invoked the aid of the goddess: 'Isis, Great Mage, heal me and release me from all things bad and evil and belonging to Seth, from the demonic fatal illnesses, as you saved and freed your son Horus'. Isis' invention of drugs and medicines was also recognised by the classical world, who prescribed a drug named after her as a panacea to stop bleeding, cure headaches and heal ulcers, lesions, fractures and bites.

Nevertheless, Cleopatra needed to draw on all her powers when the Nile once more failed to rise sufficiently in 43 BC. As the threat of famine loomed large, not to mention the bad press, the huge grain reserves in Alexandria's royal warehouses were redistributed while anti-famine measures implemented by her epistrategos Kallimachos down in Thebes were so successful that he was honoured with statues and public festivals. And to prevent any exploitation of temple supplies, Cleopatra sent out firm reminders to her tax officials to honour the traditional tax exemptions she had made to the temples or face the consequences.

The floods of 42 and 41 BC also fell short, and disease became such a problem that Cleopatra's medical advisor Dioscurides Phakas embarked on pioneering research into bubonic plague. She herself continued to work on a more esoteric level to placate the wrath of the lioness deity Sekhmet, 'Lady of Plague', as revealed by an uninscribed stela portraying a royal figure, almost certainly Cleopatra, playing her sistrum rattles to appease the great plague bringer herself in the presence of Heka, the personification of magic.

It may have been more than coincidence that Taimhotep, wife of the Memphis high priest Pasherenptah, died in 42 BC aged only thirty-one. Following her mummification, her burial in the family vault at Sakkara was marked by a large funerary stela inscribed with the lengthiest and 'most explicit laments over death' known from Egypt, composed by her brother Horemhotep. The dead woman told her husband, 'do not weary of drinking, eating, getting drunk and making love – make holiday and follow your heart day and night!' Her words were accompanied by exquisite images of Taimhotep worshipping Isis and Osiris, Horus and his fellow gods, including the Apis bull, in what were 'perhaps the finest examples of private relief ever made in the Ptolemaic period'.

It is certainly true that Cleopatra's subjects could employ the very best artists, the great revival in native art exemplified by such masterpieces as a colossal black diorite statue head that quite possibly represented Pasherenptah and a handsome young Egyptian man with unruly curls carved with consummate skill in green schist. With such quality even exceeded in royal imagery, a superb bronze figurine of a

Greek-style Horus made in Alexandria most likely represented Caesarion; while the breathtaking Tazza Farnese bowl, made of Indian
sardonyx, featured a cameo of the Nile as a male god holding a
cornucopia alongside Isis in the royal diadem reclining nonchalantly
against the head of a sphinx and Horus carrying a bag of seed.

An allegory of Cleopatra-Isis and Caesarion-Horus uniting with the
powers of the Nile to bring much-needed fertility back to Egypt, such
artworks conveyed a further political message: Cleopatra's portrayal of
her son as Horus 'Avenger of his Father' Osiris carried with it the
underlying notion of vengeance. And since Caesarion was raised by
Cleopatra to perform his filial duties and take his father's place, they
were both drawn into the approaching storm which would engulf the
ancient world in bloodshed.

Just as Caesar had predicted, his murder sparked another civil war
as his assassins were hunted down by the two men who vied to
succeed him, his deputy Antonius, backed by Caesar's troops and
money, and his posthumously adopted heir Octavian, who had
arrived back from Macedonia in early May to claim his new name
before the Senate. Understandably, Octavian demanded the money
Caesar had left him. But Antonius, who was determined to retain
power, brushed him aside.

The two men could not have been more different in terms of
temperament, ideology and certainly outward appearance. Although
his youthful looks had been matured by his thirty-nine years,
Antonius 'had a very good and noble appearance; his beard was
well grown, his forehead large, and his nose aquiline, giving him
altogether a bold, masculine look that reminded people of the faces of
Hercules in paintings and sculptures'. This description is considerably
removed from the bull-necked gargoyle image on some of his coin
portraits, which were predominantly used to emphasise particular
qualities rather than to provide a photographic likeness. His fondness
for dressing up as Herakles was nevertheless regarded as decidedly odd
by his enemies and his emulation of Alexander the antithesis of
proper Roman behaviour, as was his devotion to Dionysos, the
Eastern god of 'deviant masculinity'.

Yet the more Antony swaggered around in his exotic if ambiguous
attire, the more his rival Octavian championed the manly garb of

Apollo and Mars. Although the idea of armed combat made him physically ill and his famously puny body fell short of the virile gods he sought to emulate, he compensated by wearing several layers of underclothes beneath his toga. Even his shoes 'had rather thick soles to make him look taller', and although it was said that 'one did not realise how small a man he was, unless someone tall stood close to him', he presumably kept his distance from the strapping Antonius whenever possible.

Octavian certainly 'lacked glamour and panache, still more the vigorous masculinity of a Mark Antony. Puny, sickly, cowardly – the type is recognisable, as is the ruthlessness which often co-exists with physical cowardice. What commands admiration is high moral courage and a firm grasp of reality.' His lack of military prowess and valour were more than overcome by a brilliant political mind, complete lack of scruples, and an incredibly fortunate legacy.

Determined to emphasise this legacy at every opportunity, the eighteen-year-old Octavian set up a statue of Caesar in the family temple of Venus Genetrix which also housed the image of Cleopatra. He won over the people by putting on public games in Caesar's honour, and the timely appearance of a comet seen an hour before sunset for seven consecutive days was identified as Caesar's soul elevated into the heavens. It was dubbed the 'sidus Iulium' in the grand tradition of Egypt's ancient stellar beliefs, in which the souls of dead pharaohs were believed to rise up from their pyramids and become 'Imperishable Stars'. The Romans claimed that Caesar's soul had been transformed into the star, thereafter shown above his head in posthumous portrayals, including his new statue in Venus' temple.

In the same way that Cleopatra maintained her own links with Caesar, Octavian used his divine connections to become 'divi filius', 'the son of a god', albeit by adoption. Although his use of Caesar's name at every opportunity clearly annoyed Antonius, who told him, 'You, boy, owe everything to your name', Octavian was nevertheless feted by the remaining Republicans as an essential counterbalance to Antonius. Still naively hoping he would restore the Republic, Cicero declared that 'Octavian is an excellent boy, of whom I personally have high hopes for the future.'

As Octavian played along to benefit from Cicero's remaining political influence and receive a good press, Antonius was continuously attacked. When he was appointed priest of Caesar's cult, Cicero denounced him as a 'loathsome man! Equally loathsome as priest of a tyrant or priest of a dead human being!' Refusing to attend the Senate meeting that Antonius had called for 1 September 44 BC, Cicero then launched into further virulent attacks in the first of a series of speeches which he dubbed the 'Philippics' after the similar diatribes that the Athenian orator Demosthenes had launched three centuries earlier against the growing powers of Alexander's father, Philip of Macedon. Yet regardless of Cicero's feelings for either of them, Antonius and Octavian initially joined forces to deal with the assassins whom Cicero had already met, encouraging Brutus and Cassius to take up minor postings in Crete and Cyrene offered by some in the Senate to get them out of Rome and away from Caesar's supporters.

Antonius continued to implement plans that Caesar had outlined for his Parthian campaign, sending the general Dolabella to Syria and his own younger brother Gaius to Macedonia to return the troops that Caesar had originally sent out there. But as Antonius set off for the port of Brundisium in early October 44 BC to meet the returning troops, Octavian realised they would only increase Antonius' already over-whelming power. So he quickly sent along his own supporters to meet the men, and by the time Antonius arrived many of the troops were already pro-Octavian.

As the two men vied for control of the various legions, Octavian marched his troops into Rome while Antonius went north to tackle Brutus' brother and fellow assassin Decimus who was holed up at Mutina (Modena). Octavian had now joined forces with Cicero and, as the pair began to win over the Senate, Cicero's barrage of Philippics continued. In the second of these speeches, completed by October 44 BC, Cicero denounced Antonius as 'a disgusting, intolerable sensualist, as well as a vicious, unsavoury crook', also ridiculing his relationship with his wife Fulvia, whose first husband's murderer Cicero had defended in court. He described one of Antonius' visits to his wife, covering his head with his mantle to deliver incognito a letter which renounced his actress mistress. Antonius apparently then 'uncovered his head and threw his arms round her neck. Depraved character!'

exclaimed Cicero, to whom such spontaneous displays of emotion were clearly unknown.

As Cicero continued his wide-ranging attacks, a spineless Senate were eventually persuaded to declare Antonius public enemy number one in April 43 BC. Faced with the combined forces of Octavian and the Senate he abandoned the siege at Mutina and, now an outlaw, marched over the Alps into southern Gaul, a region he knew well. Just as Cicero had planned, Caesar's murderers were brought back into the senatorial bosom as Decimus was ordered to pursue and attack Antonius. His brother Brutus was given the province of Macedonia while Cassius received Syria, and even Sextus Pompeius was rewarded with the admiralty of the Roman fleet with which he could control the entire Mediterranean. Caesar was surely turning in his urn as his adopted son did nothing.

Yet both Octavian and the Senate had seriously underestimated Antonius and the loyalty of his men. When faced with the troops of Gaul's governor Lepidus in May, the two armies preferred to fraternise than to fight, and although unsure of the reception he might receive, Antonius strolled nonchalantly into the enemy camp. Lepidus decided it was probably best to join with his old colleague, for which he was condemned as a traitor by his own brother in the Senate, but the balance of power had once again shifted in Antonius' favour.

Decimus' men then deserted to Antonius and after Decimus himself fled north he was killed by one of Antonius' Gallic allies, who sent him Decimus' head as a gift. Sextus Pompeius felt so mistrustful of the shifting politics he stayed away from Rome, and making the fleet his own, occupied Sicily. Cicero's influence too was on the wane. Although he still assumed that he could orchestrate events through Octavian, his protégé had discovered Cicero was telling close friends that the young man should be 'lauded, applauded, and dropped', alternatively translated as 'raised, praised and erased'. Octavian decided to act alone and go all out for power to compete with Antonius' turn in fortune.

Having been refused the consulship by the Senate, he followed Caesar's example by marching his army on Rome and seizing the public treasury until he and a minor relative were made joint consuls on 19 August 43 BC, just before his twentieth birthday. He then set up a special court to bring Caesar's murderers to justice: all were found guilty in their absence and their property confiscated. Cicero himself was implicated as a conspirator and fled the city, while Brutus and Cassius tried to establish themselves in their respective provinces, Macedonia and Syria. Yet, thanks to Cicero buying them time, they had amassed considerable powers which only the combined legions of Antonius and Lepidus could take on.

Left with little choice, Octavian was forced to revoke the two men's status as enemies of state and invited them to join him in forming the Second Triumvirate, emulating that of Caesar, Pompeius and Crassus some seventeen years earlier. At a conference near Bononia (Bologna) each received the powers of consul, a five-year limit on their arrangement heading off any accusation of dictatorship. Then they carved up the ancient world between them: Antonius demanded most of Gaul, Lepidus was given a smaller part of Gaul and Spain, and Octavian received the lesser regions of Sardinia, Sicily and Africa.

Agreeing that they could now take on Brutus and Cassius, the triumvirs needed serious money to pay the troops. A hit list was compiled of those to be condemned and their property confiscated. Although 'that which gave them all the trouble was to agree who should be put to death, each of them desiring to destroy his enemies and to save his friends', it was said that 'in the end, animosity to those they hated carried the day against respect for relations and affection for friends; Octavian sacrificed Cicero to Antony, Antony gave up his uncle Lucius Caesar and Lepidus received permission to murder his brother' who had so recently denounced him.

An original seventeen names soon expanded into hundreds, many of whom fled to save their lives. Cicero too could have escaped, but he was indecisive and merely retired to one of his many villas. On 7 December 43 BC he was executed, together with his nephew, brother and many others. Delighted by the news, Antonius asked for Cicero's head and right hand which had written the attacks against him, and 'when they were brought before him he regarded them joyfully, actually bursting out more than once into laughter . . . and ordered them to be hung up above the speaker's place in the Forum'. With the orator's head and hand nailed up in this most public place very much as Ptolemaic royalty had been known to do, Fulvia gleefully took out a sharp hairpin and, as a final response to the endless slander against two of her three husbands, drove it deep into the dead man's tongue.

Women certainly began to make their presence felt in the political crisis. Antonius' mother Julia protected her brother Lucius when the soldiers came to take him, bravely challenging them to first kill her 'who gave your general his birth', which inevitably they refused to do. Emboldened by such events, and no doubt remembering the power and influence wielded by Cleopatra during her recent residence in their city, an indignant deputation of women even marched on the Forum to protest against the triumvirs' decision to tax fourteen hundred of Rome's wealthiest women. Although objections from Antonius' mother and Octavian's sister Octavia were rebuffed by Fulvia, the delegation's leader, Hortensia, gave a rousing speech, pointing out that women had no say in government and so should be exempt from tax.

Under normal circumstances, such outspoken behaviour would have caused the same scandal as had Gaia Afrania, whose insistence on defending herself in court back in Caesar's day had made her name a byword for a woman of easy virtue. Yet Hortensia's father had been a famous orator who now 'lived again in his female offspring and inspired his daughter's words', making her role as pliant mouthpiece just about acceptable. The women's unprecedented stand did the trick and, although the demonstrators were removed by force, the number taxed was immediately reduced by a thousand.

The triumvirs' female relatives once again proved useful when it came to cementing their menfolk's alliances, and with Lepidus' son already engaged to Antonius' eldest child, Antonia, Octavian broke off his own existing engagement and agreed to marry Antonius' step-daughter Claudia, Fulvia's daughter by a previous marriage. Having effectively tied his two colleagues to him by marriage, Antonius pondered other forms of alliance. With his fellow triumvirs he now rebuilt the Isis temple, the Iseum Campense, on the Campus Martius. Dedicated 'in honour of Julius Caesar' as one of the schemes planned by Caesar and Cleopatra, and now completed to honour Caesar's memory, it would also be a means of gaining favour with Cleopatra whose support would be needed in the East in the forthcoming war against Brutus and Cassius.

In tacit acceptance of Cleopatra's removal of her younger brother Ptolemy XIV, the triumvirs recognised Caesarion's kingly status and

Cleopatra concluded an alliance with Caesar's old colleague Dolabella as he fought against Cassius for control of Syria. When the Roman legions left in Alexandria by Caesar back in 47 BC were requested by Dolabella as reinforcements, Cleopatra agreed and sent them north; unfortunately they were intercepted en route and went over to Cassius' side. Dolabella then attacked the province of Asia Minor, whose governor, Trebonius, happened to be the conspirator who had so fatally waylaid Antonius at the entrance to the Senate just prior to Caesar's murder. Dolabella captured Trebonius, decapitated him and let his troops use his head as a football.

Needing to counter Dolabella's power at sea, and unable to obtain Sextus Pompeius' fleet, Cassius requested ships from various places around the Mediterranean. Although Rhodes and Lycia would not comply, he managed to get his hands on part of the Egyptian fleet when Serapion, Cleopatra's governor of Cyprus, apparently colluding with Cyprus' former queen Arsinoe holed up in Ephesus, gave him the Egyptian ships which were stationed on the island. This gave Cassius a tremendous military advantage at sea to match the one he had on land. Although some believe that Cleopatra had unofficially ordered Serapion to do this while feigning ignorance, perhaps backing both sides so as to keep Egypt independent whoever the victors, one ancient account reveals that 'Serapion, not waiting to consult Cleopatra, sent Cassius what ships they had'.

Playing for time, Cleopatra refused Cassius' request for ships, telling him Egypt was suffering acute famine and plague and did not have the extra resources – while all the while building new warships in Alexandria's dockyards. She was also maintaining a seaborne trade with India, evidenced by an inscription from Koptos dated to 43 BC which refers to her official responsible 'for the Red and Indian Seas'. Nor could it be likely that she felt any enthusiasm for helping the man who had stabbed to death her child's father only a year before. Yet she now faced a very bleak future as Cassius' forces began to close in.

Having overpowered Dolabella, who committed suicide in July 43 BC, Brutus removed another of the triumvirs' allies by installing Hortensius Hortalus, brother of the outspoken female orator Hortensia, as governor of Macedonia, and allowed him to execute the former governor, Antonius' brother Gaius. So by 42 BC, Cassius and

Brutus were in peace talks with the Parthians and controlled all the East except Egypt.

With no legions to defend a country already weakened by famine, Cleopatra did all she could to prevent Cassius' imminent invasion from just over the border in Syria until the Triumvirs finally made their move. Leaving Lepidus in control of Rome, Antonius and Octavian set out east to tackle the assassins, so Brutus summoned Cassius north to join forces at the Hellespont.

By September 42 BC both sides were ready – as was Cleopatra, who intended to join up with the Triumvirs and provide them with the ships they needed, making amends for Serapion's apparent betrayal but also wishing to play her part against those who had murdered Caesar. Just as she had led her army from Syria into Egypt back in 48 BC, she now prepared to command her troops and, taking up Caesarion's cause as 'Avenger of his Father', sailed out of Alexandria 'with a powerful fleet to assist them, in defiance of Cassius'. Although Cassius received intelligence of her plan and sent sixty warships with archers to lie in wait for her around the Peloponnese, rough autumn seas proved her undoing, and caught up in a violent storm off the coast of Libya, she was struck by severe sea sickness and much of her new fleet was wrecked. Although she managed to struggle back to Alexandria and immediately began work on sixty new vessels, news of her attempt reached the conspirators who sent out ships to destroy any of hers that remained and report sightings of wreckage. Yet with part of the enemy fleet drawn away on this task Antonius gained enough time to ferry his legions across to Macedonia where they were eventually joined by Octavian, carried in a litter since he had already started to feel unwell at the thought of the approaching battle.

They drew up their combined forces at Philippi, named after Alexander's father Philip II. Here there was an established temple of Isis, which explains how one man was able to switch sides and reach Brutus' camp. Disguised as an Isis priest, in the long robes and mask of the jackal god Anubis, he did not attract any undue attention. The fighting began on 23 October 42 BC. Brutus soundly beat Octavian's forces and seized his camp, but when he began to look for him Octavian was nowhere to be found. Having sent out his men to do battle, Caesar's nervous great-nephew had hidden out in nearby marshland after receiving a dream warning him to avoid the fight. Or at least that was his story.

Fortunately Antonius had meanwhile broken Cassius' line and beaten him back to a rocky outcrop. Although Brutus had then sent his cavalry to assist, Cassius' poor eyesight mistook the approaching troops for those of Antonius and he hastily committed suicide. As the conflict dragged on Brutus led out his own forces again on 16 November, but this time was routed by Antonius. So many of the defeated conspirator's soldiers deserted, including the poet Quintus Horatius Flaccus, better known as Horace, that no hope was left. Brutus therefore had a friend help him commit suicide.

Although Brutus had been responsible for the deaths of both Caesar and Antonius' brother Gaius, Antonius, as a former friend of his, covered his body with his own purple cloak and ordered him a noble funeral. But Octavian was having none of it. Suddenly appearing from his marshy hideaway after a sudden recovery, he ordered Brutus' head to be cut off, sent to Rome and thrown at the feet of Caesar's statue. He then sat back to watch the execution of those conspirators who had been taken prisoner, 'his conduct so disgusting to the remainder of the prisoners they courteously saluted Antony as their conqueror, but abused [Octavian] to his face with the most obscene epithets'.

With the victory completely his, the legions saluted Antonius as 'Imperator', general, while Octavian decided to keep a low profile. Yet in his rewriting of history Octavian would claim to have won a glorious victory, his biographer adding that he had defeated Brutus and Cassius even 'though in ill-health at the time'. To avenge his brother Gaius' death, Antonius ordered Hortensius to be executed at Gaius' tomb. Then, all necessary action taken, the conspirators punished and Caesar avenged, Antonius shaved off the beard he had worn for the last two years. He also ensured that suitable thanksgivings would be made at Philippi's temple of Isis, ordering the installation of 'columns entrusting the city entirely to the goddess' guardianship as its Queen and Saviour'. This endeared him to the peoples of the East and Isis' most important representative, Cleopatra. Further acknowledgement of the Egyptian ruler's bravery at sea in the recent war may explain the origins of a mysterious marble head found in Rome. The hair is set in the familiar melon coiffure topped by a curious triangular crown, and 'the unusual arrangement of hair or head-ornament may reflect the subject's involvement in a religious cult or suggest that she should be compared to a goddess'. Although not previously identified, the headgear's incredible similarity to the ship's-prow crown worn by Berenike II and the wreath of ship's beaks awarded by the Senate for distinction in naval combat may well constitute an image of Cleopatra as Isis Pharia, patron goddess of Alexandria and Mistress of the Seas, honoured for her military achievements when avenging Caesar.

As the war against Caesar's assassins drew to an end the triumvirs carved up the empire among them, their particular characters very much reflecting the territories they chose. For although Octavian returned west and retained his control of Sardinia, Corsica and Sicily, taking Spain from Lepidus but ceding him the province of Africa, Antonius took the lion's share. Placing Gaul under his own governors, he claimed the entire East as his own, his resounding victory at Philippi legitimising him as ruler in the eyes of its Hellenised peoples. The five provinces of Macedonia, Asia Minor, Bithynia-Pontus, Cilicia and Syria, plus a host of client kingdoms, would need serious reorganisation before he could access the taxes required for his projected campaign against the Parthians. But in the meantime he spent the winter of 42–41 BC in Athens, where he had lived in his student days.

Dressed in his favourite Greek attire, he went about the cultured city attending lectures, banquets, games and the theatre, where he 'erected a scaffold in plain sight above the theatre, and roofed with green boughs, like the 'caves' built for Bacchic revels; on this he hung tambourines, fawnskins and other Dionysiac trinkets of all sorts, where he reclined in company with his friends and drank from early morning, being entertained by artists summoned from Italy, while Greeks from all parts assembled to see the spectacle'. For that extra-spectacular *son et lumiere* touch 'he even shifted the place of his revels to the top of the Acropolis, while the entire city of Athens was illuminated with torches hung from the roofs. And he gave orders that he should be recognised as Dionysus throughout all the cities.'

When spring came it was time to start work in the East, rewarding those rulers who had supported the triumvirs and punishing those who had not. Crossing into Asia, he visited Pergamon, home of the impressive library of the Attalids dominated by a huge statue of Athena, and summoned representatives from the various regions to meet with him. Following his demand for a massive ten years' worth of tax to be paid in a single year, negotiations had resulted in it being spread over two, since he would need to retain the support of the states bordering Parthia. After Antonius met with the Judaeans Hyrcanus II was reinstated as high priest in recognition of his support for Caesar in the earlier Alexandrian War, but following the death of Hyrcanus' minister Antipatros, an Edomite Arab and nominal Jew, he was replaced by his capable son Herod who Antonius made a viceroy and awarded regal status. Antonius was also called on to arbitrate between two rival kings in Cappadocia, and, despite a brief affair with the beautiful Queen Glaphyra, mother of one candidate, Antonius gave the throne to his rival before Glaphyra ultimately got her way.

Yet he was still a married man, his interests back in Rome represented by his formidable wife Fulvia, 'a woman of restless spirit and very bold' and said to be female only in body. Antonius acknowledged his wife's admirable contribution to his government by issuing coins in Gaul and Phoenicia with their joint profiles, and in some cases with Fulvia's portrait alone, the first Roman woman to be so portrayed. She worked closely alongside Antonius' remaining brother, Lucius, then consul, and the pair began to formulate plans to oust Octavian, currently facing the tricky problem of settling one hundred thousand veteran troops demanding land in Italy.

At the other side of the empire Antonius moved on to Ephesus, home of the great goddess Artemis, where the citizens who had hailed Caesar as divine and managed to keep hold of their temple treasury had also heard of Antonius' desire to be hailed as Dionysos. They sent out women 'dressed up like bacchantes and the men and boys like satyrs and fauns, and throughout the town nothing was to be seen but spears wreathed about with ivy, harps, flutes and psalteries, while Antony in their songs was Dionysus the Giver of Joy'. Such recognition provided an all-important link to Alexander, most useful propaganda if Antonius was to follow in his footsteps and take on Parthia. Like his old master Auletes, he was proclaimed 'New Dionysus', a title repeated throughout the Near East as a useful counter to Octavian's own claims to deity in the West.

Paying his respects to Artemis in the city's vast temple, Antonius must also have met its most illustrious priestess, Auletes' youngest daughter, Arsinoe, now in her mid-twenties. Following her banishment to Ephesus by Caesar, the Ephesian clergy had begun to address her by her former title, 'queen', and she may well have used the opportunity of Antonius' visit to put forward her case for restoration.

Having met Cleopatra's one remaining sibling, Antonius must have considered the various merits of the two women and the differences between them as he began to work out his strategy for approaching Cleopatra herself. He needed her assistance in his plans for the East, but would not travel to Egypt and appear as a supplicant; instead, he sent an envoy to invite her to meet him in Cilicia (modern Turkey). Exploiting her desire to keep hold of Egypt at any cost, he claimed he wanted her to explain rumours, no doubt embellished by Arsinoe, that she had secretly supported Cassius and Brutus – a claim which was patently untrue but which he felt should help gain her vital support in return for keeping her throne.

Yet he should have known that Cleopatra would prove more than his match in any such negotiations.

PART FIVE

9

The Inimitable Life: Antonius
and Conspicuous Consumption

In 41 BC Marcus Antonius, Triumvir, Imperator and victor of Philippi, requested the presence of the Egyptian pharaoh Cleopatra Thea Philopator in the ancient city of Tarsus. His envoy, the effete Quintus Dellius, was ushered into the royal presence in Alexandria and, after formally greeting the twenty-eight-year-old ruler enthroned before him, 'set himself at once to pay his court to the Egyptian . . . advising her to go to Cilicia in her best attire'.

Although responding with her usual 'adroitness and subtlety in speech', Cleopatra as an independent monarch was in no hurry to respond to Antonius' request despite 'many letters of invitation from him and his friends'. Yet she also recognised a real possibility of forming a new alliance with Rome in the person of Antonius, Caesar's closest supporter. He was a man she had known for some fourteen years, and his desire to emulate both Caesar and Alexander, combined with his well-known love of Greek culture, good living and forthright women, augured well for the future. So, regardless of her delaying tactics, Cleopatra decided she would visit Antonius in Tarsus – but in her own time, on her own terms and in her own inimitable style.

As 'she made great preparations for her journey, of money, gifts, and ornaments of value, such as so wealthy a kingdom might afford', she would use the Ptolemies' legendary love of show to transform a mundane summit meeting into a spectacular showcase of political intent. Yet the most potent weapon in Cleopatra's political armoury remained her understanding of the male ego. Fully aware of Antonius' recent declaration that he was to be addressed as Dionysos, a god identified with the Egyptian Osiris, Cleopatra would take him at his word, flattering his divine identity by appearing as his consort Isis-Aphrodite. Although she had already established her public image as the

235

Living Isis, she would use her appearance to issue a subtle invitation to a union on both the divine and human level.

Having previously worked her magic on Caesar, Cleopatra 'was to meet Antony in the time of life when women's beauty is most splendid', a beauty enhanced by a veritable army of dress designers, cosmeticians, perfumiers and hairstylists. Capable of transforming the woman into the goddess of beauty personified, the mysterious art of female adornment was traditionally regarded with some suspicion by men. It could certainly have a devastating effect when employed upon the political stage, and while some Republicans claimed that Cleopatra's face 'was painted up beyond all measure', Roman poets admitted that 'a careful toilet will make you attractive, but without such attention, the loveliest faces lose their charm, even were they comparable to those of the Idalian goddess herself', Aphrodite.

In her preparations for her meeting with Antonius Cleopatra could have drawn on all manner of cosmetic products, ranging from 'oesyspum', an oily lanolin preparation extracted from sheep's wool, to face powder made from lupin seeds or iris root. The popular white lead foundation 'cerussa' was also available in a non-toxic version made of tin oxide, sheep fat and starch, while the desired rosy hue for cheeks was obtained with powdered red ochre or the imported Indian rouge 'orchil', the colour also mixed with an oily base to create a strong reddish lipstick.

Further emphasising her expression with neatly plucked brows, Cleopatra's eyes would certainly have received detailed attention, since it was well known that the glance from a woman's eyes could fell a man as effectively as a fatal blow in battle. Although chaste Greek ladies were expected to look modestly at the floor and never directly at men, the Egyptians had always had a very different outlook, dramatically transforming their eyes with black kohl made of the finely ground lead ore galena mixed with palm oil or filtered salt solution. Decanted into practical tube containers and applied with sticks of ivory, bronze, silver or gold, kohl was an important ingredient in Greco–Roman love magic and, like all fashionable Alexandrian women of the time, Cleopatra would have emphasised and elongated her eyes, perhaps even shading her eyelids with powdered green malachite, blue lapis lazuli or yellow saffron to replicate Aphrodite's golden allure each time she blinked.

Watching in wall-mounted mirrors as her servants worked their magic, Cleopatra might also have used a hand-held version, adorned with the reef-like 'Knot of Herakles' or a handle in the form of Herakles' club wrapped in his signature lionskin. This use of Herakles' emblems on cosmetic equipment alluded to the mythical Queen Omphale of Lydia, who seduced and literally disarmed Herakles by taking his club and lionskin for herself. Since Antonius claimed to be Herakles' descendant, Cleopatra may have sought the same result as she scrutinised her own transformation.

Her choice of perfume would form another element of her multi-sensory strategy, and she had all the products of the ancient world to choose from. Cyprus, recently restored to her by Caesar, was a long-standing centre of perfume production and her royal city of Alexandria was the heart of the international perfume industry, importing exotic ingredients from Arabia, India and the Far East and blending them with Egyptian materials in the perfume factories of the Delta. Cleopatra may well have had her own signature fragrance in the manner of other ancient monarchs. The Parthian kings' perfume 'The Royal', for instance, was made from a huge number of exotic ingredients sourced from across their vast empire to emphasise the extent of their power.

The Egyptians had long used perfumes for ritual and political purposes, but Cleopatra was also fully aware that perfumes were most closely associated with love and sex, the domain of Hathor-Aphrodite, whose sacred flowers were myrtle and rose. This made it likely she would have selected Myrtinum, myrtle oil, or Rhodinon, rose oil. These substances were applied liberally to both skin and hair, and it was recommended so 'that your oiled tresses may not injure your splendid silk dresses, let this pin fix your twisted hair and keep it up.'

Hair care was yet another area of ritual importance and was regarded as an act of worship in which devotees 'with ivory combs in their hands . . . combing the goddess's royal hair' offered combs and hairpins to Isis-Aphrodite. The goddess' hair was usually shown pinned up in the same no-nonsense bun as Cleopatra's, fixed firmly in place with gold and silver hairpins. Although women's hair was generally secured in public, some men admitted that in private 'I love to see it fall in floating tresses about your shoulders'. So for her meeting with Antonius, Cleopatra may have left sections of her hair to fall loosely about her shoulders in the manner of Isis-Aphrodite whose 'long thick hair fell in tapering ringlets on her lovely neck'.

Such ringlets were generally created with heated metal tongs, then set with a resin or wax-based styling mixture, although hairpieces could also provide extra length, detail and colour. The red hair of the Germanic tribes conquered by Caesar was particularly prized for this purpose. It was a shade favoured by fashionable Alexandrian women, including some in the royal household. Presumably Cleopatra's own auburn hair had set the trend, maybe enhanced with a vegetable colorant such as henna (*Lawsonia inermis*). Long used in Egypt through-out society, even by the pharaohs, the shrub was common around Canopus near Alexandria, although the best-quality henna came from Askalon, Cleopatra's former refuge in Judaea.

Yet for her actual choice of costume Cleopatra almost certainly chose a Greek-style chiton. Aphrodite's chiton was usually portrayed slipping down to reveal one shoulder, so women were advised to 'leave uncovered the top of your shoulder and the upper part of your left arm. That is especially becoming to women who have a white skin. At the mere sight of it, I should be mad to cover all I could touch with kisses', since 'to kindle in us the fires of love, dress is more potent than the dread arts of the magician'.

Cleopatra's chiton on this occasion was perhaps made from the same gauzy linen which had revealed her 'white breasts' before Caesar, or from the silk imported from the Greek island of Cos, or even from the finest-quality silk sourced from as far afield as China. Fashion-conscious Alexandrian redheads displayed a clear preference for blues and greens. From 'azure blue like a clear sky' to 'water-green from the colour that it imitates, I could easily imagine that the Nymphs were clothed in such apparel'. Cleopatra dressed her most beautiful female attendants in the robes of Nereids and Graces to accompany her to Tarsus.

No doubt to complement her own choice of sea-green silky robes as the goddess born from the ocean spray Cleopatra would have worn numerous pearls from her fabulous collection. These items would also have conveyed a political message as the ultimate symbols of Eastern wealth, which might soon be made available to Antonius. Portrayed on coins with pearl-tipped hairpins to lend gleaming lustre to her hair, Cleopatra also wore a long pearl necklace wound twice, flapper-style, around her neck. Yet her most famous jewels were her enormous earrings made from the two largest pearls 'in the whole of history'. Having 'come down to her through the hands of the Kings of the East', presumably a reference to Mithridates' seizure of the Ptolemies' treasury which Caesar is likely to have returned to her, they were worth a staggering 10 million sesterces each. She wore them to great effect during her time in Rome: women who copied her were said to be discontented unless the value of several estates hung from each lobe.

She may also have combined her huge creamy pearls with vivid green Egyptian emeralds, whose intense colour, so loved by her Ptolemaic predecessors, was intimately linked with the green-faced fertility god Osiris and his Greek equivalent Dionysos. Pearls and gems were even added to footwear of the time. Cleopatra's adoption of Aphrodite's trademark gilded sandals may even have had the cork platform soles worn by fashion-conscious Alexandrian women – certainly an asset in a world where physical stature was all-important for a head of state.

Suitably bejewelled from perfumed head to gilded foot, then, Cleopatra could finally take her place aboard her golden ship to begin her voyage north past Cyprus, then east to the Cilician coast. Her arrival from the direction of the legendary island birthplace of golden Aphrodite would confirm her identity before she herself had even come into view.

As 'word went round that Aphrodite was coming to revel with Dionysos for the good of Asia', exactly as she had planned, the incredible ship reached the mouth of the river Kydnos where crowds began to mass along its crocus-filled banks to witness one of the most dramatic entrances in history. For Cleopatra 'sailed up the river Kydnos in a gold-prowed barge, with purple sails spread, and rowed along by silver oars to the sound of the flute mingled with pipes. She lay beneath a gold-spangled canopy, adorned like Aphrodite in a picture, and young boys, like Cupids in pictures, stood on either side and fanned her. The most beautiful of her serving maids, wearing the robes of Nereids and of Graces, stood by the rudders and by the bulwarks. Wonderful scents from many types of incense permeated the river-banks. Some of the populace escorted her on either side from the river mouth, and others came down from the city for the spectacle. The crowd in the market place poured out, until Antony himself, seated on his tribunal [seat], was left alone.'

While he waited in increasingly solitary splendour in the empty forum, his royal guest had no intention of setting foot on his territory and remained within her canopy as a goddess veiled within her shrine. For this was a battle of wills which she fully intended to win, refusing Antonius' invitation to dinner but inviting him and his officers to dine with her on her ship. Left with little choice, Antonius agreed, and from that moment, she had him.

As his torch-lit escort arrived on the riverbank where her golden ship continued to glow long after sunset, hundreds of carefully arranged lights twinkled like stars among the rigging in 'a spectacle that has seldom been equalled for beauty'. Evoking the well-known light festivals of Isis, Antonius' formal welcome was illuminated for everyone to see. When finally allowed into her presence he 'was amazed at her wit, as well as her good looks, and became her captive as though he were a young man, although he was forty years of age'.

In the great state dining room, hung with gold and purple tapestries, Cleopatra had 'arranged in his honour a royal symposium, in which the service was entirely of gold and jewelled vessels made with exquisite art'. Although he was 'overwhelmed with the richness of the display', Cleopatra 'quietly smiled and said that all these things were a present for him'.

Following the formality of this all-important meeting at which she robustly defended her actions in the recent conflict, Cleopatra invited Antonius and his party to dine with her again the following evening and 'on this occasion she provided an even more sumptuous symposium by far, so that she caused the vessels which had been used on that first occasion to appear paltry; and once used she presented him with these also. As for the officers, each was allowed to take the couch on which he had reclined; even the sideboards, as well as the spreads for the couches, were divided among them. And when they departed, she furnished litters for the guests of high rank, with bearers, while for the greater number she provided horses gaily caparisoned with silver-plate harness, and for all she sent along Ethiopian slaves to carry the torches.'

For their final evening on board ship Cleopatra repeated the performance, this time filling the dining room with rose petals to a depth of several feet. And only when she was satisfied by the cumulative effects of such sensory overload did she finally accept his invitation to dinner, since 'he was very desirous to outdo her as well in magnificence as contrivance; but he found he was altogether beaten in both, and was so well convinced of it that he was himself the first to jest and mock at his poverty of wit and his rustic awkwardness'. For, despite his Greek education and love of Greek culture, Antonius was always a rather blunt soldier at heart, and, realising she would have to engage with him on his level, she did so 'without any sort of reluctance or reserve' before embarking on her plan to raise his political aspirations in line with her own.

For Cleopatra was about to revive the plans she had made with Caesar, once again turning to the ambiguous words of the Sibylline Oracle which stated that an Immortal King would join with a widowed Queen to subdue Rome. Then 'the whole wide world under a woman's hand ruled and obeying everywhere shall stand . . . the Widow shall be queen of the whole wide world' in a new golden age of East–West unity. Having manufactured her visit to Tarsus as the tangible arrival of this new golden age, Cleopatra offered Antonius a glittering future with all the resources he would need to take on Parthia and assume sole command of the Roman world. In return, he would remove her remaining enemies.

Following reports of 'Queen' Arsinoe claiming to be the true ruler of Egypt from her base at Ephesus, Cleopatra's revelation that it had been Arsinoe who had persuaded Egypt's Cypriot governor, Serapion, to help Cassius meant that Antonius agreed to her immediate execution. And 'whatever Cleopatra ordered was done, regardless of laws, human or divine. While her sister Arsinoe was a suppliant in the temple of Artemis, Antony sent assassins thither and put her to death' in the temple which had long been the slaughterhouse for all the city's meat and now for a former queen of Egypt.

Although Cleopatra asked for clemency for the temple clergy who had hailed Arsinoe queen, Antonius also ordered the execution of Serapion and a young pretender claiming to be the resurrected Ptolemy XIII risen from the Nile. With all potential rivals to the Egyptian throne eliminated and Cleopatra's position secured by the stamp of approval from Rome, Antonius now matched Caesar's grant of Cyprus with the gift of Roman Cilicia. Having achieved all she had wanted and more, a jubilant Cleopatra announced her decision to return home, and invited Antonius to join her there.

After quelling a rebellion in Syria toward the end of 41 BC, he arrived in Alexandria, a city he had last seen during Auletes' bloody restoration fourteen years before. The citizens were delighted to have him back, as was Cleopatra, who 'gave him a magnificent reception . . . He went out only to the temples, the schools, and the discussions of the learned, and spent his time with Greeks, out of deference to Cleopatra, to whom his sojourn in Alexandria was wholly devoted'.

During the winter, when the rough seas were effectively closed to traffic and military campaigns were suspended, Antonius spent his time in Alexandria much as he had in Athens, as a private citizen and wearing Greek attire. He also maintained his physical prowess and when he 'exercised in arms, she was there to see'. He took her hunting, a popular royal pastime, using Indian hunting dogs, and even went sea fishing, Antonius giving 'secret orders to the fishermen to dive under water and put fishes that had been already taken upon his hooks; and these he drew so fast that the Egyptian perceived it. But feigning great admiration she told everybody how dextrous Antony was and invited them next day to come and see him again. So when a number of them had come on board the fishing boats, as soon as he had let down his hook one of her servants was before hand with his divers and fixed upon his hook a salted fish from Pontus. Antony, feeling his line give, drew up the prey, and when, as may be imagined, great laughter ensued. Said Cleopatra "Leave the fishing rod, general, to us poor sovereigns of Pharos and Canopus; your game is cities, provinces and kingdoms"', encouraging him to follow in the footsteps of Alexander and regain as much of the former Ptolemaic empire as possible.

Yet despite the fact that the seas were too rough to sail on from October to March, Cleopatra was blamed for Antonius' prolonged stay in Egypt. It was claimed that he 'was over and over again disarmed by Cleopatra, and beguiled away, while great actions and enterprises of the first necessity fell, as it were, from his hands, to go with her to the seashore at Canopus and Taphosiris, and play about'.

Canopus was regarded by the Romans as a rather 'fast' watering-place, a kind of St Tropez-meets-Lourdes. It was a cult centre of Isis and

Osiris, where huge crowds of the faithful came to celebrate Osiris' resurrection. His cult image was regularly taken out in his golden boat between Canopus and his other centre at Taposiris, and, following his Ptolemaic makeover as Serapis, the temple at Canopus had been transformed into a magnificent Serapeum: 'people of the highest renown had faith and slept within it' to receive miracle cures at the hands of the magician-like clergy of all-powerful Isis. Cleopatra herself regularly visited the place dressed as Living Isis. Canopus also housed a shrine of Herakles where Antonius, dressed in the attire of his divine ancestor, looked like 'Herakles in the picture where Omphale is seen removing his club and stripping him of his lion skin' to wear herself before presenting him with items of female dress.

Such behaviour, perhaps hinting at the way Cleopatra and Antonius may have swapped roles for amusement or as part of some dramatic performance, would inevitably be criticised back in Rome, with Antonius 'forgetting his nation, his name, his toga' to become Cleopatra's 'cymbal player from Canopus'. Yet he was actually taking part in traditional Egyptian rites and honouring his Greek ancestry, a role Cleopatra acknowledged by commissioning a highly refined portrait bust in darkest green Egyptian basalt, set up at Canopus' cult centre to celebrate Antonius' identification as Dionysos-Osiris personified.

In nearby Alexandria where they spent most of the winter, a shared love of drama would have seen them visit the city's grandest theatre, connected to the palace by a covered gallery which ran between water gardens and the wrestling arena. The theatre was the place where 'the Artists of Dionysos' wrote and performed plays. Dionysos' counterpart, Osiris, had long been honoured by drama performed in temples, while Egyptian tales, rather like Greek comedies, were also performed in secular surroundings by masked actors who wore a tie-on phallus and were popular among Alexandrians for their 'over-ready tongue and impudent wit'.

The Egyptian royals themselves had even been known to take part in dramatic performances, from the Seleucid Antiochos IV who was known to fling off his robes and dance around naked to Auletes' love of costume dramas. Cleopatra and Antonius employed performers such as Chelidon, dubbed a 'performer of improper dances' by the Romans, who were even more shocked to hear that Antonius' friend Lucius

Munatius Plancus, Rome's governor of Syria, dressed as a sea god, 'performing a dance in which his naked body was painted blue and his head encircled with reeds, whilst he wore a fish's tail and crawled upon his knees'.

Clearly enjoying life within the self-contained world of the innermost palace quarter, the couple would probably also have spent time at the palace on the island of Antirrhodos, so named because of its similarity in shape to the larger Greek island of Rhodes where Antonius had been educated. It was the perfect hideaway, with a private quayside giving access to a palace built by the early Ptolemies but later remodelled, quite possibly by Cleopatra herself. Some sixty thousand square feet of white limestone esplanade supported a palace of red granite, quartzite and basalt, its colonnades interspersed with statues of monarchs and gods, from marble figures of Thoth-Hermes, naked except for a himation cloak slung over his shoulder, to 15-foot-high granite figures of Cleopatra and Caesarion and granite and diorite sphinxes bearing the face of Auletes.

Within such magnificent surroundings Cleopatra and Antonius are said to have been inseparable, enjoying the gaming table where 'she played at dice with him', together with chess, backgammon, knucklebones and a new game created in Alexandria which used ivory counters decorated with city landmarks and royal portraits for a reality version of snakes and ladders. Yet the highlight of each day was the sumptuous banquet attended by a small elite group of friends including Plancus, who flattered Cleopatra outrageously, and another who spent so much time in Antonius' company that he called himself 'the Parasite'. They formed their own exclusive club called the Amimetobioi, the 'Inimitables', whose 'members entertained one another daily in turn, with an extravagance of expenditure beyond measure or belief'. This was far more than simply having a few friends round to dinner, for the cost of such extravagant banquets followed by all-night drinking symposia could be astronomical.

Because they were a means of displaying status, Cleopatra used her legendary banquets to demonstrate her regard for Antonius, a man who so appreciated good food that he once rewarded his cook with a splendid house after a particularly fine meal in Athens. With the whole of the known world scoured for exotic produce in her attempt to better each banquet and retain her ability to amaze, peacocks and cranes were brought from Samos and Melos, tuna and sturgeon from Chalcedon and Rhodes, preserved fish from Pontus, scallops from Tarentum and shellfish from the Red Sea and maybe even Britain, whose oysters were popular in Rome. Alexandria's own seafood was also available in abundance, the mussels, clams and cockles found in the waters right outside the palace sweet and succulent in contrast to the acornlike flavour of those found in deeper waters beyond the harbours.

The Ptolemies certainly enjoyed locally caught fish and imported smoked varieties, along with a wide range of meat from wild game to domestic fowl. An acquaintance of one of Cleopatra's chefs was taken into the royal kitchens where he 'admired the prodigious variety of all things; but particularly, seeing eight wild boars roasting whole, says he, "surely you have a great number of guests". The cook laughed at his simplicity, and told him that there were not above 12 to sup, but that every dish was to be served up just roasted to a turn, and if anything was but one minute ill-timed, it was spoiled. "And" he said "maybe Antony will sup just now, maybe not this hour, maybe he will call for wine, or begin to talk, and will put it off. So that" he continued "it is not one but many suppers must be had in readiness, as it is impossible to guess at his hour". '

There would certainly have been a considerable amount of wine consumed within the palace that winter, as Cleopatra, proud of the quality of the wines served at her table, ensured a continuous supply in honour of Antonius as Living Dionysos. As the ultimate wine connoisseur, Dionysos was said to have a clear preference for Greek wines, although Italian wines had also been greatly improved by Greek expertise. Falernian and Caecuban vintages were exported in cork-stoppered pottery amphorae whose porous interiors sealed with pine resin resulted in a retsina-like product.

Wines were also produced in Gaul's Rhône valley, in Spain, Cyprus, Syria, Phoenicia and Egypt itself, where the Ptolemies had expanded a millennia-old industry to meet the demands of a Greek population and lucrative foreign markets. Although the vineyards closest to the palaces were among the very best, those around Lake Mareotis were 'so good that Maroitic wine is racked off with a view to ageing it'. High-quality wines were also produced in the central Delta, Thebes and the western oases of Bahariya, Khargeh and Farafra.

As regions associated with Alexander, the Egyptian wine-producing areas had particular significance for Cleopatra's dynasty whose Ptolemaia festival celebrating the divinity of their royal house invoked Dionysos in an alcohol-fuelled extravaganza. Great floats featured a giant wine press in which grapes were trod to produce wine as the procession moved along. Another supported 30,000 gallons of wine in a huge wine skin made from the pelts of hundreds of leopards, Dionysos' sacred creatures. They were followed by a massive silver mixing bowl holding a further 6000 gallons, flanked by sixteen hundred boys wearing ivy and pine cone wreaths and carrying gold and silver wine jugs.

Although wine-drinking formed a key part of the royal lifestyle, the monarchy's fondness for it was a charge often laid against them. The teetotal orator Demosthenes had railed against Philip II's drinking habits and Cicero had claimed the same of Antonius, whose 'house rang with the din of drunkards, the pavements swam with wine, the walls dripped with it'. He told him, 'you are a drink-sodden, sex-ridden wreck!', even claiming that he had tried to crown Caesar king when 'soaked in wine'. Antonius had been forced to publish a written defence called *On His own Drunkenness*.

Yet the damage had been done and, although he was remembered as 'a great man of notable ability', Antonius was apparently 'turned to alien ways and unroman vices by his love of drink and his equal passion for Cleopatra'. Later Roman sources would also claim that 'the Egyptian woman demanded the Roman Empire from the drunken general as the price of her favours', and was herself accused of excessive drinking, her mind 'swimming in Mareotic wine' and her speech slurred by 'a tongue submerged by incessant wine'.

Given that alcohol consumption by Roman women was restricted by law, Cleopatra's drinking habits were far more subtle than the limited understanding of her critics might suggest. Temple liturgy encouraged Egypt's monarchs, as part of the royal and ritual identity, to 'take to yourself the wine from Khargeh, from Farafra, the wine from Khargeh and Bahariya, and may your mouth be opened by it', and with Philae's ritual texts promising 'drunkenness upon drunkenness without end', inebriation allowed direct communion with the gods.

Marble head of Alexander the Great capturing his tousled hair, distinctive tilt of the head and upward gaze to emphasise his divinity. It was produced between the second and first century BC in Alexandria, the city he had founded and where he was buried.

One of the marble heads of Cleopatra VII from Rome, often regarded as her most flattering portrait. Close links with Alexander have been suggested on the basis of its slight tilt of the head and wavy hair, here swept up into the 'melon coiffure'.

A marble bust of Gaius Julius Caesar sculpted c.20 BC and apparently based on an original of 44 BC. Such portraits appear to underplay the extent of his receding fair hair which he is said to have combed forward toward his brow.

Bronze figurine of an elite Alexandrian woman c. second century BC. Her body is swathed in a voluminous sheet-like mantle and although most of her face is veiled, her elongated eyes are made up Egyptian-style and her hair is swept back in a bun

One of the marble heads of Cleopatra VII from Rome, with the 'melon' hairstyle topped by the broad royal diadem. It is thought to be a copy of her golden statue, which Caesar set up in his temple of Venus Genetrix in the city's Forum.

Marble head of a Ptolemaic royal female from first century BC Rome. The vulture headdress and wig of stylised curls replicate Cleopatra's appearance in Egyptian temple scenes, and the head possibly represents Cleopatra as Living Isis to complement Caesar's own moves toward divinity.

The marble head of a woman 'resembling' Cleopatra VII from first century BC Rome. Remains of its unusual angular headgear possibly represent a crown of ships' prows awarded for naval success, suggesting Cleopatra was a recipient.

A mosaic image from Mendes portraying third century BC Ptolemaic pharaoh Berenike II as the personification of Alexandria. Her ships' prow crown and anchor-shaped brooch emphasised her key role in naval successes during her joint reign with husband Ptolemy III.

Reproduction of the mosaic from the temple of Isis-Fortuna at Palestrina portraying the Nile landscape, possibly commissioned by Cleopatra to commemorate her cruise with Caesar. It has been suggested that her image was once shaded by the red and gold parasol preserved in seventeenth century drawings of a missing part of the lower right temple scene.

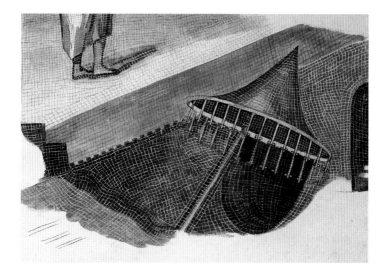

One of the Ptolemaic limestone statues of the bull-headed war god Montu from his temple at Medamud, originally paired with companion figures of his female consort Rattawy, 'Female Sun of the Two Lands'. Montu was represented by his cult animal the Buchis bull which was honoured by Cleopatra at the start of her reign.

One of the large granite statues of the falcon god Horus at Edfu temple flanking the front pylon of Cleopatra's father Ptolemy XII Auletes. The small royal figure protected by the falcon god was recently interpreted as Cleopatra's eldest son Caesarion.

The rear wall of Dendera temple portraying Cleopatra and Caesarion at either end of the wall offering to the gods. Further images of Cleopatra on the temple's interior walls and subterranean crypts were balanced by her ritual activities within the chapels located high on the temple's roof.

Sculpted head of Marcus Antonius from Rome featuring his thick-set, Herakles-like features – one of the few to escape the destruction of Antonius' statuary ordered by Octavian.

Gold ring with skilfully carved red jasper intaglio of Marcus Antonius, made c.40–30 BC for use as both a seal and for adornment.

Painted image from a villa at Herculaneum portraying a red-haired woman whose facial features, royal diadem and hairstyle adorned with fine pearl-studded hairpins suggest a posthumous portrait of Cleopatra VII.

Sandstone dyad of two divine children from Dendera, perhaps representing Cleopatra's twins Alexander Helios and Cleopatra Selene. The boy's sidelock of hair is topped by the sun disc and the girl's coiffure adorned by the lunar crescent, both figures guarded by the Eye of Horus and two large protective serpents.

Papyrus document dated 23 February 33 BC granting tax breaks to Roman general Canidius Crassus. The addition of the phrase 'let it be done' at the end of the document was recently identified as Cleopatra's own handwriting.

Limestone stela from the Fayum set up by Wennefer, chief priest of Isis, on 2 July 51 BC 'on behalf of the female king Cleopatra, the goddess Philopator'. She is shown on the right as a traditional pharaoh in the double crown and linen kilt with a flat bare torso as she makes offerings to Isis seated on the left.

Bronze eighty drachma coin of Cleopatra VII from her Alexandrian mint, portraying her distinctive profile, royal diadem, and 'melon' coiffure with wavy curls around her forehead.

Silver denarius of Cleopatra VII and Antonius c.32 BC, her image here on the obverse featuring her trademark melon coiffure and diadem enhanced with pearl jewellery. Yet her masculine-looking profile emphasising her ability to rule is now regarded by some as evidence she was not the famous beauty of legend

Marble head of Cleopatra VII set up by her daughter Cleopatra Selene in her capital Iol Caesarea (modern Algeria). The curly hair appearing beneath her mantle is very similar to the way Alexander was represented at this time and was perhaps a means of maintaining connections with their great ancestor.

Ptolemaic priestesses described as 'braided, beauteous, tressed, high bosomed, richly adorned, all drunk with wine' reiterated the theme of thousand-year-old hymns claiming, 'How happy is the temple of Amun, even she that spends her days in festivity with the king of the gods within her . . . she is like a drunken woman, who sits outside the chamber with braided hair and beauteous breasts.' And despite translations of 'loosened' rather than 'braided' hair to suggest dishevelment and nudity, the combination of carefully dressed hair, an attractive cleavage and drunken demeanour were all characteristics of the goddess Hathor. Similar misinterpretations surround the Ptolemaic statue of a woman seated on the ground with a wine jug and generally known as *The Old Drunken Woman*; she is usually dismissed as an elderly destitute. Yet her costume and jewellery suggest a woman of means, most likely one of the thousands of Alexandrian women attending the festivals of Dionysos, even 'perhaps a famous drinker whose statue could be properly placed within a precinct of the god of wine'.

So with Cleopatra's consumption sanctioned by ritual expectation as the Lady of Drunkenness quaffing with the Living Dionysos, Cleopatra was a 'philopotes' or 'lover of drinking' in the mould of Alexander's mother Olympias. She was leader of Dionysos' female devotees, whose states of inebriation could lead to bloody sacrifice; their rites recalled the way Egypt's own Hathor-Sekhmet was sent to earth to destroy mankind, revelling in the bloodbath she brought forth and growing drunk in the process.

Although the notion of female aggression was completely unacceptable to the Romans, especially if fuelled by alcohol, wine and beer were staple beverages in many ancient cultures and drinking 'nothing less than a symbol of Greek cultural identity'. Based on the belief that 'no man who is a wine-lover can be of low character', the symposium drinking party, maintaining friendships and alliances, was central to Greek social life.

These occasions were based on the consumption of wine within a controlled social environment. The wine, first mixed with water in a bowl (*krater*), was ladled into a jug, often decorated with images of the Ptolemaic royal women holding cornucopiae. Then it was poured into cups – the classic drinking vessel, the *rhyton*, was a miniature cornucopia usually made of highly glazed pottery. More substantial silver cups were manufactured at Memphis, and Cleopatra's tableware was 'entirely of gold'; she also had 'jewelled vessels made with exquisite art'. Her personal drinking cup, set with a large amethyst as the symbol of sobriety which was believed to offset intoxication, was complemented by the large violet amethyst she wore on her finger.

As she and the Inimitables reclined each evening, enjoying a wide range of entertainment in honour of Dionysos, flute players, dancers and acrobats performed to 'the latest vaudeville numbers, the slinkiest hits from the Nile!' They played drinking games such as *kottabos*, in which wine dregs were flicked at specific targets, and their drinking songs invoked Dionysos and his fellow gods, for 'Apollo is here for the dance, I hear his lyre playing and I sense the Cupids, and Aphrodite herself. . . He who madly joins the all-night dancing, staying awake 'til dawn comes, will receive the prize of honey cakes for playing the *kottabos* game, and he may kiss whom he will of all the girls and whomever he wants of the boys.'

Some of Cleopatra's exploits capture a little of the atmosphere pervading her late-night soireés within the palace. On occasion she ventured out into the city, covered and disguised as she had been for her first meeting with Caesar. Now, in Antonius' company, 'she would go rambling with him to disturb and torment people at their doors and windows, dressed like a servant-woman, for Antony also went in servant's disguise, and from these expeditions he often came home very scurvily answered, and sometimes even beaten severely, though most people guessed who he was. However, the Alexandrians in general liked it all well enough, and joined good-humouredly and kindly in his frolic and play, saying they were much obliged to Antony for acting his tragic parts at Rome and keeping his comedy for them.'

A state of playful drunkenness was the aim, rather than total stupefaction. Three bowls of wine were regarded as the limit for any gathering, since Dionysos himself claimed 'the fourth *krater* is mine no longer, but belongs to hubris; the fifth to shouting, the sixth to revel, the seventh to black eyes, the eighth to summonses, the ninth to bile and the tenth to madness and people tossing furniture about'. At one infamous Greek party involving too much wine the participants believed they were sailing rough seas, throwing furniture out of the window to lighten the load and still feeling 'seasick' the next day.

Yet along with its recreational and ritual uses, wine had long been used for therapeutic purposes and blended with medicinal ingredients in both Egypt and Greece. It is said that Zeus' daughter, Helen of Troy, had added 'Egyptian drugs' to the wine she presented to her husband Menelaus and his men when stranded on the island of Pharos, and as every lover of Homer knew, 'into the bowl in which their wine was mixed she slipped a drug that had the power of robbing grief and anger of their sting and banishing all painful memories. No one that swallowed this dissolved in wine could shed a single tear that day . . . This powerful anodyne was one of many useful drugs which had been given to the daughter of Zeus [Helen] by an Egyptian lady, Polydamna, the wife of Thon. For the fertile soil of Egypt is most rich in herbs, many of which are wholesome in solution, though many are poisonous. And in medical knowledge the Egyptian leaves the rest of the world behind.'

This drug was possibly from the opium poppy (*Papaver somniferum*); its main constituent, morphine, is an analgesic, narcotic, stimulant and euphoric. Opium was certainly used as a sedative in the classical world, stored in small poppy-shaped jugs. The ancient Egyptian 'shepen' sometimes identified as poppy was 'used to produce beer, and shepen occurs in medical texts' in a remedy to stop a child crying and still has a reputation as an aphrodisiac in modern Egypt. The Egyptians also used lotus flowers 'to produce a narcotic-laced wine', and Cleopatra herself suggested her banquet guests 'should drink their chaplets' which were traditionally made from lotus flowers. It is therefore quite intriguing to think that Homer's reference to a Greek daughter of the gods adding mood-enhancing drugs to the wine of her warrior partner became a reality under the well-read and medically astute Cleopatra. Drink spiking was certainly not unknown. One marriage contract was signed by a bride who swore by Isis, Osiris, Horus and Zeus that 'I shall not prepare love charms against you, whether in your beverages or in your food.' Yet Cleopatra did just this when creating her own magical potion, enhancing her image as Aphrodite and winning a bet with Antonius all at the same time.

After a challenge to stage the most costly banquet ever, she wagered that she personally could consume 10 million sesterces at a single sitting – a claim which caused great amusement until she unhooked one of her huge pearl earrings, 'that remarkable and truly unique work of nature. Antony was full of curiosity to see what in the world she was going to do', and along with everyone present watched as she held up her amethyst–studded drinking cup. After its contents had been replenished at a prearranged signal, she dropped the huge pearl into the liquid and, as the contents began to fizz, offered up a toast to Antonius and drank the whole lot down, the ultimate in conspicuous consumption.

Although many have doubted the exact details of the story, assuming that Cleopatra simply swallowed the pearl 'knowing that it could be recovered later on', her gesture was based on a sound knowledge of chemistry. For pearls are largely made of calcium carbonate and dissolve in acidic solutions. Although normal wine would have been insufficient to dissolve a pearl so quickly, sour wine or 'vinum acer', modern vinegar, at around 5–7 per cent acetic acid would certainly have done the job. As the calcium dissolved in the vinegar's water content and fizzed up into bubbles of carbon dioxide the pearl would have acted like an indigestion tablet, neutralising the acid to make Cleopatra's pearl and vinegar cocktail quite palatable. As she acted out the chemical formula

$$CaCO_3 + 2CH_3COOH \rightarrow Ca(CH_3COO)_2 + H_2O + CO_2$$

Cleopatra's grasp of hard science also tipped over into the esoteric, since the potion she created was known as 'magistery', a renowned aphrodisiac linked with Aphrodite-Venus as goddess of love.

As she prepared to treat her remaining earring in the same way and presumably offer it to Antonius, Plancus stepped in and declared her the outright winner of the bet. Antonius then had to pay a forfeit and so, 'at a great banquet in front of many guests, he had risen up and rubbed her feet, to fulfil some wager or promise'. Although Egyptian courtiers had long anointed the royal feet as part of state ceremonials, Cleopatra's choice of forfeit reveals a witty side to her character, since it was traditional Greek practice that men at drinking parties had their feet rubbed by women, one such guest exclaiming, 'what you are doing now to me, rubbing my feet with your lovely soft hands, it is quite magnificent.'

Such intimacy was certainly achieved by the end of 41 BC, since the couple were already lovers. As a founder member of the 'Inimitable Livers', Antonius liked to think of himself as 'the Inimitable Lover', and, as with Caesar before him, the opportunity to possess Alexander's living descendant must surely have been a tremendous attraction – particularly a descendant whose credentials as the Living Aphrodite must have proved irresistible.

Egyptian images of Aphrodite portrayed her virtually naked but for a luxuriant hairstyle, pins removed to allow her hair to fall around her shoulders. Her skimpy costume might often be little more than a breast-band, a garment she was often shown removing to emphasise 'the erotic charge unleashed even then by lingerie, which helped women look their best for their lovers'. In addition to her bra-like garment, Aphrodite was also portrayed in necklaces, bracelets, anklets and long chains crossed over her body, worn singly or in pairs. These developed into a kind of jewelled harness, the 'kestos himas' in which Aphrodite herself claimed 'all my power resides'. It was not dissimilar in composition to the heavy gold girdles, necklaces and lavish gold 'kekryphalos' hairnets worn by the highest-status women at the Ptolemaic court.

Such jewellery was often all that was worn during sex. One woman was portrayed on an engraved mirror case, wearing an elaborate bun hairstyle, body chain, anklet and precious little else, in her boudoir next to a bedside table bearing a wine jug, the erotic paintings on the walls typical of the way elite Alexandrians displayed 'in their homes lustful embraces of their gods. People who reckon sexual excess to be piety . . . ornament their bedrooms with small painted pictures, hanging up rather high, like offerings in a temple. While lying in bed in the midst of their sensual pleasure they can feast their eyes on a naked Aphrodite locked in sexual union with Ares', the Roman war god Mars.

Blatant sexual imagery of this kind had been part of Egypt's non-prudish culture for centuries, and the palace at Alexandria would certainly have contained its fair share of erotic images. Yet centre stage in Cleopatra's own sumptuous quarters would have been her golden bed, its comfortable, feather-stuffed mattress covered in hima-tion-type linen sheets, perhaps topped by an exquisite Egyptian bed-spread described as 'delicate, well-woven, glistening, beautifully coloured, covered with many flowers, covered with ornaments, purple, dark green, scarlet, violet, rich with scarlet blooms, purple bordered, shot with gold, embroidered with figures of animals, gleaming with stars'. The soft glow of oil lamps flickering gently at the bedside, combined with kyphi incense sprinkled on the gold brazier, would have created a suitably restful yet seductive atmosphere as the earthly forms of Aphrodite and Dionysos finally came together in well-upholstered comfort.

Although Antonius, still married to Fulvia, seems to have had no qualms about committing adultery, Cleopatra was single, and within the cosmopolitan and non-prudish atmosphere of Alexandria sex was simply another enjoyable pastime. So-called *symplegma* ('knot') figurines portrayed improbable sexual positions, while the royal library is known to have contained a wide variety of sex-themed works from improper stories to self-help manuals. One such manual, written by Philaenis of Samos, contained the advice, 'Concerning seductions: accordingly, the seducer should be unadorned and uncombed, so he does not seem to the woman to be too concerned about the matter in hand.' This was followed by tips on flattery, 'saying that the plain woman is a goddess, the ugly woman charming, the elderly one like a young girl', then a chapter 'Concerning Kisses' and another 'Concerning Sexual Positions'.

Similarly revealing details were featured in Ovid's *Art of Love*, deemed unsuitable for married ladies. It detailed sexual positions based on mythical couples, from the 'Hector and Andromache', featuring the man on top, to the 'Milanion and Atlanta', requiring the woman's legs to be placed on the man's shoulders. The poet also advised each woman 'to know herself, and to enter upon love's battle in the pose best suited to her charms. If a woman has a lovely face, let her lie upon her back; if she prides herself upon her hips let her display them to the best advantage . . . . If you are short, let your lover be the steed . . . . Love has a thousand postures . . . . So, then, my dear ones, feel the pleasure in the very marrow of your bones; share it fairly with your lover, say pleasant, naughty things the while. And if Nature has withheld from you the sensation of pleasure, then teach your lips to lie and say you feel it all. But if you have to pretend, don't betray yourself by over-acting. Let your movements and your eyes combine to deceive us, and, gasping, panting, complete the illusion.'

The intensity of sex was certainly captured in a Ptolemaic spell likening penetration to alchemy, 'this mysterious fire, all fire, all nape-of-neck, all sigh, all pliant, all you forge in this stove of fire, breathe it also into the heart and liver, into the woman's loins and belly; lead her into the house of the man, let her give to his hand what is in her hand, to his mouth what is in her mouth, to his body what is in her body, to his wand what is in her womb. Quickly, quickly, at once, at once!' Magic too was employed during intercourse. Male stamina could be maintained with a decoction of celery and rocket sacred to the highly phallic Min, while Dionysos' help might be invoked with a blend of pine cones, wine and pepper; carrot juice rubbed on the penis was claimed to prevent premature ejaculation.

Similar combinations of ingredients such as alum, brine or vinegar were recommended as contraception. Aristotle advocated cedar oil, white lead or frankincense to be smeared on the female genitals, while Dioscorides recommended an application of peppermint, alum or cedar gum, a 'miraculous' contraceptive when rubbed on the penis. Although all were commodities easily available to Cleopatra, she clearly had no intention of using any of them and presumably, as she had planned, by February 40 BC she was once again pregnant.

The timing was somewhat unfortunate, however, for the news coincided with sudden military crises in both East and West to threaten all that Antonius had so far achieved. Despite accusations that, trapped in a state of inertia that the Romans regarded as an Egyptian vice, he had simply been 'squandering and fooling away in enjoyments that most costly of all valuables, time', Antonius nevertheless reacted swiftly to the news, leaving his pregnant lover whom he would not see again for more than three years.

Although Cleopatra all but disappeared from the Roman records during this period, Egyptian sources reveal the way she maintained control over her expanded kingdom and growing family. In 40 BC, her eleventh regnal year, priestly records at Sakkara reveal that the mother-of-Apis cow, which had died while she had been at Tarsus, was buried following its lengthy mummification process in the Iseum vaults high on the desert plateau of Sakkara. In her pregnant state embodying the divine spirit of the sacred cow, another aspect of Isis, Cleopatra no doubt paid a state visit and made suitable offerings to the great goddess for the protection of her unborn offspring.

Yet the divine cow was not the only passing at Memphis that year, which also saw the death of the forty-nine-year-old high priest Pasherenptah III. As he posthumously stated in his funerary inscription, 'it came to pass under the majesty, the sovereign, Lady of the Two Lands, Cleopatra and her son Caesarion, in regnal year 11, 15th Epep, the day on which I landed forever. I was placed in the West and all the rites for my august mummy were carried out for me'. His elaborate seventy-day mummification was followed by interment beside his wife, Taimhotep in the Sakkara necropolis.

He was succeeded by their only son, Petubastis III, born after his parents had invoked Imhotep in their attempts to have a son to continue the priestly line. The boy had been born in Cleopatra's sixth regnal year (46–45 BC), the same year as Caesarion. So at the tender age of seven young Petubastis became High Priest of Memphis, his position within the Egyptian administration neatly balancing that of the equally youthful pharaoh Caesarion. Presumably he was installed by Cleopatra and Caesarion at the same type of grand ceremonials in Alexandria which had marked his father's elevation to office, and the youthful priest's basalt statue was set up in the city's great Serapeum as a clear mark of royal favour.

Keen to keep a close watch on matters beyond Egypt too, Cleopatra had been following Antonius' progress after he had left Alexandria for Tyre to tackle the Parthians and their new allies, the remaining Roman Republicans. Having invaded Asia Minor to take Cilicia and Caria, the Parthians had simultaneously invaded Syria, seized Antioch and driven Antonius' client king, Herod, from Judaea. Yet they were only part of Antonius' troubles.

During his absence impregnating the irresistible ruler of Egypt, his wife Fulvia, perhaps in a misguided attempt to regain her husband's attention, had joined forces with his remaining brother Lucius to take on Octavian. They wanted to exploit the chaos he had caused throughout Italy by trying to evict landowners in order to settle some of his many thousand veteran troops. When Lucius set out north to try and join up with Antonius' men in Gaul, Octavian had sent out his secret weapon, his colleague Marcus Vipsanius Agrippa, who managed to surround the famously balding Lucius inside the town of Perugia. His men fired volleys of specially made sling shots inscribed, 'Lucius Antonius, you're dead, baldy. Victory of Gaius Caesar [Octavian]'. Other slogans revealed that their target was Fulvia's genitals – crude threats inspired by Octavian's poem about his battle against a woman whose only feminine attribute was her anatomy.

Indeed, when Lucius' male allies had all deserted him, the indefatigable Fulvia raised a private army of veterans until, meeting with little success, Lucius surrendered. As a consul and Antonius' brother he was pardoned and sent to Spain as governor, although the unfortunate citizens of Perugia were not so lucky and their town was given over to Octavian's soldiers to plunder. Unfortunately the cremation of one of the inhabitants accidentally set fire to the town and destroyed the booty, whereupon Octavian took three hundred leading citizens, some of whom he knew personally, and telling them 'you must die', on the Ides of March 40 BC had each one sacrificed on an altar dedicated to the deified Julius Caesar.

Having firmly established himself in the West, Octavian also reached an understanding with Pompeius' remaining son Sextus, self-styled King of the Seas, who wore a blue cloak as son of Neptune-Poseidon. He was made ruler of Sicily, Sardinia and Corsica by the Senate on condition that he kept Rome's grain supply flowing from the province of North Africa. Octavian broke off his unconsummated union with Fulvia's daughter Claudia, which had originally sealed the Triumvirate, and instead married Scribonia, an aunt of Sextus' wife. And although somewhat older than her twenty-four-year-old husband, Scribonia soon became pregnant.

Given the disastrous consequences of her political intervention, Fulvia broke down and in failing health fled to Athens with her sons Antyllus and Iullus and Antonius' mother, Julia. In the spring of 40 BC, in the midst of the Parthian crisis, a furious Antonius arrived from Tyre for a stormy meeting, hearing the full story before leaving Fulvia and his family in Greece while he went to deal with Octavian in Italy.

Although Octavian's troops would not let him land, Antonius besieged Brundisium (Brindisi) even though neither army wanted to fight fellow soldiers. After much negotiation, Octavian and Antonius decided to reconcile their differences, drawing up the treaty of Brundisium which was signed in September that year. Both men would share Italy as a common recruitment ground, and with Octavian receiving Gaul, Spain, Dalmatia and Sardinia and Lepidus retaining Africa Nova, Antonius kept everything from Macedonia to the Euphrates.

Following Fulvia's death in Greece Antonius was once more a single man, so the treaty was sealed by his diplomatic marriage to Octavian's recently widowed older sister Octavia. The standard ten-month mourning period ensuring the paternity of any child born during that period was waived by the Senate to allow this particular marriage of convenience to take place. As the vital lynchpin in the balance of power between Octavian and Antonius, Octavia was an interesting character. Likely to have been far more devious than history likes to imagine when setting her virtues against Cleopatra's apparent vices, she was of similar age to Cleopatra, a patron of intellectuals and already the mother of several children. She is also generally described as beautiful, even if her coin images sometimes give a contradictory impression, and with a bun, a nodus topknot over her forehead and soft tendrils left loose about her neck her brother's supporters waxed lyrical about her hair which was praised for being natural, presumably in contrast to Cleopatra's more artfully crafted appearance.

About the time that Octavia married Antonius in Rome, where Octavian's wife Scribonia was about to give birth to Octavian's only child Julia, Cleopatra herself went into labour. In October 40 BC she gave birth to a daughter and a son. The unusual occurrence of twins was quite a feat, although she was not the first royal Ptolemy to produce dual offspring or even the first Cleopatra to do so, since Cleopatra Tryphaena, eldest daughter of Ptolemy Physkon and his niece Cleopatra III, had produced twin boys for the Seleucid king Antiochos Grypus. A second occurrence of twins among the first-century BC Egyptian elite also supports the idea that another of Physkon's daughters, Princess Berenike, had indeed married into the Egyptian family of the high priests of Memphis, since the princess' twenty-four-year-old great-granddaughter Berenike, eldest daughter of Taimhotep and the high priest Pasherenptah III, also produced twins, a boy and girl who seem to have died soon afterwards along with their mother.

With mixed-sex twins more rare than same-sex ones, Cleopatra's achievement was particularly special since 'live twin births will have been fewer and survival through infancy of one or both lower still'. And although the ancient Egyptians did not practice the infanticide of Egypt's Greek population and parts of modern Egypt where girls in mixed-sex pairs are sometimes 'not fed', this was certainly not the fate of Cleopatra's twin children.

Greatly cherished on a dynastic as well as a maternal level, the archetypal mixed-sex twins were the creator deities Shu and Tefnut, parents of twins Geb and Nut, who in turn gave birth to quads or two pairs of twins, Isis and Nephthys, 'the divine sister pair', and their brothers Osiris and Seth. Yet actual twin births were highly unusual, and their mysterious nature bestowed special status on them; the twin architects Suty and Hor said of each other, 'he came from the womb with me the same day'. Some also believe that their contemporaries, co-rulers Akhenaten and Nefertiti, were also biological twins – they were certainly portrayed as the twin gods Shu and Tefnut. During the Ptolemaic period when same-sex twins Castor and Pollux were associates of Isis, Ptolemy II had a mistress named Didyme, 'the twin'. The female twins Taues and Taous worked as 'didymai' when representing Isis and Nephthys in Apis rites at Sakkara during the reign of Ptolemy VI, whose title 'twin of the living Apis' revealed the prestigious nature of twin status.

As Cleopatra considered the many layers of symbolism associated with her two special children, she knew their names would be of paramount importance. So she named them after Alexander and his sister Cleopatra. The additional epithets Helios and Selene, Sun and Moon, the heavenly bodies whom the Greeks regarded as twins, also supported Cleopatra's identification with the Divine Mother Isis who was said to have given birth to the sun.

It is unthinkable that Cleopatra did not mark this particularly impressive achievement in some way. A little-known sandstone statue group (*dyad*) from Dendera portraying 'two deities whose exact identity is not certain' quite possibly represents Cleopatra's new offspring, a boy and a girl who are shown embracing. The boy's sidelock of hair is topped by the sun disc and the girl's coiffure is adorned by the lunar crescent, while the amulet-like eyes of Horus on each crown bestow vital protection. They are both surrounded by the great coils of two protective serpents, the spirits of Isis and Serapis, who guarded Alexandria and all members of the royal house, and the back of the sculpture is spangled with stars.

Yet their celestial names and attributes were also guided by the prophecies of the Sibylline Oracle which had already revealed that Rome would be defeated by the East, led by a mistress who would usher in a golden age of love and reconciliation. This united empire of East and West would be ruled over by a divine boy whose coming would be announced by a star. A further prophecy known as 'the Battle of the Stars' claimed that the Bull, identified with Dionysos-Antonius, would kill Capricorn, the badge of Octavian, whereupon 'the Virgin changed the fate of her Twins in the constellation of the Ram' – an ambiguous passage which may well have been interpreted as a reference to Isis-Cleopatra, her new twin children and Alexander as the 'sacred ram of Amun'. As revealed by the great Zodiac ceiling that she created at Dendera, Cleopatra and her astrologers used such prophecies and oracles as a means of manipulating the present and anticipating the future. The practice was highlighted by the earliest horoscope found in Egypt, dated precisely to 4 May 38 BC: the name 'Per-at', 'female pharaoh', was followed by a technical listing of 'Sun: Taurus 4: Jupiter in Cancer. Moon: Capricorn 20 and a half . . .'.

While Cleopatra's royal astrologers were busy predicting the future for herself and her children, she used the same methods to keep informed of matters in Rome, where astrology was also used to predict births, marriages and deaths. Antonius himself seems to have had some interest in such matters, and an Egyptian astrologer was part of his retinue in Rome. But while predicting a glorious future for Antonius, he also warned that his spirit would always be overshadowed by that of Octavian, from whom he was advised to keep a distance – the astrologer was perhaps in Cleopatra's pay as a means of interpreting the stars to her own advantage while keeping a connection between them.

Cleopatra and Antonius are certainly known to have corresponded, for it was later said that 'he had frequently at the public audience of kings and princes received amorous messages written in tablets made of onyx and crystal, and read them openly'. Although the letters contents were never divulged, their 'amorous' nature presumably reflected Cleopatra's state of mind, and although almost every word in classical literature dealing with love and passion was penned by men, a rare female perspective is provided by one Egyptian woman writing to her husband, 'you must know that I did not see the sun because you are out of my sight; for I have no other sun but you'. Even more dramatically, the lyrics of a popular Ptolemaic song conveyed feelings of abandonment, claiming that 'pain grips me whenever I remember how he used to kiss me, all the while treacherously intending to desert me . . . beloved stars and Mistress Night, my partner in passion, now escort me once again to him toward who Aphrodite drives me, I who am betrayed . . . Be warned – I have an unconquerable will when I am enraged, when I remember I will sleep alone.'

It may even be the case that Cleopatra employed magic to influence Antonius during their long separation; her alter-ego Isis was certainly well known as Mistress of Magic 'who arose in the beginning as Magician', and spells of the time often begin, 'I call upon thee Lady Isis, with thy many names and many forms.' These might include Aphrodite, Venus, Demeter and Hekate, a moon deity from Thrace, and with spells often performed facing the moon as Isis' celestial symbol, magical equipment included sinuous, long bronze wands in the form of cobras, bronze divination bowls and amulets, and charms inscribed with a combination of hieroglyphs, Greek letters and Hebrew formulae.

Among a whole range of love spells, one claimed to attract 'men to women and women to men and makes virgins rush out of their homes'. A particularly sinister curse from Cleopatra's reign asked a love rival, 'are you a burning woman, an abominable fire, a scorching woman? You should bathe yourself in blood, you should wash yourself with urine, one should set a suit of nettles on your body. Go! No one will find enough water in the sea, you sow, for washing off your face. Your day of death is at hand.' Such words were spoken over wax or pottery figurines with the victim's hair attached or even impaled with nails.

Yet regardless of her personal feelings for Antonius and indeed for Octavia, it was clear that Cleopatra was deeply concerned by political matters closer to home after the Parthians forced Antonius' client king Herod from Judaea. He travelled south to Alexandria to seek help from

Cleopatra, who formally received him as Antonius' ally and in the same way that previous Ptolemaic royals had employed Jewish generals offered him command of her army. Turning her down, he instead requested a ship to take him to Rome, where he was declared ruler of Judaea and King of the Jews by the Senate, who saw him as a vital counter to Cleopatra's growing powers in the East. With official sanction from Rome Herod went into military overdrive, returning to Judaea to oust the Parthians, kill off all remaining rivals to his throne and deal with fundamentalist Jews who regarded him as a Roman collaborator. Yet his expansion into Samaria, Galilee and much of Syria also earned him Cleopatra's bitter enmity, since these were all territories she wanted for herself in order to restore the Ptolemies' former empire.

She must also have been seriously unimpressed with news that Octavia was pregnant with Antonius' child. When the couple's first daughter, Antonia, was born in the autumn of 39 BC they moved to Athens for the winter to prepare for Antonius' forthcoming invasion of Parthia. There they issued coins featuring their joint profiles, and with the Athenians honouring the couple as 'Beneficent Gods' Antonius underwent sacred marriage to the city's patron goddess Athena Polias, who on this occasion was identified with Octavia. And as the wily Octavia tried to eclipse her rival on a divine as well as an earthly level, this incursion into territory previously occupied by Cleopatra must have outraged her – presumably as intended.

Nevertheless Antonius' political fortunes were in the ascendant. Herod's success against the Parthians was matched by that of Antonius' forces, led by his capable deputy Publius Ventidius Bassus, one of Caesar's men and part of the old guard. The Parthian advance into Asia Minor and Syria was beaten back and their crown prince killed in battle near Antioch in June 38 BC. His severed head was sent on a tour of the provinces to ram home the point.

Having finally beaten the Parthians to restore Rome's honour fifteen years after they had defeated Crassus, Antonius celebrated the victories in Greece while Ventidius was given a Triumph of his own in Rome. Yet such success clearly upstaged Octavian: despite the fact that had married into the family of Sextus Pompeius, Sextus himself remained a rallying point for rebels. His powerful fleet controlled Rome's all-important grain supply and this power was a threat to the Triumvirs' plans.

Left with little choice, Octavian had to take him on, and began by divorcing Scribonia, mother of his only child. Claiming as the reason 'I could not bear the way she nagged me', Octavian had already spotted a much younger model. Almost immediately after his divorce in January 38 BC he made nineteen-year-old Livia Drusilla divorce her husband to marry him in 'indecent haste', according to Antonius, particularly since she was then pregnant with her second child. Nevertheless, their enduring union was probably the most important alliance Octavian ever made, based on Livia's impressive family's connections, her outstanding advice and her political, some claimed murderous, man-oeuvrings behind the scenes.

Although Octavian then launched his attack against Sextus, he was twice defeated and was forced to ask Antonius for help. So in the spring of 37 BC Antonius brought him the ships he needed. He was met at Tarentum by Octavian and a large retinue including Quintus Horatius Flaccus (Horace) and Publius Vergilius Maro (Virgil), two poets appointed as Octavian's spin doctors to promote his public image and rewrite history when necessary.

As Antonius and Octavian continued to dominate Rome's fortunes, Octavia's presence was vital in negotiating the uneasy peace between husband and brother, two men of wildly differing character who never actually liked each other. Nevertheless, she managed to persuade Antonius to loan Octavian 130 ships, promising that her brother would return the favour by providing Antonius with twenty thousand more troops for his forthcoming campaign of retribution against Parthia. And since the original Triumvirate had lapsed, it was renewed for another five years with the treaty of Tarentum, sealed by the betrothal of Antonius' eldest son, nine-year-old Antyllus, to Octavian's two-year-old daughter Julia.

After business was concluded in autumn 37 BC, Octavian returned to Rome to maintain a high public profile as the model Roman leader while Antonius left Italy for the East. He was accompanied by Octavia, pregnant with their second child, but she became ill on reaching Corcyra (Corfu) and, rather than risk her health, Antonius sent her back to her brother's care in Rome where she lived with their daughter Antonia, his two sons by Fulvia and Octavia's two sons by a previous marriage.

Meanwhile Antonius travelled on to Syria to reorganise the Eastern provinces following the Parthian invasions. Over the winter of 37–36 BC which he spent in Antioch, he drew up new plans for controlling the East. Reducing the previous five provinces down to three, namely Syria, Asia (referring to Asia Minor) and Bithynia, he also amalgamated the scattered client kingdoms into fewer, larger regions in order to create a chain of allies stretching from Thrace in the north right down the eastern Mediterranean to Egypt in the south. He placed each in the hands of his most trusted supporters. Herod would remain in Judaea, backed by a Roman garrison to suppress Jewish unrest, while hand-picked new men included Amyntas, secretary to a previous client king and now promoted to ruler of Galatia, and Polemon, son of a Phrygian politician, who gained Pontus. Cappadocia went to Archelaos Sisinnes, son of Antonius' one-time lover Glaphyra and Archelaos, short-lived consort of Cleopatra's eldest sister, Berenike IV.

Yet, with no sign of the legions promised by Octavia and her brother, Antonius would need the support and wealth of Cleopatra more than ever. But he had not seen his lover for almost four years, nor the twins she had borne him. And since in the meantime he had married and fathered two children by Octavian's sister, he knew he would need to make some serious concessions to win back the support of the woman who held his future in her hands.

IO

Goddess of the Golden Age:
the Restoration of Empire

In autumn 37 BC, Antonius once more sent his envoy to Alexandria to request the presence of Cleopatra in Antioch. He must have presented her with a most attractive offer in return for her support, an offer suggested by the choice of venue. The great Seleucid city had long played a crucial role in Ptolemaic politics, from Ptolemy III's expansion in the 240s BC to the great ceremony of 145 BC when the people of Antioch had offered Ptolemy VI the Seleucid throne and diadem. His adoption of the combined Ptolemaic and Seleucid diadems demonstrated his control of both empires in a form of dual regalia which must surely have appealed enormously to Cleopatra. It had also been at Antioch where Antonius had taken up his post as Gabinius' cavalry commander back in 55 BC, setting out to meet the teenage Cleopatra and escort her back to Egypt with her father Auletes. Eighteen years later, he prepared to meet her again as she finally arrived in a city filled with meaning for them both.

Royal protocol aside, it must have been a deeply emotional moment for the couple as Cleopatra presented Antonius with his three-year-old twins for the very first time. Although he already had at least five other children, his twins by Cleopatra gave him a dynastic link to Alexander the Great. So, whereas his other children all bore their father's name, from his eldest child Antonia, his two sons Marcus Antonius Antyllus and Iullus Antonius and, most recently, two daughters again both named Antonia, he acknowledged Cleopatra's children as his own while confirming their names as Alexander Helios and Cleopatra Selene.

Names and their associations would be an important part of his propaganda campaign. Since the Greeks regarded the sun and moon as twin companions of Victory there was a great portent for the forthcoming campaign against Parthia, whose king was traditionally regarded as 'Brother of the Sun and Moon': Antonius' paternity made him 'Father of the Sun and Moon'. The children's names equally reflected Cleopatra's ambitions, since Alexander Helios, named after Alexander the Great as the sun god Helios in his distinctive sunray crown, had been the role model of Ptolemy III who had extended Ptolemaic power to its greatest extent. The same king had also sent Isis' statue to Antioch and the goddess' powers were now invoked in the name Cleopatra Selene, whose namesake had ruled over much of the region during four marriages within the Ptolemaic and Seleucid houses. As likely mother of Auletes, Selene was also the child's great-grandmother, so this was a most appropriate name to conjure with in Cleopatra's attempted reunification of Egypt and Syria under her own control.

Taking up residence with her precious children in Antioch's royal palace, set among groves of laurel and cypress trees, Cleopatra was at last reunited with Antonius when the thirty-one-year-old pharaoh officially married her forty-six-year-old Roman lover in the winter of 37 BC.

Their marriage was recognised in Egyptian law and Antonius' status as royal consort referred to in demotic texts; ancient sources refer to Cleopatra 'who married the Roman general, Antony'. He himself announced 'uxor mea est', 'she is my wife', and although he was already married in Roman law, which forbade marriage to a non-Roman citizen, Antonius certainly regarded marriage between Roman and non-Roman citizens as legally binding, since he married his eldest child, Antonia, to a wealthy Asiatic. Although polygamy was likewise banned under Roman law, Alexander, Ptolemy I and Ptolemy Physkon had all been married to several women at once. So too had Caesar, marrying Cleopatra while he was still married to Calpurnia and even planning new laws to legalise the move. So, given his intention to follow in Caesar's footsteps, Antonius himself wed Cleopatra, his sacred marriage to the goddess Athena in Athens repeated in Syria when Dionysos-Osiris finally married Aphrodite-Isis to usher in the prophesied Golden Age.

No doubt he was attired for the ceremony in the manner of a Greek groom, richly clothed and perfumed; Roman men did little more than put on a clean toga and comb their hair. Yet the bride in both Greek and Roman tradition had to undergo a whole variety of rites prior to marriage. After being bathed, perfumed and made up, the Greek 'nymphokomos' would be on hand to oversee every detail of the bride's appearance as a means of expressing her family's status; the Roman wedding garment, on the other hand, based on an ancient Etruscan noble's tunic, would be woven by the bride to prove her domestic abilities.

Although Cleopatra's attire would have been manufactured by dressmakers and arranged by her attendants to transform her into black-robed Isis, she may have adopted the traditional Roman bridal belt of ewe wool to symbolise fertility. It was tied firmly in place with the complex knot of Herakles, Antonius' ancestor; the knot was a popular motif in gold jewellery and is likely to have appealed to Cleopatra alongside her trademark pearls and diadem.

Of paramount importance in Roman wedding preparations, the bride's hair was styled with a spear as a reminder that the first Roman marriages were associated with warfare when women of the neighbouring Sabines were carried off to Rome for marriage. A spear which had taken life was felt best able to tackle the dangerous sexual powers believed to lurk in women's hair. Its tip was used to part the hair into six sections which were then wrapped around the head to create the 'six-tressed coiffure' of the Vestal Virgins which 'commits the bride's chastity to their husbands'.

Then, with heads bound by fragrant laurel, myrtle or marjoram flowers, Greek and Roman brides traditionally wore a veil, dyed with costly saffron to create the orange-red 'flame colour' believed to promote fertility. Both the Greeks and Romans associated red with births, marriages and deaths: it was the colour of sacrifice from the woman sacrificing her virginity to her husband to the blood of childbirth, and the mother of Zeus' twins, Leto, was known as 'Leto of the red veil'. So, as mother of divine twins herself, Cleopatra may well have worn a red veil as part of her bridal outfit, fitting as it did with the fiery Egyptian goddess Hathor-Sekhmet, dubbed 'Lady of the Red Linen' after her propensity for violence and blood-letting. A red veil would certainly have complemented the black robes of Isis, whose temples were a venue for marriage where couples could 'exchange vows with the goddess as our witness'. So it seems quite possible that

Cleopatra and Antonius made use of Antioch's own temple of Isis, whose cult statue, dating back to 241 BC, had been sent from Egypt by Ptolemy III to mark the extent of Egyptian control.

Although scenes from Antioch's 'House of the Isis Mysteries' show the goddess standing beside a male initiate wearing nothing but a red cloth over his shoulder, the actual marriage ceremony differed widely throughout the ancient world. Traditional Egyptian marriage required little more than cohabitation followed by equal legal rights to property and divorce, whereas Greek and Roman women were handed from father to husband as property. The original Roman marriage which symbolised the seizure of the bride by force with the words 'Thus, beloved, I seize you' was eventually superseded by a ceremony based more on Eastern customs in which the bride announced, 'Where you are Gaius, I am Gaia.' And as the couple clasped right hands, a ring might be placed on the third finger of the bride's left hand – usually gold in the case of the wealthy, perhaps set with a precious stone carved with an image of deities or hands clasping in union. Certainly, Antonius was sufficiently impressed with the work of the Athens-based engraver Gaius Avianius Evander to bring him to Alexandria: a gold ring adorned with a red jasper intaglio of Antonius' portrait was perhaps a type deemed appropriate for his new wife Cleopatra.

The ceremonials were generally followed by a wedding feast, which in the case of royal marriages was held in a great pavilion of the sort used at the nuptials of Alexander, Ptolemy and their successors. Roses and narcissi formed the backdrop for specially composed wedding songs and speeches, followed by the groom revealing his wife's face to the guests by lifting her veil before the happy couple were taken in nocturnal procession to the groom's home. He carried his new wife over the threshold to prevent her stumbling and bringing bad luck, and they were showered with dried fruit and nuts to bring fertility before being led to the bridal chamber with its saffron-coloured hangings. Then, behind closed doors, the husband undertook the final unveiling of his bride, untying the complex Herakles knot of her bridal belt in a symbolic unlocking of her chastity.

Although the extent to which such customs were employed during Antonius' marriage to Cleopatra is impossible to gauge, she regarded the event as so important that she renumbered her regnal years to make 'Year 16 which is also Year 1'. Yet this was no mere declaration of love, since her marriage had been accompanied by one of the most generous wedding presents of all time – nothing less than the restoration of virtually all the Ptolemies' former empire – and it was this major achievement which Cleopatra wished to announce to the world.

As the couple prepared to rule the East together, coins issued at Antioch, Damascus and Askelon provide the only known images of Cleopatra at the time of her marriage. With her usual melon coiffure topped with the royal diadem and embellished with small curls carefully arranged over her brow, her chlamys robe adorned by a necklace of round pearls wrapped twice about her neck, the thirty-one-year-old appears younger than her gaunt face on coins from her late teens and early twenties. So perhaps her rejuvenation was part of this 'new beginning', in the same way that images of certain pharaonic predecessors had grown younger during their reigns. She was literally backed by her new husband Antonius, who appeared on the coins' reverse. His increasingly Eastern ways were balanced by the apparent Westernisation of Cleopatra who was 'made to look Roman, almost like Antony in drag', an amusing notion not so far from the truth, since their images emphasised their combined powers noted on the coins' inscriptions.

With Antonius named 'Imperator for the third time and triumvir', Cleopatra was 'Basilissa', female version of the Greek 'king', followed by the title 'Kleopatra Thea Neotera', 'the new Cleopatra Thea', after her great-great-aunt the first Cleopatra Thea. Daughter of one monarch, sister of two, wife of three (two of whom took on Parthia) and mother of four (virtually the same tally as Cleopatra VII herself), Egyptian-born Thea had ruled in her own right as the only Seleucid royal woman ever to issue her own coins. And it was her example Cleopatra VII chose to follow as she restored the Ptolemies' former empire across the East.

Believing that 'the greatness of the Roman empire consisted more in giving than in taking', Antonius made land grants to his new wife stretching right down the eastern Mediterranean coast, from Cilicia, through Syria and Phoenicia, large parts of Judaea, Lebanon and the Arab state of Ituraea. Confirmed as ruler of Cyprus, she also received estates on Crete and regained Cyrene. All these regions were rich in a range of natural resources which Egypt had intermittently controlled for the previous three millennia. Lebanon's timber supplies, in particular, would be vital for building the ships needed to patrol the eastern Mediterranean during Antonius' forthcoming Parthian campaign, particularly since he had given 130 of his ships to Octavian in return for troops which had still not materialised.

Although Cleopatra did not receive all of Judaea, which she wanted but which Antonius had previously given to the militarily useful Herod, she did receive Herod's lands around Jericho containing groves of the shrubs which produced the precious Balm of Gilead (*Commiphora gileadensis* and *Pistacia lentiscus*), of which it was said that 'every scent ranks below balsam'. Only growing in these limited areas, the balm was so rare that it was incredibly expensive, and since it was regarded as 'the most precious drug that there is', a key ingredient in medicine, incense and perfumes, this land was a most valuable gift. Nor was Herod the only one of Antonius' dependants left seriously out of pocket by Cleopatra's gains, for the Nabatean Arabs of Jordan were ordered to hand over control of their trade in Dead Sea bitumen 'which serves as no small source of income. . . . the barbarians export the tar to Egypt and sell it for embalming the dead, for if this material is not mixed into the other substances the cadaver will not last long'. And whereas the mighty Seleucid army had failed to take the bitumen trade by force, the Nabateans were forced to hand it over to Cleopatra without a fight.

So not only had her restoration of almost all the Ptolemies' empire been achieved without bloodshed, it had made Cleopatra an incredibly wealthy woman; and to crown her amazing success, she now discovered she was pregnant with her fourth child. It must therefore have been with the most tremendous sense of satisfaction that she left Antioch in the spring of 36 BC, taking her leave of Antonius at Zeugma on the Euphrates to return to Alexandria in a grand royal progress overland. Taking the opportunity to view her new territories and show herself to her new subjects, she travelled from the Seleucid city of Apamea and the religious centre of Emesa down toward the mountains of Lebanon to arrive at Ituraea with its famous shrine of Zeus at Baalbek. After a rapturous reception at the great city of Damascus where her image was placed on the coinage, she moved on to Judaea and was received by Herod at his capital, Jerusalem.

Housed in suitably regal splendour in his newly built fortified palace, she toured the balsam groves which had once been his, ordering cuttings to be taken back to Egypt for planting in Heliopolis, the ancient centre of Egypt's incense-fuelled sun worship. Then the consummate businesswoman agreed to lease the groves back to him for the huge annual rent of 200 talents. Apart from these financial reverses Herod was also unsettled by Cleopatra's friendship with his new mother-in-law Alexandra, whose daughter he had recently married when he became king and adopted the Jewish faith. Because he was an Idumaean Arab by birth, however, he was unable to fulfill the accompanying role of Jewish high priest; but equally he claimed that Alexandra's popular sixteen-year-old son Aristobulus was too young for the office. This so outraged Alexandra that she appealed directly to Cleopatra and Antonius, whereupon Aristobulus was made high priest regardless of Herod's opinion.

So, with his detested enemy now his guest, Herod planned Cleopatra's assassination. But when his advisers pointed out Antonius' likely reaction to the murder of 'a woman who held the greatest position of any living at that time' he settled for character assassination instead, claiming she had tried to seduce him in order to discredit him with Antonius and acquire his entire kingdom. The story is certainly consistent with the tactics of a king who killed one of his ten wives, three of his sixteen sons, an uncle, his unfortunate brother-in-law Aristobulus when his plan to escape to Egypt with his mother was discovered, and all first-born boys in Judaea so as to eliminate the long-awaited 'King of the Jews' prophesied across the ancient world. Yet, in contrast to the unfortunate Aristobulus and Alexandra, Jesus and his mother Mary escaped Herod's wrath by their flight into Egypt, a journey that Cleopatra and her unborn child also undertook when 'instead of having her murdered, he plied her with gifts and escorted her on the way to Egypt'.

It must surely have been a spectacular homecoming as the pregnant monarch made her triumphal return to Alexandria after restoring virtually all the Ptolemies' fabled empire. It was an achievement she marked by taking the unique title 'Philopatris', 'Fatherland Loving', usually assumed to refer to Cleopatra as a lover of Egypt. Yet this Greek title is equally likely to have referred to Macedonia, homeland 'of Alexander and Egypt's dynastic family. She was a Macedonian . . . and since Cleopatra's patris [homeland] was Macedon, she was looking back to old Greece and to the home of her forefathers'. But given her ability to appear as all things to all people, the title may have been intentionally ambiguous as she reached out across vast swathes of territory to pursue Alexander's own achievements, announcing her intentions in her titles 'New Thea, Father Loving and Fatherland Loving', Cleopatra, 're-nowned in her ancestry'.

In September 36 BC the thirty-three-year-old gave birth to her fourth child, whom she named Ptolemy Philadelphus. Again she was using the magical power of names, since the baby's namesake, Ptolemy II Philadelphus, had ruled the territories she gained at her marriage, the time when her child had been conceived. And with her children by Antonius a key part of her foreign policy, her eldest child Caesarion remained her co-ruler within Egypt and, in 36 BC, aged eleven, was elevated to the throne as full co-regent.

As Cleopatra revelled in her glorious renaissance in Alexandria, Antonius was already on the long march to Parthia with a force so great it 'made all Asia shake'. Having brought together a force of a hundred thousand comprising sixty thousand Roman soldiers, ten thousand Celtic and Spanish cavalry and thirty thousand infantry provided by his Eastern allies, he had made a decision to set out following the news that the Parthian king had just been assassinated by his brother Phraates. During the ensuing purge of rivals to the throne, the Parthian governor Monaises came over to Antonius' side; having installed him as his client king east of Antioch, Antonius followed Caesar's original plans by sending his forces north to Armenia. After his general Publius Canidius Crassus defeated the Armenian king Artavasdes, bringing him over to the Roman cause as an ally, Antonius and the bulk of the army continued south into the Parthian vassal state of Media (modern Azerbaijan), from where they would launch their ultimate attack on the Parthian heartland.

But, as their cumbersome baggage train travelled on behind, guarded by troops under Antonius' officer Oppius and the new Armenian ally Artavasdes, a surprise attack by the turncoat Monaises and fifty thousand mounted archers destroyed all their supplies and siege equipment. At this setback, Artavasdes withdrew his own forces to Armenia. All this was unknown to Antonius, who waited in vain outside Media's fortified capital for the siege engines he needed in order to attack the city. Stuck in a barren landscape with no supplies, against an enemy who refused to face him on the field, he was eventually forced to return west where twenty thousand of his men fell victim to dysentery, hunger and repeated attacks. And on the retreat over the Armenian mountains to Syria, another eight thousand were lost in severe blizzards at the onset of a bitter winter.

Yet at that same moment at the other end of the Roman world, deploying the ships loaned by Antonius, Octavian was celebrating victory over Sextus Pompeius. Octavian himself had been too ill to take part, and 'could not even stand up to review his fleet when the ships were already at their fighting stations; but lay on his back and gazed up at the sky, never rising to show that he was alive until his admiral Marcus Agrippa had routed the enemy'. As Sextus fled east and many of his troops were crucified – a traditional form of Roman execution – the elimination of his senatorial support so alarmed Lepidus that he feared he might be next. He therefore seized Sicily, but Octavian's men easily retook the island and Lepidus was stripped of his powers, losing both Sicily and Africa Nova to Octavian. With the three-way power base now reduced to two-way, world politics were suddenly polarised between East and West, between Alexandria and Rome, and between the two remaining triumvirs, Antonius and Octavian.

Octavian now returned to Rome a hero, having freed the seas, brought an end to civil war and finally secured peace. The contrast with Antonius' situation could not have been more stark. Having lost more than a quarter of his entire force as a result of bad weather and treachery, the dejected triumvir finally reached the Phoenician coast, once more summoning Cleopatra to come and meet him with money and supplies. Even though she had recently given birth and it was the middle of winter, when rough seas normally closed the Mediterranean to traffic, Cleopatra bravely set sail. Antonius waited so impatiently he 'could not hold out long at table, but in the midst of the drinking would often rise or spring up to look out, until she put into port'. After they returned to Alexandria in early 35 BC, the couple received news that the king of Media had quarrelled with his overlord Phraates over the division of Roman booty, and was now offering them an alliance to include the use of his deadly cavalry when Antonius renewed the invasion. New plans were drawn up. Cleopatra would take responsibility for the navy needed to guard the Mediterranean. But Antonius still needed to augment his reduced land forces, since the twenty thousand men Octavia and her brother had promised him never materialised. A mere two thousand were eventually sent out only as far as Athens in the spring of 35 BC, along with just seventy of the 130 ships that Antonius had originally lent him. And Octavian sent these reinforcements in the company of his most deadly weapon, his sister Octavia.

Keen to take back her husband in order to restore her position as wife and mother while competing with Cleopatra's contribution to the war effort, Octavia was the ultimate political pawn whose role as 'dutiful wife', so skilfully exploited by her brother, created an obvious trap. If Antonius went to Athens to accept the troops and Octavia, he would risk losing Cleopatra's vital support. Yet the small number of soldiers on offer made this an unlikely scenario, and it seems that Octavian wanted him to repudiate Octavia. In so doing Antonius would be casting himself in an even weaker position following his recent military defeat.

While Antonius considered his options Cleopatra is said to have resorted to hysterical tactics, declaring undying love, feigning tears, throwing tantrums and apparently starving herself, 'bringing her body down by slender diet'. Although later sources claimed that such unlikely behaviour decided the matter for Antonius, he could surely weigh up the two clear choices before him. For in the West were Octavia, their two daughters and a brother-in-law whose very existence threatened all that Antonius wanted to achieve. Against this in the East were Cleopatra and their three children, all descendants of Alexander whom he might still emulate through his military abilities. And in the Octavian-free East, Antonius could be his own man. Since his future as an independent force clearly lay with Cleopatra, Antonius wrote to Octavia in Athens, telling her to send him the troops, the ships and Antyllus, his eldest son by Fulvia, while she must return to her brother in Rome and care for Antyllus' younger brother and their two daughters. As expected of any Roman wife, she obeyed her husband while he continued gathering his forces at his Syrian base, Antioch, in preparation for the renewed war against Parthia.

As Cleopatra helped fund his expedition and maintained alliances across the East, the couple had sealed their agreement with the king of Media by betrothing their son Alexander Helios to the Median princess Iotape (Jatapa). They almost accepted an alliance from Sextus Pompeius until he joined with the Parthians and continued to undermine Roman authority by setting fire to Roman shipping. Eventually, however, he was captured by one of Antonius' client kings and executed by Antonius' general Marcus Titius, nephew of the Syrian governor Plancus.

Antonius had also sent out his envoy Dellius to Artavasdes of Armenia, giving him a final chance to redeem himself by suggesting he once again join with them to invade Parthia. His refusal provided sufficient reason for Antonius' forces to invade Armenia in spring 34 BC. Artavasdes and his family were sent back to Egypt as prisoners, a Roman garrison installed under Canidius Crassus, and Antonius and Cleopatra issued coins bearing the news 'Armenia conquered'. Their victory had been a 'brilliant success', not only providing them with a solid base from which to take on Parthia the following summer, but opening up new markets to Roman traders and providing lands for Roman settlers. This news was so well received in Rome that it became imperative for Octavian to prove his own military abilities amidst well-founded rumours of cowardice.

Setting out with Agrippa to secure Italy's north-eastern borders against any future attacks from the east, they subdued volatile Illyricum (former Yugoslavia) as far as the Macedonian border and seized large amounts of booty. By injuring his knee, Octavian could finally claim to have received 'honourable wounds' in battle. When he returned to Rome in late 34 BC the Senate awarded Octavian a Triumph, which he postponed to allow public celebrations for Antonius' Armenian campaign and the death of Sextus. This was no magnanimous gesture, but aimed to draw maximum public attention to Antonius' continuing absence from Rome and from Octavia. The Senate set up public statues of Antonius and Octavian in the Forum and voted similar honours to their Roman wives Octavia and Livia. Both women were elevated to the rank of Vestal Virgin, the highest status a Roman woman could attain. Their modestly swathed statues would have proved a stark contrast to that of Cleopatra standing in Caesar's temple of Venus. The same comparisons were drawn between their menfolk, who similarly divided public opinion: images of their alter-egos Apollo and Herakles battling it out adorned the temple of Apollo on the Palatine Hill, where Octavian set up his own cult to counter the divine aura fostered by Antonius and Cleopatra. As Octavian knew full well, Antonius would not return to Rome to celebrate a traditional Triumph, for he had travelled back to Alexandria in the autumn of 34 BC to be greeted as the second Alexander by an adoring public led by Cleopatra.

The couple celebrated their military success by reviving the great Ptolemaia festival initiated to honour her dynasty's lineage from both Alexander and Dionysos through displays of Eastern wealth. Painted scenes of Alexander at Narmouthis in the Fayum portrayed him Dionysos-like in triumphant procession, an image Caesar chose to repeat in his own Ptolemaic-style Triumph in Rome and which now Antonius was reviving, playing his favourite role of Dionysos to the hilt. Preceded by a vast retinue of celebrants, divine statuary and exotic spoils, Antonius appeared before the crowds, having given orders that he should be called Dionysos, his head bound with the ivy wreath, his person enveloped in the saffron robe of gold and wielding Dionysos' pinecone-topped thyrsos wand.

Riding down the great central highway of Alexandria in a splendid gold chariot, Antonius may well have replicated the route of the previous 'Neos Dionysos', Auletes. He was described as 'coming forth in procession around the temple of Isis by his war chariot . . . to alight at the temple of Isis, lady of the Mound-of-Egypt', presumably referring to the Serapeum complex which was built on high ground, its walls sheathed in gleaming metal atop a great sweep of one hundred white stone steps. The black-robed Cleopatra sat enthroned above the proceedings to receive the conquering hero. As he formally presented her with all the spoils of war, including the Armenian king and his fellow prisoners secured in chains of silver as befitted their regal status, the entire city would have bowed down before her in thanksgiving in rites overseen by the youthful high priest Petubastis, who may also have led further celebrations to confirm the marriage of a couple who were now portrayed by artists as Isis and Dionysos. Yet the great triumphal procession was only a preliminary to the main event known to history as the 'Donations of Alexandria'.

It was the culmination of everything that Cleopatra and Antonius had so far achieved. Surviving details suggest a spectacle initiated by Antonius but almost certainly stage-managed by Cleopatra. Taking place in Alexandria's huge Gymnasion stadium, traditional stage of the Ptolemaia festival, it featured displays of lavish wealth that demonstrated to all the power of this ultimate celebrity couple and their growing dynasty, and repeated the same ceremony of 52 BC when Auletes presented his own four children to the Alexandrians.

At the centre of the proceedings a two-tiered platform of gleaming silver held six gold thrones, the two largest, on the higher tier, occupied by the glittering couple themselves. The royal consort Antonius, in full Roman military dress as Triumvir, Imperator and commander of the eastern provinces, was flanked by Roman legionary standards and a Roman bodyguard beneath a fine linen canopy topped by the twin Ptolemaic eagles; his wife Cleopatra 'was then, as at other times when she appeared in public, dressed in the habit of the goddess Isis and gave audience to the people under the name of the New Isis'. With her black robes sharply defined against the Gymnasion's brilliant white marble walls and the colourful costumes of those around her, she was accompanied by her four children each enthroned on the second tier: the thirteen-year-old pharaoh Caesarion, the six-year-old twins Helios and Selene, and two-year-old Ptolemy Philadelphus.

Rising to address the massed ranks of Alexandrians, calling on oratorial skills so effectively employed at Caesar's funeral ten years earlier, Antonius addressed them in his capacity as Caesar's high priest, telling them in their shared Greek tongue that he spoke in honour of the deified Julius. Reiterating that 'the greatness of the Roman empire consisted more in giving than in taking', he named each of his three children by Cleopatra and proceeded to list the territories he now bestowed on each of them in the name of Rome.

Stating that 'his own sons by Cleopatra were to have the style of "kings of kings"', he presented the eldest, Alexander Helios, with Armenia, Media and Parthia to give him all the lands east of the Euphrates as far as India, the furthest extent of Alexander the Great's own empire. With the boy's betrothal to the king of Media's only daughter Iotape confirming his status, six-year-old 'Alexander was brought out before the people in Median costume, the tiara and upright peak'. A superb bronze figurine of a chubby young boy from late first-century BC Alexandria, dressed in the same Median dress, is highly likely to depict this child: he is standing on tiptoes, stretching out his hand to take his newly awarded territories.

Antonius then presented his younger son, two-year-old Ptolemy, with Phoenicia, Syria and Cilicia. The toddler was brought out like his older brother but dressed in the purple mantle, Macedonian boots and distinctive Macedonian cap known as the *kausia*, 'done about with the diadem; for this was the habit of the successors of Alexander'. As the two boys then turned to acknowledge their parents formally, no doubt after a considerable amount of practice, 'one was received by a guard of Macedonians, the other one by one of Armenians' as a mark of their status.

Then came Cleopatra's only daughter, six-year-old Cleopatra Selene, who received the huge territory of Cyrene (eastern Libya) combined with Crete. The girl herself is perhaps represented on a bronze plaque showing twins Selene-Isis and Helios-Horus holding long sceptres alongside a double cornucopia, quite possibly the moment when the young twins were presented with their own sceptres at the great event.

Yet in light of the childrens' young age, Cleopatra was made regent for them all. She was now proclaimed 'Cleopatra Thea Neotera Philopator Philopatris', 'the New Thea, Father Loving and Fatherland Loving,' Ruler of Egypt, Cyprus, Libya and Coele-Syria, while the Latin inscription on the couple's Roman-style coins announced, 'Cleopatrae reginae regum filiorum regum', 'Cleopatra, Queen of Kings, and her sons who are kings'.

Finally came her eldest child and co-ruler Caesarion, bearing the pharaonic regalia of crook and flail and dressed in robes of finest linen. Hailing him as 'Ptolemy Caesar, King of Kings', to share senior rank with his mother over her three youngest children, Antonius declared the thirteen-year-old pharaoh sole legitimate heir of Julius Caesar. It was political dynamite.

It was certainly too much for Octavian, who, on becoming consul for a second time in January 33 BC, finally went public with his attacks on Antonius. In a brilliant PR campaign targeting the couple whose coherent policy of ruling the East would surely soon move westwards, Octavian's allegations became all the more plausible the longer Antonius stayed away from Rome. He seized on rumours of his rival's marriage to Cleopatra, and it was later said that Antonius 'by marrying two wives at once, did a thing which no Roman had ever allowed himself', even though Caesar had begun to change the laws of Rome to accommodate his own polygamy.

So, in contrast to the saintly Octavia, Cleopatra became 'Aegyptia coniunx', 'the Egyptian wife', following her 'filthy marriage', and the lands that Antonius had awarded his faithful ally two years earlier were reduced to the gifts of a besotted lover. With the Donations dismissed as 'a theatrical piece of insolence and contempt of his country', the Ptolemaic procession preceding them was misrepresented as a Roman Triumph held outside Rome, scandalising many Romans 'because they felt he had made a present to the Egyptians of the honourable and sacred traditions of his fatherland for the sake of Cleopatra', even though pharaohs had processed in golden chariots to celebrate military victories centuries before Rome was even founded. And despite the fact that Cleopatra had funded this particular 'Roman' conquest, Octavian claimed that the spoils of the war had been dedicated to Egypt's Isis rather than Rome's Capitoline Zeus, conjuring up images of the corrupt Eastern monarch enjoying her ill-gotten gains while his virtuous sister sat at home on a par with the Vestal Virgins and did her weaving.

Giving Agrippa the powers to banish anyone who might voice an alternative opinion or hold pro-Egyptian sympathies, Octavian decided to compete with Alexandria by rebuilding Rome. Funded by spoils from the Illyrian war and using some of the plans Caesar had drawn up with Cleopatra's help, Agrippa was appointed 'Commissioners for public works,' and under his direction old temples were restored, roads repaired and public halls and colonnades constructed along with new aqueducts, drains and bath-houses. And as grand games and financial incentives won over the people, Octavian kept up his attacks on Antonius in the Senate, accusing him of needless cruelty in the death of Sextus Pompeius, even though he himself had crucified many of Sextus' troops, and highlighting the captivity of the Armenian king, despite the fact that his life had been spared in contrast to the several hundred Perugians whom Octavian had dispatched as human sacrifices.

Understandably riled by such hypocrisy, Antonius robustly defended himself by letter, and although Octavian mocked his opponent's literary style, his use of 'antique diction' and 'nonsensicalities of those garrulous Asiatic orators', which his own limited knowledge of Greek failed to grasp, Antonius continued to fire his vivid missives north. Pointing out that Octavian had unlawfully seized Lepidus' territories, given land out to only his veteran troops, retained almost half the ships loaned to him and sent a mere tenth of the troops promised in return, Antonius' most fascinating defence tackled the main issue, his relationship with Cleopatra.

In a startlingly frank letter, Antonius asked Octavian, 'What's come over you? Do you object to my sleeping with Cleopatra? She is my wife! And it isn't as if this were anything new – the affair started nine years ago! And what about you? Are you faithful to Livia Drusilla? My congratulations if, when this letter arrives, you have not already been to bed with Tertullia or Terentilla or Rufilla or Salvia Titisiena – or all of them. Does it really matter so much where, or with whom, you get your erections?' For behind his carefully honed public image, Octavian kept at least one mistress and had numerous affairs with his colleagues' wives and daughters, albeit claiming that they were undertaken purely 'for reasons of state, not simple passion' to find out what his enemies were up to. Yet his methods were unsubtle even by the standards of Antonius, who accused Octavian of 'hauling an ex-consul's wife from her husband's dining room into the bedroom – before his eyes, too! He brought the woman back, says Antonius, blushing to the ears and with her hair in disorder.'

Yet the real reason for Octavian's attacks was Antonius' public declaration of Caesarion's paternity, both at the Donations and in a report to the Senate announcing that Caesar had acknowledged Caesarion as his son to several colleagues, including Gaius Oppius. Clearly this undermined Octavian's adopted status, and Oppius was persuaded to publish a retraction. Antonius' supporters then accused Octavian of homosexuality, sacrilege and cowardice. As the two factions became increasingly hostile, Octavian's propaganda machine was forced to work flat out to counter a couple who had the support of most of the Greek-speaking nations and a considerable number of Romans. For Alexandria was already home to Plancus, one of the couple's regular dinner guests, and Dellius the one-time envoy, the senator Quintus Ovinius who managed Cleopatra's woollen mills and the Greek-born Roman officer Gaius Julius Papeios, who led a party of Roman and Greek troops down to Philae in spring 32 BC to pay homage to Isis and their monarch.

With Rome's legionary standards flanking Cleopatra's great throne room and her royal insignia emblazoned on the shields of the Roman guard ordered to obey her commands, her court was also home to increasing numbers of artists, scholars and craftsmen appointed by Antonius. They also 'collected for Cleopatra the masterpieces of the East', from antique bronze statue groups to ancient paintings and Pergamon's great royal library, which must have delighted Cleopatra above all else for she was said to have derived 'a positively sensuous pleasure from literature'. The gesture had tremendous political significance, for not only did it enable Antonius to fulfil his duties as Caesar's successor by replacing works lost during the Alexandrian War, it allowed Cleopatra to fulfil yet another of the Ptolemies' long-held dreams, acquiring the vast library of former rivals to acknowledge her control of their former kingdom. The vast cargo of two hundred thousand books was transferred from Pergamon's temple of Athena-Isis to Alexandria's Serapeum close to the Isis temple, and the new library initiated another wave of cultural growth as Cleopatra's scholars began to register and collate the avalanche of new information.

Ever mindful of the need for a thorough education for her children as future monarchs, Cleopatra appointed the Damascus-born philosopher and historian Nikolaus as tutor to the twins Alexander and Cleopatra and young Ptolemy Philadelphus, who were also cared for by a tutor named Euphronios. Their older half-brother Caesarion was taught by the scholar Rhodon, while Theodorus was tutor to Antonius' eldest son Antyllus – Antonius' legal heir, according to Roman law. Although he had not been direct part of the Donations ceremony, the ten-year-old appeared with his father on coinage, and he enjoyed the same luxurious lifestyle as his half-siblings. His personal physician, Philotas, recalled how young Antyllus had once rewarded him for a witty comment by giving him all the plate on the sideboard until advised he might be better accepting its value in money, 'for there may be amongst the rest some antique or famous piece of workmanship which Antony would be sorry to part with'. The number of children in the royal household was increased in 33 BC by the arrival of the infant Princess Iotape of Media, future bride of six-year-old Alexander Helios. The royal children also seem to have been close to their twelve-year-old cousin Petubastis, a familiar figure at court, whose statuary was set up at the Serapeum.

Such statuary was also part of the Caesareum temple, where Antonius as Caesar's high priest would have led the sacred rites. Cleopatra commissioned a further shrine in honour of Antonius as Dionysos-Osiris, and in keeping with the Ptolemies' re-erection of ancient obelisks in honour of their partners she set up a red granite one in the square adjoining Antonius' monument. There were also bronze statues of Antonius set on basalt bases, one erected on 28 December 34 BC to mark the Donations and inscribed in Greek 'Antonius the great, lover without peer, Parasitos set this up to his own god and benefactor, 29th day of Khoiak, year 19 which is also year 4.'

As Cleopatra continued to use this system of double dating in her administration, assisted by those capable of maintaining government during her regular absence abroad – her Syrian adviser Alexas, her secretary Diomedes, her finance minister Seleucus, the eunuch Mardion and a second Potheinos who may have been her prime minister – she had also begun to prepare for the inevitable conflict with Octavian which she realised was fast approaching. Still sixty ships short following Antonius' loan to the man who was now her enemy, she had imported great quantities of timber from Syria and Lebanon to build new warships, maybe redeploying some of her trading vessels which normally operated in the Red Sea to create an impressive fleet of over two hundred. Drawing on revenue generated through long-term trade with India and the recent acquisition of the balm and bitumen trade, she brought together the huge sums needed to pay the army and foreign supporters, but required another way of maintaining support from those within Egypt. So, instead of doling out money as her father had done, she set up a system of tax breaks such as the one which Antonius' general Canidius received in February 33 BC, informing him that

We have granted to Publius Canidius and his heirs the annual exportation of 10,000 artabas of wheat and the annual importation of 5,000 Coan amphoras of wine without anyone exacting anything in taxes from him or any other expense whatsoever. We have also granted tax exemption on all the land he owns in Egypt on the understanding that he shall not pay any taxes, either to the state account or to the special account of us and others, in any way in perpetuity. . . . Let it be written to whom it may concern, so that knowing it they can act accordingly. Let it be done!

This is a fascinating insight into Cleopatra's financially astute mind, but what really makes this document come to life is the addition of the Greek phrase γινεσθω, meaning 'let it be done', personally added at the end of the document in the hand of Cleopatra herself and thus representing the closest tangible link to the woman yet found.

Meanwhile Antonius had once more travelled north and, after meeting with their ally the Median king, wrote to the Senate to explain the true nature of the Donations in order to counter Octavian's accusations. He then arrived in Ephesus, where he sent for Cleopatra and prepared for New Year's Eve. This was the date when the second Triumvirate came to an end: at midnight on 31 December 33 BC.

As East and West held their breath, waiting for the two ex-triumvirs to make their next move following the bitter war of words which had raged throughout 33 BC, Antonius gained the upper hand when his powerful colleagues Gnaeus Domitius Ahenobarbus and Gaius Sosius were both appointed consul for 32 BC. Having received Antonius' report regarding his command of the East and the Donations, Ahenobarbus was unwilling to divulge its potentially inflammatory contents. But Sosius took the initiative, finally reading it out in February before a packed Senate who learned that the Donations were simply the confirmation of territories already awarded in Antonius policy of governing the East. Antonius then played his trump card by offering to lay down his powers if Octavian would do the same. Left with little room to manoeuvre, Octavian and his supporters began to insult the consuls, intimidating them with an armed guard whose presence in the Senate was illegal. The meeting broke up amid volatile scenes recalling those which had followed the murder of Caesar.

But then an extraordinary thing happened. Both consuls and almost half the Senate publicly aligned themselves with Antonius, and some three to four hundred men left Rome to set up a new Senate in Ephesus. The harbour there was suddenly swamped by ships 'coming in from all quarters to form the navy'. Cleopatra herself arrived in her royal flagship *Antonias* at the head of a personal squadron of sixty ships followed by 140 warships, to be hailed as monarch by the Ephesian people.

When Canidius Crassus appeared with his legions from Armenia the commanders reassembled their mighty force of 75,000 legionaries, the vast majority drawn from the Greek-speaking nations, together with 25,000 infantry, 12,000 cavalry, 500 warships and 300 smaller vessels, all largely funded by Cleopatra who had brought with her the royal war chest containing 20,000 talents in bullion. The couple's mint in Lebanon was now able to produce the coins needed to pay their troops; each legion was to be paid in coinage featuring their own legionary standard backed by the image of a war galley. Such resources far outweighed those of Octavian, who was forced to levy a deeply unpopular 25 per cent income tax across Italy where Antonius and Cleopatra had already begun distributing well-placed funds to their remaining supporters. If they had marched into Italy during the spring of 32 BC they would surely have been victorious, but they did not yet make their move.

Residing at Antonius' Ephesus HQ which he referred to as 'the Palace', Cleopatra maintained the same high public profile as she would have had in Alexandria: 'she visited the market place [forum] with Antony, presided with him over festivals and the hearing of lawsuits, rode around with him on horseback even in the cities, or else was carried in a litter'. She was also present at Antonius' planning meetings as she almost certainly had been at Caesar's, but some newly arrived allies began to voice objections, complaining that women surely belonged in the home and their presence in camp would bring bad luck. The peculiarly aggressive behaviour of swallows nesting in the stern of Cleopatra's flagship was regarded as a bad omen. Perhaps nervous that she would uncover certain financial irregularities regarding her money, Plancus and his nephew Titius were among those muttering against her; Ahenobarbus even refused to use her royal form of address, curtly referring to her as 'Cleopatra' and bluntly requesting that she return to Egypt.

Yet she was having none of it. She was backed by the other consul, Sosius, an admiral who recognised the crucial importance of the ships she contributed, but her strongest support came from Canidius Crassus, commander of the land forces, who claimed that her presence was needed to sustain the morale of their Egyptian troops. He also told his fellow officers that 'it was not just that one that bore so great a part in their charge of the war should be robbed of her share of glory', especially as she was in no way inferior 'in prudence to any one of the kings that were serving with him; she had long governed a great kingdom by herself alone, and long lived with him [Antonius], and gained experience in public affairs'. So, regardless of any dissent, Cleopatra was staying where she was.

In April 32 BC, as the campaign season fast approached, she and Antonius travelled to the island of Samos, summoning to join them 'all kings, princes and governors, all nations and cities within the limits of Syria, the Maeotid Lake, Armenia and Illyria'. Each was told to provide troops, provisions and 'theatrical artists' – the couple's preparations for war involved several weeks of Ptolemaic-style 'high festivities' in honour of Dionysos, personified by their supreme commander Antonius who led the procession as 'this one island for some days resounded with piping and harping, theatres filling and choruses playing. Every city sent an ox as its contribution to the sacrifice and the kings that accompanied Antonius competed who should make the most magnificent feasts and the greatest presents' to gain divine support for the war ahead. Plans were already in place for their forthcoming Triumph, which would, like Julius Caesar's, feature Roman-style games with gladiators to celebrate Octavian's defeat. In May the couple left Samos for the Greek mainland, the border between their world and that of Octavian and the place where all their fates would soon be decided.

On two previous occasions Antonius had fought and won here to decide Rome's future, first with Caesar against Pompeius at Pharsalus, and then with a largely absent Octavian against Brutus and Carsius at Philippi. He must have felt the gods were surely with him for a third time as he and Cleopatra viewed their vast force and equally impressive navy.

Sending their fleet west around the Peloponnese to create a line of defence, the couple themselves travelled on to Athens to pass the summer of 32 BC. As Antonius' former home and a place that Cleopatra seems to have visited as a girl, the city had close links to the Ptolemies whose statues stood on the Acropolis. The Athenians now set up Cleopatra's statue as Isis alongside a companion figure of Antonius as Osiris, and, holding court in Antonius' sumptuous Athenian home as she had done in Caesar's Roman villa twelve years earlier, Cleopatra 'courted the favour of the people with all sorts of attentions. The Athenians in requital, having decreed her public honours, deputed several of the citizens to wait upon her at her house; amongst whom went Antony as one, he being an [honorary] Athenian citizen and he it was that made the speech'.

After paying great honours to the wife who sat before him he initiated divorce proceedings against the other, and 'sent orders to Rome to have Octavia removed from his house. She left it, we are told, accompanied by all his children, except the eldest by Fulvia, who was then with his father.' Amidst much 'weeping and grieving that she must be looked upon as one of the causes of the war', it was said they 'pitied not so much her as Antonius himself, and more particularly those who had seen Cleopatra, whom they could report to have no way the advantage of Octavia either in youth or in beauty' – the classic responses to a jilted woman. Having replaced Octavia as the face of female divinity in Athens, and now as Antonius' sole wife, Cleopatra must have been ecstatic. Nevertheless she must have realised that Antonius' decision finally to divorce Octavia was first and foremost a political move designed to sever dramatically the last remaining tie with his bitter enemy Octavian. Later it was claimed that Antonius 'drove away his lawful Roman wife to please the foreign and unlawful woman. And so . . . Antony procured his ruin by his marriage'.

Just as intended, the divorce of his sister provoked Octavian into action, making him appear the aggressor and presenting him with a real problem. For having only just made a name for himself as the great saviour who had personally ended Rome's civil war, he could hardly resume hostilities against a fellow Roman. And so he initiated moves to sideline Antonius and target Cleopatra as the 'enemy without'. She was a foreigner, a monarch and a woman, each guaranteed to repel much of the Roman establishment, so Octavian cast himself as her brave opponent and, despite the fact that the cities of Bononia (Bologna) and Palaestrina remained loyal to Antonius and Cleopatra, Octavian would claim that 'all Italy took a personal oath to me voluntarily, demanding me as their leader in the war'.

Exploiting Rome's long-standing suspicion of the East, he told his fellow citizens they faced the gravest of dangers, since Cleopatra and her Eastern hordes could at any moment swarm into their city and destroy their very way of life. In line with the Sibylline Oracle's prophecy 'O Rome . . . the Queen crops off your delicate head of hair and uttering judgements will hurl you to earth from the sky', Octavian's poets claimed that Cleopatra wanted 'to demolish the Capitol, and topple the empire.'

So the noble, masculine West prepared to embark on its great crusade against the corrupt and feminised East, and all memory of the unpopular war tax receded as Octavian's henchman Calvisius described the corrupt lifestyle that Cleopatra had forced upon Antonius. As a result of her influence he had unlawfully seized the Library of Pergamum to give to her, had forced the Ephesians to salute her as monarch and had read her love letters in the presence of leading statesmen. Inferring that he paid more attention to a woman's words, it was asserted that he had once lost interest in a speech being made by a leading Roman orator simply at the sight of her and had even been seen rubbing her feet in public.

Although some dismissed Calvisius' take on such events, the orator Marcus Valerius Messala published a booklet duplicating his claims and adding that Antonius used a golden chamber pot of 'an enormity that even Cleopatra would have been ashamed'. It was also claimed that he ran behind her litter in Eastern dress, as emasculated as the court eunuchs, described as 'her squalid pack of diseased half-men'; Octavian even commented that 'the generals they would have to fight would be Mardion the eunuch, Pothinus, Eiras, Cleopatra's hair-dressing girl and Charmion, who were Antony's chief state-councillors'.

When the couple's former ally, the 'pathologically treacherous' Plancus came over to Octavian, claiming that Cleopatra's presence in meetings had upset his sensibilities – but failing to mention that he had once painted himself blue and crawled naked along the floor to amuse her – he too enumerated Antonius' apparent crimes before the Senate. He also claimed to know the contents of his will, which had apparently been sent back to Rome and deposited with the Vestal

Virgins. After the chief priestess refused to hand it over, Octavian seized it by force.

With the reading out of wills, genuine or otherwise, something in which Roman statesmen had long specialised in their dealings with Ptolemaic Egypt, Octavian made a great show of reading out edited highlights from the last will and testament of Marcus Antonius. Reaffirming Caesarion as the legitimate son of Caesar, something Antonius had already done at the Donations, he then stated his apparent wish to leave generous legacies to his children by Cleopatra, even though Roman law did not allow children of a non-Roman citizen to inherit – something Antonius knew full well. This clause was almost certainly invented by Octavian, who then added with a final flourish that, if Antonius were to die in Rome, he had requested burial with Cleopatra in Alexandria.

Even if he had voiced such a wish privately, it hardly seems credible that Antonius would have provided written proof in the very city controlled by his great adversary. Yet despite those who were outraged at the violent treatment of the sacred Vestals and the disclosure of such a private document, Octavian's masterful propaganda hit the mark. Whether his audience believed him or not they were smart enough to realise the tide might well be turning, regardless of the methods used to turn it. So, as defections to Octavian's cause began, Antonius' supporters attempted damage limitation. They concluded that the only way to silence Octavian was to remove Cleopatra from the equation.

Gaius Geminius was sent to Athens to speak urgently with Antonius, but Cleopatra was immediately suspicious and kept him waiting. When finally made to state his business over dinner, he answered that he would explain himself on a more sober occasion, although 'one thing he had to say, whether sober or drunk, was that all would go well if Cleopatra would return to Egypt'. Despite Antonius' angry response, Cleopatra is said to have simply congratulated him, with the words, 'You have done well, Geminius, to tell your secret without being put on the rack.'

Antonius' remaining support in Rome now began to fall away, while claims that Cleopatra wanted to move the capital to Alexandria developed into the widespread belief that she wished to become 'queen of Rome'. She was said to have referred to the day when 'I shall one day give judgement on the Capitol', the sacred heart of Rome itself, and such stories gained sufficient support from the remaining members of the Senate to allow Octavian's plans to be pushed through.

Stripping the absent Antonius of his remaining powers and 'denying him the authority which he had let a woman exercise in his place', Octavian finally denounced Cleopatra as an enemy of the state in the autumn of 32 BC. Formally declaring war on the thirty-seven-year-old mother of four, he processed through Rome to the Field of Mars and the temple of the war goddess Bellona where he made a vitriolic speech against her. Then, taking up a blood-smeared javelin, he hurled it east into land representing enemy territory, if not the enemy herself, Cleopatra the 'fatale monstrum' or deadly force. It has famously been stated that 'Rome, who had never condescended to fear any nation or people, did in her time fear two human beings; one was Hannibal, and the other was a woman.'

As Rome remained in a state of high alert waiting for Cleopatra and her hordes to cross the Adriatic, the time had long passed for any invasion of Italy to be successful – since Cleopatra, as a foreign invader, would turn Antonius' remaining Roman supporters against him. So Greece would remain the battleground. Having left Athens in the autumn, Antonius and Cleopatra moved west to Corinth to keep watch over the Gulf of Corinth. Linked to the fortress at Methone on the southernmost tip of the Peloponnese, it was part of Antonius' defensive chain stretching from Corcyra (Corfu) in the north down to Cyrene in the south, a means of keeping Egypt and the East safe while also forming a vital supply route to Alexandria.

Yet the bulk of their forces were concentrated around the Bay of Ambracia, the perfect harbour for more than four hundred warships ornamented with bronze prows representing Isis, armed Athena and centaurs together with brass spikes, forked prows and multiple rams. Armed with grappling irons, incendiary devices and catapults, each had a standard contingent of 120 soldiers plus a detachment of archers, while as many as 600 rowers, mixed crews of Egyptians, Phoenicians, Indians, Arabs and Sabaeans, were needed to manoeuvre up to ten banks of oars.

Late in 32 BC, Antonius and Cleopatra arrived to make their winter camp at Aktion (Actium) on the bay's southern promotory, looking west to await Octavian. They were unaware that a traitor had been among them until Dellius defected to Octavian's side and, having made claims that Cleopatra had taken against him, revealed the couple's position and their battle plans. This allowed Agrippa to seize Methone and other key sites in Antonius' defensive network so that the vital supply chain from Alexandria fell apart.

As Octavian, Agrippa and some eighty thousand men made their camp only half a mile away north of the bay at a place named Toryne, meaning 'ladle', Antonius was cut off from his land forces strung out further north to protect the coast. With his advisers clearly alarmed at this situation, Cleopatra is said to have commented tersely 'we may be frightened if Octavian has got hold of the ladle', mocking those still voicing their disapproval of her continued presence.

Such sentiments were certainly voiced in Octavian's camp where soldier-poet Horace claimed that 'amid the soldiers' standards the sun shines on the shameful Egyptian pavilion', asking how any Roman could bring himself to 'bear weapons at a woman's behest'. For Octavian would be facing Antonius 'and – shocking! – accompanied by an Egyptian wife', spurring on her troops by shaking her 'native sistrum' to summon up 'all kinds of monstrous gods' as she challenged Rome's Neptune, Minerva and Venus. As these were all deities she herself worshipped and in one case even personified, claims that 'lecherous Canopus' prostitute queen dared to oppose her yapping Anubis against our Jupiter' likewise fell short of historical accuracy, since the couple's own coins bore the head of Jupiter, embellished with the rams' horns of Amun.

Then Octavian, having adopted the unprecedented title 'Commander Caesar, son of the god' both to dismiss the existence of Caesarion and take on Living Isis, publicly prayed for victory to Mars before addressing his troops. He described Cleopatra as 'this pestilence of a woman,' and Antonius as her effeminate, impotent appendage – 'let nobody consider him a Roman, but rather an Egyptian; let us not call him Antony but rather Serapis'. Then he dismissed the Egyptians as nothing but a 'rabble' who 'worship reptiles and beasts as gods, they embalm their bodies to make them appear immortal, they are most forward in effrontery, but most backward in courage. Worst of all, they are not ruled by a man, but are the slaves of a woman.'

Although he had only half as many ships as Antonius, he had Agrippa as his admiral, who on the basis of Dellius' intelligence was able to bring his fleet around to block the bay and trap most of the couple's ships. Yet despite the sparse nature of the surviving evidence, Antonius won a series of military encounters after crossing over to the north of the bay; one of these victories was revealed on coins, which named him 'Imperator' for the fourth time as a title awarded by troops following a successful battle.

When Octavian turned down his offer of single combat, preferring an assassination attempt which nevertheless failed, simply played a waiting game as the summer temperatures rose. With most of their food supplies cut off, Antonius' men grew weaker. Then disease struck the camp: dysentery and malaria from marshy ground wiped out hundreds, until there were insufficient rowers to man the ships. Antonius was forced to burn 140 vessels to prevent them falling into enemy hands. Morale plummeted. Defections to Octavian included the consul Ahenobarbus, about whom Antonius joked that he must be missing his mistress. So, despite Cleopatra's fury, he sent his old comrade his staff and equipment, which he received shortly before he expired from fever.

Faced with this growing crisis, late in August 31 BC Antonius called a council of war in an attempt to find the best way out of a no-win situation. Since most preferred a land-based solution, Canidius Crassus advised them to abandon the fleet, send Cleopatra back to Alexandria and then retreat inland north to Macedonia, joining with the Dacians to attack Octavian by land. Yet this was an all-or-nothing strategy that Cleopatra felt was too risky. Unwilling to hand over the fleet to give Octavian control of the sea, she believed they should try to save as many of their ships as possible, using the afternoon's offshore winds to break out, sail to Egypt and regroup to fight again. She was accused of forcing this strategy on Antonius against his better judgement, but he knew the opposition too would prefer a land battle; by using the element of surprise, they could still break out of the bay and turn to fight at sea, taking out as many of Octavian's ships as possible in the process.

So, ordering Canidius Crassus to take the army back to Egypt via Asia Minor, Antonius press-ganged unfortunate locals to fill the short-fall of rowers while the sails usually left ashore during fighting were taken on board for the flight ahead. And with the war chest loaded on to Cleopatra's flagship by night, they waited for a spell of rough sea to subside. When the morning of 2 September 31 BC dawned calmly, Antonius, resplendent in his purple cloak, urged his men to fight on board ship as well as they did on land. Then as he boarded his flagship, Cleopatra, 'rich in gaudy robes' and highly visible, boarded hers to await the breeze, which began to build up toward noon.

As their remaining fleet of around 240 ships moved slowly out of the bay, Cleopatra's squadron kept to the rear while Antonius, with his admiral, Sosius, to his left, sailed out towards Agrippa's ships on the right. Although they did not respond, he had little choice but to launch his attack to break the stalemate. For several hours the air was thick with arrows, javelins, spears, catapult missiles and fire-balls. It was said that 'from the fifth to the seventh hour it raged with terrific losses on both sides', and with 'Roman corpses floating in the sea', increasing quantities of debris were washed ashore as ships on both sides succumbed to the onslaught.

Although Octavian spent the battle laid low with sea-sickness, his ships drew Sosius out and, as a gap developed in the fighting, Cleopatra, keeping to the prearranged plan to escape and regroup, saw her chance and headed for open sea. Yet, surrounded by the smaller, lighter vessels of the enemy, Antonius could not go after her and was forced to transfer to a smaller craft to do so. The rest of their fleet, caught up in heavy fighting, were unable to follow and in rising seas had little choice but to surrender.

It was claimed that in the thick of battle Antonius decided suddenly to chase after his fickle wife who, 'as a woman and as an Egyptian', had treacherously fled to save herself. Despite the fact that the sails each vessel carried clearly indicated that she was acting according to plan, Cleopatra has been condemned as a coward ever since and Antonius taken to be so besotted that he simply followed. Later compared to the Trojan prince Paris in his love for Helen of Troy, Antonius, 'like another Paris, left the battle to fly to her arms; or rather, to say the truth, Paris fled when he was already beaten; Antony fled first, and, following Cleopatra, abandoned his victory', a tragic tale of doomed love yet complete nonsense.

The couple had broken out with around a hundred ships as opposed to 'hardly one' as claimed by the enemy. Aktion had been 'no heroic battle but a series of skirmishes on land and a few exchanges at sea', and although later transformed into legend by Octavian's poets, their subsequent eulogies were clearly 'out of proportion with the actual events', since the poorly reported encounter had been no resounding victory or defeat for either side.

Octavian may have won by default, but Cleopatra and Antonius had succeeded in their plan for escape and lived to fight another day. And as her flagship pressed on south, the pragmatic Cleopatra was already making plans for the next stage in a war she still fully intended to win.

PART SIX

The Final Year: Defeat, Death and Eternal Life

Having pulled off their successful escape from Aktion, Cleopatra and Antonius headed south down the coast of the Peloponnese. Still planning their next move, they reached Cape Taenarum after three days' sailing and despatched orders to Canidius Crassus who was leading the army overland to Egypt. But soon they received devastating news.

Although the men had followed orders as far as Macedonia, they had been intercepted by Octavian's forces and, during week-long negotiations, had wavered when offered a deal which included returning to their Italian homeland – something Antonius could never offer them. Despite Canidius' refusal to betray Antonius, his men finally switched sides. While he and his fellow officers made their escape to Egypt, Octavian claimed they had simply chosen to abandon their troops whose surrender he accepted.

The news that his men had deserted was far more of a disaster for Antonius than the shambolic encounter at Aktion, and as Cleopatra's flagship resumed its journey south over the Mediterranean he spent the crossing in silence at the prow of the ship. Although her servants did what they could to bring the couple together to eat and sleep, he slid into a deep depression while Cleopatra maintained her steely determination. Given that they still had troops in the East, together with part of their fleet, she was fully aware that the Mediterranean need not be the only theatre of operations, nor was it Egypt's only coastline. And having survived previous situations when her very life had hung in the balance, New Isis came increasingly to the fore in the face of her husband's increasing inertia.

Before heading for Alexandria, the couple sailed 125 miles west to the key communications base at Paraetonium (Mersa Matruh) on Egypt's western border, from where they intended to organise a counter-attack. Yet not only did they receive confirmation that their forces in Greece had defected, they discovered that their four remaining legions in Cyrene had also gone over to Octavian whose name had already begun to appear on Cyrene's coinage. To prevent the turncoat legions being sent over the border into Egypt, Antonius decided to remain at Paraetonium and do what he could to fortify the region. Since this was the place from which Alexander had launched his trailblazing expedition to Siwa, the Ptolemies had created a subterranean shrine here in his honour, and filled it with ancestral portraits including images of Cleopatra's grandfather Ptolemy IX. It seems highly likely that she followed Ptolemaic tradition by invoking the powers of her great ancestor to help restore Antonius' spirit.

Leaving him with around forty of their remaining ships, she took her sixty-strong squadron east to Alexandria, sailing into harbour with purple sails unfurled. With garlands about her prow, and flying the flags of victory to deny any rumour of defeat, she disembarked to flute music and hymns, 'The Glorification of Cleopatra Philopator' honouring the 'divine protectress of the country'.

Her confident façade allowed her to resume control of the administration. It was said that 'as soon as she reached safety, she slew many of the foremost men, since they had always been displeased with her and were now elated over her disaster'. No doubt the recent betrayals by Dellius, Plancus and Ahenobarbus were foremost in her mind as she eliminated those within the Alexandrian elite who wished to exploit her weakened position. The most prominent victim of her purge was Artavasdes, former king of Armenia, who had not only betrayed Antonius during the first Parthian campaign but refused to pay her homage. She sent his head as a gift to his sworn enemy the king of Media, whose young daughter was already betrothed to Cleopatra's son Alexander Helios.

As she continued to renew alliances with Antonius' remaining vassals, no doubt unsurprised that Herod of Judaea, who had once named his palace 'Antonia', was already planning his harbour city of Caesarea in honour of his new overlord Octavian, the latter was still in no position to invade Egypt since Aktion had not been as decisive as was later claimed. There were still centres of fierce resistance: the community of gladiators the couple had established at Cyzicus in Asia

Minor marched south through Syria, for as soon as they heard what had happened they started for Egypt to help their rulers – and if necessary would fight to the death. So, needing to secure Greece and counter the couple's remaining popularity, Octavian began to work back through the couple's recent itinerary from Athens to Samos until he received news of serious rebellion in Italy. Although a conspiracy led by the son of the former triumvir Lepidus had been put down and its leader executed, Agrippa was sent back to maintain calm and the thousands of soldiers who had been promised so much by Octavian were now demanding their rewards.

Left with little choice, Octavian was forced to return to Italy in winter seas so stormy they claimed the life of his personal physician. When he finally reached Brundisium he was met by the Senate, but his hero's welcome was marred by jeering crowds of angry veterans demanding payment. Although temporarily appeasing them with land previously awarded to Antonius' troops, Octavian knew that in the long term he desperately needed the fabled wealth of the Ptolemies which Cleopatra still possessed and planned to use.

To augment the 20,000 talents remaining in her war chest, later sources claimed she 'plundered her country's gods and her ancestors' sepulchres' and 'did not exempt even the most holy shrines' in a charge of sacrilege which has long been accepted even though she had a tradition of funding the temples as a means of maintaining native support. And clearly the Egyptians did continue to support her, since a delegation from southern Egypt demonstrated their willingness to bear arms on her behalf to defend their country against Octavian, and her statues continued to be venerated in temples throughout the land by a clergy headed by her royal relative, the high priest Petubastis. So if temple funds were indeed forthcoming, they must have taken the form of voluntary contributions.

Certainly one of Cleopatra's very first acts after returning home was to honour Isis and Min in their joint temple at Koptos, with a stone stela dated 21 September 31 BC inscribed 'year 22 which is equivalent of year 7, first month of akhet, day 22 of the female pharaoh, the bodily daughter of kings who were on their part kings born of kings, Cleopatra, the beneficent father-loving goddess and of pharaoh Ptolemy called Caesar, the father and mother loving god'. Only Caesarion was portrayed, perhaps promoted alone in case anything should happen to his mother and co-ruler. The text then referred to royal payments to the Buchis bull cult and the wages for local linen weavers who prepared the creature's funerary wrappings. Yet such royal favour may well have been prompted by the fact that Koptos was the main access point from the Nile to the Red Sea, the route guarded by Min and Isis whose assistance Cleopatra sought in her forthcoming plans to safeguard her treasure, her children and herself.

For while Egypt was surrounded to the east, west and north, the south remained free, and this is where Cleopatra planned her next move. Having accepted that the Mediterranean belonged to Octavian, she decided against moving to Spain to join Pompeius' few remaining supporters and instead staked her future on Egypt's other coastline. As a region beyond Octavian's reach yet familiar to the Ptolemies, particularly to Cleopatra who spoke many of its languages, the Red Sea region encompassed much of southern Egypt — even if enemy forces invaded the Delta, the south would continue to regard itself as an independent region strongly supportive of her regime. Relocation to an area on the direct sea route with India would also offer new opportunities for travel and trade. A fine bronze figurine of Isis' son Harpokrates with his characteristic sidelock and the crown of Upper and Lower Egypt, manufactured in Alexandria but found in the Punjab, was perhaps advance propaganda for plans she began to implement by means of 'a most bold and wonderful enterprise'.

What she did was transport her remaining fleet of sixty ships, which were presumably far too large to pass through the existing canal, 'over the small space of land which divides the Red Sea from the sea near Egypt'. It was said that 'the narrowest place is not much above 300 furlongs [about 40 miles] across' so 'over this neck of land Cleopatra had formed a project of dragging her fleet and setting it afloat in the Arabian Gulf', using Egyptian-style wooden rollers or perhaps a wheeled transporter system like one she may have recently seen in Corinth in which ships were transported overland.

But although the plan gave real scope for the future, it ended in sudden disaster when her great ships were destroyed by 'the Arabians of Petra' led by their ruler Malchus. Having long resented the Ptolemies' territorial incursions and trade links, the Arabs had never forgiven

Cleopatra's seizure of their lucrative bitumen trade. Their devastating arson attack, supported by Octavian's newly appointed governor of Syria and Herod of Judaea, settled some old scores.

If Antonius' lowest point had been the defection of his land forces, the destruction of her fleet, which had offered them all a means of survival, was surely Cleopatra's darkest hour. Yet even through this she remained active, for while she still had her treasure she had her power. With Antonius back from Paraetonium, having done what he could to safeguard the western routes into Egypt, Cleopatra gave orders that the eastern approach via Pelusium was to be secured while she prepared to take on Octavian, using the treasury he so desperately needed as a bargaining tool. Deciding to split the wealth, she would keep half in Alexandria within her vault-like mausoleum while entrusting the rest to her teenage co-ruler Caesarion who would in due course be sent abroad, far away from Octavian who was already on his way.

By spring 30 BC he was already in Rhodes, where Cleopatra sent word she was willing to abdicate on condition that her children were allowed to rule Egypt. She accompanied her message with a large bribe and the royal insignia of an Eastern monarch, in much the same way that Rome had once sent Ptolemy IV a toga in place of his favoured Dionysiac garb – no doubt making a point to Octavian, who famously insisted on the toga as a means of emphasising the difference between Romans and effete Easterners. Although he kept the money, and presumably the exotic ensemble, his response was non-commital and it was repeated when she sent the tutor Euphronios with another bribe to put the same request.

While Cleopatra and her children continued to live in the palace at Alexandria, quite possibly on Antirrhodos, a despondent Antonius preferred his own company in the light of continuing defections which had even included his old ally Herod. Sharing the sentiments of the misanthrope Timon of Athens and his famous epitaph 'here I am laid, my life of misery done, ask not my name, I curse you every one', Antonius gave form to his feelings by extending a promontory into the sea to build the Timoneum, a granite and marble retreat close to Cleopatra's palace on Antirrhodos to the west but completely separated by water, allowing her to see him but not to reach him.

He sent Octavian his son Antyllus, once engaged to Octavian's infant daughter Julia; the boy passed on the message that his father simply wanted to live as a private citizen in Alexandria, or in Athens if that were not possible. Although Octavian kept the money accompanying his request, he sent his answer back only to Cleopatra, telling her 'there was no reasonable favour which she might not expect, if she put Antonius to death or expelled him from Egypt'.

Although Antonius then offered to kill himself on condition Cleopatra would be spared, it was jealousy that finally roused him from his inertia. Octavian's handsome young freedman Thyrsos was enjoying such prolonged audiences with Cleopatra that he gave orders for Thyrsos to be flogged for his impertinence. Sending him back to Octavian with a note claiming his 'busy impertinent ways had provoked him', Antonius added that Octavian could even the score by flogging Antonius' own freedman Hipparchus, who had recently gone over to Octavian's side.

Finally leaving his self-imposed exile, Antonius decided to enjoy what was left of his life and 'was received by Cleopatra in the palace and set the whole city into a course of feasting, drinking and presents'. Although she kept her own thirty-ninth birthday celebrations purposefully low-key, she must have been deeply relieved to have him back, insisting that his fifty-second was celebrated on 14 January 30 BC with such magnificence 'that many of the guests who sat down in want went home wealthy men'.

To make a symbolic severance from the traitors Plancus, Titius and Dellius, the couple formally dissolved 'The Inimitable Livers' and in its place founded the 'Synapothanoumenoi', 'Those who will die together' or 'The Suicide Club'. Made up of hard-core supporters who wore chaplets of poisoned flowers, each vowed they would die with the couple when the time came, including Canidius Crassus who had bravely defied Octavian and made it back to Egypt.

Wishing to find a painless means to end her life should the need arise, Cleopatra was determined to follow the example of her uncle Ptolemy of Cyprus who had commited suicide when the Romans had taken his kingdom. At all costs she wished to avoid the fate of her half-sister Arsinoe who had been forced to walk in chains through Rome, the city she herself had once ruled with Caesar. With no intention of ever returning, certainly not in any Triumph of Octavian, Cleopatra adamantly declared, 'I will not be shown in a Triumph'.

So to this end, 'her daily practice' involved research within the Mouseion on the subject of toxicology, and 'busied in making a collection of all varieties of poisonous drugs and in order to see which of them were the least painful in the operation, she had them tried upon prisoners condemned. But finding that the quick poisons always worked with sharp pains and that the less painful were slow, she next tried venomous animals, and watched with her own eyes whilst they were applied, one creature to the body of another.' Alexandria's first librarian Demetrios of Phaleron was said to have chosen to die by the bite of an asp, a form of execution used in Alexandria and considered by the Greek doctor Galen a humane method. Indeed, it was said that 'she pretty well satisfied herself that nothing was comparable to the bite of the asp, which without convulsion or groaning brought on a heavy drowsiness and lethargy with a gentle sweat on the face, the sense being stupefied by degrees; the patient, in appearance, being sensible of no pain, but rather troubled to be disturbed or awakened like those that are in a profound natural sleep'. So she kept snakes and 'other reptiles to end her life', no doubt in the royal zoo.

Having chosen the perfect means to pass over into the afterlife with the dignity befitting her status, Cleopatra was equally keen to complete the place in which she would be buried – her mausoleum begun early in her reign in accordance with pharaonic tradition. Having nevertheless broken with tradition by opting out of burial in the Soma, she had created 'several tombs and monuments' for herself and immediate family as an independent complex. It was described as 'joining the temple of Isis', a phrase which could refer to any one of the city's many Isis temples, including a round temple in the easterly Hadra quarter with its royal statuary and 'large edifice'; however, a further reference to 'the tomb which she was building in the grounds of the palace' suggests it was next to the temple of Isis on the Lochias promontory beside the sea.

Surviving descriptions of the tombs' 'wonderful height' also mention that they were 'very remarkable for their workmanship', recalling Cleopatra's magnificent Birth House at Hermonthis whose 'luxuriant decoration represented an excellent example of the baroque style of [Ptolemaic] architecture. The daring roof construction of the entrance kiosk, the play of light and shadows at the capitals, and the effect of the

huge, window-like openings that created beautiful connections between interior and exterior spaces must have been stunning.'

Possibly accessed by means of an 'ingenious double system of
trapdoor and sliding portcullis' as used in other Ptolemaic tombs,
Cleopatra's is known to have been a two-storeyed construction with
a windowless ground floor and an upper storey reached by at least one
internal staircase. Windows set high up in the building would let in
both light and sound, from the lapping of the sea to the daily rituals in
the adjoining temple, allowing her remains to be venerated as sacred
relics in the manner of Alexander and perpetuating her status as a
goddess with the powers of resurrection. There may even have been an
ancient-style false door on the wall between temple and tomb, a feature
Cleopatra had incorporated into her Hermonthis Birth House to enable
the living to communicate with the dead. Contemporary tombs in
Alexandria even had antechamber-style dining areas where the living
could eat with the dead, among surroundings decorated in a blend of
classical and Egyptian-style décor, where Greek gods, cupids and
dolphins appeared alongside Isis, Osiris and jackal-headed Anubis,
bending over the mummy on the funerary bier.

Although the first four Ptolemaic couples had been cremated
following Macedonian custom, their ashes placed in gold chests or
urns within the Soma, increasing royal patronage of native practices and
burial 'Egyptian fashion' had led to the revival of royal mummification
by 180 BC. This was something that Cleopatra VII would almost
certainly have demanded for herself, following Alexander's example:
mummification was central to her identity as Isis and a crucial step
toward resurrection and eternal life.

Surviving mummies of Ptolemaic officials reveal evidence of high-
quality preservation. Cleopatra's distant cousin Pasherenptah III
claimed in his funerary inscription that his body was 'placed in the
West and all the rites for my august mummy were carried out', much in
the manner described in the only two remaining literary sources,
Herodotus and Cleopatra's contemporary Diodorus. Beneath the
watchful eye of the chief funerary priest, masked as the jackal god
Anubis, the body would be laid out on a stone embalming table and the
brain removed down the nose or from the base of the skull. The cavity
would then be sealed with warm resin. After the 'paraschistes' or

'cutter-up' embalmer had opened the left side of the abdomen with a black obsidian blade to remove the entrails, then been ritually chased away for inflicting damage to the body, the 'taricheutai' or 'salters' used natron salts to dry out the body and reduce its weight by 75 per cent. When the cavity had been rinsed with sterilising date palm wine and spices, the dessicated entrails were replaced inside the body which was then washed and 'made beautiful with unguent, myrrh and incense', together with 'sefy' (juniper oil) 'kedros' (cedar oil) and small amounts of Dead Sea bitumen, 'for if this material is not mixed into the other substances the cadaver will not last long'. Finally the skin was sealed with a layer of resin and warm beeswax, both key ingredients in Egyptian embalming along with antibacterial honey, as used in the embalming of Alexander.

Having left instructions for her own mummification, Cleopatra must also have selected the appropriate jewellery and amulets, chief among which would be her royal diadem as insignia of the Ptolemaic royal house. In contrast to Roman burials, forbidden by law to contain any gold other than 'the teeth of the deceased if fastened with gold', Egyptian burials were legendary for their wealthy contents. The mummy of one of Cleopatra's priestly relatives was said to have been 'made of funerary raiment, gold and silver ornaments with protective amulets of all sorts of genuine precious stones.'

Presumably she would have left orders to be laid out with her arms crossed over her chest in the regal pose of pharaohs, and adorned with the same large quantities of rings and bracelets. Gold snakes for her forearms would have been based on the creatures' importance in the worship of both Isis and Dionysos, whose female devotees had live snakes coiled about their arms. A pair of gold serpent bracelets dated c.40–20 BC adorned with pearls and emeralds seem particularly appropriate: the emeralds' vivid green, the colour of new life, associated them with Osiris, whose own burial had featured the traditional broad-collar necklace subsequently placed over the chest of every mummy as a potent amulet.

As the texts in Cleopatra's rooftop Osiris chapel at Dendera revealed, no fewer than 104 separate amulets were required during the mummification process. Her preparations for the burial of the Buchis bull she had installed at the beginning of her reign included a wide assortment of amulets in feldspar, porphyry, lapis lazuli and red jasper to give him the 'best burial' of any of the bulls at Hermonthis when his time came. As in human mummification each amulet would be placed at a specific point on the body and activated by appropriate spells from the *Book of the Dead* funerary texts before being covered in multiple layers of finest linen sealed with warmed resin. Then, after being covered in an outer shroud and bead net to symbolise the starry sky, the funerary mask protecting the head would assimilate the deceased with a specific deity. The mask of Cleopatra would surely be the face of Isis, manufactured to the very highest specifications in gold and precious gems.

As tradition dictated, the masked mummy was ultimately intended for its coffin which in the case of pharaohs was often made of gold. Although Alexander's anthropoid (body-shaped) coffin of beaten gold had been replaced in 89 BC by the 'glass' one familiar to Cleopatra, it was said that 'the most highly valued glass is colourless and transparent, as closely as possible resembling rock crystal'. Given that terms could be interchangeable, perhaps Alexander's casket had actually been made of rock crystal obtained from the coast of modern Sudan and Eritrea. Certainly when a Persian delegation visited the region, they 'were taken to see the coffins. . . . said to be made of crystal, and the method the Ethiopians follow is first to dry the corpse, either by the Egyptian process or some other . . . they then enclose it in a shaft of crystal which has been hollowed out, like a cylinder, to receive it. The stuff is easily worked, and is mined in large quantities. The corpse is plainly visible inside the cylinder; there is no disagreeable smell, or any other cause of annoyance, and every detail can be distinctly seen as if there were nothing between one's eyes and the body.'

Perhaps the inspiration behind Cleopatra's choice of casket, the fact that such crystal 'is to be found also on an island called Necron, or Island of the Dead, in the Red Sea facing Arabia' was known by at least one of her relatives. The type obtained from 'an island in the Red Sea 60 miles from the city of Berenike' was also 'known as "iris" in token of its appearance, for when it is struck by the sunlight in a room it casts the appearance and colours of a rainbow on the walls near by, continually altering its tints and ever causing more and more astonishment because of its extremely changeable effects . . . and in full sunlight it scatters the beams that shine upon it, and yet at the same time lights up adjacent objects by projecting a kind of gleam in front of itself'.

The qualities of such a stone seemingly brought to life by the sun must have appeared quite magical and made it a highly appropriate material in which to place a body which would remain perfectly visible within. Perhaps, following Egyptian tradition, Cleopatra even commissioned a gold shrine to cover her coffin. Alexander's shrine had a gold and jewelled roof, and even Caesar's body had been laid in state beneath a gilded shrine modelled on his temple of Venus, the 'Roman counterpart of Hathor'. She certainly planned to surround her burial with lavish funerary equipment which may have included *Book of the Dead* funerary texts, figurines of the gods, Greek-style vases, wine amphorae and all her personal possessions from thrones and couches, precious plate and jewelled vessels to her lavish ward-robe, cosmetics chests, perfumes and magnificent jewellery collection. For it was certainly said that, once she had completed her tomb, 'thither she removed her treasure, her gold, silver, emeralds, pearls, ebony, ivory [and] cinnamon'.

She also let it be known that the burial goods included 'a great quantity of torchwood and tow', which, as intended, greatly alarmed Octavian who 'began to fear lest she should in a desperate fit set all these riches on fire' in a huge funerary pyre. So, as as he travelled south through Syria, he repeatedly stressed his good intentions and the offer of a fair hearing – but on condition she killed Antonius. Yet despite countless claims Cleopatra had used and manipulated men throughout her life to achieve her own ends, her husband's death was something she would not consider, even as a means of self-preservation. And having made all possible preparation for her own death, she turned her attentions to the continuity of her dynasty.

In 30 BC, four years after the Donations ceremony had been held as part of the great Ptolemaia celebrations, the time had come for the festival to be held again. So in another great spectacle in the Gymnasion stadium, Cleopatra reaffirmed the succession with public celebrations for Caesarion, her heir and co-ruler, as he reached his sixteenth birthday, 'in honour of which the citizens of Alexandria did nothing but feast and revel for many days'. No doubt his transition into adult society was marked by undergoing the 'mallokouria', when his sidelock of hair was cut off. This rite of passage was described by one Alexandrian father who stated that 'my son Theon had his long hair cut off in honour of the city on the 15th Tybi in the Great Serapeum in the presence of the priests and officials'. Then, following custom, Caesarion was formally 'registered among the youths' of Alexandria and publicly acknowledged a man, Cleopatra wanting everyone to see King Ptolemy XV as a capable pharaoh, emerging from her shadow to stand on his own royal feet. Public celebrations were also held for Antyllus, Antonius' eldest son and heir, who at fourteen underwent a Roman rite of passage, exchanging his boy's toga with its purple stripe for the all-white toga *virilis* as he too became a man in the eyes of Roman society.

Although these were standard events in the lives of all Egyptian and Roman boys, the celebrations were a means for Cleopatra to highlight the power of her dynasty and demonstrate her own procreative abilities in contrast to those of her enemy. Octavian, after all, had had only a single daughter with his former wife Scribonia and had been unable to father children with Livia – who had still managed to produce two sons by a previous husband. Cleopatra wished to show to the world her son by Caesar, her three children by Antonius, and the eldest of his four boys, Antyllus.

Having made her point in the most public manner, she began to put her survival plan into action and, securing one part of her treasure in her mausoleum, entrusted the rest to Caesarion. For in June 30 BC, 'at the eve of a favourable monsoon', mother and son made their farewells at the harbourside as the young pharaoh and his tutor Rhodon embarked on their journey upriver to Koptos. From here they took the long desert road to the Red Sea port of Berenike, presumably making the 220-mile camel journey by night to escape the heat. Then, having safely reached the port after twelve days, they waited for favourable conditions to take them by ship to India and to safety, intending to meet up with Cleopatra at some future time.

Meanwhile Alexander, Cleopatra and Ptolemy, the three youngest children, were also evacuated in the care of their tutor Euphronios. They were believed to have been taken south to Cleopatra's supporters in Thebes, from where arrangements may have been made for Alexander Helios and the Median princess Iotape to travel out to her homeland at a later date. The children's departure cannot have been too soon, as Octavian's forces had begun to close in.

To the west Gaius Cornelius Gallus, friend of Octavian's spin doctor poet Virgil, was already sailing toward the African coast, and although Antonius set out with the couple's remaining forty ships to take him on he was beaten back and the ships were lost, enabling Gallus' fleet to press on toward Alexandria. To the north-east, Octavian had reached Phoenicia by the summer, collecting new allies en route including Herod of Judaea who added his military support to the advance on Egypt. Soon the invaders were able to seize the well-fortified border town of Pelusium with little resistance, following collusion by the garrison commander, Seleucus. Cleopatra gave immediate orders for the execution of Seleucus' wife and daughter to punish the man who had so readily allowed Octavian into Egypt.

Moving swiftly around the Delta coast, Octavian's forces pressed on to the resort of Canopus and were soon at the gates of the royal city. But, as their cavalry began an advance, Antonius was ready and, leading his remaining forces out of the Canopic Gate, beat them back against all the odds. Returning to the palace in triumph, he went straight to Cleopatra and 'armed as he was, he kissed her, and commending to her favour one of his men who had most signalised himself in the fight'. As a reward for the man's courage and for defending her kingdom against enemy attack, Cleopatra presented him with a golden breastplate and helmet. That same evening the soldier defected to Octavian.

As he began to undermine the couple's support within Egypt, Octavian knew it was vital that any native force should be dealt with as soon as possible. Hearing that Cleopatra's subjects had offered to march north and help in the armed struggle, he acted swiftly to eliminate their figurehead and spiritual leader, the high priest of Memphis. As Egypt's highest native authority, its members related to the crown, the Memphite dynasty offered unwavering support for the monarchy which made it the natural focus for native unrest. So, regardless of his young age, Petubastis had to be removed. Although classical sources are completely silent on a domestic matter of no particular interest to them, Egyptian evidence reveals that the sixteen-year-old high priest met his untimely death on 6th Mesore, 31 July 30 BC, a date which seems far too coincidental for this not to have been an assassination. With the Memphite dynasty effectively terminated, there remained only the monarchy in Alexandria, where Cleopatra was determined to retain her treasure. Antonius was equally determined to fight, but his offer of hand-to-hand combat with Octavian was once again refused and the suggestion made that Antonius might prefer to find some other way to die.

So that was it. There would be no life in exile, and there was now only one option for Antonius. But as a true soldier he would fight to the last, so he planned his last battle on land and sea with their remaining troops. On the evening of 31 July, the 'Synapothanoumenoi' met for the last time. As the die-hard members of the Suicide Club gathered for a final great banquet, Antonius revealed he could never hope to win and simply desired an honourable death. He may even have contemplated Cleopatra's suggestion they take flowers she had already poisoned from their hair and drop them into their wine, 'having gathered the fragments of his chaplet into his cup'.

In the sombre atmosphere of that hot summer night, the city had already fallen quiet when an unearthly music was heard, 'the sound of all sorts of instruments, and voices singing in tune, and the cry of a crowd of people shouting and dancing, like a troop of bacchanals on its way'. The disembodied procession seemed to pass through the centre of the city and out through the eastern gate, then suddenly grew very loud before disappearing into the distance towards the enemy camp. Interpreted as Dionysos leading his ghostly band of revellers away from the palace for the last time as Antonius' god finally deserted him, the event was in fact far more ominous: Dionysos was abandoning the very dynasty he had for so long protected.

At dawn on 1 August, the Egyptian 8th Mesore, Cleopatra and Antonius made what they believed to be their final farewell. Having briefed the remaining fleet, Antonius reviewed the troops and defiantly led them out of the eastern Canopic Gate and up to rising ground. From there they overlooked the enemy camp, watching as the fleet moved out towards the rising sun to engage Octavian's ships.

Yet there was to be no engagement. Hopelessly outnumbered, the couple's remaining ships simply pulled alongside the enemy, saluted them, and became part of the larger fleet which then advanced as one towards the city. Having seen their naval comrades defect, Antonius' cavalry did likewise; only the small infantry force attempted a half-hearted attack before they too began to melt away, leaving Antonius alone. Unable to gain any satisfaction from Octavian, he had no choice but to return to the palace as Alexandria formally surrendered.

As the remnants of her once mighty fleet joined with the enemy, Cleopatra assumed the worst and, believing Antonius had been killed, told her remaining servants to report to any enquiry that she too was dead. Taking up her dagger she went straight to her tomb, accompanied by Charmion and Eiras, perhaps also her attendant Mardion. Once inside they would have operated the mechanism to seal the great stone entrance as they presumably prepared to take their lives.

Yet Antonius was still very much alive. As he returned to the palace to search for Cleopatra, he was told that she had gone to her tomb. With her personal physician Olympus providing an eyewitness account of the unfolding drama, Antonius apparently mused aloud, 'Why delay any longer? Fate has snatched away the only thing for which I still wanted to live. I'm not so troubled, Cleopatra, that you have gone, for I shall soon be with you. But it distresses me that so great a general should be found to be less courageous than a woman.' Passing into his personal chambers, he stripped off his armour and handed his sword to his servant Eros, who instead turned the weapon on himself and fell dead at Antonius' feet. 'Well done, Eros, well done, you've shown your master how to do what you hadn't the heart to do yourself', he declared as he drove the blade into his stomach.

Antonius lay down to wait for the end, but it did not come quickly and, in considerable pain, he called out for someone to finish him off. Although the servants had already scattered in fear, one had evidently informed Cleopatra that Antonius was alive, so she had sent orders via her secretary Diomedes that he should be brought to her. At the news that she too was still alive, Antonius insisted he go to her, and with assistance managed to reach the tomb.

With its entrance already sealed, Cleopatra looked down from one of the high windows and, with the help of her two women, let down rope winches, either left over from building work or left in place to manoeuvre her heavy coffin into position. As they hauled up the wounded Antonius, 'it was no easy task for the women; and Cleopatra, with all her force, clinging to the rope, and straining with her head to the ground, with difficulty pulled him up, while those below encouraged her with their cries, and joined in all her efforts and anxiety'. Although he was bleeding heavily, he was successfully brought into the tomb, 'still holding up his hands to her, and lifting up his body with the little force he had left'. Eyewitnesses claimed that 'nothing was ever more sad than this spectacle', which even now was being reported to Octavian.

With the dying Antonius helped to a bed which was presumably part of the funerary furniture, Cleopatra covered him in her sheet-like mantle and began to mourn in traditional fashion, 'beating her breast with her hands, lacerating herself, and disfiguring her own face with the blood from his wounds, she called him her lord, her husband, her emperor, and seemed to have pretty nearly forgotten all her own evils, she was so intent upon his misfortunes'. As he did his best to calm her, he ordered wine from the funerary stocks and, after drinking his last, advised her to put her trust in Gaius Proculeius, one of Octavian's staff but an honourable man. Reminding her that he had lived a full life and had been the most illustrious and powerful of men, he told her not to grieve but to remember their past happiness together. And then he died in her arms.

Panicking that the distraught Cleopatra would kill herself and torch her treasure, Octavian sent for Proculeius and ordered him to get her out alive. Unable to gain access via the sealed entrance, Proculeius requested she came out, to which she agreed providing Octavian would allow Caesarion to rule Egypt. Assuring her she could trust Octavian, Proculeius then had his colleague Cornelius Gallus keep her talking while he and the freedman Epaphroditus used scaling ladders to gain entrance through one of the upper-storey windows. As her servants shouted out to warn her of the men's arrival, Cleopatra pulled out her dagger to stab herself but was forcibly seized by Proculeius who removed the weapon. And, given her well-known interest in toxicology, or perhaps following a tip-off, he then 'shook her dress to see if there were any poisons hid in it'.

Taken prisoner, she was escorted back to the palace with Epaphroditus as her guard, and, although allowed to keep her retinue, was placed under house arrest in quarters which had no doubt been thoroughly searched for any means by which she might harm herself. This action may also have been influenced by the suicide of her eunuch attendant Mardion, who 'had of his own accord delivered himself up to the serpents at the time when Cleopatra had been seized . . . and after being bitten by them had leaped into a coffin prepared for him'.

Meanwhile, Octavian himself finally entered Alexandria, promising his troops a financial incentive if they did not sack the city. Clearly unsure of the reception he might receive from the notoriously violent citizens, he decided to appear with the Alexandrian philosopher Arius Didymus, his newly appointed adviser on Egyptian affairs, 'holding him by the hand and talking with him' as Octavian called a public meeting in the Gymnasion. The citizens of Alexandria had mixed feelings for Cleopatra as a Roman collaborator, and now listened as their new Roman master, flanked by his massed ranks of troops, told them they were all free of blame. Of the Roman supporters of Cleopatra's regime Canidius Crassus, Quintus Ovinius and various others had been summarily executed, and only the admiral and former consul Sosius spared. But Octavian declared he would spare the citizens too because their city was so large and beautiful, because of his feelings for his new friend Didymus and, he announced, for the sake of the great Alexander, whose tomb Didymus now took him to see.

Apparently visiting the Soma to pay his respects – while seeing how much of the Ptolemies' famous wealth remained there – Octavian entered the subterranean burial chamber and 'had the sarcophagus containing Alexander the Great's mummy removed from the mausoleum . . . and, after a long look at its features, showed his veneration by crowning the head with a golden diadem and strewing flowers on the trunk'. Unfortunately while viewing the body he 'actually touched it, with the result that a piece of the nose was broken off, so the story goes. Yet he was unwilling to look at the remains of the Ptolemies, although the Alexandrians were very anxious to show them; Octavian commented, "I wished to see a king, not corpses".'

Presumably unimpressed that the famous treasure was no longer present, save for Alexander's gold breastplate which it would have been impolitic to take, Octavian declined the offer to visit the city's temples. Instead he sent his troops into the Caesareum, the great temple of his adoptive father Julius Caesar, following a tip-off from Antyllus' tutor Theodorus that Antonius' son had taken refuge there. When the fourteen-year-old was found cowering at the feet of Caesar's statue he was 'dragged from the image of the god Julius, to which he had fled, with vain pleas for mercy'. He was then beheaded, allowing his tutor to steal the necklace from what remained of Antyllus' neck before he was captured himself and crucified on the orders of Octavian in punishment for having tried to steal from the body and perhaps to silence him too.

Troops were sent south to seek out Caesarion and his three half-siblings. The three youngest were tracked down to their hiding place in Thebes and sent back to Alexandria under guard while Caesarion, trying to leave the country with a large amount of treasure, was persuaded by his tutor Rhodon to return to Alexandria and negotiate his future. Hearing that the pharaoh was making his way back to the royal city, Octavian 'sent cavalry in pursuit' to bring him back under guard too.

Having seized one half of Cleopatra's treasure from Caesarion, Octavian turned his attentions to the rest and, after managing to reopen the tomb, began to remove its precious contents. Chief among these was the body of Antonius which Octavian wished to see for himself. Well known for according full honours to his own fallen enemies, news of his death made such an impact on his former allies that 'many kings and great commanders made petition to [Octavian] for the body of Antonius to give him his funeral rites, but he would not take the corpse away from Cleopatra by whose hands he was buried with royal splendour and magnificence, it being granted to her to employ what she pleased on his funeral'.

With no further details known, she presumably ordered his body to be washed and laid out 'in state, clothed in splendid raiment'. Although Roman tradition favoured cremation, as had been done for Caesar, there is no mention of this for Antonius who, the ancient sources claim, was 'embalmed'. Yet since his burial 'is not likely to have been delayed more than one or two days' after his death, the standard seventy-day procedure would have been impossible. So either his body was left untreated and simply interred in Cleopatra's mausoleum in a sarco-phagus already in situ, or she made arrangements for the body to be handed over to the embalmers who would then have begun their ten-week task, perhaps within her funerary complex, while she initiated the mourning rites which traditionally lasted for the duration of the embalming process.

Isis incarnate, now the archetypal grieving widow, genuinely mourned her dead Osiris-Dionysos, savagely tearing her face and chest as she lamented the death of Antonius and the end of their dreams. Black eye paint running down her bloodied cheeks would have mingled with the dust she threw over her head until, completely breaking down, she was taken back to the palace, still under guard, her physician Olympus reporting that 'in this extreme of grief and sorrow' she had 'inflamed and ulcerated her breasts with beating them'. Yet, regardless of his treatment, 'she fell into a high fever' between 3 and 8 August and, refusing all food and drink, simply wished to die, asking Olympus to help her do so.

At this point Octavian intervened, and, using 'menacing language about her children', informed her that death was not an option. She must eat and take suitable medication since, so the ancient sources claim, he wanted her alive so that she and her remaining family could appear in Rome to star in his Triumph. Although the reality of a widowed mother and her children might not quite measure up to the terrifying character he had created, some believe he simply wanted her to disappear as soon as possible with no blame on his part. Her execution would certainly damage his reputation for clemency, while, if allowed to live, she would always be a figurehead for rebellion. Yet the ancient sources were almost certainly correct in their belief that she was to feature in his Triumph, for if Octavian had truly wanted her dead he could simply have allowed her to die as she had wished instead of threatening her children.

The sources also claim that Octavian himself visited her around 8 August to check on her recovery, and although some authorities doubt whether such a meeting ever took place and are of the opinion that it was simply invented for dramatic effect, it may well be that direct contact was made if both parties were now residing within the same palace complex, particularly if one was anxious to gain a full picture of all the wealth the other still had in her possession. It is said that, when Octavian was admitted, Cleopatra was lying in bed with Olympus still in attendance, but immediately rose up and fell at his feet, playing along as conquered victim 'as if she desired nothing more than to prolong her life'. Although the recent mourning had left 'her hair and face looking wild and disfigured, her voice quivering, and her eyes sunk in her head', she nevertheless retained 'her old charm and the boldness of her youthful beauty' and 'still sparkled from within'. Some even claimed she had 'dressed herself with studied negligence – indeed, her appearance in mourning wonderfully enhanced her beauty', presumably in spite of the self-inflicted gouges; having had Caesar and Antonius, they claimed, she now tried to seduce Octavian, only 'the chastity of the princeps [Octavian] was too much for her'.

This is a risible claim in the light of Octavian's known promiscuity, and in any case it is hard to believe that Cleopatra could have demonstrated any such reaction to this rather mundane-looking little man whose sole intent was to make an inventory of her remaining assets. For, as the sources do in fact reveal, 'having had by her a list of her treasure, she gave it into his hands', until her finance minister, Seleucus, pointed out that certain articles seemed to have been omitted. At this she is said to have grabbed her minister by the hair and struck him before admitting that she had indeed kept back a few 'women's toys' – pieces of jewellery she had selected as gifts for Livia and Octavia.

Cleopatra had convinced Octavian that she did indeed intend to live, and so, reassured that she was fit to travel to Rome, he withdrew, satisfied that he had deceived her, 'but in fact, was himself deceived.' Already well aware of his plans for the Triumph, Cleopatra was determined to avoid this at all costs; she would literally rather die. Octavian's poets claimed, accurately for once, that 'she, seeking to die more nobly, showed no womanish fear of the sword . . . resolved for death, she was brave indeed. She was no docile woman but truly scorned to be taken away in her enemy's ships, deposed, to an overweening triumph'. When she was informed by Octavian's officer Publius Cornelius Dolabella that Octavian was about to leave for Syria, while she herself would be sent to Rome in three days' time, Cleopatra put her final plan into action.

On 10 August, she requested to be allowed out of her quarters in order to pay her final respects to Antonius before she left Egypt for ever. Still too weak to walk, she was carried in her litter to her funerary complex in the company of Eiras and Charmion and on arrival made appropriate offerings for his soul, perhaps favourites such as 'pure wine and fragrant oil of spikenard, balsam too, and crimson roses'. As she prayed to Antonius' spirit, she told him 'no further offerings or libations expect from me; these are the last honours that Cleopatra can pay your memory . . . But if the gods below, with whom you now are, either can or will do anything, suffer not your living wife to be abandoned; let me not be led in triumph to your shame, but hide me and bury me here with you, since amongst all my bitter misfortunes nothing has afflicted me like this brief time that I have had to live without you.'

When she returned to the palace, passing Epaphroditus and the guards, she withdrew behind the emerald-studded doors into her private quarters, ordering her attendants to prepare her a bath. After she had bathed and perfumed herself, Eiras styled her hair into its usual melon coiffure, carefully braiding each section, pulling it back and securing it in a bun at the back of her head with several large hairpins. Then, with Charmion's help, 'she put on her finest robes' and reclined to eat a splendid lunch, no doubt accompanied by the very finest of wines and polished off with a few large figs brought in fresh from the country.

She then called for a writing tablet and stylus, and in a final missive to Octavian echoed Antonius' desire that they should be buried together in the same tomb. After she had sealed the letter with her signet ring, it was passed out to Epaphroditus who sent it by messenger to Octavian. She dismissed all her staff except Eiras and Charmion, her two most trusted servants, who had supported her through much of her eventful life and would now play their parts in Cleopatra's final performance. Yet it would be a performance which is even now still shrouded in mystery. For, despite the famous snakebite scenario, the ancient sources admit that 'no one knows for certain by what means she perished' since 'what really took place is known to no one'.

Certainly Cleopatra's famous asp can be dismissed as a work of fiction based on her caricature-like effigy with snakes coiling up both arms in the manner of the goddess Isis. When the effigy was later paraded around Rome it was described by Octavian's poets Virgil, Propertius and Horace, who pictured 'the pair of asps in wait for her' and as she 'handled fierce snakes, her corporeal frame drank their venom.' Like so much else they produced, an historical inaccuracy. But the image for which they are responsible – the tragic Cleopatra expiring with at least one asp in tow, an image endlessly recycled by artists down the centuries – is now firmly lodged in history.

Although some later sources claim that 'an asp was brought in amongst those figs and covered with the leaves', and that when Cleopatra saw it she simply said, ' "So here it is" and held out her bare arm to be bitten', the presence of such a snake raises a considerable number of problems. The term 'asp' is used to describe any snake capable of puffing wide its neck and can be applied to several kinds of North African viper, including *Vipera aspis*, the horned viper (*Cerastes cornutus*) and *Cerastes vipera*, which has even gained the nickname 'Cleopatra's asp'. Yet a viper's bite causes an intense reaction: burning pains spread throughout the body, the blood clots, creating disfiguring purple blotches and swellings, and vomiting and incontinence precede the final loss of consciousness.

Since such a snake would have been completely unsuited to Cleopatra's known desire for a dignified end, it has therefore been suggested that the 'asp' was in fact the Egyptian cobra, *Naja haje*, whose poison acts rapidly on the nerves. Other than two small marks from the fangs, there is no damage to the skin. A slight drowsiness leads to gradual paralysis of the body, ending in a fatal coma in full accordance with the ancient description of Cleopatra's choice of snake-based poison 'which without convulsion or groaning brought on a heavy drowsiness and lethargy with a gentle sweat on the face, the sense being stupefied by degrees; the patient, in appearance, being sensible of no pain, but rather troubled to be disturbed or awakened like those that are in a profound natural sleep'.

Almost a century ago it was also suggested that Cleopatra's choice of the cobra may have been based on symbolic reasons, since snakes in general and cobras in particular were an integral part of Egyptian, Greek and Roman symbolism from Alexandria's 'good spirit' Agathos Daimon to the classical 'ourouboros' representing the beginning and end of all things. Alexander himself was believed to have been conceived by means of a sacred snake which could also be the bringer of death. Isis and her consort Osiris-Serapis were both worshipped as snakes; Isis as the great magician Weret-Hekau appeared as a cobra, and the goddess' acolytes carried snakes in much the same way as did devotees of Dionysos. Yet it is the cobra's identification with the sacred uraeus serpent of ancient Egypt which seems to have generated most interest in terms of Cleopatra's motivation. It was worn as an emblem on the crown of all Egyptian pharaohs, and it is claimed that Cleopatra would have regarded this symbol of divine kingship as the perfect means of achieving immortality and most fitting to her status as the last pharaoh of Egypt.

Yet this ingenious explanation ignores the fact that the uraeus was meant to spit venom at the pharaoh's enemies and not at the monarch – not to mention the fact that she already regarded herself as immortal in the form of the Living Isis. And having done all she could in life to guarantee the succession of her son Caesarion, she could surely never have wanted to depict herself as the last of her line.

The use of a cobra also fails from a logistical point of view; because all its venom is discharged in the first bite, a single cobra could never have supplied the means for all three women to take their lives at the same time. Several snakes would therefore be required; in addition, cobras containing sufficient venom to kill a single human are around six feet in length. To conceal three such snakes would require a basket of figs so large that it could surely never have been smuggled past the guards – an unlikely scenario recalling the way in which Cleopatra herself is usually believed to have been smuggled into the palace by a late-night carpet salesman in another episode of creative embellishment.

To circumvent the problem, the ancient sources suggest that a snake may already have been well hidden within Cleopatra's quarters, 'kept in a vase, and that she vexed and pricked it with a golden spindle till it seized her arm'. As a tale which grew in the telling, it was eventually claimed that she had actually been killed by a 'two-headed serpent capable of bounding several feet in the air', and after biting her it had hidden in a pot-plant until Octavian arrived, when it jumped out and bit him too.

The popular desire to believe in a snake-induced suicide seems to ignore the fact that a snake itself did not have to be physically present for its poison to be employed, particularly by a woman apparently so well versed in toxicology. With cobra venom providing a relatively pain-free death without unfortunate side-effects on the body, it was surely simply a matter of hiding its poison prior to use, perhaps blended into some form of ointment as mentioned in one source compiled only a few years after the event. Furthermore, little notice seems to have been paid to several ancient sources which claim that 'she had smeared a pin with some poison whose composition rendered it harmless if the contact were external, but which, if even the smallest quantity entered the bloodstream, would quickly prove fatal, although also painless; according to this theory, she had previously worn the pin in her hair as usual', for 'it was also said she carried poison in a hollow bodkin, about which she wound her hair'.

Such pins would have been a key part of her trademark melon coiffure, tucked away within the hair mass, their portrayal in sculpted images or in the hair of female mummies of the time revealing how such a lethal object could be secreted innocuously about the person. And since female hair was in many ways regarded as inviolable in Roman culture, the Roman soldiers who searched her for concealed weapons and even shook her robes for poisons seem never to have considered investigating her hairstyle. Given that Cleopatra chose to die in the company of her hairdresser Eiras, a woman whom Octavian himself had ridiculed as 'Cleopatra's hair-dressing girl' alongside other courtiers and eunuchs deemed to be incapable of any significant deeds, it must have been with a tremendous sense of satisfaction that Eiras now provided the very means by which Octavian was deprived of his greatest triumph.

In a final flourish, Cleopatra had even directed the layout of this final tableau which would be played out for greatest effect to an audience who would throw open the doors at any time once Octavian had read the letter. Perhaps pausing for a last look out at the sea, the domain of Isis Pharia which stretched out far beyond her window, Cleopatra lay down upon her golden bed and 'with majestic grace, took in her hands all the emblems of royalty'. After neatly arranging Cleopatra's robes about her, Charmion took her place at the head of the bed as Eiras took hers at the foot – specific positions at either end of the body which were the traditional places of Isis and Nephthys as chief guardians of the deceased. With Charmion the royal dresser taking the place of Nephthys, the goddess responsible for the linen which decked out the dead, Isis' close association with the hairdresser's art meant that Eiras was equally well placed to perform this sacred duty as she handed over the hollow hairpin with its lethal contents.

Cleopatra 'made a slight scratch on her arm and had dipped the pin in the blood'. Since the skin was slightly broken, the venomous contents were rapidly absorbed intravenously. As the poison began to take effect, Cleopatra closed her eyes and a gradual numbness crept across her body. The last sounds she heard would have been the low voices of her two women preparing to follow, and the steady lapping of the waves, growing increasingly distant until vanishing completely.

The silence would only have been broken by the sound of hobnailed soles against the palace's marble floors as Octavian's men hurried through the ante-rooms and flung open the doors, to find Cleopatra dead, 'lying upon a bed of gold, set out in all her royal ornaments. Eiras, one of her women, lay dying at her feet, and Charmion, just ready to fall, scarce able to hold up her head, was adjusting her mistress's diadem' inherited from Alexander as her symbol of power. Clearly stunned by the calculated effect of the stage-managed sight before them, one of the men asked angrily, 'Was this well done of your lady, Charmion?' 'Extremely well done,' she answered defiantly with her final breath, 'and as befitting the descendant of so many kings.'

12

Epilogue: the Aftermath

As soon as Octavian received Cleopatra's letter requesting burial with Antonius, he rushed to her quarters since 'he was so anxious to save Cleopatra as an ornament for his triumph'. Ordering specialist physicians to try to revive her, the men were unable to find any obvious cause of death, and no signs of violence: 'the only marks that were found on her body were tiny pricks on the arm'.

Paying little attention to any hairpins scattered around or indeed reinserted into the hair, they assumed that such marks must have been made by a snake. Yet of the three large cobras which would have been needed to kill all three women, not a single snake was found, 'only something like the trail of it was said to have been noticed on the sand by the sea, on the part towards which the building faced and where the windows were'. Nevertheless, it was said that Octavian 'actually summoned Psyllian snake-charmers to suck the poison from her self-inflicted wound, supposedly from the bite of an asp'. Renowned for their ability 'if sent for immediately, to suck out the venom of any reptile before the victim dies', some of these Libyan Psylli presumably practised in Alexandria.

Their Egyptian equivalents were priests of the scorpion goddess Selket, experts in the treatment of scorpion stings and snakebites, who employed complex rites set down in the medical texts. A Ptolemaic treatment specifically for snakebite listed twenty-one types of snake and the different gods associated with them, followed by a prognostic test to find out 'Will the patient live or die?' Treatment then involved cutting out the bite and applying natron salt to reduce swelling, in the way that magnesium sulphate might be used today; alternatively the wound might be treated with various combinations of onion, beer, carob, terebinth, kyphi, mustard or a decoction of mandrake root.

Certainly some form of emergency treatment was administered to Cleopatra, since Octavian 'not only came to see her body, but called in the aid of drugs and of the Psylli in an attempt to revive her', their reciting of the correct incantation an equally vital part of such treatment. For, as one Ptolemaic spell stated, 'the poison does not enter the heart here, nor burn the breast here . . . Osiris' sword destroys the poison, it cools the burn, when the snakes – merbu, wartet, ketet – come out!' Such spells also listed the traditional gods Selket, Ra and Horus, although the deity most often invoked was Isis, consummate physician and the expert healer in cases of snakebite.

Yet despite every medical and magical attempt to revive her, it was too late. Cleopatra had escaped. She had defiantly predicted, 'I will not be shown in a Triumph', and it is said that Octavian 'was bitterly chagrined on his own account, as if all the glory of his victory had been taken away from him'.

But he also realised that, to be seen as her legal successor by the Egyptians, some of whom rose up in revolt at news of her death, he must give his predecessor proper burial. So, honouring her last wishes, he ordered her tomb to be completed and her body to be buried alongside that of Antonius, presumably handing her body over to the embalmers since the sources maintain that the couple 'were both embalmed in the same manner and buried in the same tomb'.

The timing of Cleopatra's funerary rites was certainly significant from a ritual point of view, for, only two days after her death on 10 August, the Egyptians celebrated the Birthday of Isis, the Lychnapsia or 'Festival of Lights' to commemorate the time when Isis searched the darkness by torchlight for the body of Osiris. So, as every Isis temple across Egypt and beyond blazed with light, the body of Living Isis was laid out in her tomb beside the goddess' temple on Alexandria's Lochias peninsula, her devotees taking comfort in the legend that the goddess could never die. For, unlike her husband Osiris, Isis herself had never suffered death but was perceived as a human queen who had simply passed into another dimension in order to resurrect the dead. A later literary work, based on the pharaonic Ancestor Ritual, had Cleopatra describing how the dead await the waters of rebirth to be reborn, and the idea that Isis' temples allowed the souls of the dead to be revived was reflected in the belief that at least one of her shrines was 'full of ghosts'.

Accompanying their mistress into the beyond were Charmion and Eiras, whose loyalty became proverbial in Alexandria. Octavian ordered that 'her women also received honorable burial by his directions', presumably within Cleopatra's mausoleum following the age-old practice of burying servants with those they had served in life during Egypt's earliest periods. Statues of the two serving women were also set up at the burial site. However, claims that Octavian gave orders for Cleopatra to receive a burial 'with royal splendour and magnificence' failed to mention that she was nevertheless deprived of her vital, albeit precious funerary equipment. It is said that 'great quantities of treasure were found in the palace', and in his rampant asset-stripping, Octavian melted down the royal plate and all the precious metals he could find, sending back to Rome all Cleopatra's other treasures including her personal jewellery and her remaining great pearl worth around 10 million sesterces. And although his biographer was keen to point out that he only kept for himself 'a single agate cup', he somehow found sufficient funds to purchase the ultimate status symbol, his own island, when he bought himself Capri the following year.

The Egyptian wealth sent back to Rome ended thirteen years of economic depression overnight as 'the rate of interest fell from 12 to 4%'. Octavian could also now guarantee huge supplies of Egyptian grain each year, and was finally able to give his troops their long overdue back pay. One later Roman source claimed that he 'seduced the army with bonuses, and his cheap food policy was successful bait for civilians. Indeed, he attracted everybody's goodwill by the enjoyable gift of peace', eliminating all possible opposition as 'war or judicial murder had disposed of all men of spirit' and clearly one woman.

Following Cleopatra's death on the 17th day of Mesore, to 10 August, Egypt was apparently ruled by her children for a period of some three weeks until Octavian's regime began on the first day of the following month, 1st Thoth, 31 August 30 BC, when Egypt was formally annexed by Rome. Having made himself Cleopatra's legitimate heir by ordering her burial and completing her tomb, Octavian ordered the execution of her eldest son and co-regent Caesarion, the fifteenth and final Ptolemy whose dynasty had ruled Egypt for almost three hundred years.

Agreeing with Arius' opinion that 'it is bad to have too many Caesars', paraphrasing a line from the Iliad, Octavian had finally made himself sole heir of Julius Caesar, ordering work to be carried out on the Caesarium which Cleopatra had created in Caesar's honour and which he rededicated in honour of himself. He nevertheless continued with Cleopatra's plans by ordering the pair of granite obelisks she had selected from Heliopolis to be set up at either side of the huge entrance way. Each stood on the back of four giant bronze crabs whose claws, inscribed in Greek and Latin, announced that they had been set up on the orders of Octavian; the obelisks, however, eventually taken to London and New York, are still quite rightly known as 'Cleopatra's Needles'.

The Caesarium's interior was home to numerous statues in keeping with Egypt's long tradition of ancestor worship, but Octavian now set up marble statues of himself to replace those of the previous regime. Female images were required to compete with those of Cleopatra, so statues of his wife Livia were set up together with those of other female relatives. The bust of a young woman recently found in Alexandria's harbour had been identified on the basis of her hairstyle as Octavia's youngest daughter, Antonia Minor.

Yet there were no such favours for her father Antonius, whose statues were pulled down and smashed wherever they were found. The obelisk that Cleopatra had erected in his honour was rededicated to Rome's conquest of Egypt, and, with his name chiselled out of every official inscription, Octavian declared 14 January, the day of Antonius' birth, to be 'nefastus' or unholy.

The destruction of Cleopatra's own statues was only prevented when 'Archibius, one of her friends, gave [Octavian] two thousand talents to save them'. Such a sum would support the Roman army for a whole year, and it was an offer that even Octavian could not refuse. Although Archibius is generally assumed to have been a courtier with more money than sense, only the temples would have been capable of finding such an extraordinary sum, particularly since they would have needed Cleopatra's statuary to remain intact as a vital part of Egypt's divine ancestor cult. And given that Archibius' Egyptian name was Horemakhbyt, it has been plausibly suggested that he was spokesman for the Egyptian clergy following the death of the teenage high priest Petubastis.

Not only had the high priest's death seriously affected national administration, it had deeply changed matters within the ancient Egyptian capital, Memphis, where new rulers of Egypt were traditionally confirmed and crowned by the hereditary high priest. This was now no longer possible since 'the Memphite dynasty was extinguished at the same moment as the House of the Ptolemies'. The Egyptian records even suggest that Octavian's forces had ransacked the tomb of the previous high priest, Pasherenptah III, for although he had died ten years before and been buried alongside his wife Taimhotep, his body had to be remummified and reburied in 30 BC, presumably following its desecration. So, to prevent the body of his unfortunate son and heir Petubastis sharing the same fate, it was kept in the embalmers' workshop for a staggering seven years before it was felt sufficiently safe to bury his mummy with its 'gold and silver ornaments with protective amulets of all sorts of genuine precious stones'.

Having secured Alexandria, Octavian moved on to Memphis where the high priest's nearest living relative, Psenamun of Letopolis, had to be drafted in to become Octavian's high priest, designated 'divus filius', 'divine son' of Julius Caesar, or 'god and son of a god' in Egyptian. Although he was worshipped as such within the great temple complex of Memphis, it is perhaps telling that Psenamun was the first and last high priest of Octavian. After the unfortunate Petubastis was finally buried seven years after his death, priestly records ceased in 23 BC.

Refusing to follow his female predecessor's enthusiasm for native religion, Octavian 'would not go out of his way, however slightly, to honour the divine Apis bull'. He claimed 'to worship gods, not cattle', and his feelings were echoed by his spin doctor poets who ridiculed the 'demented', 'deranged' Egyptians and their absurd devotion to such sacred creatures. In a complete break with Ptolemaic practices, the new regime were reluctant to pay for the animals' costly burials, and they were increasingly wrapped in recycled papyri rather than best-quality linen. A similar situation was reflected in burials of the Buchis bulls at Hermonthis. When the twenty-four-year-old bull which Cleopatra had once rowed along the Nile at the very start of her reign died soon after she did, the sandstone stela marking its burial named Octavian but lacked any accompanying titles or even a cartouche.

The Hermonthis clergy, 'the angry priests', were apparently unwilling to acknowledge the legitimacy of a successor by using his official titles, even though they had already been devised. Anti-Roman feelings are also suggested by the requirement that all temple personnel, from the highest priest to the lowliest worker, had to swear an oath that they would not abandon their posts and take part in rebellion. A surviving document from the Fayum refers to two men,

> both lamplighters in the temple of Serapis, most great god, and of the Isis shrine there, and Paapis son of Thonis and Petorisris son of Patoiphos, both lamp-lighters in the temple of Taweret, most great goddess, at Oxyrynchos. All four swear by Caesar, god and son of a god, to the overseers of the temples in the Oxyrynchos and Kynopolitye nomes, that we will superintend the lamps of the above named temples in the Oxyrynchos and Kynopolitye nomes, that we will superintend the lamps of the above named temples and will supply proper oil for the daily lamps burning in the temples signified from Thoth 1 to Mesore 5 of the present year 1 of Caesar in accordance with what was supplied up to the 22nd which was year 7 of Cleopatra; and we the aforesaid are mutually sureties and all our property is security for the performance of the duties herein written.

Yet clearly such oaths proved ineffective, so in reaction to ongoing native unrest which, as always, focused on the temples, Octavian confiscated all temple lands and placed the clergy under the 'high priest of Alexandria and all Egypt', a new appointee responsible for enforcing strict rules concerning everything from priestly dress to their behaviour. He also gave orders for his statuary to be set up throughout the country, a giant bronze image erected in the far south at Aswan embellished with large, inlaid eyes to reflect his own which gleamed 'like those of horses, the whites being larger than usual'; it was also a means of keeping a symbolic watch over the border with Nubia, home of the nomadic Blemmyes and Nobatae.

These volatile peoples were devotees of Isis too, which perhaps explains why, regardless of his true feelings towards Egypt and its gods, Octavian was keen to have himself portrayed at Philae in full pharaonic garb, bringing myrrh, wine and all good things to Isis and her fellow gods. He was even named 'beloved of Ptah and Isis'. Further south at

Kalabsha in Nubia, he ordered towering figures of Cleopatra and Caesarion offering to Isis on a 23-foot-high gateway to be recarved as himself, accompanied by cartouches naming him 'the Roman' and 'Caesar the god, son of the god'.

Although Octavian was portrayed as a traditional pharaoh on Egypt's monuments in order to conform to a culture built entirely around the central figure of a king, the country was soon ruled in absentia when he left Egypt for Syria, finally returning to Italy in the summer of 29 BC. Although he and his Roman successors would continue to use the traditional pharaonic titles 'King of Upper and Lower Egypt, Lord of the Two Lands, son of Ra', they added the additional phrase 'he whose power is incomparable in the City par excellence that he loves, Rome', making clear that Egypt's pharaoh no longer resided in Egypt.

Having reduced Cleopatra's fiercely independent kingdom to little more than his personal domain, he treated the Egyptians themselves differently from other subject peoples. Allowed neither to enter the Roman Senate, as they had been in Ptolemaic times, nor even to serve in the army, they were reduced to little more than serfs producing grain for Rome. And, with Egypt's borders closed to foreigners, travel was only possible by means of a special visa. Any Roman of senatorial class was forbidden to visit Egypt without his express permission, and he 'took a leaf from Alexander's book when [he] decided to keep Egypt under strict surveillance'. Fully aware of the risks associated with handing Egypt over to anyone in the Senate, Octavian appointed the lesser-ranking general Cornelius Gallus, one of the men who had arrested Cleopatra, as his 'Prefect of Egypt and Alexandria' – 'praefectus Aegypti et Alexandreae'. Having successfully dealt with rebellions in the south, Gallus commissioned celebratory inscriptions at temples such as Philae, 'caused a list of his achievements to be inscribed upon the pyramids' and even set up his own statuary throughout Egypt. Yet it is also reported Gallus 'circulated much disparaging gossip' about Octavian who prosecuted him for treason and killed himself.

Yet serious unrest would continue across much of southern Egypt, and later, in 24–23 BC, Octavian would suffer a serious defeat at in 24–23 BC at the hands of 'Queen Candace', the Meroitic Kandake or female ruler Amanirenas. As the forces of this 'second Cleopatra' marched over the border from Sudan into Egypt and overwhelmed three Roman cohorts to seize Aswan, they took many prisoners and 'even wrenched from their bases the statues of Caesar', explaining how the head of Octavian's large bronze statue with inlaid eyes ended up 470 miles south in Meroe, buried beneath temple steps to be symbolically trampled underfoot Egyptian-style by all those entering the sacred precincts.

Having already taken his leave of Egypt which he never visited again, on 13 August 29 BC Octavian had finally entered Rome. There he celebrated three lavish Triumphs to mark his victories in Illyria, Aktion and Egypt – it was said that 'all the processions presented a striking appearance on account of the spoils of Egypt'. Cleopatra's vast wealth and funerary equipment were displayed in a parade which culminated in the appearance of her eleven-year-old twins, beneath a sign naming them simply 'Sol et Luna', Sun and Moon. Any suggestion that Octavian had been relieved to be rid of Cleopatra in case he offended public opinion by displaying her in the Triumph was surely offset by his use of her children, forced to march through Rome beside a great wax image of their dead mother. This 'effigy of the dead Cleopatra lying on a couch, so that in a sense she too, together with the live captives, who included her children . . . formed a part of the pageant' even included the theatrical portrayal of asps winding bracelet-style up her arms toward her chest, revealing to the illiterate crowds her death by snake venom.

Amongst those lining the route to celebrate Cleopatra's death, the poet Propertius and his girlfriend secured such a good vantage point of the effigy he could claim 'I've seen the sacred adders' fang upon her bosom close and hang, and her whole body slowly creep on the dark road to endless sleep'. Fellow poet Horace also marked the occasion by rewriting the rather sombre poem he had written soon after Aktion, any reservations that Cleopatra still lived now replaced by joy and relief at her death. For now Rome was finally able to crack open the vintage wine and celebrate in full, his 'Cleopatra Ode' beginning 'Nunc est bibendum', 'Now is the time to drain the flowing bowl, now with unfettered foot to beat the ground with dancing, now with feasting to deck the couches of the gods, my comrades!'.

The culmination of the Triumph was the execution of prisoners in the Forum, after which the conquering hero Octavian then ascended the

Capitoline Hill to offer sacrifice in the temple of Jupiter at the summit. Since this was the religious heart of Rome, from which Cleopatra had supposedly wished to rule, Octavian distributed largesse around the Capitol's most important shrines of Jupiter (Zeus), Juno (Hera) and Minerva (Athena), each one stripped of all previous dedications and embellished with the rich spoils of Cleopatra's Egypt. He admitted that his gifts to Rome's temples 'cost me about 100,000,000 sesterces', and it is surely more than coincidence that 'the largest mass of rock crystal ever seen' weighing around 150lb (68 kg), was dedicated in the Capitol's temple complex by his wife Livia. It was just possibly the crystal that Cleopatra had intended for her Alexander-style coffin, although its astronomical value meant that this was something she would never have been permitted to keep, even after death.

Octavian built a total of ten new temples, repairing more than eighty others all 'at great expense, without any inscription of my name'. Having commissioned the great temple known as the Pantheon, he adorned it with a new statue of Venus. Keen to reclaim the goddess for Rome and to symbolise Cleopatra's defeat, he adorned his new statue with her remaining huge pearl 'cut in two pieces, so that half a helping of the jewel might be in each of the ears.' He even took for his new statue the pearl necklace she herself had placed on Caesar's statue of Venus in his family temple in the Forum.

Although mindful of his pledge to leave this, like all statues of Cleopatra, intact, Octavian nevertheless changed its immediate sur-roundings by creating a much larger Forum with a somewhat phallic layout. Two semi-circular galleries or exedrae appear to form testicles and a long projecting forecourt extended into the area of Caesar's Venus temple so that 'the buildings could be imagined as having sexual intercourse' in a very subtle, albeit disturbing, use of architectural domination.

Certainly Octavian had learned much from his time in Alexandria, and keeping to the plans Caesar himself had drawn up with Cleopatra's advice, Octavian inaugurated the new Senate House which Caesar had initiated. He could also claim that 'I found Rome built of sun dried bricks – I leave her clothed in marble', when marble was used for the first time in the city to cover Apollo's temple on the Palatine Hill. Behind doors of imported ivory, panels of North African marble and glazed relief figures of Apollo-Octavian battling Antonius-Herakles gave way to an Alexandrian-style library where 'all that men of old and new times thought, with learned minds, is open to inspection by the reader.'

In the grand tradition of Roman generals who had for centuries carted off antiquities from Greece and the East to enhance their more modest city, Octavian ordered a succession of statues and obelisks to be brought back from Egypt, initiating a trend which led to more obelisks ending up in Rome than remained in Egypt. Of two brought from the great temple of the sun god Ra at Heliopolis to symbolise his victory over Egypt, that of Seti I was set up in the centre of the Circus Maximus (now in the Piazza del Popolo) while the second, originally commissioned by the Saite king Psammetichus II, was reinscribed with Octavian's name and set up in the Campus Martius (now in Monte Citorio) in the centre of a marble and bronze pavement. Marked out in lines and an Egyptian-inspired Zodiac to create a giant sundial 100 yards across called the Solarium Augusti, 'the biggest clock of all time' was obviously influenced by the Egyptian method of using sunlight and shadow to mark time and key events. The 100-foot-high obelisk at its centre was erected in such a way that twice a year, at sunset on Octavian's birthday, 23 September (the autumn equinox), and again on 21 March (the spring equinox), its shadow fell straight across the dial and up the steps to touch the altar of the 'Peace of Augustus', inscribed with the legend that 'Augustus gave this gift to the Sun, having brought Egypt into the power of the Roman People'.

Eventually two more granite obelisks (now in the Piazza dell'Esquilino and the Piazza del Quirinale) were imported from Egypt to flank the entrance to the ambitious mausoleum that Octavian had begun to build on the Campus Martius as early as 28 BC. Quite possibly inspired by that of Cleopatra, his dynastic sepulchre, complete with gardens and trees, featured a façade as found on great royal tombs across the East. Beneath the domed top, the tomb was essentially a step pyramid in cross-section, and as Egyptomania took hold of Rome wealthy men such as Gaius Cestius even built their own pyramid-shaped tombs in the middle of the eternal city.

Although Octavian would always maintain he had restored the Republic in the face of threatened monarchy from the East, he became Rome's princeps or 'leading citizen', effectively its first emperor, in

January 28 BC, after which his totalitarian regime determined virtually every aspect of life from legislating on public morals to suppressing such undesirable cults as Isis worship. He even pronounced on dress, ordering all male citizens to wear the toga and married women the all-concealing long dress and mantle.

Such policies were simply rubber-stamped by the compliant Senate, who wished to mark his elevation to power with a new name connecting him directly with Rome. Some favoured Romulus, the founder of the city and its first king, until his advisers pointed out connotations with monarchy and tyranny. So, as a more honourable alternative, Munatius Plancus suggested the name 'Augustus', quoting an epigram which stated 'when glorious Rome had founded been, by augury august'. Although ground consecrated by the augurs was indeed known as 'august', it seems more than coincidental that Plancus, who had once danced before Cleopatra, the New Isis, would have known that another of her divine titles was 'Isis Augusta', meaning majestic and sacred. So it was that the banker's son Gaius Octavianus became Augustus Caesar in 27 BC after lifting a name from the goddess persona of Cleopatra.

It was also decided that a month should be named to celebrate Octavian's new name in the same way that the fifth month, Quinctilis, had been renamed July in honour of Julius Caesar's birth month. Yet instead of selecting his own birth month, September, the newly named Augustus claimed Sextilis as the month of Augustus, ordering 'that the month renamed in his honour should be the one in which he brought down Cleopatra' and the first day of August, the day Alexandria had surrendered, was declared a public holiday.

From that time onwards avoiding any reference to Cleopatra, Antonius or the civil war, Octavian simply stated 'Aegyptum imperio populi Romani adieci', 'I added Egypt to the empire of the Roman people', even though he had made Egypt his personal possession. After first isolating its people from the rest of the ancient world by forbidding any Roman to visit Egypt or any Egyptian to visit Rome, he made sure that his version of events was never contradicted by implementing a policy of mass censorship. Thousands of contradictory or incriminating texts, from the Sibylline books to the writings of Julius Caesar, were burnt. A brief missive to his Surveyor of Libraries ordered the removal of any works deemed 'unsuitable' for public consumption, replacing them with his own rewriting of history, greatly enhanced by the pens of his eloquent poets.

Yet despite such drastic measures, some sources did survive. When the royal archives in Alexandria were taken over and countless official documents binned as waste paper, some were recycled as mummy cartonnage and only discovered two thousand years later when Cleopatra's handwriting came to light. The funerary inscriptions of the high priests of Memphis, concealed beneath Sakkara's drifting sands, were only rediscovered and translated in modern times, while the complexities of Ptolemaic hieroglyphs on temple walls 'were enough to safeguard embarrassing facts and dangerous sentiments' from the eyes of Octavian's agents.

The names and images of Cleopatra and Antonius also survived on their coinage, the silver currency of Antonius remaining in circulation for some 250 years, far longer than the softer gold coins of Octavian which lasted a century at most. And, like his coinage, Antonius' genes too proved the more durable. Fathering only a single child, Julia, Octavian repeatedly used her for his own political ends, first betrothing her to Antonius' son Antyllus and then, after his execution, to the distinctly non-Roman king of the Getae in contradiction of Roman law. She was finally married off to her cousin, Octavia's son Marcellus, in 25 BC, and on his premature death she was passed on to the elderly Agrippa in belated thanks for winning Octavian his many battles. Despite the twenty-five-year age gap they had two sons, Gaius and Lucius, who became Octavian's heirs. At Agrippa's death Julia was forced to marry Livia's son Tiberius to provide a father figure for the boys, yet, with neither party keen on the marriage, Julia had a number of affairs. Following her relationship with Antonius' youngest son, Iullus, he was forced to commit suicide by Octavian while Julia was charged with promiscuity under her father's strict moral laws, exiled to the small island of Pandateria and even denied burial in the family tomb. Since her sons also mysteriously died young, Octavian was left with little choice but to adopt his adult stepson Tiberius as his successor when he himself finally passed away in AD 14 aged seventy-five, some say poisoned by Livia who wanted her ageing son as emperor.

Yet, in contrast to Octavian's distinct lack of success as a dynast,

Antonius' descendants were prolific and widespread. In the East, his half-Asiatic granddaughter Pythodoris was married off to his former client kings, first Polemon of Pontus and then Archelaus of Cappadocia. In the West, his grandson Claudius and great-grandsons Caligula and Nero were the three emperors who succeeded Octavian and Tiberius.

Under their successive reigns so much Eastern splendour was revived that there were once again rumours that Alexandria would replace Rome as the capital of the empire. Antonius' memory was rehabilitated by his great-grandson Caligula, who ordered the obelisk that Cleopatra had set up in Antonius' honour to be brought from Alexandria and set up close to Rome's centre of Isis worship (now in the Piazza di San Pietro outside the Vatican). Caligula gave Isis' cult state recognition after its violent suppression under the previous regime, fostered his own divinity based on mysteries related to Isis' cult and even pursued a Ptolemaic-style marriage to his sister. As an admirer of Alexander the Great, he also had suitable offerings presented to Alexander's mummy, taking its golden breastplate for himself and very nearly adopting the Ptolemic-style royal diadem when dining with foreign kings.

After his distinctly un-Roman behaviour hastened his assassination Caligula was succeeded by Antonius' grandson Claudius, who continued to support the Isis cult by commissioning the elaborate altar known as 'the mensa Isiaca', decorated with images of Isis and the sacred bulls. Claudius' military tribune Gaius Stertimius Xenophon was also a priest of Isis and Serapis, and though Octavian and his immediate family had all been cremated according to Roman custom and their ashes placed within the family mausoleum, their urns gave way to sarcophagi when at least one member of the imperial family chose to be embalmed Egyptian-style.

As Egypt's influence continued to spread through Rome, helped by such courtiers as Chaeremon, a former librarian at Alexandria and expert on Egyptian civilisation, the writing of 'Aigyptiaka', books about Egypt, became a popular literary pastime. As a noted historian and author of works on Etruscan and Carthaginian history, Claudius himself began a modern history of Rome beginning with Caesar's murder in 44 BC, until his grandmother Livia strongly advised him to leave out events before 30 BC and any mention of Cleopatra, for even he as emperor 'would not be allowed to publish a free and unvarnished report on the intervening period'. With the censorship supported by Claudius' mother Antonia, Antonius' daughter by Octavia, Antonius' daughter by Cleopatra conversely did all she could to keep her parents' legacy very much alive, for Cleopatra Selene was 'totally her mother's daughter'.

Although many historians like to believe that all three of the couple's children had been spared, based on the claim that Octavian 'brought them up no less tenderly than if they had been members of his own family, and gave them the education their rank deserved', seven-year-old Ptolemy Philadelphos was not mentioned as part of the Triumph of 29 BC and may well have succumbed to his first cold winter in Rome. The Triumph was also, ominously, the last official sighting of Alexander Helios, who died 'before military and marriageable age'. His bride-to-be, Iotape, now surplus to requirements, was sent back to her father Artavasdes, who was pardoned by Octavian and made client king of Armenia. Iotape herself was married off to a fellow client king in Commagene.

As the only surviving child of Cleopatra, eleven-year-old Cleopatra Selene was sent to live with the saintly Octavia whose household consisted of her own teenage sons by her first marriage, her two daughters by Antonius, the two Antonias, aged nine and six, and thirteen-year-old Iullus, Antonius and Fulvia's remaining son after Octavian had beheaded his older brother Antyllus. The children were raised and educated to become the means of creating political alliances, and Selene was part of Octavian's plan for North Africa. She was now betrothed to Prince Juba, who had lived in Rome ever since Caesar had brought him back from North Africa as a four-year-old, been granted Roman citizenship, taken the name Gaius Julius Juba and remained with Caesar, presumably meeting Cleopatra VII during her time in Rome. Then, taking up residence in Octavia's household, the bookish prince was made client king of Mauritania and Numidia in 25 BC and married to Selene.

Although officially only queen of Mauritania and Numidia, Selene had been awarded Cyrene by her parents in the Donations ceremony, while her status as sole remaining child of Cleopatra VII meant she must surely have regarded herself as ruler of Egypt by birth. As heirs to the whole of North Africa, in theory if not in practice, Juba and Selene ruled their kingdom from their coastal capital, Iol. They renamed it

Caesarea (modern Cherchel), which may have applied as much to Julius Caesar as to Octavian, and re-created Cleopatra's court within a luxurious palace complex embellished with superb mosaics, marble walls and swathes of rich purple fabrics produced at Juba's dye factories at Mogador. The palace was filled with relief carvings of sphinxes, bronze figures of Dionysos and lamps of Alexandrian design, and large quantities of statuary were imported from Egypt. There were 1500-year-old statues of the pharaohs Tuthmosis I, and Tuthmosis III, a giant uraeus snake and a head of Amun, perhaps sourced from Thebes to perpetuate the dynastic link with Alexander and his divine father.

Within a veritable 'gallery of ancestors', stunning marble busts of the very handsome, curly-haired Juba stood alongside images of the equally attractive Selene, whose sculpted portraits carried all 'the marks of her devotion and love for her mother country'. Inheriting her mother's love of pearls and lush fabrics, she honoured her memory by adopting her trademark melon hairstyle, albeit adorned with more defined snail-like curls to frame her somewhat fuller face.

Another piece of family statuary set up by the couple was an image of Ptolemy I, together with a basalt statue of the last high priest of Memphis, Petubastis III, a half-cousin who appears to have been close to the royal family. The statue was inscribed with the sixteen-year-old Petubastis' death date, 31 July 30 BC, when, just like Selene's half-brothers Caesarion and Antyllus, he had been killed on Octavian's orders.

Yet the most spectacular piece the couple set up was a large marble statue of Cleopatra VII herself. A world away from the somewhat soft-focus, unthreatening portraits of Cleopatra made during her stay in Rome as a young woman, 'the veiled head shows perhaps a different portrait type of Cleopatra VII'. This veritable tour de force captures the essence of this vital, spirited woman whose subsequent achievements were celebrated by the daughter who presumably commissioned it. The head was partly covered by her mantle, and both ears were pierced to take earrings which were likely to be new versions of her famous pearls; the way the curling hair was carved over the brow strongly resembles that of a Roman period head of Alexander the Great also from North Africa, quite possibly Selene's way of reinforcing her mother's connections with their dynasty's renowned ancestor. Indeed, this face of Cleopatra with its 'prominent but beautiful nose' is so very strong that some have even claimed it represents a man; given its strong similarities to Cleopatra's masculine-style coin images and the tremendous achievements influencing its creation, such confusion seems unsurprising.

The new court also seems to have inspired silverware of equally astonishing quality: a stunning silver dish featuring a central female figure is quite likely to be Selene herself. Her tousled curls above the brow are 'arranged in no recognisable coiffure', just as on the marble head she created of her mother, and the same type of pierced ears are visible beneath the elephant-skin cap of Alexander, surrounded by all the emblems of Ptolemaic Egypt from the sistrum and cobra to the cornucopia. Selene's own crescent moon emblem was coupled with the image of Helios in memory of her brother Alexander Helios, while images of the lyre, grapes and pine cones of Dionysos together with the club and quiver of Herakles paid tribute to her father Antonius.

Like Antonius and Cleopatra, Selene and Juba used their coinage to put across a political message: Rex Juba appeared on one side and Basilissa Cleopatra on the other. Her portraits suggest that she 'inherited her mother's strong prominent nose but leave us with the impression that she was probably prettier than Cleopatra VII' — or at least less threatening-looking. Often representing Isis by means of the crescent moon emblem, Selene's coins also featured the Egyptian sistrum, crown of double plumes and sun disc and the image of a crocodile as a characteristic emblem of Egypt. The couple certainly kept live crocodiles within the capital's great Isis temple, adorned with statuary of the goddess, and the cult was sufficiently popular to inspire Apuleius, a Romanised North African (from modern Algeria) whose famous second-century AD work *Metamorphoses* is the only complete Roman 'novel' to have survived, complete with superb details of the workings of the Isis cult.

The strong continuity with Selene's homeland of Egypt was also reflected in the architects, painters, writers and scholars who flocked to her court, while Juba's personal physician Euphorbus was the brother of Antonius' Greek freedman Antonius Musa. Both were leading practitioners in hydrotherapy treatments, presumably carried out in Caesarea's luxurious bath complex which was supplied by a colossal aqueduct. The couple also built a grand theatre and hippodrome alongside a great library which developed as a centre of learning.

Juba himself was described as being 'even more distinguished for his renown as a student than for his royal sovereignty', and his passion for philology, history and geography was reflected by the expeditions the couple sent out across their sphere of influence. These travelled as far west as the Atlantic islands dubbed 'Canaria' (from Latin *canis*) after the large dogs to be found there and brought back a pair of hounds for Juba himself; the Canary Islands' date palms and papyrus evoked Selene's homeland while sophisticated forms of mummification also developed.

In trying to forge ever stronger connections with Egypt, they also sent out an expedition to find the mysterious source of the Nile. Herodotus had claimed that Egypt's great river ran horizontally west to east across North Africa, Alexander's tutor Aristotle had suggested that its source might indeed lie to the west, and it had been a problem that Juba's protector Caesar had once wrestled with himself. Obviously keen to find out for themselves, the couple despatched their explorers who believed they had discovered the source of the Nile in the mountains of their kingdom of Mauretania, 'so far as King Juba was able to ascertain'.

Apparently separating North Africa from Ethiopia, since 'the Nile above the 3rd cataract, together with its tributary, the Atbara, can indeed be envisaged as dividing Ethiopia from Egypt', this apparent discovery was referred to by the poet Crinagoras of Mytilene. In his epigram to celebrate Juba and Selene's marriage, he announced, 'Great neighbour regions of the world, which the full stream of Nile separates from the black Aethiopians, you have made common kings for both by marriage, making a single race of Egyptians and Libyans. May the king's children hold from their fathers in their turn firm dominion over both mainlands.'

When Selene and Juba had their first child some time between 13 and 9 BC they named him Ptolemy. Although few personal details have survived, Selene clearly exerted a powerful influence given the overtly Egyptian style of her court and 'the unusually elevated status of women at Caesaraea in the centuries following her death', when educated women such as the grammarian Volusia Tertullina were part of a prominent female elite. When Selene died aged around thirty-five, perhaps in childbirth, her passing was linked to a lunar eclipse. Once more inspired, the poet Crinagoras claimed that 'when she rose the moon herself grew dark, veiling her grief in night, for she saw her lovely namesake Selene bereft of life and going down to gloomy Hades. With her she had shared her light's beauty, and with her death she mingled her own darkness.'

Presumably mummified in the manner of her dynasty, Cleopatra Selene was buried in the royal necropolis some 20 miles east of the capital Iol Caesarea within 'the public memorial of the royal family'. This was most likely the huge circular tomb which Juba II is believed to have built, measuring over 200 feet in diameter. Its exterior façade set with sixty Ionic columns featured at each of the cardinal points an elegantly carved 'false door', recalling a traditional Egyptian feature favoured by Cleopatra VII herself and above which a series of stone steps of diminishing diameter rose 75 feet towards the summit.

By combining the Eastern circular mausoleum with ancient Egyptian funerary architecture, Juba and Selene had created a step pyramid with a twist. The tomb's concealed entrance, located below the false door on the eastern side to face the rising sun, opened onto a vaulted passage which led through to a rectangular ante-chamber, from which seven steps gave access to a circular, vaulted gallery running anti-clockwise for some 500 feet. At the end of the gallery as it spiralled back towards the centre of the tomb, an Egyptian-style sliding limestone portcullis mechanism sealed the burial chamber 'which could have held only two or three inhumation burials'; although ransacked at some time in antiquity, the chamber entered in 1885 still contained traces of the original contents, from carnelian beads and an Egyptian pendant to a few scattered pearls, so beloved of Selene's famous mother.

Juba long outlived his wife, travelling around the East and briefly remarrying before returning to Mauretania in AD 5. In AD 21 he took as his co-regent his son Ptolemy, who following Juba's death in AD 23, became king of Mauretania in his own right. His titles were confirmed by Tiberius and the Senate, who declared him a 'friend and ally of the Roman people', while a senatorial delegation presented him with an ivory sceptre and the triumphal purple toga known as the 'toga picta', embroidered with stars.

A superb marble head from the royal capital reveals Ptolemy to have been as handsome as his father Juba, his lightly bearded face and neat hairstyle clearly influenced by his Roman contemporaries. Although little is known about Ptolemy's personal life, with no official records of a wife or children, mention of 'Regina Urania', assumed to be a court lady with royal pretensions, may perhaps refer to a royal relative who chose to follow her illustrious Ptolemaic predecessors by taking the name 'Ourania' by which Aphrodite herself was known.

Having apparently amassed great wealth, Ptolemy felt sufficiently independent of Rome by his eighteenth regnal year to issue gold coins featuring his triumphal regalia and ivory sceptre, perhaps reflecting his success in dealing with intermittent rebellions within his kingdom. He also spent time abroad, travelling to Greece and being honoured at Athens with a statue inscribed 'son of King Juba and descendent of king Ptolemy', which was set up in the Gymnasion of the early Ptolemies.

Then in AD 39 he was summoned by his cousin the emperor Caligula to Rome, perhaps in his capacity as grandson of the Living Isis, to celebrate the consecration of the new Isis temple on the Campus Martius. The ancient sources claim that Ptolemy's appearance in a resplendent purple cloak, perhaps worn over the star-studded toga picta he had been awarded by the Senate, 'attracted universal admiration', and that, greatly disliking being upstaged in this way, Caligula had Ptolemy arrested and executed.

Since he was the only client king whom Caligula dispatched in this manner, there was probably more to it than Ptolemy's flashy dress sense: the story may perhaps conceal the fact that Ptolemy had been implicated in a major plot against the emperor led by one Gaetulicus, whose father had been an ally of Ptolemy's own father, Juba. Ptolemy may have hoped that, if the conspiracy was successful, he would regain territory including the emperor's personal domain of Egypt. Or maybe he had simply become too powerful and wealthy to be a mere client king and Caligula wanted to make Mauretania a Roman province.

When Caligula himself was assassinated in AD 41 his successor, Claudius, did absorb Mauretania back into the Roman empire, but, sufficiently moved by the death of Ptolemy who had been his cousin through their common grandfather Antonius, ordered statues of both Ptolemy and Juba II to be set up in their capital, Caesarea. Both were dedicated to Venus in the goddess' temple in the city as Claudius' knowledge of history perpetuated a practice which kept faith with their shared predecessor Julius Caesar.

It seems quite ironic that the last known descendant of Cleopatra the

Great, her grandson Ptolemy, should have been executed by the self-confessed Isis devotee Caligula, himself a great-grandson of Antonius. Yet Cleopatra VII's influence was very much kept alive, both through her Isis persona and quite possibly through other royal descendants. Although details are sparse, with only seven Mauretanian royals known by name over a sixty-five-year period, Selene and Juba II are known to have had a daughter some time around 8 BC since she is mentioned in an honorary inscription set up in Athens. Roman sources also refer to a granddaughter of Cleopatra and Antonius named Drusilla who married Tiberius Claudius Felix, a freedman of the emperor Claudius, who in the fifties AD became procurator (revenue official) of Judaea, the kingdom Cleopatra VII had so desired for herself.

Drusilla's husband was also an associate of Paul of Tarsus, the very place where Cleopatra had sailed to meet Antonius in the guise of Aphrodite, and, like Antioch and Ephesus, a cult centre of Isis. Following Paul's conversion to the new faith of Christianity, his zealous missionary work throughout Syria, Asia Minor and Greece brought him into close contact with Isis' many devotees who remained a dominant religious power in the ancient world; even the ship in which he sailed from Malta to Puteoli and Syracuse was an Alexandrian vessel named the *Dioskuri*, the divine twins Castor and Pollux who had been 'made saviours' by Isis herself. And as her worship had spread way beyond Egypt, transcending ethnic and political barriers as far as Britain, the image of mother Isis with her divine son was adopted by the early Christians as they attempted to compete with her all-embracing appeal.

Although Drusilla herself seems to have died some time in the thirties AD, legend claims that the line carried on for several more centuries to emerge again in the third century AD as the forceful figure Zenobia of Palmyra. Known in Syrian inscriptions as Bat-Zabbai, 'the one with beautiful long hair', the twenty-seven-year-old Zenobia had become regent for her son following the death of her husband in AD 267. Famed for her intellect and beauty, she claimed descent from Cleopatra, and, emulating this great role model, is even said to have owned a collection of her predecessor's drinking cups, presumably obtained from their shared city of Antioch.

When the self-styled 'New Cleopatra' challenged the power of Rome, adopting the royal diadem and taking imperial titles including the name 'Augusta', the Roman Senate appealed to the emperor Claudius Augustus to 'set us free from Zenobia' as she expanded her Syrian territories into Asia Minor. She then invaded Egypt. The fighting which accompanied her invasion of Alexandria in AD 272 caused such destruction that 'walls were torn down and it lost the greater part of the area known as the Brucheion', the Palace Quarter, when the Great Library itself may even have been destroyed.

Her rebellion was eventually crushed in battles at Antioch and Palmyra by Claudius' successor Aurelian, and the jewel-bedecked Zenobia is said to have been brought to Rome, bound in golden chains, to walk in Aurelian's Triumph. She was then spared and allowed to live out the rest of her days on Aurelian's estate near Tivoli. Yet Arab tradition ignored the Romans and had Zenobia escape her enemy 'King Amr' by committing suicide, consuming poison she had concealed in a hollow ring while declaring 'bi-yadi la bi-yad Amr' – 'I die by my own hand, not that of Amr', a widely used Arab proverb.

The conflation of Zenobia's fate with that of Cleopatra, even down to the concealment of fatal poison within a form of adornment, very much reflects the long-lasting influence of Cleopatra VII for centuries after her death. With her gold statue still standing in the temple of Venus in Rome's Forum as late as AD 220, Cleopatra remained a figure of veneration in Egypt and was worshipped throughout the country, from Alexandria to Hermopolis and beyond. Egypt was said to praise and extol 'her Cleopatra', whose statuary remained a focus of veneration in the furthest southern reaches as late as AD 373, when a temple scribe could write 'I overlaid the figure of Cleopatra with gold' within Isis' cult centre Philae.

As the last Egyptian temple to remain active in the face of Christianity well into the sixth century AD, Philae's monarch-goddess maintained a tremendous appeal. In AD 453, when the people of the region concluded a treaty with Rome which allowed them to take the temple's cult statue across the Nile in celebration of the annual 'Sailing of Isis' Ship', they were re-enacting the journeys of Egypt's greatest female pharaoh as she travelled the world in pursuit of her dream, the restoration of the empire of Alexander the Great.

As the last of his Successors, her suicide had proved to be a turning point for western civilisation. Having come so very close to achieving her goal, accommodating Rome in order to keep Egypt independent while using the Romans themselves to help her do so, Cleopatra had proved so terrifying to her enemies that their hostility still resonates to this day. Yet despite all attempts to erase her story, she had proved too memorable a figure to be so easily destroyed and, like Alexander himself, became a legend. Even her most venomous critics were forced to admire the sheer courage of this legendary descendant of so many kings, Cleopatra the Great, whose spirit, inherited from Alexander himself, had ultimately proved unbreakable.

Notes

Introduction

1 'her celebrity seems to have been due primarily to the fact that she slept with both Julius Caesar and Mark Antony – the two most powerful men of her day – and that she was credited with being extremely ambitious'. Garland 2005, p.30.

2 'a blacked-out landscape illuminated by occasional flashes of lightning when Egypt impinges upon world events'. Skeat 1962, p.100.

2 'torn away the deceptive web which the hate of her enemies had spun around Cleopatra, and ascertained the truth'. Volkmann 1958, p.176.

2 For the 1988 exhibition *Cleopatra's Egypt: Age of the Ptolemies* see Brooklyn 1988 and more recent version, Walker and Higgs (eds.,) 2001. Although for some Cleopatra's story still depends 'on a perilous series of deductions from fragmentary or flagrantly unreliable evidence' (Beard 2003), others claim that 'for nearly half a century, the confrontation between literary testimonies and new documentary evidence . . . has continually revised the history of Queen Cleopatra VII . . . Every day we find . . . Cleopatra further upstream from her myth'. Bingen 2007, p.63. Hermonthis' Birth House demolished in 1861, Alexandria's royal quarters only recently located, see Empereur 1998 and 2002, Goddio (ed.) 1998 etc.

4 Debate over coin portraits created headline 'Ugly? Our Cleopatra was a real beauty, not like your Queen: Egyptians hit back at slur'. *Sunday Express* 15.4.01, p.44.

4 'Nefertiti is a face without a queen, Cleopatra is a queen without a face'. Malraux 1969 in Goudchaux 2001.b, p.210.

4 'a figure whose brilliance and charisma matched Alexander's own'. Green in Getty 1996, p.19.

5 'far more significant was Hatshepsut, a female pharaoh who reigned for nearly twenty years in the 15th century BC'. Roehrig et al. 2006, front flap of dust jacket.

7 'great potentate'. Sandys 1615 p.99.
7 'a lass unparalleled'. Shakespeare 1988, Act V, Scene II, p.183

Chapter 1

11 Alexander's mummy and tomb in Saunders 2006 and Chugg 2004; the tomb 'returned to the centre-stage of world history in the time of Cleopatra'. Chugg 2004, p.x.

13–14 Relationship between Greece and Egypt in Philips 1996, Wachsmann 1987 and Vasunia 2001; 'Peoples of the Sea' in Sandars 1985; First millennium BC in Kitchen 1996 and Myliwiec 2000.

14 'the Sea of the Greeks'. Fourth-century BC stela, Lichtheim 1980, p.88.

14 'where the houses are furnished in the most sumptuous fashion'. Homer, *Odyssey* IV.120–37, Rieu trans., p.66–7, also Homer, *Iliad* IX.381, Rieu trans., p.171.

16 'fond of his joke and his glass, and never inclined to serious pursuits', Herodotus II.174, de Selincourt trans., p.198.

17 Origins of 'Nile' in Smith 1979, pp.163–4; Egypt as 'gift of the river' in Griffiths 1966.

17 'the Egyptians themselves in their manners and customs seem to have reversed the ordinary practices of mankind'. Herodotus, II.33, de Selincourt trans., p.142.

17 'are employed in trade while the men stay at home and do the weaving'. Herodotus, II.33, de Selincourt trans., p.142.

17 'women pass water standing up, men sitting down'. Herodotus II.33, de Selincourt trans., p.142; Greeks' descriptions in Wyke 2002, p.210, Vasunia 2001, Harrison 2003, p.148.

18 'the corpse had been embalmed and would not fall to pieces under the blows, Cambyses ordered it to be burnt'. Histories III.16, de Selincourt trans., p.210.

18 'Do you call that a god, you poor creatures?' Herodotus III.28–30, de Selincourt trans., p.215.

18 For camels see Bovil 1956 and Rowley-Conwy 1988.

18 Homeric style battle epics such as Story Cycle of Pedubastis in Lichtheim 1980, p.151–6.

19 'hereditary princess, held in high esteem, favoured with sweet love, the mistress of Upper and Lower Egypt, of gracious countenance, beautiful with the double feather, great royal consort, Lady of the Two Lands'. Kuhlmann 1981, pp.267–79.

19 'a magic defence'. Arnold 1999, p.124.

20 'renowned in her ancestry'. Whitehorne 2001, p.1.

22 'terrified the male spectators as they raised their heads from the wreaths of ivy . . . or twined themselves around the wands and garlands of the women'. Plutarch, *Alexander 2*, trans. 1973, p.254.

22 'fair-skinned, with a ruddy tinge'. Plutarch, *Alexander 4*, trans. 1973, p.255.

22 'ever to be best and stand far above all others'. Homer, *Iliad* VI, in Lane Fox 1973, p.66, alternatively 'Let your motto be I lead. Strive to be the best', Homer, *Iliad* VI, Rieu trans., p.122.

22 'talked freely with them and quite won them over, not only by the friendliness of his manner but also because he did not trouble them with any childish or trivial inquiries, but questioned them about the distances they had travelled by road, the nature of the journey into the interior of Persia, the character of the king, his experience in war, and the military strength and prowess of the Persians'. Plutarch, *Alexander 5*, trans. 1973, p.256.

23 'a wise man should fall in love, take part in politics and live with a king'. Diogenes, *Laertius* 5.31, in Lane Fox, 1973, p.53.

23 'great souled man'. Aristotle, *Ethics* IV.3, in Howland 2002, p.27.

23 'as if friends and relatives, and to deal with the barbarians as with beasts or plants', Aristotle, in Green 1970, p.40; women's high voices in Aristotle in *Physiognomics* 807a, in Llewellyn-Jones 2003, p.267.

23 'animated tools'. Aristotle, *Politics* I.iv.1253b23, trans. Sinclair, pp.63–4.

23 'courtesans we keep for pleasure, concubines for attending day-by-day to the body and wives for producing heirs, and for standing trusty guard on our household property'. Apollodorus, in Davidson 1997, p.77.

23 'the Macedonians consider Ptolemy to be the son of Philip, though putatively the son of Lagus, asserting that his mother was with child when she was married to Lagus by Philip'. Pausanias 1.6.2 in Chugg 2004, p.52.

23 'Ptolemy was a blood relative of Alexander and some believe he was Philip's son'. Curtius 9.8.22 in Chugg 2004, p.52.
'Olympias, too, had made it clear that Ptolemy had been fathered by Philip'. Alexander *Romance*, in Chugg, 2004 p.52; Bingen 2007 p.18 suggests Ptolemy started the rumour himself.

24 'Wreathed is the bull. All is done. The sacrificer awaits'. Pausanias 8.7.6 in Green 1970, p.65.

25 'was neither hereditary nor was it produced by natural causes. On the contrary, it was said that as a boy he had shown an attractive disposition and displayed much promise, but Olympias was believed to have given him drugs which impaired the functions of his body and irreparably injured his brain'. Plutarch, *Alexander* 77, trans. 1973, p.334.

26 'You are invincible my son!'. Plutarch Alexander 14, trans., 1973, p.266.

26 'Alexander, the son of Philip, and all the Greeks with the exception of the Spartans won these spoils of war from the barbarians who dwell in Asia'. Plutarch, *Alexander* 16, trans. 1973, p.270.

27 'in military matters the feeblest and most incompetent of men'. Arrian III. 22, de Selincourt trans., p.185.

27 'led the race for safety'. Arrian II.11, in de Selincourt trans., p.120.

27 Persian casualties 'remained unequalled until the first day of the Somme'. Levi 1980, p.179.

27 'full of many treasures, luxurious furniture and lavishly dressed servants' and 'the whole room marvellously fragrant with spices and perfumes'. Plutarch, *Alexander* 20, trans. 1973, p.274.

29 'to match the greatest of the pyramids of Egypt'. Hypomnemata in *Andronicos* 1988, p.229.

29 'in Egypt, it is not possible for a king to rule without the help of the priests'. Plato, *Politics* 290.d Vasunia 2001, p.266.

30 'in the Throne Chamber of the Temple of Ptah'. Pseudo-Kallisthenes, Witt 1971, p.290, note 5.

31 'By order of Peukestas: no-one is to pass. The chamber is that of a priest'. Bowman 1986, p.57.

31 'there is an island called Pharos in the rolling seas off the mouth of the Nile, a day's sail out for a well-found vessel with a roaring wind astern. In this island is a sheltered cove where sailors come to draw their water from a well and can launch their boats on an even keel into the deep sea'. Homer, *Odyssey* IV, 354–60, Rieu trans., p.73.

32 'the top of a bull's head with two straight peninsular horns jutting out into the open sea just beyond the two ends of the island'. MacLeod, (ed.) 2002, p.36

32 'at once struck by the excellence of the site, and convinced that if a city were built upon it, it would prosper. Such was his enthusiasm that he could not wait to begin the work; he himself designed the general layout of the new town, indicating the position of the market square, the number of temples to be built and which gods they should serve – the gods of Greece and the Egyptian Isis – and the precise limits of its outer defences'. Arrian III.2, de Selincourt trans., p.149.

32 'generally sunny, but sometimes rather cold and rainy in winter, and not intolerably hot in summer, there being an almost continuous northern breeze from the sea'. Weigall 1928, pp.123–4.

34 'Oh, son of god'. Plutarch, *Alexander* 27, trans. 1973, pp.283–4.

34 'phallic-looking mummy . . . draped in cloths and jewels'. Levi 1980, p.178.

34 'the answer which his heart desired'. Arrian 4, de Selincourt trans., p.153.

34 'the high priest commanded him to speak more guardedly, since his father was not a mortal'. Plutarch, Alexander 27, trans. 1973, p.283.

Chapter 2

38 Alexander 'had probably entered a deep, terminal coma due to the onset of cerebral malaria'. Chugg 2004, p.34.

38 'made of hammered gold, and the space about the body they filled with spices such as could make the body sweet-smelling and incorruptible'. Diodorus XVIII.26, Geer trans., p.89.

38 'was appointed to govern Egypt and Libya and those lands of the Arabs that were contiguous to Egypt; and Kleomenes who had been made governor by Alexander, was subordinated to Ptolemy'. Arrian, *History of Events after Alexander* 156.F1,5, in Walbank 1981, p.100.

39 'Alexander's real body was sent ahead without fuss and formality by a secret and little used route. Perdikass found the imitation corpse with the elaborate carriage and halted his advance, thinking he had laid hands on the prize. Too late he realized he had been deceived'. Aelian, *Varia Historia*, in Chugg 2004, p.43.

39 'proceeded to bury with Macedonian rites in Memphis'. Pausanias 1.6.3, in Saunders 2006, p.40; 'Alexander was interred in Memphis'. FGrH.239 in Saunders 2006, p.40; philosophers' statues in Ridgway 1990, pp.132–3; Nectanebo II sarcophagus in Chugg 2004, pp.55–65.

40 'this great governor searched for the best thing to do for the gods of Upper and Lower Egypt'. 'Stela of the Satrap', Cairo CG.22181 in Dunand and Zivie-Coche 2004, p.200.

41 'girdlewearers'. Romer and Romer 1995, p.75.

42 'was the most powerful of Ptolemy I's wives and the one with the most virtues and intelligence'. Plutarch, *Pyrrhus* 4.4 in Rowlandson (ed.) 1998, p.26; Dryden trans., p.315.

42 'brought down from Memphis the corpse of Alexander'. Pausanias in Chugg 200, p.76; for alabaster tomb see Empereur 1998, p.144–53.

43 Ptolemaic royal women 'played the same role as kings' and 'eliminated gender hierarchy for a brief period in Classical antiquity'. Pomeroy 1984, pp.xviii-xix; they 'much more closely resembled their pharaonic predecessors than they did Greek women of any class'. Springborg 1990, p.198.

43 Reaction to marriage in Athenaeus XIV.621, Gulick trans., p.345; Cimon

of Athens married his half-sister, see Pomeroy 1975, p.241; the 'Egyptians also made a law . . . contrary to the general custom of mankind, permitting men to marry their sisters, this being due to the success attained by Isis in this respect'. Diodorus 1.27.1–2 in Oldfather trans., p.85.

43 'Daughter of Ra'. Troy 1986, p.178.

43 Cameo (Vienna Kunsthistoriches Museum) in Hölbl 2001, fig.2.1; blond hair in Theocritus XVII.103 in Grant 1972, p.5; features in Thompson 1973, p.82; goitre in Hinks 1928, p.242.

44 Myrtle wreath as slang for genitals in Whitehorne 2001, p.1.

44 'rising from the flashing sea and laughing, striking lightning from her lovely face'. Collecteana Alexandrina, after Thompson 1973, p.84.

44 'that must be a very dirty get-together. For the assembly can only be that of a miscellaneous mob who have themselves served with a stale and utterly unseemly feast'. Athenaeus, *Deipnosophists*, in Wilkins and Hill 2006, p.104.

44 Ptolemy II 'probably owed a good deal of his efficiency in war and in administrative ideas to his sister-wife Arsinoe II'. Thompson 1973, p.3.

45 'myrrh and calamus for the temple of the gods of Egypt'. Simpson (ed.) 2002, p.91.

45 'not heaped up to lie useless, as if the wealth of ever-industrious ants; much is lavished on the shrines of the gods'. Theocritus, Idyll 17, in Dunand and Zivie-Coche 2004, p.204; 100 talents for sacred cow burial in P.Zen.Pestman 50, in Rowlandson (ed.) 1998, p.49.

46 'the Romans, pleased that one [sic] so far away should have thought so highly of them'. Cassius Dio 10.41 in Walker and Higgs 2001, p.14 and trans., Cary, pp.367–9.

46 Alexandria as 'New York of the ancient world' in Ray in Walker and Higgs (eds.,) 2001 p.36; inventors' role to 'beautify cities, serve the army and mystify worshippers'. Hodges 1973, pp.182–3.

47 Ptolemy II 'caused the philosophy of the Egyptians (before alone peculiar to the priests) to be divulged in Greeke for the benefit of students'. Sandys 1615, p.111.

47 'they cut open criminals received out of the kings' prisons, and they studied whilst the breath of life remained in them'. Celsus, *De Medicina* I in MacLeod, (ed.) 2002, p.111.

47 'the most august of all princes and devoted, if any one ever was, to culture and learning'. Athenaeus *Deipnosophists* XII.536, Gulick trans., p.425.

47 'and concerning the number of books, the establishing of libraries, and the collection in the Hall of the Muses, why need I even speak, since they are in all men's memories'. Athenaeus, *Deipnosophists* V.203, Gulick trans., pp.420–1.

48 'marble figures, a hundred in all, the work of foremost artists . . . and paintings by artists of the Sicyonian school alternating with a great variety of selected portraits'. Athenaeus *Deipnosophists* V.196, Gulick trans., p.391.

48 'Come on! Get your cloak. Let's go to the house of the king, rich Ptolemy. I hear the queen has done a beautiful job of decorating it . . . And when you've seen it, what won't you be able to say to someone who hasn't!'. Theocritus, Idyll 15, exc. G. in Thompson 1964, p.157.

48 'everything in Egypt was play-acting and painted scenery'. Plutarch, *Aratus*, 15.2 in Walbank 1979, p.182.

48 'the form of the Egyptian Bes the dancer, who trumpets forth a shrill note when the spout is opened for the flowing wine'. Athenaeus, *Deipnosophists* XI.497, Gulick trans., p.219.

49 'that her statue be set up in all the temples. This pleased their priests for they were aware of her noble attitude toward the gods and of her excellent deeds to the benefit of all people . . . Beloved of the Ram'. Mendes Stela Cairo CG.22181 in Brooklyn 1988, p.43.

49 'where bitch-mounting goats go mating with the women'. Strabo, in Lindsay 1963, p.6.

49 'a goat tupped a woman, in full view of everyone – a most surprising event'. Herodotus, II.46, de Selincourt trans., p.148.

49 'I will make you a god [sic] at the head of the gods on earth'. Brooklyn 1988, p.43.

49 'a man of wit and taste, partial to the ladies'. Theocritus, Idylls 14.58–68, in Lewis 1986, p.11.

50 'Unlucky devil that I am! To think I cannot even be one of those fellows'. Athenaeus *Deipnosophists* XII.536, Gulick trans., p.425.

50 Berenike II's exploits in Callimachus' 'Victory of Berenike' in Ashton 2003, p.59; Egyptian epithet describing her bravery, strength and courage in Troy 1986, p.179.

50 'deep-set long eyes, a nose wide at the nostrils, a ball-chin – a face slightly reminiscent of Nefertiti . . . it looks as though the Hellenistic Greeks, like the moderns, admired the Nefertiti profile'. Thompson 1973, p.86, p.105, note 5.

50 Berenike II's hair in Brooklyn 1988, p.182, Thompson 1973, p.86 and Nachtergael 1980, 1981; crown in Empereur 2002, p.12; perfumes in Athenaeus, *Deipnosophists* XV.689.a, Griffin 1976, p.93.

50 'ta per-aat Bereniga . . . the pharaoh Berenike'. Hölbl 2001, p.85.

50 'perceived as the equivalent of an Egyptian king. There could be nothing clearer than the idea of a female Horus'. Tait 2003, p.7; her role in Aelian VH.14.43, in Thompson 1973, p.87, and female vizier in Troy 1986, p.179.

51 'a sacred statue for her, of gold and set with precious stones'. Canopus Decree in Rowlandson (ed.) 1998, p.32; veiled Berenike II statue in Ashton 2003, fig.10, p.82.

51 'adorned with great columned halls and statuary which seems almost alive'. Ammianus Marcellinus in MacLeod (ed.) 2002, p.71.

51 'constant concern, combined with heavy outlay and expense, for Apis and Mnevis and the other renowned sacred animals in the land'. Canopus Decree in Rowlandson (ed.) 1998, p.31.

51 'the one who has his being before the ancestors'. Ibrahim 1979, pp.170–1; Edfu was 'the memorial of Egypt's national King Horus and the country's archives of religious traditions and beliefs'. Reymond and Barns 1977, p.7.

51 'offerings shall be made in your shrine, O Falcon, O you of the dappled plumage! . . . shespu er shespet ek shenbet sab-shuwt'. Watterson 1979. p.167.

52 'Nekhbet stabs him who violates your inviolable soil . . . shatat her shemy shash shaw ek shata'. Watterson 1979, p.169.

52 'I hold my harpoon! I drive back the hidden ones, I stab their bodies, I cut them up, I deflect their attack against Horus of the dappled plumage', temple texts based on Wilson's translation in Quirke (ed.) 1997, p.183.

52 'strong protector of the gods and mighty wall for Egypt'. Hölbl 2001, p.80.

52 'a loose, voluptuous, and effeminate prince, under the power of his pleasures and his women and his wine . . . while the great affairs of state were managed by Agathoklea, the king's mistress, [and] her mother and pimp Oinanthe'. Plutarch, *Kleomenes*, Dryden trans., p.669.

52 'an eyewitness of the sickness of the realm'. Plutarch, *Kleomenes*, in Walbank 1979 p.182; three Greek ambassadors all died in Ptolemy IV's ninth year, in Walker and Higgs (eds.,), 2001, p.117.

53 Arsinoe III presenting hair lock in Nachtergael 1980; spear-wielding 'heroine of the battle of Raphia' in Thompson 1973, p.26.

53 'taking presents to the king and queen to commemorate and renew their friendship'. Livy 27.4.10 in Maehler 2003, p.203; also in Moore trans., p.215.

53 'Neos Dionysos'. Hölbl 2001, p.171.

53 'carrying a timbrel and taking part in the show'. Plutarch, Dryden trans., p.669.

53 'built in the middle of the city a memorial building which is now called the Sema [tomb] and he laid there all his forefathers together with his mother, and also Alexander the Macedonian'. Zenobius, in Chugg 2004, p.80.

54 'the Soma also, as it is called, is part of the royal district. This was the walled enclosure which contained the burial places of the kings and that of Alexander'. Strabo 17.1.8 in Chugg 2004, p.81.

54 'worthy of the glory of Alexander in size and construction'. Diodorus XVIII.28, Geer trans., p.95.

54 'his shameful philanderings and incoherent and continuous bouts of drunkenness, not surprisingly found in a very short space of time both himself and his kingdom to be the object of a number of conspiracies'. Polybius 5.34.4–10 in Walker and Higgs (eds.,) 2001, p.18.

55 'some bit them, some stabbed them, others cut out their eyes. Whenever one of them fell, they ripped their limbs apart, until they had in this way mutilated them all. For a terrible savagery accompanies the angry passions of the people who live in Egypt'. Polybius XV.27, 29, 33 in Rowlandson (ed.) 1998, p.34.

55 'had them slain on the wood'. Rosetta Stone, trans., Simpson in Parkinson 1999, p.199.

55 'god, the son of a god and goddess and being like Horus, son of Isis and Osiris'. Rosetta Stone, trans., Simpson in Parkinson 1999, p.198.

56 'sacred animals that are honoured in Egypt'. Rosetta Stone, trans., Simpson in Parkinson 1999, p.199.

56 'Female Horus'. Hölbl 2001, p.167; female vizier in Troy 1986, p.179, epithet 'her bravery and strength is that of Hathor in her great love' in Troy 1986, p.179.

56 'Ptolemy and Cleopatra, rulers of Egypt'. Livy 37.3.9 in Sage trans., p.299.

56 'brought the only important intrusion of foreign blood'. Mahaffy 1915, p.2.

56 'ill-favoured looks and boxers' noses'. Whitehorne 2001, p.83.

57 'the Pharaohs Cleopatra the mother the manifest goddess and Ptolemy son of Ptolemy the manifest god'. Whitehorne 2001, p.86.

57 'Don't hesistate to name the little one 'Cleopatra', your little daughter'. P.Münch III.57, Rowlandson (ed.) 1998, p.292.

57 'following Egyptian custom'. Porphyry, in Hölbl 2001, p.147.

58 'was brought in by the mime performers entirely wrapped up . . . when the symphony sounded, he would leap up and dance naked and act with the clowns'. Athenaeus *Deipnosophists* V.195, in Gulick trans., p.387.

58 'should always consider the trust and good will of the Roman people the supreme defence of their kingdom'. Livy 45.13.7 in Maehler 2003, p.204 and Schlesinger trans., p.287.

59 'Theoi Philometores'. Hölbl 2001, p.183.

60 'genealogical cobweb'. Rice 1999, p.21.

59 'in his mother's arms'. Justin XXXVIII.8.4, in Hölbl 2001, p.194.

60 'murdered many of the Alexandrians; not a few he sent into exile, and filled the islands and towns with men who had grown up with his brother'. Athenaeus *Deipnosophists* IV.184, Gulick trans., pp.312–13; for 'cultural fallout' see Whitehorne 2001, p.109.

60 'Benefactor'. . . Malefactor', Athenaeus, *Deipnosophists* XII.549, Gulick trans., p.493, 'Physkon . . . Fatty', Athenaeus, *Deipnosophists* XII.549, Gulick trans., p.492, note b.

60 'the Alexandrians have already got one thing from our visit. Thanks to us they've finally seen their king walking!' Plutarch, *Moralia* 201.A in Whitehorne 2001, p.108.

60 'utterly corrupted with fat and with a belly of such size that it would have been hard to measure it with one's arms'. Athenaeus, *Deipnosophists* XII.549, Gulick trans., p.493.

60 'astonished at the number of inhabitants of Egypt and the natural advantages of the countryside . . . a mighty power could be sustained if this kingdom ever found capable leaders'. Diodorus 28b.3 in Walker and Higgs 2001, p.20.

61 Marriage between royals and priests in Vienna Stela No.82, Reymond and Barns 1977, p.10–11, p.17.

61 'the Two Horus'. Hölbl 2001, p.195.

62 'whichever of her sons she would make co-regent'. Maehler 1983, p.1.

63 'we know of none of the kings so hated by his mother'. Pausanias 1.9.1 in Rowlandson (ed.) 1998, p.35.

63 Cleopatra III as Alexander's priest in Hölbl 2001, p.208; wearing Alexander's elephant headdress in Whitehorne 2001, pl.5; as human-headed sphinx in Ashton 2003, p.141.

64 'Female Horus, Lady of Upper and Lower Egypt, Mighty Bull'. Troy 1986, p.179.

64 'to become both king and queen, both god and goddess'. Whitehorne 2001, p.147.

64 'the scarlet one'. Green 1990, p.877, note4; Whitehorne 2001, p.130.

64 'women's ornaments'. Appian, *Mithridatic War*, 23, in White trans., p.281.

64 'when it came to the rounds of dancing at a drinking party he would jump from a high couch barefoot as he was and perform the figures in a livelier fashion than those who had practiced them'. Poseidonius quoted in Athenaeus *Deipnosophists* XII.550, Gulick trans., pp.495–7.

64 'Kokke's child'. Strabo 17.797C in Whitehorne 2001, p.221, no.22.

65 'the younger sister of the King Ptolemy men called Alexander'. Vienna funerary stela No. 82 in Reymond 1981, p.132.

65 'drank in the presence of the king. He [the king] handed out unto him the golden crook, mace, robe of linen from the southern house and the leather garment according to the ritual of Ptah's festivals and solemn processions. He [the king] placed his golden ornaments on his head according to the custom of his forefathers in the 17th year of his age'. Reymond 1981 pp.132–3.

65 'a first-class and remarkable temple, one of the most ancient and most famous'. Dunand and Zivie-Coche 2004, pp.209–10.

65 'Ptolemy X Alexander I removed the gold sarcophagus of Alexander the Great and substituted one of glass'. Strabo XVII.1.8 (794.C) in Broughton 1942, p.330.

66 'extremely popular with the Alexandrians'. Cicero in Whitehorne 2001, p.175.

66 'the greatest god, Soter the king, has reached Memphis, and that Hierax has been despatched with considerable forces to bring Thebes under control. We wanted to inform you so that you, knowing this, take courage. Farewell'. Maehler 1983, p.2.

66 'great expenses in collecting Greek art'. Griffin 1976, p.91, note51.

66 'filthy lucre' . . . 'loose foreign morals'. Juvenal, *Satires* VI.297–99, trans., Green, p.138.

67 Elder prince Ptolemy became Ptolemy XII Auletes; his mother most likely Ptolemy XI's sister-wife Cleopatra Selene, though others believe she 'was a concubine', (Foss 1997) p.81, perhaps Syrian or Greek (Grant 1972, p.5) or even elite Egyptian (Reymond and Barns 1977, p.27, Hölbl 2001, p.222); 'there is unanimity amongst genealogists that the identification, and hence ethnicity, of the maternal grandmother of Cleopatra VII is currently not known'. Bianchi 2003, p.13

67 'our god and lord the king'. Orientis Graeci Inscriptiones Selectae 741 in Grant 1972, p.22.

68 'not a man but a piper [auletes] and magician [magos]'. Athenaeus, *Deipnosophists* V.206.d in Grant 1972, p.21; in Gulick translation, 'magos' is 'juggler', p.433.

68 'degenrarunt'. Livy 38.17.11, Sage trans., pp.58–9.

68 'The king himself halted his war chariot. He arrayed my head for me with the glorious chaplet of gold and all the genuine precious stones, the royal effigy being in its midst. I was made his prophet'. BM.EA.886, in Reymond 1981, p.148.

68 'It is me who placed the uraeus upon the king on the day of Uniting-the-Two-Lands for him and also carried out for him all the ceremonies in the Mansion of the Jubilee. It is me who conducted all the offices concealad from the public eye'. Stela BM.EA.886, in Reymond 1981, p.148.

69 'with his courtiers, his wives, the royal children with his lordly possessions were sitting at meal and were spending a pleasant time while
assisting at festivals of all gods and goddesses'. BM.886, in Reymond
1981, pp.148–9.

69 'legitimate'. Strabo XVII. 796, in Barns 1977 p.29; for redundancy of
claims see Bingen 2007, p. 55, p.67.

69 Removal of Cleopatra V Tryphaena from records in Huss 1990, p.196
and Hölbl 2001, p.223.

Chapter 3

73 Although Huss 1990 and Hölbl 2001, p.223 suggest Cleopatra VII's
mother was Egyptian, others believe she 'came from the highest Macedonian aristocracy'. (Bingen 2007, p.66); some claim Cleopatra was a black
African, whereas others note 'how unlikely it is that the queen was black in
any sense that could be recognized in the United States today', (Hamer
1996, p.88) and 'if she was black, no one mentioned it' (Foss 1997, p.82).

73 Estimation as '32 parts Greek, 27 parts Macedonian and 5 parts Persian' in
Foss 1997, p.82.

73 'Our lords and greatest gods'. Grant 1972, p.22.

73 Egyptian ruler as Alexander's priest since 116 BC in Whitehorne 2001.

73 'the eyes of the king of Upper Egypt the ears of the king of Lower Egypt'.
Stela BM.EA.147, in Lichtheim 1980, p.61 and Reymond 1981, pp.165–
77.

74 'god's beloved and friend of the King'. Stela BM.EA.147, in Lichtheim
1980 p.61 and Reymond 1981, pp.165–77.

74 'military overseer of the Red and Indian Seas' in Goudchaux 2003,
p.109.

75 'one of the Romans killed a cat and the multitude rushed in a crowd to
his house, neither the officials sent by the king to beg the man off nor the
fear of Rome which all the people felt were enough to save the man from
punishment, even though his act had been an accident'. Diodorus
1.83.8–9, Oldfather trans., p.287.

75 'friend and ally of the Roman people'. Maehler 1983, p.3; also Caesar in
Civil Wars, III.107, Peskett trans., p.349.

76 Strabo states Auletes had three daughters (XVII. 796 in Barns 1977,
p.29), whereas Porphyry (in Whitehorne 2001, p.182) later claimed four
when assuming Berenike IV and Cleopatra Tryphaena were both his
daughters.

76 'one of his daughters' on Athenian epitaph in Grant 1972, pp.15–16, Goudchaux 2001, p.131.

76 'even lying on the ground it is a marvel'. Pliny XXXIV.18.41–42 in Loeb trans., p.159.

77 'Cato neither went forward to meet him, nor so much as rose up to him, but saluting him as an ordinary person, bade him sit down. This at once threw Ptolemy into some confusion'. Plutarch, *Cato*, Dryden trans., p.633, latrine mentioned in Grant 1972, p.15.

77 'by force'. Tertullian, *Ad Nationes* I.1.17–18 in Maehler 2003, p.205.

79 'at first sight', 'he had fallen in love with her at first sight long ago when she was still a girl and he was serving as master of horse under Gabinius'. Appian *Roman History* V.8, trans., White, p.389.

79 'in his rage and spite against the Egyptians'. Plutarch, *Antony*, Dryden trans., p.749.

79 'he left behind him a great name among the Alexandrians'. Plutarch, *Antony*, Dryden trans., p.749.

80 'thieving, effeminate ballet boy in curlers'. Cicero in Grant 1969, p.96.

80 'the home of all tricks and deceits'. Cicero, *Pro. Rab. Post.* 35, reported in Wyke 2002, p.211.

81 'sage'. el-Daly 2005, p.131.

81 'the most illustrious and wise among women . . . great in herself and in her achievements in courage and strength'. John of Nikiou 67, in Hughes-Hallett 1990, p.70; el-Daly 2005, p.132.

81 'the last of the wise ones of Greece'. El-Masudi in Hughes-Hallett, 1990, p.70

81 'the virtuous scholar'. El-Daly 2005, p.131

81 'who elevated the ranks of scholars and enjoyed their company'. El-Masudi in el-Daly 2005, p.133.

81 'the dead lying in Hades, waiting for the waters of rebirth to come and revive them so they can be reborn and flower again in the springtime'. Roberts 2000, p.202.

81 'there is no Royal Road to geometry'. Euclid, in MacLeod (ed.) 2002, p.4.

81 'wrote books on medicine, charms and cosmetics in addition to many other books ascribed to her which are known to those who practiced medicine'. El-Masudi in el-Daly 2005, p.133.

82 Toxicological interest in Plutarch, *Antony*, Dryden trans., p.774; Cassius Dio 51.11 in Scott-Kilvert trans., p.72; *De Bello Aegyptiaco* in Volkmann 1953, p.193; Ibn Wahshiya in el-Daly 2005, p.134.

82 'scribe of the god'. El-Daly 2005, p.134.

82 'a worthy young woman, skilled in speech, whose advice is bright'. Stela BM.EA.147, in Reymond 1981, p.174.

82 Egypt's female monarchs in Fletcher 2004, pp.186–225; Manetho's list in Gardiner 1964, pp.429–53; Memphite womenfolk in Reymond 1981.

84 'Strong Bull beloved of Maat, Daughter of Ra, beloved of Amun.' Callender 2004, p.94.

84 'in whose time Troy was taken'. Gardiner 1964, p.445.

84 'Philadelphos' in Bingen 2007, p.66, with children hailed 'Philadelphoi', OGIS II.741 in Bingen 2007, p.66, note 9.

84 'the thirtieth year which is also the first'. Skeat 1960, p.91.

84 Head of teenage Cleopatra(?) in Bianchi 2003, pl.6, p.20; Ptolemy XII's head in Brooklyn 1988 No.57, p.154; both 'stress their Macedonian origins' in Brooklyn 1988, p.155; similarity of features in Brooklyn 1988 p.154; Dendera crypt images in Bianchi 2003, pl.1b, p.14.

85 'one copy of the will had been taken to Rome by his envoys to be placed in the treasury, but had been deposited with Pompeius because it had not been possible to place it there owing to the embarrassments of the state; a second duplicate copy was left sealed for production at Alexandria'. Caesar, *Civil War* III.108, trans., Peskett, p.351.

85 'prophet of King Ptolemy, justified'. BM.EA.147, in Lichtheim 1980, p.64.

86 'King of Upper and Lower Egypt'. Lepsius in Brooklyn 1988, p.52.

86 'Female Horus, the Great One, Mistress of Perfection, Brilliant in Counsel, Lady of the Two Lands, Cleopatra, the Goddess who loves her Father, the Image of her Father'. Tait 2003, p.4.

86 "Upper Egyptian King of the land of the white crown, Lower Egyptian King of the land of the red crown'. Troy 1986, p.179.

87 Image of red-haired woman from Herculaneum villa, Naples Museo Nazionale Archeologico 90778 in Ward-Perkins and Claridge 1976, no.24 and Walker and Higgs (eds.,) 2001, No.325, p.314.

87 Isis' cult statue clothed in vulture feathers in Aelian in Witt 1971, p.91; see also Brooklyn 1988, no.17, p.107 and Riefstahl 1944, p.47.

87 'gave audience to the people under the name of the New Isis . . . appeared in public dressed in the habit of the goddess Isis'. Plutarch, *Antony*, Dryden trans., p.768.

87 'the black-robed queen . . . black raiment'. Plutarch in Witt 1971, p.147; 'Wearers of Black'. Plutarch 52 in Witt 1971, p.97.

88 'many-coloured robe was of finest linen . . . but what caught and held my eye more than anything else was the deep black lustre of her mantle. She wore it slung across her body from the right hip to the left shoulder, where it was caught in a knot resembling the boss of a shield; but part of it hung in innumerable folds, the tasseled fringe quivering'. Apuleius, Graves trans., p.270.

88 'Isis the Great, Mother of the God, the Great One, the powerful, sovereign of the gods without whom no-one accedes to the palace, it is at her command the king ascends the throne'. Dunand and Zivie-Coche 2004, p.237.

88 'Myrionymos'. Witt 1971, p.127.

88 'male gods united in a bull'. Mond and Myers, II pp.25, 46–9.

89 'soul on body'. Mond and Emery 1929, p.4

89 'the living spirit of Ra born of the great Cow united with the creator gods, he is Amun who goes on his four feet, the image of Montu, lord of Thebes, the father of fathers, the mother of mothers, who renews the life of every one of the gods'. after Mond and Myers 1934, I p.14, II, pp.11–12.

89 'changes colour every hour and is shaggy with hair which sprouts outward contrary to the nature of all animals'. Macrobius, *Saturnalia* I.21 in Mond and Myers, 1934, II, p.27.

89 'only women may look at it; these stand facing it and pulling up their garments show their genitals'. Diodorus I.85 in Oldfather trans., p.291.

89 'anasyrmenê'. Montserrat 1996, p.167; also Herodotus II.60, de Selincourt trans., p.153; Nefertiti in Vergnieux and Gondran 1997, p.89.

89 'took his phallus in his fist and ejaculated'. Spell 527, Faulkner 1969, p.198.

89 'Hail Min who fecundates his mother, how secret is that which you have done to her in the darkness'. Roberts 1995, p.89.

90 'Bull who copulates with fair ladies'. Spell 420, Faulkner 1977, p.68.

90 'bukolion'. Gordon and Schwabe 2004, p.47.

90 Nineteenth-century use of statue Louvre N.390 reported by Maspero in Montserrat 1996, p.168.

90 'generative light falling strongly from the moon'. Plutarch, *de Iside* XLIII in Mond and Myers 1934, I, p.11.

90 'the Lady of the Two Lands, the goddess Philopator, rowed him in the barque of Amun, together with the royal boats, all the inhabitants of Thebes and Hermonthis and the priests being with him and he reached Hermonthis, his dwelling-place'. Buchis Stela No.13, Copenhagen, in Mond and Myers 1934, I, p.14, II, pp.11–12; Tarn 1936, p.188, Skeat 1962, p.101 and Brooklyn 1988, no.107, p.213.

91 'Hermonthis and beautiful Thebes were united in drunkenness and the noise was heard in heaven'. Mond and Myers 1934, I, p.13.

91 'as for the ruler, everyone was able to see her'. Buchis Stela No.13, Copenhagen in Goudchaux 2001, p.133.

91 'I adore thy majesty and give praise to your soul, O great god, self created'. Lepsius in Mond and Myers, 1934 II, pp.25, 46–49.

91 'on behalf of the female king [basilissa] Cleopatra, goddess Philopator'. Louvre E.27113, in Rowlandson (ed.) 1998, p.38; same portrayal of Hatshepsut see Fletcher 2004, p.218; stela of Berenike IV 'whose principal decoration is a bearded bust wearing a nemes [king's headcloth]' in Brooklyn 1988, p.188.

92 Astronomical ceiling study in Andreu et al. 1997, pp.210–11; Cleopatra travelling to inauguration in Goudchaux 2001, p.133.

92 'on pain of death'. Pap. BGU 1730 in Skeat 1962, p.104.

93 'Pharaoh Ptolemy and Pharaoh Cleopatra, the gods who love their father'. Chaveau 2002, p.25.

93 'year 1 which is also year 3'. Hölbl, 2001 p.231.

93 Apis burial ritual in Vos 1993, pp.144–5; Cleopatra's funding in Goudchaux 2001, p.133.

93 Stela with Isis in red crown in Farag 1975, p.166, pl.XXIII.1.

94 'grew up a very beautiful youth'. Plutarch *Antony*, Dryden trans., p.749.

94 'the firebrand and tornado of the age'. Lucius Annaeus Florus in Lindsay 1970, p.478.

94 'gladiatorial strength'. Cicero, Second Philipic in Grant 1960 trans., p.129.

94 'this is a new way of conquering, to strengthen one's position by kindness and generosity'. Caesar in Barry 2005, p.14.

95 'Caesar wrote admirably: his memoirs are cleanly, directly and gracefully composed, and divested of all rhetorical trappings'. Cicero in Suetonius, *Julius Caesar* 56, in Graves trans., p.34.

95 'I earnestly invite you to join with me in carrying on the government of Rome. If, however, timidity makes you shrink from the task I shall trouble you no more. For in that case I shall govern it myself'. Caesar in Grant 1968, p.148.

95 Cleopatra 'was driven from her throne by her brother Ptolemy'. Livy, *Summaries* CXI, Schlesinger trans., p.139; Ptolemy removed Cleopatra 'from the throne by the help of his relations and friends'. Caesar, *Civil War* III, 103 in Peskett trans., pp.343–4; 'others blame the minister Pothinus . . . he had banished Cleopatra'. Plutarch, *Caesar* XLVIII.5, Dryden trans., p.596.

96 'Pharaoh Cleopatra'. Chaveau 2002, p.25; her retreat south in Malalas XI.279, in Hölbl 2001, p.232.

96 'took up residence in Arabia and Palestine'. Walker and Higgs (eds.,) 2001, p.24.

96 Askalon coins in Walker and Higgs (eds.,) 2001, p.234 'bear a striking relationship to her father and even evoke the likeness of Ptolemy I Soter'. Brooklyn 1988, p.184.

96 Caesar refers to 'King Ptolemy, a boy in years, waging war with large forces against his sister Cleopatra', *Civil War,* III, 103, Peskett trans., pp.343–5; Cleopatra 'was collecting an army in Syria'. Appian, *Roman History* II.84, in White trans., p.381.

96 'descended from Ares [Roman Mars] and Aphrodite [Venus] and Saviour of Mankind', based on Hölbl 2001, p.289.

97 'reckon descent from the goddess Venus . . . can claim both the sanctity of kings who reign supreme among mortals, and the reverence due to gods, who hold even kings in their power'. Suetonius, *Julius Caesar* 6, Graves trans., p.11.

98 'a dead man cannot bite'. Plutarch, *Pompey*, Dryden trans., p.537.

98 'he learns of the death of Pompeius'. Caesar, *Civil Wars* III.106, Peskett trans., p.349; alternatively 'he burst into tears'. Livy, *Summaries* CXII, Schlesinger trans., p.141.

99 'undaunted, with looks that ever masked his fears'. Lucan, *Civil War* 10.14–20, Duff trans., p.591.

99 'amazing building complex comprised multiple colonnaded courts of different shapes and dimensions'. Polybius 15.25 in Grimm 2003, p.45; also described as 'luxuriant groves and gardens and with many-coloured lodges. Below, there lies a constructed harbour out of view, which the kings used – and also Antirrhodos, an isle nearby, with a palace and small harbour of its own . . . The Sema or Tomb of Alexander is also embodied in the palace-system'. Strabo in Lindsay 1963, pp.3–4.

99 'visited the temples of the gods and the ancient shrines of divinity which attest the former might of Macedonia. No thing of beauty attracted him, neither the gold and ornaments of the gods, nor the city walls; but in eager haste he went down into the vault hewn out for a tomb. There lies the mad son of Macedonian Philip'. Lucan, *Civil War* 10.14–20, Duff trans., p.591.

100 Caesar declared 'King Ptolemy and his sister Cleopatra should disband the armies they controlled and should settle their disputes by process of law before himself rather than by armed force between themselves'. Caesar, *Civil Wars* III.107, in Peskett trans., p.351.

Chapter 4

101 'was at a loss at how to get in undiscovered'. Plutarch, *Caesar* XLIX, Dryden trans., p.596.

101 'piquant wrapper'. Forster 1982, p.26, referring to 'a bale of oriental carpets'.

101 'she thought of putting herself into the coverlet of a bed and lying at length, whilst Apollodorus tied up the bedding and carried it on his back through the gates to Caesar's apartments'. Plutarch, *Caesar* XLIX, Dryden trans., p.596.

101 'linen bag of the kind used to carry carpets'. Canfora 1990, p.66.

101 'bed–linen sack'. Walker and Higgs, (eds.,) 2001, p.24.

102 Himation in Llewellyn-Jones 2003, p.77.

102 'coverlets and bedclothes were considered as clothing by the Romans'. Croom 2000, p.30.

102 'wrap their heads in their himatia such that the garment seems to cover the whole face like a little mask; the eyes alone peep out; all the other parts of the face are covered by the mantles'. Herakleides, in Galt 1931, pp.382–3; origins of face veiling in Vogelsang-Eastwood 1996; dedication of 'face veil', Anth.Pal. 6.207 in Llewellyn-Jones 2003, p.218.

102 'by law, only my eyes should see you'. Sebesta 1997, p.535; Plutarch states veil imposed by husbands hiding wives from other men, Moralia 232.C, in Galt 1931, p.373.

102 Bronze figurine MMA.1972.118.95 (the 'Baker Dancer') in Thompson 1950 and Galt 1931.

102 'fluid and like a whirlwind', Thompson 1950, p.380; imagery of veiling and sea in Homer, *Odyssey* 5.351–3, Rieu trans., p. 97, *Iliad* 24.93–96 in Rieu trans., p.439; Isis emerging from sea in mantle in Apuleius XI, Graves trans. 1950, p.270.

103 'I am that which is, which hath been, and which shall be, and none have ever lifted the veil that hides my Divinity from mortal eyes'. Plutarch, *De Iside et Osiride*, see Witt 1971, p.67.

103 Unveiling gesture 'anakalypteria' signified surrender of virginity in Sebesta 1997, p.535; 'unveiling oneself in public, or in front of a man to whom you were not related, is not part of the image or daily habit of a modest woman . . . the gesture of unveiling is alien to the Greek concept of femininity'. Llewellyn-Jones 2003, p.110.

104 'white breasts were revealed by the fabric of Sidon'. Lucan, *Civil War* 10.141, in Duff trans., p.601.

104 'could see her whole body in it, and his desire grew even greater than it had been before'. P.Cairo 30646, trans., Tait in Rowlandson (ed.) 1998, p.365.

104 'her beauty was not in and for itself incomparable'. Plutarch, *Antony* 27, in Goudchaux 2001(b), p.210; see also Dryden trans., p.757.

104 'the power of her beauty', Plutarch, *Antony*, Dryden trans., p.775.

104 'she was a woman of surpassing beauty, and at that time, when she was in the prime of her youth, she was most striking. Being brilliant

to look upon and to listen to, with the power to subjugate every one, even a love-sated man already past his prime, she thought that it would be in keeping with her role to meet Caesar, and she reposed in her beauty all her claims to the throne'. Cassius Dio, 42.34, Cary trans., p.169.

000 For doubts on identity, 'Elizabeth Taylor must be the most genuine existing portrait of Cleopatra' claims Johansen 2003 p.75; 'a web of the most highly educated guesswork has been woven to secure the image of Cleopatra'. Hamer 1993, p.3.

104 Rarity of inscribed statues in Bianchi 1980, p.19; images sufficiently distinct that 'we feel that we would recognize them on the colonnaded streets of Alexandria'. Thompson 1973, p.78.

105 'she is beautiful'. Davidson 1997, pl.8.

105 'pretty neither by the standards of [her] own day nor by those of ours'. Hughes-Hallett 1990, p.17.

105 'whilst it does not flatter her it bears a close relationship to the portraits of Alexander the Great'. Southern 2001, p.121, commenting on Berlin Staatliche Museen Preussischer Kulturbesitz Antikenmuseum no.1976.10.

105 'suggests her great physical beauty'. Bowman 1986, p.25.

105 'is infinitely more beautiful than the unflattering coin portrait, and it does convey an image of the great queen's personality'. Maehler 1983, p.8; 'these [coin] images are often cited to show that Cleopatra was not as beautiful as the myths surrounding her would suggest, but such judgements are invariably made on the basis of the taste of modern scholars, rather than any contemporary evidence, and miss the point of numismatic portraiture', states Wilfong 1997, pp.37–8; coins suggesting 'witch-like face' far more graceful when cleaned and given 'acid peel', states Goudchaux 2001(b), p.211.

105 'even the famously attractive Kleopatra VII of Egypt is shown with a flabby neck that suggests a goitre'. Prag and Neave 1997, p.78.

105 'in drag'. Hamer 1996, p.84

105 'a cruel, hook-nosed hag'. Girling 2001, p.33.

105 'attractive . . . radiant'. Goudchaux 2001(b), p.211.

105 'contact of her presence, if you lived with her, was irresistible; the attraction of her person, joining with the charm of her conversation, and the character that attended all she said or did, was something bewitching'. Plutarch, *Antony* 27, Dryden trans., p.757.

105 'a most delicious voice'. Plutarch, *Antony* 27, Foster trans., in Saylor 2004, p.352, compared with high pitch described by Aristotle in *Physiognomics* 807a, in Llewellyn-Jones 2003, p.267.

105 'silence is the ornament of women'. Sophocles, *Ajax* 293, in Llewellyn-Jones 2003, p.268.

106 'she had the facility of atuning her tongue, like an instrument with many strings, to whatever language she wish(ed.) There were few foreigners she had to deal with through an interpreter, and most she herself gave her replies without an intermediary – to the Ethiopians, Troglodytes, Hebrews, Arabs, Syrians, Medes and Parthians. It is said she knew languages of many other peoples too, although the preceding kings had not tried to master even the Egyptian tongue, and some had indeed ceased to speak Macedonian'. Plutarch, *Antony* 27, in Rowlandson, (ed.) 1998, p.40.

106 'narcisstic personality seems consistently to be the best description for her', – Orland et al. 1990, p.174.

106 'muffled his head with a cloak and secretly put to sea in a small boat, alone and incognito'. Suetonius *Julius Caesar* 58, Graves trans., p.35.

107 'his dress, it seems, was unusual: he had added wrist-length sleeves with fringes to his purple-striped senatorial tunic, and the belt which he wore over it was never tightly fastened – hence Sulla's warning to the aristocratic party "Beware of that boy with the loose clothes". Suetonius, *Caesar* 45.3, in Graves trans., p.29.

107 'Do you know of any man who, even if he has concentrated on the art of oratory to the exclusion of all else, can speak better than Caesar? Or anyone who makes so many witty remarks? Or whose vocabulary is so varied and yet so exact?". Cicero in Suetonius, *Caesar* 55, Graves trans., p.33.

108 'On the Ocean' by Pytheas in Cunliffe 2002; for Ptolemaic ship reaching Britain see Levi 1980, p.187.

108 'because he knew that in almost all the Gallic campaigns the Gauls had received reinforcements from the Britons. Even if there was no time for a campaign that season, he thought it would be of great advantage to him merely to visit the island, to see what its inhabitants were like, and to make himself acquainted with the lie of the land, the harbours and the landing-places'. Caesar, *Conquest of Gaul* V.I, Handford trans., p.119.

108 'gives them a more terrifying appearance in battle'. Caesar, *Conquest of Gaul* V.2, Handford trans., p.136.

109 'embalm in cedar-oil and carefully preserve in a chest, and these they exhibit to strangers'. Diodorus V.29, in Oldfather trans., p.175.

109 'astonishing masses of cliff'. Cicero, in Weigall 1926, p.26.

109 'he weighed with his own hand to judge their value'. Suetonius, Caesar 47, Graves trans., p.30.

110 'sky-blue Britons'. Martial *Epigrams* XI.liii in Carr 2005, appendix, and Ottaway 2004, p.59.

110 'azure beauty'. Propertius, *Elegies* II.18b in Carr 2005, appendix.

110 'so high were the prices he paid on slaves of good character and attainments that he became ashamed of his extravagance and would not allow the sums to be entered in his accounts'. Suetonius, *Caesar* 47, in Graves trans., p.30.

110 'always led his army, more often on foot than in the saddle'. Suetonius, *Caesar* 57, Graves trans., p.35.

110 'keep a close eye on me!' Suetonius, *Caesar* 65, Graves trans., p.37.

110 'my men fight just as well when they are stinking of perfume'. Suetonius *Caesar* 67, Graves trans., p.37.

110 'he used to comb the thin strands of his hair forward from his poll . . . a disfigurement which his enemies harped upon, much to his exasperation'. Suetonius, *Caesar* 45, Graves trans., p.29.

110 'tall, fair and well built with a rather broad face and keen dark brown eyes'. Suetonius, *Caesar* 45, Graves trans., p.29.

111 'discovered his disposition which was very susceptible, to such an extent that he had his intrigues with ever so many other women – with all, doubtless, who chanced to come his way'. Cassius Dio 42.34.2, Cary trans., p.167.

111 'his affairs with women are commonly described as numerous and extravagant: among those of noble birth who he is said to have seduced were Servius Sulpicius' wife Postumia; Aulus Gabinius's wife Lollia; Marcus Crassus' wife Tertulla; and even Gnaeus Pompeius's wife Mucia'. Suetonius, *Caesar* 50, Graves trans., p.31.

111 'Caesar's wife must be above suspicion'. Plutarch, *Caesar* 9, Dryden trans., p.581.

111 'Home we bring our bald whoremonger, Romans lock your wives away! All the bags of gold you lent him went his Gallic tarts to pay!'. Suetonius, *Caesar* 51, Graves trans., p.31.

111 'Caesar was led by Nicomedes's attendants to the royal bedchamber, where he lay on a golden couch, dressed in a purple shift . . . So this decendant of Venus lost his virginity in Bithynia'. Cicero in Suetonius, *Caesar* 49, Graves trans., p.30.

111 'pansy Romulus'. Grant 1968, p.101.

112 'every woman's husband and every man's wife'. Suetonius, *Caesar* 52, Graves trans., p.32.

112 'without Caesar's knowledge – the disgrace of Egypt, promiscuous to the harm of Rome'. Lucan *Civil War* 10.58–60 in Maehler 2003, p.211.

112 'lecherous prostitute queen . . . worn among her own household slaves'.

Propertius, III.11, Shepherd 1985 in Maehler 2003, pp.209–10; also 'a woman of insatiable sexual appetite'. Cassius Dio 51.15, Scott-Kilvert trans., p.76.

112 'became so debauched that she often sold herself as a prostitute; but she was so beautiful that many men bought a night with her at the price of their own death'. Aurelius Victor in Lovric 2001, p.52.

112 'the power of the courtesan – and she exploited it professionally'. Forster 1982, pp.25–6.

112 'willing to use her body to gain her political ends'. Watterson 1998, p.28, although 'the image of Cleopatra . . . who pays with her body the price of the power she wants to keep . . . is a reduced image and, in many points of view, completely falsified'. Bingen 2007, pp.53–4.

112 Although Cleopatra's descent from Alexander is currently doubted, Romans believed it (e.g. Curtius 9.8.22 in Chugg 2004, p.52; Propertius III.11 in Maehler 2003, p.210, 215).

112 'was particularly desirous of settling the disputes of the princes [sic] as a common friend and arbitrator'. Caesar, *Civil Wars* III.109, Peskett trans., p.351; yet 'his actions were obviously inspired by a genuine romantic attachment'. Hölbl 2001, p.236.

114 'it is a good thing for me to sit down with Tanous so that she may be my wife'. Rowlandson (ed.) 1998, p.318, stating marriage was 'brought about by 2 people living together', p.319.

114 'the surge of the breakers was ever to be heard in its airy halls'. Weigall 1928, p.122.

114 Ptolemies' palatial features in Athenaeus, *Deipnosophists* V.195–197, Gulick trans., pp.386–93.

114 'the rafters were hidden beneath a thick coating of gold. The walls shone with marble'. Lucan, *Civil War* 10.112–115 in Duff trans., p.599; see also Empereur 2002, p.45–47; Burn 2004, p.105; paintings 'graced the courts of . . . the Ptolemies of Egypt' in Ward-Perkins and Claridge 1976, p.69; cinnabar and gold leaf in Laing 1997, p.106, Edwards et al. 1999.

114 Hobnailed caliga footwear worn up to centurion rank and report of slipping in Josephus, *Bellum Judaicum* 6.1.8, both in Goldman 2001, p.122.

115 'while stationed abroad, he always had dinner served in two separate rooms: one for his officers and Greek friends, the other for Roman citizens and the more important provincials'. Suetonius, *Caesar* 48, Graves trans., p.30; Macedonian palace dining rooms divided 'into grades of differing importance, for which there is clear evidence in 2nd century Ptolemaic Egypt'. Tomlinson 1970, p.314.

116 'her baleful beauty painted up beyond all measure: covered with the

spoils of the Red Sea, she carried a fortune round her neck and in her hair, and was weighed down by her ornaments'. Lucan *Civil War* 10.137–141, Duff trans., p.601.

116 'take the food with the tips of your fingers; and you must know eating is itself an art . . . to eat a little less than you feel inclined to . . . don't drink more than your head will stand. Don't lose the use of your head and feet; and never see two things when only one is there'. Ovid, *Art of Love* III, Lewis May trans., p.100.

116 'like an extraordinarily beautiful meadow'. Athenaeus, *Deipnosophists* V.196, Gulick trans., p.391.

116 'Rose-breasted Lady'. Witt 1971, p.298, note71.

116 'in honour of lady Isis'. Witt 1971, p.164.

116 'pleasant social intercourse and conviviality'. Witt 1971, p.164.

116 'so fair haired that Caesar said he had never seen hair so red in the Rhine country'. Lucan *Civil War* 10.129–131, in Duff trans., p.599.

116 'he once put his baker in irons for giving him a different sort of bread from that served to his guests'. Suetonius, *Caesar* 48, Graves trans., p.30.

117 'walnut and rue at the start of the meal counter all poisons'. Galen, in Wilkins and Hill 2006, p.236.

117 'the only sober man who ever tried to wreck the Constitution'. Suetonius, *Caesar* 53, Graves trans., p.32.

117 'not even his enemies denied that he drank abstemiously', Suetonius, Caesar 53, Graves trans., p.32.

117 'he often feasted with her until dawn'. Suetonius, *Caesar* 52, Graves trans., p.32.

118 'slay our cruel mistress in her very bed . . . take Caesar's life'. Lucan, *Civil War* 10.373–375, Duff trans., p.619.

118 'it was possible that the blood of Caesar might be shed over the king's drinking cups and his head fall upon the table'. Lucan, *Civil War* 10.421–424, Duff trans., p.621–3.

118 'a busy listening fellow whose excessive timidity made him inquisitive into everything . . . Caesar, upon the first intelligence of it, set a guard upon the hall where the feast was kept and killed Pothinus'. Plutarch, *Caesar*, Dryden trans., p.596.

118 'he burnt all those ships and the rest that were in the docks'. Caesar, *Civil Wars* III.111, Peskett trans., p.357; evidence that Caesar did not destroy Great Library in Empereur 2002, p.43.

120 'sacred emblems'. Caesar, Alexandrian War 32, in Way trans., p.63.

121 'Julius Caesar made a pillar of brass for the Jews at Alexandria and declared publicly that they were citizens of Alexandria'. Josephus, *Antiq.* xiv.188, in Davis 1951, p.99; also *Cont. Ap* ii.37, in Davis 1951, p.99.

121 'the elder of the two boys – the late king – being now no more, Caesar assigned the kingdom to the younger one and to Cleopatra, the elder of the two daughters, who had remained his loyal adherent'. Caesar, *Alexandrian War* 33, Way trans., p.63.

121 'according to Egyptian rites'. Southern 2001, p.123.

121 'fell in love with her, married her and had a son with her'. John of Nikiou, in el-Daly 2005, p.132.

121 Chalcedony intaglio with Caesar's image in Grant 1972, pp.81–2.

Chapter 5

125 'could have been scarcely more than a day trip'. Hughes-Hallett 1990, p.19.

125 'are related more particularly in my Egyptian history'. Appian, *Roman History* II.90, White trans., p.393.

125 'through the whole country, and back to Memphis where he attended the performance of religious festivities and was on that occasion escorted by his nobles, his wives, and his royal children'. Reymond and Barns 1977, p.13.

125 'ascended the Nile with 400 ships, exploring the country in company with Cleopatra and generally enjoying himself with her'. Appian, *Roman History* II.90, White trans., p.393.

126 'saloons for dining parties, with berths, and with all the other conveniences of living'. Athenaeus, *Deipnosophists* V.204, Gulick trans., pp.425–7.

126 'bulged as they ascended, and the drums differed, one being black and the other white, placed alternately. Some of their capitals were circular . . . resembling rose blossoms slightly opened . . . calyxes of water-lilies and the fruit of freshly-budded date-palms'. Athenaeus, *Deipnosophists* V.206, in Gulick trans., p.431.

126 'immense and superb vessels with rooms and gardens and fountains, ornamented with marbles and precious metals and rare woods, all shining with gold and purple'. *Antiquity* 1927 (b), p.221; see also Carlson 2002.

127 Cleopatra's purple sails in Plutarch *Antony* 26–27, Dryden trans., p.757 and Pliny, *Natural History* XIX.V.22, Loeb trans., p.435.

128 'god's beloved and friend of the King'. Stela BM.EA.147, in Lichtheim 1980 p.61 and Reymond 1981, pp.165–77.

128 'the Ox Mneuis kept in a sanctuary as a god'. Strabo in Lindsay 1963, p.7.

128 'a display of vain toil with nothing pleasing or picturesque about it'. Strabo in Lindsay 1963, p.7.

129 'pleased with the Pyramids'. Milne 1916 (b), p.p77–78.

129 'every person who is Greek shall worship the son of Ptah, Imouthes'. Witt 1971, p.156.

129 'large and populous, ranks next after Alexandria, and is made up of mixed races like those who have settled together at Alexandria. Lakes stretch before the city and palaces'. Strabo in Lindsay 1963, pp.8–9.

129 Memphis temple where Isis 'passed from among mankind' in Witt 1971, p.101.

130 'the altars where incense is offered to the sacred Cow of Memphis'. Ovid, *Art of Love* III, Lewis May trans., p.94.

130 'the bull Apis is kept in a sort of sanctuary, regarded as a god. His forehead and certain other parts of his body are marked with white, but the rest is black, and it is by these marks that they always choose the bull suitable for the succession after the death of the one holding the honour. Before his sanctuary lies a court, in which there is another sanctuary allocated to the bull's mother'. Strabo, in Lindsay 1963, p.8.

130 'the bull with the beautiful horns . . . standing sideways by him, it licked his robe'. Palatine Anthology 7.7hh in Vasunias 2001, p.299.

130 'popping and hissing noises'. Pinch 1994, p.164; alliterative texts in Watterson 1979; alchemy furnace described by Zosimus of Panopolis (Akhmim) in Pinch 1994, p.169.

131 'sitting at meal and spending a pleasant time while assisting at festivals of all the gods and goddesses'. BM.886, in Reymond 1981, p.149.

131 'elegant and decorated . . . its floor decorated with genuine lapis and genuine turquoise. There was a great deal of furniture in it, which was covered with royal linen, and there were numerous gold cups on the sideboard . . . incense was put on the brazier, and perfume was brought'. Pap. Cairo 30646, trans., Tait in Rowlandson (ed.) 1998, pp.364–5.

131 'a noble resplendent of possessions of every kind. To me belongs a harem of fair maidens'. BM.886, in Reymond 1981, p.149.

131 Taimhotep claimed 'I was pregnant by him 3 times but did not bear a male child, only 3 daughters' on stela BM.EA.147, in Lichtheim 1980, pp.59–65, Reymond 1981, pp.165–77.

131 'fluid of conception' and Arab pharmacopoeia in Dunand and Zivie-Coche 2004, p.313.

131 'who gives a son to him who has none'. Reymond 1981, p.175.

131 Ptolemaic bull statues Louvre N.390 in Louvre 1981, p.XI, Cleveland 1969.118 in Berman 1999, p.466; statue of Ptolemy IX identified by Maehler 1983, p.10.

132 'Know that Hesat is Isis!'. Pap. Zen. Pestman 50, in Rowlandson (ed.) 1998, p.49.

132 'its development for it alone is planted with olives, of which there are many large trees bearing fine fruit'. Strabo 17.1.35, in Alston 1995, p.17; for Caesar considering scheme for Rome, see Seton-Williams 1978, p.10.

132 'from every shivering fit and fever'. Scheidel 2001, p.77.

132 Fayum stela Louvre E.27113 in Rowlandson (ed.) 1998, p.38, Brooklyn 1988, p.189.

132 Hymns in Dunand and Zivie-Coche 2004, p.233; Cleopatra's buildings in Maehler 1983, p.7; crocodile burials in Chaveau 2133, p.108; temple crocodile in Houlihan 1996, p.119.

133 'putting rings made of glass or gold into its ears and bracelets round its front feet'. Herodotus, II. 69, de Selincourt trans., p.156.

133 'make ready guest-chambers and landing-stages and presents, and to take every care that he should be satisfied'. Pap. Tebtunis 33 in Milne 1916(b), p.78.

133 'fed on grain and bits of meat and wine, which are always offered to it by visiting foreigners . . . we came upon the creature as it lay on the edge of the lake and when the priests went up to it some of them opened its mouth and another put the cake in, then the meat, and poured the honey-mixture down'. Strabo in Lindsay 1963, p.10.

133 Crocodile handlers in Pliny, *Natural History* VIII.38.92–93, trans., pp.67–9; statue BM.GR.1805.7–3.6 in Walker and Higgs (eds.,) 2001, p.339.

133 'Wet-nurse of the Crocodile'. Tiradritti 1998, p.14.

134 'a satirical reference to Cleopatra VII of Egypt'. BM.GR.Q.100, Johns 1989, fig.91, p.110.

134 'a large statue of Serapis, 9 cubits high, made of smaragdus'. *Natural History* Pliny XXXVII.76, Loeb trans., p.225.

135 'a mixture of religious buildings in traditional Egyptian style rubbing shoulders with the classically designed public buildings that defined the Greek polis – the bath complex, the gymnasium and the theatre. But on leaving the centre, one would have moved into a large and dirty Egyptian village showing comparatively little change from previous eras'. Montserrat 1996, p.80.

136 Greek graffiti seen in 1824 'at which time they had not been visited by any modern traveller'. Gardner Wilkinson in Davies 1903, p.3; dog cemetery in Kemp 2006, p.22.

137 'only by loud screaming can one lead one another's way'. Ibn Gubayr in Arnold 1999, p.164.

137 'To Theon. Let the relevant persons be told that the temple of Isis built on behalf of our well-being by Kallimachos the military commander south of Ptolemais is to be tax-free and inviolable together with the

houses built around it as far as the wall of the city. Let it be done'. based on van Minnen 2003, p.43.

137 'remarkable structure of solid stone'. Strabo in Lindsay 1963, p.11.

137 'Memnonion'. Kemp in Rutherford 2003, p.174.

138 'the gods in Abydos'. Rutherford 2003, p.179.

138 'to my mind, she is too short'. Eady 1983, p.17.

138 Osiris' rites in Herodotus' II.62, de Selincourt trans., p.153 and in Plutarch, see Witt 1971, p.213, Dunand and Zivie-Coche 2004, p.239 and Gillam 2004, pp.55–9, 104.

139 'older than her mother'. Witt 1971, p.292, note 4.

139 temple's east wall conceals 'suites of rooms, called crypts, and a staircase within its thickness. The lowest set of crypts is below ground, contained within foundations about 10 metres deep . . . in the ground-level and upper crypts are access holes . . . all were concealed within the decoration'. Baines and Malek 1980 p.64; 'the only female monarch depicted in the relief decoration at Dendera is Cleopatra VII'. Bianchi 2003, p.14.

139 'the naos shrine of Hathor resplendent in silver, gold and every kind of precious stone without measure . . . the statue of Isis which is hidden, made of finest gold'. Shore 1979, p.149.

140 'I give you happiness daily, without distress for your majesty . . . drunkenness upon drunkenness without end'. Poo 1995, p.143.

140 'nigro tibicine'. Juvenal XV.49 in Maehler 2003, p.212.

140 'Pharaoh comes to dance and comes to sing, Mistress, see his dancing, see the skipping! He offers the wine jug to you, Mistress, see his dancing, see the skipping! His heart is pure, no evil in his body, Mistress, see his dancing, see the skipping! O Golden One, how fine is the song, like the song of Horus himself, which Ra's son sings as the finest singer. He is Horus, the musician! He hates to see sorrow in your soul, he hates the bright goddess to be sad! Oh beautiful One, Great Cow, Great Magician, Glorious Lady, Gold of the gods, he comes to dance, comes to sing with his sistrum [sacred rattle] of gold and his menat [ritual necklace] of malachite, his feet rush toward the Mistress of Music as he dances for her and she loves all he does!' After Lichtheim 1980, pp.107–9.

141 'I hope that you are in good health, and without cease, for you, I worship close to the hair at Koptos'. Pap. Michigan VIII.502, in Nachtergael 1981, p.593.

141 Female performers in Smith and Hall 1984, p.15; gazelle as 'Isis' plaything'. Witt 1971, p.33.

141 Cleopatra's limestone statue UC.14521 in Walker and Higgs (eds.,) 2001, p.171.

141 'Lady of the Two Lands, Cleopatra Philopator, beloved of Min of

Koptos, King's Daughter, King's Wife'. Ashton 2003(b), pp.25–6, with barque shrine in Arnold 1999, p.221 and Ashton 2003(b), pl.1, p.25.

142 'Come, Golden Goddess . . . it is good for the heart to dance! Shine on our feast at the hour of retiring, and enjoy the dance at night. Come! The procession takes place at the site of drunkenness, drunks play tambourines for you in the cool night, and those they awaken bless you'. Based on Drioton in Manniche 1991, p.61.

142 'Female Sun of the Two Lands'. Louvre 1981, p.325.

142 'lord of Medamud, Thebes, Tod and Hermonthis'. Mond and Myers 1934, II, pp.25, 46–49.

143 'deliberately made by one of the men standing all around and near the base'. Strabo XVII.1.46 in Lindsay 1963, p.12; Gardiner 1961 p.92.

143 'considered to be Memnon and a talking stone'. Manetho in Gardiner 1961 p.98; 'Memnon's legs . . . recall the visitors' books that are to be found in many tourist resorts'. Milne 1916(b), p.80.

144 'tomb of Osymandyas'. Diodorus I.47–49, Oldfather trans., pp.167–75.

144 'marvelously devised, a spectacle worth seeing'. Strabo XVII.1.46 in Lindsay 1963, p.12; Gardiner 1961, p.92.

144 'those who have not seen this place have never seen anything: blessed are they who visit this place'. Milne 1916(b), p.80.

144 Menkare's son buried in sarcophagus of Ankhnesneferibre. James and Davis 1983, p.54.

145 'magnificent'. Macrobius, *Saturnalia* I.21 in Mond and Myers 1934, II, p.27.

145 'King of Upper and Lower Egypt'. Lepsius in Brooklyn 1988, p.52.

145 'Female Horus'. Tait 2003, p.4.

146 'was there because Cleopatra wanted her to be there'. Ray 2003, p.11.

146 'luxuriant decoration represented an excellent example of the baroque style of [Ptolemaic] architecture'. Arnold 1999, p.224; layout duplicating that at Dendera in Arnold 1999, p.346; Cleopatra's Hermonthis mammisi 'a principal shrine in its own right'. Ray 203, p.10.

146 'the play of light and shadows at the capitals, and the effect of the huge, window-like openings that created beautiful connections between interior and exterior spaces must have been stunning'. Arnold 1999, p.224.

146 Birthing scenes in Brooklyn 1988, p.35; eighteenth-century 'bull' reference in Mond and Myers 1934 II, p.49.

146 'the egg in the bodies of women, to provide the country with younger generations for the favour of the King of Upper and Lower Egypt, beloved of Khnum'. Gillam 2005, p.119.

147 'Female Horus, Lady of Upper and Lower Egypt and Mighty Bull', 'it was Cleopatra III who had provided her with her inspiration'. Whitehorne 2001, pp.147–8.

147 'as a giant sundial'. Arnold 1999, p.220.

148 'kyphi'. Plutarch, *Moralia* 383.d in Montserrat 1996, p.70; 'best quality oil'. Watterson 1979, p.168; 'sacred oils', myrrh, unguents for statues etc. in Manniche 1999, pp.40–1, 45, 108.

148 'Festival of the Beautiful Union'. Gillam 2005, p.122 and Watterson 1998, pp.105–11.

148 'for anointing the Golden Goddess Hathor'. Manniche 1999, p.41.

148 'the faraway conquering god' which was 'an excellent metaphor, in Egyptian terms, for Caesar'. Ray 2003, p.9.

148 'I am Horus whom Isis has brought forth and whose protection was guaranteed in the egg'. Witt 1971, p.214; protection rituals in Gillam 2005, pp.98–9.

149 'his being before the ancestors'. Ibrahim 1979, pp.170–1.

150 'would have sailed together in her state barge nearly to Ethiopia had his soldiers consented to follow him'. Suetonius, *Caesar*, 52, in Graves trans., p.32.

150 Cleopatra's Kom Ombo images in Höbl 2001, p.272; crocodile pool with 'an elaborate fountain system'. Arnold 1999, p.220.

150 'the victorious crowd, gnawing his bones, ate all of him'. Juvenal XV.80–81 in Maehler 2003, p.212.

151 'Island from the time of Ra'. Wilkinson 2000, p.213.

151 'Queen of the South'. Witt 1971, p.61; Arsinoe II's crown 'differed from the traditional queen's crown, and was modeled on the crown of Hatshepsut'. Rowlandson (ed.) 1998, p.29.

151 'Mistress of Life, as she dispenses life. Men live by the command of her soul' After Dunand, and Zivie-Coche 2004, p.237.

152 'pure mound'. Shaw and Nicholson 1995, p.223.

152 Cleopatra's statue in Hölbl, p.310; Caesar's time on the Nile 'served to show him how important was the cult of the sovereigns, dead or alive'. Goudchaux 2001, p.134.

Chapter 6

153 Caesar states he 'was compulsorily detained by the etesian winds, which blow directly counter to those sailing from Alexandria'. Caesar, *Civil Wars* III.107, Peskett trans., p.349.

154 'Kaisaros Epibaterios . . . Embarking Caesar'. Grimm 2003, p.48.

155 'Reliever of the birth pangs of women'. Apuleius, Graves trans., p.269.

155 'I have brought forth the new-born baby at the tenth orbit of the moon –

fit light for the deed that is consummated'. Andros Hymn in Witt 1971, p.148.

155 'celibate spear'. Pliny *Natural History*.28.33–34, Loeb trans., p.25.

155 'measuring the courses of the heavenly bodies; he urged her not to hurry in giving birth. At the same time he jumbled up the cosmic elements by the use of his magic powers, discovered what lay hidden in them and said to her 'woman, contain yourself and struggle against the pressure of Nature'. Alexander Romance, in Jasnow 1997, p.98.

156 'literate with her wits about her . . . sound of limb, robust and according to some endowed of long slim fingers and short nails . . . She will be unperterbed, unafraid in danger and able to state clearly the reasons for her measures, bringing reassurance to her patients and be sympathetic . . . She must also keep her hands soft, abstaining from wool working which would make them hard, and she must acquire softness by means of ointments if it is not present naturally'. Soranus in Jackson 1988, pp.96–7.

157 'injected seed . . . to appease the soul . . . one must not pay attention to the popular saying that it is necessary to provide food for two organisms'. Soranus in Jackson 1988, p.95.

157 'if the bulk of the abdomen is hanging down under its weight'. Soranus in Jackson 1988, p.95.

158 'fastening an amulet about herself'. Plutarch, *De Iside et Osiride*, in Witt 1971, p.213.

158 'one should not forbid their use, for even if the amulet has no direct effect, still through hope it will possibly make the patient more cheerful'. Soranus in Jackson 1988, p.88.

158 'god of the House of Birth who opens the vagina'. Ritner 1984, p.215.

158 'greatest god of the womb of women'. Ritner 1984, p.217.

158 'bring down the womb or placenta to be said 4 times over a dwarf of clay tied to the woman's head'. Pinch 1994, p.129; Egyptian-made birth amulet from Britain in Wilson and Wright 1964.

158 Birth bricks in Wegner 2002; birth stool in Jackson 1988, p.97; Olympias 'on the birth stool' in Alexander Romance in Jasnow 1997, p.98.

158 'should beware of fixing her gaze steadfastedly on the genitals of the labouring woman, lest being ashamed, her body becomes contracted'. Jackson 1988, p.99.

158 'make every effort to expel the child'. Galen, *On the Natural Faculties* III.ii, in Jackson 1988, p.97.

159 'warm water in order to cleanse all parts; sea sponges for sponging off; pieces of wool in order for a woman's parts to be covered; bandages to swaddle the new born; a pillow to place the newborn infant below the woman until the afterbirth has also been taken care of; and things to

smell, such as pennyroyal, apple and quince'. Soranus in Jackson 1988, p.97.

159 'before surgical operations and punctures to produce anesthesia'. Pliny, *Natural History*, XXV.44.150 in Loeb trans., p.243.

159 'mothers and children'. Zias in Rimon 1997, p.16; see also Nunn 1996, p.156.

159 'remarkable power to increase the force of uterine contractions, concomitant with a significant reduction of labour pain'. Zias et al. 1993, p.215.

159 'caesus'. Grant 1969, p.23 and Ellis 1978, p.74.

159 'expertly-made precision instruments'. Jackson 1988, p.93.

160 'one should do everything gently and without bruising'. Soranus in Jackson 1988, p.104.

160 'Who died here? Herois. How and when? Heavy-wombed in pained labour she set down her burden – a mother she was for a moment, but the child died also. Light may the earth be on her, may Osiris bestow cool water'. Lichtheim 1980, p.7.

160 'on receiving my letter please be so good as to come home promptly because your poor daughter Herennia has di(ed.) And to think she had already come safely through a miscarriage. For she gave birth to a still-born child in the 8th month, but herself survived 4 days, and only after that did she die . . . so if you come and you so wish, you can see her'. Pap. Fuad 75, in Montserrat 1997, p.37.

161 'Great Mother of the Gods'. Witt 1971, p.131.

161 'Ptuwlmis djed tuw en ef Kisrs . . . Ptolemaios named Caesar'. Hölbl 2001, p.238, with 'pharaoh Caesar' on demotic stela Louvre 335 in Hölbl 2001, p.238.

161 'the child's parentage was not in doubt. He combined Egypt and Rome in his lineage'. Southern 2001, p.123.

162 Caesar's news and plans for new law in Suetonius, *Caesar* 52 in Graves trans., p.32.

162 'the Sun Child'. Ray 2003, p.10; Isis gave birth to sun in Plutarch, *Moralia* 354.C in Tarn 1932, p.146; Caesar as Montu and Amun in Goudchaux 2001 p.133 and Ray 2003, p.11, who also states child equated with Alexander.

163 'Female Horus, the Great One, Lady of the Two Lands . . . the Goddess who loves her father . . . Image of her father'. After Tait 2003, p.4.

163 Mammisi's false door in Arnold 1999, p.223; false door of Dendera mammisi in Arnold 1999, p.231 and Hölbl 2001, p.270.

163 'keeping dreadful death far away when in labour'. Anth. Pal.6.270, after Llewellyn-Jones 2003, p.218.

163 'From your mother, greetings. We received the letter from you in which you announce that you have given birth to your child. I kept praying to the gods every day on your behalf. Now that you have escaped, I am spending my days in the greatest joy. I sent you a flask full of olive oil and several pounds of dried figs'. Pap. Münch III.57, in Rowlandson (ed.) 1998, p.292.

163 'Cleopatras Basilisses', 'of Cleopatra the female king' on coin BM.Cleopatra VII.3 in Walker and Higgs (eds.,) 2001, no.186, p.178, and Wyke 2002, fig.6.1, p.203.

164 'she had caused to be built joining the temple of Isis several tombs and monuments of wonderful height and very remarkable for their workmanship'. Plutarch, *Antony*, Dryden trans., p.775.

164 For tomb's location in Hadra quarter see Ashton 2003(b) p.28 and Ashton 2003 pp.120–2.

164 'the tomb which she was building in the grounds of the palace'. Cassius Dio 51.8 in Scott-Kilvert trans., p.69

164 'actually formed part of the temple buildings; and if this be so Cleopatra must have had it in mind to be laid to rest within the precincts of the sanctuary of the goddess with whom she was identified'. Weigall 1914, pp.289–90.

164 'Came. Saw. Conquered'. Suetonius, *Caesar* 37, Graves trans., p.25; 'such a victory transported Caesar with incredible delight'. Caesar, *Alexandrian War* 77, Way trans., p.133.

165 'courteous, insincere conversations in which the two men specialised'. Grant 1969, p.181.

165 'Africa! I have tight hold of you!'. Suetonius, *Caesar* 59, Graves trans., p.35.

165 'a very rare occurance'. Gillam 2004, p.104.

165 'springs from the Eye of Ra . . . from the left eye of Osiris . . . from the eye of Thoth'. Manniche 1999, p.26.

166 'with the best of myrrh on all her limbs'. Breasted 1988, p.113.

166 'green eye paint for the right eye and black kohl for the left eye'. Wilson in Quirke (ed.) 1997, p.190.

166 'many-colored robe . . . part was glistening white, part crocus-yellow, part glowing red and along the entire hem a woven border of flowers and fruit clung swaying in the breeze . . . in innumerable folds, the tasseled fringe quivering. It was embroidered with glittering stars on the hem and everywhere else, and in the middle beamed a full and fiery moon'. Apuleius, based on Graves trans. p.270.

166 'Black-robed Queen'. Plutarch in Witt 1971, p.97, p.147; devotees' vestments in Apuleius XI, Graves trans., p.286; priests' studded stoles in Riggs 2002, p.98.

166 'fell in tapering ringlets on her lovely neck'. Apuleius, Graves trans., p.270.

166 'shone a round disc like a mirror . . . vipers rising from the left-hand and right-hand partings of her hair'. Apuleius, based on Graves trans., p.270.

167 'which sang shrilly when she shook the handle'. Apuleius, based on Graves trans. p.270.

167 'filled with every kind of real precious stones, every kind of perfume, every kind of grain'. Shore 1979 p.149.

167 'Ptolemy living forever beloved of Ptah . . . Lady of Dendera, Lady of Heaven, Mistress of All Gods'. After Shore 1979, pp.138–41.

167 'Festival Scent . . . Madjet'. Manniche 1999, p.108; 'secret unguent'. Manniche 1999, p.45; 'for anointing the golden goddess Hathor, great mistress of Dendera'. Manniche 1999, pp.40–1.

168 'may have had a performative function'. Gillam 2004, p.108.

169 'generative light falling strongly from the moon'. Plutarch, in Mond and Myers 1934 I, p.11.

169 'your sister Isis comes to you, rejoicing in love for you, she placed your phallus on her vulva and your seed issues into her, she being as alert as a star'. Spell 632a–633b, based on Benard and Moon (eds) 2169, p.228.

169 'the Moon'. Cassius Dio 50.5, Scott-Kilvert trans., p.39.

169 'at this secret hour that the Moon-goddess, sole sovereign of mankind, is possessed of her greatest power and majesty. She is the shining deity by whose divine influence not only all beasts, wild and tame, but all inanimate things as well, are invigorated; whose ebbs and flows control the rhythm of all bodies whatsoever, whether in the air, on earth, or below the sea'. Apuleius, Graves trans., p.268.

171 Two hundred and forty gold pieces in Suetonius, *Caesar* 38, Graves trans., p.26; 60,000 gold pieces = 1,500,000 denarii based on Suetonius, *Caesar* 50, Graves p.31, so 240 gold pieces = 6,000 denarii.

171 'chanting ribald songs as they were privileged to do, this was one of them – "Gaul was brought to shame by Caesar, by King Nicomedes he. Here comes Caesar, wreathed in Triumph for his Gallic victory"'. – Suetonius, *Caesar* 49 in Graves trans., p.31.

172 'between two lines of elephants, 40 in all, which acted as his torch-bearers'. Suetonius, *Caesar* 37, in Graves trans., p.25.

173 'see how easily an old man slips . . . the man who many fear must also fear many himself'. Decimus Laberius in Grant 1969, p.192 and Volkmann 1958, p.83.

173 'he was a gladiator'. Juvenal, *Satires* VI.110 in Green trans., p.13.

174 'what modesty can be looked for in some helmeted hoyden, a renegade from her sex, who thrives on masculine violence'. Juvenal, *Satires*

VI.254–257, in Green trans., p.136; female gladiator with Anubis lamps in Kennedy 2000, p.11; Amazons as Isis devotees in Lichtheim 1980, pp.151–56.

174 'a display recorded to have been thought more wonderful even than the show of gladiators which he gave'. Pliny *Natural History* XIX.22, in Loeb trans., p.435.

174 'to sleep in tents pitched along the streets or roads, or on rooftops'. Suetonius, *Caesar* 39, Graves trans., p.27.

175 'an overnight celebrity'. Garland 2005, p.28.

Chapter 7

179 Cleopatra's correspondence with Theon dated 7 March 46 BC and 14 March 46 BC, stating 'Theon, to the city of the Ptolemaeans, greetings. Subjoined is a copy of the proclamation transmitted to us, together with the command in response, so that you may know it and deposit it in your public archives as fitting. Take care of yourselves, so you may be well, Farewell, year 6, phamenoth 12'. Van Minnen 2003, p.43.

179 'he was born in regnal year 6, day 15 of Epiphi, in the 8th hour of the day under the majesty of the Sovereign, Lady of the Two Lands, Cleopatra. The child's appearance was like that of the son of Ptah and there was jubilation over him by the people of Memphis. He was called Pedubastis and all rejoiced over him'. After Reymond 1981, pp.165–77; Lichtheim 1980, pp.59–65; Brooklyn 1988, No.122, p.230; Walker and Higgs (eds.,) 2001, p.187.

179 'the sea of the Greeks'. Lichtheim 1980, p.88.

180 'extraordinarily well proportion(ed.) Wonderful also was the adornment of the vessel besides; for it had figures at stern and bow not less than 18 feet high, and every available space was elaborately covered with encaustic painting; the entire surface where the oars projected, down to the keel, had a pattern of ivy leaves and Bacchic wands . . . by a crowd to the accompaniment of shouts and trumpets'. Athenaeus, *Deipnosophists* V.204, in Gulick trans., p.423, see also Goddio and Bernard 2004, p.162.

180 'Navigium Isidis' in James and O'Brien 2006, p.247, Witt 1971, pp.165–84; Isis' temples in Caputo 1998, p.247, Puteoli's Isis temple in Ward-Perkins and Claridge 1976, pp.15–16.

181 Suggestion she visited temple 'to thank the divinity linked to Isis for having given her Caesar's son' in Goudchaux 2001, p.133; recent interpretation of mosaic in Walker and Higgs (eds) 2001, p.333, with

detail of Cleopatra(?) with parasol in drawings at Windsor Royal Library (Pf.Z.19214) in Walker and Higgs (eds) 2001, p.335.

181 'decreed that from sunrise until dusk, no transport, cart wagon or chariot of any form would be allowed within the precincts of Rome . . . no exceptions to this order'. Hagen 1967, p.274.

182 'high titles and rich presents'. Suetonius, *Caesar* 52, Graves trans., p.32.

182 'worth 60,000 gold pieces'. Suetonius, *Caesar* 50, in Graves trans., p.31.

182 Suggestion that pearls could be those Mithridates seized is supported by reference to them coming to her 'through the hands of the Kings of the East'. Pliny *Natural History* IX.121–122, Loeb trans., p.243.

182 'do not think they have a real villa unless it rings with many resounding Greek names'. Varro, in Farrar 1998, p.22; ridicule by Cicero, *De Leg*.II.2 in Walker and Higgs (eds) p.288; water features in Ward-Perkins and Claridge 1976, nos 81–8; gardens in Farrar 1998; excavations of gardens in Pinto-Guillame 2002.

183 Egyptian-themed wall scenes in Kleiner 2005 pp.172–4, Walker and Higgs (eds.,) pp.286–7, Ward-Perkins and Claridge 1976, p.69, Matyszak 2003, p.156.

184 'he carried tessellated and mosaic pavements with him on his campaigns'. Suetonius, *Caesar* 46, in Graves trans., p.29.

184 'tossae Britannicae'. Bowman 2003, p.67, describing 'some kind of rug' which is 'referred to in a famous third-century inscription from Thorigny as tossae Britannicae'.

184 Priests' wooden headrests in Witt 1971, pp.94–5.

184 'a keen collector of gems, carvings, statues and Old Masters'. Suetonius, *Caesar* 47, Graves trans., p.30.

185 'crammed with gold and silver vessels from Delos and Corinth, an "automatic cooker" which he had bought at an auction, embossed silver, coverlets, pictures, statues and marbles'. Cicero, in Earl 1968, p.99.

185 'used the official residence on the Sacred Way'. Suetonius, Caesar 46, Graves trans., p.29.

185 'villae marittimae'. Ward-Perkins and Claridge 1976, p.16.

185 'more imposing than any known palace or villa of contemporary Hellenistic kings'. Trevelyan 1976, p.19; Alexander mosaic in Grant 1976, pp.175–6, 185.

185 Isis' images in Ward-Perkins and Claridge 1976, No.186, p.57; Isis' Italian temples in Witt 1971, figs 22–3, 25–7; 'House of Mysteries' in Ward-Perkins and Claridge 1976, No.204; Piso's villa in Trevelyan 1976, p.45 and Grant 1976, p.137; Laurentum villa in Weigall 1928, pp.241–3.

186 'Cleopatra's Baths'. El-Daly 2005, p.137; Aphrodite bathing on crocodile in Roveri et al. 1988, p.123.

186 'people regard baths fit only for moths if they haven't been arranged so that they receive the sun all day long through the widest of windows, if men cannot bath and get a tan at the same time and if they cannot look out from their bath tubs over stretches of land and sea'. Seneca, *Epist.*86, 4–13 in Hoss 2005, p.20.

186 'surrounded by glass windows overlooking the sea'. Weigall 1928, pp.241–3.

186 'masses of water that fall crashing down from level to level'. Seneca *Epist.*86, 4–13 in Hoss 2005, p.20.

187 'oeno'. Dioscorides in Manniche 1999, p.131; soap in P.Enteux 82, in Rowlandson (ed.) 1998, pp.172–4; brechu discussed by Dioscorides in Manniche 1999, p.132.

187 'not without its use to a wrinkled body'. Martial, *Epigrams* XIV.60, 1871 trans., p.612; lomentum in d'Ambrosio 2001, p.8 and Pliny, *Natural History* XXII.156, trans., p.405.

187 'the glutinous matter wherewith the Halcyon cements its nest' as 'certain cure for spots and pimples' in Ovid, *Art of Beauty* 76–78, Lewis May trans., p.115; see also *Metro News* 2007.

187 'creta fullonica'. D'Ambrosio 2001, p.8; 'nitrum' in Martial, *Epigrams* VI.93 in Jackson 1988, p.50.

187 'freshens her complexion with asses' milk'. Juvenal, *Satires* VI.469–70, Green trans., p.145; milk for wrinkles in Pliny, *Natural History* XXVIII.183, trans., p.125; emulsion in Manniche 1999, p.135.

187 'ancient form of chemical peel, the cosmetic procedure used to straighten out wrinkles or even out pigmentation'. *Chemistry World* 2006, p.22.

188 'his head carefully trimmed and shaved'. Suetonius *Caesar* 45, in Graves trans., p.29.

188 'see that your legs are not rough with bristles'. Ovid, *Art of Love* III.193–9, Lewis May trans., p.91.

188 'medicines for hair loss are recorded in her own words, more or less as follows. 'Against hair loss: make a paste of realgar [arsenic monosulphide] and blend it into oak gum, apply it to a cloth and place it where you have already cleaned as thoroughly as possible with natron [salts]'', adding that 'I myself have added foam to natron to the above recipe, and it worked nicely'. Galen, *De compositione medicamentorum secundum locos* XII.403–404 in Rowlandson (ed.) 1998, p.41.

188 'she put her wig on back-to-front in her confusion'. Ovid, *Art of Love III*, 243–6, after d'Ambrosio 2001, p.18; Egyptian and Roman wigs in Fletcher 2005; German hair in Ovid, *Amores* 1.14, Lewis May trans., p.31, Indian hair in Parker 2002, pp.41–2.

188 'on no account let your lover find you with a lot of 'aids to beauty' boxes

about you. The art that adorns you should be unsuspected . . . So let your servants tell us you are still asleep, if we arrive before your toilet's finish(ed.) You will appear all the more lovely when you've put on the finishing touch. Why should I know what it is that makes your skin so white? Keep your door shut, and don't let me see the work before it's finish(ed.) There are a whole host of things we men should know nothing about!'. Ovid, *Art of Love* III.209–210, 225–229, Lewis May trans., p.91.

189 Antonius 'rubbed her feet'. Plutarch, Antony, Dryden trans., p.769; Mendesian unguent used for feet and Cleopatra's 400-denarii hand cream in Manniche 1999, p.63; 400 denarii = 1lb perfume in Pliny *Natural History* XIII.20, trans., p.111.

189 'seductively brings on sleep, so that without getting drunk, the sorrows and tensions of daily anxieties are loosened and untied like tangled knots'. Plutarch, *Concerning Isis and Osiris* 80 = *Moralia* 383.d in Montserrat 1996, p.70.

189 'foreign essences' in Pliny *Natural History* XIII.24, trans., p.113; promotion of perfumes by Arsinoe II and Berenike II in Athenaeus, *Deipnosophists* XV.689.a in Griffin 1976, p.93.

189 'Aphrodite's Elixir', 'Bloom of Youth' in Smith 1992, pp.163–7.

190 'Rose breasted Lady'. Witt 1971, p.298, note 71; 'the finest extract of roses in the world was made at Cyrene while the great Berenice was alive'. Athenaeus, *Deipnosophists* XV.689.a, see Griffin 1976, p.93; roses introduced to Egypt by Ptolemies in Carter 1940, p.252.

190 Egyptian rock crystal bottles in Rogers et al. 2001, pp.81–2; Cleopatra's agate vessels in Suetonius, *Augustus* 71, Graves trans., p.90, see also Cleveland 1964.92 in Berman 1999, p.484; blue glass vessels in Ward-Perkins and Claridge 1976, nos. 231, 234.

190 'one cannot escape the conclusion that on some occasions, Roman soldiers were pleasantly sweet-smelling!'. Ottaway 2004, p.56, recalling Caesar's men 'stinking of perfume'. Suetonius, *Caesar* 67 in Graves trans., p.37.

190 Ostia toilets in Hodges 1974 fig.229, p.199; Isis' latrine image in Ward-Perkins and Claridge 1976, p.57; Amasis' gold pot in Herodotus, II.172–4, de Selincourt trans., p.197; Ptolemaic chamber pot in Pliny, XXXIII.50, Loeb trans., p.41; Alexandria's drains in Empereur 1998, pp.125–43.

190 'bands of the behinds' in Hall 1986, p.55 and 'rhakos', 'a sort of tampon made of wool or linen', in Milanezi 2005, p.78.

191 'Unswept Hall' mosaic in Davidson 1998, p.xv; skeleton mosaic in Ward-Perkins and Claridge 1976, no.18; seafood mosaic in Ward-Perkins and Claridge 1976, no.253.

191 'a man for whom such a dinner sufficed had no need of gold' in Wilkins and Hill 2006, p.200.

192 'Puls Punica' and 'lagana' tagliatelle enjoyed by Cicero, see Jarrat and Jarrat in Grant 1999, p.39, 65; for typical wealthy Roman menu see Jones 2006.

192 'the eel you consider the greatest divinity, and we the greatest dish'. Davidson 1997, p.8.

192 'pale skin, slender figures and large eyes'. Hyperides in Davidson 1997, p.9.

192 'opsomanes', 'gunaikomanes'. Chrysippus in Davidson 1997, p.9.

192 'see the red fish playing between my fingers'. Cairo JE.25218/IFAO 1266 based on Manniche 1987, p.88.

192 Venus in Juvenal, *Satires* VI.300 in Green trans., p.138; 'oysters from Kent and Essex became very popular in Rome, and perhaps in Alexandria too; and it may be that they were already known to the Inimitables'. Weigall, 1928 p.128.

192 'Numidian birds'. *Satyricon*, 55 in Parker 2002, p.58.

193 Cleopatra's figs in Plutarch, *Antony* 85 in Rowlandson (ed.) 1998, pp.40–1; Egyptian fruit sent to Italy in Empereur 2002, p.35; Alexander's ice dessert in Fagan (ed.) 2004, p.119.

193 'the Roman equivalent of the modern champagne'. Rackham 1916, p.223.

193 'perfumed singer and musical virtuoso'. Volkmann 1958, p.88.

194 'worse still is the well-read menace, who's hardly settled for dinner before she starts . . . , comparing, evaluating rival poets . . . she's so determined to prove herself eloquent, learned . . . Avoid a dinner partner with an argumentative style . . . choose someone rather who doesn't understand all she reads. I hate these authority-citers . . . who with antiquarian zeal quote poets I've never heard of'. Juvenal, *Satires* VI.434–56, Green trans., p.144.

194 Her effect on Caesar 'is not to be underestimated. Influenced by his relationship with her, he began to act more and more like a Hellenistic ruler'. Hölbl 2001, p.239.

194 'the home of all tricks and deceits'. Cicero, *Pro. Rab. Post.* 35 in Wyke 2002, p.211; Cicero's 'problem' with women in Grant 1972, p.96.

195 'dirty little Greek'. Grant 1972, p.64; ' queen' as term of contempt in Bingen 2007, p.45, also 'Cleopatra is "Aegyptia", "Egyptian", for Romans who wanted to offend or stigmatise her', p.60.

195 'charming in conversation, yet her conduct was appropriate. She kept house, she made wool'. Pomeroy 1975 p.199; with 'no place for a woman in the strictly patriarchal Roman system of power' (Bingen 2007,

p.45), one 'on display as head of state . . . was therefore in itself transgressive and untranslatable, except in terms of sexual availability' (Hamer 1993, p.20); as symbol of equality male clothing 'could not be worn by mature women with aspiration to power'. Davies 2005, p.128.

195 'our ancestors established the rule that all woman, because of their weakness of intellect, should be under the power of [male] guardians'. Cicero, *Pro Murena* 27 in Allason-Jones 1990, p.16.

195 'I hate the queen! And the man who vouches for her promises, Ammonius, knows I have good reason to do so; although the gifts she promised me were of a literary nature and not beneath my dignity – the sort I should not have minded proclaiming in public. Her man Sara too, beside being a rogue, I have found impertinent towards myself. Once, and only once, have I seen him in my house; and then, when I asked him politely what he wanted, he said he was looking for Atticus. And the queen's insolence, when she was living in Caesar's house in the gardens across the Tiber, I cannot recall without indignation. So no dealings with that lot!'. Cicero, in Grant 1972, p.96; 'Sara' as shortening of Serapion see Grant 1972, p.261.

196 'loathsome man'. Cicero, Second Philipic, Graves trans., p.149.

196 'phaikasion'. MacLeod (ed.) 2002, p.52.

196 'and also by the fashion of his dress. For whenever he had to appear before large numbers, he wore his tunic girt low about the hips, a broadsword on his side, and over all a large coarse mantle'. Plutarch, *Antony*, Dryden trans., p.749.

196 'Antonius started up and left them in the middle of their cause, to follow at her side and attend her home'. Plutarch, *Antony*, in Dryden trans., p.769.

196 'push-cart'. Soranus', *Gynaecology* II.45–54 in Allason-Jones 1990, p.38; Caesarion's resemblence to Caesar in Suetonius, *Caesar* 52 in Graves trans., p.32.

197 'Cleopatra look'. Walker and Higgs (eds.,) 2001, pp.143–44, 208–209.

198 'a beautiful image of Cleopatra by the side of the goddess'. Appian, *Roman History* II.102, White trans., p.417; also Cassius Dio 51.22.3 in Scott-Kilvert trans., p.83.

198 'polite' (based on 'had even politely adorned his new temple of Venus with a statue of her') in Grant 1969, p.217.

198 'open acknowledgement of marriage between a descendant of a prestigious dynasty and the daughter of a god'. Walker and Higgs (eds.) 2001, p.277.

198 'Vatican Head' in Vatican Museum 38511 in Walker and Higgs (eds.,) 2001, No.196, p.218; Brooklyn 1988, No.76, pp.184–6; Kleiner 2005, p.152, fig.9.8 etc.

198 'a lotus crown or uraeus, or even the remains of a large knotted lock of hair'. Higgs in Walker and Higgs (eds.,) 2001, p.218; 'top-knot' in Walker and Higgs (eds.,) 2001, no.337, p.320.

198 For 'blemish' as child's finger see Bianchi 2003, p.19.

199 'slightly more flattering portrayal'. Walker and Higgs (eds.,) 2001, p.220 referring to Berlin Staatliche Museen Preussischer Kulturbesitz Antikenmuseum 1976.10, in Brooklyn 1988 No.77, p.187, Walker and Higgs (eds.,) 2001, No.198, pp.220–1, Hamer 1993, pl.1.2, p.4 etc.

199 'perhaps the finest and most beautiful portrait sculpture'. Maehler in Smith and Hall 1984, p.96.

199 'speaks for itself . . . it is infinitely more beautiful than the unflattering coin portrait, and it does convey an image of the great queen's personality'. Maehler 1983, p.8.

199 'great physical beauty'. Bowman 1986, p.25; Johansen 2003, p.77.

199 'whilst it does not flatter her, it bears a close relationship to the portraits of Alexander the Great'. Southern 2001, p.121.

199 Capitoline Head in Capitoline Museum Rome Inv.1154/S in Walker and Higgs (eds.,) 2001, pp.144–5, 217; same image on rings, see Walker and Higgs (eds.,) 2001, p.217.

200 For Iseum Campense dedicated to Julius Caesar see Cassius Dio XLVII.15.4 in Maehler 2003, p.205; 1987 discovery of priest's statue in Walker and Higgs (eds.,) p.329.

200 'temples, altars and divine images and a priest of his own cult'. Suetonius, Julius Caesar 76, in Graves trans., p.41.

200 'to the Unvanquished God'. Cassius Dio XLIII.45, in Goudchaux 2001, p.134.

200 Plans 'to constrain the Tiber to tolerate Nile's threats' in Propertius III.11, trans., Shepherd 1985 in Maehler 2003, pp.209–10; canal to drain marshes in Seton-Williams 1978, p.10, Grant 1972, pp.89–90.

200 'as crowded, probably, as modern Bombay or Calcutta'. Storey 1997, p.976, referring to census of 69 BC which gave city's population at 900,000.

201 It was said she 'spread her disgusting gauze on Tarpeia's rocks'. Propertius III.11, trans., Shepherd 1985 in Maehler 2003, pp.209–10; scale as eastern tradition in Grant 1968, p.196.

204 'a son being subsequently born to himself'. Suetonius, Caesar 83 in Graves trans., p.46, see also Chaveau 2002, p.32.

204 'a formidable guest, yet no regrets! For everything went very pleasantly indeed . . . On the 19th he stayed with Philippus until one o'clock and let no one in – I believe he was doing accounts with Balbus. Then he went for a walk on the shore. After two he had a bath . . . He had an oil-massage and

then sat down to dinner . . . His entourage were very lavishly provided for in three other rooms. Even the lower-ranking ex-slaves and the slaves lacked for nothing; the more important ex-slaves I entertained in style. In other words, we were human beings together. Still, he was not the sort of guest to whom you would say, "do please come again on your way back". Once is enough!'. Cicero in Grant trans., p.89.

204 Clues to second pregnancy based on Cicero's comments in *Letters to Atticus* XIV.20, 2, Grant 1972 p.95, combined with provision for 'a son being subsequently born to himself'. Suetonius, *Caesar* 83 in Graves trans., p.46, also Chaveau 2002, p.32.

204 'only a king can conquer the Parthians'. Suetonius, *Caesar* 80, Graves trans., p.43.

205 'Parens Patriae . . . Father of the Fatherland'. Walker and Higgs (eds.,) 2001, p.224.

205 'Long live the King!'. Suetonius, *Caesar* 79, Graves trans., p.43.

205 'it is likely that Cleopatra made her contribution, even if she was not present'. Goudchaux 2001, p.135.

205 'your colleague sat on the rostra, wearing his purple toga, on his golden chair, his garland on his head. Up you come, approaching the chair . . . you display a diadem. Groans all over the Forum! Where did the diadem come from? You hadn't found it in the gutter. No, you'd brought it with you, a planned, premeditated crime. You made to place the diadem on Caesar's head amid the lamentations of the people – he kept refusing it, and the people applaud(ed.) You had been urging Caesar to make himself king, you wanted him your master rather than your colleague'. Cicero, *Philippics* 2.XXXIV.85–86 in Heskel 2001, p.137; he also asked 'where did this diadem come from? . . . It was a premeditated crime in advance'. Cicero, Philippics 2.XXXI.85 in Goudchaux 2001, p.135.

206 'got up, took off his mantle and shouted that he was ready to have his throat slit if someone wanted to do it'. Plutarch, *Antony* 12 in Goudchaux 2001, p.135.

206 'a tendency to nightmares'. Suetonius, *Caesar* 45, in Graves trans., p.29.

206 'no doubt'. Grant 1972, p.93.

Chapter 8

207 'Brutus was elected consul when he sent the kings away, Caesar sent his consuls packing and Caesar is our king today'. Suetonius, *Caesar* 80, Graves trans., p.44.

297 'If only you were alive now!'. Suetonius, *Caesar* 80, Graves trans., p.44.

208 'no longer refuses to be called a tyrant, in fact he practically demands it, and that is exactly what he is'. Cicero, *Letters to Atticus*, in Grant 1968, p.148.

208 'either through the agencies of his enemies, or of himself'. Cicero, in Grant 1968, p.150.

208 'It is more important for Rome than for myself that I should survive. I have long been sated with power and glory; but should anything happen to me, Rome will enjoy no peace. A new civil war will break out under far worse conditions than the last'. Suetonius, *Caesar* 86, Grant trans., p.48.

209 'the best sort of death . . . 'let it come swiftly and unexpectedly'. Suetonius, *Caesar* 87, Graves trans., p.48.

209 'the Ides of March have come' . . . 'Ay, they have come, but they have not yet gone'. Suetonius, *Caesar* 81, Graves trans., p.45.

209 'This is violence!'. Suetonius, *Caesar* 82, Graves trans., p.45.

210 'you too my son?'. Suetonius, *Caesar* 82, Graves trans., p.46.

210 'our heroes most splendidly and gloriously achieved everything that was in their power'. Cicero, *Letter to Atticus*, in Graves trans., p.91.

211 'armed neutrality, whilst Antonius carried on the government along Caesarian lines'. Southern 2001, p.151.

211 'a son being subsequently born to himself'. Suetonius, *Caesar* 83, Graves trans., p.46 and Chaveaux 2002, p.32.

212 'modelled on the temple of Venus Genetrix'. Springborg 1990, p.204; for effigy turned by mechanical device see Toynbee 1996, p.58.

212 'did I save these men that they might murder me?'. Suetonius, *Caesar* 84, Graves trans., p.47.

212 'the torches which charred the very body of Caesar'. Cicero in Grave's trans., p.141.

212 'divine forms, perhaps the Twin Brethren . . . javelin at hand and sword at thigh to set light to the pyre' Suetonius, *Caesar* 84, Graves trans., p.47.

213 'I myself carried the man away, leaving only his image behind: what fell by the sword was Caesar's shade'. Ovid *Calendar* 3.697–704 in Springborg 1990, p.205.

213 'we must give place to fortune; I think we must leave Italy and go to Rhodes or somewhere else. If the best happens we shall return to Rome. If ordinary fortune, we shall live in exile, if the worst, we shall employ the last resort'. Earl 1968, p.19–20.

214 'I am hoping it is true about the queen and *that* Caesar'. Cicero, *Letters to Atticus* XIV.20, 2 in Grant 1972, p.95; Caesar's non-Roman 'children' in Lucan, *Civil War* 10.76 in Duff trans., p.595.

214 'I see nothing to object to in the flight of the queen'. Cicero, *Letters to Atticus* XIV.8.1 in Grant 1972 p.95.

214 'ricinium' in Sebesta 2001, p.46; Homer's description of Demeter's mourning attire in Llewellyn-Jones 2003, p.306.

215 Cleopatra's murder of brother in Porphyry FGH.260 and Josephus *Contra Apion* II.58, both in Grant 1972, p.98; Josephus claimed she poisoned him, previous Ptolemy poisoning courtier in Diodorus XXVIII.14, Walton trans., p.241.

215 'Isis lived with her brother [and husband] Osiris, and when he died she vowed she would never accept the partnership of another man. She avenged her husband's murder and continued thereafter to rule entirely according to the laws. In sum, she was responsible for the most and greatest benefactions to all mankind'. Diodorus 1.27.1–2, in Rowlandson (ed.) 1998, p.50.

215 'I have acted as a man although I was a woman in order to make Osiris' name survive on earth'. Pap. Louvre 3079 I, col.110 in Benard and Moon (eds.) 2000, p.228.

215 'she has made the power of women equal to that of men'. Witt 1971, p.110.

215 'in her role as supreme magician slaying Osiris' enemies'. Etienne 2003, p.98; snake bracelets in D'Auria et al. 1988, p.198; Ptolemies' images on jewellery in Clark 1935; ring with Caesar's portrait BM.GR.1873.10–20.4 in Walker and Higgs (eds.,) 2001, p.223.

216 Cleopatra's Needles in Grimm 2003, p.48, Empereur 1998, pp.111–23 (now in London and New York).

216 'the like of which had never been seen before'. John of Nikiou in el-Daly 2005, p.132.

216 'there is elsewhere no precinct like this temple, situated on an elevation facing the harbours renowned for their excellent moorage; it is huge and conspicuous, decorated on an unparalleled scale with dedicated offerings, surrounded by a girdle of pictures and statues in silver and gold, forming a precinct of enormous breadth, embellished with porticoes, libraries, chambers, groves, gateways, broad walks and courts and everything adorned with the beauty that the most lavish expenditure could provide'. Philo, *Legatio ad Gaium* XXII.151, in MacLeod (ed.) 2002, p.42.

216 '. . . when climbing the second staircase, below the right-hand portico, next to the temple of Venus, in which stood a marble statue of the goddess . . .', in Grimm 2003, p.48.

217 'the image of the god Julius'. Suetonius, *Augustus* 17, in Graves trans., p.59; schist statue Berlin Staatliche Museen, Antikensammlung R.9 in Walker and Higgs (eds.,) 2001, p.222.

217 'Cleopatra's Baths'. El-Daly 2005, p.137, with Cleopatreion in Hölbl 2001, p.310.

217 'on the orders of the female king and the male king'. Thompson 2003, p.33, stating in note 26 that the decree could refer to Alexandria or Leontopolis (Tell el-Yahudiya).

217 Lions' entertainment in Aelian, *De Natura Animalium* XII, 6–7 in el-Weshahy 2002, p.1223; stela Copenhagen Museum A.756 dated to 'the late Ptolemaic Period – more specifically the reign of Ptolemy XV and Cleopatra VII'. El-Weshahy 2002, p.1230.

218 'Uniter of the Two Lands'. Ray 2003, p.9; for Cleopatra's relationship with dead Caesar and arrangement of royal images see Bingen 2007, p.54–55.

218 'live, Osiris, live! May the listless one rise up – I am Isis! . . . Horus comes at your call Osiris, you will be placed upon his arms, you will be safe in your power'. Richards and Wilfong 1994, p.15.

218 Granite stela Turin Museum 1764 in Porter and Moss 1989, p.714, and Hölbl 2001, p.240.

218 Caesar as Amun-Ra impregnating Cleopatra in Goudchaux 2001 p.133; stages of Hermonthis' contruction in Arnold 1999, pp.223–4.

219 Figure protected by granite falcons identified as Caesarion by Goudchaux 2001, p.139.

219 'carries off mostly children up to age of 10'. Celsus in Jackson 1988, p.103.

219 'body lies in the sand, but his soul has gone to its own land'. Dunand and Zivie-Coche 2004, p.330.

219 'Isis, Great Mage, heal me and release me from all things bad and evil and belonging to Seth, from the demonic fatal illnesses, as you saved and freed your son Horus'. Ebers Papyrus, based on Witt 1971, p.187.

220 Tax decree in Thompson 2003, p.33, Bingen 2007, pp.141–54, Chaveau 2002, p.36.

220 Dioscurides Phakas in Galen XIX.63, in Grant 1972, p.181; stela in Foreman 1999, p.75.

220 'most explicit laments over death'. Lichtheim 1980 pp.59–60.

220 'do not weary of drinking, eating, getting drunk and making love – make holiday and follow your heart day and night!'. BM.EA.147 after Reymond 1981, p.177; Lichtheim 1980 pp.59–60.

220 'perhaps the finest examples of private relief ever made in the Ptolemaic period'. Brooklyn 1988, p.231; 'it is indeed strange that in the days of the last Ptolemies and the last Cleopatra there should have been produced native Egyptian sculpture in a quantity and of a uniformly high level of quality such as had not been known for nearly one hundred years'. Bothmer 1960, p.171.

220 Black statue head Brooklyn 58.30 in Brooklyn 1988, p.138; man with curls BM.EA.55253 in Walker and Higgs (eds) 2001, p.246; Tazza Farnese bowl Naples Museum 27611 in Dwyer 1992; bronze figurine of Greek-style Horus Cleveland 1972.6 in Berman 1999, p.474.

221 'had a very good and noble appearance; his beard was well grown, his forehead large, and his nose aquiline, giving him altogether a bold, masculine look that reminded people of the faces of Hercules in paintings and sculptures'. Plutarch, *Antony*, Dryden trans., p.749.

221 'deviant masculinity'. Hales 2005, p.135.

222 'had rather thick soles to make him look taller'. Suetonius, *Augustus* 73, Graves trans., p.92.

222 'one did not realize how small a man he was, unless someone tall stood close to him'. Suetonius, *Augustus* 79, Graves trans., p.95.

222 'lacked glamour and panache, still more the vigorous masculinity of a Mark Antony. Puny, sickly, cowardly – the type is recognizable, as is the ruthlessness which often co-exists with physical cowardice. What commands admiration is high moral courage and a firm grasp of reality'. Earl 1968, p.192.

222 'You, boy, owe everything to your name'. Cicero, Philippics 13.24, in Walker and Higgs 2001, p.190.

222 'Octavian is an excellent boy, of whom I personally have high hopes for the future'. Cicero, *Letter to Trebonius*, in Graves trans. 1960, p.98.

223 'loathsome man! Equally loathsome as priest of a tyrant or priest of a dead human being!'. Cicero, Second Philippic, Graves trans., p.149.

223 'a disgusting, intolerable sensualist, as well as a vicious, unsavoury crook'. Second Philippic in Graves trans., p.109.

223 'uncovered his head and threw his arms round her neck. Depraved character!' Cicero, Second Philippic, in Graves trans., p.135.

224 'lauded, applauded, and dropped'. Cicero in Graves trans., p.96.

224 'raised, praised and erased' Matyszak 2003, p.215.

225 'that which gave them all the trouble was to agree who should be put to death, each of them desiring to destroy his enemies and to save his friends . . . in the end, animosity to those they hated carried the day against respect for relations and affection for friends; Octavian sacrificed Cicero to Antony, Antony gave up his uncle Lucius Caesar and Lepidus received permission to murder his brother'. Plutarch, *Antony*, Dryden trans., p.754.

225 'when they were brought before him he regarded them joyfully, actually bursting out more than once into laughter . . . and ordered them to be hung up above the speaker's place in the Forum'. Plutarch, *Antony*, Dryden trans., p.754; for Fulvia's actions see Flamarion 1997, p.58.

226 'who gave your general his birth'. Plutarch, *Antony*, Dryden trans., p.754.

226 'lived again in his female offspring and inspired his daughter's words'. Valerius Maximus in Flaschenriem 1999, p.36.

226 'in honour of Julius Caesar'. Ashton 2003, p.143.

227 'Serapion, not waiting to consult Cleopatra, sent Cassius what ships they had'. Appian, *Roman History* IV.61, White trans., p.243.

227 'for the Red and Indian Seas'. Tarn in Goudchaux 2003 p.109.

228 'with a powerful fleet to assist them, in defiance of Cassius'. Appian *Roman History* V.8, in White trans., p.389.

229 'his conduct so disgusting to the remainder of the prisoners they courteously saluted Antony as their conqueror, but abused [Octavian] to his face with the most obscene epithets'. Suetonius, Augustus 13, Graves trans. p.57.

229 'though in ill-health at the time'. Suetonius, *Augustus* 56 Graves trans., p.56.

229 'columns entrusting the city entirely to the goddess' guardianship as its Queen and Saviour'. Witt 1970, p.327.

229 'the unusual arrangement of hair or head-ornament may reflect the subject's involvement in a religious cult or suggest that she should be compared to a goddess'. Walker and Higgs (eds.,) 2001, No.212, Rome Museo Capitolini 3356, p.231.

230 'erected a scaffold in plain sight above the theatre, and roofed with green boughs, like the 'caves' built for Bacchic revels; on this he hung tambourines, fawnskins and other Dionysiac trinkets of all sorts, where he reclined in company with his friends and drank from early morning, being entertained by artists summoned from Italy, while Greeks from all parts assembled to see the spectacle . . . he even shifted the place of his revels to the top of the Acropolis, while the entire city of Athens was illuminated with torches hung from the roofs. And he gave orders that he should be recognised as Dionysus throughout all the cities'. Athenaeus, *Deipnosophists* IV. 148, Gulick trans., pp.176–7.

231 'a woman of restless spirit and very bold'. Plutarch, *Antony*, Dryden trans., p.758.

231 'dressed up like bacchantes and the men and boys like satyrs and fauns, and throughout the town nothing was to be seen but spears wreathed about with ivy, harps, flutes and psalteries, while Antony in their songs was Dionysus the Giver of Joy'. Plutarch, *Antony*, Dryden trans., p.756.

Chapter 9

235 'set himself at once to pay his court to the Egyptian . . . advising her to go to Cilicia in her best attire'. Plutarch, *Antony* 25, Dryden trans., p.756.

235 'adroitness and subtlety in speech'. Plutarch, *Antony* 25, Dryden trans., p.756.

235 'many letters of invitation from him and his friends'. Plutarch, *Antony* 26–27 in Rowlandson (ed.) 1998, p.39.

235 'she made great preparations for her journey, of money, gifts, and ornaments of value, such as so wealthy a kingdom might afford'. Plutarch, *Antony* 25, Dryden trans., p.756.

236 'was to meet Antony in the time of life when women's beauty is most splendid'. Plutarch *Antony* 25, Dryden trans., p.756.

236 'painted up beyond all measure'. Lucan, *Civil War* 10.137–141 Duff trans., p.601

236 'a careful toilet will make you attractive, but without such attention, the loveliest faces lose their charm, even were they comparable to those of the Idalian goddess herself'. Ovid, *Art of Love* III. 105–106, Lewis May trans., p.89.

236 'oesyspum' in Allason-Jones 1990, p.130; lead toxicity in Vitruvius, *De Architectura* VIII in Jackson 1988, p.45; non-toxic cream in Evershed et al. 2004; orchil in Parker 2002, pp.41–42.

236 Female stare like death blow or 'loosening the knees' in Llewellyn-Jones 2003, p.263.

237 'The Royal'. Pliny *Natural History* XIII.18, Loeb trans., p.109.

237 'that your oiled tresses may not injure your splendid silk dress, let this pin fix your twisted hair, and keep it up'. Martial, *Epigrams* XIV.24 in 1871 trans., p.608.

237 'with ivory combs in their hands . . . combing the goddess's royal hair'. Apuleius XI.9, Graves trans., p.275.

237 'I love to see it fall in floating tresses about your shoulders'. Ovid *Art of Love* III.235–8, in Lewis May trans., p.91.

238 'long thick hair fell in tapering ringlets on her lovely neck'. Apuleius, Graves trans., p.270.

238 'leave uncovered the top of your shoulder and the upper part of your left arm. That is especially becoming to women who have a white skin. At the mere sight of it, I should be mad to cover all I could touch with kisses'. Ovid, *Art of Love* III.307–310, Lewis May trans., p.93; Aphrodite's chiton revealing left shoulder in Walker and Higgs (eds.,) 2001, p.312.

238 'to kindle in us the fires of love, dress is more potent than the dread arts of the magician'. Ovid, *Art of Beauty* 35–36, Lewis May trans., p.114.

238 'white breasts'. Lucan, *Civil War* 10.141, Duff trans., p.601.

238 'azure blue like a clear sky . . . water-green from the colour that it imitates, I could easily imagine that the Nymphs were clothed in such apparel'. Ovid, *Art of Love III*, 173–178, Lewis May trans., p.90; also Empereur 2002, p.29.

239 'in the whole of history . . . come down to her through the hands of the Kings of the East'. Pliny, IX.121–122, Loeb trans., p.243; references to 'her gold, silver, emeralds, pearls' in Plutarch, *Antony*, Dryden trans., p.775.

239 'word went round that Aphrodite was coming to revel with Dionysos for the good of Asia'. Plutarch, *Antony* 26–27, in Rowlandson (ed.) 1998, p.39.

239 'sailed up the river Kydnos in a gold-prowed barge, with purple sails spread, and rowed along by silver oars to the sound of the flute mingled with pipes and flutes. She lay beneath a gold-spangled canopy, adorned like Aphrodite in a picture, and young boys, like Cupids in pictures, stood on either side and fanned her. So too the most beautiful of her serving maids, wearing the robes of Nereids and of Graces, some stood by the rudders and some by the bulwarks. Wonderful scents from many types of incense permeated the riverbanks. Some of the populace escorted her on either side from the river mouth, and others came down from the city for the spectacle. The crowd in the market place poured out, until Antony himself, seated on his tribunal [seat], was left alone'. Plutarch, *Antony* 26–27, in Rowlandson (ed.) 1998, p.39.

240 'a spectacle that has seldom been equalled for beauty'. Plutarch, *Antony* 27, Dryden trans., p.757.

240 'was amazed at her wit as well as her good looks, and became her captive as though he were a young man, although he was forty years of age'. Appian, *Roman History* V.8, White, trans., p.389.

240 'arranged in his honour a royal symposium, in which the service was entirely of gold and jewelled vessels made with exquisite art . . . overwhelmed with the richness of the display . . . quietly smiled and said that all these things were a present for him'. Athenaeus, *Deipnosophists* IV.147, Gulick trans., pp.174–5.

240 Cleopatra's defence of her actions in Appian, *Roman History* V.8, White, trans., p.389.

240 'on this occasion she provided an even more sumptuous symposium by far, so that she caused the vessels which had been used on that first occasion to appear paltry; and once used she presented him with these

also. As for the officers, each was allowed to take the couch on which he had reclined; even the sideboards, as well as the spreads for the couches, were divided among them. And when they departed, she furnished litters for the guests of high rank, with bearers, while for the greater number she provided horses gaily caparisoned with silver-plate harness, and for all she sent along Ethiopian slaves to carry the torches'. Athenaeus, *Deipnosophists* IV.147–148, Gulick trans., pp.174–7.

241 'he was very desirous to outdo her as well in magnificence as contrivance; but he found he was altogether beaten in both, and was so well convinced of it that he was himself the first to jest and mock at his poverty of wit and his rustic awkwardness'. Plutarch, *Antony* XXVI, Dryden trans., p.757.

241 'without any sort of reluctance or reserve'. Plutarch, *Antony* XXVI, Dryden trans., p.757.

241 'the whole wide world under a woman's hand ruled and obeying everywhere shall stand . . . the Widow shall be queen of the whole wide world'. *Oracula Sibyllina* III.79 in Grant 1972, p.173.

241 'whatever Cleopatra ordered was done, regardless of laws, human or divine. While her sister Arsinoe was a suppliant in the temple of Artemis . . . Antony sent assassins thither and put her to death'. Appian, *Roman History* V, White trans., p.389.

242 'she gave him a magnificent reception . . . He went out only to the temples, the schools, and the discussions of the learned, and spent his time with Greeks, out of deference to Cleopatra, to whom his sojourn in Alexandria was wholly devoted'. Appian *Roman History* V.11 White trans., pp.393–5.

242 'exercised in arms, she was there to see'. Plutarch, *Antony* in Dryden trans., p.758.

242 'secret orders to the fishermen to dive under water and put fishes that had been already taken upon his hooks; and these he drew so fast that the Egyptian perceived it. But feigning great admiration she told everybody how dextrous Antony was and invited them next day to come and see him again. So when a number of them had come on board the fishing boats, as soon as he had let down his hook one of her servants was before hand with his divers and fixed upon his hook a salted fish from Pontus. Antony, feeling his line give, drew up the prey, when, as may be imagined, great laughter ensu(ed.) Said Cleopatra 'Leave the fishing rod, general, to us poor sovereigns of Pharos and Canopus; your game is cities, provinces and kingdoms'. Plutarch, *Antony* Dryden trans., p.758.

242 'was over and over again disarmed by Cleopatra, and beguiled away, while great actions and enterprises of the first necessity fell, as it were, from his hands, to go with her to the seashore at Canopus and Taphosiris,

and play about'. Plutarch, *Antony and Demitrius Compared*, Dryden trans., p.780.

242 'fast watering-place'. Milne 1916(b), p.78; 'dizzy combination of Lourdes and St. Tropez'. Montserrat 1996, p.164.

243 'people of the highest renown had faith and slept within it'. Strabo 17.801 in Milne 1916(b), p.78.

243 'Herakles in the picture where Omphale is seen removing his club and stripping him of his lion skin'. Plutarch, *Antony and Demitrius Compared*, Dryden trans., p.780.

243 'forgetting his nation, his name, his toga'. Florus II.21.2–3 in Walker 2003, p.197; Maehler 2003, p.213.

243 'cymbal player from Canopus'. Cassius Dio 50.27, Scott-Kilvert trans., p.54; portrait bust in Bankes Collection in Walker and Higgs (eds.,) 2001, p.241.

243 'over-ready tongue and impudent wit'. Statius, Silvae V.5.66–68 in Maehler 2003, p.213, with a 'taste for the grotesque and sexual that characterises other aspects of Alexandrian art'. MacLeod (ed.) 2002, pp.122–3.

243 'performer of improper dances'. Seneca in Grant 1972, p.179.

244 'performing a dance in which his naked body was painted blue and his head encircled with reeds, whilst he wore a fish's tail and crawled upon his knees'. Velleius *Paterculus*, II.83.2 in Grant 1972, p.178.

244 'she played at dice with him'. Plutarch, *Antony* Dryden trans., p.758; counter game in Ward-Perkins and Claridge 1976, no. 239 and Walker and Higgs (eds) pp.316–17.

244 'the Parasite'. Fraser 1957, pp.71–3; Walker and Higgs (eds) 2001, p.232.

244 'members entertained one another daily in turn, with an extravagance of expenditure beyond measure or belief'. Plutarch, *Antony*, Dryden trans., p.757.

245 'admired the prodigious variety of all things; but particularly, seeing eight wild boars roasting whole, says he, "surely you have a great number of guests". The cook laughed at his simplicity, and told him that there were not above 12 to sup, but that every dish was to be served up just roasted to a turn, and if anything was but one minute ill-timed, it was spoil(ed.) "And" he said "maybe Antony will sup just now, maybe not this hour, maybe he will call for wine, or begin to talk, and will put it off. So that" he continued "it is not one but many suppers must be had in readiness, as it is impossible to guess at his hour". Plutarch, *Antony*, Dryden trans., p.757.

245 'so good that Maroitic wine is racked off with a view to ageing it'. Strabo,

Geography 17.1.14, in Empereur 1997, p.217; Oases' wines in Poo 1995, p.20, 99; Ptolemaia festival in Athenaeus, *Deipnosophists* V.198, trans., pp.400–1.

246 'house rang with the din of drunkards, the pavements swam with wine, the walls dripped with it'. Cicero, Second Philippic, Graves trans., p.147.

246 'you are a drink-sodden, sex-ridden wreck!'. Cicero, Second Philippic, Graves trans., p.105.

246 'soaked in wine'. Cicero, Thirteenth Philippic, 31, in Heskel 2001, p.137.

246 'a great man of notable ability . . . turned to alien ways and unroman vices by his love of drink and his equal passion for Cleopatra'. Seneca in Lindsay 1970 p.478.

246 'the Egyptian woman demanded the Roman Empire from the drunken general as the price of her favours'. Lucius Annaeus Florus in Lovric, p.72.

246 'swimming in Mareotic wine'. Horace I.37.14 in Maehler 2003, p.210.

246 'a tongue submerged by incessant wine'. Propertius III.11, trans., Shepherd 1985 in Maehler 2003, p.210.

246 'take to yourself the wine from Khargeh, from Farafra, the wine from Khargeh and Bahariya, and may your mouth be opened by it'. Poo 1995, pp.20, 99.

246 'drunkenness upon drunkenness without end'. Poo 1995, p.143.

247 'braided, beauteous, tressed, high bosomed, richly adorned, all drunk with wine'. Cairo JE.29310, based on Lichtheim 1980, p.56.

247 'How happy is the temple of Amun, even she that spends her days in festivity with the king of the gods within her . . . she is like a drunken woman, who sits outside the chamber with braided hair and beauteous breasts'. Fletcher 1995, p.56 (based on Davies and Gardiner).

247 'perhaps a famous drinker whose statue could be properly placed within a precinct of the god of wine'. Ridgway 1990, p.337.

247 'nothing less than a symbol of Greek cultural identity'. Davidson 1997, p.40.

247 'no man who is a wine-lover can be of low character'. Alexis, in Davidson 1997, p.52.

248 'entirely of gold . . . jewelled vessels made with exquisite art'. Athenaeus, *Deipnosophists* IV.147, Gulick trans., pp.174–5; amethysts in Pliny Natural History XXXVII.124, Loeb trans., p.265 and Parker 2002, p.47.

248 'the latest vaudeville numbers, the slinkiest hits from the Nile!'. Ovid, *Art of Love* III.316–318, in Montserrat 1996, p.117.

248 'Apollo is here for the dance, I hear his lyre playing and I sense the

Cupids, and Aphrodite herself . . . He who madly joins the all-night dancing, staying awake til dawn comes, will receive the prize of honey cakes for playing the kottabos game, and he may kiss whom he will of all the girls and whomever he wants of the boys'. Montserrat 1996, p.179; Thompson 1964, p.163.

248 'she would go rambling with him to disturb and torment people at their doors and windows, dressed like a servant-woman, for Antony also went in servant's disguise, and from these expeditions he often came home very scurvily answered, and sometimes even beaten severely, though most people guessed who he was. However, the Alexandrians in general liked it all well enough, and joined good-humouredly and kindly in his frolic and play, saying they were much obliged to Antony for acting his tragic parts at Rome and keeping his comedy for them'. Plutarch, *Antony*, Dryden trans., p.758.

248 'the fourth krater is mine no longer, but belongs to hubris; the fifth to shouting, the sixth to revel, the seventh to black eyes, the eighth to summonses, the ninth to bile and the tenth to madness and people tossing furniture about'. Eubulus, in Davidson 1997, p.44; 'sea sickness' in Davidson 1997, p.44.

249 'into the bowl in which their wine was mixed she slipped a drug that had the power of robbing grief and anger of their sting and banishing all painful memories. No one that swallowed this dissolved in wine could shed a single tear that day . . . This powerful anodyne was one of many useful drugs which had been given to the daughter of Zeus [Helen] by an Egyptian lady, Polydamna, the wife of Thon. For the fertile soil of Egypt is most rich in herbs, many of which are wholesome in solution, though many are poisonous. And in medical knowledge the Egyptian leaves the rest of the world behind'. Homer, *Odyssey* IV, Rieu trans., p.58.

249 'used to produce beer, and shepen occurs in medical texts'. Manniche 1989, p.131.

249 'to produce a narcotic-laced wine'. Nunn 1996, p.157.

249 'should drink their chaplets'. Pliny *Natural History* XXI.12, in Loeb trans., p.169.

249 'I shall not prepare love charms against you, whether in your beverages or in your food'. PSI.1.64 in Rowlandson (ed.) 1998, p.323.

250 'that remarkable and truly unique work of nature. Antony was full of curiosity to see what in the world she was going to do'. Pliny *Natural History* IX.59.119–121, Loeb trans., p.245.

250 'knowing that it could be recovered later on'. Rackham in Pliny IX, trans., p.244, note b.

250 Revised chemical formula based on $CaCO_3 + CH_3COOH \rightarrow Ca + H_2O$

+ CO_2 given at website http://penelope.uchicago.edu/grout/encyclo-paedia__romana/miscellanea/cleopatra.html; for pearls dissolving in acidic conditions see Allason-Jones 1990, p.128.

250 'at a great banquet in front of many guests, he had risen up and rubbed her feet, to fulfil some wager or promise'. Plutarch, *Antony*, Dryden trans., p.769.

250 'what you are doing now to me, rubbing my feet with your lovely soft hands, it is quite magnificent'. Antiphanes in Davidson 1997, p.162.

251 'the Inimitable Lover'. Fraser 1957, p.73.

251 'the erotic charge unleashed even then by lingerie, which helped women look their best for their lovers'. Varone, in Stafford 2005, p.106; Aphrodite removing breast band popular motif, e.g. Staatliche Anti-kensammlungen und Glyptothek München 8516 in Stafford 2005, fig.9.6, p.107.

251 'all my power resides'. Homer, *Iliad* 14.214–217, trans., Graves pp.262--3; necklace 'worn across the chest bandolier-style' in d'Ambrosio 2001, p.55; harness in Laing 1997, p.80.

251 'in their homes lustful embraces of their gods. People who reckon sexual excess to be piety . . . ornament their bedrooms with small painted pictures, hanging up rather high, like offerings in a temple. While lying in bed in the midst of their sensual pleasure they can feast their eyes on a naked Aphrodite locked in sexual union with Ares'. Clement *Protrepticus* IV.57–61.4, in Montserrat 1996, p.213.

251 'delicate, well-woven, glistening, beautifully coloured, covered with many flowers, covered with ornaments, purple, dark green, scarlet, violet, rich with scarlet blooms, purple bordered, shot with gold, embroidered with figures of animals, gleaming with stars'. Pollux of Naukratis, in Grant 1976, p.186.

252 'Concerning seductions: accordingly, the seducer should be unadorned and uncombed, so he does not seem to the woman to be too concerned about the matter in hand'. Philaenis, Montserrat 1996, p.113.

252 'saying that the plain woman is a goddess, the ugly woman charming, the elderly one like a young girl'. Philaenis in Montserrat 1996, p.114.

252 'to know herself, and to enter upon love's battle in the pose best suited to her charms. If a woman has a lovely face, let her lie upon her back; if she prides herself upon her hips let her display them to the best advantage. . . . If you are short, let your lover be the steed. . . . Love has a thousand postures. . . . So, then, my dear ones, feel the pleasure in the very marrow of your bones; share it fairly with your lover, say pleasant, naughty things the while. And if Nature has withheld from you the sensation of pleasure, then teach your lips to lie and say you feel it all. But if you have to

pretend, don't betray yourself by over-acting. Let your movements and your eyes combine to deceive us, and, gasping, panting, complete the illusion'. Ovid, *Art of Love* III.775–778, Lewis May trans., p.100.

253 'this mysterious fire, all fire, all nape-of-neck, all sigh, all pliant, all you forge in this stove of fire, breathe it also into the heart and liver, into the women's loins and belly; lead her into the house of the man, let her give to his hand what is in her hand, to his mouth what is in her mouth, to his body what is in her body, to his wand what is in her womb. Quckly, quickly, at once, at once!'. Romer and Romer 1995, p.71.

253 'squandering and fooling away in enjoyments that most costly of all valuables, time'. Plutarch, *Antony*, in Dryden trans., p.757.

254 'it came to pass under the majesty, the sovereign, Lady of the Two Lands, Cleopatra and her son Caesarion, in regnal year 11, 15th Epep, the day on which I landed forever. I was placed in the West and all the rites for my august mummy were carried out for me'. Harris Stela BM.EA.886 in Reymond 1981 pp.136–50; Walker and Higgs (eds.,) p.185 and Dunand and Zivie-Coche 2004, p.200.

254 Fulvia told 'as long as Italy remained at peace Antony would stay with Cleopatra, but that if war should break out there he would come back speedily', Appian *Roman History* V.19, White trans., p.409.

255 'Lucius Antonius, you're dead, baldy. Victory of Gaius Caesar [Octavian]'. Walker and Higgs (eds.,) 2001, p.239; threats against Fulvia in Wyke 2002, p.220.

255 'you must die'. Suetonius, *Augustus* 15, in Graves trans., p.57.

257 'live twin births will have been fewer and survival through infancy of one or both lower still'. Baines 1985, p.479.

257 'not fed'. Baines 1985, p.479.

257 'he came from the womb with me the same day'. BM EA.826. in Lichtheim 1976, p.88.

257 'twin of the living Apis'. Baines 1985, p.472.

257 'two deities whose exact identity is not certain'. Abdalla 1991, p.189, referring to Dendera dyad Cairo JE.46278.

258 'the Virgin changed the fate of her Twins in the constellation of the Ram . . . sacred ram of Amun'. Tarn 1932, pp.144–5.

258 'Per-at . . . female pharaoh . . . Sun: Taurus 4: Jupiter in Cancer. Moon: Capricorn 20 and a half.' Ashmolean Museum, in Neugebauer and Parker 1968, pp.231–4; Antonius' astrologer in Plutarch *Antony* 33, Dryden trans., p.759.

258 'he had frequently at the public audience of kings and princes received amorous messages written in tablets made of onyx and crystal, and read them openly'. Plutarch, *Antony*, Dryden trans., p.769.

259 'you must know that I did not see the sun because you are out of my sight; for I have no other sun but you'. Pap.Oxy.XLII.3059. in Montserrat 1996, p.89.

259 'pain grips me whenever I remember how he used to kiss me, all the while treacherously intending to desert me . . . beloved stars and Mistress Night, my partner in passion, now escort me once again to him toward who Aphrodite drives me, I who am betrayed. . . . Be warned – I have an unconquerable will when I am enraged, when I remember I will sleep alone'. Pap.Grenf.1.1 in Rowlandson (ed.) 1998, pp.107–8.

259 'who arose in the beginning as Magician'. Witt 1971, p.311, note 7.

259 'I call upon thee Lady Isis, with thy many names and many forms'. Witt 1971, p.193.

259 'men to women and women to men and makes virgins rush out of their homes'. PGM.XXXVI.69–71 in Montserrat 1996, p.187.

259 'are you a burning woman, an abominable fire, a scorching woman? You should bathe yourself in blood, you should wash yourself with urine, one should set a suit of nettles on your body. Go! No one will find enough water in the sea, you sow, for washing off your face. Your day of death is at hand'. O. Wien D.70 in Rowlandson (ed.) 1998, p.36.

260 Joint coins of Antonius and Octavia in Southern 1999, fig.20; Walker and Higgs (eds) 2001, nos. 249–50, p.238, no. 259, p.240.

261 'I could not bear the way she nagged me'. Suetonius, *Augustus* 62, Graves trans., p.84.

261 'indecent haste'. Suetonius, *Augustus* 69, Graves trans., p.88.

Chapter 10

264 'Brother of the Sun and Moon'. Tarn 1932 p.159.

264 'who married the Roman general, Antony'. Athenaeus, *Deipnosophists* IV, 147, Gulick trans., pp.174–5; Antonius' as consort in demotic Pap.Ash.D.39 in Reymond and Barns 1977, p.23.

264 'she is my wife'. Suetonius *Augustus* 69, Graves trans., p.89; Earl 1968 p.51; Southern 1998, p.131.

265 'commits the bride's chastity to their husbands'. Verrius Flaccus in Sebesta 1997, p.535; la Folette 2001, pp.56–60; compare with 'your red-headed wife, the one with the *seven* tressed hair'. Martial, 12.32.2–4, in la Folette 2001, p.57.

265 'flame colour'. la Follette 2001, p.55, Sebesta 2001, pp.55–6.

265 'exchange vows with the goddess as our witness'. Achilles Tatius V.14, in

Montserrat 1996, p.91; mosaic scenes from Antioch house in Witt 1971, p.161, pl.34.

266 'thus, beloved, I seize you'. La Folette 2001, p.57; ring with Antonius' portrait BM.GR.1867.5–7.724 in Walker and Higgs (eds.,) 2001, p.244.

267 'Year 16 which is also Year 1'. Fraser 1957, p.71.

267 'made to look Roman, almost like Antony in drag'. Hamer 1984, p.84.

267 'Imperator for the third time and triumvir', Cleopatra 'Basilissa', 'Thea Neotera' in Walker and Higgs (eds.,) 2001, p.234; Williams in Walker and Ashton (eds.,) 2003, pp.87–94.

267 'the greatness of the Roman empire consisted more in giving than in taking'. Plutarch, *Antony* Dryden trans., p.761.

268 'every scent ranks below balsam'. Pliny *Natural History* XII.111, Loeb trans., p.79.

268 'the most precious drug that there is'. Josephus *Jewish Antiquities* 15.4, 2 in Groom 1981, pp.128–9.

268 'which serves as no small source of income . . . the barbarians export the tar to Egypt and sell it for embalming the dead, for if this material is not mixed into the other substances the cadaver will not last long'. Diodorus 19, 98–99 in Rimon et al. 1997, p.56; Koller et al. 2005, p.610; Rullkötter and Nissenbaum 1988, also Geer trans., p.103.

269 'a woman who held the greatest position of any living at that time'. Josephus, *Jewish Antiquities* 15.97–103 in Grant 1972, p.159.

269 'instead of having her murdered, he plied her with gifts and escorted her on her on the way to Egypt'. Josephus, in Grant 1972, p.160.

269 'Philopatris . . . Fatherland Loving'. BGU.XIV.2376 in Maehler 1983 p.8.

270 'of Alexander and Egypt's dynastic family. She was a Macedonian . . . and since Cleopatra's patris was Macedon, she was looking back to old Greece and to the home of her forefathers'. Thompson 2003, p.31, see also Bingen 2007, p.62.

270 'made all Asia shake'. Plutarch, *Antony*, Dryden trans., p.761.

271 'could not even stand up to review his fleet when the ships were already at their fighting stations; but lay on his back and gazed up at the sky, never rising to show that he was alive until his admiral Marcus Agrippa had routed the enemy'. Suetonius, *Augustus* 16, Graves trans., p.58.

271 'could not hold out long at table, but in the midst of the drinking would often rise or spring up to look out, until she put into port'. Plutarch, *Antony* 51.2, in Rice 1999, p.57.

272 'bringing her body down by slender diet'. Plutarch, *Antony* in Dryden trans., p.767.

273 'brilliant success'. Chaveau 2002, p.58.

273 'honourable wounds'. Earl 1968, p.50.

274 'given orders that he should be called Dionysus . . . his head bound with the ivy wreath, his person envelopped in the saffron robe of gold'. Velleius Paterculus II.82, in Grant 1972, p.161.

274 'coming forth in procession around the temple of Isis by his war chariot . . . to alight at the temple of Isis, lady of the Mound-of-Egypt'. BM.EA.886, in Reymond 1981, p.148.

275 'was then, as at other times when she appeared in public, dressed in the habit of the goddess Isis and gave audience to the people under the name of the New Isis'. *Antony*, Dryden, trans., p.768.

275 'the greatness of the Roman empire consisted more in giving than in taking'. Plutarch, *Antony* Dryden trans., p.761.

275 'his own sons by Cleopatra were to have the style of "kings of kings"'. Plutarch, Antony, Dryden trans., p.768.

276 'Alexander was brought out before the people in Median costume, the tiara and upright peak'. Plutarch, *Antony*, Dryden trans., p.768; bronze figurine in Median dress MMA.GR.49.11.3 in Smith 1917; Walker and Higgs (eds.,) p.139, 250.

276 'done about with the diadem; for this was the habit of the successors of Alexander'. Plutarch, *Antony*, Dryden trans., p.768.

276 'one was received by a guard of Macedonians, the other one by one of Armenians'. Plutarch, *Antony*, Dryden trans., p.768.

276 Bronze plaque in Thompson 1973, p.65, pl.LXX.b; double cornucopiae 'appears on the coins of Mark Antony . . . and smacks of the taste of Alexandria'. Thompson 1973, pp.64–5.

276 'Kleopatrae reginae regum filiorum regum' in Southern 1999, p.115.

277 'by marrying two wives at once, did a thing which no Roman had ever allowed himself'. Plutarch, *Antony and Demetrius Compared*, Dryden trans., p.780.

277 'Aegyptia coniunx . . . 'the Egyptian wife'. Virgil, Aeneid VIII.688, in Maehler 2003, p.208.

277 'filthy marriage'. Propertius III.11, trans., Shepherd 1985 in Maehler 2003, pp.209–10.

277 'a theatrical piece of insolence and contempt of his country'. Plutarch, *Antony*, Dryden trans., p.768.

277 'because they felt he had made a present to the Egyptians of the honourable and sacred traditions of his fatherland for the sake of Cleopatra'. Plutarch, *Antony* 50 in Walker and Higgs (eds.,) 2001, p.195.

278 'antique diction . . . nonsensicalities of those garrulous Asiatic orators'. Suetonius, *Augustus* 86 Graves trans., p.97.

278 'What's come over you? Do you object to my sleeping with Cleopatra?

She is my wife! And it isn't as if this were anything new – the affair started 9 years ago! And what about you? Are you faithful to Livia Drusilla? My congratulations if, when this letter arrives, you have not already been to bed with Tertullia or Terentilla or Rufilla or Salvia Titisiena – or all of them. Does it really matter so much where, or with whom, you get your erections?'. Suetonius, *Augustus* 69, based on Graves trans., p.89; Earl 1968, p.51; Southern 1998, p.131.

278 'for reasons of state, not simple passion'. Suetonius, *Augustus* 69, Graves trans., p.88.

278 'hauling an ex-consuls wife from her husband's dining room into the bedroom – before his eyes, too! He brought the woman back, says Antonius, blushing to the ears and with her hair in disorder'. Suetonius, *Augustus* 69, Graves trans., p.88.

279 'collected for Cleopatra the masterpieces of the East'. Griffin 1977, p.23.

279 'a positively sensuous pleasure from literature'. Flavius Philostratus, in Grant 1972, p.181.

280 'for there may be amongst the rest some antique or famous piece of workmanship which Antony would be sorry to part with'. Plutarch, *Antony*, Dryden trans., p.758.

280 'Antonius the great, lover without peer, Parasitos set this up to his own god and benefactor, 29th day of Khoiak, year 19 which is also year 4'. Walker and Higgs (eds.,) 2001 p.232; Fraser 1957, p.73.

280 For Red Sea trade vessels redeployed see Goudchaux 2003, p.111; rowing crews including 'Arabians and Bactrians' in Virgil Aeneid VIII.705–706, in Dryden trans., p.223.

281 'We have granted to Publius Canidius and his heirs the annual exportation of 10,000 artabas of wheat and the annual importation of 5,000 Coan amphoras of wine without anyone exacting anything in taxes from him or any other expense whatsoever. We have also granted tax exemption on all the land he owns in Egypt on the understanding that he shall not pay any taxes, either to the state account or to the special account of us and others, in any way in perpetuity . . . Let it be written to whom it may concern, so that knowing it they can act accordingly. Let it be done'. Pap.Berolinensis 25.239 in Ägyptisches Museum und Papyrussammlung, Berlin, in van Minnen 2003, pp.35, 44; Walker and Higgs (eds.,) 2001, no.188, p.180; handwriting of Ptolemies IX and X in van Minnen 2003, p.35 and Reeves 2000, p.213.

282 'coming in from all quarters to form the navy'. Plutarch *Antony*, Dryden trans., p.768.

282 'the Palace . . . she visited the market place [forum] with Antony, presided with him over festivals and the hearing of lawsuits, rode around

with him on horseback even in the cities, or else was carried in a litter'. Cassius Dio 50.5, Scott–Kilvert trans., p.38.

283 'it was not just that one that bore so great a part in their charge of the war should be robbed of her share of glory', especially as she was in no way inferior 'in prudence to any one of the kings that were serving with him; she had long governed a great kingdom by herself alone, and long lived with him, and gained experience in public affairs'. Plutarch, *Antony*, Dryden trans., p.768.

283 'all kings, princes and governors, all nations and cities within the limits of Syria, the Maeotid Lake, Armenia and Illyria . . . this one island for some days resounded with piping and harping, theatres filling and choruses playing. Every city sent an ox as its contribution to the sacrifice and the kings that accompanied Antonius competed who should make the most magnificent feasts and the greatest presents'. Plutarch, *Antony*, Dryden trans., p.769.

284 'courted the favour of the people with all sorts of attentions. The Athenians in requital, having decreed her public honours, deputed several of the citizens to wait upon her at her house; amongst whom went Antony as one, he being an [honorary] Athenian citizen and he it was that made the speech'. Plutarch, *Antony*, Dryden trans., p.769.

284 'sent orders to Rome to have Octavia removed from his house. She left it, we are told, accompanied by all his children, except the eldest by Fulvia, who was then with his father . . . weeping and grieving that she must be looked upon as one of the causes of the war . . . pitied not so much her as Antonius himself, and more particularly those who had seen Cleopatra, whom they could report to have no way the advantage of Octavia either in youth or in beauty'. Plutarch, *Antony*, Dryden trans., p.769.

284 'drove away his lawful Roman wife to please the foreign and unlawful woman. And so . . . Antony procured his ruin by his marriage'. Plutarch, *Antony and Demetrius Compared*, Dryden trans., p.780.

285 'all Italy took a personal oath to me voluntarily, demanding me as their leader in the war'. Augustus, *Res Gestae* 25, in Walker and Higgs (eds.,) 2001, p.193.

285 'O Rome . . . the Queen crops off your delicate head of hair and uttering judgements will hurl you to earth from the sky'. Lindsay 1970, p.356.

285 'to demolish the Capitol and topple the empire'. Horace, Ode I.37 in Maehler 2003, p.206.

285 'an enormity that even Cleopatra would have been ashamed'. Pliny, *Natural History* XXXIII.50, Loeb trans., p.41, replicating Herodotus'

earlier account of Saite court in *Histories* II. 172, de Selincourt trans., p.197.

285 'her squalid pack of diseased half-men'. Horace, Ode I.37 in Grant 1972, p.214; 'the minion of withered eunuchs'. Horace, Epode IX.12–15, Bennett trans., p.387.

285 'the generals they would have to fight would be Mardion the eunuch, Pothinus, Eiras, Cleopatra's hair-dressing girl and Charmion, who were Antony's chief state-councillors'. Plutarch, *Antony*, Dryden trans., p.770.

285 'pathologically treacherous'. Velleius Pateruclus, in commentary to Cicero, trans., Grant, p.98.

286 'one thing he had to say, whether sober or drunk, was that all would go well if Cleopatra would return to Egypt . . . You have done well, Geminius, to tell your secret without being put on the rack'. Plutarch, *Antony*, after Dryden trans., p.770.

286 'I shall one day give judgement on the Capitol'. Cassius Dio 50.5 in Scott-Kilvert trans., p.39.

287 'denying him the authority which he had let a woman exercise in his place'. Plutarch *Antony* Dryden trans., p.770; Antonius' acceptance of gynaikokratia 'feminine rule' in Plutarch, *Antony*, Dryden trans., p.751, and Wyke 2002, p.220.

287 'fatale monstrum'. Horace, Ode I.37.21 in Bennett trans., p.100; 'a monster capable of forcing fate'. Bingen 2007, p.44, see also Luce 1963, p.255 and Maehler 2003, p.207.

287 'Rome, who had never condescended to fear any nation or people, did in her time fear two human beings; one was Hannibal, and the other was a woman'. Tarn 1934, p.111.

288 'we may well be frightened if Octavian has got hold of the ladle'. Plutarch, *Antony*, Dryden trans., p.771.

288 'amid the soldiers' standards the sun shines on the shameful Egyptian pavilion'. Horace, Epode IX.16, Bennett trans., p.386.

288 'bear weapons at a woman's behest'. Horace, Epode IX.12–15, Bennett trans., p.387.

288 'and – shocking! – accompanied by an Egyptian wife'. Virgil, *Aeneid* VIII.688, in Maehler 2003 p.208; see also Bingen 2007, p.45 – 'behind him, o scandal, his Egyptian wife!'.

288 'native sistrum . . . all kinds of monstrous gods and barking Anubis'. Virgil, *Aeneid* VIII.698–700 in Maehler 2003, p.208.

288 'lecherous Canopus' prostitute queen dared to oppose her yapping Anubis against our Jupiter'. Propertius III.11, trans., Shepherd 1985 in Maehler 2003, pp.209–10.

288 'this pestilence of a woman'. Cassius Dio 50.24, Scott-Kilvert trans., p.53.

288 'let nobody consider him a Roman, but rather an Egyptian; let us not call him Antony but rather Serapis'. Cassius Dio, 50.27, Scott-Kilvert trans., p.54.

288 'rabble . . . worship reptiles and beasts as gods, they embalm their bodies to make them appear immortal, they are most forward in effrontery, but most backward in corage. Worst of all, they are not ruled by a man, but are the slaves of a woman'. Cassius Dio, 50.24, Scott-Kilvert trans., p.53.

289 'Imperator'. Southern 1998, p.139.

290 'rich in gaudy robes'. Virgil, *Aeneid* VIII, Dryden trans., p.223.

290 'from the fifth to the seventh hour it raged with terrific losses on both sides'. Paulus Orosius, in Lovric 2001, p.84.

290 'Roman corpses floating in the sea'. Propertius II.15, in Griffin 1977, p.26.

290 'as a woman and as an Egyptian'. Cassius Dio 50.33, in Scott-Kilvert trans., p.59.

290 'like another Paris, left the battle to fly to her arms; or rather, to say the truth, Paris fled when he was already beaten; Antony fled first, and, following Cleopatra, abandoned his victory'. Plutarch, *Antony and Demtrius Compared*, Dryden trans., p.780.

290 'hardly one'. Horace, Ode I.37, in Davis 1969, p.92; 'scarce a single galley' in Bennet trans., p.99.

291 'out of proportion with the actual events'. Southern 1998, p.137.

Chapter 11

296 'divine protectress of the country'. Brooklyn 1988, pp.51–2.

296 'as soon as she reached safety, she slew many of the foremost men, since they had always been displeased with her and were now elated over her disaster'. Cassius Dio 51.5 in Grant 1972, p.217; also Scott-Kilvert trans., p.67.

297 'as soon as they heard what happened they started for Egypt to help their rulers'. Cassius Dio 51.7, Scott-Kilvert trans., p.68.

297 'plundered her country's gods and her ancestors' sepulchres'. *Contra Apion* 2.58, in Chugg 2004, p.110.

297 'did not exempt even the most holy shrines'. Cassius Dio 51.5.3–5, Scott-Kilvert trans., p.67, stockpiling repeated in Cassius Dio 51.17, Scott-Kilvert trans., p.78.

297 'year 22 which is equivalent of year 7, first month of akhet, day 22 of the

female pharaoh, the bodily daughter of kings who were on their part kings born of kings, Cleopatra, the beneficent father-loving goddess and of pharaoh Ptolemy called Caesar, the father and mother loving god'. BM.EA.1325 in Walker and Higgs (eds.,) 2001, p.175.

298 Harpokrates figurine from Punjab in Wheeler 1954, frontispiece and p.158.

298 'a most bold and wonderful enterprise'. Plutarch, Antony, Dryden trans., p.773.

298 'over the small space of land which divides the Red Sea from the sea near Egypt . . . the narrowest place is not much above 300 furlongs across' . . . 'over this neck of land Cleopatra had formed a project of dragging her fleet and setting it afloat in the Arabian Gulf'. Plutarch, *Antony*, Dryden trans., p.773; for Corinth system see Goudchaux 2003, p.111.

298 'the Arabians of Petra'. Plutarch, *Antony*, Dryden trans., p.773.

299 'here I am laid, my life of misery done, ask not my name, I curse you every one'. Plutarch *Antony*, Dryden trans., p.774.

300 'there was no reasonable favour which she might not expect, if she put Antonius to death or expelled him from Egypt'. Plutarch, *Antony*, Dryden trans., p.775.

300 'busy impertinent ways had provoked him'. Plutarch, *Antony*, Dryden trans., p.775.

300 'was received by Cleopatra in the palace and set the whole city into a course of feasting, drinking and presents'. Plutarch, *Antony*, Dryden trans., p.774.

300 'that many of the guests who sat down in want went home wealthy men'. Plutarch, *Antony*, Dryden trans., p.775.

300 'The Suicide Club'. Forster 1982, p.29; poisoned chaplets in Pliny *Natural History* XXI.12, trans., pp.169–71.

300 'I will not be shown in a Triumph'. Livy CXXXIII.54, trans., Schlesinger 1959, p.223.

301 'her daily practice' . . . a collection of all varieties of poisonous drugs and in order to see which of them were the least painful in the operation, she had them tried upon prisoners condemn(ed.) But finding that the quick poisons always worked with sharp pains and that the less painful were slow, she next tried venomous animals, and watched with her own eyes whilst they were applied, one creature to the body of another'. Plutarch, *Antony*, Dryden trans., p.774; also *De Bello Aegyptiaco* in Volkman 1953, p.193 and Pliny *Natural History* XXI.12, trans., p.171.

301 'she pretty well satisfied herself that nothing was comparable to the bite of the asp, which without convulsion or groaning brought on a heavy

drowsiness and lethargy with a gentle sweat on the face, the sense being stupefied by degrees; the patient, in appearance, being sensible of no pain, but rather troubled to be disturbed or awakened like those that are in a profound natural sleep'. Plutarch, *Antony*, Dryden trans., p.774.

301 'other reptiles to end her life'. Cassius Dio 51.11, Scott-Kilvert trans., p.72.

301 'several tombs and monuments . . . joining the temple of Isis'. Plutarch, *Antony*, Dryden trans., p.775.

301 'large edifice'. Ashton 2003(b.) p.28; also Ashton 2003, pp.120–2.

301 'the tomb which she was building in the grounds of the palace'. Cassius Dio 51.8, Scott-Kilvert trans., p.69.

301 'wonderful height . . . very remarkable for their workmanship'. Plutarch, *Antony*, Dryden trans., p.775.

301 'luxuriant decoration represented an excellent example of the baroque style of [Ptolemaic] architecture. The daring roof construction of the entrance kiosk, the play of light and shadows at the capitals, and the effect of the huge, window-like openings that created beautiful connections between interior and exterior spaces must have been stunning'. Arnold 1999, p.224.

302 'ingenious double system of trapdoor and sliding portcullis'. Habachi 1957, p.54; tomb structure in Grimm 2003, p.48.

302 'Egyptian fashion'. PSI XII.1263.7–8 in Montserrat 1997, p.33.

302 'placed in the West and all the rites for my august mummy were carried out'. Harris Stela BM.EA.886 in Reymond 1981 pp.136–50.

303 Removal of bodies in first-century BC Alexandria by 'archiatros'. Amundsen and Ferngren 1978, p.341; Athenagoras 'presided over an elaborate organisation for preserving mummies'. Grant 1972, p.181; First-century BC embalmers archive in Reymond 1973.

303 'made beautiful with unguent, myrrh and incense'. BM.EA.188, in Reymond 1981, p.221.

303 'for if this material is not mixed into the other substances the cadaver will not last long'. Diodorus 19.98–99 in Rimon et al. 1997, p.56; Koller et al. 2005, p.610; Geer trans., p.103.

303 'the teeth of the deceased if fastened with gold'. Cicero *De Legibus* II.24, after Jackson 1988, p.120.

303 'made of funerary raiment, gold and silver ornaments with protective amulets of all sorts of genuine precious stones'. Stela BM.EA.188 in Reymond 1981, pp.218, 221.

303 Snake bracelets with emeralds and pearls Boston Museum of Fine Arts No. 1981.287.288 in D'Auria et al. p.198; broad collars in Riggs 2001, p.63.

304 'best burial'. Mond and Myers 1934 I, p.173.

304 'the most highly valued glass is colourless and transparent, as closely as possible resembling rock crystal'. Pliny, *Natural History* XXXVI.198, trans., p.157.

304 'were taken to see the coffins . . . said to be made of crystal, and the method the Ethiopians follow is first to dry the corpse, either by the Egyptian process or some other . . . they then enclose it in a shaft of crystal which has been hollowed out, like a cylinder, to receive it. The stuff is easily worked, and is mined in large quantities. The corpse is plainly visible inside the cylinder; there is no disagreeable smell, or any other cause of annoyance, and every detail can be distinctly seen as if there were nothing between one's eyes and the body'. Herodotus III.24, de Selincourt trans., p.213.

304 'is to be found also on an island called Necron, or Island of the Dead, in the Red Sea facing Arabia'. Juba II in Pliny *Natural History* XXXVII.23–29, trans., p.181.

304 'an island in the Red Sea 60 miles from the city of Berenike . . . known as "iris" in token of its appearance, for when it is struck by the sunlight in a room it casts the appearance and colours of a rainbow on the walls near by, continually altering its tints and ever causing more and more astonishment because of its extremely changeable effects . . . and in full sunlight it scatters the beams that shine upon it, and yet at the same time lights up adjacent objects by projecting a kind of gleam in front of itself'. Pliny, *Natural History* XXXVII.136, trans., pp.275–6.

305 'Roman counterpart of Hathor'. Springborg 1990, p.204.

305 'thither she removed her treasure, her gold, silver, emeralds, pearls, ebony, ivory [and] cinnamon'. Plutarch, *Antony*, Dryden trans., p.775.

305 'a great quantity of torchwood and tow'. Plutarch, *Antony*, Dryden trans., p.775.

305 'began to fear lest she should in a desperate fit set all these riches on fire'. Plutarch, *Antony*, Dryden trans., p.775.

305 'in honour of which the citizens of Alexandria did nothing but feast and revel for many days'. Plutarch, *Antony*, Dryden trans., p.774.

305 'mallokouria'. Montserrat 1991.

306 'my son Theon had his long hair cut off in honour of the city on the 15th Tybi in the Great Serapeum in the presence of the priests and officials'. Pap. Oxy.XLIX.3463, based on Montserrat 1996, p.40.

306 'registered among the youths'. Plutarch, *Antony*, Dryden trans., p.774.

306 'at the eve of a favourable monsoon'. Goudchaux 2003, p.109.

306 'for the Red and Indian Seas'. Tarn in Goudchaux 2003 p.109.

307 'armed as he was, he kissed her, and commending to her favour one of his

men who had most signalised himself in the fight'. Plutarch, *Antony*, Dryden trans., p.775.

307 Petubastis' death on statue Cherchell Museum S.75 in Roller 2002 p.143; see also Reymond and Barns 1977, p.14.

308 'gathered the fragments of his chaplet into his cup'. Pliny *Natural History* XXI.12, trans., pp.169–71.

308 'the sound of all sorts of instruments, and voices singing in tune, and the cry of a crowd of people shouting and dancing, like a troop of bacchanals on its way'. Plutarch, *Antony* Dryden trans., p.775; ethereal music in Cassius Dio 51.17, Scott-Kilvert trans., p.78.

309 'Why delay any longer? Fate has snatched away the only thing for which I still wanted to live. I'm not so troubled, Cleopatra, that you have gone, for I shall soon be with you. But it distresses me that so great a general should be found to be less courageous than a woman'. After Plutarch, *Antony*, Dryden trans., p.776.

309 'Well done, Eros, well done, you've shown your master how to do what you hadn't the heart to do yourself'. After Plutarch, *Antony* Dryden trans., p.776.

309 'it was no easy task for the women; and Cleopatra, with all her force, clinging to the rope, and straining with her head to the ground, with difficulty pulled him up, while those below encouraged her with their cries, and joined in all her efforts and anxiety'. Plutarch, *Antony* Dryden trans., p.776.

310 'still holding up his hands to her, and lifting up his body with the little force he had left', eyewitnesses claiming 'nothing was ever more sad than this spectacle'. Plutarch, *Antony* Dryden trans., p.776.

310 'beating her breast with her hands, lacerating herself, and disfiguring her own face with the blood from his wounds, she called him her lord, her husband, her emperor, and seemed to have pretty nearly forgotten all her own evils, she was so intent upon his misfortunes'. Plutarch, *Antony*, Dryden trans., p.776.

310 'shook her dress to see if there were any poisons hid in it'. Plutarch, *Antony*, Dryden trans., p.776.

310 'had of his own accord delivered himself up to the serpents at the time when Cleopatra had been seized . . . , and after being bitten by them had leaped into a coffin prepared for him'. Cassius Dio 51.14, Scott-Kilvert trans., p.75.

311 'holding him by the hand and talking with him'. Plutarch, *Antony*, Dryden trans., p.776.

311 'had the sarcophagus containing Alexander the Great's mummy removed from the mausoleum at Alexandria and, after a long look at its features,

showed his veneration by crowning the head with a golden diadem and strewing flowers on the trunk'. Suetonius, *Augustus* 18, Graves trans., pp.59–60.

311 'actually touched it, with the result that a piece of the nose was broken off, so the story goes. Yet he was unwilling to look at the remains of the Ptolemies, although the Alexandrians were very anxious to show them; Octavian commented, "I wished to see a king, not corpses" '– Cassius Dio, 51.16, Scott-Kilvert trans., p.77.

311 'dragged from the image of the god Julius, to which he had fled with vain pleas for mercy'. Suetonius, *Augustus* 17, Graves trans., p.59.

312 'sent cavalry in pursuit'. Suetonius, *Augustus* 17, Graves trans., p.59.

312 'many kings and great commanders made petition to [Octavian] for the body of Antonius to give him his funeral rites, but he would not take the corpse away from Cleopatra by whose hands he was buried with royal splendour and magnificence, it being granted to her to employ what she pleased on his funeral'. Plutarch, *Antony*, Dryden trans., p.777.

312 'in state, clothed in splendid raiment'. Lucian, *On Funerals* IV, Loeb trans., p.119.

312 'embalmed'. Cassius Dio 51.15, Scott-Kilvert trans., p.75.

312 'is not likely to have been delayed more than one or two days'. Skeat 1953, p.98.

313 'in this extreme of grief and sorrow . . . inflamed and ulcerated her breasts with beating them . . . she fell into a high fever . . . menacing language about her children'. Plutarch, *Antony*, Dryden trans., p.777

313 'as if she desired nothing more than to prolong her life'. Plutarch, *Antony*, Dryden trans., p.778.

313 'her hair and face looking wild and disfigured, her voice quivering, and her eyes sunk in her head'. Plutarch, *Antony*, Dryden trans., p.778.

313 'her old charm and the boldness of her youthful beauty . . . still sparkled from within'. Plutarch, *Antony*, Dryden trans., p.778.

314 'dressed herself with studied negligence – indeed, her appearance in mourning wonderfully enhanced her beauty'. Cassius Dio, 51.12, Scott-Kilvert trans., p.73.

314 'the chastity of the princeps [Octavian] was too much for her'. Florus 2.21.9–10 in Whitehorne 2001, p.225, note 8.

314 'having had by her a list of her treasure, she gave it into his hands . . . women's toys . . . but in fact, was himself deceived'. Plutarch, *Antony*, Dryden trans., p.778

314 'she, seeking to die more nobly, showed no womanish fear of the sword . . . resolved for death, she was brave inde(ed.) She was no docile woman but truly scorned to be taken away in her enemy's ships, deposed,

to an overweening triumph'. Horace, Ode 1.37.21–32, in Maehler 2003, p.207.

314 'pure wine and fragrant oil of spikenard, balsam too, and crimson roses'. based on Ausonius, Epit. XXXI, in Toynbee 1971, p.63.

314 'no further offerings or libations expect from me; these are the last honours that Cleopatra can pay your memory . . . But if the gods below, with whom you now are, either can or will do anything, suffer not your living wife to be abandoned; let me not be led in trumph to your shame, but hide me and bury me here with you, since amongst all my bitter misfortunes nothing has afflicted me like this brief time that I have had to live without you'. Plutarch, *Antony*, Dryden trans., p.778.

315 'she put on her finest robes'. Cassius Dio, 51.13, Scott-Kilvert trans., p.74.

315 'no one knows for certain by what means she perished'. Cassius Dio, 51.14, Scott-Kilvert trans., p.74; death discussed by Griffith 1961 and Whitehorne 2001, chapter 15; effigy of Cleopatra as Isis with snakes on arms in Etienne 2003, p.98.

315 'what really took place is known to no-one'. Plutarch, *Antony*, Dryden trans., p.779.

315 'the pair of asps in wait for her'. Virgil, *Aeneid* VIII.697 in Grant 1972, p.227; Dryden trans., p.223.

315 'handled fierce snakes, her corporeal frame drank in their venom'. Horace, *Odes* 1.37.26–28, in Maehler 2003, p.207.

315 'an asp was brought in amongst those figs and covered with the leaves . . . ' "So here it is" and held out her bare arm to be bitten'. Plutarch, *Antony*, Dryden trans., p.779.

316 'asp' defined in Hölbl 2003, p.293.

316 'which without convulsion or groaning brought on a heavy drowsiness and lethargy with a gentle sweat on the face, the sense being stupefied by degrees; the patient, in appearance, being sensible of no pain, but rather troubled to be disturbed or awakened like those that are in a profound natural sleep'. Plutarch, *Antony*, Dryden trans., p.774.

317 Cobra suggested by Spiegelberg in 1925 for 'an end which was not indeed the easiest, but yet the most sacred'. Griffiths 1961 p.113; 'while the introduction of one snake is perhaps credible, the mind soon begins to boggle at this Medusa-like proliferation of reptiles'. Whitehorne 2001, p.192.

317 'kept in a vase, and that she vexed and pricked it with a golden spindle till it seized her arm'. Plutarch, *Antony*, Dryden trans., p.779.

317 'two-headed serpent capable of bounding several feet in the air'. El-Masudi in Hughes-Hallet, 1990, p.72.

317 Poisoned ointment mentioned by Strabo XVII.296 in Grant 1972, p.226.

317 'she had smeared a pin with some poison whose composition rendered it harmless if the contact were external, but which, if even the smallest quantity entered the bloodstream, would quickly prove fatal, although also painless; according to this theory, she had previously worn the pin in her hair as usual'. Cassius Dio, 51.14, Scott-Kilvert trans., pp.74–5.

318 'it was also said she carried poison in a hollow bodkin, about which she wound her hair'. Plutarch, *Antony* 82, Dryden trans., p.779.

318 Hairpins in sculpture see Bartman 2001, fig.10, p.12; in mummy hair see Bowman 1996, pl.6; Roman attitude to female hair in la Folette 2001, p.57, Sebesta 1997, p.535.

318 'Cleopatra's hair-dressing girl'. Plutarch, *Antony*, Dryden trans., p.770.

318 'with majestic grace, took in her hands all the emblems of royalty'. Cassius Dio 51.14, Scott-Kilvert trans., p.74.

318 Hairpins' ability to pierce skin in Ovid, *Art of Love* III.240–245, Lewis May trans., p.91; Apuleius VIII, Grant trans., p.191.

318 'made a small scratch her arm and caused the poison to enter her blood'. Cassius Dio, 51.14, in Scott-Kilvert trans., p.75; 'she bit herself and then poured the poison of a viper into the wound'. Galen, *De Theriacis ad Pisonem* 7, in von Wertheimer 1931, p.318.

319 'lying upon a bed of gold, set out in all her royal ornaments. Eiras, one of her women, lay dying at her feet, and Charmion, just ready to fall, scarce able to hold up her head, was adjusting her mistress's diadem'. Plutarch, *Antony* 82, Dryden trans., p.779.

319 'Was this well done of your lady, Charmion?' . . . and as befitting the descendant of so many kings'. Plutarch, *Antony* 85, Dryden trans., p.779; Rowlandson (ed.) 1998, pp.40–1.

Chapter 12

320 'he was so anxious to save Cleopatra as an ornament for his triumph'. Suetonius, *Augustus* 17, Graves trans., p.59.

320 'the only marks that were found on her body were tiny pricks on the arm'. Cassius Dio 51.14, Scott-Kilvert trans., p.74.

320 'only something like the trail of it was said to have been noticed on the sand by the sea, on the part towards which the building faced and where the windows were'. Plutarch, *Antony* 82, Dryden trans., p.779.

320 'actually summoned Psyllian snake-charmers to suck the poison from her self-inflicted wound, supposedly from the bite of an asp'. Suetonius *Augustus* 17, Graves trans., p.59.

320 'if sent for immediately, to suck out the venom of any reptile before the victim dies'. Cassius Dio 51.14, Scott-Kilvert trans., p.75.

320 'Will the patient live or die?'. After Nunn 1996, p.188.

321 'not only came to see her body, but called in the aid of drugs . . . in an attempt to revive her'. Cassius Dio 51.14 Scott-Kilvert trans., p.75.

321 'the poison does not enter the heart here, nor burn the breast here . . . Osiris' sword destroys the poison, it cools the burn, when the snakes – merbu, wartet, ketet – come out!' After Andreu et al. 1997, p.204.

321 'I will not be shown in a triumph'. Livy CXXXIII.54, trans., Schlesinger 1959, p.223.

321 'was bitterly chagrined on his own account, as if all the glory of his victory had been taken away from him'. Cassius Dio 51.14, Scott-Kilvert trans., p.75.

321 'were both embalmed in the same manner and buried in the same tomb'. Cassius Dio 51.15, Scott-Kilvert trans., p.75.

321 'full of ghosts'. Pausanias 10.32.17, in Witt 1971, p.66.

322 'her women also received honorable burial by his directions'. Plutarch, *Antony*, Dryden trans., p.779.

322 'with royal splendour and magnificence'. Plutarch, *Antony* 85, Dryden trans., p.779.

322 'great quantities of treasure were found in the palace'. Cassius Dio 51.17, Scott-Kilvert trans., p.78.

322 'a single agate cup'. Suetonius, *Augustus* 71, Graves trans., p.90.

322 'the rate of interest fell from 12 to 4%'. Earl 1968, p.55.

322 'seduced the army with bonuses, and his cheap food policy was successful bait for civilians. Indeed, he attracted everybody's goodwill by the enjoyable gift of peace . . . war or judicial murder had disposed of all men of spirit'. Tacitus, *Annals* 1.2, Grant trans., p.29–30.

322 Interregnum mentioned by Clement in Skeat 1953, pp.98–100; Whitehorne 2001, p.197.

323 'it is bad to have too many Caesars'. Plutarch, *Antony*, in Grant 1972, p.229, paraphrasing Odysseus' speech in Homer, *Iliad* II.204, Graves trans., p.45.

323 Bust identified as Antonia Minor on basis of hairstyle, 'always a precious clue regarding identity'. Goddio and Bernard 2004, p.135.

323 'Archibius, one of her friends, gave [Octavian] two thousand talents to save them'. Plutarch, *Antony* 82, Dryden trans., p.779; interpretation in Goudchaux 2001, p.129.

324 'the Memphite dynasty was extinguished at the same moment as the House of the Ptolemies'. Reymond and Barns 1977, p.14.

324 'gold and silver ornaments with protective amulets of all sorts of genuine precious stones'. BM.EA.188. in Reymond 1981, p.218.

324 'would not go out of his way, however slightly, to honour the divine Apis bull'. Suetonius, *Augustus* 93, Graves trans., p.100.

324 'to worship gods, not cattle'. Cassius Dio 51.16, Scott-Kilvert trans., p.77.

324 'deranged . . . demented'. Juvenal, *Satires* XV.1–2, 2–8, 44 in Maehler 2003, p.212; similarly 'yapping Anubis'. Propertius III.11, trans., Shepherd 1985 in Maehler 2003, p.209–210; 'monstrous gods and barking Anubis'. Virgil, *Aeneid* VIII.698–700 in Maehler 2003, p.208.

324 'the angry priests'. Lindsay 1970, p.485, deliberately omitting cartouche from Buchis Stela No.13 in Mond and Myers I p.14, II pp.11–12; Tarn 1936 p.188; Brooklyn 1988, no.107, p.213.

325 'both lamp-lighters in the temple of Serapis, most great god, and of the Isis shrine there, and Paapis son of Thonis and Petorisris son of Patoiphos, both lamp-lighters in the temple of Taweret, most great goddess, at Oxyrynchos. All four swear by Caesar, god and son of a god, to the overseers of the temples in the Oxyrynchos and Kynopolitye nomes, that we will superintend the lamps of the above named temples and will supply proper oil for the daily lamps burning in the temples signified from Thoth 1 to Mesore 5 of the present year 1 of Caesar in accordance with what was supplied up to the 22nd which was year 7 of Cleopatra; and we the aforesaid are mutually sureties and all our property is security for the performance of the duties herein written'. Oxyrynchus Papyrus, after Lindsay 1970, p.485–6.

325 'high priest of Alexandria and all Egypt'. Dunand and Zivie-Coche 2004, p.211–13.

325 'like those of horses, the whites being larger than usual'. Pliny, *Natural History* XI.143, Loeb trans., p.521; bronze statue GR 1911.9–1.1 in Bosanquet 1911, p.69; Huskinson (ed.) 2000, p.289.

325 'beloved of Ptah and Isis'. Witt 1971, p.63.

326 'the Roman . . . Caesar the god, son of the god'. Rowlandson (ed.) 1998, p.50.

326 'he whose power is incomparable in the City par excellence that he loves, Rome'. Dunand and Zivie-Coche 2004, p.201.

326 'took a leaf from Alexander's book when [he] decided to keep Egypt under strict surveillance'. Arrian III.6, de Selincourt trans., p.155; Octavian's Egyptian policy in Cassius Dio 51.17, Scott-Kilvert trans., p.77.

326 'praefectus Aegypti et Alexandreae'. Berman 1999, p.465.

326 'caused a list of his achievements to be inscribed upon the pyramids . . . circulated much disparaging gossip'. Cassius Dio 53.23, Scott-Kilvert trans., p.146.

326 'second Cleopatra'. Reeves 2326, p.36; suppression of defeat in Huskinson (ed.) 2000, p.288.

327 'even wrenched from their bases the statues of Caesar'. Strabo in Bosanquet 1911, p.70.

327 'all the processions presented a striking appearance on account of the spoils of Egypt'. Cassius Dio 51.21, Scott-Kilvert trans., p.82.

327 'an effigy of the dead Cleopatra lying on a couch, so that in a sense she too, together with the live captives, who included her children . . . formed a part of the pageant'. Cassius Dio 51.21, Scott-Kilvert trans., p.82.

327 'I've seen the sacred adders' fang upon her bosom close and hang, and her whole body slowly creep on the dark road to endless sleep', Propertius III.11.51–54 in Grant 1972, p.227; also Maehler 2003, p.210.

327 'Now is the time to drain the flowing bowl, now with unfettered foot to beat the ground with dancing, now with feasting to deck the couches of the gods, my comrades!' Horace, Ode 1.37.1–4, Bennett trans., p.99; compare with sombre Epode IX 'After Actium', Bennett trans., p.387–9.

328 'cost me about 100,000,000 sesterces', *Res Gestae* in Earl 1968, pp.101–2.

328 'the largest mass of rock crystal ever seen', Pliny, *Natural History* XXXVII, 23–29, Loeb trans., p.183.

328 'at great expense, without any inscription of my name' *Res Gestae*, in Earl 1968, pp.101–2.

328 'cut in two pieces, so that half a helping of the jewel might be in each of the ears'. Pliny *Natural History* IX.59.119–121, Loeb trans., p.247; see also Hales 2005, p.137.

328 'the buildings could be imagined as having sexual intercourse'. Montserrat in Huskinson (ed.) 2000, p.169.

328 'I found Rome built of sun dried bricks – I leave her clothed in marble'. Suetonius, *Augustus* 28, Graves trans., p.66.

329 'all that men of old and new times thought, with learned minds, is open to inspection by the reader'. Ovid, *Tristia* III.1.63, in Earl 1968, p.103.

329 'the biggest clock of all time'. Hamer 1993, p.22.

329 Octavian's mausoleum in Toynbee 1996, fig.14; Cestius' pyramid in Toynbee 1996, pl.33.

330 'when glorious Rome had founded been, by augury august'. Suetonius, *Augustus* 7, Graves trans., p.54.

330 'Isis Augusta'. Witt 1971, p.81; 'the title "Augustus" definitely connoted

monarchical power. We might paraphrase as "His Majesty'". White's commentary in Appian, *Roman History* I.5, White trans., p.13, note 1.

330 'that the month renamed in his honour should be the one in which he brought down Cleopatra'. Hamer 1993, p.xvii; discussion of 'Augustan' in Hamer 1996, p.81.

330 'I added Egypt to the empire of the Roman people'. *Res Gestae* 27.1 in La'da 2003, p.158.

331 'were enough to safeguard embarrassing facts and dangerous sentiments'. Reymond and Barns 1977, p.30.

331 Coins' durability in Walker and Higgs (eds) 2001, p.240; Antonius' claim that 'the way to carry noble blood through the world was by begetting in every place a new line and series of kings' in Plutarch, Antony 36.3–4, Dryden trans., p.761.

332 Alexandria replacing Rome in Suetonius, *Caligula* 49, Graves trans., p.173; Caligula 'turned to Cleopatra's Alexandria for a sense of courtly life as it was never lived in the days of the first citizen of the restored Republic'. Walker 2003.(b) p.85.

332 Obelisk for Antonius in Habachi p.131; Caligula's attitude to Isis in Walker and Higgs (eds) 2001, p.286, 288, and to 'Moon goddess' in Suetonius, *Caligula* 22, Graves trans., p.159.

332 'mensa Isiaca' in Tiradritti 1998, fig.23; priest of Isis and Serapis in Witt 1971, p.317, note 17; Poppaea's embalmment in Tacitus, *Annals* XVI.6 in Toynbee 1971, p.41.

332 'would not be allowed to publish a free and unvarnished report on the intervening period'. Suetonius, *Claudius* 41. 2, Graves trans., p.205.

333 'totally her mother's daughter'. Roller 2003, p.90.

333 'brought them up no less tenderly than if they had been members of his own family, and gave them the education their rank deserved'. Suetonius, *Augustus* 17, Graves trans., p.59.

333 Fates of Ptolemy and Alexander Helios in Roller 2003, p.84 and Hamer 1993, p.21.

333 'before military and marriageable age'. Roller 2003, p.84.

334 Statue of Tuthmosis I, Cherchel Museum S.74 in Roller 2002, p.142; Tuthmosis III in Scott 1933, p.175; uraeus Cherchel Museum S.86 in Roller 2003, p.142; Amun/Ammon, Cherchel Museum 66 in Roller 2002, p.142.

334 'gallery of ancestors'. Hölbl 2001, p.251.

334 Images of Juba II, e.g. Ny Carlsberg Glyptotek 1591, in Roller 2002, fig.19, p.147; Cherchel Museum S.166 in Sennequier and Colonna (eds) 2003, no.165, p.148.

334 'the marks of her devotion and love for her mother country'. Walker and

Higgs (eds) 2001, p.219 referring to Cherchel S.66; see also Louvre MA.3500 in Higgs and Walker 2003, p.71.

334 Statue of Ptolemy I, Cherchel Museum 50 in Roller 2002, p.142; statue of Petubastis III, Cherchel S.75 in Roller 2002, p.143.

334 'the veiled head shows perhaps a different portrait type of Cleopatra VII'. Cherchel Museum S.65 (28), in Higgs in Walker and Higgs (eds) 2001, p.208; see also Grant 1968, p.172; Brogan 1966, p.242.

334 Alexander the Great bust from second-century AD North Africa, National Museum of Denmark Inv.ABb97, in Chugg 2004, p.56.

334 'prominent but beautiful nose'. Brogan 1966, p.242; claim head is male by Ferroukhi in Walker and Higgs (eds) 2001, p.242.

335 'arranged in no recognizable coiffure'. Walker and Higgs (eds) 2001, p.312, in reference to silver dish Louvre Bj.1969.

335 'inherited her mother's strong prominent nose but leave us with the impression that she was probably prettier than Cleopatra VII'. Whitehorne 2001, p.199.

335 'even more distinguished for his renown as a student than for his royal sovereignty'. Pliny, *Natural History* V.16, in Loeb trans, p.231.

336 'Canaria'. Roller 2002, p.197; discussion of Egyptian-style mummification in Prahl 2004, pp.80–92 and Fletcher 2004, p.136.

336 'so far as King Juba was able to ascertain'. Pliny, *Natural History* V.51–53, in Loeb trans., p.257.

336 'the Nile above the 3rd cataract, together with its tributary, the Atbara, can indeed be envisaged as dividing Ethiopia from Egypt'. Braund 1984, p.177.

336 'Great neighbour regions of the world, which the full stream of Nile separates from the black Aethiopians, you have made common kings for both by marriage, making a single race of Egyptians and Libyans. May the king's children hold from their fathers in their turn firm dominion over both mainlands'. *Anth.Pal.9*.235, in Braund 1984, p.175.

336 'the unusually elevated status of women at Caesaraea in the centuries following her death'. Roller 2003, p.257.

336 'when she rose the moon herself grew dark, veiling her grief in night, for she saw her lovely namesake Selene bereft of life and going down to gloomy Hades. With her she had shared her light's beauty, and with her death she mingled her own darkness. Crinagoras 18/*Anth. Pal.* 7.633 in Whitehorne 2001, p.201.

337 'the public memorial of the royal family'. Pomponius Mela in Scott 1933, p.169; Sennequier and Colonna (eds) 2003, p.109.

337 'which could have held only two or three inhumation burials'. Toynbee 1971, p.159, with remains of looted contents in Scott 1933, p.173.

337 'toga picta'. Barrett 1989, p.116.

337 Statue of Ptolemy of Mauretania Louvre MA.1887 in Roller 2003, p.149; Sennequier and Colonna 2003, pp.143, 149.

337 'Regina Urania'. Roller 2003, p.252, note 41.

338 'son of King Juba and descendant of King Ptolemy'. Braund 1984, p.178.

338 'attracted universal admiration'. Suetonius, Gaius Caligula 35.2, Graves trans., p.166–67; Cassius Dio 59.21 in Barrett 1989, pp.116–18; possibility 'he hoped for an enlarged kingdom in North Africa, even including mighty Egypt itself' in Braund 1984, p.178.

339 'Drusilla, granddaughter of Cleopatra and Antonius'. Tacitus, *Histories* 5.9–10, Wellesley trans., p.285; see also Roller 2003, pp.251–2.

339 'the Dioscuri'. Acts 28.11 in Witt 1971, p.293, note.5.

339 'made saviours'. Witt 1971, p.70.

339 'the one with beautiful long hair'. Scarre 1995, p.182; Zenobia claiming descent from Cleopatra in Roller 2003, p.255, note 65; 'New Cleopatra' in Hölbl 2001, p.310.

340 'set us free from Zenobia'. *Historia Augusta*, Claud. 4.4 in Zahran 2003, p.i.

340 'walls were torn down and it lost the greater part of the area known as the Brucheion'. Ammianus Marcellinus in MacLeod (ed.) 2002, pp.72–73.

340 'bi-yadi la bi-yad 'Amr . . . 'I die by my own hand, not that of Amr'. El-Daly 2005, p.136; Zahran 2003, p.16.

340 Cleopatra 'appears in gold in the temple of Venus'. Cassius Dio 51.22.3, Scott-Kilvert trans., p.83; claim Egypt praised 'her Cleopatra' by Ammianus Marcellinus, *Roman History* XXVIII.4.9, in Bowersock 1969, p.254; Cleopatra's cult sites in Hölbl 2001, p.310, el-Daly 2005, p.137.

340 'I overlaid the figure of Cleopatra with gold'. Hölbl 2001, p.310; treaty and festival in Witt 1971, pp.62, 165 and Bowman 1986, p.51.

Bibliography

Although many more works were consulted, these were the main titles used for reference:

Abdalla, A. 1991,' A Graeco-Roman Group Statue of Unusual Character from Dendera', *Journal of Egyptian Archaeology* 77, pp.189–93

Africa, T.W. 1963, 'Herodotus and Diodorus on Egypt', *Journal of Near Eastern Studies* 22 (4), pp.254–58

Aldred, C. 1963, 'Valley Tomb No.56 at Thebes', *Journal of Egyptian Archaeology* 49, pp.176–8

Aldred, C. 1971, *Jewels of the Pharaohs*, London (Thames & Hudson)

Allason-Jones, L. 1990, *Women in Roman Britain*, London (BMP)

Alston, R. 1995, *Soldier and Society in Roman Egypt: a Social History*, London (Routledge)

d'Ambrosio, A. 2001, *Women and Beauty in Pompeii*, Los Angeles (Getty Museum)

Amundsen, D.W. and Ferngren, G.B. 1978, 'The Forensic Role Of Physicians in Ptolemaic and Roman Egypt', *Bulletin of the History of Medicine* 52, pp.336–53

Andreu, G., Rutschowscaya, M. and Ziegler, C. 1997, *Ancient Egypt at the Louvre*, Paris (Hachette)

Andrews, C. 1981, *The Rosetta Stone*, London (BMP)

Andrews, C. 1994, *Amulets of Ancient Egypt*, London (BMP)

Andrews, C. 1990, *Ancient Egyptian Jewellery*, London (BMP)

Andronicos, M. 1988, *Vergina: the Royal Tombs and the Ancient City*, Athens (Ekdotike Athenon)

Antiquity 1927, 'News and Notes: The Lakes of Nemi', *Antiquity* 1 (2), pp.221-3

Appian, trans., White, H. 1912, *Roman History II: the Mithridatic Wars*, London (Heinemann)

Appian, trans., White, H. 1913, *Roman History III–IV: the Civil Wars*, London (Heinemann)

Apuleius, trans., Adlington, W. 1996, *The Golden Ass*, Ware (Wordsworth)

Apuleius, trans., Graves., R. 1951, *The Golden Ass: The Transformations of Lucius*, Harmondsworth (Penguin)

Aristotle, trans., Sinclair, T.A. 1984, *The Politics*, Harmondsworth (Penguin)

Arnold, D. 1999, *Temples of the Last Pharaohs*, London (OUP)

Arrian, trans., de Selincourt, A. 1958, *The Campaigns of Alexander*, Harmondsworth (Penguin)

Ashton, S. 2003, *The Last Queens of Egypt*, London (Pearson)

Ashton, S. 2003(b), 'Cleopatra: Goddess, Ruler or Regent?' *Cleopatra Reassessed, British Museum Occasional Paper No.103* (eds Walker, S. and Ashton, S.), London (BMP), pp.25–30

Athenaeus trans., Gulick, C.B. 1928–33, *The Deipnosophists* II and V, London (Heinemann)

Badawy, A. 1957, 'A Sepulchral Chapel of Greco-Roman Times at Kom Abu Billo (Western Delta)', *Journal of Near Eastern Studies* 16 (1), pp.52–4

Bailey, D.M. 2000, Roman Egypt: Province of an Empire', *Egyptian Treasures from the Egyptian Museum in Cairo* (Tiridatti F., (ed.)), Vercelli, pp.378–87 (White Star) p.378–87

Baines, J. 1985, 'Egyptian Twins', *Orientalia* 54(4), pp. 461–482

Baines, J. and Malek, J. 1980, *Atlas of Ancient Egypt*, Oxford (Equinox)

Baldwin, B. 1964, 'The Death of Cleopatra', *Journal of Egyptian Archaeology* 50, pp.181–2

Barrett, A.A. 1989, *Caligula: the Corruption of Power*, London (Guild)

Barry, J.M. 2005, *Fides in Julius Caesar's Bellum Civile: a Study in Roman Political Ideology at the Close of the Republican Era,* unpublished dissertation, University of Maryland

Bartman, E. 2001, 'Hair and the Artifice of Roman Female Adornment', *American Journal of Archaeology* 105 (1), pp.1–26

Bartosiewicz, l. and Dirjec, J. 2001, 'Camels in Antiquity: Roman Period Finds from Slovenia', *Antiquity* 75 (288), pp.279–85

Beard, M.L. 2003, 'Cleopatra: from history to myth', *Guardian* (18.3.03)

Bell, L. 1985, Luxor Temple and the Cult of the Royal Ka, *Journal of Near Eastern Studies* 44, pp. 251–94

Benard, E. and Moon, B. (eds) 2000, *Goddesses Who Rule*, Oxford (OUP)

Berman, L. 1999, *The Cleveland Museum of Art: Catalogue of Egyptian Art*, New York (Hudson Hills Press)

Bianchi, R.S. 1980, 'Not the Isis Knot', *Bulletin of the Egyptological Seminar* No.2, pp.9–31

Bianchi, R.S. (ed.) 1988, *Cleopatra's Egypt: The Age of the Ptolemies*, New York (The Brooklyn Museum)

Bianchi, R.S. 2003, 'Images of Cleopatra VII Reconsidered', *Cleopatra Reassessed, British Museum Occasional Paper No.103*, (eds Walker, S. and Ashton, S.), London (BMP), pp.13–23

Bierbrier, M. (ed.) 1997, *Portraits and Masks: Burial Customs in Graeco-Roman Egypt*, London (BMP)

Bietak, M. 1992, 'Minoan Wall-Paintings Unearthed at Ancient Avaris', *Egyptian Archaeology* 2, pp.26–28

Bingen, J. 2007, *Hellenistic Egypt: Monarchy, Society, Economy, Culture*, Edinburgh (EUP)

Boardman, J., Griffin, J. and Murray, O. (eds) 1991, *The Oxford History of the Classical World*, Oxford (OUP)

Borg, B. 1997, 'The Dead as Guests at Table? Continuity and Change in the Egyptian Cult of the Dead, *Portraits and Masks: Burial Customs in Graeco-Roman Egypt* (ed.) Bierbrier, M.), London (BMP), pp.26–32

Bosanquet, R.C. 1911, 'Second Interim Report on the Excavations at Meroë in Ethiopia: III, On the Bronze Portrait Head', *Annals of Archaeology and Anthropology* IV (2–3), pp.66–71

Bothmer, B. 1960, *Egyptian Sculpture of the Late Period, 700 B.C. to A.D.100*, Brooklyn

Bovill, E.W. 1956, 'The Camel and the Garamantes', *Antiquity* 117, pp.19–21

Bowersock, G.W. 1969, 'Review: Das Bild der Cleopatra in der griechischen und lateinischen Literatur', *American Journal of Philology* 90(2), pp.252–4 (Ayer Co.)

Bowman, A. 1986, *Egypt after the Pharaohs, 332* BC – AD 642, London (BMP)

Bowman, A.K. 2003, *Life and Letters on the Roman Frontier: Vindolanda and Its People*, London (BMP)

Bradford, E. 1971, *Cleopatra*, London (Hodder & Stoughton)

Braund, D. 1984, '*Anth.Pal*.9.235: Juba II, Cleopatra Selene and the Course of the Nile', *The Classical Quarterly* 34 (1), pp. 175–8

Breasted, J.H. 1988, *Ancient Records of Egypt: Historical Documents from the Earliest Times to the Persian Conquest*, I-IV, Chicago

Brogan, O. 1966, 'Review: Roman Africa in Colour', *Antiquity* 40 (159), pp.242–3

Brooklyn Museum, 1988, *Cleopatra's Egypt: Age of the Ptolemies*, Brooklyn (Brooklyn Museum)

Broughton, T.R.S., 1942, 'Cleopatra' and 'The Treasure of the Ptolemies'", *American Journal of Philology* 63 (3), pp. 328–332

Broughton, T.R.S. 1985, 'Cleopatra and "The Treasure of the Ptolemies"': a Note, *American Journal of Philology* 106 (1), pp.115–16

Buckley, S.A. and Evershed, R. 2001, 'The Organic Chemistry of Embalming Agents in Pharaonic' and Graeco-Roman Mummies', *Nature* (vol.413, issue 6858), pp.837–41

Buckley, S., Fletcher, J., al–Thour, K., Basalama, M. and Brothwell, D. 2007, 'A Preliminary Study on the Materials Employed in Ancient Yemeni Mummification and Burial Practices', *Proceedings for the Seminar for Arabian Studies 37,* London (Archaeopress), pp.37–41

Burn, L. 2004, *Hellenistic Art: from Alexander the Great to Augustus*, London (BMP)

Bushnell, G.H. 1928, 'The Alexandrian Library', *Antiquity* 2 (6), pp.196–204

Caesar, Julius, trans., Way, A.G. 1955, *Alexandrian, African and Spanish Wars*, London (Heinemann)

Caesar, Julius, trans., Peskett, A.G. 1914, *The Civil Wars*, London (Heinemann)

Caesar, Julius, trans. Handford 1951, *The Conquest of Gaul*, Harmondsworth (Penguin)

Callender, V.G. 2004, 'Queen Tausert and the End of Dynasty 19', *Studien zur altägyptischen Kultur* 32, pp.81–104

Canfora, L. 1990, *The Vanished Library: a Wonder of the Ancient World*, Berkeley (University of California Press)

Cappers, R. 2006, *Roman Foodprints at Berenike: archaeobotanical evidence of subsistence and trade in the Eastern Desert of Egypt*, Los Angeles (University of California)

Caputo, P. 1998, 'Aegyptiaca Cumana: new evidence for Isis' cult in Campania: the site', *Proceedings of the Seventh International Congress of Egyptologists* (Eyre ed. C.), Leuven, Peeters, pp.245–53

Carlson, D. 2002, 'Caligula's Floating Palaces', *Archaeology* 55 (No.3), pp.26–31

Carter, J.M. 1970, *The Battle of Actium: the Rise and Triumph of Augustus Caesar*, London (Hamilton)

Carter, W.L. 1940, 'Roses in Antiquity', *Antiquity* 14 (55), pp.250–6

Cassius Dio, trans., Cary, E. 1914–24, *Roman History I–VII,* London (Heinemann)

Cassius Dio, trans., Scott-Kilvert, I. 1987, *The Roman History: the Reign of Augustus*, Harmondsworth (Penguin)

Casson, L. 2001, *Libraries in the Ancient World,* New Haven (Yale University Press)

Chanler, B. 1934, *Cleopatra's Daughter,* London (Putnam)

Charlesworth, M.P. 1933, 'Some Fragments of the Propaganda of Mark Antony', *Classical Quarterly* 27 (3–4), pp. 172–7

Chaveau, M. 2000, *Egypt in the Age of Cleopatra,* Ithaca (Cornell University Press)

Chaveau, M. 2002, *Cleopatra: Beyond the Myth,* Ithaca (Cornell University Press)

Chemistry World 2006, News Section, *Chemistry World,* Vol.3 (3), p.22

Chugg, A.M. 2004, *The Lost Tomb of Alexander the Great,* London (Richmond Editions/Periplus)

Cicero, trans. Grant, M., 1960, *Selected Works,* Harmondsworth (Penguin)

Clark, C.R. 1928, 'Egyptian Granular Jewelry', *Metropolitan Museum of Art Bulletin* 23 (10), pp.249–53

Clark, C.R. 1935, 'Ptolemaic Jewelry', *Metropolitan Museum of Art Bulletin* 30 (8), pp.161–4

Clark, C.R. 1951, 'Egyptian Jewelry', *Metropolitan Museum of Art Bulletin,* New Series 10 (3), pp.110–12

Corbelli, J.A. 2006, *The Art of Death in Graeco-Roman Egypt,* Aylesbury (Shire)

Corteggiani, J.P. 1986, *The Egypt of the Pharaohs at the Cairo Museum,* London

Crawford, A. 2007, 'Who Was Cleopatra?' *Smithsonian.com, http://www.smithsonianmag.com/history-archaeology/cleopatra.html*

Crook, J. 1957, 'A Legal Point about Mark Antony's Will', *Journal of Roman Studies* 47 (1–2), pp.36–8

Croom, A.T. 2000, *Roman Clothing and Fashion,* Stroud (Tempus)

Cunliffe, B. 2002, *The Extraordinary Voyage of Pytheas the Greek,* New York (Walker)

el-Daly, O. 2005, *Egyptology: the Missing Millennium,* London (UCL Press)

D'Auria, S., Lacovara, P. and Roehrig, C. 1988, *Mummies and Magic: the Funerary Arts of Ancient Egypt,* Boston (Boston Museum of Fine Arts)

Davidson, J. 1997, *Courtesans and Fishcakes: the Consuming Passions of Classical Athens,* London (Fontana)

Davies, G. 2005, 'What made the Roman toga virilis?' *Proceedings from The Clothed Body in the Ancient World* (ed. Cleland, L. et al.), Oxford (Oxbow Books), pp.121–30

Davies, S. and Smith, H.S. 1997, 'Sacred Animal Temples at Sakkara', *The Temple in Ancient Egypt* (ed. Quirke S.,), pp.112–131

Davis, A.T. 1969, 'Cleopatra Rediviva', *Greece and Rome,* 2nd Ser., Vol. 16 (1), pp. 91–4

Davis, S. 1951, *Race-Relations in Ancient Egypt: Greek, Egyptian, Hebrew, Roman*, London (Methuen)

Davis, T.M. 2001, *The Tomb of Siptah with The Tomb of Queen Tiyi*, London (Duckworth)

Dayagi-Mendels, M. 1989, *Perfumes and Cosmetics in the Ancient World*, Jerusalem

Debrohun, J.B. 1994, 'Redressing Elegy's Puella: Propertius IV and the Rhetoric of Fashion', *Journal of Roman Studies* 84, pp. 41–63

Depuydt, L. 1995, 'Murder in Memphis: The Story of Cambyses's Mortal Wounding of the Apis Bull (c. 523 BCE)', *Journal of Near Eastern Studies* 54 (2), pp.119–26

Desmond, A.C. 1971, *Cleopatra's Children*, New York (Dodd, Mead)

Diodorus Siculus, trans., Oldfather, C.H. 1936–47, *Diodorus of Sicily I–III*, London (Heinemann)

Diodorus Siculus, trans., Geer, R.M. 1947–54, *Diodorus of Sicily IX–X*, London (Heinemann)

Diodorus Siculus, trans., Walton, F.R. 1957, *Diodorus of Sicily XI*, London (Heinemann)

Donato, G. and Seefried, M. 1989, *The Fragrant Past: Perfumes of Cleopatra and Julius Caesar*, Rome (Istituto Poligrafico e Zecca Dello Stato)

Dunand, F. and Zivie-Coche, C. 2004, *Gods and Men in Egypt: 3000 BCE to 395 CE*, London (Cornell University Press)

Dwyer, E. 1992, 'The Temporal Allegory of the Tazza Farnese', *American Journal of Archaeology* 96 (2), pp.255–82

Earl, D. 1968, *The Age of Augustus*, London (Elek)

Edwards, H.G.M., Farwell, D.W. and Rozenberg, S. 1999, 'Raman Spectroscopic Study of Red Pigment and Fresco Fragments from King Herod's Palace at Jericho, *Journal of Raman Spectroscopy* 30, pp.361–6

Ellis, O.C. de C. 1947, *Cleopatra in the Tide of Time*, London (Williams & Norgate)

Ellis, P.B. 1978, *Caesar's Invasion of Britain*, London (Book Club Associates)

Ellis, S.P. 1992, *Graeco-Roman Egypt*, Princes Risborough (Shire)

Empereur, J. 1998, *Alexandria Rediscovered*, London (BMP)

Empereur, J. 2002, *Alexandria: Jewel of Egypt*, London (Thames & Hudson)

Englert, J. and Long, T. 1973, 'Functions of Hair in Apuleius' Metamorphoses', *CJ* 68, pp.236–9

Etienne, M. 2003, 'Queen, Harlot or Lecherous Goddess? An Egyptological Approach to a Roman Image of Propaganda', *Cleopatra Reassessed, British*

Museum Occasional Paper No.103 (eds Walker, S. and Ashton, S.), London (BMP), pp.95–100

Evans, P. 2000, 'La Dolce Vita on the Delta', *Sunday Times Magazine* 20.8.00, p.40–43

Evershed, R., Berstan, R., Grew, F., Copley, M., Charmant, A., Barham, E., Mottram, H. and Brown, G. 2004, 'Formulation of a Roman cosmetic', *Nature* 432, pp.35–6

Fagan, G.G. 2004, 'Bathing and Sanitation', *The Seventy Great Inventions of the Ancient World*, (ed.) Fagan, B. London (Thames & Hudson), pp.84–7

Fakhry, A. 1973, *Siwa Oasis*, Cairo (AUC Press)

Farag, S. 1975, 'Two Serapeum Stelae', *Journal of Egyptian Archaeology* 61, pp.165–7

Farrar, L. 1998, *Ancient Roman Gardens*, Stroud (Sutton)

Faulkner, R.O. 1936, 'The Bremner-Rhind Papyrus I', *Journal of Egyptian Archaeology* 22, pp.121–40

Faulkner, R.O. 1969, *The Ancient Egyptian Pyramid Texts*, Warminster (Aris & Phillips)

Faulkner, R.O. 1977, *The Ancient Egyptian Coffin Texts* II, Warminster (Aris & Phillips)

Fay, B. 1984, *Egyptian Museum Berlin,* Mainz (von Zabern)

Fazzini, R. 1975, *Images for Eternity: Egyptian Art from Berkeley and Brooklyn*, New York (The Brooklyn Musuem)

Fazzini, R.A., Bianchi, R.S., Romano, J.F. and Spanel, D.B. 1989, *Ancient Egyptian Art in the Brooklyn Museum*, Brooklyn (The Brooklyn Museum)

Ferroukhi, M. 2003, 'Les Deux Portraits de Chercell, dits de Cléopâtre VII', *Cleopatra Reassessed, British Museum Occasional Paper No.103* (eds Walker, S. and Ashton, S.), London (BMP), pp.103–8

Fielding, S. (ed.) Johnson, C.D.) 1757, *The Lives of Cleopatra and Octavia*, Lewisburg (Bucknell University Press) (originally published London, Millar)

Fildes, A. and Fletcher, J. 2001, *Son of the Gods: Alexander the Great*, London (DBP)

Flamarion, E. 1997, *Cleopatra: from history into legend*, New York (Thames & Hudson)

Flanagan, M. 2001, The Myth of Cleopatra, *Art Quarterly* (Spring), pp.46–53

Fleming, S., Fishman, B., O'Connor, D. and Silverman, D. 1980, *The Egyptian Mummy: Secrets and Science*, Philadelphia (Philadelphia University Museum)

Fletcher, J. 1998, *Oils and Perfumes of Ancient Egypt*, London (BMP)

Fletcher, J. 2004, *The Search for Nefertiti*, London (Hodder & Stoughton)

Fletcher, J. 2005, 'The Decorated Body in Ancient Egypt: hairstyles, cosmetics and tattoos', *Proceedings from The Clothed Body in the Ancient World* (ed.) Cleland, L. et al.), Oxford (Oxbow), pp.3–13

la Folette, L. 2001, 'The Costume of the Roman Bride', *The World of Roman Costume* (eds Sebesta, J.L. and Bonfante, L.), Wisconsin (University of Wisconsin Press), pp.54–64

Foreman, L. 1999, *Cleopatra's Palace: in Search of a Legend*, London (Discovery Books)

Forster, E.M. 1982, *Alexandria: a History and a Guide*, London (Michael Haag)

Foss, M. 1997, *The Search for Cleopatra*, London (Michael O'Mara)

de Franciscis, A. 1964, *Forma e Colore: la Pittura Pompeiana*, Florence (Sadea)

Fraser, P.M. 1956, 'A Temple of Hathor at Cusae', *Journal of Egyptian Archaeology* 42, pp.97–8

Fraser, P.M. 1957, 'Mark Antony in Alexandria – A Note', *Journal of Roman Studies* 47 (1–2), pp. 71-73

Fraser, P.M. 1961, 'The *ΔΙΟΛΚΟΣ* of Alexandria', *Journal of Egyptian Archaeology* 47, pp.134–8

Fraser, P.M. 1972, *Ptolemaic Alexandria*, Oxford (OUP)

Fredricksmeyer, E.A. 1991, 'Alexander, Zeus Ammon, and the Conquest of Asia', *Transactions of the American Philological Association* 121, pp.199–214

Friedman, F.D. (ed.) 1998, *Gifts of the Nile: Ancient Egyptian Faience*, London (Thames & Hudson)

Fuller, J.F.C. 1998, *Julius Caesar: Man, Soldier, Tyrant*, Ware (Wordsworth)

Galt, C. 1931, 'Veiled Ladies', *American Journal of Archaeology* 35 (4), pp.373–93

Gardiner, A.H. 1961, 'The Egyptian Memnon', *Journal of Egyptian Archaeology* 47, pp.91–9

Gardiner, A. 1964, *Egypt of the Pharaohs*, Oxford (OUP)

Garland, R. 2005, 'Celebrity in the Ancient World', *History Today* 55 (3), pp.24–30

Getty Museum 1996, *Alexandria and Alexandrianism: Papers delivered at a Symposium organized by the J.Paul Getty Museum and the Getty Center for the History of Art and Humanities April 22–25, 1993*, Malibu (Getty Museum)

Gillam, R. 2005, *Performance and Drama in Ancient Egypt*, London (Duckworth)

Girling, R. 2001, 'Riddle of the Minx', *Sunday Times Magazine* 25.3.01, pp.28–35

Goddio, F. (ed.) 1998, *Alexandria: the Submerged Royal Quarters Surveys and Excavations 1992–97*, London (Periplus)

Goddio, F. and Bernard, A. 2004, *Sunken Egypt: Alexandria*, London (Periplus)

Goldman, N. 2001, 'Roman Footwear', *The World of Roman Costume* (Sebesta,

J.L. and Bonfante, L.), Wisconsin (University of Wisconsin Press), pp.101–29

Gordon, A.H. and Schwabe, C.W. 2004, *The Quick and the Dead: Biomedical Theory in Ancient Egypt*, Leiden (Brill)

Goudchaux, G.W. 2001, 'Cleopatra's Subtle Religious Strategy', *Cleopatra of Egypt* (eds Walker, S. and Higgs, P.) London (BMP), pp.128–41

Goudchaux, G.W. 2001.(b), 'Was Cleopatra Beautiful? The conflicting answers of numismatics, *Cleopatra of Egypt* (eds Walker, S. and Higgs, P.) London (BMP), pp.210–14

Goudchaux, G.W. 2003, 'Cleopatra the Seafarer Queen: Strabo and India', *Cleopatra Reassessed, British Museum Occasional Paper No.103*, (eds. Walker, S. and Ashton, S.), London (BMP), pp.109–12

Goudsmit, J. and Brandon-Jones, D. 1999, 'Mummies of Olive Baboons and Barbary Macaques in the Baboon Catacomb of the Sacred Animal Necropolis at North Saqqara, *Journal of Egyptian Archaeology* 85, pp.45–54

Grajetzki, W. 2003, 'Ptolemaic Egypt: the Hellenistic World and Egyptian Beliefs', in *Burial Customs in Ancient Egypt: Life in Death for Rich and Poor*, London (Duckworth) pp.123–6

Grajetzki, W. 2005, *Ancient Egyptian Queens: A Hieroglyphic Dictionary*, London (Golden House Publications)

Grant, M. 1969, *Julius Caesar*, London (Chancellor Press)

Grant, M. 1972, *Cleopatra*, London (Dorset)

Grant, M. 1976, *Cities of Vesuvius: Pompeii and Herculaneum*, London (Penguin)

Grant, M. 1982, *From Alexander to Cleopatra*, London (Weidenfeld & Nicolson)

Grant, M. 1999, *Roman Cookery: Ancient Recipes for Modern Kitchens*, London (Serif)

Green, P. 1970, *Alexander the Great*, London (Book Club Associates)

Green, P. 1990, *Alexander to Actium: The Hellenistic Age*, London (Weidenfeld & Nicolson)

Green, P. 1996, 'Alexander's Alexandria', *Alexandria and Alexandrianism: Papers delivered at a Symposium organized by the J.Paul Getty Museum and the Getty Center for the History of Art and Humanities April 22–25, 1993*, Malibu (Getty Museum), p.3–25

Griffin, J. 1976, Augustan Poetry and the Life of Luxury, *Journal of Roman Studies* 66, p.87–105

Griffin, J. 1977, Propertius and Antony, *Journal of Roman Studies* 67, p. 17–26

Griffiths, J.G. 1961, 'The Death of Cleopatra VII', *Journal of Egyptian Archaeology* 47, pp.113–18

Griffiths, J.G. 1965, 'The Death of Cleopatra VII', *Journal of Egyptian Archaeology* 51, pp.209–10

Griffiths, J.G. 1966, 'Hecataeus and Herodotus' on "A Gift of the River", *Journal of Near Eastern Studies*, 25 (1), pp.57–61

Griffiths, J.G. 1970, *Plutarch's De Iside et Osiride*, Swansea (University of Wales Press)

Griffiths, J.G. 1979, 'Egyptian Nationalism in the Edfu Temple Texts', *Glimpses of Ancient Egypt: Studies in Honour of H.W. Fairman* (eds Ruffle, J., Gaballa, G.A. and Kitchen K.A.), Warminster (Aris & Philips), pp.174–79

Grimm, G. 1996, 'City Planning?' *Alexandria and Alexandrianism: Papers delivered at a Symposium organized by the J. Paul Getty Museum and the Getty Center for the History of Art and Humanities April 22–25, 1993*, Malibu (Getty Museum), pp.55–74

Grimm, G. 2003, 'Alexandria in the time of Cleopatra', *Cleopatra Reassessed, British Museum Occasional Paper No.103* (eds Walker, S. and Ashton, S.), London (BMP), pp.45–9

Groom, F. 1981, *Frankincense and Myrrh: A Study of the Arabian Incense Trade*, London (Longman)

Haas, N., Toppe, F. and Henz, B.M. 2005, 'Hairstyles in the Arts of Greek and Roman Antiquity' *Journal of Investigative Dermatology Symposium Proceedings* 100 (3), pp.298–300

Habachi, L. 1984, *The Obelisks of Egypt: Skyscrapers of the Past*, Cairo (AUC)

von Hagen, V. 1967, *The Roads That led to Rome*, London (Weidenfeld & Nicolson)

Hales, S. 2005, 'Men are Mars, Women are Venus: Divine Costumes in Imperial Rome', in *Proceedings from The Clothed Body in the Ancient World* (ed.) Cleland, L. et al.), Oxford (Oxbow), pp.131–42

Hall, R. 1986, *Egyptian Textiles*, Aylesbury (Shire)

Hamer, M. 1993, *Signs of Cleopatra: History, Politics, Representations*, London (Routledge)

Hamer, M. 1996, 'Queen of Denial', *Transition*, 72, pp.80–92

Hammond, N.G.L. 1989, *Alexander the Great: King, Commander and Statesman*, Bristol (Bristol Chemical Press)

Harlow, M. 2005, 'Dress in the Historia Augusta: the role of dress in historical narrative', *Proceedings from The Clothed Body in the Ancient World* (ed.) Cleland, L. et al.), Oxford (Oxbow), pp.143–53

Harrell, J.A. and Lewan, M.D. 2002, 'Sources of Mummy Bitumen in Ancient Egypt and Palestine', *Archaeometry* 44 (2), pp.285–93

Harrison, T. 2003, 'Upside Down and Back to Front: Herodotus and the Greek Encounter with Egypt', *Ancient Perspectives on Egypt* (eds Matthews, R. and Roemer, C.), London (UCL Press), pp.145–55

Havelock, C.M. 1982, 'A Portrait of Cleopatra II(?) in the Vassar College Art Gallery', *Hesperia*, Vol. 51, No. 3., pp. 269–76

Hepper, F.N. 1987, *Planting a Bible Garden*, London (HMSO)

Hepper, F.N. 1987, 'Trees and shrubs yielding gums and resins in the ancient Near East', *Bulletin on Sumerian Agriculture* 3, pp.107–14

Herodotus, trans., de Selincourt, A. 1959, *The Histories*, Harmondsworth (Penguin)

Heskel, J. 2001, 'Cicero as Evidence for Attitudes to Dress in the Late Republic', *The World of Roman Costume* (eds Sebesta, J.L. and Bonfante, L.), Wisconsin (University of Wisconsin Press), pp.133–54

Heuer, K. 1972, *City of the Stargazers: The Rise and Fall of Ancient Alexandria*, New York (Scribner & Sons)

Higgs, P. 2003, 'Resembling Cleopatra: Cleopatra VII's Portraits in the Context of Late Hellenistic Female Portraiture', *Cleopatra Reassessed, British Museum Occasional Paper No.103*, (eds Walker, S. and Ashton, S.), London (BMP), pp.57–70

Higgs, P. and Walker, S. 2003, 'Cleopatra VII at the Louvre', *Cleopatra Reassessed, British Museum Occasional Paper No.103* (eds Walker, S. and Ashton, S.), London (BMP), pp.71-74

Hinks, R. 1928, 'A Portrait of an Egyptian Queen', *Journal of Hellenic Studies* 48, pp. 239–42

Hodges, H. 1974, *Technology in the Ancient World*, London (Book Club Associates)

Hogarth, D.G., Lorimer, H.L. and Edgar, C.C. 1905, 'Naucratis 1903', *Journal of Hellenic Studies* 25, pp.105–36

Hölbl, G. 2001, *A History of the Ptolemaic Empire*, London (Routledge)

Holmes, W. 1959, *She Was Queen of Egypt*, London (Bell)

Holt, F.L. 1994, 'A History in Silver and Gold', *Aramco World* 45(3), pp.2–13

Holt, F. 2006, 'Ptolemy's Alexandrian Postscript', *Saudi Aramco World* (SIC) 57(6), p.4–9

Homer, trans., Rieu, E.V. 1946, *Odyssey*, Harmondsworth (Penguin)

Homer, trans., Rieu, E.V. 1954, *Iliad*, Harmondsworth (Penguin)

Horace, trans., Bennett, C.E. 1914, *The Odes and Epodes*, London (Heine-mann)

Hoss, S. 2005, *Baths and Bathing: the culture of bathing and the baths and thermae in Palestine from the Hasmoneans to the Moslem Conquest*, BAR International Series 1346, Oxford (Archaee Press)

Howland, J. 2002, 'Aristotle's Great-Souled Man', *Review of Politics* 64 (1), pp.27–56

Hughes-Hallett, L. 1990, *Cleopatra: Histories, Dreams and Distortions*, London (Bloomsbury)

Huskinson, J. (ed.) 2000, *Experiencing Rome: Culture, Identity and Power in the Roman Empire*, London (Routledge)

Huss, W. 1990, 'Die Herkunft der Cleopatra Philopator', *Aegyptus* 70, pp.191–203.

Huzar, E.G. 1985, 'Mark Antony: Marriages vs. Careers', *Classical Journal* 81 (2), pp.97–111

Ibrahim, M. el-D. 1979, 'The God of the Great Temple of Edfu', *Glimpses of Ancient Egypt: Studies in Honour of H.W. Fairman* (eds Ruffle, J., Gaballa, G.A. and Kitchen, K.A.), Warminster (Aris & Phillips), pp.170–3

Jackson, R. 1988, *Doctors and Diseases in the Roman Empire*, London (BMP)

James, P. 2000, 'The Language of Dissent', *Experiencing Rome: Culture, Identity and Power in the Roman Empire* (ed. Huskinson, J.), London (Routledge), pp.277–303

James, P. and O'Brien, M. 2006, 'To Baldly Go: a last look at Lucius and his counter humiliation strategies', *Lectiones Scrupulosae VI: Essays on the Text and Interpretation of Apuleius' Metamorphoses in Honour of Maaike Zimmerman*, Groningen (Barkhuis Publishing), pp.234–51

James, T.G.H. and Davies, V. 1983, *Egyptian Sculpture*, London (BMP)

Janssen, R. M. 1996, 'Soft Toys from Egypt', *Journal of Roman Archaeology Supplement No.19: Archaeological Research in Roman Egypt*, (ed.) Bailey, D. M. pp. 231–39

Jasnow, R. 1997, 'The Greek Alexander Romance and Demotic Egyptian Literature', *Journal of Near Eastern Studies*, 56 (2), pp.95–103

Jensen, L.B. 1963, 'Royal Purple of Tyre', *Journal of Near Eastern Studies*, 22 (2), pp.104–18

Johansen, F. 2003, 'Portraits of Cleopatra – do they exist?' *Cleopatra Reassessed, British Museum Occasional Paper No.103* (eds Walker, S. and Ashton, S.), London (BMP), pp.75–7

Johns, C. 1989, *Sex or Symbol? Erotic Images of Greece and Rome*, London (BMP)

Johnson, J.H. 1986, 'The Role of the Egyptian Priesthood in Ptolemaic Egypt', *Egyptological Studies in Honor of Richard A. Parker*, (ed. L.H. Lesko) Hanover (Brown University Press), pp.70–84

Jones, C.P. 1987, 'Stigma: Tattooing & Branding in Graeco-Roman Antiquity', *Journal of Roman Studies* 77, pp.139–55

Jones, R. 2006, *An Invitation to Dinner at the House of the Vestals*, Anglo-American Project in Pompeii, *http://www.brad.ac.uk/archsci/field__proj/anampomp/index.htm*

Jones, W.H.S. 1909, 'Dea Febris: a study of malaria in ancient Italy', *Annals of Archaeology and Anthropology* II (3), pp.97–124

Juvenal, trans., Green, P. 1967, *The Satires*, Harmondsworth (Penguin)

Kemp, B. J. 1993. 'Amarna's other period', *Egyptian Archaeology* 3, pp.13–14

Kemp, B.J. 2006, *The 2005/6 season at Tell el-Amarna: Interim Report*

Kennedy, M. 2000, 'Roman Grave believed to be Female Gladiator's', *Guardian* 13.9.00, p.11

Kessler, D. and Nur el-Din, A.H. 2002, 'Inside the Ibis Galleries of Tuna el-Gebel', *Egyptian Archaeology* 20, pp.36–8

El-Khachab, A.el-M. 1964, 'Some Recent Acquisitions in the Cairo Museum: a Golden Girdle from Ptolemaic Egypt', *Journal of Egyptian Archaeology* 50, p.144

Kitchen, K.A. 1996, *The Third Intermediate Period in Egypt (1100–650 BC)*, Warminster (Aris & Phillips)

Kleiner, D.E.E. 2005, *Cleopatra and Rome*, Cambridge (Mass.), Harvard University Press

Koller, J., Baumer, U., Kaup, Y. and Weser, U. 2005, 'Herodotus' and Pliny's Embalming Materials Identified on Ancient Egyptian Mummies', *Archaeometry* 47 (3), pp.609–28

Kuhlmann, K. 1981, 'Ptolemais: Queen of Nectanebo I. Notes on the Inscription of an Unknown Princess of the XXXth Dynasty', *MDAIK* 37, pp.267–79

La'da, C.A. 2003, 'Encounters with Ancient Egypt: the Hellenistic Greek Experience, *Ancient Perspectives on Egypt* (eds Matthews, R. and Roemer, C.), London (UCL Press), pp.157–69

Laing, J. 1999, *Art and Society in Roman Britain*, Stroud (Sutton)

Lane Fox, R. 1973, *Alexander the Great*, Harmondsworth (Penguin)

Lee, M. 2005, 'Constru(ct)ing Gender in the Feminine Greek Peplos', *Proceedings from The Clothed Body in the Ancient World* (ed.) Cleland, L. et al.), Oxford (Oxbow), p.55–64

Levi, P. 1980, *Atlas of the Greek World*, Oxford (Phaidon)

Lewis, N. 1986, *Greeks in Ptolemaic Egypt: Case Studies in the Social History of the Hellenistic World*, Oxford (Clarendon Press)

Lichtheim, M. 1973, *Ancient Egyptian Literature, I: The Old and Middle Kingdoms*, Berkeley (University of California Press)

Lichtheim, M. 1976, *Ancient Egyptian Literature, II: The New Kingdom*, Berkeley (University of California Press)

Lichtheim, M. 1980, *Ancient Egyptian Literature, III: The Late Period*, Berkeley (University of California Press)

Lindsay, J. 1963, *Daily Life in Roman Egypt*, London (Muller)

Lindsay, J. 1970, *Cleopatra*, London (Constable)

Lister, R.P. 1979, *The Travels of Herodotus*, London (Gordon & Cremonesi)

Livy, trans., Moore, F. 1950, *Livy VII*, London (Heinemann)

Livy, trans., Sage, E.T. 1935–6, *Livy X–XI*, London (Heinemann)

Livy, trans., Schlesinger, A.C. 1951, *Livy XIII*, London (Heinemann)

Livy, trans., Schlesinger, A.C. 1959, *Summaries, Fragments and Obsequens XIV*, London (Heinemann)

Llewellyn-Jones, L. 2003, *Aphrodite's Tortoise: The Veiled Woman of Ancient Greece*, (Classical Press of Wales)

Lloyd, A.B. 1976, *Herodotus Book II, Commentary 1–98*, Leiden

Lloyd, A.B. 1977, 'Necho and the Red Sea: some considerations', *Journal of Egyptian Archaeology* 63, pp.142–55

Lohwasser, A. 2001, 'Queenship in Kush: Status, Role and Ideology of Royal Women', *JARCE* 38, pp.61–76

Louvre 1981, *Un Siècle de Fouilles Françaises en Égypte 1880–1980*, Paris (IFAO)

Lovric, M. 2001, *Cleopatra's Face: Fatal Beauty*, London (British Museum Press)

Lucan, trans., Duff, J.D. 1928, *The Civil War I–X*, London (Heinemann)

Lucas, A. (rev. Harris, J.R.), 1989, *Ancient Egyptian Materials and Industries*, London (Histories and Mysteries of Man)

Luce, J.V. 1963, 'Cleopatra as Fatale Monstrum (Horace, Carm. 1. 37. 21)', *Classical Quarterly* 3 (2), pp.251–7

Luce, J.V. 1979, *Homer and the Heroic Age*, London (Thames & Hudson)

Lucian, trans., Harmon, A.M. 1925, *The Works of Lucian IV*, London (Heinemann)

Ludwig, E. 1959, *Cleopatra: the Story of a Queen*, London (Bantam)

Lunde, P. and Porter, A. (eds) 2004, *Trade and Travel in the Red Sea Region: Proceedings of Red Sea Project I*, Oxford (BAR)

MacLeod, R. (ed.) 2002, *The Library of Alexandria: Centre of Learning in the Ancient World*, London (I.B.Tauris)

MacQuitty, W. 1976, *Island of Isis: Philae, Temple of the Nile*, London (MacDonald)

Macurdy, G.H. 1927, 'Queen Eurydice and the Evidence for Woman Power in Early Macedonia', *American Journal of Philology* 48 (No. 3), pp. 201–14

Macurdy, G.H. 1936, 'Iotape', *Journal of Roman Studies* 26 (1), pp.40–2

Maehler, H. 1983, 'Egypt under the Last Ptolemies', *Institute of Classical Studies Bulletin* 30, pp.1–16

Maehler, H. 2003, 'Roman Poets on Egypt', *Ancient Perspectives on Egypt* (eds Matthews, R. and Roemer, C.), London (UCL Press), pp.203–15

Mahaffy, J.P. 1899, *A History of Egypt IV: the Ptolemaic Dynasty*, London (Methuen)

Mahaffy, J.P. 1915, 'Cleopatra VI', *Journal of Egyptian Archaeology* II (I), pp.1–4

Manniche, L. 1987, *Sexual Life in Ancient Egypt*, London (Kegan Paul)

Manniche, L. 1989, *An Ancient Egyptian Herbal*, London (BMP)

Manniche, L. 1991, *Music and Musicians in Ancient Egypt*, London (BMP)

Manniche, L. 1999, *Sacred Luxuries: Fragrance, Aromatherapy and Cosmetics in Ancient Egypt*, London (Opus)

Martial, trans., various, 1871, *The Epigrams of Martial translated into English prose*, London (Bell & Daldy)

Martin, G.T. 1981, *The Sacred Animal Necropolis at North Saqqâra: the southern dependencies of the main temple complex*, London (Egypt Exploration Society)

Matthews, R. and Roemer, C. (eds) 2003, *Ancient Perspectives on Egypt*, London (UCL Press)

Mattingly, H. 1950, 'Zephyritis', *American Journal of Archaeology* 54 (No. 2), pp.126–8

Matyszak, P. 2003, *Chronicle of the Roman Republic: the Rulers of Ancient Rome from Romulus to Augustus*, London (Thames & Hudson)

Meiklejohn, K.W. 1934, 'Alexander Helios and Caesarion', *Journal of Roman Studies* 24, pp.191–5

Metro News, 2007, 'Bird poo used for beauty face mask', *Metro News* (28.5.07)

Milanezi, S. 2005, 'Beauty in Rags: on rhakos in Aristophanic theatre', *Proceedings from The Clothed Body in the Ancient World* (ed.) Cleland, L. et al.), Oxford (Oxbow), p.75–86

Milne, J.G. 1916, 'Ptolemaic Seal Impressions', *Journal of Hellenic Studies* 36, pp.87–101

Milne, J.G. 1916(b), 'Greek and Roman Tourists in Egypt', *Journal of Egyptian Archaeology* 3 (II-III), pp.76–80

Milton, J. 1986, *Sunrise of Power: Alexander and the World of Hellenism*, Boston (Boston Publishing Company)

van Minnen, P. 2003, 'A Royal Ordinance of Cleopatra and Related

Documents', *Cleopatra Reassessed, British Museum Occasional Paper No.103*, (eds. Walker, S. and Ashton, S.), London (BMP), pp.35–42

Moioli, M.L. 2000, 'Inside the Crocodiles: Tebtunis gods were stuffed with ancient documents', *Discovering Archaeology* 2, 2, p.65

Mond, R. and Emery, W.B. 1929, 'A preliminary report on the excavations at Armant', *Annals of Archaeology and Anthropology* 16 (1–2), pp.3–12

Mond, R. and Myers, O.H. 1934, *The Bucheum* I amd II, London (Egypt Exploration Society)

Montserrat, D. 1991, 'Mallocouria and Therapeuteria: Rituals of Transition in a Mixed Society?' *Bulletin of the Amercian Society of Papyrologists* 28, pp.43–9

Montserrat, D. 1996, *Sex and Society in Graeco-Roman Egypt*, London (Kegan Paul)

Montserrat, M. 1997, 'Death and Funerals in the Roman Fayum', *Portraits and Masks: Burial Customs in Graeco-Roman Egypt*, (ed.) Bierbrier, M.), London (BMP), pp.33–44

Montserrat, D. 2000, 'Reading Gender in the Roman World', *Experiencing Rome: Culture, Identity and Power in the Roman Empire* (ed.) Huskinson, J.), London (Routledge), pp.153–81

Morris, E. 1984, *Fragrance: The Story of Perfume from Cleopatra to Chanel*, New York (Scribner & Sons)

Morkot, R.G. 2003, *Historical Dictionary of Ancient Egyptian Warfare*, Oxford (Scarecrow Press)

Moyer, I.S. 2002, 'Herodotus and an Egyptian Mirage: The Genealogies of the Theban Priests', *Journal of Hellenic Studies* 122, pp.70–90

Murray, M.A. 1934, 'The Temples of Edfu and Dendera', *Wonders of the Past* 46–47, pp.1099–1109

Myliwiec, K. 2000, *The Twilight of Ancient Egypt: First Millenium BCE,* Ithaca (Cornell University Press)

Nachtergael, G. 1980, 'Bérénice II, Arsinoé III et l'offrande de la boucle', *Chronique d'Égypte* 55, pp.240–53

Nachtergael, G. 1981, 'La Chevelure d'Isis', *Antiquité Classique* 50, pp.584–606

Naville, E. 1913, *The XI Dynasty Temple at Deir el-Bahari III*, London (Egypt Exploration Society)

Neugebauer, O and Parker, R.A. 1968, 'Two Demotic Horoscopes', *Journal of Egyptian Archaeology* 54, pp.231–5

Nicholson, P. 1996, 'The North Ibis Catacomb at North Saqqara', *Egyptian Archaeology* 9, pp.16–17

Nunn, J. 1996, *Ancient Egyptian Medicine*, London (BMP)

Orland, R.M., Orland, F.J. and Orland, P.T. 1990, 'Psychiatric assessment of Cleopatra: a challenging evaluation', *Psychopathology* 23 (3), pp.169–75

Ottaway, P. 2004, *Roman York*, Stroud (Tempus)

Ovid, trans., Lewis May, J. 2006, *The Love Books of Ovid (The Loves, The Art of Love, Love's Cure and the Art of Beauty)*, Stilwell (Digireads.com Publishing)

Ovid, trans., Mozley, J.H. 1939, *The Art of Love and other poems*, London (Heinemann)

Özeren, Ö. 1992, *Ephesus*, Istanbul (Keskin)

Paglia, C. 1990, *Sexual Personae: Art and Decadence from Nefertiti to Emily Dickinson*, London (Yale University Press)

Parker, G. 2002, 'Ex Oriente Luxuria: Indian Commodities And Roman Experience', *Journal of the Economic and Social History of the Orient* 45 (1), pp. 40–95

Parker, R.A. 1950, *The Calendars Of Ancient Egypt, Studies in Ancient Oriental Civilization No.25*, Chicago (University of Chicago Press)

Parkinson, R. 1999, *Cracking Codes: the Rosetta Stone and Decipherment*, London (BMP)

Peacock, D. and Williams, D. (eds) 2007, *Food for the Gods: New Light on the Ancient Incense Trade*, Oxford (Oxbow)

Petrie, W.M.F, 1889, *Hawara, Biahmu and Arsinoe*, London (Field & Tuer)

Petrie, W.M.F., 1896, *Koptos,* London (Quartich)

Philips, J. 1996, 'Aegypto-Aegean Relations up to the 2nd millennium B.C.' *Interregional Contacts in the Later Prehistory of Northeastern Africa*, Poznan, (Poznan Archaeological Museum) pp.459–70

Pinch, G. 1993, *Votive Offerings to Hathor*, Oxford (OUP)

Pinch, G. 1994, *Magic in Ancient Egypt*, London (BMP)

Pinto-Guillaume, E.M. 2002, 'Mollusks from the Villa of Livia at Prima Porta (Rome): Swedish Garden Archaeological Project, 1996–1999', *American Journal of Archaeology* 106 (1), pp.37–58

Pliny, trans., Rackham, H. and Jones, W.H.S. 1947–1963, *Natural History*, London (Heinemann)

Plutarch 1952, *The Lives of the Noble Grecians and Romans: the Dryden Translation*, Chicago (William Benton)

Plutarch 1973, *The Age of Alexander: Nine Greek Lives by Plutarch*, Harmondsworth (Penguin)

Pomeroy, S.B. 1975, *Goddesses, Whores, Wives and Slaves: Women in Classical Antiquity*, New York (Schocken Books)

Pomeroy, S.B. 1984, *Women in Hellenistic Egypt*, New York (Wayne State University Press)

Poo, M. 1995, *Wine and Wine Offering in the Religion of Ancient Egypt*, London (Kegan Paul)

Porter, B. and Moss, R. 1989, *Topographical Bibliography of Ancient Egyptian Hieroglyphic Texts, Reliefs and Paintings I: The Theban Necropolis, part II. Royal Tombs and Smaller Cemeteries*, Oxford (Griffith Institute)

Prag, A.J.N.W., Musgrave, J.H. and Neave, R.A.H. 1984, 'The Skull from Tomb II at Vergina: King Philip II of Macedon', *Journal of Hellenic Studies* 104, pp.60–78

Prag, J. and Neave, R. 1997, *Making Faces: Using Forensic and Archaeological Evidence*, London (BMP)

Prahl, R. 2004, 'The Origin of the Guanches – Parallels with Ancient Egypt?' *Migration and Diffusion* 5 (19), pp.80–92

Priese, K. et al. 1993, *The Masterpieces of the Pergamon and Bode Museum*, Mainz (Philipp von Zabern)

Quaegebeur, J. 1971, 'Documents concerning a Cult of Arsinoe Philadelphos at Memphis', *Journal of Near Eastern Studies*, 30 (4), pp.239–70

Quirke, S. 1990, *Who Were the Pharaohs? A History of Their Names with a List of Their Cartouches*, London (BMP)

Quirke, S. (ed.) 1997, *The Temple in Ancient Egypt: New Discoveries and Recent Research*, London (BMP)

Rackham, H. 1916, 'Notes on Horace', *The Classical Review* 30 (8), pp.223–4

Ray, J. 2001, *Reflections of Osiris: Lives from Ancient Egypt*, London (Profile Books)

Ray, J. 2003, 'Cleopatra in the Temples of Upper Egypt: the evidence of Dendera and Armant', *Cleopatra Reassessed, British Museum Occasional Paper No.103*, (eds Walker, S. and Ashton, S.), London (BMP), pp.9–11

Redford, D.B. 1986, 'The Name Manetho', *Egyptological Studies in Honor of Richard A. Parker*, (ed. Lesko, L.H.), Hanover (Brown University Press), p.118–21

Redford, D. B. 1992, *Egypt, Canaan, and Israel in Ancient Times*, Princeton (Princeton University Press)

Reeves, C.N. 1990, *Valley of the Kings: the decline of a royal necropolis*, London (Kegan Paul)

Reeves, C.N. 2000, *Ancient Egypt: The Great Discoveries: A Year-by-year Chronicle*, London (Thames & Hudson)

Reid, H. 1999, *In Search of the Immortals*, London (Hodder Headline)

Reymond, E.A.E. 1973, *Catalogue of Demotic Papyri in the Ashmolean Museum I:*

Embalmers' Archives from Hawara including Greek Documents and Subscriptions, Oxford (Griffith Institute)

Reymond, E.A.E. 1981, *From the Records of a Priestly Family from Memphis* I, Wiesbaden (Verlag Harrassowitz)

Reymond, E.A.E. and Barns, J.W. 1977, 'Alexandria and Memphis: Some Historical Observations', *Orientalia* 46 (1), pp.1–33

Reymond, E.A.E. 1969, *The Mythical Origin of the Egyptian Temple*, Manchester (Manchester University Press)

Rice, E.E. 1999, *Cleopatra*, London (Alan Sutton)

Richards, J.E. and Wilfong, T. 1994, *Preserving Eternity: modern goals, ancient intentions: Egyptian Funerary Artifacts in the Kelsey Museum of Archaeology*, Ann Arbor (Kelsey Museum)

Richardson, G.W. 1937, 'Actium', *Journal of Roman Studies* 27 (2), pp.53–164

Ridgway, B.S. 1990, *Hellenistic Sculpture I: the Styles of ca. 331–200* BC, Madison (University of Wisconsin Press)

Riefstahl, E. 1944, *Patterned Textiles in Pharaonic Egypt*, Brooklyn (Brooklyn Institute of Arts and Sciences)

Riggs, C. 2001, 'Forms of the wesekh collar in funerary art of the Graeco-Roman Period', *Chronique d'Égypte* 76, pp.57–68

Riggs, C. 2002, 'Facing the dead: recent research on the funerary art of Ptolemaic and Roman Egypt', *American Journal of Archaeology* 106 (1), pp.85–101

Rimon, O. et al. 1997, *Illness and Healing in Ancient Times*, Haifa (University of Haifa)

Ritner, R.K. 1984, A Uterine Amulet in the Oriental Institute Collection', *Journal of Near Eastern Studies*, 43 (3), pp. 209–21

Roberts, A. 1995, *Hathor Rising: the Serpent Power of Ancient Egypt*, Rottingdean (Northgate Publishers)

Roberts, A. 2000, *My Heart, My Mother: Death and Rebirth in Ancient Egypt*, Rottingdean (Northgate Publishers)

Roehrig, C. (ed.) 2005, *Hatshepsut – from Queen to Pharaoh*, New York (MMA)

Rogers, P.W., Jørgensen, L.B. and Rast-Eicher, A. (eds) 2001, *The Roman Textile Industry and its Influence*, Oxford (Oxbow)

Roller, D.W. 2003, *World of Juba II and Cleopatra Selene*, London (Routledge)

Romer, J. and Romer, E. 1995, *The Seven Wonders of the World*, London (Michael O'Mara)

Rotroff, S.I. and Lamberton, R.D. 2006, *Women in the Athenian Agora*, Athens (American School of Classical Studies at Athens)

Roveri, A.M.D. et al. 1988, *The Egyptian Museum Turin,* Milan (Federico Garolla Editore)

Rowlandson, J. (ed.) 1998, *Women and Society in Greek and Roman Egypt: a sourcebook,* Cambridge (Cambridge University Press)

Rowley-Conwy, P. 1988, 'The camel in the Nile Valley: new radiocarbon accelerator dates from Qasr Ibrim', *Journal of Egyptian Archaeology* 74, pp.245–8

Royal Commission on Historical Monuments 1962, *An Inventory of the Historical Monuments in the City of York: Vol.I, Eburacum: Roman York,* London, HMSO

Rullkötter, J. and Nissenbaum, A. 1988, 'Dead Sea asphalt in Egyptian mummies: molecular evidence', *Naturwissenschaften* 75, pp.618–21

Rutherford, I. 2003, 'Pilgrimage in Greco-Roman Egypt: New Perspectives on Graffiti from the Memnonion at Abydos', *Ancient Perspectives on Egypt* (eds Matthews, R. and Roemer, C.), London (UCL Press), pp.171–89

Saleh, M. and Sourouzian, H. 1987, *The Egyptian Museum Cairo,* Mainz (Philipp von Zabern)

Salem, M.S. 1937, 'The "Lychnapsia Philocaliana" and the Birthday of Isis', *Journal of Roman Studies* 27 (2), pp. 165–7

Samson, J. 1990, *Nefertiti and Cleopatra: Queen-Monarchs of Ancient Egypt,* London (Rubicon)

Sandars, N. 1985, *The Sea Peoples: Warriors of the Ancient Mediterranean,* London (Thames & Hudson)

Sandys, G. 1615, *The Relation of a Journey begun an.Dom 1610, in Four Books,* London (W. Barrat)

Saunders, N.J. 2006, *Alexander's Tomb: the Two Thousand Year Obsession to Find the Lost Conqueror,* New York (Basic Books)

Saylor, S. 2004, Author's note, *The Judgement of Caesar: a Mystery of Ancient Rome,* London (Constable), pp.351–6

Scarre, C. 1995, *Chronicle of the Roman Emperors: the Reign-by-reign Record of the Rulers of Imperial Rome,* London (Thames & Hudson)

Scheidel, W. 2001, *Death on the Nile: Disease and the Demography of Roman Egypt,* Leiden (Brill)

Scott, A.M. 1933, 'Algeria's Amazing Tombs: the Medrassen and the Tomebeau de la Chrétienne', *Wonders of the Past* (7–8), pp.169–75

Scott, P. 2006, 'Millennia of Murex', *Aramco World* (July/August), pp.30–7

Scullard, H.H. 1976, *From the Gracchi to Nero,* London (Methuen)

Sebesta, J.L. 1997, 'Women's Costume & Feminine Civic Morality in Augustan

Rome', 'Gender & the Body in Mediterranean Antiquity', (ed.) Wyke, M.
Gender & History Vol.9, No.3, Oxford (Blackwell), pp.529–41

Sebesta, J.L. 2001, 'Symbolism in the Costume of the Roman Woman and
Tunica Ralla, Tunica Spissa: the Colours and Textiles of Roman Costume',
The World of Roman Costume (eds Sebesta, J.L. and Bonfante, L.), Wisconsin
(University of Wisconsin Press), pp.46–53, 65–76

Sennequier, G. and Colonna, C. (eds) 2003, *L'Algérie au temps des royaumes
numides: Ve siècle avant J.-C – 1er siècle après J.-C* , Paris (Somogy Éditions
d'Art)

Seton-Williams, V. 1978, *Ptolemaic Temples*, London (Waterloo Printing Co.)

Shakespeare, W. 1988, *Antony and Cleopatra*, Harmondsworth (Penguin)

Shaw, I. and Nicholson, P. 1995, *British Museum Dictionary of Ancient Egypt*,
London (BMP)

Shore, A.F. 1979, 'Votive Objects from Dendera of the Graeco-Roman
Period', *Glimpses of Ancient Egypt: Studies in Honour of H.W. Fairman* (eds
Ruffle, J. et al.), Warminster (Aris & Phillips), pp.138–160

Simpson, S. (ed.) 2002, *Queen of Sheba: Treasures from Ancient Yemen*, London
(BMP)

Skeat, T.C. 1953, 'The Last Days of Cleopatra: a chronological problem', *JRS*
43, pp.98–100

Skeat, T.C. 1960, 'Notes on Ptolemaic Chronology I', *Journal of Egyptian
Archaeology* 46, pp.91–4

Skeat, T.C. 1961, 'Notes on Ptolemaic Chronology II', *Journal of Egyptian
Archaeology* 47, pp.107–12

Skeat, T.C. 1962, 'Notes on Ptolemaic Chronology III', *Journal of Egyptian
Archaeology* 48, pp.100–5

Skeat, T.C. 1966, 'A fragment on the Ptolemaic perfume monopoly', *Journal of
Egyptian Archaeology* 52, pp.179–80

Smith, A.H. 1917, 'A Bronze Figure of a Youth in Oriental Costume', *Journal
of Hellenic Studies*, Vol. 37, pp.135–9

Smith, H.S. 1974, *A Visit to Ancient Egypt: Life at Memphis and Saqqara (c.500–
30 BC)*, Warminster (Aris & Phillips)

Smith, H.S. 1979, 'Varia Ptolemaica', *Glimpses of Ancient Egypt: Studies in
Honour of H.W. Fairman* (eds, Ruffle, J., Gaballa, G.A. and Kitchen, K.A.),
Warminster (Aris & Phillips), p.161–6

Smith, H.S. and Hall, R. 1984, *Ancient Centres of Egyptian Civilisation*, London
(Egyptian Culture Bureau)

Smith, R.H. 1992, '"Bloom of Youth": a Labelled Syro-Palestinian Unguent
Jar', *Journal of Hellenic Studies* 112, pp.163–7

Southern, P. 1998, *Mark Antony*, Stroud (Tempus)

Southern, P. 1999, *Cleopatra*, Stroud (Tempus)

Southern, P. 2001, *Julius Caesar*, Stroud (Tempus)

Springborg, P. 1990, 'Ptolemaic Queens, Greek daimon, the Roman Emperor and his genius', in *Royal Persons: Patriarchal Monarchy and the Feminine Principle*, London (Unwin Hyman), pp.194–214

Stafford, E.J. 2005, 'Viewing and Obscuring the Female Breast: glimpses of the ancient bra', *Proceedings from The Clothed Body in the Ancient World*, Oxford (Oxbow), pp.96–110

Steuer, R.O. and Saunders, J.B. de C.M. 1959, *Ancient Egyptian and Cnidian Medicine: the Relationship of their Aetiological Concepts of Disease*, Berkeley (University of California Press)

Stevens, C.E. 1947, '55 B.C. and 54 B.C', *Antiquity* 21 (81), pp.3–9

Storey, G.R. 1997, 'The population of ancient Rome', *Antiquity* 71 (274), p.966–966

Stout, A.M. 2001, 'Jewelry as a Symbol of Status in the Roman Empire', *The World of Roman Costume* (eds Sebesta, J.L. and Bonfante, L.), Wisconsin (University of Wisconsin Press), pp.77–100

Stuart, M. 1944, 'A Faience Head of Augustus', *American Journal of Archaeology* 48 (2), pp. 171–5

Suetonius, trans., Graves, R. 1957, *The Twelve Caesars*, Harmondsworth (Penguin)

Sumner, G. 2002, 'Wicker, wool, leather and linen: the Roman Soldier on Campaign', *Exercitus: the Bulletin of the Ermine Street Guard* 3 (4), pp.83–8

Tacitus, trans., Grant, M. 1965, *The Annals of Imperial Rome,* Harmondsworth (Penguin)

Tacitus, trans., Wellesley, K. 1995, *The Histories*, Harmondsworth (Penguin)

Tacitus, trans., Mattingly, H. 1954, *Tacitus on Britain and Germany: a New Translation of the 'Agricola' and the 'Germania'*, Harmondsworth (Penguin)

Tait, J. 2003, 'Cleopatra by Name', *Cleopatra Reassessed, British Museum Occasional Paper No.103*, (eds Walker, S. and Ashton, S.), London (BMP), pp.3–7

Tanner, J. 2003, 'Finding the Egyptian in Early Greek Art', *Ancient Perspectives on Egypt* (eds Matthews, R. and Roemer, C.), London (UCL Press), pp.115–43

Tarn, W.W. 1931, 'The Battle of Actium', *Journal of Roman Studies*, Vol. 21, pp.73–199

Tarn, W.W. 1932, 'Antony's Legions', *The Classical Quarterly* 26 (2), pp. 75–81

Tarn, W.W. 1934, *Cambridge Ancient History* X, Cambridge Chapters 2–4 (CUP)

Tarn, W.W. 1936, 'The Bucheum Stelae: a Note', *Journal of Roman Studies* 26 (2), pp.187–9

Tarn, W.W. 1932, 'Alexander Helios and the Golden Age', *Journal of Roman Studies* 22 (2), pp.135–60

Taylor, J.H. 2001, *Death and the Afterlife in Ancient Egypt*, London (BMP)

Tchernia, A. and Brun, J-P. 1999, *Le Vin Romain Antique*, Grenoble, Éditions Glénat

Theophrastus trans., Hort, A. 1999, *Enquiry Into Plants and Minor Works on Odours and Weather Signs I–II*, London

Thompson, D.B, 1950, 'A Bronze Dancer from Alexandria', *American Journal of Archaeology* 54 (4), pp. 371–5

Thompson, D.B. 1964, *ΠΑΝΝΥΧΙΣ*, *Journal of Egyptian Archaeology* 50, pp.147–63

Thompson, D. B. 1973, *Ptolemaic Oinochoai and Portraits in Faience; Aspects of the Ruler-Cult*, Oxford (Clarendon Press)

Thompson, D.J. 2003, 'Cleopatra VII: The Queen in Egypt', *Cleopatra Reassessed, British Museum Occasional Paper No.103*, (eds Walker, S. and Ashton, S.), London (BMP), pp.31–4

Thucydides, trans., Warner, R. 1954, *The Peloponnesian War*, Harmondsworth (Penguin)

Tiradritti, F. 1998, *Isis, the Egyptian Goddess who Conquered Rome*, Exhibition Catalogue, Cairo (SCA)

Tomber, R. 2000, 'Indo-Roman trade: the ceramic evidence from Egypt', *Antiquity* 74 (285), p.624–631

Tomlinson, R.A. 1970, 'Ancient Macedonian Symposia', *Ancient Macedonia: papers read at the first international symposium held in Thessaloniki, 26–29 August 1968* (eds Laourdas, B. and Makaronas, C.J.), Thessalonica (Institute for Balkan Studies), pp.308–15

Toynbee, J.M.C. 1996, *Death and Burial in the Roman World* Baltimore (Johns Hopkins)

Trevelyan, R. 1976, *The Shadow of Vesuvius: Pompeii AD.79*, London (Michael Joseph)

Troy, L. 1986, *Patterns of Queenship in Ancient Egyptian Myth and History*, Uppsala (Almquist & Wiksel International)

Troy, L. 1993, 'Creating a God: the Mummification Ritual', *BACE* 4, pp.55–81

Vasunia, P. 2001, *The Gift of the Nile: Hellenizing Egypt from Aeschylus to Alexander*, Berkeley (University of California Press)

Vergnieux, R. and Gondran, M. 1997, *Aménophis IV et les pierres du soleil: Akhénaten retrouvé*, Paris (Arthaud)

Virgil, trans., Dryden, J. 1968, *Virgil's Aeneid*, New York (Airmont)

Vogelsang-Eastwood, G. 1996, *For Modesty's Sake?* Tilburg (Syntax)

Volkmann, H. 1958, *Cleopatra: a study in Politics and Propaganda*, London (Elek)

Vörös, G. 2002, 'The Taposiris Magna Mosaic in the Museum of Palestrina', *Egyptian Museum Collections around the World II* (eds Eldamaty, M. and Trad, M.), Cairo (AUC Press), pp.1209–20

Vos, R.L. 1993, *The Apis Embalming Ritual, P.Vindob.3873*, Leuven (Peeters)

Wace, R. and Andrews, C. 2004, *Pharaoh's Creatures: Animals from Ancient Egypt*, London (Rupert Wace Ancient Art Publications)

Wachsmann, S. 1987, *Aegeans in Theban Tombs*, Leuven (Peeters)

Walbank, F.W. 1979, 'Egypt in Polybius', *Glimpses of Ancient Egypt: Studies in Honour of H.W. Fairman* (eds Ruffle, J., Gaballa, G.A. and Kitchen, K.A.), Warminster (Aris & Phillips), pp.180–9

Walbank, F.W. 1981, *The Hellenistic World*, London (Fontana)

Walker, S. 2003, 'Carry-on at Canopus: the Nilotic Mosaic from Palestrina and Roman Attitudes to Egypt', *Ancient Perspectives on Egypt* (eds Matthews, R. and Roemer, C.), London (UCL Press), pp.191–202

Walker, S. 2003.(b.) 'From Empire to Empire', *Cleopatra Reassessed, British Museum Occasional Paper No.103*, (eds Walker, S. and Ashton, S.), London (BMP), pp.81–6

Walker, S. and Bierbrier, M. 1997, *Ancient Faces: Mummy Portraits from Roman Egypt*, London (BMP)

Walker, S. and Ashton, S. (eds) 2003, *Cleopatra Reassessed, British Museum Occasional Paper No.103*, London (BMP)

Walker, S. and Higgs, P. (eds) 2001, *Cleopatra of Egypt: from History to Myth*, London (BMP)

Walters, E.J. 1988, *Attic Grave Reliefs that Represent Women in the Dress of Isis, Hesperia Supplement XXII*, Princeton (American School of Classical Studies at Athens)

Ward-Perkins, J. and Claridge, A. 1976, *Pompeii AD.79*, Bristol (Imperial Tobacco Ltd.)

Watterson, B. 1979, 'The Use of Alliteration in Ptolemaic', *Glimpses of Ancient Egypt: Studies in Honour of H.W. Fairman* (eds. Ruffle, J. et al.), Warminster (Aris & Phillips), pp.167–9

Watterson, B. 1998, *The House of Horus at Edfu*, Stroud (Tempus)

Webster, G. 1959, 'Roman Windows and Grilles', *Antiquity* 33 (129), p.10–14

Wegner, J. 2002, 'A decorated birth-brick from South Abydos', *Egyptian Archaeology* 21, pp.3–4

Weigall, A. 1914, *The Life and Times of Cleopatra*, London (Thornton Butterworth)

Weigall, A. 1926, *Wanderings in Roman Britain*, London (Thornton Butterworth)

Weigall, A. 1928, *Flights into Antiquity*, London (Hutchinson)

Weigall, A. 1934, 'The Alexandria of Antony and Cleopatra', *Wonders of the Past* 52, pp.1234–8

Welles, C.B. 1962, 'The discovery of Sarapis and the Foundation of Alexandria', *Historia* 11, pp.271–89

von Wertheimer, O. 1931, *Cleopatra: a Royal Voluptuary*, London (Harrap)

el-Weshahy, M. 2002, 'Ptolemaic Lion-god Stelae at Cairo and Copenhagen Museums', *Egyptian Museum Collections around the World II* (eds Eldamaty, M. and Trad, M.), Cairo (AUC Press), pp.1221–34

Westermann, W.L. 1929, *Upon Slavery in Ptolemaic Egypt*, New York (Columbia University Press)

Westermann, W.L. 1955, *Slave Systems of Greek and Roman Antiquity*, Philadelphia (American Philosophical Society)

Wheeler, R.E.M. 1954, *Rome beyond the Imperial Frontiers*, London (Bell)

Wheeler, M. 1968, *Flames over Persepolis: Turning Point in History*, London (Weidenfeld & Nicolson)

White, R.E. 1898, 'Women in Ptolemaic Egypt', *Journal of Hellenic Studies* 18, pp.238–66

Whitehorne, J. 2001, *Cleopatras*, London (Routledge)

Wild, R.A. 1981, *Water in the Cultic Worship of Isis and Sarapis*, Leiden (Brill)

Wilfong, T. 1997, *Women and Gender in Ancient Egypt: from Prehistory to Late Antiquity*, Ann Arbor (Kelsey Museum of Archaeology)

Wilkins, J. and Hill, S. 2006, *Food in the Ancient World*, London (Blackwell)

Wilkinson, R.H. 2000, *The Complete Temples of Ancient Egypt*, London (Thames & Hudson)

Williams, G. 1958, 'Some Aspects of Roman Marriage Ceremonies and Ideals', *Journal of Roman Studies* 48 (1–2), pp. 16–29

Williams, E.R. 1985, 'Isis Pelagia and a Roman Marble Matrix from the Athenian Agora', *Hesperia* 54 (2), pp.109–19

Williams, D. and Ogden, J. 1994, *Greek Gold: Jewellery of the Classical World*, London (BMP)

Williams, E.W. 1959, 'The Oracle of Dodona: A Postscript', *Greece and Rome* 6 (2), p. 204

Wilson, D.R. and Wright, R.P. 1964, 'Roman Britain in 1963: I. Sites Explored: II. Inscriptions', *Journal of Roman Studies* 54 (1–2), pp.152–85

Wilson, P. 1997, 'Slaughtering the Crocodile at Edfu and Dendera', *The Temple in Ancient Egypt: New Discoveries and Recent Research,* (ed. S.Quirke S.), London pp.179–203

Witt, R.E. 1970, 'The Egyptian Cults in Macedonia', *Ancient Macedonia: papers read at the first international symposium held in Thessaloniki, 26–29 August 1968* (ed.) Laourdas, B. and Makaronas, C.J.), Thessalonica (Institute for Balkan Studies), pp. 324–33

Witt, R.E. 1971, *Isis in the Ancient World*, Baltimore (Johns Hopkins University Press)

Wyke, M. (ed.) 1997, 'Gender and the Body in Mediterranean Antiquity', *Gender and History* Vol.9 (3), Oxford (Blackwell)

Wyke, M. 2002, *The Roman Mistress: Ancient and Modern Representations*, Oxford (OUP)

Wynne-Thomas, J. 1979, *Proud-voiced Macedonia*, London (Springwood)

Zabkar, L.V. 1963, 'Herodotus and the Egyptian Idea of Immortality', *Journal of Near Eastern Studies*, 22 (1), pp.57–63

Zahran, Y. 2003, *Zenobia between Reality and Legend*, BAR International Series 1169, Oxford (Archaeopress)

Zias, J., Stark, H., Seligman J., Levy, R., Werker, E., Breuer, A. and Mechoulam, R. 1993, 'Early Medical Use of Cannabis', *Nature* 363, p.215

Acknowledgements

Of the many, many people who have provided help, information and support over the years has taken to create this book, I'd particularly like to thank David Beaumont & family; Ints Birzkops; Juliet Brightmore; Rita Britton; Prof. Don Brothwell; Dr. Stephen Buckley; Christine Carruthers; Julie and Adam Chalkley; Prof. Matthew Collins; Dr. Vanessa Corby; James Stevens Cox; Sian Edwards Davies; Dr. David Depraetere; Dr. David Dixon; Nicola Doherty; Mel Dyke; Elaine Edgar; Prof. Earl Ertman; Ceryl Evans; Janice Eyres; Prof. Mahmoud Ezzamel; Vanessa Fell; Alan Fildes and family; Michael Fletcher; Dr. Diane France; Pam and Barry Gidney; Marilyn Griffiths; Lynn & Barry Harper; Dr. Bernard Hephrun; Andrea Hirst-Gee; Kerry Hood; Dr. David Howard; Teresa Hull; Duncan James; Dr. Paula James; Nicola and Michael Jamieson; Dr John Kane; Prof. Barry Kemp; Mary Kershaw; Dr. Sandra Knudsen; Leight Kroeger; Rupert Lancaster; Shirley Lancaster; Duncan Lees; Jackie Ligo; Mark Lucas; Sarah Lucas; Joan Allgrove McDowell; Joan McMahon; Prof. Herwig Maehler; David Moss; Gillian Mosely; Richard Nelson; Prof. Terry O'Connor; Geoffrey Oates; Delia Pemberton; Michael and Jane Pickering; Jan Picton; Rod Poole; Tim Radford; Magdy el-Rashidy; Dr. Howard Reid; Annie Roddam; Carol Rowbotham; Filippo Salamone; Dr. Kip Sambu; Julia Samson; Emma Sargeant; Dr. Nick Saunders; Dr. Otto Schaden; Ian Scorah; Gillian Scott; Phyl and Gordon Semley; Ali Hassan Sheba and family; Bryan Sitch; Alastair Smith; Penny Smith; Alex Tapia; Angela Thomas; Jean Thompson; 'Tracey'; David and Carole Walker; Alison Walster; Ros Watson; Rowena Webb; Dr. Andy Wilson; Bob Wilson – but most of all, Garry and Susan, Kate, Stephen, Eleanor and Django!

Note on Spellings

In the spelling of names, the original Greek-style 'Kleopatra' was amended to the more familiar spelling 'Cleopatra', although Eurydice is Eurydike, Callisthenes is Kallisthenes, Cassander is Kassandros and Berenice is Berenike etc. Alongside the familiar name Julius Caesar, Mark Antony is referred to as Marcus Antonius and Pompey as Pompeius.

Picture Acknowledgements

Index